Representative Plays by American Dramatists

Edited with
Historical and Critical Introductions

By Montrose J. Moses

In Three Volumes

Volume I 1765–1819
Volume II 1815–1858
Volume III 1856–1917

REPRESENTATIVE PLAYS

By AMERICAN DRAMATISTS

THE

C O N T R A S T,

A

C O M E D Y;

IN FIVE ACTS:

Boston Museum

WRITTEN BY A

CITIZEN OF THE *UNITED STATES;*

Performed with Applause at the Theatres in NEW-YORK,
PHILADELPHIA, and MARYLAND;

AND PUBLISHED *(under an Assignment of the Copy-Right)* BY

THOMAS WIGNELL.

Primus ego in patriam
Aonio——deduxi vertice Musas.
                                        VIRGIL.
(Imitated.)

First on our shores I try THALIA's powers,
And bid the *laughing, useful* Maid be ours.

PHILADELPHIA:

FROM THE PRESS OF *PRICHARD & HALL,* IN MARKET STREET,
BETWEEN SECOND AND FRONT STREETS.

M. DCC. XC.

FAC-SIMILE TITLE-PAGE OF THE FIRST EDITION
(*From the Original, owned by Dr. F. W. Atkinson*)

Representative Plays by American Dramatists

Edited, with an Introduction to Each Play

By MONTROSE J. MOSES

1765-1819

ARNO PRESS

A New York Times Company

New York • 1978

First published by E. P. Dutton & Co. Inc., 1918,
Copyright renewed by Mrs. Leah H. Moses, 1946
Reissued by Benjamin Blom, Inc. 1964
by arrangement with Mrs. L. H. Moses.

Reprint Edition 1978 by Arno Press Inc.
LC78-55602
ISBN 0-405-08804-3
Manufactured in the United States of America.

To

DR. FRED W. ATKINSON

In grateful recollection of his encouragement
and aid in the preparation of
this volume.

Table of Contents

INTRODUCTION

The present collection of "Representative Plays by American Dramatists" is the first of its kind to be offered to the general reader. In its scope, it covers a period from 1765–1911, and in its plan of selection, it strives to show the advance in playwriting during successive periods of American history.

Because of this scheme, the choice of plays for the Colonial and Revolutionary sections necessarily includes several which, while written for the stage, are not authentically located as far as production is concerned. There is no indication that Robert Rogers's "Ponteach" was ever accepted by any of the theatrical companies of the time, and there is no positive proof that Mrs. Mercy· Warren's "The Group" was ever done, although there are casual references to the fact that performances were given at Amboyne. Nor have we any right to believe that Samuel Low's "The Politician Out-witted" received other than scant treatment from the managers to whom it was submitted; it was published rather to please the readers of the closet drama. Nevertheless, it has been thought essential to include these plays because they are representative of the spirit of the times, and help to give a more comprehensive view of the subjects which were treated in dramatic form by the early American playwrights.

From the moment the American writer ceased to be an Englishman, and became fully aware of his national consciousness, American drama, following the trend of the development of American literature, began to feel its way for the proper expression of national characteristics.

And so, in the second and third volumes of this series, the reader will find plays which, while not wonderful in their literary value, are, nevertheless, very distinctive, as reflecting the theatrical tastes of the time, and the very crude, but none the less sincere, technical effort of the playwrights. All the dramas included in the second and third volumes have had their stage productions, and are thus representative of characteristics which mark the abilities of certain actors, whose claims to originality are found in the special types they created.

It has been the present editor's object so to arrange the successive order of these plays that the reader may not only be able to judge the change in stagecraft and technique, but, likewise, may

note the change in social idea and in historical attitude toward
certain subjects. For example, "The Contrast" contains the first
American Stage Yankee—a model for a succession of Stage
Yankees to follow. But, whereas Royall Tyler's *Jonathan* was
not especially written to exploit the peculiar abilities of Mr.
Wignell, the comedian, most of the Yankee plays of a later date
were written to exploit the peculiar excellences of such actors as
G. H. Hill and James H. Hackett.

In no way can the reader better sense the change in social customs and ideals than by reading a series of plays written in successive generations and reflecting the varying customs of the
time. In some respects "The Contrast" may be considered our
very earliest drama of social manners, even though Royall Tyler
was not over-successful in stamping the small talk of his women
as being distinctively American. Rather is it the direct imitation
—without the brilliancy—of the small talk in "The School for
Scandal." But, nevertheless, "The Contrast" does attempt to
deal with society in New York before the nineteenth century, and
in Mrs. Mowatt's "Fashion," in Mrs. Bateman's "Self," in Bronson Howard's "Saratoga" (which has been published), in Clyde
Fitch's "The Moth and the Flame," and in Langdon Mitchell's
"The New York Idea," we are given a very significant and
sharply defined panoramic view of the variations in moral and
social attitudes.

The plays included in this series have very largely been selected
because of their distinct American flavour. The majority of the
dramas deal directly with American subjects. But it seemed unwise and unrepresentative to frame one's policy of selection too
rigidly on that score. Had such a method been adhered to, many
of the plays written for Edwin Forrest would have to be omitted
from consideration. It would have been difficult, because of this
stricture, to include representative examples of dramas by the
Philadelphia and Knickerbocker schools of playwrights. Robert
T. Conrad's "Jack Cade," John Howard Payne's "Brutus,"
George Henry Boker's "Francesca da Rimini," and Nathaniel P.
Willis's "Tortesa, the Usurer," would thus have been ruled from
the collection. Nevertheless are they representative plays by
American dramatists. Another departure from the American at-
mosphere is in the case of Steele Mackaye; here in preference to
"Hazel Kirke," I have selected "Paul Kauvar," farthest away
from American life, inasmuch as it deals with Nihilism, but

written at a time when there was a Nihilistic fever in New York City.

No editor, attempting such a comprehensive collection as this, can be entirely successful in including everything which will enrich his original plan. There are always limitations placed upon him by the owners of copyrights, and by gaps in the development, due to loss of manuscripts. It was naturally my desire to have all the distinctive American playwrights represented in the present collection. Therefore, in justice, the omissions have to be indicated here, because they leave gaps in a development which it would have been well to offer unbroken and complete.

When the collection was first conceived, there was every indication that permission would be granted me to reproduce at least one of the Robert Montgomery Bird manuscripts, now owned by the University of Pennsylvania. Naturally, a collection of representative plays should include either Bird's "The Gladiator," or one of his other more or less oratorical and poetical pieces, written under the inspiration of Edwin Forrest. The intention to include John Augustus Stone's "Metamora" brought to light, after correspondence with the Forrest Home in Philadelphia, that either the manuscript of that play has irrevocably been destroyed, or else has been preserved so carefully that no one remotely connected with the actor Forrest has thus far been able to locate it. Only a few well remembered speeches and isolated scenes are seemingly left of a play which increased so largely the fame of Mr. Forrest.

In the selection of *types* my attention naturally became centered on the characters of *Colonel Mulberry Sellars*, and *Judge Bardwell Slote*, the former in a dramatization of "The Gilded Age," by Mark Twain and Charles Dudley Warner, and the latter, in a play by Benjamin E. Woolf, called "The Mighty Dollar." Extended investigation revealed the fact that, even if the plays are not lost, they are still unlocated, by the literary executors of Mark Twain on the one hand, and by the family of Mr. Woolf on the other. It is well to mention these instances, because, until the recent interest in the origins of American drama, manifest on all sides, there has been a danger that many most valuable manuscript plays would be lost to the student forever.

At a revival of individual scenes from distinctive American plays, given in New York, on January 22, 1917, considerable difficulty was experienced before the stock-company manuscript of Frank E. Murdoch's "Davy Crockett" was procured. This play, old-fashioned in its general development, is none the less representative of old-time melodramatic situation and romantic manipulation, and there is every reason to believe that, with the tremendous changes in theatrical taste, unless this play is published in available printed form, it will be lost to the student of ten years from now. The play would have been included in the present edition if space had allowed.

When I came to a consideration of the modern section, there were many omissions which had to be made, due very largely to the fact that authors and owners of copyright were loath to forego their rights. A collection of this kind should undoubtedly have the name of James A. Herne represented in its contents, inasmuch as none of Mr. Herne's plays have heretofore been published, and two of his most distinctive dramas in original manuscript, "Margaret Fleming" and "Griffith Davenport," have been totally destroyed by fire. But representatives of Mr. Herne's family have declined, at the present time, to allow his plays to be published. This is to be regretted, inasmuch as nearly all of the most prominent American playwrights are represented, either in the publication of isolated plays or in definitive editions. I should have liked to end this collection with the inclusion of Mr. Eugene Walter's "The Easiest Way;" at the present time, that play, which was once issued in an edition privately printed, is to be found in the *Drama League Series* of plays.

From the standpoint of non-copyright material, two interesting conditions have been revealed through investigation. The first published play, in America, was "Androboros," by Governor Robert Hunter, written in collaboration with Chief Justice Lewis Morris.[1] Only one copy of that play is in existence, owned by Mr. H. E. Huntington, of New York, having formerly been a valued possession in the library of the Duke of Devonshire; and having descended from the private ownership of David Garrick and John Kemble, the English actors. Naturally, the private collector is loath, in view of the rarity of his edition, to allow it, at present, to be reprinted.

Some scholars, however, point to "Les Muses de la Nouvelle-France," printed in Paris in 1609, where the third piece is "Le

[1] The title-page of "Androboros" reads: "Androboros"/ A/Bographical [*Sic.*] Farce/In Three Acts, Viz./The Senate,/The Consistory,/and/The Apotheosis./ By Governour Hunter./Printed at Moropolis since 1st August, 1714. [Taken from Huntington Copy. Moropolis means Fool's Town.]

Théâtre de Neptune en la Nouvelle-France." According to Marc Lescarbot, this was "représentée sur les flots du Port-Royal le quatorzième de Novembre, mille six cens six, au retour de Sieur de Poutrincourt du pais des Armouchiquois." This may be regarded as example of the first play written and acted on North American soil, it, however, being in French, and not given within what is now the United States, but rather at Port Royal, in Acadia. (See two interesting letters, 1° W. J. Neidig, *Nation*, 88:86, January 28, 1909; 2° Philip Alexander Bruce, *Nation*, 88:136, February 11, 1909.)

It was my further desire, as an example of college playwriting, to include the text of Barnabas Bidwell's "The Mercenary Match," written at Yale, and played by the students of Yale.[1] Only one copy of that play is, thus far, known to be in existence, owned by Mr. Evert Jansen Wendell, and its inclusion in the present collection is debarred for the same reason.

Were this collection—Representative Plays by American Dramatists—encyclopedic in its scope, rather than a suggestive arrangement of a limited number of plays for the purpose of illustrating certain phases of playwriting in American theatrical history, it would have been necessary for the editor to intersperse, here and there, between the plays, certain minor forms of dramatic writing, characteristic of the work done in this country. For example, plays and dialogues written at colleges at a period ante-dating 1800, and likewise ante-dating the Revolution, are a distinctive development in themselves, and would form an interesting contrast with the work being done at the colleges since the beginning of the present so-called dramatic renaissance (1917). These dialogues, in their proper place, will be dealt with in the introductions to a few of the plays. But it is well to indicate here that such illustrations of very definite forms of dramatic expression have been omitted.

In all cases the texts used have been carefully collated with the first editions of the published dramas and, wherever possible, the original casts have been given with the Dramatis Personæ. Interest in American drama consists very largely in the elements of comparison and contrast which certain definite dramas suggest. Even if there is no manuscript of "Metamora" extant, there is sufficient data relating to the character of *Metamora* to

[1] The/Mercenary Match,/A Tragedy./By Barna Bidwell./New Haven:/Printed by Meigs, Bowen and Dana,/In Chapel-Street./(1785.)

contrast the play with Robert Rogers's "Ponteach." Even though Mrs. Warren's "The Group" might be ruled out as an acting drama, none the less is it definitely reflective of the revolutionary temper of Revolutionary times. A comparison of other types of plays will be made as they occur in the course of the three volumes. I emphasize the point here, because I wish to suggest that such a collection as this offers infinite possibilities in the study of the historical, social, and economic evolution of America.

Most of these plays have been revived. There will be noted, later, performances of "The Prince of Parthia," of "The Contrast," of Dunlap's "André," and of Mrs. Mowatt's "Fashion," according to our modern methods of acting. These plays may often seem verbose and lacking in continuous development and interest. This would lead us to believe that possibly the early actor had means at his disposal of overcoming these defects by a method of dramatic technique unknown to the present player. In reading these dramas, one must be able to bear in mind the differences which exist between the theatre of to-day and the theatre of yesterday, between the tradition of the actor of to-day and of the actor of yesterday. The technique, for example, in the characterization of *Jonathan*, and in the characterization of *Solon Shingle*, is different from the technique which characterizes the work of Clyde Fitch or which is to be found in David Belasco's "Peter Grimm." In other words, in such a collection, one asks, not the judgment of the highest literary standards, but the judgment of an historical appreciation of the changes in dramatic taste.

* * *

This, the first volume of "Representative Plays by American Dramatists," contains dramas which measure the tastes and inclinations of Colonial and Revolutionary life. In the proper understanding of their atmosphere, it is necessary to know something of the general spirit of the theatre of the period; to measure the conditions, customs, and social peculiarities of the provincial actors and audiences. For that reason, it would be well for the general reader beforehand to obtain a bird's-eye view of the history of the American theatre—a view which will comprise some consideration of the first playhouse in this country, of the conditions which confronted Hallam, Henry, and Douglass, the first actors to be at the head of what, in Williamsburg, Virginia, was known as the Virginia Comedians, and in New York and Philadelphia, as the American Company.

No more fascinating study could be imagined than following the trials and tribulations of the actors in America at this early day, who, as soon as they reached Philadelphia, or as soon as they attempted to invade Boston, were confronted by the Puritanical and sectarian prejudices, against which the early history of the American theatre had to struggle. The personalities of the Hallams, of Douglass and Hodgkinson, are picturesque and worth while tracing in all aspects of their Thespian careers in the Colonies. So, too, the persons of Thomas Wignell, the Comedian, and of Mrs. Merry, are of especial interest. Wignell, at the John Street Theatre, in New York, and at the Southwark Theatre, in Philadelphia, was wont to amuse George Washington, who, on careful examination of his Journals and expense accounts, looms up as the one big theatre-goer of the time.

The reader who follows the effect open hostility with England had upon the American theatre, will find most interesting material relating to the dramatic activities of the soldiers under the leadership of Generals Burgoyne and Howe. In fact, no account of dramatic writings in this country can ignore the fact that General Burgoyne, apart from the farce which incited Mrs. Mercy Warren, was himself a serious dramatist, who took his work seriously, and whose dramas may be obtained at any large reference library. The Red-Coats, as actors, amused their Tory public with such plays as "Tamerlane," "The Busybody," and "Zara;" and when they invaded the Southwark Theatre, around 1777, Major André, the presiding genius of the English soldier-actors, turned to good account his ability as a scene-painter, and painted a backdrop which was preserved in Philadelphia until 1821, when it was destroyed by fire. We have, however, a description of the scene, taken from Durang's "History of the Philadelphia Stage."

"It was a landscape," he writes, "presenting a distant *champagne* country, and a winding rivulet, extending from the front of the picture to the extreme distance. In the foreground and centre was a gentle cascade—the water exquisitely executed— overshadowed by a group of majestic forest trees. The perspective was excellently preserved; the foliage, verdure, and general colouring artistically toned and glazed. It was a drop scene, and André's name was inscribed on the back of it in large black letters."

The early American theatre was nothing more than the theatre of England transplanted to a more provincial atmosphere. We have a record of dramatic performances being given at Williams and Mary College before the Royal Governor, in 1702, and, in 1736, the students were presenting Addison's "Cato." In 1714, in Massachusetts, Chief Justice Samuel Sewall, famed for his witchcraft injunctions, protested against acting in Boston, and warned the people in this fashion: "Let not Christian Boston goe beyond Heathen Rome in the practice of Shameful Vanities."

Evidently the actors who had appeared in New York from the West Indies, in 1702, were, by an ill wind, blown into the sharp-prejudiced atmosphere of New England. Some authorities are inclined to believe that Thomas Kean's appearance on March 5, 1750, in New York, when, as noted by the *Weekly Postboy*, he gave a performance of "Richard III," with permission of Governor Clinton, really begins the history of legitimate theatrical performances in America. This, however, is not historically accurate, for, in South Carolina, it is noted that the first dramatic production occurred in 1734 or 1735, January 18th, although the first Charleston theatre was afterwards erected in 1773, the third regular theatre to be established in the Colonies. (See *The Nation*, 99:278–279; Yates Snowden, "South Carolina Plays and Playwrights," *The Carolinian*, November, 1909.)

The disputed point as to the first theatre in America has also been very thoroughly discussed by Judge Charles P. Daly in his brochure, "The First Theatre in America." (Dunlap Society, New Series, No. 1, 1896.)

In 1755, the Reverend Samuel Davies, whose eloquence made him quite as much an actor as a divine, complained of conditions in Virginia, declaring that plays and romances were more read than "the history of the Blessed Jesus."

The real narrative of Colonial acting, however, begins with William Hallam's appearance in Williamsburg in "The Merchant of Venice," on September 5, 1752; thereafter, as is so excellently traced in Seilhamer, the American Theatre, with its different itinerant companies, began to flourish.

The theatre was such a recreation to the Colonial people that, in many ways, it figured as the one source of official entertainment; especially on occasions when the Royal Governor had to show hospitality to visiting people. For example, the *Maryland Gazette* for November 17, 1752, declares that "The Emperor of the Cherokee nation, with his Empress and their son, the young Prince, attended by several of his warriors and Great Men, and their Ladies, were received at the Palace by his Honour the Governor, attended by such of the Council as were in Town on Thursday, the 9th instant, with all the Marks of Courtesy and Friendship, and were that Evening entertained at the Theatre with the Play (the Tragedy of 'Othello'), and a Pantomime Performance which gave them great surprise, as did the fighting with naked swords on the Stage, which occasioned the Empress to order some about her to go and prevent them killing one another."

The spirit of the theatre-going at this period has been excellently suggested by John Esten Cook in his novel, "The Virginia Comedians," but the reader who will consult rare files of Colonial newspapers will find therein many advertisements which will throw light on some of the social details of the theatre. It is enough here to suggest that, in the reading of the different plays here offered, some consideration be paid to the general theatrical atmosphere which created and fostered them.

In several of the Introductions the editor has had occasion to mention the exercises and dialogues and plays given in the colleges before the Revolution. These were the distinctive forms which time and occasion created; otherwise the early American dramatist framed his pieces in imitation of English and German tradition. However, as soon as the national period began, another interesting dramatic experiment was put into effect. This has been noted by W. W. Clapp, in his chapter written for Justin Winsor's "Commemorative History of Boston." He says:

"[It was] the custom in the earlier days of the theatre to signalize passing events by such appropriate notice as the resources of the stage would permit."

In other words, the event called forth from the Manager, because of commercial possibilities, certain spectacular scenes to attract the patriotic notice of the people. Manager Hodgkinson, on September 20, 1797, celebrated the launching of the frigate *Constitution*.[1] On January 8, 1800, at the New York Theatre, an "Ode on the Death of General Washington" was recited by Mr. Hodgkinson, written by Samuel Low. It is interesting here to note likewise that Royall Tyler pronounced a Eulogy on Washington at Bennington, Vermont, on February 22, 1800.

A patriotic effusion, celebrating the capture of the British frigate *Guerrière*, was produced on October 2, 1812. In 1813, to

[1] Dunlap, himself atune to the hour, wrote "Yankee Chronology; or, Huzza for the Constitution"—"a musical Interlude, in One Act, to which are added, The Patriotic Songs of the Freedom of the Seas, and Yankee Tars," produced at the Park Theatre, New York, 1812. Dunlap wrote many pieces of like character.

commemorate the victory of Perry, a piece was mounted, entitled, "Heroes of the Lake; or, the Glorious Tenth of September." Another piece, equally as suggestive in its title, was "The Sailor's Return; or, Constitution Safe in Port."

When the Marquis de Lafayette visited the United States in 1825, and was taken to the theatre, the occasion was celebrated by an appropriate "drop." In other words, the Manager, even in those days, had the commercial instinct fully developed.

* * *

In the preparation of the present collection, the editor wishes to thank those who have been generous in their advice and appreciation of the work in hand. Being a pioneer effort, the original research necessitated has been of an extensive character. I have had, in order to verify my data, to correspond extensively, not only with the members of the families of the different playwrights, but with many historical societies and libraries. I have likewise had the advantage of being able to consult with Dr. F. W. Atkinson, of the Brooklyn Polytechnic, whose collection of American Drama is probably one of the richest in the country, and with Professor Brander Matthews, whose interest in all drama makes the historian continually in his debt. Certain information concerning Royall Tyler has been furnished me by members of the Tyler family, including Mrs. E. L. Pratt, of Boston. In their proper places, when the plays occur, certain credits and references will be found, but it is a pleasure for me here to thank Mr. Percy Mackaye, Mr. David Belasco, Mr. Langdon Mitchell, Mr. Augustus Thomas, the Clyde Fitch Estate, and the Bronson Howard Estate, for their generous coöperation in bringing the present collection to a successful issue. The privilege is also mine to thank Mr. L. Nelson Nichols, of the Americana Division, and Mr. Victor H. Paltsits, in charge of the Manuscript Division, of the New York Public Library, together with other officials of that Library, of Columbia University, and of the Library Company of Philadelphia, and Miss Z. K. Macdonald, for their unfailing courtesy and untiring efforts in my behalf.

In order to preserve uniformity of style throughout the text of the plays certain modifications in punctuation and spelling have been adopted.

MONTROSE J. MOSES.

February 22, 1917.

BIBLIOGRAPHY OF GENERAL WORKS

Some of the most important works on the history of the American Drama and the American Theatre are given herewith. Under each author, there will be found short individual bibliographies, and in the succeeding volumes of the Collection, other general references will be given which will throw light on the theatrical conditions of the particular theatre periods. Naturally, books relating to modern conditions will be reserved for the third volume.

ALLIBONE, S. AUSTIN. A Critical Dictionary of English Literature and British and American Authors. (3 vols.) Philadelphia: J. B. Lippincott & Co. 1874. (Supplement to Allibone. By John Foster Kirk. Lippincott, 1891, 2 vols.)

ATKINSON, F. W. List of American Drama in the Atkinson Collection. 1756–1915. Brooklyn, January 1, 1916.

BATES, ALFRED. Drama. Vols. XIX, XX. For American Drama.

BECKS. Collection of Prompt Books in the New York Public Library. *Bulletin*, February, 1906, pp. 100–148.

BROWN, T. ALLSTON. A.History of the New York Stage. From the First Performance in 1732 to 1901. (3 vols.) New York: Dodd, Mead & Co. 1903.

BURTON, RICHARD. The New American Drama. New York: Thomas Y. Crowell Co. 1913.

CLAPP, WILLIAM W., JR. A Record of the Boston Stage. Boston: James Munroe and Company. 1853.

CLARK, BARRETT H. The British and American Drama of To-day. New York: Henry Holt & Co. 1915.

CRAWFORD, MARY CAROLINE. The Romance of the American Theatre. Boston: Little, Brown & Co. 1913.

DALY, HON. CHARLES P. First Theatre in America: When Was the Drama First Introduced in America? An Inquiry. Dunlap Soc. Pub., n. s. 1, 1896.

DICKINSON, THOMAS H. The Case of American Drama. Boston: Houghton Mifflin Co. 1915.

DUNLAP, WILLIAM. History of the American Theatre. London: Richard Bentley. 1833.

DURANG, CHARLES. History of the Philadelphia Stage. 1749–1855. (Published serially in the *Philadelphia Dispatch*.)

DUYCKINCK, EVERT A. and GEORGE L. The Cyclopedia of American Literature: From the Earliest Period to the Present Day. Philadelphia: William Rutter & Co. 1877. (2 vols.)

EVANS, CHARLES. American Biography. 8 vols. Privately Printed.

FAXON, FREDERICK W. Dramatic Index. Boston Book Co. 1909 *seq.*

FORD, PAUL LEICESTER. The Beginnings of American Dramatic Literature. *New England Magazine*, n. s. 9: 673–687, February, 1894.

FORD, PAUL LEICESTER. Some Notes Toward an Essay on the Beginnings of American Dramatic Literature. 1606–1789.

FORD, PAUL LEICESTER. Washington and the Theatre. Dunlap Soc. Pub., n. s. 8, 1899.

GAISFORD, JOHN. Drama in New Orleans. New Orleans. 1849.

GRISWOLD, RUFUS WILMOT. Female Poets of America, With Additions by R. H. Stoddard. New York, 1843–1873.

GRISWOLD, RUFUS WILMOT. Prose Writers of America. Philadelphia: Parry & McMillan. 1854.

HARRIS, C. FISKE. Index to American Poetry and Plays in the Collection of. Providence, 187–.

HARRISON, GABRIEL. History of the Drama in Brooklyn.

HASKELL, DANIEL C. (Compiler.) American Dramas, A List of, in the New York Public Library. New York, 1916. (See also *Bulletin of the New York Public Library*, October, 1915.)

HILDEBURN, CHARLES R. The Issues of the Press in Pennsylvania. Philadelphia, 1886.

HUTTON, LAURENCE. Curiosities of the American Stage. New York: Harper & Bros. 1891.

IRELAND, JOSEPH N. Records of the New York Stage, from 1750 to 1860. (2 vols.) New York: T. H. Morrell, Publisher. 1866.

LUDLOW, N. M. Dramatic Life as I Found It: A Record of Personal Experience with an Account of the Drama in the West and South. St. Louis: G. I. Jones & Co. 1880.

MATTHEWS, J. B. American on the Stage. *Scribner*, 28: 321.

MATTHEWS, J. B. A Book About the Theatre. New York: Charles Scribner's Sons. 1916.

MOSES, MONTROSE J. The American Dramatist. Boston: Little, Brown & Co. 1917.

MOSES, MONTROSE J. Famous Actor - Families in America. New York: Thomas Y. Crowell & Co. 1906.

PENCE, JAMES HARRY. (Compiler.) The Magazine and the Drama. An Index. New York: The Dunlap Society. 1896.

PHELPS, H. P. Players of a Century. A Record of the Albany Stage. Albany, 1880.

REES, J. The Dramatic Authors of America. Philadelphia, 1845.

RODEN, ROBERT F. Later American Plays. 1831–1900. New York: The Dunlap Society. (1900, n. s. 12.)

SABIN, JOSEPH. Dictionary of Books Relating to America. From Its Discovery to the Present Time. Vol. 1, *seq.* New York: 1868 *seq.*

SABINE, LORENZO. Biographical Sketches of Loyalists of the American Revolution. (2 vols.) Boston: Little, Brown & Co. 1864.

SCHARF, J. THOMAS, and WESTCOTT, THOMPSON. History of Philadelphia. 1609–1884. Philadelphia: L. H. Everts & Co. 1884.

SEARS, ALONZO. American Literature in the Colonial and National Periods. Boston: Little, Brown & Co. 1902.

SEILHAMER, GEORGE O. I. History of the American Theatre Before the Revolution. Philadelphia, 1888. II. History of the American Theatre During the Revolution and After. Philadelphia, 1889. III. History of the American Theatre: New Foundations. Philadelphia, 1891.

SIMPSON, HENRY. The Lives of Eminent Philadelphians, Now Deceased. Collected from Original and Authentic Sources. Philadelphia: William Brotherhead. 1859.

SMITH, SOLOMON FRANKLIN. Theatrical Management in the West and South for Thirty Years, with Anecdotal Sketches. New York: Harper & Bros. 1868.

SONNECK, OSCAR GEORGE THEODORE. Catalogue of Opera Librettos Printed Before 1800. (2 vols.) Washington: Government Printing Office. 1914.

SONNECK, O. G. T. Early Opera in America. New York: G. Schirmer. 1915.

SONNECK, O. G. T. Report on the Star-Spangled Banner, Hail Columbia, America, and Yankee Doodle. Washington: Government Printing Office. 1909.

STONE, HENRY DICKINSON. Personal Recollections of the Drama. Albany, 1873.

Times, New York. The Early Theatre. December 15, 1895, p. 13.

TOMPKINS, EUGENE, and KILBY, QUINCY. History of the Boston Theatre. Boston: Houghton Mifflin Co. 1908.

TYLER, MOSES COIT. The Literary History of the American Revolution. 1763–1783. (2 vols.) New York: G. P. Putnam's Sons. 1897.

WEGELIN, OSCAR. The Beginning of the Drama in America. *Literary Collector*, 9:177–181, 1905.

WEGELIN, OSCAR. Early American Plays. 1714–1830. New York: The Literary Collector Press. 1905. (See Dunlap Soc. Pub., n. s. 10, 1900; also the *Literary Collector*, 2:82–84.)

WEMYSS, F. C. Chronology of the American Stage from 1752 to 1852. New York: Wm. Taylor & Co.

WEMYSS, F. C. Twenty-six Years of the Life of an Actor and Manager. (2 vols.) New York: Burgess, Stringer & Co. 1847.

WILKINS, FREDERICK H. Early Influence of German Literature in America. *Americana Germanica*, 3:103–205, 1899.

WILLARD, GEORGE O. History of the Providence Stage. 1762–1891. Providence: R. I. News Co. 1891.

WILSON, JAMES GRANT. (Editor.) The Memorial History of the City of New York. (4 vols.) New York History Co. 1892 *seq.*

WINSOR, JUSTIN. The Memorial History of Boston, including Suffolk Co., Mass. 1630–1880. Boston: Ticknor & Co. 1880.

WINTER, WILLIAM. The Wallet of Time. (2 vols.) New York: Moffat, Yard & Co. 1913.

WOOD, WILLIAM B. Personal Recollections of the Stage. Embracing Notices of Actors, Authors, and Auditors, During a Period of Forty Years. Philadelphia: Henry Carey Baird. 1855.

INDIVIDUAL BIBLIOGRAPHIES FOR PLAYS

Only essential references are given, and wherever possible the author's name is indicated, rather than the title. In such cases, the full title of the reference may be had by consulting the General Bibliography.

THOMAS GODFREY, JR.

William Allen, American Biographical Dictionary; Dunlap, i, 50; Seilhamer, i, 185; Tyler, Consult Index; Journal of William Black; Journal of Sarah Eve, Extracts from the: Written while living near the City of Philadelphia in 1772–1773 (Philadelphia, 1881); *American Museum*, 471–472; *Journal National Institute Sciences*, i: 165, 1915; *Nation*, 100:415, April 15, 1915.

MAJOR ROBERT ROGERS

Allibone; Appleton's Cyclopedia of American Biography; Dictionary of National Biography; Duyckinck; Ryerson, American Loyalists; Sabin; Sabine, American Loyalists; Tyler; Winsor. Ellis P. Oberholtzer, Literary History of Philadelphia (1906); Sears. *Canadian Magazine*, 1914, 42:316–318; *Dial* (Chicago), 59:68–69; 97, 1915; *Historical Magazine* (New York), April, 1860, 127; *New England Magazine*, 1894, n. s. 9:678; Royal Society of Canada Proceedings and Transactions, ser. 2, vol. 6, sec. 2, pp. 49–59, Ottawa, 1900. The reader is also referred to the Nevins re-issue of "Ponteach," in which full bibliographies are given; also to Parkman's "History of the Conspiracy of Pontiac." Consult Caleb Stark's "Memoir and Official Correspondence of Gen. John Stark, with Notices of Several other Officers of the Revolution. Also, a Biography of Capt. Phinehas Stevens, and of Colonel Robert Rogers" (1860).

MRS. MERCY WARREN

Alice Brown, "Mercy Warren" (*Women of Colonial and Revolutionary Times*). New York: Scribner's, 1896; Duyckinck; Ellet, Women of the American Revolution; Fiske, John, American Revolution; Griswold, Female Poets of America; Mrs. Hale, Woman's Record; Rees, 132; Seilhamer, ii, 3; Winsor, Boston; Wegelin. Adams, Works of John—ed. by Charles Francis Adams.—Consult Index; *Blackwood Magazine*, xvii, 203; Correspondence Relating to Mrs. Warren's History of the American Revolution, *Mass. Hist. Coll.*, ser. 5, v. 4, 315–511; *Harper's Magazine*, 1884, 68:749; *New England Magazine*, 1894, n. s. 9:680; *North American Review*, lxviii, 415. In studying first editions of plays, the reader is referred to the Bibliographies of Charles Evans and Charles Hildeburn.

HUGH HENRY BRACKENRIDGE

Allibone; Duyckinck; Victor H. Paltsits, A Bibliography of the Separate and Collected Works of Philip Freneau (including Brackenridge)—New York: Dodd, Mead & Co., 1903; 1846 edition of Brackenridge's "Modern Chivalry," containing a biographical sketch by his son; Oberholtzer; Tyler; *United States Magazine* (in the collection of the Historical Society of Pennsylvania). The reader is also referred to Mary S. Austin's "Philip Freneau, the Poet of the Revolution: A History of his Life and Times" (1901); F. L. Pattee's "The Poems of Philip Freneau: Poet of the American Revolution"—Edited for the Princeton Historical Association, 3 volumes, 1902–1907; Samuel Davies Alexander's "Princeton College during the Eighteenth Century;" James Madison's Correspondence while at College; W. C. Armor's "Lives of the Governors of Pennsylvania," for a picture and an account of the administration of Governor Thomas Mackean. Consult also, for college atmosphere, the Journals of Philip Fithian, and the Correspondence of the Rev. Ezra Stiles, Letter of July 23, 1762, published by the Yale Press. (Styles encouraged "The Mercenary Match," by Barnabas Bidwell.)

JOHN LEACOCK

Durang; Duyckinck; Hildeburn; Ford; Sabin; Seilhamer, ii, 10; Tyler; "New Travels through North-America." Translated from the Original of the Abbé Robin [Claude C.], one of the Chaplains to the French Army in America, 1783. (Observations made in 1781); Sonneck's "Early Opera in America;" Watson's "Annals of Philadelphia;" Philadelphia Directories as mentioned in text.

SAMUEL LOW

Dunlap; Duyckinck; Sabin; Seilhamer, ii, 284; Stedman-Hutchinson, Cyclopedia of American Literature; New York Directories as mentioned.

ROYALL TYLER

Allibone; Appleton's Cyclopedia of American Biography; Dunlap, i, 137; Duyckinck; Ireland, i, 76; Stedman-Hutchinson, Library of American Literature; Winsor; "Memoirs of the Hon. Royall Tyler: Late Chief Justice of Vermont. Compiled from his Papers by his son, Thomas Pickman Tyler, 1873" (Unpublished). According to information (1917), this manuscript, incomplete, is being brought to a close by Helen Tyler Brown, great-granddaughter of the Judge. There is likewise a life of Mary Tyler, unpublished, written by herself when quite an old woman.

Consult also: J. T. Buckingham's "Personal Memoirs and Recollections," 2 vols., 1852; J. T. Buckingham's "Specimens of Newspaper Literature," 2 vols., 1850; Vermont Bar Association Proceedings, 1878–1886, vol. i, pp. 44–62, an article by the Rev. Thomas P. Tyler, D.D., of Brattleboro; Harold Milton Ellis's "Joseph Dennie and His Circle: A Study in American Literature from 1792 to 1812."—Studies in English, No. 1, *Bulletin of the University of Texas*, No. 40, July 15, 1915; John Trumbull's "Autobiographical Reminiscences and Letters, 1756–1841." The correspondence relating to Shays's Rebellion is to be found in "Brattleboro, Wyndham Co., Vermont, Early History, with Biographical Sketches. Henry Burnham."—Edited by Abby Maria Hemenway (Includes an excellent picture of Royall Tyler); William Willis's "The Law, the Courts and the Lawyers of Maine"(1863). Further references to Tyler are contained in Rees, 131; Mitchell, American Lands; John Adams' Works; Sonneck's "Opera in America," under "May-day in Town;" Seilhamer, ii, 227; *Delineator* (New York), 85:7; *New England Magazine*, 1894, n. s. 9:674; *North American Review*, July, 1858, 281.

Among Tyler's works, other than those mentioned in the Introduction, may be recorded:

1. "The Algerine Captive; or, The Life and Adventures of Dr. Updike Underhill, Six Years a Prisoner Among the Algerines." 2 vols. Walpole, N. H., 1797.
2. "Moral Tales for American Youths." Boston, 1800.
3. "The Yankee in London: A Series of Letters, written by an American Youth during Nine Months of Residence in the City of London." New York, 1809.
4. Tyler wrote for the newspapers with Joseph Dennie, Walpole, N. H., and published selections from his contributions under the title of "The Spirit of the Farmer's Museum and Lay Preacher's Gazette." He also contributed poems to the *Farmer's Weekly Museum*, to the *Portfolio*, to the Columbia

Centinel, to the *New England Galaxy*, and to the *Polyanthus*.
Prose works were likewise included therein. Some of his contributions to the *Farmer's Museum* were gathered together in
1798 under the title of "Colon and Spondee Papers," and
issued by the pioneer American printer, Isaiah Thomas.

WILLIAM DUNLAP

The reader is referred to Dunlap's own "History of the American Theatre," and to his numerous other prose works, notably
his Lives of Charles Brockden Brown and George Frederjck
Cooke. The Dunlap Society's Reprints of "André" (iv. 1887),
"Darby's Return" (n. s. 8, 1899), and "The Father" (ii, 1887)
contain biographical data. See Oscar Wegelin's "William Dunlap
and His Writings," *Literary Collector*, 7:69–76, 1904; O. S.
Coad's "William Dunlap: A Study of his Life and Writings, and
of Contemporary Culture" (scheduled for issuance by the Dunlap
Society in 1917); Dunlap's Diary, in the Library of the New
York Historical Society: Vol. 14, July 27–Dec. 13, 1797; vol.
15, Dec. 14, 1797–June 1, 1798; vol. 24, Oct. 15, 1819–April 14,
1820; vol. 30, June 27, 1833–Dec. 31, 1834. Consult also
Duyckinck; Rees, 76; Stedman-Hutchinson, Library of American Literature; Seilhamer, Index; Wood, Personal Recollections; Sonneck's "The Musical Side of George Washington;"
Analytical Magazine, i, 404, 466; *New England Magazine*, 1894,
n. s. 9, 684. See Wegelin, Evans, Hildeburn.

JAMES NELSON BARKER

Dunlap, ii, 307; Durang; Ireland; Rees; Diary of Manager
Wood, in possession of the University of Pennsylvania. Also
Griswold's "Poets and Poetry of America;" Oberholtzer's "Literary History of Philadelphia;" Simpson. Barker's political
writings were extensive.

MORDECAI MANUEL NOAH

Dunlap, ii, 316; Ireland, i, 356; Jewish Encyclopedia; Na-
tional Cyclopedia of American Biography. See also Allibone;
Duyckinck; P. K. Foley's "American Authors;" Oberholtzer's
"Literary History of Philadelphia;" Rees; Scharf and Westcott;
James Grant Wilson's "Fitz-Green Halleck;" *International
Magazine*, iii, 282; *American Jewish Historical Society Pub.*,
No. 6, 1897, 113–121; *Lippincott*, i, 665; J. T. Trowbridge's "My
Own Story. With Recollections of Noted Persons" (1903).

THE
PRINCE OF PARTHIA

A TRAGEDY

THOMAS GODFREY, JR.

(1736–1763)

Thomas Godfrey, Jr., was born in Philadelphia, on December 4, 1763, the son of a man who himself won fame as an inventor of the Quadrant. Godfrey, Senior, was a friend of Benjamin Franklin, the two probably having been drawn together by their common interest in science. When Godfrey, Senior, died, December, 1749, it was Franklin who wrote his obituary notice.[1]

Young Godfrey was a student at the College or Academy of Philadelphia, and when his education was completed, he became apprenticed to a watch-maker, remaining in that profession until 1758. As a student at the Academy, he came under the special influence of Dr. William Smith, the first Principal or Provost of that institution,[2] and it was Dr. Smith who not only obtained for Godfrey a lieutenancy with the Pennsylvania troops in 1758, which sent him in the expedition against Fort Duquesne, but who, likewise, as the Editor of *The American Magazine*, was only too glad to accept and publish some of Godfrey's poetical effusions.

That the young man was popular, and that he associated with some of the most promising figures of the time, will be seen from the fact that, although he was only twenty-seven when he died, he was counted among the friends of Benjamin West and John Green, both portrait painters, of Francis Hopkinson, who was a student at the College of Philadelphia, and of Nathaniel Evans, a young minister whose loyalty found outlet after Godfrey's death in the Memorial Edition of Godfrey's works. Evans himself wrote poems and dialogues. In his confirmation of the fact that, as a poet, Godfrey was regarded favourably by the Philadelphians of the time, he quotes from the diary of one Miss Sarah Eve, who referred to him as "our poet."

[1] A notice appeared in the Pennsylvania *Gazette*, December 19, 1749. See Scharf and Westcott's "History of Philadelphia" for references to Godfrey, Sr. Therein is given a picture of his house in Germantown, Pa. Barlow mentions him in his "Columbiad." A monument to his memory was erected in Laurel Hill Cemetery, Philadelphia, 1843. Note that David Rittenhouse, an American dramatist who translated, from the German, "Lucy Sampson; or, The Unhappy Heiress" (1789), was likewise a mathematical genius.

[2] Accounts of Dr. Smith are to be found in Henry Simpson's "Eminent Philadelphians"; Scharf & Westcott's "History of Philadelphia," ii, 1126. Dr. Smith's "Life and Correspondence," by Horace Wemyss Smith, was issued in 2 vols., 1879.

Godfrey's reputation, as a young man with musical talents and a decided taste for painting, has come down to us. Certain it is that, during all of this time of varied occupation as a watchmaker and a soldier, he must have been courting the poetic Muse. There are some who speculate, without authority, on his having been a theatre-goer, and having become inspired as a playwright by the work of the American Company, in Philadelphia; especially by the good work of Douglass. Because of insufficient evidence, that is a question which remains unproven. Nevertheless, it is certain, from an extant letter written by Godfrey on November 17, 1759, and quoted by Seilhamer, that he must have had his attention turned to playwriting as a special art. He says to his correspondent, writing from North Carolina:

By the last vessel from this place, I sent you the copy of a tragedy I finished here, and desired your interest in bringing it on the stage; I have not yet heard of the vessel's safe arrival, and believe if she is safe it will be too late for the company now in Philadelphia. [Meaning, of course, Douglass's company.]

There are two facts to be noted in this communication: first, that it was written from North Carolina, where, in 1759, Godfrey had gone on some plantation business—probably as factor; and second, that it must have been penned with the idea of immediate production by the actors in Philadelphia. According to Seilhamer, Godfrey remained in North Carolina for three years. He did not write the entire manuscript of "The Prince of Parthia" while living in the South but, as he definitely states in his letter, finished it soon after his arrival.

There is no evidence as to why Godfrey sailed to the Island of New Providence in the last year of his life, and then returned to Wilmington, N. C. There is no definite statement as to whether he contracted fever and had a sunstroke on that expedition, or after his return home. But, nevertheless, he did contract the fever and have a sunstroke; with the result that he succumbed to his illness, and died near Wilmington, North Carolina, on August 3, 1763.[1]

After his death, Godfrey's friends decided among themselves that the young man was too much of a genius for them to allow his productions to remain scattered and unrecognized. Evidently, correspondence regarding this must have taken place between Dr. Smith, Nathaniel Evans, the young minister, and John

[1] Visitors to Wilmington, N. C., will be taken to Old St. James's Church-yard, where Godfrey lies buried.

Green, the portrait painter. For, in 1765, a book was published, entitled "Juvenile Poems on Various Subjects, with the Prince of Parthia," printed in Philadelphia by one Henry Miller.[1] The volume contained a life written by Evans, a critical estimate written by Dr. Smith, of the College of Philadelphia, and an Elegy from the pen of John Green, who had been previously complimented by Godfrey in a poem entitled "A Night Piece." The whole spirit of the publication was one of friendly devotion and of firm belief in the permanency of Godfrey's position in the literary world. As was the custom of the time, the Edition was issued under the patronage of subscribers, a list being included. We know, for example, that Benjamin Franklin subscribed for twelve copies, his own private, autographed copy having been put on sale a few years ago.

As yet, no concerted effort had been made for the production of Godfrey's "The Prince of Parthia." We do not know if, during this time, the American Company had any claim on the manuscript, or whether, after Godfrey's death, it was again submitted to the theatrical people. But this much we do know, that, very hastily, the American Company, headed by David Douglass, who was playing at the Southwark Theatre in Philadelphia, decided that they would put on "The Prince of Parthia" in place of "The Disappointment; or, the Force of Credulity," a comic opera which will be noted in my introduction to John Leacock's "The Fall of British Tyranny." This musical piece had actually been put into rehearsal in 1767, when it was withdrawn. Immediately, the *Pennsylvania Journal and Weekly Advertiser* for April 23, 1767, contained an advertisement of the forthcoming production; it ran as follows:

By Authority./Never Performed before./By the American Company,/at the New Theatre, in Southwark,/On Friday, the Twenty-fourth of April, will be/presented, A Tragedy written by the late ingenious/Mr. *Thomas Godfrey*, of this city, called the/Prince of Parthia./The Principal Characters by Mr. Hallam,/Mr. Douglass, Mr. Wall, Mr. Morris,/Mr. Allyn, Mr. Tomlinson, Mr. Broad/belt, Mr. Greville, Mrs. Douglass,/Mrs. Morris, Miss Wainwight, and/ Miss Cheer./To which will be added, A Ballad Opera called/The Contrivances./To begin exactly at *Seven o'clock.—Vivant Rex &* *Regina./*

[1] Juvenile Poems/on/Various Subjects./With the/Prince of Parthia./A/Tragedy,/ By the Late/Mr. Thomas Godfrey, Junr./of Philadelphia./To which is prefixed,/ Some Account of the Author and his Writings./Poeta nascitur non fit. Hor./Phila-delphia,/Printed by Henry Miller, in Second-Street./M DCC LXV.

In the *Pennsylvania Gazette*, for the same date, appears an advertisement, without the cast of characters.

The production occurred on April 24, 1767.

Seilhamer gives a probable cast of characters, although only the list of actors is given in the advertisement. Apart from this, little is known of the production: whether or not it pleased the theatre-goers of the time. We can judge, however, from the reading of the play itself, that there was little of extreme dramatic excellence in the situations, the chief claim, from the actor's point of view, being the opportunity to deliver certain very highly coloured, poetical lines modelled after the manner of the Elizabethan drama.

In the publication of "The Prince of Parthia," we have the first printed American tragedy in existence, and in its production we have one of only two plays, written by Americans, and presented on the stage before the Revolution. The other play is George Cockings's "The Conquest of Canada; or, The Siege of Quebec," printed for the author in 1766, and presented in Philadelphia in 1773. We note, in Dr. F. W. Atkinson's estimable Bibliography of American Plays in his possession, that Cockings later described himself as "Camillo Querno, Poet Laureate to Congress."

The interest in the early history of the American drama, which has become evident within recent years, and nowhere more evident than among the student body in our American colleges, induced the Zelosophic Literary Society, encouraged by the University of Pennsylvania, to revive "The Prince of Parthia," which was written by one of their alumni. The production was consummated on March 26, 1915. Even though we have no statement as to the actual manner in which the Douglass Company presented the play originally, we are given every evidence, by those who witnessed the revival, that the play, while containing many excellences, was not of a dramatic character according to modern ideas of stage effectiveness.

The only portrait of Godfrey known to have been in existence was that painted by Benjamin West, in his earlier years. It is interesting to note that in commemoration of the one hundred and fiftieth anniversary of the original production of this play, Dr. Archibald Henderson, of the University of North Carolina, issued an *édition de luxe* of "The Prince of Parthia," with an extended introduction, historical, biographical and critical (Boston: Little, Brown & Co., 1917).

JUVENILE POEMS

ON

VARIOUS SUBJECTS.

WITH THE

PRINCE OF PARTHIA,

A

T R A G E D Y.

BY THE LATE

M: *THOMAS GODFREY*, Jun:

of PHILADELPHIA.

To which is prefixed,

Some ACCOUNT of the *AUTHOR* and his *WRITINGS*.

Poeta nafcitur non fit.   HOR.

PHILADELPHIA,
Printed by HENRY MILLER, in Second-Street.
M DCC LXV.

FAC-SIMILE OF ORIGINAL TITLE-PAGE TO FIRST EDITION

ADVERTISEMENT

Our Author has made Use of the *licentia poetica* in the Management of this Dramatic Piece; and deviates, in a particular or two, from what is agreed on by Historians: The Queen *Thermusa* being not the Wife of King *Artabanus*, but (according to *Tacitus*, *Strabo* and *Josephus*) of *Phraates; Artabanus* being the fourth King of *Parthia* after him. Such Lapses are not unprecedented among the Poets; and will the more readily admit of an Excuse, when the Voice of History is followed in the Description of Characters.

DRAMATIS PERSONÆ

MEN.

ARTABANUS, King of Parthia.

ARSACES,
VARDANES, } his Sons.
GOTARZES,

BARZAPHERNES, Lieutenant-Generales, under Arsac.

LYSIAS,
PHRAATES, } Officers at Court.

BETHAS, a Noble Captive.

WOMEN.

THERMUSA, the Queen.
EVANTHE, belov'd by Arsaces.
CLEONE, her Confident.
EDESSA, Attendant on the Queen.

Guards and Attendants.

SCENE, *Ctesiphon.*

THE PRINCE OF PARTHIA

A TRAGEDY

ACT I.

SCENE I. *The Temple of the Sun.*

GOTARZES *and* PHRAATES.

GOTARZES.

He comes, Arsaces comes, my gallant Brother
(Like shining Mars in all the pomp of conquest)
Triumphant enters now our joyful gates;
Bright Victory waits on his glitt'ring car,
And shews her fav'rite to the wond'ring croud;
While Fame exulting sounds the happy name
To realms remote, and bids the world admire.
Oh! 'tis a glorious day:—let none presume
T'indulge the tear, or wear the gloom of sorrow;
This day shall shine in Ages yet to come,
And grace the Parthian story.

PHRAATES.

                Glad Ctes'phon
Pours forth her numbers, like a rolling deluge,
To meet the blooming Hero; all the ways,
On either side, as far as sight can stretch,
Are lin'd with crouds, and on the lofty walls
Innumerable multitudes are rang'd.
On ev'ry countenance impatience sate
With roving eye, before the train appear'd.
But when they saw the Darling of the Fates,
They rent the air with loud repeated shouts;
The Mother shew'd him to her infant Son,
And taught his lisping tongue to name Arsaces:
E'en aged Sires, whose sounds are scarcely heard,
By feeble strength supported, tost their caps,
And gave their murmur to the gen'ral voice.

GOTARZES.

The spacious streets, which lead up to the Temple,
Are strew'd with flow'rs; each, with frantic joy,
His garland forms, and throws it in the way.
What pleasure, Phraates, must swell his bosom,
To see the prostrate nation all around him,
And know he's made them happy! to hear them
Tease the Gods, to show'r their blessings on him!
Happy Arsaces! fain I'd imitate
Thy matchless worth, and be a shining joy!

PHRAATES.

Hark! what a shout was that which pierc'd the skies!
It seem'd as tho' all Nature's beings join'd,
To hail thy glorious Brother.

GOTARZES.

            Happy Parthia!
Now proud Arabia dreads her destin'd chains,
While shame and rout disperses all her sons.
Barzaphernes pursues the fugitives,
The few whom fav'ring Night redeem'd from slaughter;
Swiftly they fled, for fear had wing'd their speed,
And made them bless the shade which saf'ty gave.

PHRAATES.

What a bright hope is ours, when those dread pow'rs
Who rule yon heav'n, and guide the mov'ments here,
Shall call your royal Father to their joys:
In blest Arsaces ev'ry virtue meets;
He's gen'rous, brave, and wise, and good,
Has skill to act, and noble fortitude
To face bold danger, in the battle firm,
And dauntless as a Lion fronts his foe.
Yet is he sway'd by ev'ry tender passion,
Forgiving mercy, gentleness and love;
Which speak the Hero friend of humankind.

GOTARZES.

And let me speak, for 'tis to him I owe
That here I stand, and breath the common air,
And 'tis my pride to tell it to the world.

One luckless day as in the eager chace
My Courser wildly bore me from the rest,
A monst'rous Leopard from a bosky fen
Rush'd forth, and foaming lash'd the ground,
And fiercely ey'd me as his destin'd quarry.
My jav'lin swift I threw, but o'er his head
It erring pass'd, and harmless in the air
Spent all its force; my falchin then I seiz'd,
Advancing to attack my ireful foe,
When furiously the savage sprung upon me,
And tore me to the ground; my treach'rous blade
Above my hand snap'd short, and left me quite
Defenceless to his rage; Arsaces then,
Hearing the din, flew like some pitying pow'r,
And quickly freed me from the Monster's paws,
Drenching his bright lance in his spotted breast.

PHRAATES.

How diff'rent he from arrogant Vardanes?
That haughty Prince eyes with a stern contempt
All other Mortals, and with lofty mien
He treads the earth as tho' he were a God.
Nay, I believe that his ambitious soul,
Had it but pow'r to its licentious wishes,
Would dare dispute with Jove the rule of heav'n;
Like a Titanian son with giant insolence,
Match with the Gods, and wage immortal war,
'Til their red wrath should hurl him headlong down,
E'en to destruction's lowest pit of horror.

GOTARZES.

Methinks he wears not that becoming joy
Which on this bright occasion gilds the court;
His brow's contracted with a gloomy frown,
Pensive he stalks along, and seems a prey
To pining discontent.

PHRAATES.

       Arsaces he dislikes,
For standing 'twixt him, and the hope of Empire;
While Envy, like a rav'nous Vulture, tears
His canker'd heart, to see your Brother's triumph.

GOTARZES.

And yet Vardanes owes that hated Brother
As much as I; 'twas summer last, as we
Were bathing in Euphrates' flood, Vardanes
Proud of strength would seek the further shore;
But ere he the mid-stream gain'd, a poignant pain
Shot thro' his well-strung nerves, contracting all,
And the stiff joints refus'd their wonted aid.
Loudly he cry'd for help, Arsaces heard,
And thro' the swelling waves he rush'd to save
His drowning Brother, and gave him life,
And for the boon the Ingrate pays him hate.

PHRAATES.

There's something in the wind, for I've observ'd
Of late he much frequents the Queen's apartment,
And fain would court her favour, wild is she
To gain revenge for fell Vonones' death,
And firm resolves the ruin of Arsaces.
Because that fill'd with filial piety,
To save his Royal Sire, he struck the bold
Presumptuous Traitor dead; nor heeds she
The hand which gave her Liberty, nay rais'd her
Again to Royalty.

GOTARZES.

                    Ingratitude,
Thou hell-born fiend, how horrid is thy form!
The Gods sure let thee loose to scourge mankind,
And save them from an endless waste of thunder.

PHRAATES.

Yet I've beheld this now so haughty Queen,
Bent with distress, and e'en by pride forsook,
When following thy Sire's triumphant car,
Her tears and ravings mov'd the senseless herd,
And pity blest their more than savage breasts,
With the short pleasure of a moment's softness.
Thy Father, conquer'd by her charms (for what
Can charm like mourning beauty), soon struck off
Her chains, and rais'd her to his bed and throne.
Adorn'd the brows of her aspiring Son,

The fierce Vonones, with the regal crown
Of rich Armenia, once the happy rule
Of Tisaphernes, her deceased Lord.

GOTARZES.

And he in wasteful war return'd his thanks,
Refus'd the homage he had sworn to pay,
And spread Destruction ev'ry where around,
'Til from Arsaces' hand he met the fate
His crimes deserv'd.

PHRAATES.

As yet your princely Brother
Has scap'd Thermusa's rage, for still residing
In peaceful times, within his Province, ne'er
Has fortune blest her with a sight of him,
On whom she'd wreck her vengeance.

GOTARZES.

She has won
By spells, I think, so much on my fond father,
That he is guided by her will alone.
She rules the realm, her pleasure is a law,
All offices and favours are bestow'd,
As she directs.

PHRAATES.

But see, the Prince, Vardanes,
Proud Lysias with him, he whose soul is harsh
With jarring discord. Nought but madding rage,
And ruffian-like revenge his breast can know,
Indeed to gain a point he'll condescend
To mask the native rancour of his heart,
And smooth his venom'd tongue with flattery.
Assiduous now he courts Vardanes' friendship,
See, how he seems to answer all his gloom,
And give him frown for frown.

GOTARZES.

Let us retire,
And shun them now; I know not what it means,
But chilling horror shivers o'er my limbs,
When Lysias I behold.—

SCENE II. VARDANES *and* LYSIAS.

LYSIAS.

That shout proclaims   [*Shout.*

Arsaces' near approach.

VARDANES.

Peace, prithee, peace,
Wilt thou still shock me with that hated sound,
And grate harsh discord in my offended ear?
If thou art fond of echoing the name,
Join with the servile croud, and hail his triumph.

LYSIAS.

I hail him? By our glorious shining God,
I'd sooner lose my speech, and all my days
In silence rest, conversing with my thoughts,
Than hail Arsaces.

VARDANES.

Yet, again his name,
Sure there is magic in it, Parthia's drunk
And giddy with the joy; the houses' tops
With gaping spectators are throng'd, nay wild
They climb such precipices that the eye
Is dazzl'd with their daring; ev'ry wretch
Who long has been immur'd, nor dar'd enjoy
The common benefits of sun and air,
Creeps from his lurking place; e'en feeble age,
Long to the sickly couch confin'd, stalks forth,
And with infectious breath assails the Gods.
O! curse the name, the idol of their joy.

LYSIAS.

And what's that name, that thus they should disturb
The ambient air, and weary gracious heav'n
With ceaseless bellowings? Vardanes sounds
With equal harmony, and suits as well
The loud repeated shouts of noisy joy.
Can he bid Chaos Nature's rule dissolve,
Can he deprive mankind of light and day,
And turn the Seasons from their destin'd course?
Say, can he do all this, and be a God?

If not, what is his matchless merit? What dares he,
Vardanes dares not? blush not, noble Prince,
For praise is merit's due, and I will give it;
E'en 'mid the croud which waits thy Brother's smile,
I'd loud proclaim the merit of Vardanes.

VARDANES.

Forbear this warmth, your friendship urges far.
Yet know your love shall e'er retain a place
In my remembrance. There is something here—
[Pointing to his breast.
Another time and I will give thee all;
But now, no more.—

LYSIAS.

You may command my services,
I'm happy to obey. Of late your Brother
Delights in hind'ring my advancement,
And ev'ry boaster's rais'd above my merit,
Barzaphernes alone commands his ear,
His oracle in all.

VARDANES.

I hate Arsaces,
Tho' he's my Mother's son, and churchmen say
There's something sacred in the name of Brother.
My soul endures him not, and he's the bane
Of all my hopes of greatness. Like the sun
He rules the day, and like the night's pale Queen,
My fainter beams are lost when he appears.
And this because he came into the world,
A moon or two before me: What's the diff'rence,
That he alone should shine in Empire's seat?
I am not apt to trumpet forth my praise,
Or highly name myself, but this I'll speak,
To him in ought, I'm not the least inferior.
Ambition, glorious fever! mark of Kings,
Gave me immortal thirst and rule of Empire.
Why lag'd my tardy soul, why droop'd the wing,
Nor forward springing, shot before his speed
To seize the prize?—'Twas Empire—Oh! 'twas Empire—

LYSIAS.

Yet, I must think that of superior mould
Your soul was form'd, fit for a heav'nly state,
And left reluctant its sublime abode,
And painfully obey'd the dread command,
When Jove's controuling fate forc'd it below.
His soul was earthly, and it downward mov'd,
Swift as to the center of attraction.

VARDANES.

It might be so—But I've another cause
To hate this Brother, ev'ry way my rival;
In love as well as glory he's above me;
I dote on fair Evanthe, but the charmer
Disdains my ardent suit, like a miser
He treasures up her beauties to himself:
Thus is he form'd to give me torture ever.—
But hark, they've reach'd the Temple,
Didst thou observe the croud, their eagerness,
Each put the next aside to catch a look,
Himself was elbow'd out?—Curse, curse their zeal—

LYSIAS.

Stupid folly!

VARDANES.

                    I'll tell thee, Lysias,
This many-headed monster multitude,
Unsteady is as giddy fortune's wheel,
As woman fickle, varying as the wind;
To-day they this way course, the next they veer,
And shift another point, the next another.

LYSIAS.

Curiosity's another name for man,
The blazing meteor streaming thro' the air
Commands our wonder, and admiring eyes,
With eager gaze we trace the lucent path,
'Til spent at length it shrinks to native nothing.
While the bright stars which ever steady glow,
Unheeded shine, and bless the world below.

SCENE III. QUEEN *and* EDESSA.

QUEEN.

Oh! give me way, the haughty victor comes,
Surrounded by adoring multitudes;
On swelling tides of praise to heav'n they raise him;
To deck their idol, they rob the glorious beings
Of their splendour.

EDESSA.

My royal Lady,
Chace hence these passions.

QUEEN.

Peace, forever peace,
Have I not cause to hate this homicide?
'Twas by his cursed hand Vonones fell,
Yet fell not as became his gallant spirit,
Not by the warlike arm of chief renown'd,
But by a youth, ye Gods, a beardless stripling,
Stab'd by his dastard falchin from behind;
For well I know he fear'd to meet Vonones,
As princely warriors meet with open daring,
But shrunk amidst his guards, and gave him death,
When faint with wounds, and weary with the fight.

EDESSA.

With anguish I have heard his hapless fate,
And mourn'd in silence for the gallant Prince.

QUEEN.

Soft is thy nature, but, alas! Edessa,
Thy heart's a stranger to a mother's sorrows,
To see the pride of all her wishes blasted;
Thy fancy cannot paint the storm of grief,
Despair and anguish, which my breast has known.
Oh! show'r, ye Gods, your torments on Arsaces,
Curs'd be the morn which dawn'd upon his birth.

EDESSA.

Yet, I intreat—

QUEEN.

Away! for I will curse—
Oh! may he never know a father's fondness,
Or know it to his sorrow, may his hopes
Of joy be cut like mine, and his short life
Be one continu'd tempest; if he lives,
Let him be curs'd with jealousy and fear,
And vext with anguish of neglecting scorn;
May tort'ring hope present the flowing cup,
Then hasty snatch it from his eager thirst,
And when he dies base treach'ry be the means.

EDESSA.

Oh! calm your spirits.

QUEEN.

Yes, I'll now be calm,
Calm as the sea when the rude waves are laid,
And nothing but a gentle swell remains;
My curse is heard, and I shall have revenge;
There's something here which tells me 'twill be so,
And peace resumes her empire o'er my breast.
Vardanes is the Minister of Vengeance;
Fir'd by ambition, he aspiring seeks
T'adorn his brows with Parthia's diadem;
I've fann'd the fire, and wrought him up to fury,
Envy shall urge him forward still to dare,
And discord be the prelude to destruction,
Then this detested race shall feel my hate.

EDESSA.

And doth thy hatred then extend so far,
That innocent and guilty all alike
Must feel thy dreadful vengeance?

QUEEN.

Ah! Edessa,
Thou dost not know e'en half my mighty wrongs,
But in thy bosom I will pour my sorrows.

EDESSA.

With secrecy I ever have repaid
Your confidence.

QUEEN.

I know thou hast; then hear:
The changeling King who oft has kneel'd before me,
And own'd no other pow'r, now treats me
With ill dissembl'd love mix'd with disdain.
A newer beauty rules his faithless heart,
Which only in variety is blest;
Oft have I heard him, when wrapt up in sleep,
And wanton fancy rais'd the mimic scene,
Call with unusual fondness on Evanthe,
While I have lain neglected by his side,
Except sometimes in a mistaken rapture
He'd clasp me to his bosom.

EDESSA.

Oh! Madam,
Let not corroding jealousy usurp
Your Royal breast, unnumber'd ills attend
The wretch who entertains that fatal guest.

QUEEN.

Think not that I'll pursue its wand'ring fires,
No more I'll know perplexing doubts and fears,
And erring trace suspicion's endless maze,
For, ah! I doubt no more.

EDESSA.

Their shouts approach.

QUEEN.

Lead me, Edessa, to some peaceful gloom,
Some silent shade far from the walks of men,
There shall the hop'd revenge my thoughts employ,
And sooth my sorrows with the coming joy.

SCENE IV. EVANTHE *and* CLEONE.

EVANTHE.

No, I'll not meet him now, for love delights
In the soft pleasures of the secret shade,

And shuns the noise and tumult of the croud.
How tedious are the hours which bring him
To my fond, panting heart! for oh! to those
Who live in expectation of the bliss,
Time slowly creeps, and ev'ry tardy minute
Seems mocking of their wishes. Say, Cleone,
For you beheld the triumph, 'midst his pomp,
Did he not seem to curse the empty show,
The pageant greatness, enemy to love,
Which held him from Evanthe? haste, to tell me,
And feed my gready ear with the fond tale—
Yet, hold—for I shall weary you with questions,
And ne'er be satisfied—Beware, Cleone,
And guard your heart from Love's delusive sweets.

CLEONE.

Is Love an ill, that thus you caution me
To shun his pow'r?

EVANTHE.

The Tyrant, my Cleone,
Despotic rules, and fetters all our thoughts.
Oh! wouldst thou love, then bid adieu to peace,
Then fears will come, and jealousies intrude,
Ravage your bosom, and disturb your quiet,
E'en pleasure to excess will be a pain.
Once I was free, then my exulting heart
Was like a bird that hops from spray to spray,
And all was innocence and mirth; but, lo!
The Fowler came, and by his arts decoy'd,
And soon the Wanton cag'd. Twice fifteen times
Has Cynthia dipt her horns in beams of light,
Twice fifteen times has wasted all her brightness,
Since first I knew to love; 'twas on that day
When curs'd Vonones fell upon the plain,
The lovely Victor doubly conquer'd me.

CLEONE.

Forgive my boldness, Madam, if I ask
What chance first gave you to Vonones' pow'r?
Curiosity thou know'st is of our sex.

EVANTHE.

That is a task will wake me to new sorrows,
Yet thou attend, and I will tell thee all.
Arabia gave me birth, my father held
Great Offices at Court, and was reputed
Brave, wise and loyal, by his Prince belov'd.
Oft has he led his conqu'ring troops, and forc'd
From frowning victory her awful honours.
In infancy I was his only treasure,
On me he wasted all his store of fondness.
Oh! I could tell thee of his wond'rous goodness,
His more than father's love and tenderness.
But thou wouldst jeer, and say the tale was trifling;
So did he dote upon me, for in childhood
My infant charms, and artless innocence
Blest his fond age, and won on ev'ry heart.
But, oh! from this sprung ev'ry future ill,
This fatal beauty was the source of all.

CLEONE.

'Tis often so, for beauty is a flow'r
That tempts the hand to pluck it.

EVANTHE.

          Full three times
Has scorching summer fled from cold winter's
Ruthless blasts, as oft again has spring
In sprightly youth drest nature in her beauties,
Since bathing in Niphates'[1] silver stream,
Attended only by one fav'rite maid;
As we were sporting on the wanton waves,
Swift from the wood a troop of horsemen rush'd,
Rudely they seiz'd, and bore me trembling off,
In vain Edessa with her shrieks assail'd
The heav'ns, for heav'n was deaf to both our pray'rs.
The wretch whose insolent embrace confin'd me
(Like thunder bursting on the guilty soul),
With curs'd Vonones' voice pour'd in my ears
A hateful tale of love; for he it seems
Had seen me at Arabia's royal court,
And took those means to force me to his arms.

[1] The Tigris.

CLEONE.

Perhaps you may gain something from the Captives
Of your lost Parents.

EVANTHE.

                    This I meant to try,
Soon as the night hides Nature in her darkness,
Veil'd in the gloom we'll steal into their prison.
But, oh! perhaps e'en now my aged Sire
May 'mongst the slain lie welt'ring on the field,
Pierc'd like a riddle through with num'rous wounds,
While parting life is quiv'ring on his lips,
He may perhaps be calling on his Evanthe.
Yes, ye great Pow'rs who boast the name of mercy,
Ye have deny'd me to his latest moments,
To all the offices of filial duty,
To bind his wounds, and wash them with my tears,
Is this, is this your mercy?

CLEONE.

                    Blame not heav'n,
For heav'n is just and kind; dear Lady, drive
These black ideas from your gentle breast;
Fancy delights to torture the distress'd,
And fill the gloomy scene with shadowy ills,
Summon your reason, and you'll soon have comfort.

EVANTHE.

Dost thou name comfort to me, my Cleone,
Thou who know'st all my sorrows? plead no more,
'Tis reason tells me I am doubly wretched.

CLEONE.

But hark, the music strikes, the rites begin,
And, see, the doors are op'ning.

EVANTHE.

                    Let's retire;
My heart is now too full to meet him here,
Fly swift ye hours, till in his arms I'm prest,
And each intruding care is hush'd to rest.

SCENE V.

The Scene draws and discovers, in the inner part of the Temple, a large image of the Sun, with an altar before it. Around Priests and Attendants.

KING, ARSACES, VARDANES, GOTARZES, PHRAATES, LYSIAS, *with* BETHAS *in chains.*

HYMN.

Parent of Light, to thee belong
Our grateful tributary songs;
Each thankful voice to thee shall rise,
And chearful pierce the azure skies;
While in thy praise all earth combines,
And Echo in the Chorus joins.

All the gay pride of blooming May,
   The Lily fair and blushing Rose,
To thee their early honours pay,
   And all their heav'nly sweets disclose.
The feather'd Choir on ev'ry tree
   To hail thy glorious dawn repair,
While the sweet sons of harmony
   With Hallelujahs fill the air.

'Tis thou hast brac'd the Hero's arm,
And giv'n the Love of praise to warm
His bosom, as he onward flies,
And for his Country bravely dies.
Thine's victory, and from thee springs
Ambition's fire, which glows in Kings.

KING [*coming forward*].

Thus, to the Gods our tributary songs,
And now, oh! let me welcome once again
My blooming victor to his Father's arms;
And let me thank thee for our safety: Parthia
Shall thank thee too, and give her grateful praise
To her Deliverer.

OMNES.

All hail! Arsaces!

KING.

Thanks to my loyal friends.

VARDANES [*aside*].

               Curse, curse the sound,
E'en Echo gives it back with int'rest,
The joyful gales swell with the pleasing theme,
And waft it far away to distant hills.
O that my breath was poison, then indeed
I'd hail him like the rest, but blast him too.

ARSACES.

My Royal Sire, these honours are unmerited,
Beneath your prosp'rous auspices I fought,
Bright vict'ry to your banners joyful flew,
And favour'd for the Sire the happy son.
But lenity should grace the victor's laurels,
Then, here, my gracious Father—

KING.

           Ha! 'tis Bethas!
Know'st thou, vain wretch, what fate attends on those
Who dare oppose the pow'r of mighty Kings,
Whom heav'n delights to favour? sure some God
Who sought to punish you for impious deeds,
'Twas urg'd you forward to insult our arms,
And brave us at our Royal City's gates.

BETHAS.

At honour's call, and at my King's command,
Tho' it were even with my single arm, again
I'd brave the multitude, which, like a deluge,
O'erwhelm'd my gallant handful; yea, wou'd meet
Undaunted, all the fury of the torrent.
'Tis honour is the guide of all my actions,
The ruling star by which I steer thro' life,
And shun the shelves of infamy and vice.

KING.

It was the thirst of gain which drew you on;
'Tis thus that Av'rice always cloaks its views,
Th' ambition of your Prince you gladly snatch'd
As opportunity to fill your coffers.

It was the plunder of our palaces,
And of our wealthy cities, fill'd your dreams,
And urg'd you on your way; but you have met
The due reward of your audacity.
Now shake your chains, shake and delight your ears
With the soft music of your golden fetters.

BETHAS.

True, I am fall'n, but glorious was my fall,
The day was brav'ly fought, we did our best,
But victory's of heav'n. Look o'er yon field,
See if thou findest one Arabian back
Disfigur'd with dishonourable wounds.
No, here, deep on their bosoms, are engrav'd
The marks of honour! 'twas thro' here their souls
Flew to their blissful seats. Oh! why did I
Survive the fatal day? To be this slave,
To be the gaze and sport of vulgar crouds,
Thus, like a shackl'd tyger, stalk my round,
And grimly low'r upon the shouting herd.
Ye Gods!—

KING.

Away with him to instant death.

ARSACES.

Hear me, my Lord, O, not on this bright day,
Let not this day of joy blush with his blood.
Nor count his steady loyalty a crime,
But give him life, Arsaces humbly asks it,
And may you e'er be serv'd with honest hearts.

KING.

Well, be it so; hence, bear him to his dungeon;
Lysias, we here commit him to thy charge.

BETHAS.

Welcome my dungeon, but more welcome death.
Trust not too much, vain Monarch, to your pow'r,
Know fortune places all her choicest gifts
On ticklish heights, they shake with ev'ry breeze,
And oft some rude wind hurls them to the ground.
Jove's thunder strikes the lofty palaces,

While the low cottage, in humility,
Securely stands, and sees the mighty ruin.
What King can boast, to-morrow as to-day,
Thus, happy will I reign?   The rising sun
May view him seated on a splendid throne,
And, setting, see him shake the servile chain.

[*Exit guarded.*

SCENE VI.

KING, ARSACES, VARDANES, GOTARZES, PHRAATES.

GOTARZES.

Thus let me hail thee from the croud distinct,
For in the exulting voice of gen'ral joy
My fainter sounds were lost, believe me, Brother,
My soul dilates with joy to see thee thus.

ARSACES.

Thus let me thank thee in this fond embrace.

VARDANES.

The next will be my turn, Gods, I had rather
Be circl'd in a venom'd serpent's fold.

GOTARZES.

O, my lov'd Brother, 'tis my humble boon,
That, when the war next calls you to the field,
I may attend you in the rage of battle.
By imitating thy heroic deeds,
Perhaps, I may rise to some little worth,
Beneath thy care I'll try my feeble wings,
Till taught by thee to soar to nobler heights.

KING.

Why, that's my boy, thy spirit speaks thy birth,
No more I'll turn thee from the road to glory,
To rust in slothfulness, with lazy Gownsmen.

GOTARZES.

Thanks, to my Sire, I'm now completely blest.

ARSACES.

But, I've another Brother, where's Vardanes?

KING.

Ha! what, methinks, he lurks behind the croud,
And wears a gloom which suits not with the time.

VARDANES.

Doubt not my Love, tho' I lack eloquence,
To dress my sentiments and catch the ear,
Tho' plain my manners, and my language rude,
My honest heart disdains to wear disguise.
Then think not I am slothful in the race,
Or, that my Brother springs before my Love.

ARSACES.

Far be suspicion from me.

VARDANES.

                So, 'tis done,
Thanks to dissembling, all is well again.

KING.

Now let us forward, to the Temple go,
And let, with chearful wine, the goblets flow;
Let blink-ey'd Jollity his aid afford,
To crown our triumph, round the festive board:
But, let the wretch, whose soul can know a care,
Far from our joys, to some lone shade repair,
In secrecy, there let him e'er remain,
Brood o'er his gloom, and still increase his pain.

End of the First Act.

ACT II.

SCENE I. *A Prison.*

LYSIAS [*alone*].

The Sun set frowning, and refreshing Eve
Lost all its sweets, obscur'd in double gloom.
This night shall sleep be stranger to these eyes,
Peace dwells not here, and slumber flies the shock;
My spirits, like the elements, are warring,
And mock the tempest with a kindred rage—
I, who can joy in nothing, but revenge,

Know not those boasted ties of Love and Friendship;
Vardanes I regard, but as he give me
Some hopes of vengeance on the Prince Arsaces—
But, ha! he comes, wak'd by the angry storm,
'Tis to my wish, thus would I form designs,
Horror should breed beneath the veil of horror,
And darkness aid conspiracies—He's here—

SCENE II. VARDANES *and* LYSIAS.

LYSIAS.

Welcome, my noble Prince.

VARDANES.

        Thanks, gentle friend;
Heav'ns! what a night is this!

LYSIAS.

        'Tis fill'd with terror;
Some dread event beneath this horror lurks,
Ordain'd by fate's irrevocable doom;
Perhaps Arsaces' fall—and angry heav'n
Speaks it, in thunder, to the trembling world.

VARDANES.

Terror indeed! it seems as sick'ning Nature
Had giv'n her order up to gen'ral ruin;
The Heav'ns appear as one continu'd flame,
Earth with her terror shakes, dim night retires,
And the red lightning gives a dreadful day,
While in the thunder's voice each sound is lost;
Fear sinks the panting heart in ev'ry bosom,
E'en the pale dead, affrighted at the horror,
As tho' unsafe, start from their marble goals,
And howling thro' the streets are seeking shelter.

LYSIAS.

I saw a flash stream thro' the angry clouds,
And bend its course to where a stately pine
Behind the garden stood, quickly it seiz'd,
And wrapt it in a fiery fold, the trunk
Was shiver'd into atoms, and the branches
Off were lopt, and wildly scatter'd round.

VARDANES.

Why rage the elements, they are not curs'd
Like me? Evanthe frowns not angry on them,
The wind may play upon her beauteous bosom
Nor fear her chiding, light can bless her sense,
And in the floating mirror she beholds
Those beauties which can fetter all mankind.
Earth gives her joy, she plucks the fragrant rose,
Pleas'd takes its sweets, and gazes on its bloom.

LYSIAS.

My Lord, forget her, tear her from your breast.
Who, like the Phœnix gazes on the sun,
And strives to soar up to the glorious blaze,
Should never leave Ambition's brightest object,
To turn, and view the beauties of a flow'r.

VARDANES.

O, Lysias, chide no more, for I have done.
Yes, I'll forget this proud disdainful beauty;
Hence, with vain love—Ambition, now, alone,
Shall guide my actions, since mankind delights
To give me pain, I'll study mischief too,
And shake the earth, e'en like this raging tempest.

LYSIAS.

A night like this, so dreadful to behold,
Since my remembrance's birth, I never saw.

VARDANES.

E'en such a night, dreadful as this, they say,
My teeming Mother gave me to the world.
Whence by those sages who, in knowledge rich,
Can pry into futurity, and tell
What distant ages will produce of wonder,
My days were deem'd to be a hurricane;
My early life prov'd their prediction false;
Beneath a sky serene my voyage began,
But, to this long uninterrupted calm,
Storms shall succeed.

LYSIAS.

Then haste, to raise the tempest;
My soul disdains this one eternal round,
Where each succeeding day is like the former.
Trust me, my noble Prince, here is a heart
Steady and firm to all your purposes,
And here's a hand that knows to execute
Whate'er designs thy daring breast can form,
Nor ever shake with fear.

VARDANES.

And I will use it,
Come to my bosom, let me place thee here,
How happy am I clasping so much virtue!
Now, by the light, it is my firm belief,
One mighty soul in common swells our bosoms,
Such sameness can't be match'd in diff'rent beings.

LYSIAS.

Your confidence, my Lord, much honours me,
And when I act unworthy of your love
May I be hooted from Society,
As tho' disgraceful to the human kind,
And driv'n to herd among the savage race.

VARDANES.

Believe me, Lysias, I do not know
A single thought which tends toward suspicion,
For well I know thy worth, when I affront it,
By the least doubt, may I be ever curs'd
With faithless friends, and by his dagger fall
Whom my deluded wishes most would favour.

LYSIAS.

Then let's no longer trifle time away,
I'm all impatience till I see thy brows
Bright in the glories of a diadem;
My soul is fill'd with anguish when I think
That by weak Princes worn, 'tis thus disgrac'd.
Haste, mount the throne, and, like the morning Sun,
Chace with your piercing beams those mists away,
Which dim the glory of the Parthian state:

Each honest heart desires it, numbers there are
Ready to join you, and support your cause,
Against th' opposing faction.

VARDANES.

Sure some God,
Bid you thus call me to my dawning honours,
And joyful I obey the pleasing summons.
Now by the pow'rs of heav'n, of earth and hell,
Most solemnly I swear, I will not know
That quietude which I was wont to know,
'Til I have climb'd the height of all my wishes,
Or fell, from glory, to the silent grave.

LYSIAS.

Nobly resolv'd, and spoken like Vardanes,
There shone my Prince in his superior lustre.

VARDANES.

But, then, Arsaces, he's a fatal bar—
O! could I brush this busy insect from me,
Which envious strives to rob me of my bloom,
Then might I, like some fragrant op'ning flow'r,
Spread all my beauties in the face of day.
Ye Gods! why did ye give me such a soul
(A soul, which ev'ry way is form'd for Empire),
And damn me with a younger Brother's right?
The diadem would set as well on mine,
As on the brows of any lordly He;
Nor is this hand weak to enforce command.
And shall I steal into my grave, and give
My name up to oblivion, to be thrown
Among the common rubbish of the times?
No: Perish first, this happy hated Brother.

LYSIAS.

I always wear a dagger, for your service,
I need not speak the rest—
When humbly I intreated of your Brother
T' attend him as Lieutenant in this war,
Frowning contempt, he haughtily reply'd,
He entertain'd not Traitors in his service.

True, I betray'd Orodes, but with cause,
He struck me, like a sorry abject slave,
And still withheld from giving what he'd promis'd.
Fear not Arsaces, believe me, he shall
Soon his Quietus have—But, see, he comes,—
What can this mean? Why at this lonely hour,
And unattended?—Ha! 'tis opportune—
I'll in, and stab him now. I heed not what
The danger is, so I but have revenge,
Then heap perdition on me.

VARDANES.

Hold, awhile—
'Twould be better could we undermine him,
And make him fall by Artabanus' doom.

LYSIAS.

Well, be it so—

VARDANES.

But let us now retire,
We must not be observ'd together here.

SCENE III.

ARSACES [alone].

'Tis here that hapless Bethas is confin'd;
He who, but yesterday, like angry Jove,
When punishing the crimes of guilty men,
Spread death and desolation all around,
While Parthia trembl'd at his name; is now
Unfriended and forlorn, and counts the hours,
Wrapt in the gloomy horrors of a goal.—
How dark, and hidden, are the turns of fate!
His rigid fortune moves me to compassion.
O! 'tis a heav'nly virtue when the heart
Can feel the sorrows of another's bosom,
It dignifies the man: The stupid wretch
Who knows not this sensation, is an image,
And wants the feeling to make up a life—
I'll in, and give my aid to sooth his sorrows.

SCENE IV.

VARDANES *and* LYSIAS.

LYSIAS.

Let us observe with care, something we, yet,
May gather, to give to us the vantage;
No matter what's the intent.

VARDANES.

How easy 'tis
To cheat this busy, tattling, censuring world!
For fame still names our actions, good or bad,
As introduc'd by chance, which ofttimes throws
Wrong lights on objects; vice she dresses up—
In the bright form, and goodliness, of virtue,
While virtue languishes, and pines neglected,
Rob'd of her lustre—But, let's forward, Lysias—
Thou know'st each turn in this thy dreary rule,
Then lead me to some secret stand, from whence,
Unnotic'd, all their actions we may view.

LYSIAS.

Here, take your stand behind—See, Bethas comes.

[*They retire.*

SCENE V.

BETHAS [*alone*].

To think on Death in gloomy solitude,
In dungeons and in chains, when expectation
Join'd with serious thought describe him to us,
His height'n'd terrors strike upon the soul
With awful dread; imagination rais'd
To frenzy, plunges in a sea of horror,
And tastes the pains, the agonies of dying—
Ha! who is this, perhaps he bears my fate?
It must be so, but, why this privacy?

SCENE VI.

ARSACES *and* BETHAS.

ARSACES.

Health to the noble Bethas, health and joy!

BETHAS.

A steady harden'd villain, one experienc'd
In his employment; ha! where's thy dagger?
It cannot give me fear; I'm ready, see,
My op'ning bosom tempts the friendly steel.
Fain would I cast this tiresome being off,
Like an old garment worn to wretchedness.
Here, strike for I'm prepar'd.

ARSACES.

      Oh! view me better,
Say, do I wear the gloomy ruffian's frown?

BETHAS.

Ha! 'tis the gallant Prince, the brave Arsaces,
And Bethas' Conqueror.

ARSACES.

      And Bethas' friend,
A name I'm proud to wear.

BETHAS.

      Away—away—
Mock with your jester to divert the court,
Fit Scene for sportive joys and frolic mirth;
Think'st thou I lack that manly constancy
Which braves misfortune, and remains unshaken?
Are these, are these the emblems of thy friendship,
These rankling chains, say, does it gall like these?
No, let me taste the bitterness of sorrow,
For I am reconcil'd to wretchedness.
The Gods have empty'd all their mighty store,
Of hoarded Ills, upon my whiten'd age;
Now death—but, oh! I court coy death in vain,
Like a cold maid, he scorns my fond complaining.
'Tis thou, insulting Prince, 'tis thou hast dragg'd
My soul, just rising, down again to earth,
And clogg'd her wings with dull mortality,
A hateful bondage! Why—

ARSACES.

      A moment hear me—

BETHAS.

Why dost thou, like an angry vengeful ghost,
Glide hither to disturb this peaceful gloom?
What, dost thou envy me my miseries,
My chains and flinty pavement, where I oft
In sleep behold the image of the death I wish,
Forget my sorrows and heart-breaking anguish?
These horrors I would undisturb'd enjoy,
Attended only by my silent thoughts;
Is it to see the wretch that you have made;
To view the ruins of unhappy Bethas,
And triumph in my grief? Is it for this
You penetrate my dark joyless prison?

ARSACES.

Oh! do not injure me by such suspicions.
Unknown to me are cruel scoffs and jests;
My breast can feel compassion's tenderness,
The warrior's warmth, the soothing joys of friendship.
When adverse bold battalions shook the earth,
And horror triumph'd on the hostile field,
I sought you with a glorious enmity,
And arm'd my brow with the stern frown of war.
But now the angry trumpet wakes no more
The youthful champion to the lust for blood.
Retiring rage gives place to softer passions,
And gen'rous warriors know no longer hate,
The name of foe is lost, and thus I ask
Your friendship.

BETHAS.

    Ah! why dost thou mock me thus?

ARSACES.

Let the base coward, he who ever shrinks,
And trembles, at the slight name of danger,
Taunt, and revile, with bitter gibes, the wretched;
The brave are ever to distress a friend.
Tho' my dear country (spoil'd by wasteful war,
Her harvests blazing, desolate her towns,
And baleful ruin shew'd her haggard face)
Call'd out on me to save her from her foes,

And I obey'd, yet to your gallant prowess,
And unmatch'd deeds, I admiration gave.
But now my country knows the sweets of safety,
Freed from her fears; sure now I may indulge
My just esteem for your superior virtue.

BETHAS.

Yes, I must think you what you would be thought,
For honest minds are easy of belief,
And always judge of others by themselves,
But often are deceiv'd; yet Parthia breeds not
Virtue much like thine, the barb'rous clime teems
With nought else but villains vers'd in ill.

ARSACES.

Dissimulation never mark'd my looks,
Nor flatt'ring deceit e'er taught my tongue,
The tale of falsehood, to disguise my thoughts:
To Virtue, and her fair companion, Truth,
I've ever bow'd, their holy precepts kept,
And scann'd by them the actions of my life.
Suspicion surely ne'er disturbs the brave,
They never know the fears of doubting thoughts;
But free, as are the altars of the Gods,
From ev'ry hand receive the sacrifice.

SCENE VII.

ARSACES, BETHAS, EVANTHE *and* CLEONE.

EVANTHE.

Heav'ns! what a gloom hangs round this dreadful place,
Fit habitation for the guilty mind!
Oh! if such terrors wait the innocent,
Which tread these vaults, what must the impious feel,
Who've all their crimes to stare them in the face?

BETHAS.

Immortal Gods! is this reality?
Or mere illusion? am I blest at last,
Or is it to torment me that you've rais'd
This semblance of Evanthe to my eyes?
It is! it is! 'tis she!—

ARSACES.

                    Ha!—what means this?—
She faints! she faints! life has forsook its seat,
Pale Death usurps its place—Evanthe, Oh!
Awake to life!—Love and Arsaces call!—

BETHAS.

Off—give her to my arms, my warm embrace
Shall melt Death's icy chains.

CLEONE.

                    She lives! she lives!—
See, on her cheeks the rosy glow returns.

ARSACES.

O joy! O joy! her op'ning eyes, again,
Break, like the morning sun, a better day.

BETHAS.
                    Evanthe!—
EVANTHE.
                    Oh! my Father!—

ARSACES.
                    Ha!—her Father!

BETHAS.

Heav'n thou art kind at last, and this indeed
Is recompense for all the ills I've past;
For all the sorrows which my heart has known,
Each wakeful night, and ev'ry day of anguish.
This, this has sweet'n'd all my bitter cup,
And gave me once again to taste of joy,
Joy which has long been stranger to this bosom.
Hence—hence disgrace—off, ignominy off—
But one embrace—I ask but one embrace,
And 'tis deny'd.

EVANTHE.

                    Oh, yes, around thy neck
I'll fold my longing arms, thy softer fetters,
Thus press thee to my happy breast, and kiss
Away those tears that stain thy aged cheeks.

BETHAS.

Oh! 'tis too much! it is too much! ye Gods!
Life's at her utmost stretch, and bursting near
With heart-swoln ecstasy; now let me die.

ARSACES.

What marble heart
Could see this scene unmov'd, nor give a tear?
My eyes grow dim, and sympathetic passion
Falls like a gushing torrent on my bosom.

EVANTHE.

O! happy me, this place, which lately seem'd
So fill'd with horror, now is pleasure's circle.
Here will I fix my seat; my pleasing task
Shall be to cherish thy remaining life.
All night I'll keep a vigil o'er thy slumbers,
And on my breast repose thee, mark thy dreams,
And when thou wak'st invent some pleasing tale,
Or with my songs the tedious hours beguile.

BETHAS.

Still let me gaze, still let me gaze upon thee,
Let me strain ev'ry nerve with ravishment,
And all my life be center'd in my vision.
To see thee thus, to hear thy angel voice,
It is, indeed, a luxury of pleasure!—
Speak, speak again, for oh! 'tis heav'n to hear thee!
Celestial sweetness dwells on ev'ry accent;—
Lull me to rest, and sooth my raging joy.
Joy which distracts me with unruly transports.
Now, by thy dear departed Mother's shade,
Thou brightest pattern of all excellence,
Thou who in prattling infancy hast blest me,
I wou'd not give this one transporting moment,
This fullness of delight, for all—but, ah!
'Tis vile, Ambition, Glory, all is vile,
To the soft sweets of love and tenderness.

EVANTHE.

Now let me speak, my throbbing heart is full,
I'll tell thee all—alas! I have forgot—
'T 'as slipt me in the tumult of my joy.
And yet I thought that I had much to say.

BETHAS.

Oh! I have curs'd my birth, indeed, I have
Blasphem'd the Gods, with unbecoming passion,
Arraign'd their Justice, and defy'd their pow'r,
In bitterness, because they had deny'd
Thee to support the weakness of my age.
But now no more I'll rail and rave at fate,
All its decrees are just, complaints are impious,
Whate'er short-sighted mortals feel, springs from
Their blindness in the ways of Providence;
Sufficient wisdom 'tis for man to know
That the great Ruler is e'er wise and good.

ARSACES.

Ye figur'd stones!
Ye senseless, lifeless images of men,
Who never gave a tear to others' woe,
Whose bosoms never glow'd for others' good,
O weary heav'n with your repeated pray'rs,
And strive to melt the angry pow'rs to pity,
That ye may truly live.

EVANTHE.

Oh! how my heart
Beats in my breast, and shakes my trembling frame!
I sink beneath this sudden flood of joy,
Too mighty for my spirits.

ARSACES.

My Evanthe,
Thus in my arms I catch thy falling beauties,
Chear thee; and kiss thee back to life again:
Thus to my bosom I could ever hold thee,
And find new pleasure.

EVANTHE.

O! my lov'd Arsaces,
Forgive me that I saw thee not before,
Indeed my soul was busily employ'd,
Nor left a single thought at liberty.
But thou, I know, art gentleness and love.
Now I am doubly paid for all my sorrows,
For all my fears for thee.

ARSACES.

Then, fear no more:
Give to guilty wretches painful terrors:
Whose keen remembrance raises horrid forms,
Shapes that in spite of nature shock their souls
With dreadful anguish: but thy gentle bosom,
Where innocence beams light and gayety,
Can never know a fear, now shining joy
Shall gild the pleasing scene.

EVANTHE.

Alas! this joy
I fear is like a sudden flame shot from
Th' expiring taper, darkness will ensue,
And double night I dread enclose us round.
Anxiety does yet disturb my breast,
And frightful apprehension shakes my soul.

BETHAS.

How shall I thank you, ye bright glorious beings!
Shall I in humble adoration bow,
Or fill the earth with your resounding praise?
No, this I leave to noisy hypocrites,
A Mortal's tongue disgraces such a theme;
But heav'n delights where silent gratitude
Mounts each aspiring thought to its bright throne,
Nor leaves to language aught; words may indeed
From man to man their sev'ral wants express,
Heav'n asks the purer incense of the heart.

ARSACES.

I'll to the King, ere he retires to rest,
Nor will I leave him 'til I've gain'd your freedom;
His love will surely not deny me this.

SCENE VIII.

VARDANES *and* LYSIAS *come forward.*

LYSIAS.

'Twas a moving scene, e'en my rough nature
Was nighly melted.

VARDANES.

                    Hence coward pity—
What is joy to them, to me is torture.
Now am I rack'd with pains that far exceed
Those agonies, which fabling Priests relate,
The damn'd endure: The shock of hopeless Love,
Unblest with any views to sooth ambition,
Rob me of all my reas'ning faculties.
Arsaces gains Evanthe, fills the throne,
While I am doom'd to foul obscurity,
To pine and grieve neglected.

LYSIAS.

                    My noble Prince,
Would it not be a master-piece, indeed,
To make this very bliss their greatest ill,
And damn them in the very folds of joy?

VARDANES.

This I will try, and stretch my utmost art,
Unknown is yet the means—We'll think on that—
Success may follow if you'll lend your aid.

LYSIAS.

The storm still rages—I must to the King,
And know what further orders ere he sleeps:
Soon I'll return, and speak my mind more fully.

VARDANES.

Haste, Lysias, haste, to aid me with thy council;
For without thee, all my designs will prove
Like night and chaos, darkness and confusion;
But to thy word shall light and order spring.—
Let coward Schoolmen talk of Virtue's rules,
And preach the vain Philosophy of fools;
Court eager their obscurity, afraid
To taste a joy, and in some gloomy shade
Dream o'er their lives, while in a mournful strain
They sing of happiness they never gain.
But form'd for nobler purposes I come,
To gain a crown, or else a glorious tomb.

End of the Second Act.

ACT III.

SCENE I. *The Palace.*

QUEEN *and* EDESSA.

QUEEN.

Talk not of sleep to me, the God of Rest
Disdains to visit where disorder reigns;
Not beds of down, nor music's softest strains,
Can charm him when 'tis anarchy within.
He flies with eager haste the mind disturb'd,
And sheds his blessings where the soul's in peace.

EDESSA.

Yet, hear me, Madam!

QUEEN.

Hence, away, Edessa,
For thou know'st not the pangs of jealousy.
Say, has he not forsook my bed, and left me
Like a lone widow mourning to the night?
This, with the injury his son has done me,
If I forgive, may heav'n in anger show'r
Its torments on me—Ha! isn't that the King!

EDESSA.

It is your Royal Lord, great Artabanus.

QUEEN.

Leave me, for I would meet him here alone,
Something is lab'ring in my breast—

SCENE II.

KING *and* QUEEN

KING.

This leads
To fair Evanthe's chamber—Ha! the Queen.

QUEEN.

Why dost thou start? so starts the guilty wretch,
When, by some watchful eye, prevented from
His dark designs.

KING.
Prevented! how, what mean'st thou?

QUEEN.
Art thou then so dull? cannot thy heart,
Thy changeling heart, explain my meaning to thee,
Or must upbraiding 'wake thy apprehension?
Ah! faithless, tell me, have I lost those charms
Which thou so oft hast sworn could warm old age,
And tempt the frozen hermit from his cell,
To visit once again our gayer world?
This, thou hast sworn, perfidious as thou art,
A thousand times; as often hast thou sworn
Eternal constancy, and endless love,
Yet ev'ry time was perjur'd.

KING.
Sure, 'tis frenzy.

QUEEN.
Indeed, 'tis frenzy, 'tis the height of madness,
For I have wander'd long in sweet delusion.
At length the pleasing Phantom chang'd its form,
And left me in a wilderness of woe.

KING.
Prithee, no more, dismiss those jealous heats;
Love must decay, and soon disgust arise,
Where endless jarrings and upbraidings damp
The gentle flame, which warms the lover's breast.

QUEEN.
Oh! grant me patience heav'n! and dost thou think
By these reproaches to disguise thy guilt?
No, 'tis in vain, thy art's too thin to hide it.

KING.
Curse on the marriage chain!—the clog, a wife,
Who still will force and pall us with the joy,
Tho' pow'r is wanting, and the will is cloy'd,
Still urge the debt when Nothing's left to pay.

QUEEN.
Ha! dost thou own thy crime, nor feel the glow
Of conscious shame?

KING.

                    Why should I blush, if heav'n
Has made me as I am, and gave me passions?
Blest only in variety, then blame
The Gods, who form'd my nature thus, not me.

QUEEN.

Oh! Traitor! Villain!

KING.

                   Hence—away—
No more I'll wage a woman's war with words.   [*Exit.*

QUEEN.

Down, down ye rising passions, give me ease,
Or break my heart, for I must yet be calm—
But, yet, revenge, our Sex's joy, is mine;
By all the Gods! he lives not till the morn.
Who slights my love, shall sink beneath my hate.

SCENE III.

QUEEN *and* VARDANES.

VARDANES.

What, raging to the tempest?

QUEEN.

              Away!—away!—
Yes, I will rage—a tempest's here within,
Above the trifling of the noisy elements.
Blow ye loud winds, burst with your violence,
For ye but barely imitate the storm
That wildly rages in my tortur'd breast—
The King—the King—

VARDANES.

            Ha! what?—the King?

QUEEN.
Evanthe!

VARDANES.

You talk like riddles, still obscure and short,
Give me some cue to guide me thro' this maze.

QUEEN.

Ye pitying pow'rs!—oh! for a poison, some
Curs'd deadly draught, that I might blast her beauties,
And rob her eyes of all their fatal lustre.

VARDANES.

What, blast her charms?—dare not to think of it—
Shocking impiety;—the num'rous systems
Which gay creation spreads, bright blazing suns,
With all th' attendant planets circling round,
Are not worth half the radiance of her eyes.
She's heav'n's peculiar care, good spir'ts hover
Round, a shining band, to guard her beauties.

QUEEN.

Be they watchful then: for should remissness
Taint the guard, I'll snatch the opportunity,
And hurl her to destruction.

VARDANES.

    Dread Thermusa,
Say, what has rous'd this tumult in thy soul?
What dost thou rage with unabating fury,
Wild as the winds, loud as the troubl'd sea?

QUEEN.

Yes, I will tell thee—Evanthe—curse her—
With charms—Would that my curses had the pow'r
To kill, destroy, and blast where e'er I hate,
Then would I curse, still curse, till death should seize
The dying accents on my falt'ring tongue.
So should this world, and the false changeling man
Be buried in one universal ruin.

VARDANES.

Still err'st thou from the purpose.

QUEEN.

    Ha! 'tis so—
Yes I will tell thee—for I know fond fool,
Deluded wretch, thou dotest on Evanthe—
Be that thy greatest curse, be curs'd like me,
With jealousy and rage, for know, the King,
Thy father, is thy rival.

SCENE IV.

VARDANES [*alone*].
Ha! my rival!
How knew she that?—yet stay—she's gone—my rival,
What then? he is Arsaces' rival too.
Ha!—this may aid and ripen my designs—
Could I but fire the King with jealousy,
And then accuse my Brother of Intrigues
Against the state—ha!—join'd with Bethas, and
Confed'rate with th' Arabians—'tis most likely
That jealousy would urge him to belief.
I'll sink my claim until some fitter time,
'Til opportunity smiles on my purpose.
Lysias already has receiv'd the mandate
For Bethas' freedom: Let them still proceed,
This harmony shall change to discord soon.
Fortune methinks of late grows wond'rous kind,
She scarcely leaves me to employ myself.

SCENE V.

KING, ARSACES, VARDANES.

KING.

But where's Evanthe? Where's the lovely Maid?

ARSACES.

On the cold pavement, by her aged Sire,
The dear companion of his solitude,
She sits, nor can persuasion make her rise;
But in the wild extravagance of joy
She weeps, then smiles, like April's sun, thro' show'rs.
While with strain'd eyes he gazes on her face,
And cries, in ecstacy, "Ye gracious pow'rs!
"It is too much, it is too much to bear!"
Then clasps her to his breast, while down his cheeks
Large drops each other trace, and mix with hers.

KING.

Thy tale is moving, for my eyes o'erflow—
How slow does Lysias with Evanthe creep!

So moves old time when bringing us to bliss.
Now war shall cease, no more of war I'll have,
Death knows satiety, and pale destruction
Turns loathing from his food, thus forc'd on him.
The triffling dust, the cause of all this ruin,
The trade of death shall urge no more.—

SCENE VI.

KING, ARSACES, VARDANES, EVANTHE, LYSIAS.

KING.

Evanthe!—
See pleasure's goddess deigns to dignify
The happy scene, and make our bliss complete.
So Venus, from her heav'nly seat, descends
To bless the gay Cythera with her presence;
A thousand smiling graces wait the goddess,
A thousand little loves are flutt'ring round,
And joy is mingl'd with the beauteous train.

EVANTHE.

O! Royal Sir, thus lowly to the ground
I bend, in humble gratitude, accept
My thanks, for this thy goodness, words are vile
T' express the image of my lively thought,
And speak the grateful fulness of my heart.
All I can say, is that I now am happy,
And that thy giving hand has made me blest.

KING.

O! rise, Evanthe rise, this lowly posture
Suits not with charms like thine, they should command,
And ev'ry heart exult in thy behests;—
But, where's thy aged Sire?

EVANTHE.

This sudden turn
Of fortune has so wrought upon his frame,
His limbs could not support him to thy presence.

ARSACES.

This, this is truly great, this is the Hero,

Like heav'n, to scatter blessings 'mong mankind
And e'er delight in making others happy.
Cold is the praise which waits the victor's triumph
(Who thro' a sea of blood has rush'd to glory),
To the o'erflowings of a grateful heart,
By obligations conquer'd: Yet, extend
Thy bounty unto me.   *[Kneels.*

KING.

Ha! rise Arsaces.

ARSACES.

Not till you grant my boon.

KING.

Speak, and 'tis thine—
Wide thro' our kingdom let thy eager wishes
Search for some jewel worthy of thy seeing;
Something that's fit to show the donor's bounty,
And by the glorious sun, our worship'd God,
Thou shalt not have denial; e'en my crown
Shall gild thy brows with shining beams of Empire.
With pleasure I'll resign to thee my honours,
I long for calm retirement's softer joys.

ARSACES.

Long may you wear it, grant it bounteous heav'n,
And happiness attend it; 'tis my pray'r
That daily rises with the early sweets
Of nature's incense, and the lark's loud strain.
'Tis not the unruly transport of ambition
That urges my desires to ask your crown;
Let the vain wretch, who prides in gay dominion,
Who thinks not of the great ones' weighty cares,
Enjoy his lofty wish, wide spreading rule.
The treasure which I ask, put in the scale,
Would over-balance all that Kings can boast,
Empire and diadems.

KING.

Away, that thought—
Name it, haste—speak.

ARSACES.

For all the dang'rous toil,
Thirst, hunger, marches long that I've endur'd,
For all the blood I've in thy service spent,
Reward me with Evanthe.

KING.

Ha! what said'st thou?—

VARDANES.

The King is mov'd, and angry bites his lip.—
Thro' my benighted soul all-cheering hope   [*Aside.*
Beams, like an orient sun, reviving joy.

ARSACES.

The stern Vonones ne'er could boast a merit
But loving her.

KING.

Ah! curse the hated name—
Yes, I remember when the fell ruffian
Directed all his fury at my life;
Then sent, by pitying heav'n, t' assert the right
Of injur'd Majesty, thou, Arsaces,
Taught him the duty he ne'er knew before,
And laid the Traitor dead.

ARSACES.

My Royal Sire!

LYSIAS.

My Liege, the Prince still kneels.

KING.

Ha!—rebel, off—   [*Strikes him.*
What, Lysias, did I strike thee? forgive my rage—
The name of curs'd Vonones fires my blood,
And gives me up to wrath.—

LYSIAS.

I am your slave,
Sway'd by your pleasure—when I forget it,
May this keen dagger, which I mean to hide
Deep in his bosom, pierce my vitals thro'.   [*Aside.*

KING.

Didst thou not name Evanthe?

ARSACES.

I did, my Lord!
And, say, whom should I name but her, in whom
My soul has center'd all her happiness?
Nor canst thou blame me, view her wond'rous charms,
She's all perfection; bounteous heav'n has form'd her
To be the joy, and wonder of mankind;
But language is too vile to speak her beauties.
Here ev'ry pow'r of glowing fancy's lost:
Rose blush secure, ye lilies still enjoy
Your silver whiteness, I'll not rob your charms·
To deck the bright comparison; for here
It sure must fail.

KING.

He's wanton in her praise—   [*Aside.*
I tell thee, Prince, hadst thou as many tongues,
As days have wasted since creation's birth,
They were too few to tell the mighty theme.

EVANTHE.

I'm lost! I'm lost!   [*Aside.*

ARSACES.

Then I'll be dumb for ever.

KING.

O rash and fatal oath! is there no way,
No winding path to shun this precipice,
But must I fall and dash my hopes to atoms?
In vain I strive, thought but perplexes me,
Yet shews no hold to bear me up—now, hold
My heart a while—she's thine—'tis done.

ARSACES.

In deep
Prostration, I thank my Royal Father.

KING.

A sudden pain shoots thro' my trembling breast—
Lend me thy arm Vardanes—cruel pow'rs!

SCENE VII.

ARSACES *and* EVANTHE.

EVANTHE [*after a pause*].

E'er since the dawn of my unhappy life
Joy never shone serenely on my soul;
Still something interven'd to cloud my day.
Tell me, ye pow'rs, unfold the hidden crime
For which I'm doom'd to this eternal woe,
Thus still to number o'er my hours with tears?
The Gods are just I know, nor are decrees
In hurry shuffl'd out, but where the bolt
Takes its direction justice points the mark.
Yet still in vain I search within my breast,
I find no sins are there to shudder at—
Nought but the common frailties of our natures.
Arsaces,—Oh!—

ARSACES.

Ha! why that look of anguish?
Why didst thou name me with that sound of sorrow?
Ah! say, why stream those gushing tears so fast
From their bright fountain? sparkling joy should now
Be lighten'd in thine eye, and pleasure glow
Upon thy rosy cheek;—ye sorrows hence—
'Tis love shall triumph now.

EVANTHE.

Oh!   [*Sighs.*

ARSACES.

What means that sigh?
Tell me why heaves thy breast with such emotion?
Some dreadful thought is lab'ring for a vent,
Haste, give it loose, ere strengthen'd by confinement
It wrecks thy frame, and tears its snowy prison.
Is sorrow then so pleasing that you hoard it
With as much love, as misers do their gold?
Give me my share of sorrows.

EVANTHE.

Ah! too soon
You'll know what I would hide.

ARSACES.

            Be it from thee—
The dreadful tale, when told by thee, shall please;
Haste, to produce it with its native terrors,
My steady soul shall still remain unshaken;
For who when bless'd with beauties like to thine
Would e'er permit a sorrow to intrude?
Far hence in darksome shades does sorrow dwell,
Where hapless wretches thro' the awful gloom,
Echo their woes, and sighing to the winds,
Augment with tears the gently murm'ring stream;
But ne'er disturbs such happiness as mine.

EVANTHE.

Oh! 'tis not all thy boasted happiness,
Can save thee from disquietude and care;
Then build not too securely on these joys,
For envious sorrow soon will undermine,
And let the goodly structure fall to ruin.

ARSACES.

I charge thee, by our mutual vows, Evanthe,
Tell me, nor longer keep me in suspense:
Give me to know the utmost rage of fate.

EVANTHE.

Then know—impossible!—

                   ARSACES.

             Ha! dost thou fear

To shock me?—

                   EVANTHE.

Know, thy Father—loves Evanthe.—

ARSACES.

Loves thee?

                   EVANTHE.

             Yea, e'en to distraction loves me.
Oft at my feet he's told the moving tale,
And woo'd me with the ardency of youth.
I pitied him indeed, but that was all,
Thou would'st have pitied too.

ARSACES.

I fear 'tis true;
A thousand crouding circumstances speak it.
Ye cruel Gods! I've wreck'd a Father's peace,
Oh! bitter thought!

EVANTHE.

Didst thou observe, Arsaces,
How reluctant he gave me to thy arms?

ARSACES.

Yes, I observ'd that when he gave thee up,
It seem'd as tho' he gave his precious life.
And who'd forego the heav'n of thy love?
To rest on thy soft swelling breast, and in
Sweet slumbers sooth each sharp intruding care?
Oh! it were bliss, such as immortals taste,
To press thy ruby lips distilling sweets,
Or circl'd in thy snowy arms to snatch
A joy, that Gods——

EVANTHE.

Come, then, my much-lov'd Prince,
Let's seek the shelter of some kind retreat.
Happy Arabia opens wide her arms,
There may we find some friendly solitude,
Far from the noise and hurry of the Court.
Ambitious views shall never blast our joys,
Or tyrant Fathers triumph o'er our wills:
There may we live like the first happy pair
Cloth'd in primeval innocence secure.
Our food untainted by luxurious arts,
Plain, simple, as our lives, shall not destroy
The health it should sustain; while the clear brook
Affords the cooling draught our thirsts to quench.
There, hand in hand, we'll trace the citron grove,
While with the songsters' round I join my voice,
To hush thy cares and calm thy ruffl'd soul:
Or, on some flow'ry bank reclin'd, my strains
Shall captivate the natives of the stream,
While on its crystal lap ourselves we view.

ARSACES.

I see before us a wide sea of sorrows,
Th' angry waves roll forward to o'erwhelm us,
Black clouds arise, and the wind whistles loud.
But yet, oh! could I save thee from the wreck,
Thou beauteous casket, where my joys are stor'd,
Let the storm rage with double violence,
Smiling I'd view its wide extended horrors.

EVANTHE.

'Tis not enough that we do know the ill,
Say, shall we calmly see the tempest rise,
And seek no shelter from th' inclement sky,
But bid it rage?—

ARSACES.

        Ha! will he force thee from me?
What, tear thee from my fond and bleeding heart?
And must I lose thee ever? dreadful word!
Never to gaze upon thy beauties more?
Never to taste the sweetness of thy lips?
Never to know the joys of mutual love?
Never!—Oh! let me lose the pow'r of thinking,
For thought is near allied to desperation.
Why, cruel Sire—why did you give me life,
And load it with a weight of wretchedness?
Take back my being, or relieve my sorrows—
Ha! art thou not Evanthe?—Art thou not
The lovely Maid, who bless'd the fond Arsaces?—   [*Raving.*

EVANTHE.

O, my lov'd Lord, recall your scatter'd spir'ts,
Alas! I fear your senses are unsettl'd.

ARSACES.

Yes, I would leave this dull and heavy sense.
Let me grow mad; perhaps, I then may gain
Some joy, by kind imagination form'd,
Beyond reality.—O! my Evanthe!
Why was I curs'd with empire? born to rule?—
Would I had been some humble Peasant's son,
And thou some Shepherd's daughter on the plain;

My throne some hillock, and my flock my subjects,
My crook my sceptre, and my faithful dog
My only guard; nor curs'd with dreams of greatness.
At early dawn I'd hail the coming day,
And join the lark the rival of his lay;
At sultry noon to some kind shade repair,
Thus joyful pass the hours, my only care,
To guard my flock, and please the yielding Fair.

SCENE VIII.

KING.—VARDANES *behind the Scene.*

KING.

I will not think, to think is torment—Ha!
See, how they twine! ye furies cut their hold.
Now their hot blood beats loud to love's alarms;
Sigh presses sigh, while from their sparkling eyes
Flashes desire—Oh! ye bright heav'nly beings,
Who pitying bend to suppliant Lovers' pray'rs,
And aid them in extremity, assist me!

VARDANES.

Thus, for the Trojan, mourn'd the Queen of Carthage;
So, on the shore she raving stood, and saw
His navy leave her hospitable shore.
In vain she curs'd the wind which fill'd their sails,
And bore the emblem of its change away.   [*Comes forward.*

KING.

Vardanes—Ha!—come here, I know thou lov'st me.

VARDANES.

I do, my Lord; but, say, what busy villain
Durst e'er approach your ear, with coz'ning tales,
And urge you to a doubt?

KING.

                    None, none believe me.
I'll ne'er oppress thy love with fearful doubt—
A little nigher—let me lean upon thee—
And thou be my support—for now I mean
T' unbosom to thee free without restraint:

Search all the deep recesses of my soul,
And open ev'ry darling thought before thee,
Which long I've secreted with jealous care.
Pray, mark me well.

VARDANES.

　　　　I will, my Royal Sire.

KING.

On Anna thus reclin'd the love-sick Dido;
Thus to her cheek laid hers with gentle pressure,
And wet her sister with a pearly show'r,
Which fell from her sad eyes, then told her tale,
While gentle Anna gave a pitying tear,
And own'd 'twas moving—thou canst pity too,
I know thy nature tender and engaging.

VARDANES.

Tell me, my gracious Lord, what moves you thus?
Why is your breast distracted with these tumults?
Teach me some method how to sooth your sorrows,
And give your heart its former peace and joy;
Instruct thy lov'd Vardanes.—

KING.

　　　　Yes, I'll tell thee;
But listen with attention while I speak;
And yet I know 'twill shock thy gentle soul,
And horror o'er thee 'll spread his palsy hand.
O, my lov'd Son! thou fondness of my age!
Thou art the prop of my declining years,
In thee alone I find a Father's joy,
Of all my offspring: but Arsaces—

VARDANES.

Ha!

My Brother!—

KING.

　　　　Ay—why dost start?—thy Brother
Pursues me with his hate: and, while warm life
Rolls the red current thro' my veins, delights
To see me tortur'd; with an easy smile
He meets my suff'rings, and derides my pain.

VARDANES.

Oh!

KING.

What means that hollow groan?—Vardanes, speak,
Death's image fits upon thy pallid cheek,
While thy low voice sounds as when murmurs run
Thro' lengthen'd vaults—

VARDANES.

O! my foreboding thoughts.   [*Aside.*
'Twas this disturb'd my rest; when sleep at night
Lock'd me in slumbers; in my dreams I saw
My Brother's crime—yet, death!—it cannot be—

KING.

Ha!—what was that?—

VARDANES.

O! my dread Lord, some Villain
Bred up in lies, and train'd to treach'ry,
Has injur'd you by vile reports, to stain
My Princely Brother's honour.

KING.

Thou know'st more,
Thy looks confess what thou in vain wouldst hide—
And hast thou then conspir'd against me too,
And sworn concealment to your practices?—
Thy guilt—

VARDANES.

Ha! guilt!—what guilt?—

KING.

Nay, start not so—
I'll know your purposes, spite of thy art.

VARDANES.

O! ye great Gods! and is it come to this?—
My Royal Father call your reason home,
Drive these loud passions hence, that thus deform you.
My Brother—Ah! what shall I say?—My Brother
Sure loves you as he ought.

KING.

Ha! as he ought?—
Hell blister thy evasive tongue—I'll know it—
I will; I'll search thy breast, thus will I open
A passage to your secrets—yet resolv'd—
Yet steady in your horrid villany—
'Tis fit that I from whom such monsters sprung
No more should burthen earth—Ye Parricides!—
Here plant your daggers in this hated bosom—
Here rive my heart, and end at once my sorrows,
I gave ye being, that's the mighty crime.

VARDANES.

I can no more—here let me bow in anguish—
Think not that I e'er join'd in his designs,
Because I have conceal'd my knowledge of them:
I meant, by pow'rful reason's friendly aid,
To turn him from destruction's dreadful path,
And bring him to a sense of what he ow'd
To you as King and Father.

KING.

Say on—I'll hear.

VARDANES.

He views thy sacred life with envious hate,
As 'tis a bar to his ambitious hopes.
On the bright throne of Empire his plum'd wishes
Seat him, while on his proud aspiring brows
He feels the pleasing weight of Royalty.
But when he wakes from these his airy dreams
(Delusions form'd by the deceiver hope,
To raise him to the glorious height of greatness),
Then hurl him from proud Empire to subjection.
Wild wrath will quickly swell his haughty breast,
Soon as he finds 'tis but a shadowy blessing.—
'Twas fav'ring accident discover'd to me
All that I know; this Evening as I stood
Alone, retir'd, in the still gallery,
That leads up to th' appartment of my Brother,
T' indulge my melancholy thoughts,—

KING.

Proceed—

VARDANES.

A wretch approach'd with wary step, his eye
Spoke half his tale, denoting villany.
In hollow murmurs thus he question'd me—
Was I the Prince?—I answer'd to content him—
Then in his hand he held this paper forth.
"Take this," says he, "this Bethas greets thee with,
"Keep but your word our plot will meet success."
I snatch'd it with more rashness than discretion,
Which taught him his mistake. In haste he drew,
And aim'd his dagger at my breast, but paid
His life, a forfeit, for his bold presuming.

KING.

O Villain! Villain!

VARDANES.

Here, read this, my Lord—
I read it, and cold horror froze my blood.
And shook me like an ague.

KING.

Ha!—what's this?—
"Doubt not Arabia's aid, set me but free,
"I'll easy pass on the old cred'lous King,
"For fair Evanthe's Father."—Thus to atoms—
Oh! could I tear these cursed traitors thus.

[*Tears the paper into pieces.*

VARDANES.

Curses avail you nothing, he has pow'r,
And may abuse it to your prejudice.

KING.

I am resolv'd—

VARDANES.

Tho' Pris'ner in his camp,
Yet, Bethas was attended like a Prince,
As tho' he still commanded the Arabians.
'Tis true, when they approach'd the royal city,
He threw him into chains to blind our eyes,
A shallow artifice—

KING.

That is a Truth.

VARDANES.

And, yet, he is your Son.

KING.

Ah! that indeed—

VARDANES.

Why, that still heightens his impiety,
To rush to empire thro' his Father's blood,
And, in return of life, to give him death.

KING.

Oh! I am all on fire, yes I must tear
These folds of venom from me.

VARDANES.

Sure 'twas Lysias
That cross'd the passage now.

KING.

'Tis to my wish.
I'll in, and give him orders to arrest
My traitor Son and Bethas—Now Vardanes
Indulge thy Father in this one request—
Seize, with some horse, Evanthe, and bear her
To your command—Oh! I'll own my weakness—
I love with fondness mortal never knew—
Not Jove himself, when he forsook his heav'n,
And in a brutal shape disgrac'd the God,
E'er lov'd like me.

VARDANES.

I will obey you, Sir.

SCENE IX.

VARDANES [alone].

I'll seize her, but I'll keep her for myself,
It were a sin to give her to his age—
To twine the blooming garland of the spring
Around the sapless trunks of wither'd oaks—

The night, methinks, grows ruder than it was,
Thus should it be, thus nature should be shock'd,
And Prodigies, affrighting all mankind,
Foretell the dreadful business I intend.
The earth should gape, and swallow cities up,
Shake from their haughty heights aspiring tow'rs,
And level mountains with the vales below;
The Sun amaz'd should frown in dark eclipse,
And light retire to its unclouded heav'n;
While darkness, bursting from her deep recess,
Should wrap all nature in eternal night.—
Ambition, glorious fever of the mind,
'Tis that which raises us above mankind;
The shining mark which bounteous heav'n has gave,
From vulgar souls distinguishing the brave.

End of the Third Act.

ACT IV.

SCENE I. *A Prison.*

GOTARZES *and* PHRAATES.

PHRAATES.
Oh! fly my Prince, for safety dwells not here,
Hence let me urge thy flight with eager haste.
Last night thy Father sigh'd his soul to bliss,
Base murther'd—

GOTARZES.
   Murther'd? ye Gods!—

PHRAATES.
   Alas! 'tis true.
Stabb'd in his slumber by a traitor's hand;
I scarce can speak it—horror choaks my words—
Lysias it was who did the damned deed,
Urg'd by the bloody Queen, and his curs'd rage,
Because the King, thy Sire, in angry mood,
Once struck him on his foul dishonest cheek.
Suspicion gave me fears of this, when first
I heard, the Prince, Arsaces, was imprison'd,
By fell Vardanes' wiles.

GOTARZES.

Oh! horror! horror!
Hither I came to share my Brother's sorrows,
To mingle tears, and give him sigh for sigh;
But this is double, double weight of woe.

PHRAATES.

'Tis held as yet a secret from the world.
Frighted by hideous dreams I shook off sleep,
And as I mus'd the garden walks along,
Thro' the deep gloom, close in a neighb'ring walk,
Vardanes with proud Lysias I beheld,
Still eager in discourse they saw not me,
For yet the early dawn had not appear'd;
I sought a secret stand, where hid from view,
I heard stern Lysias, hail the Prince Vardanes
As Parthia's dreaded Lord!—" 'Tis done", he cry'd,
" 'Tis done, and Artabanus is no more.
" The blow he gave me is repay'd in blood;
" Now shall the morn behold two rising suns:
" Vardanes thou, our better light, shalt bring
" Bright day and joy to ev'ry heart."

GOTARZES.

Why slept
Your vengeance, oh! ye righteous Gods?

PHRAATES.

Then told
A tale, so fill'd with bloody circumstance,
Of this damn'd deed, that stiffen'd me with horror.
Vardanes seem'd to blame the hasty act,
As rash, and unadvis'd, by passion urg'd,
Which never yields to cool reflection's place.
But, being done, resolv'd it secret, lest
The multitude should take it in their wise
Authority to pry into his death.
Arsaces was, by assassination,
Doom'd to fall. Your name was mention'd also—
But hurried by my fears away, I left
The rest unheard—

GOTARZES.

What can be done?—Reflection, why wilt thou
Forsake us, when distress is at our heels?
Phraates, help me, aid me with thy council.

PHRAATES.

Then stay not here, fly to Barzaphernes,
His conqu'ring troops are at a trivial distance;
Soon will you reach the camp; he lov'd your Brother,
And your Father with affection serv'd; haste
Your flight, whilst yet I have the city-guard,
For Lysias I expect takes my command.
I to the camp dispatch'd a trusty slave,
Before the morn had spread her blushing veil.
Away, you'll meet the Gen'ral on the road,
On such a cause as this he'll not delay.

GOTARZES.

I thank your love—

SCENE II.

PHRAATES [*alone*].
                    I'll wait behind, my stay
May aid the cause; dissembling I must learn,
Necessity shall teach me how to vary
My features to the looks of him I serve.
I'll thrust myself disguis'd among the croud,
And fill their ears with murmurs of the deed:
Whisper all is not well, blow up the sparks
Of discord, and it soon will flame to rage.

SCENE III.

QUEEN *and* LYSIAS.

QUEEN.

Haste, and shew me to the Prince Arsaces,
Delay not, see the signet of Vardanes.

LYSIAS.

Royal Thermusa, why this eagerness?
This tumult of the soul?—what means this dagger?
Ha!—I suspect—

QUEEN.

Hold—for I'll tell thee, Lysias.
'Tis—oh! I scarce can speak the mighty joy—
I shall be greatly blest in dear revenge,
'Tis vengeance on Arsaces—yes, this hand
Shall urge the shining poniard to his heart,
And give him death—yea, give the ruffian death;
So shall I smile on his keen agonies.

LYSIAS.

Ha! am I robb'd of all my hopes of vengeance,
Shall I then calmly stand with all my wrongs,
And see another bear away revenge?

QUEEN.

For what can Lysias ask revenge, to bar
His Queen of hers?

LYSIAS.

Was I not scorn'd, and spurn'd,
With haughty insolence? like a base coward
Refus'd what e'er I ask'd, and call'd a boaster?
My honour sullied, with opprobrious words,
Which can no more its former brightness know,
'Til, with his blood, I've wash'd the stains away.
Say, shall I then not seek for glorious vengeance?

QUEEN.

And what is this, to the sad Mother's griefs,
Her hope cut off, rais'd up with pain and care?
Hadst thou e'er supported the lov'd Prattler?
Hadst thou like me hung o'er his infancy,
Wasting in wakeful mood the tedious night,
And watch'd his sickly couch, far mov'd from rest,
Waiting his health's return?—Ah! hadst thou known
The parent's fondness, rapture, toil and sorrow,
The joy his actions gave, and the fond wish
Of something yet to come, to bless my age,
And lead me down with pleasure to the grave,
Thou wouldst not thus talk lightly of my wrongs.
But I delay—

LYSIAS.

To thee I then submit.
Be sure to wreck a double vengeance on him;
If that thou knowst a part in all his body,
Where pain can most be felt, strike, strike him there—
And let him know the utmost height of anguish.
It is a joy to think that he shall fall,
Tho' 'tis another hand which gives the blow.

SCENE IV.

ARSACES *and* BETHAS.

ARSACES.

Why should I linger out my joyless days,
When length of hope is length of misery?
Hope is a coz'ner, and beguiles our cares,
Cheats us with empty shews of happiness,
Swift fleeting joys which mock the faint embrace;
We wade thro' ills pursuing of the meteor,
Yet are distanc'd still.

BETHAS.

Ah! talk not of hope—
Hope fled when bright Astræa spurn'd this earth,
And sought her seat among the shining Gods;
Despair, proud tyrant, ravages my breast,
And makes all desolation.

ARSACES.

How can I
Behold those rev'rent sorrows, see those cheeks
Moist with the dew which falls from thy sad eyes,
Nor imitate distraction's frantic tricks,
And chace cold lifeless reason from her throne?
I am the fatal cause of all this sorrow,
The spring of ills,—to know me is unhappiness;—
And mis'ry, like a hateful plague, pursues
My wearied steps, and blasts the springing verdure.

BETHAS.

No;—It is I that am the source of all,
It is my fortune sinks you to this trouble;

Before you shower'd your gentle pity on me,
You shone the pride of this admiring world.—
Evanthe springs from me, whose fatal charms
Produces all this ruin.—Hear me heav'n!
If to another love she ever yields,
And stains her soul with spotted falsehood's crime,
If e'en in expectation tastes a bliss,
Nor joins Arsaces with it, I will wreck
My vengeance on her, so that she shall be
A dread example to all future times.

ARSACES.

Oh! curse her not, nor threaten her with anger,
She is all gentleness, yet firm to truth,
And blest with ev'ry pleasing virtue, free
From levity, her sex's character.
She scorns to chace the turning of the wind,
Varying from point to point.

BETHAS.

I love her, ye Gods!
I need not speak the greatness of my love,
Each look which straining draws my soul to hers
Denotes unmeasur'd fondness; but mis'ry,
Like a fretful peevish child, can scarce tell
What it would wish, or aim at.

ARSACES.

Immortals, hear!
Thus do I bow my soul in humble pray'r—
Thou, King of beings, in whose breath is fate,
Show'r on Evanthe all thy choicest blessings,
And bless her with excess of happiness;
If yet, there is one bliss reserv'd in store,
And written to my name, oh! give it her,
And give me all her sorrows in return.

BETHAS.

'Rise, 'rise my Prince, this goodness o'erwhelms me,
She's too unworthy of so great a passion.

ARSACES.

I know not what it means, I'm not as usual,
Ill-boding cares, and restless fears oppress me,

And horrid dreams disturb, and fright, my slumbers;
But yesternight, 'tis dreadful to relate,
E'en now I tremble at my waking thoughts,
Methought, I stood alone upon the shore,
And, at my feet, there roll'd a sea of blood,
High wrought, and 'midst the waves, appear'd my Father,
Struggling for life; above him was Vardanes,
Pois'd in the air, he seem'd to rule the storm,
And, now and then, would push my Father down,
And for a space he'd sink beneath the waves,
And then, all gory, rise to open view,
His voice in broken accents reach'd my ear,
And bade me save him from the bloody stream;
Thro' the red billows eagerly I rush'd,
But sudden woke, benum'd with chilling fear.

BETHAS.

Most horrible indeed!—but let it pass,
'Tis but the offspring of a mind disturb'd,
For sorrow leaves impressions on the fancy,
Which shew most fearful to us lock'd in sleep.

ARSACES.

Thermusa! ha!—what can be her design?
She bears this way, and carries in her looks
An eagerness importing violence.
Retire—for I would meet her rage alone.

SCENE V.

ARSACES *and* QUEEN.

ARSACES.

What means the proud Thermusa by this visit,
Stoops heav'n-born pity to a breast like thine?
Pity adorns th' virtuous, but ne'er dwells
Where hate, revenge, and rage distract the soul.
Sure, it is hate that hither urg'd thy steps,
To view misfortune with an eye of triumph.
I know thou lov'st me not, for I have dar'd
To cross thy purposes, and, bold in censure,
Spoke of thy actions as they merited.
Besides, this hand 'twas slew the curs'd Vonones.

QUEEN.

And darst thou insolent to name Vonones?
To heap perdition on thy guilty soul?
There needs not this to urge me to revenge—
But let me view this wonder of mankind,
Whose breath can set the bustling world in arms.
I see no dreadful terrors in his eye,
Nor gathers chilly fears around my heart,
Nor strains my gazing eye with admiration,
And, tho' a woman, I can strike the blow.

ARSACES.

Why gaze you on me thus? why hesitate?
Am I to die?

QUEEN.

Thou art—this dagger shall
Dissolve thy life, thy fleeting ghost I'll send
To wait Vonones in the shades below.

ARSACES.

And even there I'll triumph over him.

QUEEN.

O, thou vile homicide! thy fatal hand
Has robb'd me of all joy; Vonones, to
Thy Manes this proud sacrifice I give.
That hand which sever'd the friendship of thy
Soul and body, shall never draw again
Imbitt'ring tears from sorr'wing mother's eyes.
This, with the many tears I've shed, receive—
                    [*Offers to stab him.*
Ha!—I'd strike; what holds my hand?—'tis n't pity.

ARSACES.

Nay, do not mock me, with the shew of death,
And yet deny the blessing; I have met
Your taunts with equal taunts, in hopes to urge
The blow with swift revenge; but since that fails,
I'll woo thee to compliance, teach my tongue
Persuasion's winning arts, to gain thy soul;
I'll praise thy clemency, in dying accents
Bless thee for, this, thy charitable deed.

Oh! do not stand; see, how my bosom heaves
To meet the stroke; in pity let me die,
'Tis all the happiness I now can know.

QUEEN.

How sweet the eloquence of dying men!
Hence Poets feign'd the music of the Swan,
When death upon her lays his icy hand,
She melts away in melancholy strains.

ARSACES.

Play not thus cruel with my poor request,
But take my loving Father's thanks, and mine.

QUEEN.

Thy Father cannot thank me now.

ARSACES.

He will,
Believe me, e'en whilst dissolv'd in ecstacy
On fond Evanthe's bosom, he will pause,
One moment from his joys, to bless the deed.

QUEEN.

What means this tumult in my breast? from whence
Proceeds this sudden change? my heart beats high,
And soft compassion makes me less than woman:
I'll search no more for what I fear to know.

ARSACES.

Why drops the dagger from thy trembling hand?
Oh! yet be kind—

QUEEN.

No: now I'd have thee live,
Since it is happiness to die: 'Tis pain
That I would give thee, thus I bid thee live;
Yes, I would have thee a whole age a dying,
And smile to see thy ling'ring agonies.
All day I'd watch thee, mark each heighten'd pang,
While springing joy should swell my panting bosom;
This I would have—But should this dagger give
Thy soul the liberty it fondly wishes,
'Twould soar aloft, and mock my faint revenge.

ARSACES.

This mildness shews most foul, thy anger lovely.
Think that 'twas I who blasted thy fond hope,
Vonones now lies number'd with the dead,
And all your joys are buried in his grave;
My hand untimely pluck'd the precious flow'r,
Before its shining beauties were display'd.

QUEEN.

O Woman! Woman! where's thy resolution?
Where's thy revenge? Where's all thy hopes of vengeance?
Giv'n to the winds—Ha! is it pity?—No—
I fear it wears another softer name.
I'll think no more, but rush to my revenge,
In spite of foolish fear, or woman's softness;
Be steady now my soul to thy resolves.
Yes, thou shalt die, thus, on thy breast, I write
Thy instant doom—ha!—ye Gods!
                    [QUEEN *starts, as, in great fright, at hearing something.*

ARSACES.

                    Why this pause?
Why dost thou idly stand like imag'd vengeance,
With harmless terrors threatning on thy brow,
With lifted arm, yet canst not strike the blow?

QUEEN.

It surely was the Echo to my fears,
The whistling wind, perhaps, which mimick'd voice;
But thrice methought it loudly cry'd, "Forbear."
Imagination hence—I'll heed thee not—
                    [*Ghost of* ARTABANUS *rises.*
Save me—oh!—save me—ye eternal pow'rs!—
See!—see it comes, surrounded with dread terrors—
Hence—hence! nor blast me with that horrid sight—
Throw off that shape, and search th' infernal rounds
For horrid forms, there's none can shock like thine.

GHOST.

No; I will ever wear this form, thus e'er
Appear before thee; glare upon thee thus,
'Til desperation, join'd to thy damn'd crime,

Shall wind thee to the utmost height of frenzy.
In vain you grasp the dagger in your hand,
In vain you dress your brows in angry frowns,
In vain you raise your threatning arm in air,
Secure, Arsaces triumphs o'er your rage.
Guarded by fate, from thy accurs'd revenge,
Thou canst not touch his life; the Gods have giv'n
A softness to thy more than savage soul
Before unknown, to aid their grand designs.
Fate yet is lab'ring with some great event,
But what must follow I'm forbid to broach—
Think, think of me, I sink to rise again,
To play in blood before thy aching sight,
And shock thy guilty soul with hell-born horrors—
Think, think of Artabanus! and despair—   [*Sinks.*

QUEEN.
Think of thee, and despair?—yes, I'll despair—
Yet stay,—oh! stay, thou messenger of fate!
Tell me—Ha! 'tis gone—and left me wretched—

ARSACES.
Your eyes seem fix'd upon some dreadful object,
Horror and anguish clothe your whiten'd face,
And your frame shakes with terror; I hear you speak
As seeming earnest in discourse, yet hear
No second voice.

QUEEN.
    What! saw'st thou nothing?

ARSACES.
    Nothing.

QUEEN.
    Nor hear'd?—

ARSACES.
    Nor Hear'd.

QUEEN.
        Amazing spectacle!—
Cold moist'ning dews distil from ev'ry pore,
I tremble like to palsied age—Ye Gods!
Would I could leave this loath'd detested being!—
Oh! all my brain's on fire—I rave! I rave!—   [*Ghost rises again.*

Ha! it comes again—see, it glides along—
See, see, what streams of blood flow from its wounds!
A crimson torrent—Shield me, oh! shield me, heav'n.—

ARSACES.

Great, and righteous Gods!—

QUEEN.

           Ah! frown not on me—
Why dost thou shake thy horrid locks at me?
Can I give immortality?—'tis gone—   [*Ghost sinks.*
It flies me, see, ah!—stop it, stop it, haste—

ARSACES.

Oh, piteous sight!—

QUEEN.

           Hist! prithee, hist! oh death!
I'm all on fire—now freezing bolts of ice
Dart thro' my breast—Oh! burst ye cords of life—
Ha! who are ye?—Why do ye stare upon me?—
Oh!—defend me, from these bick'ring Furies!

ARSACES.

Alas! her sense is lost, distressful Queen!

QUEEN.

Help me, thou King of Gods! oh! help me! help!—
See! they envir'n me round—Vonones too,
The foremost leading on the dreadful troop—
But there, Vardanes beck'ns me to shun
Their hellish rage—I come, I come!
Ah! they pursue me, with a scourge of fire.—

                    [*Runs out distracted.*

SCENE VI.

ARSACES [*alone*].

Oh!—horror!—on the ground she breathless lies,
Silent, in death's cold sleep; the wall besmear'd
With brains and gore, the marks of her despair.
O guilt! how dreadful dost thou ever shew!
How lovely are the charms of innocence!
How beauteous tho' in sorrows and distress!—
Ha!—what noise?—   [*Clashing of swords.*

SCENE VII.

ARSACES, BARZAPHERNES *and* GOTARZES.

BARZAPHERNES.

At length we've forc'd our entrance—
O my lov'd Prince! to see thee thus, indeed,
Melts e'en me to a woman's softness; see
My eyes o'erflow—Are these the ornaments
For Royal hands? rude manacles! oh shameful!
Is this thy room of state, this gloomy goal?
Without attendance, and thy bed the pavement?
But, ah! how diff'rent was our parting last!
When flush'd with vict'ry, reeking from the slaughter,
You saw Arabia's Sons scour o'er the plain
In shameful flight, before your conqu'ring sword;
Then shone you like the God of battle.

ARSACES.

Welcome!
Welcome, my loyal friends! Barzaphernes!
My good old soldier, to my bosom thus!
Gotarzes, my lov'd Brother! now I'm happy.—
But, say, my soldier, why these threatning arms?
Why am I thus releas'd by force? my Father,
I should have said the King, had he relented,
He'd not have us'd this method to enlarge me.
Alas! I fear, too forward in your love,
You'll brand me with the rebel's hated name.

BARZAPHERNES.

I am by nature blunt—the soldier's manner.
Unus'd to the soft arts practis'd at courts.
Nor can I move the passions, or disguise
The sorr'wing tale to mitigate the smart.
Then seek it not: I would sound the alarm,
Loud as the trumpet's clangour, in your ears;
Nor will I hail you, as our Parthia's King,
'Til you've full reveng'd your Father's murther.

ARSACES.

Murther?—good heav'n!

BARZAPHERNES.

The tale requires some time;
And opportunity must not be lost;

Your traitor Brother, who usurps your rights,
Must, ere his faction gathers to a head,
Have from his brows his new-born honours torn.

ARSACES.

What, dost thou say, murther'd by Vardanes?
Impious parricide!—detested villain!—
Give me a sword, and onward to the charge,
Stop gushing tears, for I will weep in blood,
And sorrow with the groans of dying men.—
Revenge! revenge!—oh!—all my soul's on fire!

GOTARZES.

'Twas not Vardanes struck the fatal blow,
Though, great in pow'r usurp'd, he dares support
The actor, vengeful Lysias; to his breast
He clasps, with grateful joy, the bloody villain;
Who soon meant, with ruffian wiles, to cut
You from the earth, and also me.

ARSACES.

                    Just heav'ns!—
But, gentle Brother, how didst thou elude
The vigilant, suspicious, tyrant's craft?

GOTARZES.

Phraates, by an accident, obtain'd
The knowledge of the deed, and warn'd by him
I bent my flight toward the camp, to seek
Protection and revenge; but scarce I'd left
The city when I o'ertook the Gen'ral.

BARZAPHERNES.

Ere the sun 'rose I gain'd th' intelligence:
The soldiers when they heard the dreadful tale,
First stood aghast, and motionless with horror.
Then suddenly, inspir'd with noble rage,
Tore up their ensigns, calling on their leaders
To march them to the city instantly.
I, with some trusty few, with speed came forward,
To raise our friends within, and gain your freedom.
Nor hazard longer, by delays, your safety.
Already faithful Phraates has gain'd
A num'rous party of the citizens;

With these we mean t' attack the Royal Palace,
Crush the bold tyrant with surprise, while sunk
In false security; and vengeance wreck,
Ere that he thinks the impious crime be known.

ARSACES.

O! parent being, Ruler of yon heav'n!
Who bade creation spring to order, hear me.
What ever sins are laid upon my soul,
Now let them not prove heavy on this day,
To sink my arm, or violate my cause.
The sacred rights of Kings, my Country's wrongs,
The punishment of fierce impiety,
And a lov'd Father's death, call forth my sword.—

Now on; I feel all calm within my breast,
And ev'ry busy doubt is hush'd to rest;
Smile heav'n propitious on my virtuous cause,
Nor aid the wretch who dares disdain your laws.

End of the Fourth Act.

ACT V.

SCENE I. *The Palace.*

The Curtain rises, slowly, to soft music, and discovers EVANTHE
sleeping on a sofa; after the music ceases, VARDANES *enters.*

VARDANES.

Now shining Empire standing at the goal,
Beck'ns me forward to increase my speed;
But, yet, Arsaces lives, bane to my hopes,
Lysias I'll urge to ease me of his life,
Then give the villain up to punishment.
The shew of justice gains the changeling croud,
Besides, I ne'er will harbour in my bosom
Such serpents, ever ready with their stings—
But now one hour for love and fair Evanthe—
Hence with ambition's cares—see, where reclin'd,
In slumbers all her sorrows are dismiss'd,
Sleep seems to heighten ev'ry beauteous feature,
And adds peculiar softness to each grace.
She weeps—in dreams some lively sorrow pains her—
I'll take one kiss—oh! what a balmy sweetness!

Give me another—and another still—
For ever thus I'd dwell upon her lips.
Be still my heart, and calm unruly transports.—
Wake her, with music, from this mimic death.

[*Music sounds.*

SONG.

Tell me, Phillis, tell me why,
    You appear so wond'rous coy,
When that glow, and sparkling eye,
    Speak you want to taste the joy?
Prithee, give this fooling o'er,
Nor torment your lover more.

While youth is warm within our veins,
    And nature tempts us to be gay,
Give to pleasure loose the reins,
    Love and youth fly swift away.
Youth in pleasure should be spent,
Age will come, we'll then repent.

EVANTHE [*waking*].

I come, ye lovely shades—Ha! am I here?
Still in the tyrant's palace? Ye bright pow'rs!
Are all my blessings then but vis'onary?
Methought I was arriv'd on that blest shore
Where happy souls for ever dwell, crown'd with
Immortal bliss; Arsaces led me through
The flow'ry groves, while all around me gleam'd
Thousand and thousand shades, who welcom'd me
With pleasing songs of joy—Vardanes, ha!—

VARDANES.

Why beams the angry lightning of thine eye
Against thy sighing slave? Is love a crime?
Oh! if to dote, with such excess of passion
As rises e'en to mad extravagance
Is criminal, I then am so, indeed.

EVANTHE.

Away! vile man!—

VARDANES.

                If to pursue thee e'er
With all the humblest offices of love,

If ne'er to know one single thought that does
Not bear thy bright idea, merits scorn—

EVANTHE.

Hence from my sight—nor let me, thus, pollute
Mine eyes, with looking on a wretch like thee,
Thou cause of all my ills; I sicken at
Thy loathsome presence—

VARDANES.

'Tis not always thus,

Nor dost thou ever meet the sounds of love
With rage and fierce disdain: Arsaces, soon,
Could smooth thy brow, and melt thy icy breast.

EVANTHE.

Ha! does it gall thee? Yes, he could, he could;
Oh! when he speaks, such sweetness dwells upon
His accents, all my soul dissolves to love,
And warm desire; such truth and beauty join'd!
His looks are soft and kind, such gentleness
Such virtue swells his bosom! in his eye
Sits majesty, commanding ev'ry heart.
Strait as the pine, the pride of all the grove,
More blooming than the spring, and sweeter far,
Than asphodels or roses infant sweets.
Oh! I could dwell forever on his praise,
Yet think eternity was scarce enough
To tell the mighty theme; here in my breast
His image dwells, but one dear thought of him,
When fancy paints his Person to my eye,
As he was wont in tenderness dissolv'd,
Sighing his vows, or kneeling at my feet,
Wipes off all mem'ry of my wretchedness.

VARDANES.

I know this brav'ry is affected, yet
It gives me joy, to think my rival only
Can in imagination taste thy beauties.
Let him,—'twill ease him in his solitude,
And gild the horrors of his prison-house,
Till death shall—

EVANTHE.

    Ha! what was that? till death—ye Gods!
Ah, now I feel distress's tort'ring pang—
Thou canst not, villain—darst not think his death—
O mis'ry!—

VARDANES.

    Naught but your kindness saves him,
Yet bless me, with your love, and he is safe;
But the same frown which kills my growing hopes,
Gives him to death.

EVANTHE.

    O horror, I could die
Ten thousand 'mes to save the lov'd Arsaces.
Teach me the means, ye pow'rs, how to save him:
Then lead me to what ever is my fate.

VARDANES.

Not only shall he die, but to thy view
I'll bring the scene, those eyes that take delight
In cruelty, shall have enough of death.
E'en here, before thy sight, he shall expire,
Not sudden, but by ling'ring torments; all
That mischief can invent shall be practis'd
To give him pain; to lengthen out his woe
I'll search around the realm for skillful men,
To find new tortures.

EVANTHE.

    Oh! wrack not thus my soul!

VARDANES.

The sex o'erflows with various humours, he
Who catches not their smiles the very moment,
Will lose the blessing—I'll improve this softness.—[*Aside to her.*
Heav'n never made thy beauties to destroy,
They were to bless, and not to blast mankind;
Pity should dwell within thy lovely breast,
That sacred temple ne'er was form'd for hate
A habitation; but a residence
For love and gaiety.

EVANTHE.

    Oh! heav'ns!

VARDANES.
That sigh,
Proclaims your kind consent to save Arsaces.

[*Laying hold of her.*

EVANTHE.
Ha! villain, off—unhand me—hence—

VARDANES.
In vain
Is opportunity to those, who spend
An idle courtship on the fair, they well
Deserve their fate, if they're disdain'd;—her charms
To rush upon, and conquer opposition,
Gains the Fair one's praise; an active lover
Suits, who lies aside the coxcomb's empty whine,
And forces her to bliss.

EVANTHE.
Ah! hear me, hear me,
Thus kneeling, with my tears, I do implore thee:
Think on my innocence, nor force a joy
Which will ever fill thy soul with anguish.
Seek not to load my ills with infamy,
Let me not be a mark for bitter scorn,
To bear proud virtue's taunts and mocking jeers,
And like a flow'r, of all its sweetness robb'd,
Be trod to earth, neglected and disdain'd,
And spurn'd by ev'ry vulgar saucy foot.

VARDANES.
Speak, speak forever—music's in thy voice,
Still attentive will I listen to thee,
Be hush'd as night, charm'd with the magic sound.

EVANTHE.
Oh! teach me, heav'n, soft moving eloquence,
To bend his stubborn soul to gentleness.—
Where is thy virtue? Where thy princely lustre?
Ah! wilt thou meanly stoop to do a wrong,
And stain thy honour with so foul a blot?
Thou who shouldst be a guard to innocence.
Leave force to brutes—for pleasure is not found
Where still the soul's averse; horror and guilt,
Distraction, desperation chace her hence.

Some happier gentle Fair one you may find,
Whose yielding heart may bend to meet your flame,
In mutual love soft joys alone are found;
When souls are drawn by secret sympathy,
And virtue does on virtue smile.

VARDANES.

No more—
Her heav'nly tongue will charm me from th' intent—
Hence coward softness, force shall make me blest.

EVANTHE.

Assist me, ye bless't pow'rs!—oh! strike, ye Gods!
Strike me, with thunder dead, this moment, e'er
I suffer violation—

VARDANES.

'Tis in vain,
The idle pray'rs by fancy'd grief put up,
Are blown by active winds regardless by,
Nor ever reach the heav'ns.

SCENE II.

VARDANES, EVANTHE and LYSIAS.

LYSIAS.

Arm, arm, my Lord!—

VARDANES.

Damnation! why this interruption now?—

LYSIAS.

Oh! arm! my noble Prince, the foe's upon us.
Arsaces, by Barzaphernes releas'd,
Join'd with the citizens, assaults the Palace,
And swears revenge for Artabanus' death.

VARDANES.

Ha! what? revenge for Artabanus' death?—
'Tis the curse of Princes that their counsels,
Which should be kept like holy mysteries,
Can never rest in silent secrecy.
Fond of employ, some cursed tattling tongue
Will still divulge them.

LYSIAS.
> Sure some fiend from hell,
In mischief eminent, to cross our views,
Has giv'n th' intelligence, for man could not.

EVANTHE.
> Oh! ever blest event!—All-gracious heav'n!
This beam of joy revives me.

SCENE III.

VARDANES, EVANTHE, LYSIAS, *to them, an* OFFICER.

OFFICER.
> Haste! my Lord!
Or all will soon be lost; tho' thrice repuls'd
By your e'erfaithful guards, they still return
With double fury.

VARDANES.
> Hence, then, idle love—
Come forth, my trusty sword—curs'd misfortune!—
Had I but one short hour, without reluctance,
I'd meet them, tho' they brib'd the pow'rs of hell,
To place their furies in the van: Yea, rush
To meet this dreadful Brother 'midst the war—
Haste to the combat—Now a crown or death—
The wretch who dares to give an inch of ground
Till I retire, shall meet the death he shun'd.
Away—away! delays are dang'rous now—

SCENE IV.

EVANTHE [*alone*].

Now heav'n be partial to Arsaces' cause,
Nor leave to giddy chance when virtue strives;
Let victory sit on his warlike helm,
For justice draws his sword: be thou his aid,
And let the opposer's arm sink with the weight
Of his most impious crimes—be still my heart,
For all that thou canst aid him with is pray'r.
Oh! that I had the strength of thousands in me!
Or that my voice could wake the sons of men
To join, and crush the tyrant!—

SCENE V.

EVANTHE *and* CLEONE.

EVANTHE.

My Cleone—
Welcome thou partner of my joys and sorrows.

CLEONE.

Oh! yonder terror triumphs uncontroul'd,
And glutton death seems never satisfy'd.
Each soft sensation lost in thoughtless rage,
And breast to breast, oppos'd in furious war,
The fiery Chiefs receive the vengeful steel.
O'er lifeless heaps of men the soldiers climb
Still eager for the combat, while the ground
Made slipp'ry by the gushing streams of gore
Is treach'rous to their feet.—Oh! horrid sight!—
Too much for me to stand, my life was chill'd,
As from the turret I beheld the fight,
It forc'd me to retire.

EVANTHE.

What of Arsaces?

CLEONE.

I saw him active in the battle, now,
Like light'ning, piercing thro' the thickest foe,
Then scorning to disgrace his sword in low
Plebeian blood—loud for Vardanes call'd—
To meet him singly, and decide the war.

EVANTHE.

Save him, ye Gods!—oh! all my soul is fear—
Fly, fly Cleone, to the tow'r again,
See how fate turns the ballance; and pursue
Arsaces with thine eye; mark ev'ry blow,
Observe if some bold villain dares to urge
His sword presumptuous at my Hero's breast.
Haste, my Cleone, haste, to ease my fears.

Scene VI.

Evanthe [*alone*].

Ah!—what a cruel torment is suspense!
My anxious soul is torn 'twixt love and fear,
Scarce can I please me with one fancied bliss
Which kind imagination forms, but reason,
Proud, surly reason, snatches the vain joy,
And gives me up again to sad distress.
Yet I can die, and should Arsaces fall
This fatal draught shall ease me of my sorrows.

Scene VII.

Cleone [*alone*].

Oh! horror! horror! horror!—cruel Gods!—
I saw him fall—I did— pierc'd thro' with wounds—
Curs'd! curs'd Vardanes!—hear'd the gen'ral cry,
Which burst, as tho' all nature had dissolv'd.
Hark! how they shout! the noise seems coming this way.

Scene VIII.

Arsaces, Gotarzes, Barzaphernes *and* Officers, *with*
Vardanes *and* Lysias, *prisoners*.

Arsaces.

Thanks to the ruling pow'rs who blest our arms,
Prepare the sacrifices to the Gods,
And grateful songs of tributary praise.—
Gotarzes, fly, my Brother, find Evanthe,
And bring the lovely mourner to my arms.

Gotarzes.

Yes, I'll obey you, with a willing speed.　　　[*Exit* Gotarzes.

Arsaces.

Thou, Lysias, from yon tow'r's aspiring height
Be hurl'd to death, thy impious hands are stain'd
With royal blood—Let the traitor's body
Be giv'n to hungry dogs.

LYSIAS.

Welcome, grim death!—
I've fed thy maw with Kings, and lack no more
Revenge—Now, do thy duty, Officer.

OFFICER.

Yea, and would lead all traitors gladly thus,—
The boon of their deserts.

SCENE IX.

ARSACES, VARDANES, BARZAPHERNES.

ARSACES.

But for Vardanes,
The Brother's name forgot—

VARDANES.

You need no more,
I know the rest—Ah! death is near, my wounds
Permit me not to live—my breath grows short,
Curs'd be Phraates' arm which stop'd my sword,
Ere it had reach'd thy proud exulting heart.
But the wretch paid dear for his presuming;
A just reward.—

ARSACES.

He sinks, yet bear him up—

VARDANES.

Curs'd be the multitude which o'erpow'r'd me,
And beat me to the ground, cover'd with wounds—
But, oh! 'tis done! my ebbing life is done—
I feel death's hand upon me—Yet, I die
Just as I wish, and daring for a crown,
Life without rule is my disdain; I scorn
To swell a haughty Brother's sneaking train,
To wait upon his ear with flatt'ring tales,
And court his smiles; come, death, in thy cold arms,
Let me forget Ambition's mighty toil,
And shun the triumphs of a hated Brother—
O! bear me off— Let not his eyes enjoy
My agonies—My sight grows dim with death.

[*They bear him off.*

SCENE (*the Last*).

ARSACES, GOTARZES, BARZAPHERNES, *and* EVANTHE *supported.*

EVANTHE.

Lead me, oh! lead me, to my lov'd Arsaces.
Where is he?—

ARSACES.

Ha! what's this?—Just heav'ns!—my fears—

EVANTHE.

Arsaces, oh! thus circl'd in thy arms,
I die without a pang.

ARSACES.

Ha! die?—why stare ye,
Ye lifeless ghosts? Have none of ye a tongue
To tell me I'm undone?

GOTARZES.

Soon, my Brother,
Too soon, you'll know it by the sad effects;
And if my grief will yet permit my tongue
To do its office, thou shalt hear the tale.
Cleone, from the turret, view'd the battle,
And on Phraates fix'd her erring sight,
Thy brave unhappy friend she took for thee,
By his garb deceiv'd, which like to thine he wore.
Still with her eye she follow'd him, where e'er
He pierc'd the foe, and to Vardanes' sword
She saw him fall a hapless victim, then,
In agonies of grief, flew to Evanthe,
And told the dreadful tale—the fatal bowl
I saw—

ARSACES.

Be dumb, nor ever give again
Fear to the heart, with thy ill-boding voice.

EVANTHE.

Here, I'll rest, till death, on thy lov'd bosom,
Here let me sigh my—Oh! the poison works—

ARSACES.

Oh! horror!—

EVANTHE.

Cease—this sorrow pains me more
Than all the wringing agonies of death,
The dreadful parting of the soul from, this,
Its wedded clay—Ah! there—that pang shot thro'
My throbbing heart—

ARSACES.

Save her, ye Gods!—oh! save her!
And I will bribe ye with clouds of incense;
Such num'rous sacrifices, that your altars
Shall even sink beneath the mighty load.

EVANTHE.

When I am dead, dissolv'd to native dust,
Yet let me live in thy dear mem'ry—
One tear will not be much to give Evanthe.

ARSACES.

My eyes shall e'er two running fountains be,
And wet thy urn with everflowing tears,
Joy ne'er again within my breast shall find
A residence—Oh! speak, once more—

EVANTHE.

Life's just out—
My Father—Oh! protect his honour'd age,
And give him shelter from the storms of fate,
He's long been fortune's sport—Support me—Ah!—
I can no more—my glass is spent—farewell—
Forever—Arsaces!—Oh!   [*Dies.*

ARSACES.

Stay, oh! stay,
Or take me with thee—dead! she's cold and dead!
Her eyes are clos'd, and all my joys are flown—
Now burst ye elements, from your restraint,
Let order cease, and chaos be again.
Break! break, tough heart!—oh! torture—life dissolve—
Why stand ye idle? Have I not one friend
To kindly free me from this pain? One blow,
One friendly blow would give me ease.

BARZAPHERNES.

The Gods
Forefend!—Pardon me, Royal Sir, if I

Dare, seemingly disloyal, seize your sword,
Despair may urge you far—

ARSACES.

Ha! traitors! rebels!—
Hoary rev'rend Villain! what, disarm me?
Give me my sword—what, stand ye by, and see
Your Prince insulted? Are ye rebels all?—

BARZAPHERNES.

Be calm, my gracious Lord!

GOTARZES.

Oh! my lov'd Brother!

ARSACES.

Gotarzes too! all! all! conspir'd against me?
Still, are ye all resolv'd that I must live,
And feel the momentary pangs of death?—
Ha!—this, shall make a passage for my soul—

[*Snatches* BARZAPHERNES' *sword.*

Out, out vile cares, from your distress'd abode— [*Stabs himself.*

BARZAPHERNES.

Oh! ye eternal Gods!

GOTARZES.

Distraction! heav'ns!
I shall run mad—

ARSACES.

Ah! 'tis in vain to grieve—
The steel has done its part, and I'm at rest.—
Gotarzes, wear my crown, and be thou blest,
Cherish, Barzaphernes, my trusty chief—
I faint, oh! lay me by Evanthe's side—
Still wedded in our deaths—Bethas—

BARZAPHERNES.

Despair,
My Lord, has broke his heart, I saw him stretch'd,
Along the flinty pavement, in his gaol—
Cold, lifeless—

ARSACES.

He's happy then—had he heard
This tale, he'd—Ah! Evanthe chides my soul.
For ling'ring here so long—another pang
And all the world, adieu—oh! adieu!—

[*Dies.*

GOTARZES.

Oh!

Fix me, heav'n, immoveable, a statue,
And free me from o'erwhelming tides of grief.

BARZAPHERNES.

Oh! my lov'd Prince, I soon shall follow thee;
Thy laurel'd glories whither are they fled?—
Would I had died before this fatal day!—
Triumphant garlands pride my soul no more,
No more the lofty voice of war can charm—
And why then am I here? Thus then—

[*Offers to stab* **himself.**

GOTARZES.

Ah! hold,

Nor rashly urge the blow—think of me, and
Live—My heart is wrung with streaming anguish,
Tore with the smarting pangs of woe, yet, will I
Dare to live, and stem misfortune's billows.
Live then, and be the guardian of my youth,
And lead me on thro' virtue's rugged path.

BARZAPHERNES.

O, glorious youth, thy words have rous'd the
Drooping genius of my soul; thus, let me
Clasp thee, in my aged arms; yes, I will live—
Live, to support thee in thy kingly rights,
And when thou 'rt firmly fix'd, my task's perform'd,
My honourable task—Then I'll retire,
Petition gracious heav'n to bless my work,
And in the silent grave forget my cares.

GOTARZES.

Now, to the Temple, let us onward move,
And strive t' appease the angry pow'rs above.
Fate yet may have some ills reserv'd in store,
Continu'd curses, to torment us more.
Tho', in their district, Monarchs rule alone,
Jove sways the mighty Monarch on his throne:
Nor can the shining honours which they wear,
Purchase one joy, or save them from one care.

Finis.

PONTEACH

By Robert Rogers

Major Robert Rogers

MAJOR ROBERT ROGERS
(1727–1795)

Robert Rogers, a soldier of fortune, is the *Davy Crockett* of Colonial times. Born at Dumbarton, New Hampshire, on November 17th (some authorities say 1730, another 1731, while the *Dictionary of National Biography* says 1727), he was the son of James Rogers, a farmer living in a frontier cabin at Methuen, in upper Massachusetts.

Robert's boyhood was spent in an atmosphere characteristic of pioneer life. He had scarcely passed his fifteenth year (Nevins claims in 1746), when he helped withstand an attack of Indians near his home, and this may be considered his first active experience with the Red Man. From this time on, the history of the career of Robert Rogers is the history of the efforts of the Colonists against the Indians as far west as Detroit, and as far south as South Carolina. The necessity which confronted all of the Colonists made of young Rogers one of the most expert hunters of the period, and in this connection he was associated with the famous John Stark, of Green Mountain Boys reputation. In the latter's Memoir, written by Caleb Stark, we have as graphic a pen-picture of Rogers, the hunter, at twenty-two, as we have actual likenesses of Rogers in the pictures of the time.[1]

Evidently Rogers flourished financially at this period, for we find him buying land in Massachusetts in 1753. His activity as a soldier in the French and Indian War put him in command of a company, known as "Rogers' Rangers," and he participated in the Siege of Detroit against Pontiac and the French. This experience of his must have fired Rogers with the desire, after careful consideration of the condition of the Indian, to put his special plea for the cause of the Red Man in some permanent literary form, for "Ponteach" was published in 1766, after Rogers had left America, had gone to London, and thence had taken vessel for Algiers, where he fought under Dey.

By 1761, Rogers had so far advanced in worldly standing that he could afford to turn his attention to family affairs. We find

[1] These pictures were struck off on October 1, 1776. See Smith's "British Mezzotint Portraits."

him visiting Portsmouth, New Hampshire, where Elizabeth, daughter of the Reverend Arthur Browne, lived. The two were married on June 30th of that year; but evidently there was about Robert Rogers something his father-in-law did not quite relish. For, in 1763, a dispute arose between the two, because of Rogers' increasing dissipation. That they did not reach, however, any immediate open rupture, may have been due very largely to the fact that Rogers was becoming quite a land-owner in New York and New Hampshire. It was not until March 4, 1778, after Rogers had gone through many and varied experiences, not the least of which was serving a term in the Debtors' Prison in England, that his wife was granted, by the New Hampshire Legislature, a decree of divorce. She thereupon married Captain John Poach.

Naturally, most of the interest attached to Rogers is historical, not literary. His career in the French and Indian War, outlined by him in his "Journal of the French and Indian War," which was published in London in 1765; his activity in the Cherokee War in South Carolina;[1] his association with William Bird, when he had an opportunity of studying the methods of Indian guides; his political ambitions when he returned to England in 1765— all of these are matters for the historian, and have received adequate consideration by Francis Parkman and other writers. During these activities, Rogers was not idle with his pen. He kept his Journals, and they clearly reveal how much of a ranger he was. After the fashion of the times, when he returned to England, anxious to let his friends know of the conditions in America, he not only published his Journals (1769), but also a concise account of North America (1770). But there must have been something about Rogers as a soldier of fortune that was not as straight or as honest as *Davy Crockett*. We find him, for example, entrusted with the post of Governor of Mackinac, and conducting affairs so illy that he was tried for treason. He may have advanced as a soldier through the successive ranks to Major, but it would seem that the higher up he advanced in position the more unscrupulous he became.

After serving his term in the Debtors' Prison, which began on June 14, 1773, he returned to America, at the beginning of the Revolution. Among his Colonial friends, he not only counted John Stark, the ranger, but Israel Putnam as well, both of them

[1] See the South Carolina *Gazette* files for 1760, 1761.

ardent patriots and upholders of the American cause. It would seem, in 1775, that Rogers, to all outward appearance, was himself in sympathy with America. He professed being the staunch lover of those principles which America was upholding. But General Washington soon had cause to doubt his loyalty, and he was watched. With the result that his arrest was ordered, and thereupon he confessed his adherence to the Crown. Rogers then joined the forces of General Howe, bringing with him an invaluable knowledge of the land in New York and New Jersey, and adjacent territory. He was put in command of a company, known as the "Queen's Rangers," and throughout the Revolution fought bravely on the opposing side. After returning to England, he battled for further recognition, but never received the full honours he courted. He died on May 18, 1795, in South London.

"Ponteach" was probably never given in Rogers's time. There is no record of its even having been considered by any of the theatrical companies. It was published in 1766, with a London imprint on the title-page.[1] There is some slight probability that it was given an amateur production at Lake George by the summer residents there—certainly an appropriate spot to present a play by Rogers, inasmuch as the Ranger was known in that neighbourhood, and there is now familiar to all visitors a place called "Rogers's Slide," marking one of his escapades with the Indians.

In the present collection, the editor has followed the text of the 1766 edition, fully realizing the consistent changes made by Mr. Allan Nevins in his edition of the play which, with an Introduction, Biography, and invaluable historical notes, was published in 1914 by the Caxton Club of Chicago.[2]

This piece is one which is not only interesting as representative of the early type of Indian drama in America, but it is also interesting as reflective of the attitude of a dramatist with a problem to propound. "Ponteach" is our first American problem play. Parkman claims that at least part of it was written by Rogers, thus throwing doubt on his entire claim to authorship. There is not only a dignity displayed in the drawing of the main char-

[1] Ponteach:/or the/Savages of America,/A/Tragedy/[Major Robert Rogers.] London:/Printed for the Author; and Sold by J. Millan,/opposite the Admiralty, Whitehall./M.DCC.LXVI./[Price 2s. 6d.]
[2] Ponteach/or the/Savages of America/A Tragedy/By Robert Rogers/With an Introduction/and a Biography of the Author/By Allan Nevins/Chicago/The Caxton Club/1914/

acter of the Indian, but there is a very naïve attempt at subtle humour in the characters of the Englishmen.   There is no distinct excellence in depicting Indian character as such, after the romantic manner of Cooper, although Rogers, with his English tradition, has been able to lend to his dialogue a certain dignity of diction which is striking, and which gives the play a decided literary value.   Taken, however, as an historical document— and Mr. Nevins does this—one can trace in "Ponteach" the whole range of Rogers's experience as an Indian fighter.   There are constant allusions in the text to matters which Mr. Nevins has found necessary to explain in copious footnotes, and therefore to the student I would recommend this single edition of the play. "Ponteach" is published here, not from a scholarly standpoint, but simply as an example of early Indian drama.

Of these Indian dramas, there are many examples in the early history of American playwriting.   Laurence Hutton has an entertaining chapter on the subject in his "Curiosities of the American Stage," in which he enumerates such titles as "Oroloosa," "Oroonoka," "Miautoumah," to say nothing of "Hiawatha."   "Metamora; or, The Last of the Wampanoags" was brought to success through the powerful acting of Edwin Forrest, December 15, 1829.   William Wheatley, of the Park Theatre, was likewise famed for his Indian impersonations.   Among other more or less well-known plays of the species, enumerated by Wegelin, are:

F. DEFFENBACH.   "Onliata; or, The Indian Heroine."   Philadelphia.   1821.

JOSEPH DODDRIDGE.   "Logan: The Last of the Race of Skikellemus, Chief of the Cayuga Nation."   Buffalo Creek, Brooke Co., Va.   1823.

G. W. P. CUSTIS.   "The Indian Prophecy."   A National Drama in Two Acts, founded on a most interesting and romantic occurrence in the life of General Washington.   Georgetown. 1828.

NATHANIEL DEERING.   "Carrabasset; or, The Last of the Norridgewocks."   A Tragedy in Five Acts.   Portland.   1830.

W. H. C. HOSMER.   "The Fall of Tecumseh."   Avon.   1830.

PONTEACH:

OR THE

Savages of America.

A

TRAGEDY.

LONDON:

Printed for the Author ; and Sold by J. MILLAN,
oppofite the *Admiralty, Whitehall.*

M.DCC.LXVI.

[Price 2 s. 6 d.]

FAC-SIMILE TITLE-PAGE OF THE FIRST EDITION

DRAMATIS PERSONÆ

PONTEACH,	Indian Emperor on the Great Lakes.
PHILIP *and* CHEKITAN,	Sons of Ponteach.
TENESCO,	His chief Counsellor and Generalissimo.

ASTINACO,
THE BEAR,
THE WOLF,
} Indian Kings who join with Ponteach.

TORAX *and*
MONELIA
} Son and Daughter to Hendrick, Emperor of the Mohawks.

INDIAN	Conjurer.
FRENCH	Priest.

SHARP,
GRIPE,
CATCHUM,
} Three English Governors.

Colonel COCKUM,
Captain FRISK,
} Commanders at a Garrison in Ponteach's Country.

M'DOLE *and*
MURPHEY,
} Two Indian Traders.

HONNYMAN *and*
ORSBOURN.
} Two English Hunters.

Mrs. HONNYMAN,	Wife to Honnyman, the Hunter.

Warriors, Messengers, &c.

PONTEACH:
OR THE SAVAGES OF AMERICA

ACT I.

SCENE I. *An Indian Trading House.*

Enter M'DOLE *and* MURPHEY, *two Indian Traders, and their Servants.*

M'DOLE.

So, Murphey, you are come to try your Fortune
Among the Savages in this wild Desart?

MURPHEY.

Ay, any Thing to get an honest Living,
Which 'faith I find it hard enough to do;
Times are so dull, and Traders are so plenty,
That Gains are small, and Profits come but slow.

M'DOLE.

Are you experienc'd in this kind of Trade?
Know you the Principles by which it prospers,
And how to make it lucrative and safe?
If not, you're like a Ship without a Rudder,
That drives at random, and must surely sink.

MURPHEY.

I'm unacquainted with your Indian Commerce,
And gladly would I learn the Arts from you,
Who're old, and practis'd in them many Years.

M'DOLE.

That is the curst Misfortune of our Traders,
A thousand Fools attempt to live this Way,
Who might as well turn Ministers of State.
But, as you are a Friend, I will inform you
Of all the secret Arts by which we thrive,

Which if all practis'd, we might all grow rich,
Nor circumvent each other in our Gains.
What have you got to part with to the Indians?

MURPHEY.

I've Rum and Blankets, Wampum, Powder, Bells,
And such-like Trifles as they're wont to prize.

M'DOLE.

'Tis very well: your Articles are good:
But now the Thing's to make a Profit from them,
Worth all your Toil and Pains of coming hither.
Our fundamental Maxim is this,
That it's no Crime to cheat and gull an Indian.

MURPHEY.

How! Not a Sin to cheat an Indian, say you?
Are they not Men? hav'n't they a Right to Justice
As well as we, though savage in their Manners?

M'DOLE.

Ah! If you boggle here, I say no more;
This is the very Quintessence of Trade,
And ev'ry Hope of Gain depends upon it;
None who neglect it ever did grow rich,
Or ever will, or can by Indian Commerce.
By this old Ogden built his stately House,
Purchas'd Estates, and grew a little King.
He, like an honest Man, bought all by Weight,
And made the ign'rant Savages believe
That his Right Foot exactly weigh'd a Pound:
By this for many Years he bought their Furs,
And died in Quiet like an honest Dealer.

MURPHEY.

Well, I'll not stick at what is necessary:
But his Device is now grown old and stale,
Nor could I manage such a barefac'd Fraud.

M'DOLE.

A thousand Opportunities present
To take Advantage of their Ignorance;
But the great Engine I employ is Rum,

More pow'rful made by certain strength'ning Drugs.
This I distribute with a lib'ral Hand,
Urge them to drink till they grow mad and valiant;
Which makes them think me generous and just,
And gives full Scope to practise all my Art.
I then begin my Trade with water'd Rum,
The cooling Draught well suits their scorching Throats.
Their Fur and Peltry come in quick Return:
My Scales are honest, but so well contriv'd,
That one small Slip will turn Three Pounds to One;
Which they, poor silly Souls! ignorant of Weights
And Rules of Balancing, do not perceive.
But here they come; you'll see how I proceed.
Jack, is the Rum prepar'd as I commanded?

JACK.

Yes, sir, all's ready when you please to call.

M'DOLE.

Bring here the Scales and Weights immediately.
You see the Trick is easy and conceal'd.
                    [*Shewing how to slip the scales.*

MURPHEY.

By Jupiter, it's artfully contriv'd;
And was I King, I swear I'd knight th' Inventor.
—Tom, mind the Part that you will have to act.

TOM.

Ah, never fear, I'll do as well as Jack.
But then, you know, an honest Servant's Pains
Deserve Reward.

MURPHEY.

O! I'll take care of that.

Enter a number of INDIANS *with packs of fur.*

1ST INDIAN.

So, what you trade with Indians here to-day?

M'DOLE.

Yes, if my Goods will suit, and we agree.

2ND INDIAN.

'Tis Rum we want, we're tired, hot, and thirsty.

3RD INDIAN.

You, Mr. Englishman, have you got Rum?

M'DOLE.

Jack, bring a Bottle, pour them each a Gill.
You know which Cask contains the Rum.   The Rum?

1ST INDIAN.

It's good strong Rum, I feel it very soon.

M'DOLE.

Give me a Glass.   Here's Honesty in Trade;
We English always drink before we deal.

2ND INDIAN.

Good Way enough; it makes one sharp and cunning.

M'DOLE.

Hand round another Gill.   You're very welcome.

3RD INDIAN.

Some say you Englishmen are sometimes Rogues;
You make poor Indians drunk, and then you cheat.

1ST INDIAN.

No, English good.   The Frenchmen give no Rum.

2ND INDIAN.

I think it's best to trade with Englishmen.

M'DOLE.

What is your Price for Beaver Skins per Pound?

1ST INDIAN.

How much you ask per Quart for this strong Rum?

M'DOLE.

Five Pounds of Beaver for One Quart of Rum.

1ST INDIAN.

Five Pounds?   Too much.   Which is 't you call Five Pound?

M'DOLE.

This little Weight.   I cannot give you more.

1st Indian.

Well, take 'em; weigh 'em. Don't you cheat us now.

M'Dole.

No: He that cheats an Indian should be hang'd.

[Weighing the packs.

There's Thirty Pounds precisely of the Whole;
Five times Six is Thirty. Six Quarts of Rum.
Jack, measure it to them; you know the Cask.
This Rum is sold. You draw it off the best.

[Exeunt Indians to receive their rum.

Murphey.

By Jove, you've gain'd more in a single Hour
Than ever I have done in Half a Year;
Curse on my Honesty! I might have been
A little King, and liv'd without Concern,
Had I but known the proper Arts to thrive.

M'Dole.

Ay, there's the Way, my honest Friend, to live.

[Clapping his shoulder.

There's Ninety Weight of Sterling Beaver for you,
Worth all the Rum and Trinkets in my Store;
And, would my Conscience let me to the Thing,
I might enhance my Price, and lessen theirs,
And raise my Profits to an higher Pitch.

Murphey.

I can't but thank you for your kind Instructions,
As from them I expect to reap Advantage.
But should the Dogs detect me in the Fraud,
They are malicious, and would have Revenge.

M'Dole.

Can't you avoid them? Let their Vengeance light
On others' Heads, no matter whose, if you
Are but secure, and have the Cain in Hand:
For they're indiff'rent where they take Revenge,
Whether on him that cheated, or his Friend,
Or on a Stranger whom they never saw,
Perhaps an honest Peasant, who ne'er dreamt

Of Fraud or Villainy in all his life;
Such let them murder, if they will a Score,
The Guilt is theirs, while we secure the Gain,
Nor shall we feel the bleeding Victims Pain.   *[Exeunt.*

SCENE II. *A Desart.*

Enter ORSBOURN *and* HONNYMAN, *two English Hunters.*

ORSBOURN.

Long have we toil'd, and rang'd the Woods in vain,
No Game, nor Track, nor Sign of any Kind
Is to be seen; I swear I am discourag'd
And weary'd out with this long fruitless Hunt.
No Life on Earth besides is half so hard,
So full of Disappointments, as a Hunter's:
Each Morn he wakes he views the destin'd Prey,
And counts the Profits of th' ensuing Day;
Each Ev'ning at his curs'd ill Fortune pines,
And till next Day his Hope of Gain resigns.
By Jove, I'll from these Desarts hasten home,
And swear that never more I'll touch a Gun.

HONNYMAN.

These hateful Indians kidnap all the Game.
Curse their black Heads! they fright the Deer and Bear,
And ev'ry Animal that haunts the Wood,
Or by their Witchcraft conjure them away.
No Englishman can get a single Shot,
While they go loaded home with Skins and Furs.
'Twere to be wish'd not one of them survived,
Thus to infest the World, and plague Mankind.
Curs'd Heathen Infidels! mere savage Beasts!
They don't deserve to breathe in Christian Air,
And should be hunted down like other Brutes.

ORSBOURN.

I only wish the Laws permitted us
To hunt the savage Herd where e'er they're found;
I'd never leave the Trade of Hunting then,
While one remain'd to tread and range the Wood.

HONNYMAN.

Curse on the Law, I say, that makes it Death
To kill an Indian, more than to kill a Snake.
What if 'tis Peace? these Dogs deserve no Mercy;
Cursed revengeful, cruel, faithless Devils!
They kill'd my Father and my eldest Brother.
Since which I hate their very Looks and Name.

ORSBOURN.

And I, since they betray'd and kill'd my Uncle;
Hell seize their cruel, unrelenting Souls!
Tho' these are not the same, 'twould ease my Heart
To cleave their painted Heads, and spill their Blood.
I abhor, detest, and hate them all,
And now cou'd eat an Indian's Heart with Pleasure.

HONNYMAN.

I'd join you, and soop his savage Brains for Sauce;
I lose all Patience when I think of them,
And, if you will, we'll quickly have Amends
For our long Travel and successless Hunt,
And the sweet Pleasure of Revenge to boot.

ORSBOURN.

What will you do? Present, and pop one down?

HONNYMAN.

Yes, faith, the first we meet well fraught with Furs;
Or if there's Two, and we can make sure Work,
By Jove, we'll ease the Rascals of their Packs,
And send them empty home to their own Country.
But then observe, that what we do is secret,
Or the Hangman will come in for Snacks.

ORSBOURN.

Trust me for that; I'll join with all my Heart;
Nor with a nicer Aim, or steadier Hand
Would shoot a Tyger than I would an Indian.
There is a Couple stalking now this Way
With lusty Packs; Heav'n favour our Design.

HONNYMAN.

Silence; conceal yourself, and mind your Eye.

ORSBOURN.

Are you well charg'd?

HONNYMAN.

I am.   Take you the nearest,
And mind to fire exactly when I do.

ORSBOURN.

A charming Chance!

HONNYMAN.

Hush, let them still come nearer.
                    [*They shoot, and run to rifle the* INDIANS.
They're down, old Boy, a Brace of noble Bucks!

ORSBOURN.

Well tallow'd, faith, and noble Hides upon 'em.
                                    [*Taking up a pack.*
We might have hunted all the Season thro'
For Half this Game, and thought ourselves well paid.

HONNYMAN.

By Jove, we might, and been at great Expence
For Lead and Powder, here's a single Shot.

ORSBOURN.

I swear I've got as much as I can carry.

HONNYMAN.

And faith I'm not behind; this Pack is heavy.
But stop; we must conceal the tawny Dogs,
Or their blood-thirsty Countrymen will find them,
And then we're bit.   There'll be the Devil to pay,
They'll murder us, and cheat the Hangman too.

ORSBOURN.

Right.   We'll prevent all Mischief of this Kind.
Where shall we hide their savage Carcases?

HONNYMAN.

There they will lie conceal'd and snug enough—
                                    [*They cover them.*
But stay—perhaps ere long there'll be a War,
And then their Scalps will sell for ready Cash
Two Hundred Crowns at least, and that's worth saving.

ORSBOURN.

Well! that is true, no sooner said than done—[*Drawing his knife.*
I'll strip this Fellow's painted greasy Skull. [*Strips off the scalp.*

HONNYMAN.

A damn'd tough Hide, or my Knife's devilish dull—
[*Takes the other scalp.*
Now let them sleep to-night without their Caps,
And pleasant Dreams attend their long Repose.

ORSBOURN.

Their Guns and Hatchets now are lawful Prize,
For they'll not need them on their present Journey.

HONNYMAN.

The Devil hates Arms, and dreads the Smell of Powder;
He'll not allow such Instruments about him,
They're free from training now, they're in his Clutches.

ORSBOURN.

But, Honnyman, d'ye think this is not Murder?
I vow I'm shock'd a little to see them scalp'd,
And fear their Ghosts will haunt us in the Dark.

HONNYMAN.

It's no more Murder than to crack a Louse,
That is, if you've the Wit to keep it private.
And as to Haunting, Indians have no Ghosts,
But as they live like Beasts, like Beasts they die.
I've kill'd a Dozen in this self-same Way,
And never yet was troubled with their Spirits.

ORSBOURN.

Then I'm content; my Scruples are remov'd.
And what I've done, my Conscience justifies.
But we must have these Guns and Hatchets alter'd,
Or they'll detect th' Affair, and hang us both.

HONNYMAN.

That's quickly done—Let us with Speed return,
And think no more of being hang'd or haunted;
But turn our Fur to Gold, our Gold to Wine,
Thus gaily spend what we've so slily won,
And bless the first Inventor of a Gun. [*Exeunt.*

SCENE III. *An English Fort.*

Enter Colonel COCKUM *and Captain* FRISK.

COCKUM.

What shall we do with these damn'd bawling Indians?
They're swarming every Day with their Complaints
Of Wrongs and Injuries, and God knows what—
I wish the Devil would take them to himself.

FRISK.

Your Honour's right to wish the Devil his Due.
I'd send the noisy Hellhounds packing hence,
Nor spend a Moment in debating with them.
The more you give Attention to their Murmurs,
The more they'll plague and haunt you every Day,
Besides, their old King Ponteach grows damn'd saucy,
Talks of his Power, and threatens what he'll do.
Perdition to their faithless sooty Souls,
I'd let 'em know at once to keep their Distance.

COCKUM.

Captain, You're right; their Insolence is such
As beats my Patience; cursed Miscreants!
They are encroaching; fain would be familiar:
I'll send their painted Heads to Hell with Thunder!
I swear I'll blow 'em hence with Cannon Ball,
And give the Devil an Hundred for his Supper.

FRISK.

They're coming here; you see they scent your Track,
And while you'll listen, they will ne'er be silent,
But every Day improve in Insolence.

COCKUM.

I'll soon dispatch and storm them from my Presence.

Enter PONTEACH, *and other Indian* CHIEFS.

PONTEACH.

Well, Mr. Colonel Cockum, what d' they call you?
You give no Answer yet to my Complaint;
Your Men give my Men always too much Rum,
Then trade and cheat 'em. What! d' ye think this right?

COCKUM.

Tush! Silence! hold your noisy cursed Nonsense;
I've heard enough of it; what is it to me?

PONTEACH.

What! you a Colonel, and not command your Men?
Let ev'ry one be a Rogue that has a Mind to 't.

COCKUM.

Why, curse your Men, I suppose they wanted Rum;
They'll rarely be content, I know, without it.

PONTEACH.

What then? If Indians are such Fools, I think
White Men like you should stop and teach them better.

COCKUM.

I'm not a Pedagogue to your curs'd Indians.   [*Aside.*

PONTEACH.

Colonel, I hope that you'll consider this.

FRISK.

Why, don't you see the Colonel will not hear you?
You'd better go and watch your Men yourself,
Nor plague us with your cursed endless Noise;
We've something else to do of more Importance.

PONTEACH.

Hah! Captain Frisk, what! you a great man too?
My Bus'ness here is only with your Colonel;
And I'll be heard, or know the Reason why.

1ST CHIEF.

I thought the English had been better Men.

2ND CHIEF.

Frenchmen would always hear an Indian speak,
And answer fair, and make good Promises.

COCKUM.

You may be d——d, and all your Frenchmen too.

PONTEACH.

Be d——d! what's that? I do not understand.

COCKUM.

The Devil teach you; he'll do it without a Fee.

PONTEACH.

The Devil teach! I think you one great Fool.
Did your King tell you thus to treat the Indians?
Had he been such a Dunce he ne'er had conquer'd,
And made the running French for Quarter cry.
I always mind that such proud Fools are Cowards,
And never do aught that is great or good.

COCKUM.

Forbear your Impudence, you curs'd old Thief;
This Moment leave my Fort, and to your Country.
Let me hear no more of your hellish Clamour,
Or to D——n I will blow you all,
And feast the Devil with one hearty Meal.

PONTEACH.

So ho! Know you whose Country you are in?
Think you, because you have subdu'd the French,
That Indians too are now become your Slaves?
This Country's mine, and here I reign as King;
I value not your Threats, nor Forts, nor Guns;
I have got Warriors, Courage, Strength, and Skill.
Colonel, take care; the Wound is very deep,
Consider well, for it is hard to cure.   [*Exeunt* INDIANS.

FRISK.

Vile Infidels! observe their Insolence;
Old Ponteach puts on a mighty Air.

COCKUM.

They'll always be a Torment till destroy'd,
And sent all headlong to the Devil's Kitchen.
This curs'd old Thief, no doubt, will give us Trouble,
Provok'd and madded at his cool Reception.

FRISK.

Oh! Colonel, they are never worth our minding,
What can they do against our Bombs and Cannon?
True, they may skulk, and kill and scalp a few,

But, Heav'n be thank'd, we're safe within these Walls:
Besides, I think the Governors are coming,
To make them Presents, and establish Peace.

COCKUM.

That may perhaps appease their bloody Minds,
And keep them quiet for some little Term.
God send the Day that puts them all to sleep,
Come, will you crack a Bottle at my Tent?

FRISK.

With all my Heart, and drink D——n to them.

COCKUM.

I can in nothing more sincerely join.   [*Exeunt.*

SCENE IV. *An Apartment in the Fort.*

Enter Governors SHARP, GRIPE, *and* CATCHUM.

SHARP.

Here are we met to represent our King,
And by his royal Bounties to conciliate
These Indians' Minds to Friendship, Peace, and Love.
But he that would an honest Living get
In Times so hard and difficult as these,
Must mind that good old Rule, Take care of One.

GRIPE.

Ay, Christian Charity begins at home;
I think it's in the Bible, I know I've read it.

CATCHUM.

I join with Paul, that he's an Infidel
Who does not for himself and Friends provide.

SHARP.

Yes, Paul in fact was no bad Politician,
And understood himself as well as most.
All good and wise Men certainly take care
To help themselves and Families the first;
Thus dictates Nature, Instinct, and Religion,
Whose easy Precepts ought to be obey'd.

GRIPE.

But how does this affect our present Purpose?
We've heard the Doctrine; what's the Application?

SHARP.

We are intrusted with these Indian Presents.
A Thousand Pound was granted by the King,
To satisfy them of his Royal Goodness,
His constant Disposition to their Welfare,
And reconcile their savage Minds to Peace.
Five hundred's gone; you know our late Division,
Our great Expence, *Et cetera*, no Matter:
The other Half was laid out for these Goods,
To be distributed as we think proper;
And whether Half (I only put the Question)
Of these said Goods, won't answer every End,
And bring about as long a lasting Peace
As tho' the Whole were lavishly bestow'd?

CATCHUM.

I'm clear upon 't they will, if we affirm
That Half's the Whole was sent them by the King.

GRIPE.

There is no doubt but that One Third wou'd answer,
For they, poor Souls! are ign'rant of the Worth
Of single Things, nor know they how to add
Or calculate, and cast the whole Amount.

SHARP.

Why, Want of Learning is a great Misfortune.
How thankful should we be that we have Schools,
And better taught and bred than these poor Heathen.

CATCHUM.

Yes, only these Two simple easy Rules,
Addition and Subtraction, are great Helps,
And much contribute to our happiness.

SHARP.

'Tis these I mean to put in Practice now;
Subtraction from these Royal Presents makes
Addition to our Gains without a Fraction.

But let us overhaul and take the best,
Things may be given that won't do to sell.
[They overhaul the goods, &c.

CATCHUM.

Lay these aside; they'll fetch a noble Price.

GRIPE.

And these are very saleable, I think.

SHARP.

The Indians will be very fond of these.
Is there the Half, think you?

GRIPE.

It's thereabouts.

CATCHUM.

This bag of Wampum may be added yet.

SHARP.

Here, Lads, convey these Goods to our Apartment.

SERVANT.

The Indians, sir, are waiting at the Gate.

GRIPE.

Conduct them in when you've disposed of these.

CATCHUM.

This should have been new-drawn before they enter'd.
[Pulling out an inventory of the whole goods.

GRIPE.

What matters that? They cannot read, you know,
And you can read to them in gen'ral Terms.

Enter PONTEACH, *with several of his Chieftains.*

SHARP.

Welcome, my Brothers, we are glad to meet you,
And hope that you will not repent our coming.

PONTEACH.

We're glad to see our Brothers here the English.
If honourable Peace be your Desire,

We'd always have the Hatchet buried deep,
While Sun and Moon, Rivers and Lakes endure,
And Trees and Herbs within our Country grow.
But then you must not cheat and wrong the Indians,
Or treat us with Reproach, Contempt, and Scorn;
Else we will raise the Hatchet to the Sky,
And let it never touch the Earth again,
Sharpen its Edge, and keep it bright as Silver,
Or stain it red with Murder and with Blood.
Mind what I say, I do not tell you Lies.

SHARP.

We hope you have no Reason to complain
That Englishmen conduct to you amiss;
We're griev'd if they have given you Offence,
And fain would heal the Wound while it is fresh,
Lest it should spread, grow painful, and severe.

PONTEACH.

Your Men make Indians drunk, and then they cheat 'em.
Your Officers, your Colonels, and your Captains
Are proud, morose, ill-natur'd, churlish Men,
Treat us with Disrespect, Contempt, and Scorn.
I tell you plainly this will never do,
We never thus were treated by the French,
Them we thought bad enough, but think you worse.

SHARP.

There's good and bad, you know, in every Nation;
There's some good Indians, some are the reverse,
Whom you can't govern, and restrain from ill;
So there's some Englishmen that will be bad.
You must not mind the Conduct of a few,
Nor judge the rest by what you see of them.

PONTEACH.

If you've some good, why don't you send them here?
These every one are Rogues, and Knaves, and Fools,
And think no more of Indians than of Dogs.
Your King had better send his good Men hither,
And keep his bad ones in some other Country;
Then you would find that Indians would do well,
Be peaceable, and honest in their Trade;

We'd love you, treat you, as our Friends and Brothers,
And Raise the Hatchet only in your Cause.

SHARP.

Our King is very anxious for your Welfare,
And greatly wishes for your Love and Friendship;
He would not have the Hatchet ever raised,
But buried deep, stamp'd down and cover'd o'er,
As with a Mountain that can never move:
For this he sent us to your distant Country,
Bid us deliver you these friendly Belts,
                    [*Holding out belts of wampum.*
All cover'd over with his Love and Kindness.
He like a Father loves you as his Children;
And like a Brother wishes you all Good;
We'll let him know the Wounds that you complain of,
And he'll be speedy to apply the Cure,
And clear the Path to Friendship, Peace, and Trade.

PONTEACH.

Your King, I hear 's a good and upright Man,
True to his word, and friendly in his Heart;
Not proud and insolent, morose and sour,
Like these his petty Officers and Servants:
I want to see your King, and let him know
What must be done to keep the Hatchet dull,
And how the Path of Friendship, Peace, and Trade
May be kept clean and solid as a Rock.

SHARP.

Our King is distant over the great Lake,
But we can quickly send him your Requests;
To which he'll listen with attentive Ear,
And act as tho' you told him with your Tongue.

PONTEACH.

Let him know then his People here are Rogues,
And cheat and wrong and use the Indians ill.
Tell him to send good Officers, and call
These proud ill-natur'd Fellows from my Country,
And keep his Hunters from my hunting Ground.

He must do this, and do it quickly too,
Or he will find the Path between us bloody.

SHARP.

Of this we will acquaint our gracious King,
And hope you and your Chiefs will now confirm
A solid Peace as if our King was present;
We're his Ambassadors, and represent him,
And bring these Tokens of his Royal Friendship
To you, your Captains, Chiefs, and valiant Men.
Read, Mr. Catchum, you've the Inventory.

CATCHUM.

The British King, of his great Bounty, sends
To Ponteach, King upon the Lakes, and his Chiefs,
Two hundred, No [Aside] a Number of fine Blankets,
Six hundred [Aside] Yes, and several Dozen Hatchets,
Twenty thousand [Aside] and a Bag of Wampum,
A Parcel too of Pans, and Knives, and Kettles.

SHARP.

This rich and royal Bounty you'll accept,
And as you please distribute to your Chiefs,
And let them know they come from England's King,
As Tokens to them of his Love and Favour.
We've taken this long Journey at great Charge,
To see and hold with you this friendly Talk;
We hope your Minds are all disposed to Peace,
And that you like our Sovereign's Bounty well.

1ST CHIEF.

We think it very small, we heard of more.
Most of our Chiefs and Warriors are not here,
They all expect to share a Part with us.

2ND CHIEF.

These won't reach round to more than half our Tribes,
Few of our Chiefs will have a single Token
Of your King's Bounty, that you speak so much of.

3RD CHIEF.

And those who haven't will be dissatisfied,
Think themselves slighted, think your King is stingy,

Or else that you his Governors are Rogues,
And keep your Master's Bounty for yourselves.

4TH CHIEF.

We hear such Tricks are sometimes play'd with Indians.
King Astenaco, the great Southern Chief,
Who's been in England, and has seen your King,
Told me that he was generous, kind, and true,
But that his Officers were Rogues and Knaves,
And cheated Indians out of what he gave.

GRIPE.

The Devil's in 't, I fear that we're detected.   [Aside.

PONTEACH.

Indians a'n't Fools, if White Men think us so;
We see, we hear, we think as well as you;
We know there 're Lies, and Mischiefs in the World;
We don't know whom to trust, nor when to fear;
Men are uncertain, changing as the Wind,
Inconstant as the Waters of the Lakes,
Some smooth and fair, and pleasant as the Sun,
Some rough and boist'rous, like the Winter Storm;
Some are Insidious as the subtle Snake,
Some innocent, and harmless as the Dove;
Some like the Tyger raging, cruel, fierce,
Some like the Lamb, humble, submissive, mild,
And scarcely one is every Day the same;
But I call no Man bad, till such he's found,
Then I condemn and cast him from my Sight;
And no more trust him as a Friend and Brother.
I hope to find you honest Men and true.

SHARP.

Indeed you may depend upon our Honours,
We're faithful Servants of the best of Kings;
We scorn an Imposition on your Ignorance,
Abhor the Arts of Falsehood and Deceit.
These are the Presents our great Monarch sent,
He's of a bounteous, noble, princely Mind
And had he known the Numbers of your Chiefs,
Each would have largely shar'd his Royal Goodness;

But these are rich and worthy your Acceptance,
Few Kings on Earth can such as these bestow,
For Goodness, Beauty, Excellence, and Worth.

PONTEACH.

The Presents from your Sovereign I accept,
His friendly Belts to us shall be preserved,
And in Return convey you those to him.   [*Belts and furs.*
Which let him know our Mind, and what we wish,
That we dislike his crusty Officers,
And wish the Path of Peace was made more plain,
The Calumet I do not choose to smoke,
Till I see further, and my other Chiefs
Have been consulted. Tell your King from me,
That first or last a Rogue will be detected,
That I have Warriors, am myself a King,
And will be honour'd and obey'd as such;
Tell him my Subjects shall not be oppress'd,
But I will seek Redress and take Revenge;
Tell your King this; I have no more to say.

SHARP.

To our great King your Gifts we will convey,
And let him know the Talk we've had with you;
We're griev'd we cannot smoke the Pipe of Peace,
And part with stronger Proofs of Love and Friendship;
Meantime we hope you'll so consider Matters,
As still to keep the Hatchet dull and buried,
And open wide the shining Path of Peace,
That you and we may walk without a Blunder.
                                    [*Exeunt* INDIANS.

GRIPE.

Th' appear not fully satisfied, I think.

CATCHUM.

I do not like old Ponteach's Talk and Air,
He seems suspicious, and inclin'd to war.

SHARP.

They're always jealous, bloody, and revengeful,
You see that they distrust our Word and Honour;
No wonder then if they suspect the Traders,
And often charge them with downright Injustice.

GRIPE.

True, when even we that come to make them Presents,
Cannot escape their Fears and Jealousies.

CATCHUM.

Well, we have this, at least, to comfort us;
Their good Opinion is no Commendation,
Nor their foul Slanders any Stain to Honour.
I think we've done whatever Men could do
To reconcile their savage Minds to Peace.
If they're displeas'd, our Honour is acquitted,
And we have not been wanting in our Duty
To them, our King, our Country, and our Friends.

GRIPE.

But what Returns are these they've left behind?
These Belts are valuable, and neatly wrought.

CATCHUM.

This Pack of Furs is very weighty too;
The Skins are pick'd, and of the choicest Kind.

SHARP.

By Jove, they're worth more Money than their Presents.

GRIPE.

Indeed they are; the King will be no Loser.

SHARP.

The King! who ever sent such Trumpery to him?

CATCHUM.

What would the King of England do with Wampum?
Or Beaver Skins, d'ye think? He's not a Hatter!

GRIPE.

Then it's a Perquisite belongs to us?

SHARP.

Yes, they're become our lawful Goods and Chattels,
By all the Rules and Laws of Indian Treaties.
The King would scorn to take a Gift from Indians,
And think us Madmen, should we send them to him.

CATCHUM.

I understand we make a fair Division,
And have no Words nor Fraud among ourselves.

SHARP.

We throw the whole into one common Stock,
And go Copartners in the Loss and Gain.
Thus most who handle Money for the Crown
Find means to make the better Half their own;
And, to your better Judgments with Submission,
The self Neglecter's a poor Politician.
These Gifts, you see will all Expences pay; ⎞
Heav'n send an Indian Treaty every Day; ⎬
We dearly love to serve our King this way. ⎠

The End of the First Act.

ACT II.

SCENE I. *An Indian House.*

Enter PHILIP *and* CHEKITAN *from hunting, loaded with venison.*

PHILIP.

The Day's Toil's ended, and the Ev'ning smiles
With all the Joy and Pleasantness of Plenty.
Our good Success and Fortune in the Chace
Will make us Mirth and Pastime for the Night.
How will the old King and his Hunters smile
To see us loaded with the fatt'ning Prey,
And joyously relate their own Adventures?
Not the brave Victor's Shout, or Spoils of War,
Would give such Pleasure to their gladden'd Hearts.

CHEKITAN.

These, Philip, are the unstain'd Fruits of Peace,
Effected by the conqu'ring British Troops.
Now may we hunt the Wilds secure from Foes,
And seek our Food and Clothing by the Chace,
While Ease and Plenty thro' our Country reign.

PHILIP.

Happy Effects indeed! long may they last!
But I suspect the Term will be but short,

Ere this our happy Realm is curs'd afresh
With all the Noise and Miseries of War,
And Blood and Murder stain our Land again.

CHEKITAN.

What hast thou heard that seems to threaten this,
Or is it idle Fancy and Conjectures?

PHILIP.

Our Father's late Behaviour and Discourse
Unite to raise Suspicions in my Mind
Of his Designs? Hast thou not yet observ'd,
That tho' at first he favour'd England's Troops,
When they late landed on our fertile Shore,
Proclaim'd his Approbation of their March,
Convoy'd their Stores, protected them from Harm,
Nay, put them in Possession of Detroit;
And join'd to fill the Air with loud Huzzas
When England's Flag was planted on its Walls?
Yet, since, he seems displeas'd at their Success,
Thinks himself injured, treated with Neglect
By their Commanders, as of no Account,
As one subdu'd and conquer'd with the French,
As one, whose Right to Empire now is lost,
And he become a Vassal of their Power,
Instead of an Ally. At this he's mov'd,
And in his Royal Bosom glows Revenge,
Which I suspect will sudden burst and spread
Like Lightning from the Summer's burning Cloud,
That instant sets whole Forests in a Blaze.

CHEKITAN.

Something like this I have indeed perceiv'd;
And this explains what I but now beheld,
Returning from the Chace, myself concealed,
Our Royal Father basking in the Shade,
His Looks severe, Revenge was in his Eyes,
All his great Soul seem'd mounted in his Face,
And bent on something hazardous and great.
With pensive Air he view'd the Forest round;
Smote on his Breast as if oppress'd with Wrongs,
With Indignation stamp'd upon the Ground;

Extended then and shook his mighty Arm,
As in Defiance of a coming Foe;
Then like the hunted Elk he forward sprung,
As tho' to trample his Assailants down.
The broken Accents murmur'd from his Tongue,
As rumbling Thunder from a distant Cloud,
Distinct I heard, "'Tis fix'd, I'll be reveng'd;
"I will make War; I'll drown this Land in Blood."
He disappear'd like the fresh-started Roe
Pursu'd by Hounds o'er rocky Hills and Dales,
That instant leaves the anxious Hunter's Eye;
Such was his Speed towards the other Chiefs.

PHILIP.

He's gone to sound their Minds to Peace and War,
And learn who'll join the Hazards in his Cause.
The Fox, the Bear, the Eagle, Otter, Wolf,
And other valiant Princes of the Empire,
Have late resorted hither for some End
Of common Import. Time will soon reveal
Their secret Counsels and their fix'd Decrees.
Peace has its Charms for those who love their Ease,
But active Souls like mine delight in Blood.

CHEKITAN.

Should War be wag'd, what Discords may we fear
Among ourselves? The powerful Mohawk King
Will ne'er consent to fight against the English,
Nay, more, will join them as firm Ally,
And influence other Chiefs by his Example,
To muster all their Strength against our Father.
Fathers perhaps will fight against their Sons,
And nearest Friends pursue each other's Lives;
Blood, Murder, Death, and Horror will be rife,
Where Peace and Love, and Friendship triumph now.

PHILIP.

Such stale Conjectures smell of Cowardice.
Our Father's Temper shews us the reverse:
All Danger he defies, and, once resolv'd,
No Arguments will move him to relent,
No Motives change his Purpose of Revenge,

No Prayers prevail upon him to delay
The Execution of his fix'd Design:
Like the starv'd Tyger in Pursuit of Prey,
No Opposition will retard his Course;
Like the wing'd Eagle that looks down on Clouds,
All Hindrances are little in his Eye,
And his great Mind knows not the Pain of Fear.

CHEKITAN.

Such Hurricanes of Courage often lead
To Shame and Disappointment in the End,
And tumble blindfold on their own Disgrace.
True Valour's slow, deliberate, and cool,
Considers well the End, the Way, the Means,
And weighs each Circumstance attending them.
Imaginary Dangers it detects,
And guards itself against all real Evils.
But here Tenesco comes with Speed important;
His Looks and Face presage us something new.

TENESCO.

Hail, noble Youth! The News of your Return
And great Success has reach'd your Father's Ears.
Great is his Joy; but something more important
Seems to rest heavy on his anxious Mind,
And he commands your Presence at his Cabin.

PHILIP.

We will attend his Call with utmost Speed,
Nor wait Refreshment after our Day's Toil.   [*Exeunt.*

SCENE II. PONTEACH'S *Cabin.*

PONTEACH, PHILIP, CHEKITAN, *and* TENESCO.

PONTEACH.

My Sons, and trusty Counsellor Tenesco,
As the sweet smelling Rose, when yet a Bud,
Lies close conceal'd, till Time and the Sun's Warmth
Hath swell'd, matur'd, and brought it forth to View,
So these my Purposes I now reveal
Are to be kept with You, on pain of Death,

Till Time hath ripen'd my aspiring Plan,
And Fortune's Sunshine shall disclose the Whole;
Or should we fail, and Fortune prove perverse,
Let it be never known how far we fail'd,
Lest Fools shou'd triumph, or our Foes rejoice.

TENESCO.

The Life of Great Designs is Secrecy,
And in Affairs of State 'tis Honour's Guard;
For Wisdom cannot form a Scheme so well,
But Fools will laugh if it should prove abortive;
And our Designs once known, our Honour's made
Dependent on the Fickleness of Fortune.

PHILIP.

What may your great and secret Purpose be,
That thus requires Concealment in its Birth?

PONTEACH.

To raise the Hatchet from its short Repose,
Brighten its Edge, and stain it deep with Blood;
To scourge my proud, insulting, haughty Foes,
To enlarge my Empire, which will soon be yours:
Your Interest, Glory, Grandeur, I consult,
And therefore hope with Vigour you'll pursue
And execute whatever I command.

CHEKITAN.

When we refuse Obedience to your Will,
We are not worthy to be call'd your Sons.

PHILIP.

If we inherit not our Father's Valour,
We never can deserve to share his Empire.

TENESCO.

Spoke like yourselves, the Sons of Ponteach;
Strength, Courage, and Obedience form the Soldier,
And the firm Base of all true Greatness lay.

PONTEACH.

Our Empire now is large, our Forces strong,
Our Chiefs are wise, our Warriors valiant Men;
We all are furnish'd with the best of Arms,

And all things requisite to curb a Foe;
And now's our Time, if ever, to secure
Our Country, Kindred, Empire, all that's dear,
From these Invaders of our Rights, the English,
And set their Bounds towards the rising Sun.
Long have I seen with a suspicious Eye
The Strength and growing Numbers of the French;
Their Forts and Settlements I've view'd as Snakes
Of mortal Bite, bound by the Winter Frost,
Which in some future warm reviving Day
Would stir and hiss, and spit their Poison forth,
And spread Destruction through our happy Land.
Where are we now? The French are all subdued,
But who are in their Stead become our Lords?
A proud, imperious, churlish, haughty Band.
The French familiarized themselves with us,
Studied our Tongue, and Manners, wore our Dress,
Married our Daughters, and our Sons their Maids,
Dealt honestly, and well supplied our Wants,
Used no One ill, and treated with Respect
Our Kings, our Captains, and our aged Men;
Call'd us their Friends, nay, what is more, their Children,
And seem'd like Fathers anxious for our Welfare.
Whom see we now? their haughty Conquerors
Possess'd of every Fort, and Lake, and Pass,
Big with their Victories so often gain'd;
On us they look with deep Contempt and Scorn,
Are false, deceitful, knavish, insolent;
Nay, think us conquered, and our Country theirs,
Without a Purchase, or ev'n asking for it.
With Pleasure I wou'd call their King my Friend,
Yea, honour and obey him as my Father;
I'd be content, would he keep his own Sea,
And leave these distant Lakes and Streams to us;
Nay, I would pay him Homage, if requested,
And furnish Warriors to support his Cause.
But thus to lose my Country and my Empire,
To be a Vassal to his low Commanders,
Treated with disrespect and public Scorn
By Knaves, by Miscreants, Creatures of his Power;
Can this become a King like Ponteach,

Whose Empire's measured only by the Sun?
No, I'll assert my Right, the Hatchet raise,
And drive these Britons hence like frighted Deer,
Destroy their Forts, and make them rue the Day
That to our fertile Land they found the Way.

TENESCO.

No Contradiction to your great Design;
But will not such Proceeding injure us?
Where is our Trade and Commerce to be carry'd?
For they're possess'd of all the Country round,
Or whence Supplies of Implements for War?

PONTEACH.

Whence? Take them from our conquered running Foes.
Their Fortresses are Magazines of Death,
Which we can quickly turn against themselves;
And when they're driven to their destin'd Bounds,
Their Love of Gain will soon renew their Trade.
The heartless French, whene'er they see us conquer,
Will join their little Force to help us on.
Nay, many of their own brave trusty Soldiers,
In Hope of Gain, will give us their Assistance;
For Gain's their great Commander, and will lead them
Where their brave Generals cannot force their March:
Some have engag'd, when they see hope of Plunder,
In sly Disguise to kill their Countrymen.

CHEKITAN.

These Things indeed are promising and fair,
And seem a Prelude to our full Success.
But will not many Indian Chiefs refuse
To join the Lists, and hold themselves oblig'd
T' assist the Foe when hardly press'd by us?

PONTEACH.

I've sounded all their Minds; there's but a few
That are not warm and hearty in our Cause,
And those faint Hearts we'll punish at our Leisure:
For hither tends my Purpose; to subdue
The Tribes who now their annual Homage pay
To the imperious haughty Mohawk Chief,

Whose Pride and Insolence 'tis Time to curb.
He ever boasts the Greatness of his Empire,
The Swiftness, Skill and Valour of his Warriors,
His former Conquests, and his fresh Exploits,
The Terror of his Arms in distant Lands,
And on a Footing puts himself with me,
For Wisdom to contrive, and Power to do.
Such a proud Rival must not breathe the Air;
I'll die in fighting, or I'll reign alone
O'er every Indian Nation, Tribe, and Chief.
But this in solemn Silence we conceal,
Till they're drawn in to fight the common Foe,
Then from my Face, the sly Disguise I'll cast,
And shew them Ponteach to their Surprise.

TENESCO.

Thy Plan is wise, and may Success attend it;
May all the warlike numerous Tribes unite,
Nor cease to conquer while thou hast a Foe!
Then may they join and own thee for their Sovereign,
Pay full Submission to thy scepter'd Arm,
And universal Empire by thy own!

CHEKITAN.

Would you the Mohawk Emperor displease,
And wage a bloody War, by which you made
Him and his num'rous Tribes your certain Foes?

PONTEACH.

Most of his Tribes will welcome the Proposal;
For long their galled Necks have felt the Yoke,
Long wish'd for Freedom from his partial Sway,
In favour of the proud incroaching Britons.
Nay, they have oft, in spite of his Displeasure,
Rush'd forth like Wolves upon their naked Borders,
And now, like Tygers broken from their Chains,
They'll glut themselves, and revel in their Blood.

PHILIP.

Myself will undertake to make even Hendrick
Our zealous Friend against the common Foe;
His strong Attachment to them I'll dissolve,
And make him rage, and thirst for Vengeance on them.

PONTEACH.

This would be doing Honour to thyself,
And make thee worthy of thy Father's Crown.
The secret Means I will not now inquire,
Nor doubt but thus engag'd you will perform.
The Chiefs in part are knowing to my Purpose,
And think of nought but War, and Blood, and Plunder,
Till in full Council we declare our Pleasure.
But first my last Night's Dream I will relate,
Which much disturb'd my weary anxious Mind,
And must portend some signal grand Event
Of Good or Evil both to me or mine.
On yonder Plain I saw the lordly Elk
Snuffing the empty Air in seeming Sport,
Tossing his Head aloft, as if in Pride
Of his great Bulk and nervous active Limbs,
And Scorn of every Beast that haunts the Wood.
With mighty Stride he travelled to and fro,
And as he mov'd his Size was still increas'd,
Till his wide Branches reached above the Trees,
And his extended Trunk across the Plain.
The other Beasts beheld with wild Amaze,
Stood trembling round, nor dare they to approach
Till the fierce Tyger yell'd the loud Alarm,
When Bears, Cats, Wolves, Panthers, and Porcupines,
And other Beasts of Prey, with Force united
And savage Rage, attack'd the common Foe.
But as the busking Bull, when Summer Flies,
With keenest Sting disturb the grazing Herd,
Stands careless in some shady cool Retreat,
And from his Sides sweeps the envenom'd Mites,
Or shakes them with a Stamp into the Dust;
So he unmov'd amidst their Clamours stood,
Trampled and spurn'd them with his Hoofs and Horns,
Till all dispers'd in wild Disorder fled,
And left him Master of th' extended Plain.

TENESCO.

This Dream no doubt is full of some great Meaning,
And in it bears the Fate of your Design,
But whether good or ill, to me 's a Secret.

PHILIP.

It ne'er was counted ill to dream of Elks,
But aıways thought portentous of Success,
Of happy Life, and Victories in War,
Or Fortune good when we attempt the Chace.

CHEKITAN.

Such is the common Say; but here the Size
And all the Circumstances are uncommon,
And therefore can contain no common Meaning:
I fear these Things portend no Good to us,
That Mischiefs lurk like Serpents in the Grass,
Whose pois'nous deadly Bite precedes all Warning.
That this Design will end in mighty Ruin
To us and ours, Discord among our Friends,
And Triumph to our Foes.

PHILIP.

A valiant Hero!
Thou always wast a Coward, and hated War,
And lov'st to loll on the soft Lap of Peace.
Thou art a very Woman in thy Heart,
And talk'st of Snakes and Bugbears in the Dark,
Till all is Horror and Amaze about thee,
And even thy own Shadow makes thee tremble.

CHEKITAN.

Is there no Courage in delib'rate Wisdom?
Is all rank Cowardice but Fire and Fury?
Is it all womanish to re-consider
And weigh the Consequences of our Actions,
Before we desperately rush upon them?
Let me then be the Coward, a mere Woman,
Mine be the Praise of Coolness, yours of Rage.

PONTEACH.

Peace, Peace, my Sons, nor let this casual Strife
Divide your Hearts; both mean the common Good;
Go Hand in Hand to conquer and promote it.
I'll to our worthy Doctor and the Priest,
Who for our Souls' Salvation come from France;
They sure can solve the Mysteries of Fate,

And all the Secrets of a Dream explain;
Mean while, Tenesco, warn the other Chiefs
That they attend my Call within an Hour.

       [*Exeunt* PONTEACH *and* TENESCO.

PHILIP.

My Warmth perhaps has carried me too far,
But it's not in me to be cool and backward
To act or speak when Kingdoms are the Prize.
My Blood runs high at the sweet Sound of Empire,
Such as our Father's Plan ensures to us,
And I'm impatient of the least Delay.

CHEKITAN.

Thy Fire thou hast a Right to style a Virtue;
Heat is our Friend when kept within due Bounds,
But if unbridled and allowed to rage,
It burns and blisters, torments and consumes,
And, Torrent-like, sweeps every Comfort by.
Think if our Father's Plan should prove abortive,
Our Troops repuls'd, or in th' Encounter slain,
Where are our conquer'd Kingdoms then to share,
Where are our Vict'ries, Trophies, Triumphs, Crowns,
That dazzle in thy Eye, and swell thy Heart;
That nerve thy Arm, and wing thy Feet to War
With this impetuous Violence and Speed?
Crest-fallen then, our native Empire lost,
In captive Chains we drag a wretched Life,
Or fly inglorious from the conquering Foe
To barren Mountains from this fertile Land,
There to repent our Folly when too late,
In Anguish mourn, and curse our wretched Fate.

PHILIP.

But why so much of Mischiefs that may happen?
These are mere Possibilities at most;
Creatures of Thought, which ne'er can be Objections,
In valiant Minds, to any great Attempt;
They're empty Echoes of a tim'rous Soul,
Like Bubbles driv'n by the tempestuous Storm,
The Breath of Resolution sweeps them off.

Nor dost thou judge them solid from thy Heart,
I know the secret Motive in thy Breast,
Thus to oppose our Father's great Design,
And from an Undertaking to dissuade,
In which thou'lt share the Profit and the Glory.
Hendrick, the King of Mohawks, hath a Daughter,
With whom I saw you dallying in the Shade,
And thought you then a Captive to her Charms.
The bright Monelia hangs upon thy Heart,
And softens all the Passions of thy Soul;
Her thou think'st lost should we proclaim a War,
In which the King her Father will not join.

CHEKITAN.

What if I have a Value for Monelia,
Is it a Crime? Does she not merit Love
From all who see her move, or hear her speak?

PHILIP.

True, she is engaging, has a charming Air;
And if thy Love is fix'd, I will assist it,
And put thee in Possession of the Joy
That thou desirest more than Crowns and Empire.

CHEKITAN.

As how, dear Philip? Should we wage a War,
Which Hendrick disapproves, the Prize is lost.
Not Empires then could make Monelia mine;
All Hopes are dash'd upon that fatal Rock;
Nor Gold, nor Prayers, nor Tears, nor Promises,
Nor all the Engin'ry of Love at Work,
Could save a single Moment of my Joy.

PHILIP.

Yes, I will save it all, and make her thine,
Act but thy Part, and do as I prescribe,
In Peace or War thou shalt possess the Prize.

CHEKITAN.

Thy Words revive my half-despairing Heart.
What must I act? or which Way must I turn?

I'll brave all Dangers, every Ill defy,
Risk Life itself, to call Monelia mine.
Help me, my Philip, and I'll be thy Slave,
Resign my Share of Empire to thy Hand,
And lay a Claim to nothing but Monelia.

PHILIP.

Rewards I do not ask; I am thy Brother,
And hold my Kindness to thee as a Debt.
Thou know'st I have engag'd to bring King Hendrick
To join the Lists, and fight against our Foes,
To rouse him to Revenge, and Rage, and War,
And make him zealous in the common Cause.
Nay, with uncommon Fury he shall rave,
And urge his Warriors on to Blood and Murder.
When this is done, Monelia may be thine,
Hendrick will court Alliance to our Tribe,
And joy to call great Ponteach's Son his own.

CHEKITAN.

But should you fail in these Attempts, and he
Prove obstinately fix'd against the War,
Where's then Monelia? where is Chekitan?
My Hopes are blasted, all my Joys are fled,
Like the vain Phantoms of a Midnight Dream,
Are scattered like the Dust before a Whirlwind,
And all my Soul is left a Void for Pain,
Vexation, Madness, Frenzy, and Despair,
And all the Pains of disappointed Love.
Better I ne'er had flattered my fond Heart,
Nor sooth'd my Mind with Prospects of my Joy,
Than thus to perish on the Point of Hope.

PHILIP.

Leave all to me; I've so concerted Matters,
That I defy ev'n Fate to disappoint me.
Exert thyself, and to Monelia go,
Before th' assembled Chiefs in Council meet;
Urge it to her, and to her Brother Torax,
That should their Father prove refractory,
Withdraw himself, and order his Domestics

To hasten home at News of our Design;
Urge it, I say, to them; Torax loves War;
To linger here in Hopes of his Return,
Which tell them I'll effect ere twice the Sun
Has run the Circuit of his daily Race.
Here they may loiter careless, range the Woods,
As tho' the Noise of War had not been heard.
This will give full Success to both our Wishes:
Thou'lt gain the Prize of Love, and I of Wrath,
In favour to our Family and State.
Thou'lt tame the Turtle, I shall rouse the Tyger;
The one will soothe thy Soul to soft Repose,
The other prove a Terror to our Foes.

CHEKITAN.

I see the subtle Argument thou'lt use,
And how thou'lt work upon the old King's Weakness,
Thou'lt set his strong Affection for his Children
At War against his Kindness for our Foes,
By urging their Attachment to our Cause,
That they'll endure ev'n Banishment and Death,
Rather than cease to be our steadfast Friends.

PHILIP.

All this I'll urge, nay, more, I will convince him,
These Foes to us can be no Friends to him;
I'll thunder in his Ears their growing Power,
Their Villainies and Cheats upon his Subjects:
That their fair Shew of Love is foul Disguise;
That in their Hearts they hate the Name of Indians,
And court his Friendship only for their Profit;
That when no longer he subserves their Ends,
He may go whistle up some other Friends.

CHEKITAN.

This must alarm and bring him to our Mind.
I'll hasten to my Charge with utmost Speed,
Strain every Nerve, and every Power exert;
Plead, promise, swear like any Christian Trader;
But I'll detain them till our Ends are answer'd,
And you have won their Father to our Purpose.   [*Exit.*

PHILIP [*solus*].

Oh! what a wretched Thing is a Man in Love!
All Fear—all Hope—all Diffidence—all Faith—
Distrusts the greatest Strength, depends on Straws—
Soften'd, unprovident, disarm'd, unman'd,
Led blindfold; every Power denies its Aid,
And every Passion's but a Slave to this;
Honour, Revenge, Ambition, Interest, all
Upon its Altar bleed—Kingdoms and Crowns
Are slighted and condemn'd, and all the Ties
Of Nature are dissolv'd by this poor Passion:
Once have I felt its Poison in my Heart,
When this same Chekitan a Captive led
The fair Donanta from the Illinois;
I saw, admir'd, and lov'd the charming Maid,
And as a Favour ask'd her from his Hands,
But he refus'd and sold her for a Slave.
My Love is dead, but my Resentment lives,
And now's my Time to let the Flame break forth,
For while I pay this ancient Debt of Vengeance,
I'll serve my Country, and advance myself.
He loves Monelia—Hendrick must be won—
Monelia and her Brother both must bleed—
This is my Vengeance on her Lover's Head—
Then I'll affirm, 'twas done by Englishmen—
And to gain Credit both with Friends and Foes,
I'll wound myself, and say that I receiv'd it
By striving to assist them in the Combat.
This will rouse Hendrick's Wrath, and arm his Troops
To Blood and Vengeance on the common Foe.
And further still my Profit may extend;
My Brother's Rage will lead him into Danger,
And, he cut off, the Empire's all my own.
Thus am I fix'd; my Scheme of Goodness laid,
And I'll effect it, tho' thro' Blood I wade,
To desperate Wounds apply a desperate Cure,
And to tall Structures lay Foundations sure;
To Fame and Empire hence my Course I bend,
And every Step I take shall thither tend.

End of the Second Act.

Ponteach

ACT III.

SCENE I. *A Forest.*

CHEKITAN.
[*Seeing* TORAX *and* MONELIA, *coming towards them.*]

As the young Hunter, anxious in the Chace,
With beating Heart and quivering Hand espies
The wish'd for Game, and trembles for th' Event,
So I behold the bright Monelia's Steps,
Whom anxiously I've sought, approach this way—
What shall I say? or how shall I accost her?
It is a fatal Minute to mistake in.
The Joy or Grief of Life depends upon 't;
It is the important Crisis of my Fate.
I've thought a thousand things to say and do,
But know not which to say or do the first.
Shall I begin with my old Tale of Love?
Or shall I shock her with the News of War?
Must I put on the Face of Joy or Grief?
Seem unconcern'd or full of Doubts and Fears?
How unprepar'd I am for the Encounter!
I'd rather stand against an Host of Foes—
But she draws near, and Fate must guide me now,
                        [*Enter* TORAX *and* MONELIA.
Where tend your Steps with such an Air of Joy?

TORAX.

To view the Beauties of th' extended Lake,
And on its mossy Bank recline at Ease,
While we behold the Sports of Fish and Fowl,
Which in this Calm no doubt will be diverting.
And these are new Amusements to Monelia,
She never saw the Sea or Lakes before.

CHEKITAN.

I'm glad our Country's aught to give such Pleasure
To one deservedly so welcome in it.

MONELIA.

That I am welcome you have oft assur'd me.
That I deserve it you may be mistaken,

The outside Shew, the Form, the Dress, the Air,
That please at first Acquaintance, oft deceive us,
And prove more Mimickers of true Desert,
Which always brightens by a further Trial,
Appears more lovely as we know it better,
At least can never suffer by Acquaintance.
Perhaps then you To-morrow will despise
What you esteem To-day, and call deserving.

CHEKITAN.

My Love to you, Monelia, cannot change.
Your Beauty, like the Sun, for ever pleases,
And like the Earth, my Love can never move.

MONELIA.

The Earth itself is sometimes known to shake,
And the bright Sun by Clouds is oft conceal'd,
And gloomy Night succeeds the Smiles of Day;
So Beauty oft by foulest Faults is veil'd,
And after one short Blaze admir'd no more,
Loses its Lustre, drops its sparkling Charms,
The Lover sickens, and his Passion dies.
Nay, worse, he hates what he so doted on.
Time only proves the Truth of Worth and Love,
The one may be a Cheat, the other change,
And Fears, and Jealousies, and mortal Hate,
Succeed the Sunshine of the warmest Passion.

CHEKITAN.

Have I not vow'd my Love to you, Monelia,
And open'd all the Weakness of my Heart?
You cannot think me false and insincere,
When I repeat my Vows to love you still;
Each time I see you move, or hear you speak,
It adds fresh Fuel to the growing Flame.
You're like the rising Sun, whose Beams increase
As he advances upward to our View;
We gaze with growing Wonder till we're blind,
And every Beauty fades and dies but his.
Thus shall I always view your growing Charm,
And every Day and Hour with fresh Delight.

Witness thou Sun and Moon, and Stars above,
Witness ye purling Streams and quivering Lakes,
Witness ye Groves and Hills, and Springs and Plains,
Witness ye Shades, and the cool Fountain, where
I first espied the Image of her Charms,
And starting saw her on th' adjacent Bank,
If I to my Monelia prove untrue.

MONELIA.

Hoh! now your Talk is so much like a Christian's,
That I must be excus'd if I distrust you,
And think your fair Pretences all designing.
I once was courted by a spruce young Blade,
A lac'd Coat Captain, warlike, active, gay,
Cockaded Hat and Medal on his Breast,
And every thing was clever but his Tongue;
He swore he lov'd, O! how he swore he lov'd,
Call'd on his God and Stars to witness for him,
Wish'd he might die, be blown to Hell and damn'd,
If ever he lov'd woman so before:
Call'd me his Princess, Charmer, Angel, Goddess,
Swore nothing else was ever half so pretty,
So dear, so sweet, so much to please his Taste,
He kiss'd, he squeez'd, and press'd me to his Bosom,
Vow'd nothing could abate his ardent Passion,
Swore he should die, should drown, or hang himself,
Could not exist if I denied his Suit,
And said a thousand Things I cannot Name:
My simple Heart, made soft by so much Heat,
Half gave Consent, meaning to be his Bride.
The Moment thus unguarded, he embrac'd,
And impudently ask'd to stain my Virtue.
With just Disdain I push'd him from my Arms,
And let him know he'd kindled my Resentment;
The Scene was chang'd from Sunshine to a Storm,
Oh! then he curs'd, and swore, and damn'd, and sunk,
Call'd me proud Bitch, pray'd Heav'n to blast my Soul,
Wish'd Furies, Hell, and Devils had my Body,
To say no more; bid me begone in Haste
Without the smallest Mark of his Affection.
This was an Englishman, a Christian Lover.

CHEKITAN.

Would you compare an Indian Prince to those
Whose Trade it is to cheat, deceive, and flatter?
Who rarely speak the Meaning of their Hearts?
Whose Tongues are full of Promises and Vows?
Whose very Language is a downright Lie?
Who swear and call on Gods when they mean nothing?
Who call it complaisant, polite good Breeding,
To say Ten thousand things they don't intend,
And tell their nearest Friends the basest Falsehood?
I know you cannot think me so perverse,
Such Baseness dwells not in an Indian's Heart,
And I'll convince you that I am no Christian.

MONELIA.

Then do not swear, nor vow, nor promise much,
An honest Heart needs none of this Parade;
Its Sense steals softly to the list'ning Ear,
And Love, like a rich Jewel we most value,
When we ourselves by Chance espy its Blaze
And none proclaims where we may find the Prize.
Mistake me not, I don't impeach your Honour,
Nor think you undeserving my Esteem;
When our Hands join you may repeat your Love,
But save these Repetitions from the Tongue.

CHEKITAN.

Forgive me, if my Fondness is too pressing,
'Tis Fear, 'tis anxious Fear, that makes it so.

MONELIA.

What do you fear? have I not said enough?
Or would you have me swear some Christian Oath?

CHEKITAN.

No, but I fear our Love will be oppos'd,
Your Father will forbid our Hands to join.

MONELIA.

I cannot think it; you are Ponteach's Son,
Heir to an Empire large and rich as his.

CHEKITAN.

True; but your Father is a Friend to Britons,
And mine a Foe, and now is fix'd on War,
Immediate War: This Day the Chiefs assemble,
To raise the Hatchet, and to arm the Troops.

MONELIA.

Then I must leave your Realm, and bid Adieu,
In spite of your fond Passion, or my own;
For I can never disoblige my Father,
Though by it I were sure to gain an Empire.

CHEKITAN.

Then Chekitan's undone, undone for ever.
Unless your Father by kind Fate is mov'd
To be our Friend, and join the Lists with mine.

TORAX.

Nothing would please me better; I love War,
And think it time to curb the English Pride,
And give a check to their increasing Power.
The Land is ravag'd by their numerous Bands,
And every Day they're growing more our Lords.

CHEKITAN.

Are you sincere, or do you feign this Speech?

TORAX.

Indeed my Tongue does not bely my Heart;
And but my Father's wrong-turn'd Policy
Forbids, I'd instant join in War with you,
And help to set new Limits to their Power.

CHEKITAN.

'Tis plain, if they proceed, nor you nor I
Shall rule an Empire, or possess a Crown,
Our Countries all will soon become a Prey
To Strangers; we perhaps shall be their Slaves.
But will your Father be convinc'd of this?

TORAX.

I doubt he'll not. The good old Man esteems
And dotes upon them as most worthy Friends;

I've told him often that he cherish'd Serpents,
To bite his Children, and destroy his Friends.
But this he calls the Folly of my Youth,
Bids me be silent, show Respect to Age,
Nor sow Sedition in my Father's Empire.

CHEKITAN.

Stiff as he is, he yet may be subdued;
And I've a Power prepar'd that will attack him.
Should he refuse his Aid to our Design,
Retire himself, and bid his Troops to follow,
Yet Philip stands engag'd for his Return,
Ere twice the Sun has ris'n and blest the Earth.
Philip is eloquent, and so prepar'd,
He cannot fail to bend him to our Purpose.
You and Monelia have a Part to act;
To linger here, should he in Haste retreat
Till Philip follows and employs his Force.
Your Stay will add new Life to the Design,
And be of mighty Weight to gain Success.

MONELIA.

How shall we tarry midst the Noise of War,
In Danger of our Lives from Friends and Foes;
This will be deem'd a Madness by our Father,
And will deserve his most severe Rebuke.

CHEKITAN.

Myself will be a Sponsor for your Safety;
And should your Father baffle our Attempts,
Conduct you home from all the Noise of War,
Where may you long in Peace and Plenty smile,
While I return to mourn my hapless Fate.
But should Success attend on Philip's Purpose.
Your Father will not discommend your Stay,
But smiling give new Vigour to the War;
Which being ended, and our Foes subdu'd,
The happy Fruits of Peace succeed to all,
But we shall taste the greater Sweets of Love.

TORAX.

The Purport of our Stay is hid from me;

But Philip 's subtle, crafty as the Fox.
We'll give full Scope to his enticing Art,
And help him what we can to take the Prey.

MONELIA.

In your Protection then I trust myself,
Nor will delay beyond th' appointed Term,
Lest anxious Fears possess our Father's Heart,
Or Mischiefs happen that incur his Anger.

TORAX.

It is agreed; we now pursue our Walk;
Mean time consult what else may be of Use,
You're pain'd with Love, and I'm in Pain for War.   [*Exeunt.*

CHEKITAN [*solus*].

The Game is sure—Her Brother's on my Side—
Her Brother and my own—My Force is strong—
But could her Father now be rous'd to War,
How should I triumph and defy even Fate?
But Fortune favours all advent'rous Souls:
I'll now to Philip; tell him my Success,
And rouse up every Spark of Vigour in him:
He will conceive fresh Hopes, and be more zealous.

SCENE II. PONTEACH'S *Cabin.*

PONTEACH, *an Indian* CONJURER, *and French* PRIEST.

PONTEACH.

Well! have you found the Secret of my Dream,
By all your Cries, and Howls, and Sweats, and Prayers?
Or is the Meaning still conceal'd from Man,
And only known to Genii and the Gods?

CONJURER.

Two Hours I've lain within the sultry Stove,
While Floods of Sweat ran trickling from my Skin;
With Howls and Cries and all the Force of Sound
Have I invok'd your Genius and my own,
Smote on my Breast, and beat against my Head,

To move an Answer, and the Secret learn.
But all in vain, no Answer can I have,
Till I first learn what secret Purposes
And great Designs are brooding in your Mind.

PRIEST.

At our pure Virgin's Shrine I've bowed my Knees,
And there in fervent Prayer pour'd out my Soul;
Call'd on Saint Peter, call'd on all the Saints
That know the Secrets both of Heaven and Earth,
And can reveal what Gods themselves can do:
I've us'd the Arts of our most holy Mother,
Which I receiv'd when I forsook the World,
And gave myself to Holiness and Heaven;
But can't obtain the Secret of your Dream,
Till I first know the Secrets of your Heart,
Or what you hope or wish to be effected.
'Tis on these Terms we learn the Will of God,
What Good or Ill awaits on Kings or Kingdoms;
And without this, St. Peter's Self can't tell,
But at a Dream like yours would be confounded.

PONTEACH.

You're well agreed—Our Gods are much alike—
And I suspect both Rogues—What! won't they tell!
Should they betray my Scheme, the whole is blown.
And yet I fain would know.   I'll charge them first.   [*Aside.*
Look here; if I disclose a Secret to you,
Tell it to none but silent honest Gods;
Death to you both, if you reveal to Men.

BOTH.

We will, we will, the Gods alone shall know.

PONTEACH.

Know then that I have fix'd on speedy War,
To drive these new Encroachers from my Country.
For this I meant t' engage our several Tribes,
And when our Foes are driven to their Bounds,
That we may stand and hold our Rights secure,
Unite our Strength under one common Head,

Whom all these Petty Kings must own their Lord,
Not even Hendrick's self shall be excused.
This is my Purpose. Learn if it shall prosper,
Or will it end in Infamy and Shame?

CONJURER.

[*Smiting on his breast, groaning, and muttering in his cloak or blanket, falls down upon the ground, beats his head against it, and pretends to listen: then rises, and says with a rumbling hideous voice:*]

Success and Victory shall attend your Arms;
You are the mighty Elk that none can conquer,
And all the Tribes shall own you for their King.
Thus, say the Genii, does your Dream intend.

PRIEST.

[*Looking up to Heaven in a praying posture for a small space, says:*]

Had I but known you was resolv'd on War,
And War against those Heretics the English,
I need not to have ask'd a God or Saint
To signify the Import of your Dream.
Your great Design shall have a prosperous End,
'Tis by the Gods approv'd, and must succeed.
Angels and Saints are dancing now in Heaven:
Your Enemies are theirs, are hated by them,
And they'll protect and help you as their Champion,
That fights their Battles, and defends their Cause.
Our great St. Peter is himself a Warrior;
He drew his Sword against such Infidels,
And now, like him, you'll gain immortal Honour,
And Gods in Heaven and Saints on Earth will praise you.

PONTEACH.

The Gods and Genii do as you have said.
I'll to the Chiefs, and hasten them to Arms.

[*Exeunt* PONTEACH *and* CONJURER.

PRIEST [*solus*].

This, by St. Peter, goes as I would have it.
The Conjurer agreed with me to pump him,

Or else deny to solve his dubious Vision:
But, that we've so agreed in our Responses,
Is all mere Providence, and rul'd by Heaven,
To give us further Credit with this Indian.
Now he is fix'd—will wage immediate War—
This will be joyful News in France and Rome,
That Ponteach is in Arms, and won't allow
The English to possess their new-gain'd Empire:
That he has slain their Troops, destroy'd their Forts,
Expell'd them from the Lakes to their old Limits:
That he prefers the French, and will assist
To repossess them of this fertile Land.
By all the Saints, of this I'll make a Merit,
Declare myself to be the wise Projector;
This may advance me towards St. Peter's Chair,
And these blind Infidels by Accident
May have a Hand in making me a Pope—
But stop—Won't this defeat my other Purpose?
To gain the Mohawk Princess to my Wishes?
No—by the holy Virgin, I'll surprise her,
And have one hearty Revel in her Charms.
But now I'll hasten to this Indian Council;
I may do something there that's apropos.   [*Exit.*

SCENE III. *An Indian Senate-House.*

PONTEACH, TENESCO, PHILIP, ASTINACO, BEAR, WOLF, *and
French* PRIEST.

PONTEACH.

Are all the Chiefs and Warriors here assembled,
That we expect to honour this Day's Council?

TENESCO.

All are conven'd except the Mohawk King,
Who, as we are inform'd, denies his Presence.

PHILIP.

I've half succeeded with the stubborn Chief.
He will not join in Council, but hath promised,
Till further Notice, not to be our Foe:

He'll see how we unite, and what Success
Attends our Arms; in short, he gives strong Hints
That he will soon befriend the common Cause.

PONTEACH.

Do what he will, 'tis this explains my Meaning;

[*Taking up the hatchet.*

You all are well appris'd of my Design,
Which every passing Moment but confirms:
Nay, my Heart's pain'd while I withhold my Hand
From Blood and Vengeance on our hated Foes.
Tho' I should stand alone, I'll try my Power
To punish their Encroachments, Frauds, and Pride;
Yet tho' I die, it is my Country's Cause,
'Tis better thus to die than be despis'd;
Better to die than be a Slave to Cowards,
Better to die than see my Friends abus'd;
The Aged scorn'd, the Young despis'd and spurn'd.
Better to die than see my Country ruin'd,
Myself, my Sons, my Friends reduc'd to Famine,
Expell'd from hence to barren Rocks and Mountains,
To curse our wretched Fate and pine in Want;
Our pleasant Lakes and Fertile Lands usurp'd
By Strangers, Ravagers, rapacious Christians.
Who is it don't prefer a Death in War
To this impending Wretchedness and Shame?
Who is it loves his Country, Friends, or Self,
And does not feel Resentment in his Soul?
Who is it sees their growing Strength and Power,
And how we waste and fail by swift Degrees,
That does not think it Time to rouse and arm,
And kill the Serpent ere we feel it sting,
And fall the Victims of its painful Poison?
Oh! could our Fathers from their Country see
Their ancient Rights encroach'd upon and ravag'd,
And we their Children slow, supine, and careless
To keep the Liberty and Land they left us,
And tamely fall a Sacrifice to Knaves!
How would their Bosoms glow with patriot Shame,
To see their Offspring so unlike themselves?
They dared all Dangers to defend their Rights,

Nor tamely bore an Insult from a Foe.
Their plain rough Souls were brave and full of Fire,
Lovers of War, nor knew the Pain of Fear.
Rouse, then, ye Sons of ancient Heroes, rouse,
Put on your Arms, and let us act a Part
Worthy the Sons of such renowned Chiefs.
Nor urge I you to Dangers that I shun,
Or mean to act my Part by Words alone;
This Hand shall wield the Hatchet in the Cause,
These Feet pursue the frighted running Foe,
This Body rush into the hottest Battle;
There should I fall, I shall secure my Honour,
And, dying, urge my Countrymen to Vengeance
With more Success than all the Force of Words.
Should I survive, I'll shed the foremost Tear
O'er my brave Countrymen that chance to fall;
I'll be the foremost to revenge their Blood,
And, while I live, honour both them and theirs.
I add no more, but wait to hear your Minds.

TENESCO.

Tho' I'm a Warrior, and delight in Arms,
Have oft with Pleasure heard the Sound of Battle,
And oft return'd with Victory and Triumph;
Yet I'm not fond to fight without just Cause,
Or shed the Blood of Men for my Diversion;
But I have seen, with my own Eyes I've seen,
High Provocations from our present Foes,
Their Pride and Insults, Knavery and Frauds,
Their large Encroachments on our common Rights,
Which every Day increase, are seen by all,
And grown so common, they are disregarded.
What calls on us more loudly for Revenge,
Is their Contempt and Breach of public Faith.
When we complain, they sometimes promise fair;
When we grow restless, Treaties are propos'd,
And Promises are gilded then with Presents.
What is the End? Still the old Trade goes on;
Their Colonels, Governors, and mighty Men,
Cheat, lie, and break their solemn Promises,
And take no care to have our Wrongs redress'd.

Their King is distant, would he hear our Prayers:
Still we've no other Way to come at Justice,
But by our Arms to punish Wrongs like these,.
And Wrongs like these are national and public,
Concern us all, and call for public Vengeance.
And Wrongs like these are recent in our Minds.

PHILIP.

Public or private Wrongs, no matter which.
I think our Hunters ought to be reveng'd;
Their Bodies are found torn by rav'nous Beasts,
But who doubts they were kill'd by Englishmen?
Their Heads are scalp'd, their Arms and Jewels gone,
And Beasts of Prey can have no Use for these.
No, they were murdered, slyly, basely shot,
And who that has a Heart does not resent it?
Oh! how I long to tear their mangled Limbs!
Yes, I could eat their Hearts, and drink their Blood,
And revel in their Torments, Pains, and Tortures;
And, though I go alone, I'll seek Revenge.

ASTINACO.

This is the Fire and Madness of your Youth,
And must be curb'd to do your Country Service.
Facts are not always what they seem to be,
And this perhaps may be the Fault of One
Whom their Laws punish if you once detect him.
Shall we then, to revenge your Countrymen,
To recompense a Wrong by one committed,
Rouse all to Arms, and make a general Slaughter?
'Tis higher Motives move my Mind to War,
And make me zealous in the common Cause.
But hear me—'Tis no Trifle we're upon—
If we have Wisdom, it must now be used;
If we have Numbers, they must be united;
If we have Strength, it must be all exerted;
If we have Courage it must be inflamed,
And every Art and Stratagem be practis'd:
We've more to do than fright a Pigeon Roost,
Or start a timorous Flock of running Deer;
Yes, we've a strong, a warlike stubborn Foe,

Unus'd to be repuls'd and quit the Field,
Nay, flush'd with Victories and long Success,
Their Numbers, Strength, and Courage all renown'd,
'Tis little of them that you see or know.
I've seen their Capital, their Troops and Stores,
Their Ships, their Magazines of Death and Vengeance,
And, what is more, I've seen their potent King,
Who like a God sits over all the World,
And thunders forth his Vengeance thro' the Earth.
When he is pleas'd, Smiles sit upon his Face,
And Goodness flows in Rivers at his Feet;
When he's provok'd, 'tis like a fiery Tempest,
All's Terror and Amazement in his Presence,
And frighted Heroes trembling flee his Wrath.
What then is to be done? what may we hope?
At most, by secret, sly, and subtle Means
To curb these vagrant Outcasts of his Subjects,
Secure our Countries from their further Ravage,
And make ourselves of more Importance to them,
Perhaps procure a Peace to our Advantage.
In this I'll join and head my valiant Troops,
Who will not fail to act a valiant Part.

THE BEAR.

What is the Greatness of their King to us?
What of his Strength or Wisdom?   Shall we fear
A Lion chain'd, or in another World?
Or what avails his flowing Goodness to us?
Does not the ravenous Tyger feed her Young?
And the fierce Panther fawn upon his Mate?
Do not the Wolves defend and help their Fellows,
The poisonous Serpent feed her hissing Brood,
And open wide her Mouth for their Protection?
So this good King shows Kindness to his own,
And favours them, to make a Prey of others;
But at his Hands we may expect no Favour,
Look back, my Friends, to our Forefathers' Time,
Where is their Country? where their pleasant Haunts?
The running Streams and shady Forests where?
They chas'd the flying Game, and liv'd in Plenty.
Lo, these proud Strangers now possess the Whole;

Their Cities, Towns, and Villages arise,
Forests are spoil'd, the Haunts of Game destroy'd,
And all the Sea Coasts made one general Waste;
Between the Rivers Torrent-like they sweep,
And drive our Tribes toward the setting Sun.
They who once liv'd on yon delightful Plains
Are now no more, their very Name is lost.
The Sons of potent Kings, subdu'd and murder'd,
Are Vagrants, and unknown among their Neighbours.
Where will the Ravage stop? the Ruin where?
Does not the Torrent rush with growing Speed,
And hurry us to the same wretched End?
Let us grow wise then by our Fathers' Folly,
Unite our Strength, too long it's been divided,
And mutual Fears and Jealousies obtain'd:
This has encourag'd our encroaching Foes,
But we'll convince them, once, we dare oppose them.

THE WOLF.

Yet we have Strength by which we may oppose,
But every Day this Strength declines and fails.
Our great Forefathers, ere these Strangers came,
Liv'd by the Chace, with Nature's Gifts content,
The cooling Fountain quench'd their raging Thirst.
Doctors, and Drugs, and Med'cines were unknown,
Even Age itself was free from Pain and Sickness.
Swift as the Wind, o'er Rocks and Hills they chas'd
The flying Game, the bounding Stag outwinded,
And tir'd the savage Bear, and tam'd the Tyger;
At Evening feasted on the past Day's Toil,
Nor then fatigu'd; the merry Dance and Song
Succeeded; still with every rising Sun
The Sport renew'd; or if some daring Foe
Provok'd their Wrath, they bent the hostile Bow,
Nor waited his Approach, but rush'd with Speed,
Fearless of Hunger, Thirst, Fatigue, or Death.
But we their soften'd Sons, a puny Race,
Are weak in Youth, fear Dangers where they're not;
Are weary'd with what was to them a Sport,
Panting and breathless in One short Hour's Chace;
And every Effort of our Strength is feeble.

We're poison'd with the Infection of our Foes,
Their very Looks and Actions are infectious,
And in deep Silence spread Destruction round them.
Bethink yourselves while any Strength remains;
Dare to be like your Fathers, brave and strong,
Nor further let the growing Poison spread.
And would you stop it, you must resolve to conquer,
Destroy their Forts and Bulwarks, burn their Towns,
And keep them at a greater Distance from us.
Oh! 'tis a Day I long have wish'd to see,
And, aged as I am, my Youth returns
To act with Vigour in so good a Cause.
Yes, you shall see the old Wolf will not fail
To head his Troops, and urge them on to Battle.

Ponteach.

Your Minds are all for War, we'll not delay;
Nor doubt but others gladly will comply,
When they behold our Union and Success.

Tenesco.

This Holy Priest has something to propose
That may excite us all to greater Zeal.

Ponteach.

Let him be heard: 'Tis something from his Gods,
And may import the common Interest much.

Priest.
[*Coming from one side, where he hath stood listening.*]

'Tis not to shew my Eloquence of Speech,
Or drown your Senses with unmeaning Sound,
That I desire Admittance to your Council;
It is an Impulse from the Gods that moves me,
That what I say will be to your Advantage.
Oh! With what secret Pleasure I behold
So many wise and valiant Kings unite,
And in a Cause by Gods and Saints espous'd.
Heaven smiles on your Design, and it shall prosper.
You're going to fight the Enemies of God;
Rebels and Traitors to the King of Kings;

Nay, those who once betray'd and kill'd his Son,
Who came to save you Indians from Damnation—
He was an Indian, therefore they destroy'd him;
He rose again and took his flight to Heaven;
But when his Foes are slain he'll quick return;
And be your kind Protector, Friend, and King.
Be therefore brave and fight his Battles for him;
Spare not his Enemies, where-e'r you find 'em:
The more you murder them, the more you please him;
Kill all you captivate, both old and young,
Mothers and Children, let them feel your Tortures;
He that shall kill a Briton, merits Heaven.
And should you chance to fall, you'll be convey'd
By flying Angels to your King that's there
Where these your hated Foes can never come.
Doubt you the Truth of this my Declaration?
I have a Witness here that cannot lie.

                        [*Pulling out a burning glass.*

This Glass was touch'd by your great Saviour's Hand,
And after left in holy Peter's Care;
When I command, it brings down Fire from Heaven,
To witness for me that I tell no Lie.

                      [*The* INDIANS *gather round and gaze.*

Behold—Great God, send Fire, convince these Indian Kings
That I'm thy Servant, and report the Truth,

           [*In a very praying posture and solemn canting tone.*

Am sent to teach them what they ought to do,
To kill and scalp, to torture and torment
Thy murderous treacherous Foes, the hateful English.

      [*It takes fire; the* INDIANS *are amaz'd, and retreat from it.*

PONTEACH.

Who now can doubt the Justice of our Cause,
Or this Man's Mission from the King above,
And that we ought to follow his Commands?

ASTINACO.

'Tis wonderful indeed—It must be so—

TENESCO.

This cannot be a Cheat—It is from Heaven—

ALL.

We are convinc'd and ready to obey;
We are impatient to revenge our King.

PONTEACH.

[*Takes up the bloody hatchet and flourishes it round.*]

Thus do I raise the Hatchet from the Ground,
Sharpen'd and bright may it be stain'd with Blood,
And never dull'd nor rusted till we've conquer'd,
And taught proud Englishmen to dread its Edge.

ALL.

[*Flourishing their hatchets, and striking them upon a block.*]

Thus will we hew and carve their mangled Bodies,
And give them to the Beasts and Birds for Food.

PONTEACH.

And thus our Names and Honours will maintain
While Sun and Moon, Rivers and Trees remain;
Our unborn Children shall rejoice to hear
How we their Fathers made the English fear.

THE WAR SONG.

To the tune of "Over the Hills and far away," sung by TENESCO,
*the head warrior. They all join in the Chorus, and dance, while
that is singing, in a circle round him; and during the Chorus the
music plays.*

Where-e'r the Sun displays his Light,
Or Moon is seen to shine by Night,
Where-e'r the noisy Rivers flow
Or Trees and Grass and Herbage grow.—*Chorus.*

Be 't known that we this War begin
With proud insulting Englishmen;
The Hatchet we have lifted high,
[*Holding up their hatchets.*]
And them we'll conquer or we'll die.—*Chorus.*

The Edge is keen, the Blade is bright,
Nothing saves them but their Flight;
And then like Heroes we'll pursue,
Over the Hills and Valleys through.—*Chorus.*

They'll like frighted Women quake,
When they behold a hissing Snake;
Or like timorous Deer away,
And leave both Goods and Arms a Prey.—*Chorus.*

Pain'd with Hunger, Cold, or Heat,
In Haste they'll from our Land retreat;
While we'll employ our scalping Knives—
       [*Drawing and flourishing their scalping knives.*
Take off their Skulls, and spare their Lives.—*Chorus.*

Or in their Country they'll complain,
Nor ever dare return again;
Or if they should they'll rue the Day,
And curse the Guide that shew'd the Way.—*Chorus.*

If Fortune smiles, we'll not be long
Ere we return with Dance and Song,
But ah! if we should chance to die,
Dear Wives and Children do not cry.—*Chorus.*

Our Friends will ease your Grief and Woe,
By double Vengeance on the Foe;
Will kill, and scalp, and shed their Blood,
Where-e'r they find them thro' the Wood.—*Chorus.*

No pointing Foe shall ever say
'Twas there the vanquish'd Indian lay;
Or boasting to his Friends relate
The Tale of our unhappy Fate.—*Chorus.*

Let us with Courage then away
To hunt and seize the frighted Prey;
Nor think of Children, Friend, or Wife,
While there's an Englishman alive.—*Chorus.*

In Heat and Cold, thro' Wet and Dry,
Will we pursue, and they shall fly
To Seas which they a Refuge think,
And there in wretched Crowds they'll sink.—*Chorus.*
           [*Exeunt omnes singing.*

The End of the Third Act.

ACT IV.

SCENE I. *The Border of a Grove.*

Enter TENESCO *to* PHILIP *and* CHEKITAN.

TENESCO.

The Troops are all assembled, some have march'd,
Perhaps are now engag'd, and warm in Battle;
The rest have Orders where to bend their Course.
Each Tribe is headed by a valiant Chief,
Except the Bulls which fall to one of you;
The other stays to serve the State at home,
Or back us, should our Forces prove too weak.

PHILIP.

The Bulls are brave, had they a brave Commander,
They'd push the Battle home with sure Success.
I'd choose of all the Troops to be their Leader;
For tho' I'd neither Courage, Skill, nor Strength,
Honour attends the Man who heads the Brave;
Many are dubb'd for Heroes in these Times,
Who owe their Fame to those whom they commanded.

TENESCO.

But we shall ne'er suspect your Title false;
Already you've confirm'd your Fame and Courage,
And prov'd your Skill and Strength as a Commander.

PHILIP.

Still I'll endeavour to deserve your Praise,
Nor long delay the Honour you propose.

CHEKITAN.

But this will interfere with your Design,
And oversets the Scheme of winning Hendrick.

PHILIP.

Ah true—and kills your Hope—This Man 's in Love.

                                   [*To* TENESCO.

TENESCO.

Indeed! In Love with whom? King Hendrick's Daughter?

PHILIP.

The same; and I've engag'd to win her Father.

TENESCO.

This may induce him to espouse our Cause,
Which likewise you engag'd should be effected.

PHILIP.

But then I can't command as was propos'd,
I must resign that Honour to this Lover,
While I conduct and form this double Treaty.

TENESCO.

I am content if you but please yourselves
By Means and Ways not hurtful to the Public.

CHEKITAN.

Was not the Public serv'd, no private Ends
Would tempt me to detain him from the Field,
Or in his stead propose myself a Leader;
But every Power I have shall be exerted:
And if in Strength or Wisdom I should fail,
I dare presume you'll ever find me faithful.

TENESCO.

I doubt it not—You'll not delay your Charge;
The Troops are all impatient for the Battle.
                    [*Exeunt* TENESCO *and* PHILIP.

CHEKITAN [*solus*].

This is not to my Mind—But I must do it—
If Philip heads the Troops, my Hopes are blown—
I must prepare, and leave the Event to Fate
And him—'Tis fix'd—There is no other Choice;
Monelia I must leave, and think of Battles—
She will be safe—But, Oh! the Chance of War—
Perhaps I fall—and never see her more—
This shocks my Soul in spite of Resolution—
The bare Perhaps is more than Daggers to me—
To part for ever! I'd rather stand against
Embattled Troops than meet this single Thought;

A Thought in Poison dipp'd and pointed round;
Oh! how it pains my doubting trembling Heart!
I must not harbour it—My Word is gone—
My Honour calls—and, what is more, my Love.

        [Noise of MONELIA *striving behind the scene.*

What Sound is that?—It is Monelia's Voice;
And in Distress—What Monster gives her Pain?

   [Going towards the sound, the Scene opens and discovers the
PRIEST *with her.*

SCENE II. MONELIA *and* PRIEST.

CHEKITAN

What do I see? The holy Priest is with her.

MONELIA.

[Struggling with the PRIEST, *and trying to disengage herself.]*
No, I would sooner die than be dishonour'd—
Cut my own Throat, or drown me in the Lake.

PRIEST.

Do you love Indians better than us white Men?

MONELIA.

Nay, should an Indian make the foul Attempt,
I'd murder him, or kill my wretched Self.

PRIEST.

I must I can, and will enjoy you now.

MONELIA.

You must! You sha'n't, you cruel, barbarous Christian.

CHEKITAN.

Hold, thou mad Tyger—What Attempt is this?   *[Seizing him.*
Are you a Christian Priest? What do you here?   *[Pushes him.*
What was his Will, Monelia? He is dumb.

MONELIA.

May he be dumb and blind, and senseless quite,
That had such brutal Baseness in his Mind.

CHEKITAN.

Base, false Deceiver, what could you intend?

[*Making towards him.*

MONELIA.

Oh, I am faint—You have preserv'd my Honour,
Which he, foul Christian, thirsted to destroy.

[PRIEST *attempts to go.*

CHEKITAN.

Stay; leave your Life to expiate your Crime:
Your heated Blood shall pay for your Presumption.

[*Offering to strike him with a hatchet.*

PRIEST.

Good Prince, forbear your pious Hand from Blood;
I did not know you was this Maiden's Lover,
I took her for a Stranger, half your Foe.

CHEKITAN.

Did you not know she was King Hendrick's Daughter?
Did you not know that she was not your Wife?
Have you not told us, holy Men like you
Are by the Gods forbid all fleshly Converse?
Have you not told us, Death, and Fire, and Hell
Await those who are incontinent,
Or dare to violate the Rites of Wedlock?
That your God's Mother liv'd and died a Virgin,
And thereby set Example to her Sex?
What means all this? Say you such Things to us,
That you alone may revel in these Pleasures?

PRIEST.

I have a Dispensation from St. Peter
To quench the Fire of Love when it grows painful.
This makes it innocent like Marriage Vows;
And all our holy Priests, and she herself,
Commit no Sin in this Relief of Nature:
For, being holy, there is no Pollution
Communicated from us as from others;
Nay, Maids are holy after we've enjoy'd them,
And, should the Seed take Root, the Fruit is pure.

CHEKITAN.

Oh vain Pretense! Falsehood and foul Deception!
None but a Christian could devise such Lies!
Did I not fear it might provoke your Gods,
Your Tongue should never frame Deceit again.
If there are Gods, and such as you have told us,
They must abhor all Baseness and Deceit,
And will not fail to punish Crimes like yours.
To them I leave you—But avoid my Presence,
Nor let me ever see your hated Head,
Or hear your lying Tongue within this Country.

PRIEST.

Now by St. Peter I must go—He's raging.   [*Aside.*

CHEKITAN.

That Day I do, by your great dreadful God,
This Hand shall cleave your Head, and spill your Blood,
Not all your Prayers, and Lies, and Saints shall save you.

PRIEST.

I've got his Father's Secret, and will use it.
Such Disappointment ought to be reveng'd.   [*Aside.*

CHEKITAN.

Don't mutter here, and conjure up your Saints,
I value not their Curses, or your Prayers.
                   [*Stepping towards the* PRIEST *to hurry him.*

PRIEST.

By all the Saints, young Man, thou shalt repent it.

                                                           [*Exit.*

MONELIA.

Base, false Dissembler—Tyger, Snake, a Christian!
I hate the Sight; I fear the very Name.
O Prince, what has not your kind Presence sav'd me!

CHEKITAN.

It sav'd to me more than my Father's Empire;
Far more than Crowns and Worlds—It sav'd Monelia,
The Hope of whom is more than the Creation.

In this I feel the Triumph of an Hero,
And glory more than if I'd conquer'd Kingdoms.

MONELIA.

Oh, I am thine, I'm more than ever thine;
I am your Captive now, your lawful Prize:
You've taken me in War, a dreadful War!
And snatch'd me from the hungry Tyger's Jaw.
More than my Life and Service is your Due,
And had I more I would devote it to you.

CHEKITAN.

O my Monelia! rich is my Reward,
Had I lost Life itself in the Encounter;
But still I fear that Fate will snatch you from me.
Where is your Brother? Why was you alone?

Enter TORAX, *from listening to their discourse.*

TORAX.

Here am I: What would you of me?

MONELIA.

Torax!
I've been assaulted by a barbarous Man,
And by mere Accident escap'd my Ruin.

TORAX.

What Foe is here? The English are not come?

MONELIA.

No: But a Christian lurk'd within the Grove,
And every Christian is a Foe to Virtue;
Insidious, subtle, cruel, base, and false!
Like Snakes, their very Eyes are full of Poison;
And where they are not, Innocence is safe.

TORAX.

The holy Priest! Is he so vile a Man?
I heard him mutter Threat'nings as I past him.

CHEKITAN.

I spar'd his guilty Life, but drove him hence,
On Pain of Death and Tortures, never more

To tread the Earth, or breathe the Air with me.
Be warn'd by this to better tend your Charge.
You see how Mischiefs lie conceal'd about us,
We tread on Serpents ere we hear them hiss,
And Tygers lurk to seize the incautious Prey.
I must this Hour lead forth my Troops to Battle,
They're now in Arms, and waiting my Command.

MONELIA.

What Safety shall I have when you are gone?
I must not, cannot, will not longer tarry,
Lest other Christians, or some other Foe,
Attempt my Ruin.

CHEKITAN.

Torax will be your Guard.
My Honour suffers, should I now decline;
It is my Country's Cause; I've pawn'd my Word,
Prevented Philip, to make sure of you.
He stays. 'Tis all in favour to our Love;
We must at present please ourselves with Hopes.

MONELIA.

Oh! my fond Heart no more conceals its Flame;
I fear, my Prince, I fear our Fates are cruel:
There's something whispers in my anxious Breast,
That if you go, I ne'er shall see you more.

CHEKITAN.

Oh! how her Words unman and melt my Soul!
As if her Fears were Prophecies of Fate.   [Aside.
I will not go and leave you thus in Fears;
I'll frame Excuses—Philip shall command—
I'll find some other Means to turn the King;
I'll venture Honour, Fortune, Life, and Love,
Rather than trust you from my Sight again.
For what avails all that the World can give?
If you're withheld, all other Gifts are Curses,
And Fame and Fortune serve to make me wretched.

MONELIA.

Now you grow wild—You must not think of staying;
Our only Hope, you know, depends on Philip.

I will not fear, but hope for his Success,
And your Return with Victory and Triumph,
That Love and Honour both may crown our Joy.

CHEKITAN.

Now this is kind; I am myself again.
You had unman'd and soften'd all my Soul,
Disarm'd my Hand, and cowardiz'd my Heart:
But now in every Vein I feel an Hero,
Defy the thickest Tempest of the War:
Yes, like a Lion conscious of his Strength,
Fearless of Death I'll rush into the Battle;
I'll fight, I'll conquer, triumph and return;
Laurels I'll gain and lay them at your Feet.

MONELIA.

May the Success attend you that you wish!
May our whole Scheme of Happiness succeed!
May our next Meeting put an End to Fear,
And Fortune shine upon us in full Blaze!

CHEKITAN.

May Fate preserve you as her Darling Charge!
May all the Gods and Goddesses, and Saints,
If conscious of our Love, turn your Protectors!
And the great thundering God with Lightning burn
Him that but means to interrupt your Peace.   [*Exeunt.*

SCENE III. *Indian Senate-House.*

PONTEACH *and* PHILIP.

PONTEACH.

Say you that Torax then is fond of War?

PHILIP.

He is, and waits impatient my Return.

PONTEACH.

'Tis friendly in you thus to help your Brother;
But I suspect his Courage in the Field;
A love-sick Boy makes but a cow'rdly Captain.

PHILIP.

His Love may spur him on with greater Courage;
He thinks he's fighting for a double Prize;
And but for this, and Hopes of greater Service
In forwarding the Treaty with the Mohawk,
I now had been in Arms and warm in Battle.

PONTEACH.

I much commend the Wisdom of your Stay.
Prepare yourself, and hasten to his Quarters;
You cannot make th' Attempt with too much Speed.
Urge ev'ry Argument with Force upon him,
Urge my strong Friendship, urge your Brother's Love,
His Daughter's Happiness, the common Good;
The general Sense of all the Indian Chiefs,
The Baseness of our Foes, our Hope of Conquest;
The Richness of the Plunder if we speed;
That we'll divide and share it as he pleases;
That our Success is certain if he joins us.
Urge these, and what besides to you occurs;
All cannot fail, I think, to change his Purpose.

PHILIP.

You'd think so more if you knew all my Plan.　　　　[Aside.
I'm all prepar'd now I've receiv'd your Orders,
But first must speak t' his Children ere I part,
I am to meet them in the further Grove.

PONTEACH.

Hark! there's a Shout—We've News of some Success;
It is the Noise of Victory and Triumph.

　　　　　　　　　　　　　　　　[Enter a MESSENGER.

MESSENGER.

Huzza! for our brave Warriors are return'd
Loaded with Plunder and the Scalps of Christians.

　　　　　　　　　　　　　　　　[Enter WARRIORS.

PONTEACH.

What have you done? Why all this Noise and Shouting?

1ST WARRIOR.

Three Forts are taken, all consum'd and plunder'd;
The English in them all destroy'd by Fire,
Except some few escap'd to die with Hunger.

2ND WARRIOR.

We've smok'd the Bear in spite of all his Craft,
Burnt up their Den, and made them take the Field:
The mighty Colonel Cockum and his Captain
Have dull'd our Tomhocks; here are both their Scalps:
                    [*Holding out the two scalps.*
Their Heads are split, our Dogs have eat their Brains.

PHILIP.

If that be all they've eat, the Hounds will starve.

3RD WARRIOR.

These are the scalps of those two famous Cheats
Who bought our Furs for Rum, and sold us Water.
          [*Holding out the scalps, which* PONTEACH *takes.*
Our Men are loaded with their Furs again,
And other Plunder from the Villains' Stores.

PONTEACH.

All this is brave! [*Tossing up the scalps, which others catch, and
    toss and throw them about.*
This Way we'll serve them all.

PHILIP.

We'll cover all our Cabins with their Scalps.

WARRIORS.

We'll fat our Dogs upon their Brains and Blood.

PONTEACH.

Ere long we'll have their Governors in Play.

PHILIP.

And knock their grey-wig'd Scalps about this Way.

PONTEACH.

The Game is started; Warriors, hunt away,
Nor let them find a Place to shun your Hatchets.

ALL WARRIORS.

We will: We will soon shew you other Scalps.

PHILIP.

Bring some alive; I long to see them dance
In Fire and Flames, it us'd to make them caper.

WARRIORS.

Such Sport enough you'll have before we've done.   [*Exeunt.*

PONTEACH.

This still will help to move the Mohawk King.
Spare not to make the most of our Success.

PHILIP.

Trust me for that—Hark; there's another Shout;
                                [*Shouting without.*
A Shout for Prisoners—Now I have my Sport.

PONTEACH.

It is indeed; and there's a Number too.

Enter WARRIORS.

1ST WARRIOR.

We've broke the Barrier, burnt their Magazines,
Slew Hundreds of them, and pursu'd the rest
Quite to their Settlements.

2ND WARRIOR.

There we took
Their famous Hunters Honnyman and Orsbourn;
The last is slain, this is his bloody Scalp.   [*Tossing it up.*
With them we found the Guns of our lost Hunters,
And other Proofs that they're the Murderers;
Nay, Honnyman confesses the base Deed,
And, boasting, says, he's kill'd a Score of Indians.

3RD WARRIOR.

This is the bloody Hunter: This his Wife;
            [*Leading them forward, pinioned and tied together.*
With two young Brats that will be like their Father.
We took them in their Nest, and spoil'd their Dreams.

PHILIP.

Oh I could eat their Hearts, and drink their Blood,
Were they not Poison, and unfit for Dogs.
Here, you Blood-hunter, have you lost your Feeling?
You Tygress Bitch! You Breeder up of Serpents!

    [*Slapping* HONNYMAN *in the face, and kicking his wife.*

PONTEACH.

Stop—We must first consult which way to torture.
And whether all shall die—We will retire.

PHILIP [*going*].

Take care they don't escape.

WARRIOR.

They're bound secure.

    [*Exeunt* INDIANS; *manent* PRISONERS.

SCENE IV.

MRS. HONNYMAN.

Oh, Honnyman, how desperate is our Case!
There's not a single Hope of Mercy left:
How savage, cruel, bloody did they look!
Rage and Revenge appear'd in every Face.

HONNYMAN.

You may depend upon 't, we all must die,
I've made such Havoc, they'll have no Compassion;
They only wait to study out new Torments:
All that can be inflicted or endur'd,
We may expect from their relentless Hands.
Their brutal Eyes ne'er shed a pitying Tear;
Their savage Hearts ne'er had a Thought of Mercy;
Their Bosoms swell with Rancour and Revenge,
And, Devil-like, delight in others' Plagues,
Love Torments, Torture, Anguish, Fire, and Pain,
The deep-fetch'd Groan, the melancholy Sigh,
And all the Terrors and Distress of Death,
These are their Music, and enhance their Joy.
In Silence then submit yourself to Fate:

Make no Complaint, nor ask for their Compassion;
This will confound and half destroy their Mirth;
Nay, this may put a stop to many Tortures,
To which our Prayers and Tears and Plaints would move them.

MRS. HONNYMAN.

Oh, dreadful Scene! Support me, mighty God,
To pass the Terrors of this dismal Hour,
All dark with Horrors Torments, Pains, and Death!
Oh, let me not despair of thy kind Help;
Give Courage to my wretched, groaning Heart!

HONNYMAN.

Tush, Silence! You'll be overheard.

MRS. HONNYMAN.

Oh, my dear Husband! 'Tis an Hour for Prayer,
An Infidel would pray in our Distress:
An Atheist would believe there was some God
To pity Pains and Miseries so great.

HONNYMAN.

If there's a God, he knows our secret Wishes;
This Noise can be no Sacrifice to him;
It opens all the Springs of our weak Passions.
Besides, it will be Mirth to our Tormentors;
They'll laugh, and call this Cowardice in Christians
And say Religion makes us all mere Women.

MRS. HONNYMAN.

I will suppress my Grief in Silence then,
And secretly implore the Aid of Heaven.
Forbid to pray! Oh, dreadful Hour indeed!   [*Pausing.*
Think you they will not spare our dear sweet Babes?
Must these dear Innocents be put to Tortures,
Or dash'd to Death, and share our wretched Fate?
Must this dear Babe that hangs upon my Breast
                            [*Looking upon her infant.*
Be snatch'd by savage Hands and torn in Pieces!
Oh, how it rends my Heart! It is too much!
Tygers would kindly soothe a Grief like mine;

Unconscious Rocks would melt, and flow in Tears
At this last Anguish of a Mother's Soul.
                    [*Pauses, and views her child again.*
Sweet Innocent! It smiles at this Distress,
And fondly draws this final Comfort from me:
Dear Babe, no more: Dear Tommy too must die,
                    [*Looking at her other child.*
Oh, my sweet First-born! Oh, I'm overpower'd.   [*Pausing.*

HONNYMAN.

I had determin'd not to shed a Tear;   [*Weeping.*
But you have all unman'd my Resolution;
You've call'd up all the Father in my Soul;
Why have you nam'd my Children? Oh, my Son!
                    [*Looking upon him.*
My only Son—My Image—Other Self!
How have I doted on the charming Boy,
And fondly plann'd his Happiness in Life!
Now his Life ends: Oh, the Soul-bursting Thought!
He falls a Victim for his Father's Folly.
Had I not kill'd their Friends, they might have spar'd
My Wife, my Children, and perhaps myself,
And this sad, dreadful Scene had never happen'd.
But 'tis too late that I perceive my Folly;
If Heaven forgive, 'tis all I dare to hope for.

MRS. HONNYMAN.

What! have you been a Murderer indeed!
And kill'd the Indians for Revenge and Plunder?
I thought you rash to tempt their brutal Rage,
But did not dream you guilty as you said.

HONNYMAN.

I am indeed. I murder'd many of them,
And thought it not amiss, but now I fear.

MRS. HONNYMAN.

O shocking Thought! Why have you let me know
Yourself thus guilty in the Eye of Heaven?
That I and my dear Babes were by you brought
To this Extreme of Wretchedness and Woe?

Why have you let me know the solemn Weight
Of horrid Guilt that lies upon us all?
To have died innocent, and seen these Babes
By savage Hands dash'd to immortal Rest,
This had been light, for this implies no Crime:
But now we die as guilty Murderers,
Not savage Indians, but just Heaven's Vengeance
Pursues our Lives with all these Pains and Tortures.
This is a Thought that points the keenest Sorrow,
And leaves no Room for Anguish to be heighten'd.

HONNYMAN.

Upbraid me not, nor lay my Guilt to Heart;
You and these Fruits of our past Morning Love
Are innocent. I feel the Smart and Anguish,
The Stings of Conscience, and my Soul on Fire.
There's not a Hell more painful than my Bosom,
Nor Torments for the Damn'd more keenly pointed.
How could I think to murder was no Sin?
Oh, my lost Neighbour! I seduc'd him too.
Now death with all its Terrors disappears,
And all I fear 's a dreadful Something-after;
My Mind forebodes a horrid, woful Scene,
Where Guilt is chain'd and tortur'd with Despair.

MRS. HONNYMAN.

The Mind oppress'd with Guilt may find Relief.

HONNYMAN.

Oh, could I reach the pitying Ear of Heaven,
And all my Soul evaporate in Sound,
'T would ask Forgiveness! but I fear too late;
And next I'd ask that you and these dear Babes
Might bear no Part in my just Punishment.
Who knows but by pathetic Prayers and Tears
Their savage Bosoms may relent towards you,
And fix their Vengeance where just Heaven points it?
I still will hope, and every Motive urge.
Should I succeed, and melt their rocky Hearts,
I'd take it as a Presage of my Pardon,
And die with Comfort when I see you live.

[*Death halloo is heard without.*

MRS. HONNYMAN.

Hark! they are coming—Hear that dreadful Halloo.

HONNYMAN.

It is Death's solemn Sentence to us all;
They are resolv'd, and all Entreaty's vain.
Oh, horrid Scene! how shall I act my Part?
Was it but simple Death to me alone!
But all your Deaths are mine, and mine the Guilt.

Enter INDIANS *with stakes, hatchets, and firebrands.*

Oh, horrid Preparation, more than Death!

PONTEACH.

Plant down the Stakes, and let them be confin'd:
                    [*They loose them from each other.*
First kill the Tygers, then destroy their Whelps.

PHILIP.

This Brat is in our Way, I will dispatch it.
                    [*Offering to snatch the sucking infant.*

MRS. HONNYMAN.

No, my dear Babe shall in my Bosom die;
There is its Nourishment, and there its End.

PHILIP.

Die both together then, 'twill mend the Sport;
Tie the other to his Father, make a Pair;
Then each will have a Consort in their Pains;
Their sweet Brats with them, to increase the Dance.
    [*They are tied down, facing each other upon their knees, and
    their backs to the stakes.*

WARRIOR.

All now is ready; they are bound secure.

PHILIP.

Whene'er you please, their jovial Dance begins.
                    [*To* PONTEACH.

MRS. HONNYMAN.

Oh, my dear Husband! What a Sight is this!
Could ever fabling Poet draw Distress
To such Perfection! Sad Catastrophe!
There are not Colours for such deep-dyed Woe,
Nor words expressive of such heighten'd Anguish.
Ourselves, our Babes, O cruel, cruel Fate!
This, this is Death indeed with all its Terrors.

HONNYMAN.

Is there no secret Pity in your Minds?
Can you not feel some tender Passion move,
When you behold the Innocent distress'd?
True, I am guilty, and will bear your Tortures:
Take your Revenge by all the Arts of Torment;
Invent new Torments, lengthen out my Woe,
And let me feel the keenest Edge of Pain:
But spare this innocent afflicted Woman,
Those smiling Babes who never yet thought Ill,
They never did nor ever will offend you.

PHILIP.

It cannot be: They are akin to you.
Well learnt to hunt and murder, kill and rob.

PONTEACH.

Who ever spar'd a Serpent in the Egg?
Or left young Tygers quiet in their Den?

WARRIOR.

Or cherishes young Vipers in his Bosom?

PHILIP.

Begin, begin; I'll lead the merry Dance.
              [*Offering at the woman with a firebrand.*

PONTEACH.

Stop: Are we not unwise to kill this Woman?
Or Sacrifice her Children to our Vengeance?
They have not wrong'd us; can't do present Mischief.
I know her Friends; they're rich and powerful,

And in their Turn will take severe Revenge:
But if we spare, they'll hold themselves oblig'd,
And purchase their Redemption with rich Presents.
Is not this better than an Hour's Diversion,
To hear their Groans, and Plaints, and piteous Cries?

WARRIORS.

Your Counsel 's wise, and much deserves our Praise;
They shall be spar'd.

PONTEACH.

Untie, and take them hence;

> [*They untie the woman and the oldest child from* HONNYMAN,
> *and retire a little to consult his death.*

When the War ends her Friends shall pay us for it.

PHILIP.

I'd rather have the Sport than all the Pay.

HONNYMAN.

O, now, kind Heaven, thou hast heard my Prayer,
And what's to follow I can meet with Patience.

MRS. HONNYMAN.

Oh, my dear husband, could you too be freed!

[Weeping.

Yet must I stay and suffer Torments with you.
This seeming Mercy is but Cruelty!
I cannot leave you in this Scene of Woe,
'Tis easier far to stay and die together!

HONNYMAN.

Ah! but regard our Children's Preservation:
Conduct their Youth, and form their Minds to Virtue;
Nor let them know their Father's wretched End,
Lest lawless Vengeance should betray them too.

MRS. HONNYMAN.

If I must live, I must retire from hence,
Nor see your fearful Agonies in Death;
This would be more than all the Train of Torments.
The horrid Sight would sink me to the Dust;

These helpless Infants would become a Prey
To worse than Beasts, to savage, bloody Men.

HONNYMAN.

Leave me—They are prepar'd, and coming on—
Heav'n save you all! Oh, 'tis the last dear Sight!

MRS. HONNYMAN.

Oh, may we meet where Fear and Grief are banish'd!
Dearest of Men, adieu—Adieu till then.

> [*Exit, weeping with her children.*

PHILIP.

Bring Fire and Knives, and Clubs, and Hatchets all;
Let the old Hunter feel the Smart of Pain.

> [*They fall upon* HONNYMAN *with various instruments of torture.*

HONNYMAN.

Oh! this is exquisite!   [*Groaning and struggling.*

1ST WARRIOR.

Hah! Does this make you dance?

2ND WARRIOR.

This is fine fat Game!

PHILIP.

Make him caper.   [*Striking him with a club, kicking, &c.*

HONNYMAN.

O ye eternal Powers, that rule on high,
If in your Minds be Sense of human Woe,
Hear my Complaints, and pity my Distress!

PHILIP.

Ah, call upon your Gods, you faint-heart Coward!

HONNYMAN.

Oh, dreadful Racks! When will this Torment end?
Oh, for a Respite from all Sense of Pain!
'Tis come—I go—You can—no more torment.   [*Dies.*

PHILIP.

He's dead; he'll hunt no more; h' 'as done with Game.
  [*Striking the dead body, and spitting in the face.*

PONTEACH.

Drive hence his wretched Spirit, lest it plague us;
Let him go hunt the Woods; he's now disarm'd.
  [*They run round brushing the walls, &c., to dislodge the
  spirit.*

ALL.

Out, Hunter, out, your Business here is done.
Out to the Wilds, but do not take your Gun.

PONTEACH [*to the Spirit*].

Go, tell our Countrymen, whose Blood you shed,
That the great Hunter Honnyman is dead:
That we're alive, we'll make the English know,
Whene'er they dare to serve us Indians so:
This will be joyful News to Friends from France,
We'll join the Chorus then, and have a Dance.
  [*Exeunt omnes, dancing, and singing the last two lines.*

End of the Fourth Act.

ACT V.

SCENE I. *The Border of a Grove, in which* MONELIA *and* TORAX
are asleep.

Enter PHILIP [*speaking to himself*].

As a dark Tempest brewing in the Air,
For many Days hides Sun and Moon, and Stars,
At length grown ripe, bursts forth and forms a Flood
That frights both Men and Beasts, and drowns the Land;
So my dark Purpose now must have its Birth,
Long nourish'd in my Bosom, 'tis matur'd,
And ready to astonish and embroil
Kings and their Kingdoms, and decide their Fates.
Are they not here? Have I delay'd too long?
  [*He espies them asleep.*

Yes, in a Posture too beyond my Hopes,
Asleep! This is the Providence of Fate,
And proves she patronizes my Design,
And I'll show her that Philip is no Coward.

> [*Taking up his hatchet in one hand, and scalping knife in the other, towards them.*]

A Moment now is more than Years to come:
Intrepid as I am, the Work is shocking.

> [*He retreats from them.*

Is it their Innocence that shakes my Purpose?
No; I can tear the Suckling from the Breast,
And drink their Blood who never knew a Crime.
Is it because my Brother's Charmer dies?
That cannot be, for that is my Revenge.
Is it because Monelia is a Woman?
I've long been blind and deaf to their Enchantments.
Is it because I take them thus unguarded?
No; though I act the Coward, it's a Secret.
What is it shakes my firm and fix'd Resolve?
'Tis childish Weakness: I'll not be unman'd.

> [*Approaches and retreats again.*

There's something awful in the Face of Princes,
And he that sheds their Blood, assaults the Gods:
But I'm a Prince, and 'tis by me they die;

> [*Advances arm'd as before.*

Each Hand contains the Fate of future Kings,
And, were they Gods, I would not balk my Purpose.

> [*Stabs* MONELIA *with the knife.*

TORAX.

Hah! Philip, are you come? What can you mean?

> [TORAX *starts and cries out.*

PHILIP.

Go learn my Meaning in the World of Spirits;

> [*Knocks him down with his hatchet, &c.*

'Tis now too late to make a Question of it.
The Play is ended [*Looking upon the bodies*], now succeeds
the Farce.

Hullo! Help! Haste! the Enemy is here.

[Calling at one of the doors, and returning.

Help is at Hand—But I must first be wounded: [*Wounds himself.*

Now let the Gods themselves detect the Fraud.

Enter an INDIAN.

INDIAN.

What means your Cry? Is any Mischief here?

PHILIP.

Behold this flowing Blood; a desperate Wound!

[Shewing his wound.

And there's a Deed that shakes the Root of Empires.

[Pointing to the bodies.

2ND INDIAN.

Oh, fatal Sight! the Mohawk Prince is murder'd.

3RD INDIAN.

The Princess too is weltering in her Blood.

PHILIP.

Both, both are gone; 'tis well that I escap'd.

Enter PONTEACH.

PONTEACH.

What means this Outcry, Noise, and Tumult here?

PHILIP.

Oh see, my Father! see the Blood of Princes,

A Sight that might provoke the Gods to weep,

And drown the Country in a Flood of Tears.

Great was my Haste, but could not stop the Deed;

I rush'd among their Numbers for Revenge,

They frighted fled; there I receiv'd this Wound.

[Shewing his wound to PONTEACH.

PONTEACH.

Who, what were they? or where did they escape?

PHILIP.

A Band of English Warriors, bloody Dogs!

This Way they ran from my vindictive Arm, [*Pointing, &c.*
Which but for this base Wound would sure have stopp'd them.

PONTEACH.

Pursue, pursue, with utmost Speed pursue,
[*To the* WARRIORS *present.*
Outfly the Wind till you revenge this Blood;
'Tis royal Blood, we count it as our own.
[*Exeunt* WARRIORS *in haste.*
This Scene is dark, and doubtful the Event;
Some great Decree of Fate depends upon it,
And mighty Good or Ill awaits Mankind.
The Blood of Princes cannot flow in vain,
The Gods must be in Council to permit it:
It is the Harbinger of their Designs,
To change, new-mould, and alter Things on Earth:
And much I fear, 'tis ominous of Ill,
To me and mine; it happen'd in my Kingdom.
Their Father's Rage will swell into a Torrent—
They were my Guests—His Wrath will centre here;
Our guilty Land hath drunk his Children's Blood.

PHILIP.

Had I not seen the flying Murderers,
Myself been wounded to revenge their Crime,
Had you not hasten'd to pursue the assassins,
He might have thought us treacherous and false,
Or wanting in our hospitable Care:
But now it cannot but engage his Friendship,
Rouse him to Arms, and with a Father's Rage
He'll point his Vengeance where it ought to fall;
And thus this Deed, though vile and dark as Night,
In its Events will open Day upon us,
And prove of great Advantage to our State.

PONTEACH.

Haste then; declare our Innocence and Grief;
Tell the old King we mourn as for our own,
And are determin'd to revenge his Wrongs;
Assure him that our Enemies are his,
And rouse him like a Tyger to the Prey.

PHILIP.

I will with Speed; but first this bleeding Wound
Demands my Care, lest you lament me too.

[Exit, to have his wound dress'd.

PONTEACH *[solus]*.

Pale, breathless Youths! Your Dignity still lives:

[Viewing the bodies.

Your Murderers were blind, or they'd have trembled,
Nor dar'd to wound such Majesty and Worth;
It would have tam'd the savage running Bear,
And made the raging Tyger fondly fawn;
But your more savage Murderers were Christians.
Oh, the distress'd good King! I feel for him,
And wish to comfort his desponding Heart;
But your last Rites require my present Care.   *[Exit.*

SCENE II. *The Senate-House.*

PONTEACH, TENESCO, *and others.*

PONTEACH.

Let all be worthy of the royal Dead;
Spare no Expense to grace th' unhappy Scene,
And aggrandize the solemn, gloomy Pomp
With all our mournful, melancholy Rites.

TENESCO.

It shall be done; all Things are now preparing.

PONTEACH.

Never were Funeral Rites bestow'd more just;
Who knew them living, must lament them dead;
Who sees them dead, must wish to grace their Tombs
With all the sad Respect of Grief and Tears.

TENESCO.

The Mourning is as general as the News;
Grief sits on every Face, in every Eye,
And gloomy Melancholy in Silence reigns:
Nothing is heard but Sighs and sad Complaints,
As if the First-born of the Realm were slain.

PONTEACH.

Thus would I have it; let no Eye be dry
No Heart unmov'd, let every Bosom swell
With Sighs and Groans. What Shouting do I hear?

[*A shouting without, repeated several times.*

TENESCO.

It is the Shout of Warriors from the Battle;
The Sound of Victory and great Success.

[*He goes to listen to it.*

PONTEACH.

Such is the State of Men and human Things;
We weep, we smile, we mourn, and laugh thro' Life,
Here falls a Blessing, there alights a Curse,
As the good Genius or the evil reigns.
It's right it should be so.   Should either conquer,
The World would cease, and Mankind be undone
By constant Frowns or Flatteries from Fate;
This constant Mixture makes the Potion safe,
And keeps the sickly Mind of Man in Health.

Enter CHEKITAN.

It is my Son. What has been your Success?

CHEKITAN.

We've fought the Enemy, broke thro' their Ranks,
Slain many on the Spot, pursu'd the rest
Till Night conceal'd and sav'd them from our Arms.

PONTEACH.

'Tis bravely done, and shall be duly honour'd
With all the Signs and Marks of public Joy.

CHEKITAN.

What means this Gloom I see in every Face?
These smother'd Groans and stifled half-drawn Sighs;
Does it offend that I've return'd in Triumph?

PONTEACH.

I fear to name—And yet it must be known.   [*Aside.*
Be not alarm'd, my Son, the Laws of Fate
Must be obey'd: She will not hear our Dictates.

I'm not a Stranger to your youthful Passion,
And fear the Disappointment will confound you.

CHEKITAN.

Has he not sped? Has ill befell my Brother?

PONTEACH.

Yes, he is wounded but—Monelia's slain,
And Torax both. Slain by the cowardly English,
Who 'scap'd your Brother's wounded threat'ning Arm,
But are pursued by such as will revenge it.—

CHEKITAN.

Oh wretched, wretched, wretched Chekitan! [*Aside.*

PONTEACH.

I know you're shock'd—The Scene has shock'd us all,
And what we could, we've done to wipe the Stain
From us, our Family, our Land and State;
And now prepare due Honours for the Dead,
With all the solemn Pomp of public Grief,
To shew Respect as if they were our own.

CHEKITAN.

Is this my Triumph after Victory?
A solemn, dreadful pompous Shew:
Why have I 'scap'd their Swords and liv'd to see it? [*Aside.*
Monelia dead! aught else I could have borne:
I'm stupefy'd: I can't believe it true;
Shew me the Dead; I will believe my Eyes,
But cannot mourn or drop a Tear till then.

TENESCO.

I will conduct you to them—Follow me—
[*Exeunt* TENESCO *and* CHEKITAN.

PONTEACH.

This is a sad Reception from a Conquest,
And puts an awful Gloom upon our Joy;
I fear his Grief will overtop his Reason;
A Lover weeps with more than common Pain.
Nor flows his greatest Sorrow at his Eyes:
His Grief is inward, and his Heart sheds Tears,

And in his Soul he feels the pointed Woe,
When he beholds the lovely Object lost.
The deep-felt Wound admits no sudden Cure;
The festering Humour will not be dispers'd,
It gathers on the Mind, and Time alone,
That buries all Things, puts an End to this.   [*Exeunt omnes.*

SCENE III. *The Grove, with the dead bodies;* TENESCO *pointing*
CHEKITAN *to them.*

TENESCO.

There lie the Bodies, Prince, a wretched Sight!
Breathless and pale.

CHEKITAN.

A wretched Sight indeed;   [*Going towards them.*
Oh, my Monelia; has thy Spirit fled?
Art thou no more? a bloody, breathless Corpse!
Am I return'd full flush'd with Hopes of Joy,
With all the Honours Victory can give,
To see thee thus? Is this, is this my Welcome?
Is this our Wedding? Wilt thou not return?
Oh, charming Princess, art thou gone for ever?
Is this the fatal Period of our Love?
Oh! had I never seen thy Beauty bloom,
I had not now been griev'd to see it pale:
Had I not known such Excellence had liv'd,
I should not now be curs'd to see it dead:
Had not my Heart been melted by thy Charms,
It would not now have bled to see them lost.
Oh, wherefore, wherefore, wherefore do I live:
Monelia is not—What's the World to me?
All dark and gloomy, horrid, waste, and void:
The Light of the Creation is put out!—
The Blessings of the Gods are all withdrawn!
Nothing remains but Wretchedness and Woe;
Monelia's gone; Monelia is no more.
The Heavens are veil'd because she don't behold them:
The Earth is curs'd, for it hath drunk her Blood;
The Air is Poison, for she breathes no more:
Why fell I not by the base Briton's Sword?

Why press'd I not upon the fatal Point?
Then had I never seen this worse than Death,
But dying said, 'tis well—Monelia lives.

TENESCO.

Comfort, my Prince, nor let your Passion swell
To such a Torrent, it o'erwhelms your Reason,
And preys upon the Vitals of your Soul.
You do but feed the Viper by this View;
Retire, and drive the Image from your Thought,
And Time will soon replace your every Joy.

CHEKITAN.

O my Tenesco, had you ever felt
The gilded Sweets, or pointed Pains of Love,
You'd not attempt to sooth a Grief like mine.
Why did you point me to the painful Sight?
Why have you shown this Shipwreck of my Hopes,
And plac'd me in this beating Storm of Woe?
Why was I told of my Monelia's Fate?
Why wa'n't the wretched Ruin all conceal'd
Under some fair Pretence—That she had fled—
Was made a Captive, or had chang'd her Love—
Why wa'n't I left to guess her wretched End?
Or have some slender Hope that she still liv'd?
You've all been cruel; she died to torment me;
To raise my Pain, and blot out every Joy.—

TENESCO.

I fear'd as much: His Passion makes him wild—   [*Aside.*
I wish it may not end in perfect Frenzy.

CHEKITAN.

Who were the Murderers? Where did they fly?
Where was my Brother, not to take Revenge?
Show me their Tracks, I'll trace them round the Globe;
I'll fly like Lightning, ravage the whole Earth—
Kill every thing I meet, or hear, or see.
Depopulate the World of Men and Beasts,
'Tis all too little for that single Death.
                    [*Pointing to* MONELIA'S *corpse*

I'll tear the Earth that dar'd to drink her Blood;
Kill Trees, and Plants, and every springing Flower:
Nothing shall grow, nothing shall be alive,
Nothing shall move; I'll try to stop the Sun,
And make all dark and barren, dead and sad;
From his tall Sphere down to the lowest Centre,
There I'll descend, and hide my wretched Self,
And reign sole Monarch in a World of Ruin.

TENESCO.

This is deep Madness, it hath seiz'd his Brain.   [Aside.

CHEKITAN.

But first I'll snatch a parting last Embrace.
          [He touches and goes to embrace the corpse.
Thou dear cold Clay! forgive the daring Touch;
It is thy Chekitan, thy wounded Lover.
'Tis; and he hastens to revenge thy Death.
          [TORAX groans and attempts to speak.

TORAX.

Oh, oh, I did not—Philip—Philip—Oh.
                    [CHEKITAN starts.

CHEKITAN.

What—did I not hear a Groan? and Philip call'd?

TENESCO.

It was, it was, and there is Motion too.
          [Approaches TORAX, who groans and speaks again.

TORAX.

Oh! Oh! Oh! Oh! Oh! Philip—help. Oh! Oh!

TENESCO.

He is alive—We'll raise him from the Ground.
          [They lift him up, and speak to him.
Torax, are you alive? or are our Ears deceiv'd?

TORAX.

Oh. Philip, do not—do not—be so cruel.

CHEKITAN.

He is bewilder'd, and not yet himself.
Pour this into his Lips—it will revive him.
          [They give him something.

TENESCO.

This is a Joy unhop'd for in Distress.

[TORAX *revives more.*

TORAX.

Oh! Philip, Philip!—Where is Philip gone?

TENESCO.

The Murderers are pursued—He will go soon.
And now can carry Tidings of your Life.

TORAX.

He carry Tidings! he's the Murderer.

TENESCO.

He is not murder'd; he was slightly wounded,
And hastens now to see the King your Father.

TORAX.

He is false, a barbarous, bloody Man,
A Murderer, a base disguis'd Assassin.

CHEKITAN.

He still is maz'd, and knows not whom he's with

TORAX.

Yes, you are Chekitan, and that's Monelia.

[*Pointing to the corpse.*

This is Tenesco—Philip stabb'd my Sister,
And struck at me; here was the stunning Blow.

[*Pointing to his head.*

He took us sleeping in this silent Grove;
There by Appointment from himself we waited.
I saw him draw the bloody Knife from her,
And, starting, ask'd him, Why, or what he meant?
He answered with the Hatchet on my Skull,
And doubtless thought me dead and bound in Silence.
I am myself, and what I say is Fact.

TENESCO.

The English 'twas beset you; Philip ran
For your Assistance, and himself is wounded.

TORAX.

He may be wounded, but he wounded me;
No Englishman was there, he was alone.
I dare confront him with his Villainy:
Depend upon 't, he's treacherous, false, and bloody.

CHEKITAN.

May we believe, or is this all a Dream?
Are we awake? Is Torax yet alive?
Or is it Juggling, Fascination all?

TENESCO.

'Tis most surprising! What to judge I know not.
I'll lead him hence; perhaps he's still confus'd.

TORAX.

I gladly will go hence for some Relief,
But shall not change, from what I've now aver'd.

TENESCO.

Then this sad Storm of Ruin 's but begun.　　　　　[*Aside.*
Philip must fly, or next it lights on him.
　　　　　　　　[*Exeunt* TENESCO *and* TORAX *led by him.*

CHEKITAN.

And can this be—Can Philip be so false?
Dwells there such Baseness in a Brother's Heart?
So much Dissimulation in the Earth?
Is there such Perfidy among Mankind?
It shocks my Faith—But yet it must be so—
Yes, it was he, Monelia, shed thy Blood.
This made him forward to commence our Friend,
And with unusual Warmth engage to help us;
It was for this so cheerful he resign'd
To me the Honour of Command in War;
The English Troops would never come so near;
The Wounds were not inflicted by their Arms.
All, all confirms the Guilt on Philip's Head.
You died, Monelia, by my Brother's Hand;
A Brother too intrusted with our Love.
I'm stupify'd and senseless at the Thought;
My Head, my very Heart is petrify'd.

This adds a Mountain to my Weight of Woe.
It now is swell'd too high to be lamented;
Complaints, and Sighs, and Tears are thrown away,
Revenge is all the Remedy that's left;
But what Revenge is equal to the Crime?
His Life for her's! An Atom for the Earth—
A Single Fly—a Mite for the Creation:
Turn where I will I find myself confounded:
But I must seek and study out new Means.
Help me, ye Powers of Vengeance! grant your Aid,
Ye that delight in Blood, and Death, and Pain!
Teach me the Arts of Cruelty and Wrath,
Till I have Vengeance equal to my Love,
And my Monelia's Shade is satisfied. [*Exit.*

SCENE IV.

PHILIP [*solus*].

His Grief no Doubt will rise into a Rage,
To see his Charmer rolling in her Blood,
I choose to see him not till my Return;
By then the Fierceness of the Flame may cease;
Nay, he'll grow cool, and quite forget his Love,
When I report her Father's kindled Wrath,
And all the Vengeance he intends to take.
[CHEKITAN *comes in sight.*
But this is he, I cannot now avoid him;
How shall I soothe his Grief—He looks distracted—
I'm such a Stranger grown to Tears and Pity,
I fear he will not think I sympathize.

Enter CHEKITAN.

CHEKITAN.

Have I then found thee, thou false hearted Traitor?
Thou Tyger, Viper, Snake, thou worse than Christian;
Bloodthirsty Butcher, more than Murderer!
Thou every Thing but what Men ought to love!
Do you still live to breathe and see the Sun?
And face me with your savage guilty Eye?

PHILIP.

I fear'd, alas, you would run mad and rave.
Why do you blame me that I am not dead?
I risk'd my Life, was wounded for your Sake,
Did all I could for your Monelia's Safety,
And to revenge you on her Murderers.
Your Grief distracts you, or you'd thank me for 't.

CHEKITAN.

Would you still tempt my Rage, and fire my Soul,
Already bent to spill your treacherous Blood?
You base Dissembler! know you are detected,
Torax still lives, and has discover'd all.

                    [PHILIP *starts and trembles.*

PHILIP.

Torax alive!—It cannot—must not be.   [*Aside.*

CHEKITAN.

Well may you shake—You cannot mend your Blow.
He lived to see, what none but you could think of,
The bloody Knife drawn from Monelia's Breast.
Had you a thousand Lives, they'd be too few;
Had you a Sea of Blood, 't would be too small
To wash away your deep-dy'd Stain of Guilt.
Now you shall die; and Oh, if there be Powers
That after Death take Vengeance on such Crimes,
May they pursue you with their Flames of Wrath,
Till all their Magazines of Pain are spent.

           [*He attacks* PHILIP *with his hatchet.*

PHILIP.

I must defend myself [*Drawing his hatchet*], the Case is des-
        perate.   [*Fights;* PHILIP *falls.*
Fate is too hard; and I'm oblig'd to yield.
'Twas well begun—but has a wretched End—
Yet I'm reveng'd—She cannot live again.
You cannot boast to 've shed more Blood than I—
Oh, had I—had I—struck but one Blow more!   [*Dies.*

CHEKITAN.

What have I done! this is my Brother's Blood!
A guilty Murderer's Blood! He was no Brother.

All Nature's Laws and Ties are hence dissolv'd;
There is no Kindred, Friendship, Faith, or Love
Among Mankind—Monelia's dead—The World
Is all unhing'd—There's universal War—
She was the Tie, the Centre of the Whole;
And she remov'd, all is one general Jar.
Where next, Monelia, shall I bend my Arm
To heal this Discord, this Disorder still,
And bring the Chaos Universe to Form?
Blood still must flow and float the scatter'd Limbs
Till thy much injur'd love in Peace subsides.
Then every jarring Discord once will cease,
And a new World from these rude Ruins rise.   [*Pauses.*
Here then I point the Edge, from hence shall flow
                              [*Pointing his knife to his heart.*
The raging crimson Flood, this is the Fountain
Whose swift Day's Stream shall waft me to thy Arms,
Lest Philip's Ghost should injure thy Repose.   [*Stabs himself.*
I come, I come—Monelia, now I come—
Philip—away—She's mine in spite of Death.   [*Dies.*

Enter TENESCO.

TENESCO.

Oh! I'm too late, the fatal Work is done.
Unhappy Princes; this your wretched End;
Your Country's Hopes and your fond Father's Joy;
Are you no more? Slain by each other's Hands,
Or what is worse; or by the Air you breath'd?
For all is Murder, Death, and Blood about us:
Nothing safe; it is contagious all:
The Earth, and Air, and Skies are full of Treason!
The Evil Genius rules the Universe,
And on Mankind rains Tempests of Destruction.
Where will the Slaughter of the Species end?
When it begins with Kings and with their Sons,
A general Ruin threatens all below.
How will the good King hear the sad Report?
I fear th' Event; but as it can't be hid,
I'll bear it to him in the softest Terms,
And summon every Power to soothe his Grief,
And slack the Torrent of his Royal Passion.   [*Exit.*

SCENE V. *Senate-House.*

PONTEACH [*solus*].

The Torrent rises, and the Tempest blows;
Where will this rough, rude Storm of Ruin end?
What crimson Floods are yet to drench the Earth?
What new-form'd Mischiefs hover in the Air,
And point their Stings at this devoted Head?
Has Fate exhausted all her Stores of Wrath,
Or has she other Vengeance in reserve?
What can she more? My Sons, my Name is gone;
My Hopes all blasted, my Delights all fled;
Nothing remains but an afflicted King,
That might be pitied by Earth's greatest Wretch.
My Friends; my Sons, ignobly, basely slain,
Are more than murder'd, more than lost by Death.
Had they died fighting in their Country's Cause,
I should have smil'd and gloried in their Fall;
Yes, boasting that I had such Sons to lose,
I would have rode in Triumph o'er their Tombs.
But thus to die, the Martyrs of their Folly,
Involv'd in all the complicated Guilt
Of Treason, Murder, Falsehood, and Deceit,
Unbridled Passion, Cowardice, Revenge,
And every Thing that can debase the Man,
And render him the just Contempt of all,
And fix the foulest Stain of Infamy,
Beyond the Power of Time to blot it out;
This is too much; and my griev'd Spirit sinks
Beneath the Weight of such gigantic Woe.
Ye that would see a piteous, wretched King,
Look on a Father griev'd and curs'd like me;
Look on a King whose Sons have died like mine!
Then you'll confess that these are dangerous Names,
And put it in the Power of Fate to curse us;
It is on such she shews her highest Spite.
But I'm too far—'Tis not a Time to grieve
For private Losses, when the Public calls.

Enter TENESCO, *looking sorrowful.*

What are your Tidings?—I have no more Sons.

TENESCO.

But you have Subjects, and regard their Safety.
The treacherous Priest, intrusted with your Councils,
Has publish'd all, and added his own Falsehoods;
The Chiefs have all revolted from your Cause,
Patch'd up a Peace, and lend their Help no more.

PONTEACH.

And is this all? we must defend ourselves,
Supply the Place of Numbers with our Courage,
And learn to conquer with our very Looks:
This is a Time that tries the Truth of Valour;
He shows his Courage that dares stem the Storm,
And live in spite of Violence and Fate.
Shall holy Perfidy and seeming Lies
Destroy our Purpose, sink us into Cowards?

TENESCO.

May your Hopes prosper! I'll excite the Troops
By your Example still to keep the Field.   [*Exit.*

PONTEACH.

'Tis coming on. Thus Wave succeeds to Wave,
Till the Storm's spent, then all subsides again—
The Chiefs revolted:—My Design betray'd:—
May he that trusts a Christian meet the same;
They have no Faith, no Honesty, no God,
And cannot merit Confidence from Men.
Were I alone the boist'rous Tempest's Sport,
I'd quickly move my shatter'd, trembling Bark,
And follow my departed Sons to Rest.
But my brave Countrymen, my Friends, my Subjects,
Demand my Care: I'll not desert the Helm,
Nor leave a dang'rous Station in Distress;
Yes, I will live, in spite of Fate I'll live;
Was I not Ponteach, was I not a King,
Such Giant Mischiefs would not gather round me.
And since I'm Ponteach, since I am a King,
I'll shew myself Superior to them all;
I'll rise above this Hurricane of Fate,
And shew my Courage to the Gods themselves.

Enter TENESCO, *surprised and pausing.*

I am prepar'd, be not afraid to tell;
You cannot speak what Ponteach dare not hear.

TENESCO.

Our bravest Troops are slain, the rest pursu'd;
All is Disorder, Tumult, and Rebellion.
Those that remain insist on speedy Flight;
You must attend them, or be left alone
Unto the Fury of a conquering Foe,
Nor will they long expect your Royal Pleasure.

PONTEACH.

Will they desert their King in such an Hour,
When Pity might induce them to protect him?
Kings like the Gods are valued and ador'd,
When Men expect their Bounties in Return,
Place them in Want, destroy the giving Power,
All Sacrifices and Regards will cease.
Go, tell my Friends that I'll attend their Call.
                              [*Rising. Exit* TENESCO.
I will not fear—but must obey my Stars: [*Looking round.*
Ye fertile Fields and glad'ning Streams, adieu;
Ye Fountains that have quench'd my scorching Thirst,
Ye Shades that hid the Sun-beams from my Head,
Ye Groves and Hills that yielded me the Chace,
Ye flow'ry Meads, and Banks, and bending Trees,
And thou proud Earth, made drunk with Royal Blood,
I am no more your Owner and your King.
But witness for me to your new base Lords,
That my unconquer'd Mind defies them still;
And though I fly, 'tis on the Wings of Hope.
Yes, I will hence where there's no British Foe,
And wait a Respite from this Storm of Woe;
Beget more Sons, fresh Troops collect and arm,
And other Schemes of future Greatness form;
Britons may boast, the Gods may have their Will,
Ponteach I am, and shall be Ponteach still.   [*Exit.*

Finis.

THE GROUP

By Mrs. Mercy Warren

MRS. MERCY WARREN

MRS. MERCY WARREN
(1728–1814)

Most of the literature—orations as well as broadsides—created in America under the heat of the Revolution, was of a strictly satirical character. Most of the Revolutionary ballads sung at the time were bitter with hatred against the Loyalist. When the conflict actually was in progress, the theatres that regaled the Colonists were closed, and an order from the Continental Congress declared that theatre-going was an amusement from which all patriotic people should abstain. These orders or resolutions were dated October 12, 1778, and October 16. (Seilhamer, ii, 51.) The playhouses were no sooner closed, however—much to the regret of Washington—than their doors were thrown wide open by the British troops stationed in Boston, New York, and Philadelphia. A complete history of the American stage has to deal with Howe's players, Clinton's players, and Burgoyne's players.

Of all these Red-Coat Thespians, two demand our attention—one, Major André, a gay, talented actor; the other, General Burgoyne, whose pride was as much concerned with playwriting as with generalship. The latter dipped his pen in the satirical ink-pot, and wrote a farce, "The Blockade of Boston." It was this play that drew forth from a woman, an American playwright, the retort stinging. This lady was Mrs. Mercy Warren[1] who, although distinguished for being a sister of James Otis, and the wife of General James Warren, was in her own name a most important and distinct literary figure during the Revolution.

So few women appear in the early history of American Drama that it is well here to mention Mrs. Charlotte Ramsay Lennox (1720–1804) and Mrs. Susanna Rowson (1762–1824). The former has the reputation of being the first woman, born in America, to have written a play, "The Sister" (1769). The author moved to London when she was fifteen, and there it was her

---

[1] Mrs. Warren was born at Barnstable, Mass., September 25, 1728, and died at Plymouth, Mass., October 19, 1814.

piece was produced, with an epilogue by Oliver Goldsmith. She is referred to in Boswell's Life of Johnson.

Of Susanna Rowson, whose Memoir has been issued by Rev. Elias Nason, we know that, as a singer and actress, she created sufficient reputation in London to attract the attention of Wignell, the comedian. (Clapp. Boston Stage. 1853, p. 41.)

With her husband, she came to this country in 1793, and, apart from her professional duties on the stage, wrote a farce, "Volunteers" (1795), dealing with the Whiskey Insurrection in Pennsylvania, "The Female Patriot" (1794), "Slaves in Algiers; or, A Struggle for Freedom" (1794), and "Americans in England" (1796). All of these were produced. Her literary attainments were wide, her most popular novel being "Charlotte Temple, a Tale of Truth" (1790). She likewise compiled many educational works. (See Wegelin.)

The picture conjured up in our mind of Mrs. Warren is farthest away from satire. To judge by the costume she wore when she sat to Copley for her portrait, she must have been graced with all the feminine wiles of the period. Behold Mrs. Mercy Warren, satirist, as the records describe her:

Her head-dress is of white lace, trimmed with white satin ribbons. Her robe is of dark-green satin, with a pompadour waist, trimmed with point lace. There is a full plait at the back, hanging from the shoulders, and her sleeves are also of point lace. White illusion, trimmed with point lace, and fastened with a white satin bow, covers her neck. The front of the skirt and of the sleeves are elaborately trimmed with puffings of satin.

But however agreeable this picture may be, Mrs. Warren, on reading Burgoyne's farce, immediately sharpened her pen, and replied by writing a counter-farce, which she called "The Blockheads; or, the Affrighted Officers." [1] It was in the prologue to this play that the poet-dramatist wrote:

> Your pardon first I crave for this intrusion.
> The topic's such it looks like a delusion;
> And next your candour, for I swear and vow,
> Such an attempt I never made till now.
> But constant laughing at the Desp'rate fate,
> The bastard sons of Mars endur'd of late,
> Induc'd me thus to minute down the notion,

[1] The/Blockheads:/or, the/Affrighted Officers. /A/Farce. /Boston:/ Printed in Queen-Street,/M,DCC,LXXVI./

Which put my risibles in such commotion.
By yankees frighted too! oh, dire to say!
Why yankees sure at red-coats faint away!
Oh, yes—They thought so too—for lack-a-day,
Their gen'ral turned the *blockade* to a play:
Poor vain poltroons—with justice we'll retort,
And call them *blockheads* for their idle sport.

Unfortunately, we cannot test the comparative value of satire as used by Burgoyne and Mrs. Warren, because the Burgoyne play is not in existence. But, undoubtedly, our Revolutionary enthusiast knew how to wield her pen in anger, and she reflects all of the bitter spirit of the time. Not only is this apparent in "The Blockheads," but likewise in "The Group," a piece which holds up to ridicule a number of people well known to the Boston of that day.

Mrs. Warren was the writer of many plays, as well as being noted for her "History of the American Revolution" (1805), and for her slim volume of poems (1790), which follow the conventional sentiments of the conventionally sentimental English poetry of that. time.

In "The Group" we obtain her interesting impressions, in dramatic form, of North and Gage and, from the standpoint of the library, we regard with reverence the little copy of the play printed on the day before the battle of Lexington—a slim brochure, aimed effectively at Tory politicians.[1]

In fact, mention the name Tory to Mrs. Warren, and her wit was ever ready to sharpen its shafts against British life in America. That is probably why so many believe she wrote "The Motley Assembly," a farce, though some there be who claim that its authorship belongs to J. M. Sewall. Dr. F. W. Atkinson asserts that this was the first American play to have in it only American characters.[2]

The satirical farce was a popular dramatic form of the time. Mrs. Warren was particularly effective in wielding such a polemic note, for instance, when she deals with the Boston Massacre in her Tragedy, "The Adulateur" (Boston: Printed

[1] On the title-page of the Boston edition there appears the following proem: "As the great business of the polite world is the eager pursuit of amusement, and as the Public diversions of the season have been interrupted by the hostile parade in the capital; the exhibition of a new farce may not be unentertaining."

[2] The /Motley /Assembly, /A /Farce. /Published /For the /Entertainment /of the / Curious. /Boston: /Printed and Sold by Nathaniel Coverly, in /Newbury-Street, / M,DCC,LXXIX. /

and sold at the New Printing-Office,/Near Concert-Hall./ M,DCC,LXXIII./). On the King's side, however, the writers were just as effective. Such an example is seen in "The Battle of Brooklyn, A farce of Two Acts: as it was performed at Long-Island, on Tuesday, the 27th of August, 1776, By the Representatives of the Tyrants of America, Assembled at Philadelphia" (Edinburgh: Printed in the Year M.DCC. LXXVII.), in which the British ridicule all that is Continental, even Washington. This farce was reprinted in Brooklyn, 1873.

Jonathan Mitchell Sewall's (1748–1808) "A Cure for the Spleen; or, Amusement for a Winter's Evening" (1775) was another Tory protest, which carried the following pretentious subtitle: "Being the substance of a conversation on the Times, over a friendly tankard and pipe, between Sharp, a country Parson; Bumper, a country Justice; Fillpot, an inn-keeper; Graveairs, a Deacon; Trim, a Barber; Brim, a Quaker; Puff, a late Representative. Taken in short-hand by Roger de Coverly."

Mrs. Warren was the intimate friend of many interesting people. It concerns us, however, that her most significant correspondence of a literary nature was carried on with John Adams, afterwards President of the United States. This friendship remained unbroken until such time as Mrs. Warren found it necessary to picture Adams in her History of the Revolution; when he objected to the portraiture.

The student of history is beholden to Mr. Adams for many of those intimate little sketches of Revolutionary and early national life in America, without which our impressions would be much the poorer. His admiration for Mrs. Warren was great, and even in his correspondence with her husband, James Warren, he never allowed an opportunity to slip for alluding to her work as a literary force in the life of the time. I note, for example, a letter he wrote on December 22, 1773, suggesting a theme which would "become" Mrs. Warren's pen, "which has no equal that I know of in this country."

In 1775, after "The Group" was written, and, according to custom, submitted by Warren to John Adams for criticism and approval, we find him praising Mrs. Warren, and quoting from her play. So poignantly incisive was Mrs. Warren's satire that many people would not credit her with the pieces she actually wrote, and there were those who thought it incredible that a woman should use satire so openly and so flagrantly as she. The consequence is, many of her contemporaries attributed the writing of "The Group" to masculine hands, and this attitude drew from Mrs. Warren the following letter written to Mr. Adams:

My next question, sir, you may deem impertinent. Do you remember who was the author of a little pamphlet entitled, *The Group?* To your hand it was committed by the writer. You brought it forward to the public eye. I will therefore give you my reason for naming it now. A friend of mine, who lately visited the Athenæum [a Boston Library], saw it among a bundle of pamphlets, with a high encomium of the author, who, he asserted, was Mr. Samuel Barrett. You can, if you please, give a written testimony contradictory of the false assertion.

This letter was written long after the Revolution, when she was not loath to let it be known that she was the creator of this little play, and is clearly indicative of the general attitude the public had toward Mrs. Warren as an author. Her appeal instantly called forth a courteous rejoinder from Mr. Adams, who wrote:

What brain could ever have conceived or suspected Samuel Barrett, Esquire, to have been the author of "The Group"? The bishop has neither the natural genius nor the acquired talents, the knowledge of characters, nor the political principles, sentiments, or feelings, that could have dictated that pungent drama. His worthy brother, the Major, might have been as rationally suspected.

I could take my Bible oath to two propositions, 1st. That Bishop Barrett, in my opinion, was one of the last literary characters in the world who ought to have been suspected to have written "The Group." 2d. That there was but one person in the world, male or female, who could at that time, in my opinion, have written it; and that person was Madam Mercy Warren, the historical, philosophical, poetical, and ·satirical consort of the then Colonel, since General, James Warren of Plymouth, sister of the great, but forgotten, James Otis.

According to Adams, he immediately went to the Boston Athenæum, where his nephew, W. S. Shaw, was Librarian. He drew from the shelves a copy of "The Group", which had been bought from the collection of Governor Adams of Massachusetts, and forthwith, on looking it over, wrote down the original names of the people satirized therein.[1] This copy is still a valuable possession of the library.

While Mrs. Warren was writing "The Group," she sent it piecemeal to her husband, who was on the field of battle. He, being proud of the literary attainments of his wife, sent it around to his friends, under seal of secrecy. And his appeal to these friends was very significant of the pride he felt in the manuscript. Here is what he wrote to Adams, on January 15, 1775:

Inclosed are for your amusement two Acts of a dramatic performance composed at my particular desire. They go to you as they came out of the hand of the Copier, without pointing or marking. If you think it worth while to make any other use of them than a reading, you will prepare them in that way & give them such other Corrections & Amendments as your good Judgment shall suggest.

It gradually became known among Warren's friends who the real writer of the satire was, much to the consternation of Mrs. Mercy Warren. She was modest to the extreme, usually being thrust into writing on particular subjects by the enthusiasm of her friends. For example, she wrote a poem on the Boston Tea Party, and, in sending it to her husband, she confessed that it was a task

done in consequence of the request of a much respected friend. It was wrote off with little attention. . . I do not think it has sufficient merit for the public eye.

By the same post, she sent him another scene from "The Group."

Whatever you do with either of them [meaning the manuscripts], you will doubtless be careful that the author is not exposed, and hope your particular friends will be convinced of the propriety of not naming her at present.

Mrs. Warren was the author of several other plays, among them "The Adulateur" and "The Retreat," which preceded

[1] Mrs. Warren's biographer, Alice Brown, quotes the list, as follows, the persons satirized being in parentheses: Lord Chief Justice Hazlerod (Oliver); Judge Meagre (E. Hutchinson); Brigadier Hateall (Ruggles); Hum Humbug, Esq., (Jno. Erving); Sir Sparrow Spendall (Sir Wm. Pepperell); Hector Mushroom (Col. Murray); Beau Trumps (Jno. Vassall); Dick, the Publican (Lechmere); Monsieur de François (N. R. Thomas); Crusty Crowbar, Esq. (J. Boutineau); Dupe,—Secretary of State (T. Flucker); Scriblerius Fribble (Leonard); Commodore Bateau (Loring). The significance of these names will be apparent to the student of local Colonial history.

"The Group" in date of composition, and "The Sack of Rome."
The latter was contained in a volume of poems issued in 1790,
in which "The Ladies of Castile" was dedicated to President
Washington, who wrote the author a courteous note in acknowledgment.

In the preface to this volume, Mrs. Warren gives her impressions of the stage, which are excellent measure of the regard
Americans of this period had for the moral influence of the play-
house. Thus, she writes:

Theatrical amusements may, sometimes, have been prostituted
to the purposes of vice; yet, in an age of taste and refinement, lessons of morality, and the consequences of deviation, may, perhaps,
be as successfully enforced from the stage, as by modes of instruction, less censured by the severe; while, at the same time, the exhibition of great historical events, opens a field of contemplation to the
reflecting and philosophic mind.

But Mrs. Warren was not entirely given over to the serious
occupations of literary work. We find her on intimate terms
with Mrs. Adams, the two of them in their daily association
calling each other *Portia* and *Marcia*.

Who actually played in "The Group" when it was given a
performance is not recorded. We know, however, from records,
that it was given for the delectation of the audiences assembled
"nigh head quarters, at Amboyne." This evidence is on the
strength of Mrs. Warren's own statement. Sanction for the
statement appears on the title-pages of the New York, John
Anderson, issue of 1775,[1] and the Jamaica-Philadelphia, James
Humphreys, Jr., edition of the same year.

I have selected this play, "The Group," as being an excellent
example of the partisan writing done at the time of our American Revolution, and no one can afford to overlook it, although
its actable qualities, according to our present-day judgment,
are doubtful.

[1] The /Group,/ A / Farce: / As lately Acted, and to be Re-acted, to the Wonder/
of all superior Intelligences; /Nigh Head Quarters, at/ Amboyne. /In Two Acts./
New-York: / Printed by John Anderson,/ at Beekman's-Slip./ [The Boston edition
was printed and sold by Edes and Gill, in Queen-Street, 1775.]

THE

G R O U P,

A

F A R C E:

As lately Acted, and to be Re-acted, to the Wonder
of all superior Intelligences;

NIGH HEAD QUARTERS, AT

A M B O Y N E.

IN TWO ACTS.

J A M A I C A, PRINTED;
PHILADELPHIA, RE-PRINTED;
BY JAMES HUMPHREYS, junior, in Front-street.
M,DCC,LXXV.

FAC-SIMILE TITLE-PAGE OF THE FIRST EDITION

The AUTHOR has thought proper to borrow the following spirited lines from a late celebrated Poet, and offer to the public, by way of PROLOGUE, which cannot fail of pleasing at this crisis.

PROLOGUE

WHAT! arm'd for virtue, and not point the pen,
Brand the bold front of shameless guilty men,
Dash the proud gamester from his gilded car,
Bare the mean heart which lurks beneath a star,

* * *

Shall I not strip the gilding off a knave,
Unplac'd, unpension'd, no man's heir, or slave?
I will, or perish in the gen'rous cause;
Hear this and tremble, ye who 'scape the laws;
Yes, while I live, no rich or noble knave,
Shall walk the world in credit to his grave;
To virtue only, and her friends, a friend,
The world beside may murmur, or commend.

DRAMATIS PERSONÆ

Lord Chief Justice HAZLEROD,
Judge MEAGRE,
Brigadier HATEALL,
HUM HUMBUG, *Esquire,*
Sir SPARROW SPENDALL,
HECTOR MUSHROOM,—*Col.*
BEAU TRUMPS,
DICK, *the Publican,*
SIMPLE SAPLING, *Esquire,*
Monsieur de FRANÇOIS,
CRUSTY CROWBAR, *Esquire,*
DUPE,—*Secretary of State,*
SCRIBLERIUS FRIBBLE,
Commodore BATEAU,
COLLATERALIS,—*a new-made Judge.*

Attended by a swarm of court sycophants, hungry harpies, and unprincipled danglers, collected from the neighbouring villages, hovering over the stage in the shape of locusts, led by Massachusettensis in the form of a basilisk; the rear brought up by Proteus, bearing a torch in one hand, and a powder-flask in the other. The whole supported by a mighty army and navy, from Blunderland, for the laudable purpose of enslaving its best friends.

The

GROUP

A

Farce

ACT I.

SCENE I. *A little dark Parlour in Boston:*

GUARDS *standing at the door.*

HAZLEROD, CRUSTY CROWBAR, SIMPLE SAPLING, HATEALL, *and* HECTOR MUSHROOM.

SIMPLE.

I know not what to think of these sad times,
The people arm'd,—and all resolv'd to die
Ere they'll submit.——

CRUSTY CROWBAR.

I too am almost sick of the parade
Of honours purchas'd at the price of peace.

SIMPLE.

Fond as I am of greatness and her charms,
Elate with prospects of my rising name,
Push'd into place,—a place I ne'er expected,
My bounding heart leapt in my feeble breast.
And ecstasies entranc'd my slender brain.—
But yet, ere this I hop'd more solid gains,
As my low purse demands a quick supply.—
Poor Sylvia weeps,—and urges my return
To rural peace and humble happiness,
As my ambition beggars all her babes.

CRUSTY.

When first I listed in the desp'rate cause,
And blindly swore obedience to his will,
So wise, so just, so good I thought Rapatio,
That if salvation rested on his word
I'd pin my faith, and risk my hopes thereon.

HAZLEROD.

Any why not now?—What staggers thy belief?

CRUSTY.

Himself—his perfidy appears—
It is too plain he has betray'd his country;
And we're the wretched tools by him mark'd out
To seal its ruins—tear up the ancient forms,
And every vestige treacherously destroy,
Nor leave a trait of freedom in the land.
Nor did I think hard fate wou'd call me up
From drudging o'er my acres,
Treading the glade, and sweating at the plough,
To dangle at the tables of the great;
At bowls and cards to spend my frozen years;
To sell my friends, my country, and my conscience;
Profane the sacred sabbaths of my God;
Scorn'd by the very men who want my aid
To spread distress o'er this devoted people.

HAZLEROD.

Pho—what misgivings—why these idle qualms,
This shrinking backwards at the bugbear conscience;
In early life I heard the phantom nam'd,
And the grave sages prate of moral sense
Presiding in the bosom of the just;
Or planting thongs about the guilty heart.
Bound by these shackles, long my lab'ring mind,
Obscurely trod the lower walks of life,
In hopes by honesty my bread to gain;
But neither commerce, or my conjuring rods,
Nor yet mechanics, or new fangled drills,
Or all the iron-monger's curious arts,
Gave me a competence of shining ore,

Or gratify'd my itching palm for more;
Till I dismiss'd the bold intruding guest,
And banish'd conscience from my wounded breast.

CRUSTY.

Happy expedient!—Could I gain the art,
Then balmy sleep might sooth my waking lids,
And rest once more refresh my weary soul.

HAZLEROD.

Resolv'd more rapidly to gain my point,
I mounted high in justice's sacred seat,
With flowing robes, and head equip'd without,
A heart unfeeling and a stubborn soul,
As qualify'd as e'er a Jefferies was;
Save in the knotty rudiments of law,
The smallest requisite for modern times,
When wisdom, law, and justice are supply'd
By swords, dragoons, and ministerial nods,
Sanctions most sacred in the Pander's creed,
I sold my country for a splendid bribe.
Now let her sink——and all the dire alarms
Of war, confusion, pestilence, and blood,
And tenfold mis'ry be her future doom—
Let civil discord lift her sword on high,
Nay, sheath its hilt e'en in my brother's blood;
It ne'er shall move the purpose of my soul;
Tho' once I trembled at a thought so bold;
By Philalethes's arguments, convinc'd,
We may live Demons, as we die like brutes,
I give my tears, and conscience to the winds.

HATEALL.

Curse on their coward fears, and dastard souls,
Their soft compunctions and relented qualms,
Compassion ne'er shall seize my steadfast breast
Though blood and carnage spread thro' all the land;
Till streaming purple tinge the verdant turf,
Till ev'ry street shall float with human gore,
I Nero-like, the capital in flames,
Could laugh to see her glotted sons expire,
Tho' much too rough my soul to touch the lyre.

SIMPLE.

I fear the brave, the injur'd multitude,
Repeated wrongs, arouse them to resent,
And every patriot like old Brutus stands,
The shining steel half drawn—its glitt'ring point
Scarce hid beneath the scabbard's friendly cell,
Resolv'd to die, or see their country free.

HATEALL.

Then let them die—*The dogs we will keep down*—
While N——'s my friend, and G——approves the deed,
Tho' hell and all its hell-hounds should unite,
I'll not recede to save from swift perdition
My wife, my country, family, or friends.
G——'s mandamus I more highly prize
Than all the mandates of th' etherial king.

HECTOR MUSHROOM.

Will our abettors in the distant towns
Support us long against the common cause,
When they shall see from Hampshire's northern bounds
Thro' the wide western plains to southern shores
The whole united continent in arms?——

HATEALL.

They shall—as sure as oaths or bond can bind;
I've boldly sent my new-born brat abroad,
Th' association of my morbid brain,
To which each minion must affix his name,
As all our hope depends on brutal force,
On quick destruction, misery, and death;
Soon may we see dark ruin stalk around,
With murder, rapine, and inflicted pains;
Estates confiscate, slav'ry, and despair,
Wrecks, halters, axes, gibbeting and chains,
All the dread ills that wait on civil war;——
How I could glut my vengeful eyes to see
The weeping maid thrown helpless on the world,
Her sire cut off.—Her orphan brothers stand,
While the big tear rolls down the manly cheek.

Robb'd of maternal care by grief's keen shaft,
The sorrowing mother mourns her starving babes,
Her murder'd lord torn guiltless from her side,
And flees for shelter to the pitying grave
To screen at once from slavery and pain.

HAZLEROD.

But more complete I view this scene of woe,
By the incursions of a savage foe,
Of which I warn'd them, if they dare refuse
The badge of slaves, and bold resistance use.
Now let them suffer—I'll no pity feel.

HATEALL.

Nor I!—— But had I power, as I have the will,
I'd send them murm'ring to the shades of hell.

End of the First Act.

ACT II.

*The scene changes to a large dining room. The table furnished
with bowls, bottles, glasses, and cards.—— The Group appear
sitting round in a restless attitude. In one corner of the room is
discovered a small cabinet of books, for the use of the studious and
contemplative; containing, Hobbs's Leviathan, Sipthorp's Sermons, Hutchinson's History, Fable of the Bees, Philalethes on
Philanthropy, with an appendix by Massachusettensis, Hoyl
on Whist, Lives of the Stuarts, Statutes of Henry the Eighth, and
William the Conqueror, Wedderburne's speeches, and acts of
Parliament, for 1774.*

SCENE I.

HATEALL, HAZLEROD, MONSIEUR, BEAU TRUMPS, SIMPLE,
HUMBUG, SIR SPARROW, &c., &c.

SCRIBLERIUS.
——Thy toast, Monsieur,
Pray, why that solemn phiz:—
Art thou, too, balancing 'twixt right and wrong?

Hast thou a thought so mean as to give up
Thy present good, for promise in reversion?
'Tis true hereafter has some feeble terrors,
But ere our grizzly heads are wrapt in clay
We may compound, and make our peace with Heav'n.

MONSIEUR.

Could I give up the dread of retribution,
The awful reck'ning of some future day,
Like surly Hateall I might curse mankind,
And dare the threat'ned vengeance of the skies.
Or like yon apostate——

> [*Pointing to* HAZLEROD, *retired to a corner
> to read Massachusettensis.*

Feel but slight remorse
To sell my country for a grasp of gold.
But the impressions of my early youth,
Infix'd by precepts of my pious sire,
Are stings and scorpions in my goaded breast;
Oft have I hung upon my parent's knee
And heard him tell of his escape from France;
He left the land of slaves, and wooden shoes;
From place to place he sought a safe retreat,
Till fair Bostonia stretch'd her friendly arm
And gave the refugee both bread and peace:
(Shall I ungrateful 'rase the sacred bonds,
And help to clank the tyrant's iron chains
O'er these blest shores—once the sure asylum
From all the ills of arbitrary sway?)
With his expiring breath he bade his sons,
If e'er oppression reach'd the western world,
Resist its force, and break the servile yoke.

SCRIBLERIUS.

Well quit thy post; ——Go make thy flatt'ring court
To Freedom's Sons and tell thy baby fears;
Shew the foot traces in thy puny heart,
Made by the trembling tongue and quiv'ring lip
Of an old grandsire's superstitious whims.

MONSIEUR.

No,——I never can——
So great the itch I feel for titl'd place,
Some honorary post, some small distinction,
To save my name from dark oblivion's jaws,
I'll hazard all, but ne'er give up my place,
For *that* I'll see Rome's ancient rites restor'd,
And flame and faggot blaze in ev'ry street.

BEAU TRUMPS.

——That's right, Monsieur,
There's nought on earth that has such tempting charms
As rank and show, and pomp, and glitt'ring dress,
Save the dear counters at belov'd Quadril,
Viner unsoil'd, and Littleton, may sleep,
And Coke lie mould'ring on the dusty shelf,
If I by shuffling draw some lucky card
That wins the livres, or lucrative place.

HUM HUMBUG.

When sly Rapatio shew'd his friends the scroll,
I wonder'd much to see thy patriot name
Among the list of rebels to the state,
I thought thee one of Rusticus's sworn friends.

BEAU TRUMPS.

When first I enter'd on the public stage
My country groan'd beneath base Brundo's hand,
Virtue look'd fair and beckon'd to her lure,
Thro' truth's bright mirror I beheld her charms
And wish'd to tread the patriotic path
And wear the laurels that adorn his fame;
I walk'd a while and tasted solid peace
With Cassius, Rusticus, and good Hortensius,
And many more, whose names will be rever'd
When you, and I, and all the venal herd,
Weigh'd in Nemesis, just impartial scale,
Are mark'd with infamy, till time blot out
And in oblivion sink our hated names.
But 'twas a poor unprofitable path,

Nought to be gain'd, save solid peace of mind,
No pensions, place or title there I found;
I saw Rapatio's arts had struck so deep
And giv'n his country such a fatal wound,
None but his foes promotion could expect;
I trim'd, and pimp'd, and veer'd, and wav'ring stood,
But half resolv'd to shew myself a knave,
Till the Arch Traitor prowling round for aid
Saw my suspense and bade me doubt no more;—
He gently bow'd, and smiling took my hand,
And whispering softly in my list'ning ear,
Shew'd me my name among his chosen band,
And laugh'd at virtue dignifi'd by fools,
Clear'd all my doubts, and bade me persevere
In spite of the restraints, or hourly checks
Of wounded friendship, and a goaded mind,
Or all the sacred ties of truth and honour.

COLLATERALIS.

Come, 'mongst ourselves we'll e'en speak out the truth.
Can you suppose there yet is such a dupe
As still believes that wretch an honest man?
The later strokes of his serpentine brain
Outvie the arts of Machiavel himself,
His Borgian model here is realiz'd
And the stale tricks of politicians play'd
Beneath a vizard fair——
——Drawn from the heav'nly form
Of blest religion weeping o'er the land
For virtue fall'n, and for freedom lost.

BEAU TRUMPS.

I think with you——
——unparalleled his effront'ry,
When by chican'ry and specious art,
'Midst the distress in which he'd brought the city,
He found a few (by artifice and cunning,
By much industry of his wily friend
The false Philanthrop——sly undermining tool,
Who with the Syren's voice——
Deals daily round the poison of his tongue)

To speak him fair—and overlook his guilt.
They by reiterated promise made
To stand his friend at Britain's mighty court,
And vindicate his native injur'd land,
Lent him their names to sanctify his deeds.
But mark the traitor——his high crimes gloss'd o'er
Conceals the tender feelings of the man,
The social ties that bind the human heart;
He strikes a bargain with his country's foes,
And joins to wrap America in flames.
Yet with feign'd pity, and Satanic grin,
As if more deep to fix the keen insult,
Or make his life a farce still more complete,
He sends a groan across the broad Atlantic,
And with a phiz of Crocodilian stamp,
Can weep, and wreathe, still hoping to deceive,
He cries the gath'ring clouds hang thick about her,
But laughs within——then sobs——
          ——Alas! my country?

Hum Humbug.

Why so severe, or why exclaim at all,
Against the man who made thee what thou art?

Beau Trumps.

I know his guilt,—I ever knew the man,
Thy father knew him e'er we trod the stage;
I only speak to such as know him well;
Abroad I tell the world he is a saint,
But as for int'rest I betray'd my own
With the same views, I rank'd among his friends:
But my ambition sighs for something more.
What merits has Sir Sparrow of his own,
And yet a feather graces the fool's cap:
Which did he wear for what himself achiev'd,
'Twould stamp some honour on his latest heir——
But I'll suspend my murm'ring care awhile;
Come, t' other glass——and try our luck at Loo,
And if before the dawn your gold I win,
Or e'er bright Phœbus does his course begin,
The eastern breeze from Britain's hostile shore

Should waft her lofty floating towers o'er,
Whose waving pendants sweep the wat'ry main,
Dip their proud beaks and dance towards the plain,
The destin'd plains of slaughter and distress,
Laden with troops from Hanover and Hess,
It would invigorate my sinking soul,
For then the continent we might control;
Not all the millions that she vainly boasts
Can cope with Veteran Barbarian hosts;——
But the brave sons of Albion's warlike race,
Their arms, and honours, never can disgrace,
Or draw their swords in such a hated cause,
In blood to seal a N——'s oppressive laws,
They'll spurn the service;——Britons must recoil,
And shew themselves the natives of an isle
Who sought for freedom, in the worst of times
Produc'd her Hampdens, Fairfaxes, and Pyms.
   But if by carnage we should win the game,
Perhaps by my abilities and fame:
I might attain a splendid glitt'ring car,
And mount aloft, and sail in liquid air.
Like Phaëton, I'd then out-strip the wind,
And leave my low competitors behind.

Finis.

THE BATTLE OF BUNKERS-HILL

By

HUGH HENRY BRACKENRIDGE

HUGH HENRY BRACKENRIDGE

HUGH HENRY BRACKENRIDGE
(1748–1816)

The battle of Bunker's Hill was an event which stirred whatever dramatic activity there was in America at the time of the Revolution. Therefore, a play written on the subject should not be omitted from a collection supposed to be representative of the different periods in American history and in American thought. The reader has an interesting comparison to make in Hugh Henry Brackenridge's play, which the title-page declares is "A dramatic piece of five acts, in heroic measure, by a gentleman of Maryland," and a later piece entitled "Bunker Hill, or the Death of General Warren," written by John Daly Burk (1776–1808), who came to America because of certain political disturbances, and published his drama with a Dedication to Aaron Burr (1797), the year it was given in New York for the first time.[1] It will be found that the former play is conceived in a better spirit, and is more significant because of the fact that it was written so soon after the actual event.

It is natural that Hugh Henry Brackenridge should have been inspired by the Revolution, and should have been prompted by the loyal spirit of the patriots of the time. For he was the stuff from which patriots are made, having, in his early life, been reared in Pennsylvania, even though he first saw the light near Campbletown, Scotland, in 1748. His father (who moved to America in 1753) was a poor farmer, and Hugh received his schooling under precarious conditions, as many boys of that time did. We are given pictures of him, trudging thirty miles in all kinds of weather, in order to borrow books and newspapers, and we are told that, being quick in the learning of languages, he made arrangements with a man, who knew mathematics, to trade accomplishments in order that he himself might become better skilled in the science of calculation.

---

[1] Burk wrote another play, "Female Patriotism; or, The Death of Joan d'Arc," given a New York production in 1798. An interesting letter from Burk to J. Hodgkinson, who produced his "Bunker Hill," is to be found in Dunlap's "The American Theatre" (London, 1833, i, 313). The play has been reissued by the Dunlap Society (1891, no. 15), and edited, with an introduction by Brander Matthews.

At the age of fifteen, he was so well equipped that he was engaged to teach school in Maryland, at Gunpowder Falls, some of his pupils being so much larger and older than he that, at one time, he had to take a brand from the fire, and strike one of them, in order to gain ascendency over him.

At eighteen, pocketing whatever money he had saved, he went to President Witherspoon, of the College of New Jersey, arranging with that divine to teach classes in order that he might afford to remain and study. While there, among his classmates may be counted James Madison, future president of the United States, Philip Freneau, the poet, and others of later note. Aaron Burr was a Junior at the time of Brackenridge's graduation, as was William Bradford. Though he was on intimate terms with Madison, he was much more the friend of Freneau, the two writing together "The Rising Glory of America." Should one take the complete piece, which was read by Brackenridge at Commencement, and mark therein that part of the poem composed by Freneau, and included later in Freneau's published works, one might very readily understand that Brackenridge was less the poet, even though in some ways he may have been more versatile as a writer.

This piece, "The Rising Glory of America,"[1] is representative of a type of drama which was fostered and encouraged by the colleges of the time. We find Francis Hopkinson, in the College of Philadelphia, writing various dialogues, like his "Exercise: Containing a Dialogue [by the Rev. Dr. Smith] and Ode, sacred to the memory of his late gracious Majesty George II. Performed at the public commencement in the College of Philadelphia, May, 1761." Yet Hopkinson was one of the Signers of the Declaration of Independence!

What says Abbé Robin, viewing Harvard in 1781:

Their pupils often act tragedies, the subject of which is generally taken from their national events, such as the battle of Bunker's Hill, the burning of Charlestown, the death of General Montgomery, the capture of Burgoyne, the treason of Arnold, and the Fall of British Tyranny. You will easily conclude that in such a new nation as this, these pieces must fall infinitely short of that perfection to which our European literary productions of this kind are wrought up; but, still, they have a greater effect upon the mind than the best of ours would have among them, because those manners and

[1] Philadelphia:/Printed by Joseph Crukshank, for R. Aitken,/Bookseller, Opposite the London-Coffee-/House, in Front-Street./M,DCC,LXXII./

customs are delineated, which are peculiar to themselves, and the events are such as interest them above all others. The drama is here reduced to its true and Ancient origin.

Nathaniel Evans also wrote dialogues, performed at the public Commencements in Philadelphia, like the one on May 17, 1763. We have already noted that "The Prince of Parthia" was written as a college play. "The Military Glory of Great Britain" was also prepared as an entertainment by the graduates of the College of New Jersey, held in Nassau-Hall, September 29, 1762, with the authorship unknown. It was a type of play which tempted many men, who later tried their hand at more important dramatic work.

Another interesting title of the time ran as follows:

An/Exercise,/containing/a Dialogue and Ode/On the Accession of His present gracious Majesty,/George III./Performed at the public Commencement in the College of/Philadelphia, May 18th, 1762./ Philadelphia:/Printed by W. Dunlap, in Market-Street, M,DCC, LXII./

In order to understand the spirit which prompted both Brackenridge and Freneau, one needs must turn to an account of the latter's life, and learn therefrom certain facts concerning the early college spirit of Brackenridge, which was ignored by his son in the only authentic record of his life we have.

From Freneau we understand, for example, that, as early as June 24, 1769, a certain number of students banded themselves into an undergraduate fraternity, called the American Whig Society, the chief members of that association being Madison, Brackenridge, Bradford, and Freneau himself. There is a manuscript book in the possession of the Historical Society of Pennsylvania, originally owned by Bradford, and containing some of their later poetical tirades. It is called "Satires against the Whigs," and is composed of ten pastorals by Brackenridge and a number of satires by Freneau. It is strange that the intimacy between Brackenridge and Freneau did not lead to their rooming together while at College, Brackenridge giving way to James Madison. But we do know that the two were very intimately associated in early literary work, and, in the manuscript book just mentioned, there is contained the fragment of a novel written alternately by the two, and called "Father Bombo's Pilgrimage to Mecca in Arabia."

Then followed "The Rising Glory of America," which, when Brackenridge graduated, September 25, 1771, was announced on the program of events—afternoon division—as being entirely by himself. This must have been an oversight, inasmuch as Freneau had more than a mere hand in the execution of the piece, and inasmuch as we possess Brackenridge's own confession "that on his part it was a task of labour, while the verse of his associate flowed spontaneously."

The college life of the time was not devoted entirely to literary creativeness or to political discussions. There is published an address by President Witherspoon to the inhabitants of Jamaica (1772), in which he outlined the course of study to which the students were subjected. It indicates, very excellently, the classical training that Brackenridge, Freneau, and Madison had to undergo. In fact, we find, on Commencement Day, Freneau debating on "Does Ancient Poetry excel the Modern?" and throwing all his energy in favour of the affirmative argument. And Brackenridge, selected to deliver the Salutatory, rendered it in Latin, "De societate hominum." (See Pennsylvania *Chronicle;* John Maclean's "History of the College of New Jersey," i, 312; Madison's correspondence while a student; also Philip Vickers Fithian's Journal and Letters: 1764–1774. Student at Princeton College: 1770–1772. Tutor at Nomini Hall in Virginia: 1773–1774. Ed....by J. R. Williams. Princeton, 1900.) The Princeton historian points to this class of 1771 as being so patriotic that a unanimous vote was taken to appear at graduation in nothing but things of American manufacture.[1]

This much we do know regarding the early life of Brackenridge: that he was always pressed for money, that it was his indefatigableness and thirst for knowledge which carried him through the schools of the time, and through college.

His son even confesses that his father was obliged, on one occasion, to write an address which one of the students had to deliver, and to receive in payment therefor a new suit of clothes!

It was after his graduation that Brackenridge tutored in the College for a while, meantime taking up a course in theology. After this, he accepted a position as teacher in a school on the eastern shore of Maryland, because the "Academy" offered him a most flattering salary, and he could not reject it, however much

---

[1] The students of Princeton have not revived the "Battle of Bunkers-Hill," but they point still with some pride to the ivy which was planted by the class of 1771.

he may have been interested in his college work. No sooner was he established there than he wrote to his friend, Freneau, inviting him to take the second position in the Maryland Seminary. This position was accepted by Freneau, who wrote to James Madison on November 22, 1772, mentioning therein that Brackenridge was at the head of Sommerset Academy, to which he himself had come on October 18th of that year, and where he was teaching the young idea and pursuing at the same time his theological studies.

As illustration of how much Freneau was at heart in tune with the work, we note that he says, "We have about thirty students in this Academy who prey upon me like leeches."

According to Brackenridge's son, whose Memoir of his father is published in the 1846 edition of "Modern Chivalry," there must, however, have been in this part of Maryland a polished social atmosphere, which gave ample opportunity for the wit, the scholarship, and the conversational and social powers of Brackenridge to develop.

For the students of Sommerset Academy, Brackenridge wrote his play, "The Battle of Bunkers-Hill," [1] and though there is no record of this piece having been actually presented, it is generally agreed that the Principal wrote his drama as an exercise for the pupils to perform. It was published anonymously, the fashion of the day which has led to many disputes,—for example, as to the authorship claims of John Leacock and Mrs. Mercy Warren. Royall Tyler was likewise diffident about letting his name appear on the title-page of "The Contrast."

When published in 1776, Brackenridge's piece was dedicated to Richard Stockton, and its tone and temper are thoroughly indicative of the spirit that must have dominated all his writings while at College.

The year 1776 marks Brackenridge's severance from teaching work. He soon after went to Philadelphia with his small fortune of one thousand pounds, and continued his efforts to make a livelihood by editing the *United States Magazine*, which afforded him an opportunity of airing his patriotic views, and gave him the added pleasure of inviting his associate, Freneau, to become one of the leading contributors. The following year, even though

[1] The/Battle/of/Bunkers-Hill./A Dramatic Piece,/of Five Acts,/in Heroic Measure. /By a Gentleman of Maryland./—Pulcrumque mori succurrit in armis./Virgil./— 'Tis glorious to die in Battle.—/Philadelphia:/Printed and Sold by Robert Bell, in Third-Street./MDCCLXXVI./

he had never been ordained in the Church, Brackenridge, nevertheless, a licensed divine, enlisted as Chaplain in the Revolutionary Army, and there are extant a number of vigorous political sermons which it was his wont to deliver to the soldiers—the same fiery eloquence seen in his "Eulogium on the Brave Men who fell in the Contest with Great Britain," delivered in 1778.

Some time elapsed while he travelled hither and thither with a bible in his saddle-bags, according to description, and then Brackenridge took up the study of law, inasmuch as his very advanced views on religious questions would not allow him to subscribe to all the tenets of his Presbyterian faith. This drew down upon him the inimical strictures of the pulpit, but marked him as a man of intellectual bravery and certain moral daring.

Having completed his law reading in Annapolis, under Samuel Chase, afterwards Supreme Court Judge, he crossed the Alleghanies, in 1781, and established himself in Pittsburgh, where he rapidly grew in reputation, through his personal magnetism and his undoubted talents as a lawyer. He was strictly in favour of the Federal Constitution, and those who wish to fathom his full political importance should not only study his record as Judge of the Supreme Court of the State of Pennsylvania, when he was appointed by Governor McKean, but, more significant still, the part he took in the Whiskey Insurrection, which brought him in touch with Albert Gallatin. In accord with the temper of the times, he was a man of party politics, although he never allowed his prejudices to interfere with his duties on the bench. As a Judge, his term of office ran from 1800 to the day of his death, June 25, 1816.

Mr. Brackenridge, besides being the author of the dialogue and play mentioned, likewise wrote several other dramas, among them being a tragedy, "The Death of General Montgomery at the Siege of Quebec" (1777), and a number of Odes and Elegies. The historical student will find much material relating to Brackenridge's political manoeuvres, in his book on the Western Insurrection; but probably as an author he is more justly famous for his series of stories and sketches published under the title, "Modern Chivalry" (1792), and representing a certain type of prose writing distinctive of American letters of the time of Clay and Crawford. These impressions were later added to. It is a type to be compared with the literary work done in the Southern

States by J. J. Hooper, Judge Longstreet, and Judge Baldwin in ante-bellum days.

Among Brackenridge's other works may be mentioned:

An account of Pittsburgh in 1786. (Pittsburgh *Gazette*, July 29, 1786. Carnegie Library, Pittsburgh: *Monthly Bulletin*, 1902, v., 257–262, 288–290, 332–335.)

The Adventures of Captain Farrago. Philadelphia, 1856.

The Adventures of Major O'Regan. Philadelphia, 1856.

Gazette Publications. Carlisle, 1806.

Incidents of the Insurrection in the western parts of Pennsylvania. Philadelphia, 1795.

Law Miscellanies. Philadelphia, 1814.

Narrative of the late Expedition against the Indians. 1798.

An Occasional Paper by Democritus, entitled "The Standard of Liberty." 1802.

Political Miscellany. 1793.

There are many plays extant dealing specifically with events connected with the Revolution and the War of 1812. For a discussion of same, see an article by A. E. Lancaster, "Historical American Plays," *Chautauquan*, 31:359–364, 1900; also see the present editor's "The American Dramatist," Chapter III. Note the following plays particularly:

C. E. GRICE. "The Battle of New Orleans; or, Glory, Love and Loyalty." An Historical and National Drama. 1816.

W. Ioor. "The Battle of the Eutaw Springs, and Evacuation of Charleston; or, the Glorious 14th of December, 1782." A National Drama. Played in Charleston, 1817.

S. B. H. JUDAH. "A Tale of Lexington." A National Comedy, founded on the opening of the Revolution. 1823.

THE

BATTLE

O F

BUNKERS-HILL.

A DRAMATIC PIECE,

OF FIVE ACTS,

IN HEROIC MEASURE.

BY A GENTLEMAN OF MARYLAND.

—————— *Pulcrumque mori fuccurrit in armis.*
VIRGIL.

'Tis glorious to die in Battle.

PHILADELPHIA:

Printed and Sold by ROBERT BELL, in Third-Street.

MDCCLXXVI.

FAC-SIMILE TITLE-PAGE OF THE FIRST EDITION

TO

RICHARD STOCKTON, *Esquire;*

MEMBER

OF THE HONOURABLE,

THE

CONTINENTAL CONGRESS,

for the State
of

NEW-JERSEY.

SIR,

I take the Freedom to Inscribe with YOUR Name, the following short Performance in Honour of some brave MEN, who have fallen in the Cause of LIBERTY.

It was at first drawn up for an Exercise in Oratory, to a number of young Gentlemen in a southern Academy, but being now Published, may serve the same Purpose, in other AMERICAN Seminaries.

The many Civilities, received from YOUR Family, at an earlier Period of my Life, while a Student at NEW-JERSEY College, demand the warmest Gratitude; and I do continually, with the most sincere Pleasure, recollect and acknowledge them.

It is my fervent wish, that the Ruler of the Universe may Crown with Success, the Cause of FREEDOM, and speedily relieve our bleeding Country in whose Service YOU have distinguishedly exerted YOUR eminent Abilities, by assisting HER Deliberations in the grand Council of the Empire.

SIR,

I am,

With great Respect,

Your much obliged,
and most humble **Servant,**

THE AUTHOR.

PROLOGUE

to the

BATTLE

of

BUNKERS-HILL

By a Lieutenant Colonel in the CONTINENTAL ARMY.

This mighty Era big with dread alarms,
Aloud calls each AMERICAN to arms.
Let ev'ry Breast with martial ardour glow,
Nor dread to meet the proud usurping foe.
What tho' our bodies feel an earthly chain,
Still the free soul, unblemish'd and serene
Enjoys a mental LIBERTY,—a charm,
Beyond the power of fate itself to harm.
Should vict'ry crown us in the doubtful strife—
Eternal honours mark the hero's life.
Should Wounds and slaughter be our hapless doom—
Unfading laurels deck the Martyr's Tomb:
A sure reward awaits his soul on high,
On earth his memory shall never die,
For when we read the fatal story o'er,
One tear shall drop for him who is—no more,
Who nobly struggled to support our laws,
And bravely fell in freedom's sacred cause.
  Let virtue fire us to the martial deed;
We fight to conquer and we dare to bleed:
Witness ye fathers! whose protracted time,
Fruitful of story, chronicles the clime.
These howling deserts, hospitably tame,
Erst snatch'd you martyrs, from the hungry flame;
'Twas Heav'n's own cause, beneath whose shelt'ring power,
Ye grew the wonder of this present hour—

The task—be ours with unremitted toil,
To guard the rights of this dear-purchas'd soil,
From Royal plund'rers, greedy of our spoil,
Who come resolv'd to murder and enslave,
To shackle FREEMEN and to rob the brave.
The loud mouth'd cannon threaten from afar,
Be this our comfort in the storm of war—
Who fights, to take our liberty away,
Dead-hearted fights, and falls an easy prey.
Then, on my brethren to the embattl'd plain,
Who shrinks with fear, anticipates a chain.

DRAMATIS PERSONÆ

WARREN
PUTNAM   } *American Officers.*
GARDINER

GAGE
HOWE
BURGOYNE } *British Officers.*
CLINTON
LORD PIGOT

SHERWIN, *Aide-de-camp to General Howe.*

Soldiers, &c.

THE
BATTLE
OF
BUNKERS-HILL

ACT I.

SCENE I. *Camp at Cambridge.*

Enter WARREN, PUTNAM, *and* GARDINER.

WARREN.

Why thus, brave Putnam, shall we still encamp
Inactive here; and with this gentle flood,
By Cambridge murmuring, mix briny tears?
Salt tears of grief by many a parent shed,
For sons detain'd, and tender innocents
In yon fair City, famishing for bread;
For not fond mothers or their weeping babes—
Can move the hard heart of relentless Gage.
Perfidious man! Who pledg'd his oath so late,
And word of honour to those patriots
Yet in his power, that yielding him their arms,
They should receive permission to depart,
And join once more their valiant countrymen;
But now detains as hostages these men,
In low damp dungeons, and in gaols chain'd down
While grief and famine on their vitals prey.
Say, noble Putnam, shall we hear of this,
And let our idle swords rust in the sheath,
While slaves of Royal Power impeach our worth
As vain, and call our patience cowardice?

PUTNAM.

Not less, bold Warren, have I felt the pangs
Of woe severe in this calamity:

And could I with my life redeem the times,
The richest blood that circles round my heart,
Should hastily be shed.   But what avails
The genuine flame and vigour of the soul,
When nature's self, and all the strength of art,
Opposes every effort in our power?
These sons of slavery dare not advance,
And meet in equal fight our hostile arms.
For yet they well remember LEXINGTON,
And what they suffer'd on that rueful day,
When wantoning in savage rage, they march'd
Onward to CONCORD, in a firm array,
Mock music playing, and the ample flag
Of tyranny display'd; but with dire loss
And infamy drove back, they gain'd the town,
And under cover of their ships of war,
Retir'd, confounded and dismay'd.   No more
In mirthful mood to combat us, or mix
Their jocund music with the sounds of war.
To tempt no more unequal fight with men,
Who to oppose dire arbitrary sway,
Have grasp'd the sword: and resolute to brave
Death in a thousand dreary shapes, can know,
In the warm breast, no sentiment of fear.

GARDINER.

The free born spirit of immortal fire
Is stranger to ignoble deeds, and shuns
The name of cowardice.   But well thy mind,
Sage, and matur'd by long experience, weighs
The perilous attempt, to storm the town,
And rescue thence, the suff'ring citizens.
For but one pass to that peninsula,
On which the city stands, on all sides barr'd.
And here what numbers can supply the rage,
Of the all devouring, deep mouth'd cannon, plac'd,
On many a strong redoubt: while on each side,
The ships of war, moor'd, in the winding bay,
Can sweep ten thousand from the level beach,
"And render all access impregnable."

WARREN.

True, valiant Gard'ner, the attempt is vain,
To force that entrance to the sea-girt town;
Which while we hop'd for peace, and in that view,
Kept back our swords, we saw them fortify.
But what if haply, with a chosen few,
Led through the midnight shades, yon heights were gain'd,
And that contiguous hill, whose grassy foot,
By Mystic's gentle tide is wash'd.   Here rais'd,
Strong batt'ries jutting o'er the level sea,
With everlasting thunder, shall annoy
Their navy far beneath; and in some lucky hour,
When dubious darkness on the land is spread,
A chosen band may pierce their sep'rate fleet,
And in swift boats, across the narrow tide,
Pour like a flame, on their unguarded ranks,
And wither them: As when an angel smote
The Assyrian camp.   The proud Sennacherib,
With impious rage, against the hill of God,
Blasphem'd.   Low humbl'd, when the dawning light,
Saw all his host dead men: So yet I trust,
The God of battles will avouch our cause,
And those proud champions of despotic power,
Who turn our fasting to their mirth, and mock
Our prayers, naming us the SAINTS, shall yet,
Repay with blood, the tears and agonies,
Of tender mothers, and their infant babes,
Shut up in BOSTON.

PUTNAM.

Heaven, smile on us then,
And favour this attempt.   Now from our troops,
Seven hundred gallant men, and skill'd in arms,
With speed select, choice spirits of the war.
By you led on, brave Gard'ner, to the heights,
Ere yet the morn with dawning light breaks forth,
Intrench on BUNKERS-HILL; and when the day
First o'er the hill top rises, we shall join
United arms, against the assailing foe,
Should they attempt to cross the narrow tide,
In deep battalion to regain the hill.

GARDINER.

The thought is perilous, and many men,
In this bold enterprise, must strew the ground.
But since we combat in the cause of God,
I draw my sword, nor shall the sheath again
Receive the shining blade, till on the heights
Of CHARLES-TOWN, and BUNKER'S pleasant HILL,
It drinks the blood of many a warrior slain.

ACT II.

SCENE I. *Boston.*

Enter GAGE, HOWE, *and* BURGOYNE.

BURGOYNE.

How long, brave gen'rals, shall the rebel foe,
In vain arrangements, and mock siege, display
Their haughty insolence?—Shall in this town,
So many thousands, of *Britannia's* troops,
With watch incessant, and sore toil oppress'd,
Remain besieg'd? A vet'ran army pent,
In the inclosure, of so small a space,
By a disorder'd herd, untaught, unofficer'd.
Let not sweet Heav'n, the envious mouth of fame,
With breath malignant, o'er the Atlantic wave
Bear this to Europe's shores, or tell to France,
Or haughty Spain, of LEXINGTON'S retreat.
Who could have thought it, in the womb of time,
That *British* soldiers, in this latter age,
Beat back by peasants, and in flight disgrac'd,
Could tamely brook the base discomfiture;
Nor sallying out, with spirit reassum'd,
Exact due tribute of their victory?
Drive back the foe, to Alleghany hills,
In woody valleys, or on mountain tops,
To mix with wolves and kindred savages.

GAGE.

This mighty paradox, will soon dissolve.
Hear first, Burgoyne, the valour of these men,

Fir'd with the zeal, of fiercest liberty,
No fear of death, so terrible to all,
Can stop their rage. Grey-headed clergymen,
With holy bible, and continual prayer,
Bear up their fortitude—and talk of heav'n,
And tell them, that sweet soul, who dies in battle,
Shall walk, with spirits of the just. These words
Add wings to native rage, and hurry them
Impetuous to war. Nor yet in arms
Unpractised. The day of LEXINGTON
A sad conviction gave our soldiery,
That these AMERICANS, were not that herd,
And rout ungovern'd, which we painted them.

HOWE.

Not strange to your maturer thought, Burgoyne,
This matter will appear. A people brave,
Who never yet, of luxury, or soft
Delights, effeminate, and false, have tasted.
But, through hate of chains, and slav'ry, suppos'd,
Forsake their mountain tops, and rush to arms.
Oft have I heard their valour published:
Their perseverance, and untamable,
Fierce mind, when late they fought with us, and drove,
The French encroaching on their settlements,
Back to their frozen lakes. Or when with us
On Cape Breton, they stormed Louisburg.
With us in Canada, they took Quebec;
And at the Havannah, these NEW-ENGLAND MEN,
Led on·by Putnam, acted gallantly.
I had a brother once, who in that war,
With fame commanded them, and when he fell,
Not unlamented; for these warriors,
So brave themselves, and sensible of merit,
Erected him a costly monument;
And much it grieves me that I draw my sword,
For this late insurrection and revolt,
To chastise them. Would to Almighty God,
The task unnatural, had been assign'd,
Elsewhere. But since by Heaven, determined,
Let's on, and wipe the day of LEXINGTON,

Thus soil'd, quite from our soldiers' memories.
This reinforcement, which with us have fail'd,
In many a transport, from *Britannia's* shores,
Will give new vigour to the Royal Arms,
And crush rebellion, in its infancy.
Let's on, and from this siege, calamitous,
Assert our liberty; nay, rather die,
Transfix'd in battle, by their bayonets,
Than thus remain, the scoff and ridicule
Of gibing wits, and paltry gazetteers,
On this, their madding continent, who cry,
Where is the *British* valour: that renown
Which spoke in thunder, to the Gallic shores?
That spirit is evaporate, that fire;
Which erst distinguish'd them, that flame;
And gen'rous energy of soul, which fill'd
Their Henrys, Edwards, thunder-bolts of war;
Their Hampdens, Marlboroughs, and the immortal **Wolfe,**
On the Abraham heights, victorious.
Britannia's genius, is unfortunate,
And flags, say they, when Royal tyranny
Directs her arms.   This let us then disprove,
In combat speedily, and take from them,
The wantonness of this fell pride, and boasting.

GAGE.

Tho' much I dread the issue of the attempt,
So full of hazard, and advent'rous spirit;
Yet since your judgment, and high skill in arms,
From full experience, boldly prompts you on,
I give my voice, and when one day hath pass'd,
In whose swift hours, may be wrought, highly up,
The resolution, of the soldiery,
With soothing words, and ample promises,
Of rich rewards, in lands and settlements,
From the confiscate property throughout,
These rebel colonies, at length subdu'd;
Then march we forth, beat up their drowsy camp,
And with the sun, to this safe capital,
Return, rich, with the triumphs of the war.
And be our plan, that which brave Haldiman,

Ere yet recall'd, advis'd to us. Let first,
Brave Howe, and Clinton, on that western point,
Land with the transports, and mean time Burgoyne,
With the artillery, pour sharp cannonade,
Along the neck, and sweep, the beachy plain,
Which lies to Roxborough, where yon western stream,
Flowing from Cambridge, mixes with the Bay.
Thus, these AMERICANS, shall learn to dread,
The force of discipline, and skill in arms.

ACT III.

SCENE I. *Bunkers-Hill.*

Enter GARDINER, *with seven hundred men.*

GARDINER.

This is the hill, brave countrymen, whose brow
We mean to fortify. A strong redoubt,
With saliant angles, and embrasures deep,
Be speedily thrown up. Let each himself,
Not undeserving, of our choice approve,
For out of thousands, I have challeng'd you,
To this bold enterprise, as men of might,
And valour eminent, and such this day,
I trust, will honour you. Let each his spade,
And pick-axe, vig'rously, in this hard soil,
Where I have laid, the curved line, exert.
For now the morning star, bright Lucifer,
Peers on the firmament, and soon the day,
Flush'd with the golden sun, shall visit us.
Then gallant countrymen, should faithless Gage,
Pour forth his lean, and half-starv'd myrmidons;
We'll make them taste our cartridges, and know,
What rugged steel, our bayonets are made of;
Or if o'er charg'd, with numbers, bravely fall,
Like those three hundred at Thermopylæ,
And give our Country, credit in our deaths.

ACT IV.

SCENE I. *Boston.*

GAGE [*solus*].

Oh, sweet tranquillity, and peace of soul,
That in the bosom of the cottager,
Tak'st up thy residence—cannot the beams,
Of royal sunshine, call thee to my breast?
Fair honour, waits on thee, renown abroad,
And high dominion, o'er this Continent,
Soon as the spirit, of rebellious war,
Is scourg'd into obedience.   Why then, ye Gods,
This inward gnawing, and remorse of thought,
For perfidy, and breach of promises!
Why should the spouse, or weeping infant babe,
Or meek ey'd virgin, with her sallow cheek,
The rose by famine, wither'd out of it;
Or why the father, or his youthful son,
By me detain'd, from all their relatives,
And, in low dungeons, and, in Gaols chain'd down,
Affect my spirit, when the mighty cause,
Of *George* and *Britain*, is endangered?
For nobly struggling, in the cause of kings,
We claim the high, the just prerogative,
To rule mankind, and with an iron rod,
Exact submission, due, tho' absolute.
What tho' they style me, villain, murderer,
And imprecate from Heaven, dire thunderbolts,
To crush my purposes—Was that a gun,
Which thunders o'er the wave?—Or is it guilt,
That plays the coward, with my trembling heart,
And cools the blood, with frightful images.
O guilt, thy blackness, hovers on the mind,
Nor can the morning dissipate thy shades.
Yon ruddy morn, which over BUNKERS-HILL,
Advancing slowly, blushes to the bay,
And tips with gold the spires of CHARLES-TOWN.

Enter BURGOYNE.

The rebel foe, grown yet more insolent,
By that small loss, or rout, at LEXINGTON,

Prevent our purpose and the night by-past,
Have push'd intrenchments, and some flimsy works,
With rude achievement, on the rocky brow,
Of that tall hill. A ship-boy, with the day,
From the tall mast-head, of the Admiral,
Descry'd their aim, and gave the swift alarm.
Our glasses mark, but one small regiment there,
Yet, ev'ry hour we languish in delay,
Inspires fresh hope, and fills their pig'my souls,
With thoughts of holding it. You hear the sound
Of spades and pick-axes, upon the hill,
Incessant, pounding, like old Vulcan's forge,
Urg'd by the Cyclops.

Enter HOWE.

To your alarm posts, officers; come, gallant souls,
Let's out, and drive them from that eminence,
On which the foe, doth earth himself.
I relish not, such haughty neighbourhood.
Give orders, swiftly, to the Admiral,
That some stout ship heave up the narrow bay,
And pour indignant, from the full-tide wave,
Fierce cannonade, across the isthmus point,
That no assistance may be brought to them.
If but seven hundred, we can treat with them.
Yes, strew the hill, with death, and carcasses,
And offer up, this band, a hecatomb,
To *Britain's* glory, and the cause of kings.

[*Exeunt* BURGOYNE *and* HOWE.

GAGE [*solus*].

May Heaven protect us, from their rage, I say,
When but a boy, I dream'd of death in bed,
And ever since that time, I hated things
Which put him, like a pair of spectacles,
Before my eyes. The thought lies deep in fate,
Nor can a mortal see the bottom of it.
'Tis here—'Tis there—I could philosophize—
Eternity, is like a winding sheet—
The seven commandments like—I think there's seven—
I scratch my head—but yet in vain I scratch—
Oh Bute, and Dartmouth, knew ye what I feel,

You sure would pity an old drinking man,
That has more heart-ake, than philosophy.

[*Exit.*

SCENE II. HOWE *with the British Army.*

HOWE.

The day at length, propitious shews itself,
And with full beams of majesty, the sun,
Hath bless'd its fair nativity; when Heaven,
Brave soldiers, and the cause of kings,
Calls on the spirit of your loyalty,
To chastise this rebellion, and tread down,
Such foul ingratitude—such monstrous shape,
Of horrid liberty, which spurns that love—
That fond maternal tenderness of soul,
Which on this dreary coast, first planted them:
Restrain'd the rage, of murdering savages,
Which, with fierce inroad, on their settlements,
Made frequent war—struck down the arm of France,
Just rais'd, to crush them, in their infancy:
And since that time, have bade their cities grow,
To marts of trade: call'd fair-ey'd commerce forth,
To share dominion, on the distant wave,
And visit every clime, and foreign shore.
Yet this, brave soldiers, is the proud return,
For the best blood of *England,* shed for them.
Behold yon hill, where fell rebellion rears
Her snake-stream'd ensign, and would seem to brave
With scarce seven hundred, this sea-bounded Camp,
Where may be counted, full ten thousand men,
That in the war with France so late, acquir'd
Loud fame, and shook the other continent.
Come on, brave soldiers, seize your gleaming arms,
And let this day, in after times be held,
As Minden famous, and each hostile field,
Where *British* valour shone victorious.
The time moves slow, which enviously detains,
Our just resentment from these traitors' heads.
Their richest farms, and cultur'd settlements,
By winding river, or extensive bay,

Shall be your first reward. Our noble king,
As things confiscate, holds their property,
And in rich measure, will bestow on you,
Who face the frowns, and labour of this day.
He that outlives this battle, shall ascend,
In titled honour, to the height of state,
Dukedoms, and baronies, midst these our foes,
In tributary vassalage, kept down,
Shall be your fair inheritance. Come on,
Beat up th' heroic sound of war. The word
Is, *George* our sov'reign, and *Britannia's* arms.

ACT V.

SCENE I. *Bunkers-Hill.*

WARREN *with the American Army.*

WARREN.

To arms, brave countrymen, for see the foe
Comes forth to battle, and would seem to try,
Once more, their fortune in decisive war.
Three thousand, 'gainst seven hundred, rang'd this day,
Shall give the world, an ample specimen,
What strength, and noble confidence, the sound
Of Liberty inspires. That Liberty,
Which, not the thunder of Bellona's voice,
With fleets, and armies, from the *British* Shore,
Shall wrest from us. Our noble ancestors,
Out-brav'd the tempests, of the hoary deep,
And on these hills, uncultivate, and wild,
Sought an asylum, from despotic sway;
A short asylum, for that envious power,
With persecution dire, still follows us.
At first, they deem'd our charters forfeited.
Next, our just rights, in government, abridg'd.
Then, thrust in viceroys, and bashaws, to rule,
With lawless sovereignty. Now added force,
Of standing armies, to secure their sway.
Much have we suffer'd from the licens'd rage,
Of brutal soldiery, in each fair town.

Remember March, brave countrymen, that day
When BOSTON'S streets ran blood. Think on that day,
And let the memory, to revenge, stir up,
The temper of your souls.   There might we still,
On terms precarious, and disdainful liv'd,
With daughters ravished, and butcher'd sons,
But Heaven forbade the thought.   These are the men,
Who in firm phalanx, threaten us with war,
And aim this day, to fix forever down,
The galling chains, which tyranny has forg'd for us,
These count our lands and settlements their own,
And in their intercepted letters, speak,
Of farms, and tenements, secured for friends,
Which, if they gain, brave soldiers, let with blood,
The purchase, be seal'd down.   Let every arm,
This day be active, in fair freedom's cause,
And shower down, from the hill, like Heav'n in wrath,
Full store of lightning, and fierce iron hail,
To blast the adversary.   Let this ground,
Like burning Ætna or Vesuvius top,
Be wrapt in flame—The word is, LIBERTY,
And Heaven smile on us, in so just a cause.

SCENE II. Bunkers-Hill.

GARDINER [leading up his men to the engagement].
   Fear not, brave soldiers, tho' their infantry,
In deep array, so far out-numbers us.
The justness of our cause, will brace each arm,
And steel the soul, with fortitude; while they,
Whose guilt hangs trembling, on their consciences,
Must fail in battle, and receive that death,
Which, in high vengeance, we prepare for them.
Let then each spirit, to the height, would up,
Shew noble vigour, and full force this day.
For on the merit, of our swords, is plac'd,
The virgin honour, and true character,
Of this whole Continent: and one short hour,
May give complexion, to the whole event,
Fixing the judgment whether as base slaves,
We serve these masters, or more nobly live,

Free as the breeze, that on the hill-top, plays,
With these sweet fields, and tenements, our own.
O fellow soldiers, let this battle speak,
Dire disappointment, to the insulting foe,
Who claim our fair possessions, and set down,
These cultur'd-farms, and bowry-hills, and plains,
As the rich prize, of certain victory.
Shall we, the sons of MASSACHUSETTS-BAY,
NEW HAMPSHIRE, and CONNECTICUT; shall we
Fall back, dishonour'd, from our native plains,
Mix with the savages, and roam for food,
On western mountains, or the desert shores,
Of Canada's cold lakes? or state more vile,
Sit down, in humble vassalage, content
To till the ground for these proud conquerors?
No, fellow soldiers, let us rise this day,
Emancipate, from such ignoble choice.
And should the battle ravish our sweet lives,
Late time shall give, an ample monument,
And bid her worthies, emulate our fame.

SCENE III. *Boston.*

The British Army being repuls'd, SHERWIN *is dispatch'd to* GENERAL GAGE, *for assistance.*

SHERWIN, GAGE, BURGOYNE, *and* CLINTON.

SHERWIN.

Our men advancing, have receiv'd dire loss,
In this encounter, and the case demands,
In swift crisis, of extremity,
A thousand men to reinforce the war

GAGE.

Do as you please, Burgoyne, in this affair,
I'll hide myself in some deep vault beneath.

[*Exit.*

BURGOYNE.

'Tis yours, brave Clinton, to command, these men.
Embark them speedily.   I see our troops,
Stand on the margin of the ebbing flood

(The flood affrighted, at the scene it views),
And fear, once more, to climb the desp'rate hill,
Whence the bold rebel, show'rs destruction down.

[*Exeunt.*

SCENE IV.

WARREN.

Mortally wounded, falling on his right knee, covering his breast with his right hand, and supporting himself with his firelock in his left.

A deadly ball hath limited my life,
And now to God, I offer up my soul.
But O my Countrymen, let not the cause,
The sacred cause of liberty, with me
Faint or expire.   By the last parting breath,
And blood of this your fellow soldier slain,
Be now adjur'd, never to yield the right,
The grand deposit of all-giving Heaven,
To man's free nature, that he rule himself.
With these rude Britons, wage life-scorning war,
Till they admit it, and like hell fall off,
With ebbing billows, from this troubl'd coast,
Where but for them firm Concord, and true love,
Should individual, hold their court and reign.
Th' infernal engin'ry of state, resist
To death, that unborn times may be secure,
And while men flourish in the peace you win,
Write each fair name with worthies of the earth.
Weep not your Gen'ral, who is snatch'd this day,
From the embraces of a family,
Five virgin daughters young, and unendow'd,
Now with the foe left lone and fatherless.
Weep not for him who first espous'd the cause
And risking life have met the enemy,
In fatal opposition—But rejoice—
For now I go to mingle with the dead,
Great Brutus, Hampden, Sidney, and the rest,
Of old or modern memory, who liv'd,
A mound to tyrants, and strong hedge to kings,
Bounding the inundation of their rage,

Against the happiness and peace of man.
I see these heroes where they walk serene,
By crystal currents, on the vale of Heaven,
High in full converse of immortal acts,
Achiev'd for truth and innocence on earth.
Mean time the harmony and thrilling sound
Of mellow lutes, sweet viols, and guitars,
Dwell on the soul and ravish ev'ry nerve.
Anon the murmur of the tight-brac'd drum,
With finely varied fifes to martial airs,
Wind up the spirit to the mighty proof
Of siege and battle, and attempt in arms.
Illustrious group! They beckon me along,
To ray my visage with immortal light,
And bind the amarinth around my brow.
I come, I come, ye first-born of true fame.
Fight on, my countrymen, be FREE, be FREE.

SCENE V. *Charles-town.*

*The reinforcement landed, and orders given to burn Charles-town,
that they may march up more securely under the smoke.* GENERAL
HOWE *rallies his repuls'd and broken troops.*

HOWE.

Curse on the fortune, of *Britannia's* arms,
That plays the jilt with us. Shall these few men
Beat back the flower, and best half of our troops,
While on our side, so many ships of war,
And floating batt'ries, from the mystic tide,
Shake all the hill, and sweep its ridgy top?
O Gods! no time can blot its memory out.
We've men enough, upon the field today,
To bury, this small handful, with the dust
Our march excites—back to the charge—close ranks,
And drive these wizards from th' enchanted ground.
The reinforcement, which bold Clinton heads,
Gives such superiority of strength,
That let each man of us but cast a stone,
We cover this small hill, with these few foes,
And over head, erect a pyramid.
The smoke, you see, enwraps us in its shade,

On, then, my countrymen, and try once more,
To change the fortune, of the inglorious day.

SCENE VI. *Bunkers-Hill.*

GARDINER [*to the American Army*].
You see, brave soldiers, how an evil cause,
A cause of slavery, and civil death,
Unmans the spirit, and strikes down the soul.
The gallant *Englishman*, whose fame in arms,
Through every clime, shakes terribly the globe,
Is found this day, shorn of his wonted strength,
Repuls'd, and driven from the flaming hill.
Warren is fallen, on fair honour's bed,
Pierc'd in the breast, with ev'ry wound before.
'Tis ours, now tenfold, to avenge his death,
And offer up, a reg'ment of the foe,
Achilles-like, upon the Hero's tomb.
See, reinforc'd they face us yet again,
And onward move in phalanx to the war.
O noble spirits, let this bold attack,
Be bloody to their host.   GOD is our Aid,
Give then full scope, to just revenge this day.

SCENE VII. *The Bay-Shore.*

The British Army once more repuls'd, HOWE *again rallies his
flying troops.*

HOWE.
But that so many mouths can witness it,
I would deny myself an *Englishman*,
And swear this day, that with such cowardice,
No kindred, or alliance, has my birth.
O base degen'rate souls, whose ancestors,
At Cressy, Poitiers, and at Agincourt,
With tenfold numbers, combated, and pluck'd
The budding laurels, from the brows of France.
Back to the charge, once more, and rather die,
Burn'd up, and wither'd on this bloody hill,
Than live the blemish of your Country's fame,

With everlasting infamy, oppress'd.
Their ammunition, as you hear, is spent,
So that unless their looks, and visages,
Like fierce-ey'd Basilisks, can strike you dead;
Return, and rescue yet, sweet Countrymen,
Some share of honour, on this hapless day.
Let some brave officers stand on the rear,
And with the small sword, and sharp bayonet,
Drive on each coward that attempts to lag,
That thus, sure death may find the villain out,
With more dread certainty, than him who moves,
Full in the van, to meet the wrathful foe.

SCENE VIII. *Bunkers-Hill.*

GARDINER, *desperately wounded and borne from the field by two soldiers.*

GARDINER.

A musket-ball, death-wing'd, hath pierc'd my groin,
And widely op'd the swift curr'nt of my veins.
Bear me then, Soldiers, to that hollow space,
A little hence, just in the hill's decline.
A surgeon there may stop the gushing wound,
And gain a short respite to life, that yet
I may return, and fight one half hour more.
Then, shall I die in peace, and to my GOD,
Surrender up, the spirit, which He gave.

SCENE IX.

PUTNAM [*to the American Army*].

Swift-rising fame, on early wing, mounts up,
To the convexity of bending Heaven,
And writes each name, who fought with us this day,
In fairest character, amidst the stars.
The world shall read it, and still talk of us,
Who, far out-number'd, twice drove back the foe,
With carnage horrid, murm'ring to their ships.
The Ghost of Warren says, enough—I see
One thousand veterans, mingled with the dust.

Now, for our sacred honour, and the wound,
Which Gard'ner feels, once more we charge—once more,
Dear friends, and fence the obscur'd hill
With hecatombs of slain. Let every piece
Flash, like the fierce-consuming fire of Heaven,
And make the smoke, in which they wrap themselves,
"A darkness visible."—Now once again,
Receive the battle, as a shore of rock
The ocean wave. And if at last we yield,
Leave many a death, amidst their hollow ranks,
To damp the measure, of their dear-bought joy.

Scene X *and Last. Bunkers-Hill.*

The American Army overpower'd by numbers are obliged to retreat.

Enter Howe, Pigot, *and* Clinton *with the British Army.*

Richardson [*a young officer, on the parapet*].

The day is ours, huzza, the day is ours,
This last attack has forc'd them to retreat.

Clinton.

'Tis true, full victory declares for us,
But we have dearly, dearly purchas'd it.
Full fifteen hundred of our men lie dead,
Who, with their officers, do swell the list
Of this day's carnage—On the well-fought hill,
Whole ranks cut down, lie struggling with their wounds,
Or close their bright eyes, in the shades of night.
No wonder! such incessant musketry,
And fire of Cannon, from the hill-top pour'd,
Seem'd not the agency of mortal men,
But Heaven itself, with snares, and vengeance arm'd,
T' oppose our gaining it.   E'en when was spent
Their ammunition, and fierce Warren slain,
Huge stones were hurled from the rocky brow,
And war renew'd, by these inveterate;
Till Gard'ner wounded, the left wing gave way,
And with their shatter'd infantry, the whole,
Drawn off by Putnam, to the causeway fled,

When from the ships, and batt'ries on the wave
They met deep loss, and strew'd the narrow bridge,
With lifeless carcases. Oh, such a day,
Since Sodom and Gomorrah sunk in flames,
Hath not been heard of by the ear of man,
Nor hath an eye beheld its parallel.

LORD PIGOT.

The day is ours, but with heart-piercing loss,
Of soldiers slain, and gallant officers.
Old Abercrombie, on the field lies dead.
Pitcairn and Sherwin, in sore battle slain.
The gallant reg'ment of Welsh fusileers,
To seventeen privates, is this day reduc'd.
The grenadiers stand thinly on the hill,
Like the tall fir-trees on the blasted heath,
Scorch'd by the autumnal burnings, which have rush'd,
With wasting fire fierce through its leafy groves.
Should ev'ry hill by the rebellious foe,
So well defended, cost thus dear to us,
Not the united forces of the world,
Could master them, and the proud rage subdue
Of these AMERICANS.—

HOWE.

E'en in an enemy I honour worth,
And valour eminent. The vanquish'd foe,
In feats of prowess shew their ancestry,
And speak their birth legitimate;
The sons of Britons, with the genuine flame,
Of British heat, and valour in their veins.
What pity 'tis, such excellence of mind,
Should spend itself, in the fantastic cause,
Of wild-fire liberty.—Warren is dead,
And lies unburied, on the smoky hill;
But with rich honours he shall be inhum'd,
To teach our soldiery, how much we love,
E'en in a foe, true worth and noble fortitude.
Come then, brave soldiers, and take up the dead,
Majors, and Col'nels, which are this day slain,
And noble Captains of sweet life bereft.
Fair flowers shall grow upon their grassy tombs,

And fame in tears shall tell their tragedy,
To many a widow and soft weeping maid,
Or parent woe-ful for an only son,
Through mourning *Britain*, and *Hibernia's* isle.

Enter BURGOYNE *from Boston.*

Oft have I read, in the historic page,
And witnessed myself, high scenes in war:
But this rude day, unparallel'd in time,
Has no competitor—The gazing eye,
Of many a soldier, from the chimney-tops,
And spires of Boston, witnessed when Howe,
With his full thousands, moving up the hill,
Receiv'd the onset of the impetuous foe.
The hill itself, like Ida's burning mount,
When Jove came down, in terrors, to dismay
The Grecian host, enshrouded in thick flames;
And round its margin, to the ebbing wave,
A town on fire, and rushing from its base,
With ruin hideous, and combustion down.
Mean time, deep thunder, from the hollow sides
Of the artill'ry, on the hilltop hear'd,
With roar of thunder, and loud mortars play'd,
From the tall ships, and batt'ries on the wave,
Bade yon blue ocean, and wide heaven resound.
A scene like which, perhaps, no time shall know,
Till Heav'n with final ruin fires the ball,
Burns up the cities, and the works of men,
And wraps the mountains in one gen'ral blaze.

[*Exeunt.*

The End.

EPILOGUE

Written by a Gentleman of the Army.

Supposed to be spoken, immediately after the Battle; by LIEUTEN-
ANT COLONEL WEBB, *Aide-de-camp to* GENERAL PUTNAM.

The field is theirs, but dearly was it bought,
Thus long defended and severely fought.
Now pale-fac'd death sits brooding o'er the strand,
And views the carnage of his ruthless hand.
But why my heart this deep unbidden sigh,
Why steals the tear, soft trickling from the eye?
Is FREEDOM master'd by our late defeat,
Or HONOUR wounded by a brave retreat?
'Tis nature dictates; and in pride's despite,
I mourn my brethren slaughter'd in the fight.
Th' insulting foe now revels o'er the ground,
Yet flush'd with victory, they feel the wound.
Embru'd in gore, they bleed from ev'ry part,
And deep wounds rankle at *Britannia's* heart.
O fatal conquest! Speak thou crimson'd plain,
Now press'd beneath the weight of hundreds slain!
There heaps of *British* youth promiscuous lie,
Here, murder'd FREEMEN catch the wand'ring eye.
Observe yon stripling bath'd in purple gore,
He bleeds for FREEDOM on his native shore.
His livid eyes in drear convulsions roll,
While from his wounds escapes the flutt'ring soul,
Breathless and naked on th' ensanguin'd plain,
Midst friends and brothers, sons and fathers slain.
No pitying hand his languid eyes to close,
He breathes his last amidst insulting foes;
His body plunder'd, massacred, abus'd;
By Christians—Christian fun'ral rites refus'd—
Thrown as a carrion in the public way,
To Dogs, to Britons, and to Birds a prey.
Enwrapt in sulph'rous flame and clouds of smoke,

Brave Gard'ner sinks beneath the deadly stroke,
And Warren bleeds to grace the bloody strife,
And for his injur'd country gives his life.
Yet while his mighty soul ascends the skies,
On earth his blood for ten-fold vengeance cries.
Great spirit rest—by Heaven it is decreed,
Thy murd'ring tyrants by the sword shall bleed.
E'en racks and gibbets would but consecrate,
And death repeated be too kind a fate.
The sword is drawn, in peace no more to rest,
Till justice bathes it in some tyrant's breast.
Honour my weapon with the glorious task,
And let me stab, 'tis all the boon I ask.
Kind pow'rs, beneath your all-protecting shield,
I now unsheathe my sword, and take the field
Sure of success, with this sweet comfort giv'n,
Who fights for FREEDOM,—fights the cause of HEAV'N.

AN ODE

on the Battle of BUNKERS-HILL.

*Sung and Acted by a Soldier in a Military Habit, with his Firelock,
&c.*

In the Same Measure with a Sea Piece, Entitled the "Tempest."
—Cease, rude Boreas, blust'ring railer—

I.

You bold warriors, who resemble
    Flames, upon the distant hill,
At whose view, the heroes tremble,
    Fighting with unequal skill.
Loud-sounding drums now with hoarse murmurs,
    Rouse the spirit up to war,
Fear not, fear not, tho' their numbers,
    Much to ours, superior are.
Hear brave WARREN bold commanding,
    "Gallant souls and vet'rans brave,
See the enemy just landing,
    From the navy-cover'd wave.
Close the wings—advance the center—
    Engineers point well your guns—
Clap the matches, let the rent air,
    Bellow to *Britannia's* sons."

II.

Now think you see, three thousand moving,
    Up the brow of BUNKERS-HILL,
Many a gallant vet'ran shoving,
    Cowards on against their will.
The curling volumes all behind them,

Dusky clouds of smoke arise,
  Our cannon-balls, brave boys shall find them,
    At each shot a hero dies.
Once more WARREN midst this terror,
  "Charge, brave soldiers, charge again,
Many an expert vet'ran warrior
    Of the enemy is slain.
Level well your charged pieces,
  In direction to the town;
They shake, they shake, their lightning ceases,
    That shot brought six standards down."

III.

Maids in virgin beauty blooming,
  On *Britannia's* sea-girt isle,
Say no more your swains are coming,
  Or with songs the day beguile.
For sleeping sound in death's embraces,
  On their clay-cold beds they lie,
Death, grim death, alas defaces,
  Youth and pleasure which must die.
"March the right wing, GARD'NER, yonder,
  Take th' assailing foe in flank,
The hero's spirit lives in thunder,
  Close there, sergeants, close that rank.
The conflict now doth loudly call on
  Highest proof of martial skill,
Heroes shall sing of them, who fall on,
  The slipp'ry brow of BUNKERS-HILL."

IV.

Unkindest fortune, still thou changest,
  As the wind upon the wave,
The good and bad alike thou rangest,
  Undistinguish'd in the grave.
Shall kingly tyrants see thee smiling,
  Whilst the brave and just must die,
Them of sweet hope and life beguiling

In the arms of victory?
"Behave this day, my lads, with spirit,
  Wrap the hill-top as in flame;
Oh, if we fall, let each one merit,
  Immortality in fame.
From this high ground like Vesuv'us
  Pour the floods of fire along;
Let not, let not, numbers move us,
  We are yet five hundred strong."

V.

Many a widow sore bewailing
  Tender husbands, shall remain,
With tears and sorrows, unavailing,
  From this hour to mourn them slain.
The rude scene striking all by-standers,
  Bids the little band retire,
Who can live like salamanders,
  In such floods of liquid fire?
"Ah! Our troops are sorely pressed,
  Howe ascends the smoky hill,
Wheel inward, let these ranks be faced,
  We have yet some blood to spill.
Our right wing push'd, our left surrounded,
  Weight of numbers five to one,
Warren dead, and Gard'ner wounded,
  Ammunition is quite gone."

VI.

See the steely points, bright gleaming,
  In the sun's fierce dazzling ray,
Groans arising, life-blood streaming,
  Purple o'er the face of day.
The field is cover'd with the dying,
  Free-men mixt with tyrants lie,
The living with each other vying,
  Raise the shout of battle high.
Now brave Putnam, aged soldier,

"Come, my vet'rans, we must yield;
More equal match'd, we'll yet charge bolder,
  For the present quit the field.
The GOD of battles shall revisit,
  On their heads each soul that dies,
Take courage, boys, we yet sha'n't miss it,
  From a thousand victories."

A SPEECH

By GENERAL WASHINGTON, *on his entering the Town of Boston, at the head of the American Army, after the British troops were by his skilful approaches obliged to abandon it.*

Auspicious day, of happiness unmix'd!
When this fair City, without blood-shed won,
Receives to her sweet bosom, once again,
Her free-born sons, of perseverance try'd,
And noble fortitude, in deeds of arms.
Now let the father meet his infant son,
His virgin daughter, and long faithful spouse,
And kiss away all tears, but those of joy.
Now, let the ardent lover clasp his fair,
New flush the red rose in her damask cheek,
Light up the glad beam in her rolling eye,
And bid all pain and sorrowing be gone.
Oh, happy day—Shine on thou blissful sun,
And not one vapour blemish thy career,
Till from thy mid-day champaign, wheeling do
Thou in the western ocean go to rest.
O happy town—Now let thy buildings smile,
Thy streets run down, with silver floods of joy,
And from thy temples, loudly, hymn and song
Sweep the high arches of resounding Heaven.
Yes, fellow soldiers, let us bend to him
Who gave us strength, and confidence of soul, .
To meet the Battle and fierce iron war,
Urg'd on severe by the tyrannic foe,
With deadly thunder, and mischievous arms.
To him who with his tempest, bulg'd the deep,
And their full hundred war-ships, on the bay,
Chain'd, with his strong wind, to the North-east shore.
The hand of Heaven, is visible in this,
And we, O God, pour forth our souls in praise.
O fellow soldiers, let our off'rings rise,

Not in rich hecatombs, of bulls and goats,
But in true piety, and light of love,
And warm devotion, in the inward part.
Let your festivity be mix'd with thought,
And sober judgment, on this grand event.
March on, and take true pleasure to your arms,
You all are bridegrooms, to fair joy to-day.

A

MILITARY SONG
by the
ARMY:

On GENERAL WASHINGTON'S *victorious entry into the Town of Boston.*

I.

Sons of valour, taste the glories,
    Of Celestial LIBERTY,
Sing a Triumph o'er the Tories
    Let the pulse of joy beat high.

II.

Heaven this day hath foil'd the many
    Fallacies of GEORGE their King,
Let the echo reach Britan'y,
    Bid her mountain summits ring.

III.

See yon Navy swell the bosom,
    Of the late enraged sea,
Where e'er they go we shall oppose them,
    Sons of valour must be free.

IV.

Should they touch at fair RHODE-ISLAND,
    There to combat with the brave,
Driven, from each hill, and high-land,
    They shall plough the purple wave.

V.

Should they thence, to fair VIRGIN'Y
    Bend a squadron to DUNMORE,
Still with fear and ignominy,
    They shall quit the hostile shore.

VI.

To CAROLINA or to GEORG'Y,
  Should they next advance their fame,
This land of heroes shall disgorge the
  Sons of tyranny and shame.

VII.

Let them rove to climes far distant,
  Situate under Arctic skies,
Call on Hessian troops assistant,
  And the Savages to rise.

VIII.

Boast of wild brigades from Russia,
  To fix down the galling chain,
Canada and Nova Scotia,
  Shall discharge these hordes again.

IX.

In NEW-YORK State rejoin'd by CLINTON,
  Should their standards mock the air,
Many a surgeon shall put lint on
  Wounds of death received there.

X.

War, fierce war, shall break their forces,
  Nerves of tory men shall fail,
Seeing HOWE with alter'd courses,
  Bending to the western gale.

XI.

Thus, from every bay of ocean,
  Flying back, with sails unfurl'd,
Tost with ever-troubl'd motion,
  They shall quit this smiling world.

XII.

Like Satan banished from HEAVEN,
  Never see the smiling shore,
From this land so happy, driven,
  Never stain its bosom more.

The End.

THE FALL

OF

BRITISH TYRANNY

By JOHN LEACOCK

JOHN LEACOCK

Among the elusive figures of early American Drama stands John Leacock, author of "The Fall of British Tyranny,"[1] published in 1776, in Philadelphia. Even more elusive is the identification, inasmuch as his name has been spelled variously Leacock, Lacock, and Laycock. To add to the confusion, Watson's "Annals of Philadelphia," on the reminiscent word of an old resident of that town, declares that Joseph Leacock penned "The Medley."[2] "He wrote also a play, with good humour," says this authority, "called 'British Tyranny.'" On careful search of the files, no definite information in regard to Leacock has been forthcoming. The dedication to "The Fall of British Tyranny" was signed "Dick Rifle," but there is no information to be traced from this pseudonym.

Searching the Colonial Records of Pennsylvania, I discovered no less than three John Leacocks mentioned, all of whom were Coroners, as well as a Joseph Leacock, who occupied the same position. Examining the Records of the Pennsylvania Soldiers of the Revolution, I found several John Leacocks in the ranks as privates, and also one John Laycock.

Professor Moses Coit Tyler, in his "Literary History of the American Revolution" (ii, 198), giving a list of the characters in the play and the names of those supposed to be lampooned, analyzes the piece thoroughly, and says, "From internal evidence, it must be inferred that the writing of the play was finished after the publication of 'Common Sense' in January, 1776, and before the news had reached Philadelphia of the evacuation of Boston, March 17, 1776." Though Sabin takes for granted that Leacock wrote "The Fall of British Tyranny," Hildeburn, in the "Issues of the Press" (ii, 249), states that it is "said to have

---

[1] The Fall/of/British Tyranny;/or,/American Liberty/Triumphant./The First Campaign./A Tragi-Comedy of Five Acts,/as Lately Planned/at the Royal Theatrum Pandemonium,/at St. James's./The Principal Place of Action in America./Publish'd According to Act of Parliament./Quis furor ô cives! quæ tanta licentia ferri?/ Lucan. lib. I. ver. 8./What blind, detested madness could afford/Such horrid licence to the murd'ring sword?/Rowe./Philadelphia:/Printed by Styner and Cist, in Second-street,/near Arch-street. M DCC LXXVI.

[2] "The Medley; or, Harlequin Have At Ye All." A pantomime produced at Covent Garden, and published in 1778.

been written by Mr. Laycock of Philadelphia." If the John Leacock, whose name appears in the Philadelphia Directory of 1802, is the one who wrote "The Fall of British Tyranny," following that clue we find his name disappearing from the Directory in 1804. Hence, he must either have died, or have moved away from Philadelphia.

The elusive name of Leacock is to be considered also in connection with an opera entitled, "The Disappointment; or, The Force of Credulity," signed by Andrew Barton,[1] supposed to be a pseudonym, and attributed variously to "Colonel" Thomas Forrest and to John Leacock. I already have had occasion to mention "The Disappointment" in connection with Godfrey's "The Prince of Parthia." The reader will remember that in 1767 "The Disappointment" was put into rehearsal, but was suddenly withdrawn in preference to Godfrey's piece. This play has been fully and interestingly analyzed by O. G. Sonneck, who gives the reasons for the withdrawal of the play from rehearsal by the American Company of Philadelphia, 1767. These reasons are definitely stated in the *Pennsylvania Gazette* for April 16, 1767, which contains this warning in the American Company's advertisement of "The Mourning Bride": "N.B. 'The Disappointment' (that was advertised for Monday), as it contains personal Reflections, is unfit for the Stage."

The reason why this piece is attributed to "Colonel" Thomas Forrest is that there is a memorandum in substantiation on the title-page of a copy owned by the Library Company of Philadelphia.

Mr. Sonneck gives further and more extensive treatment of the subject in his excellent book on "Early Opera in America," (Schirmer, 1915) as well as in "Sammelbände der Internationale Musik Gesellschaft," for 1914–1915.

We mention the matter here, because, although Sonneck enters into a long discussion of the life of Forrest, he fails to give any satisfactory account of John Leacock. In fact, he says in closing, "If Andrew Barton, Esq., is to be a pseudonym, it seems to me that John Leacock, claimed (by Mr. Hildeburn) to have

---

[1] From Sabin, I take the following:
BARTON (A.) "The Disappointment; or, The Force of Credulity." A new American Comic Opera, of two Acts. By Andrew Barton, Esq. [Motto.] *New York, Printed in the year* M, DCC, LXVIII. 8vo, pp. v., 58. P. t. Second edition, revised and corrected, with large additions, by the Author. *Philadelphia*, Francis Shallus, 1796. 12 mo. pp. iv., 94, p. 3801. [Sabin also notes that the Philadelphia Library copy is very rare, with MS Key to the characters, who were Philadelphians. Air No. iv is Yankee Doodle (1767).]

written the tragi-comedy of 'The Fall of British Tyranny,' should not be cast aside so cheerfully in favour of Thomas Forrest."

Seilhamer and Durang, referring to the matter, mention Joseph Leacock as a claimant for the authorship of "The Disappointment," and say that he was a jeweler and a silversmith in Philadelphia; they also mention John Leacock, the Coroner. Durang, in the "History of the Philadelphia Stage," throws all weight in favour of Thomas Forrest. Sonneck says further, regarding the matter,—"We may dispose of Joseph by saying that he seems to have been among the dead when, in 1796, the second edition of 'The Disappointment,' revised and corrected by the author, was issued. On the other hand, Coroner John Leacock figures in the Philadelphia Directories even later."

So the matter stands. The play, however, is a very definite contribution, illustrating how quickly the American spirit changed in the days preceding the Revolution. Imagine, in 1762, the students of the College of New Jersey giving a piece entitled "The Military Glory of Great Britain;"[1] and so short a time afterwards, only fourteen years, in fact, a piece with the title, "The Fall of British Tyranny," being greeted by the theatre-going public! Leacock's attempt may be taken as the first example that we have of an American chronicle play. And it is likewise significant as being the first literary piece in which George Washington appears as a character. In the advertisement, the play is thus described (see Ford):

"A pleasing scene between Roger and Dick, two shepherds near Lexington.

"Clarissa, etc. A very moving scene on the death of Dr. Warren, etc., in a chamber near Boston, the morning after the battle of Bunker's Hill.

"A humorous scene between the Boatswain and a Sailor on board a man-of-war, near Norfolk in Virginia.

"Two very laughable scenes between the Boatswain, two Sailors and the Cook, exhibiting specimens of seafaring oratory, and peculiar eloquence of those sons of Neptune, touching Tories, Convicts, and Black Regulars: and between Lord Kidnapper and the Boatswain.

[1] The Title-page runs as follows:
The/Military Glory/of/Great-Britain,/an/Entertainment,/given by the late Candidates for/Bachelor's Degree,/At the close of the/Anniversary Commencement, held/in/Nassau-Hall/New-Jersey/September 29th, 1762./Philadelphia:/Printed by William Bradford, M, DCC, LXII.

"A very black scene between Lord Kidnapper and Major Cudjo.

"A religious scene between Lord Kidnapper, Chaplain, and the Captain.

"A scene, the Lord Mayor, etc., going to St. James's with the address.

"A droll scene, a council of war in Boston, Admiral Tombstone, Elbow Room, Mr. Caper, General Clinton and Earl Piercy.

"A diverting scene between a Whig and a Tory.

"A spirited scene between General Prescott and Colonel Allen.

"A shocking scene, a dungeon, between Colonel Allen and an officer of the guard.

"Two affecting scenes in Boston after the flight of the regulars from Lexington, between Lord Boston, messenger and officers of the guard.

"A patriotic scene in the camp at Cambridge, between the Generals Washington, Lee, and Putnam, etc., etc."

It is interesting to note that in the Abbé Robin's discerning remarks, concerning the effect of drama on the pupils of Harvard in 1781, and on the general appeal of drama among the American Patriots, he mentions "The Fall of British Tyranny" without giving the author's name.

The FALL

of

BRITISH TYRANNY

or,

AMERICAN LIBERTY

TRIUMPHANT.

The. FIRST CAMPAIGN.

A *TRAGI-COMEDY* of FIVE ACTS,

AS LATELY PLANNED

At the Royal Theatrum Pandemonium,
at St. James's.

THE PRINCIPAL PLACE OF ACTION IN AMERICA.

PUBLISH'D. ACCORDING TO ACT OF PARLIAMENT.

Quis furor ô cives! quæ tanta licentia ferri?
LUCAN. lib. 1. ver. 8.

What blind, detested madness could afford
Such horrid licence to the murd'ring sword?
ROWE.

PHILADELPHIA:

PRINTED BY STYNER AND CIST, IN SECOND-STREET.
NEAR ARCH-STREET. M DCC LXXVI.

FAC-SIMILE TITLE-PAGE OF THE FIRST EDITION

THE DEDICATION

To Lord Boston, Lord Kidnapper, and the innumerable and never-ending Clan of Macs and Donalds upon Donalds, and the Remnant of the Gentlemen Officers, Actors, Merry Andrews, strolling Players, Pirates, and Buccaneers in America.

My Lords and Gentlemen:

Understanding you are vastly fond of plays and farces, and frequently exhibit them for your own amusement, and the laudable purpose of ridiculing your masters (the YANKEES, *as you call 'em), it was expected you would have been polite enough to have favoured the world, or America at least (at whose expense you act them), with some of your play-bills, or with a sample of your composition.*

I shall, however, not copy your churlishness, but dedicate the following Tragi-Comedy to your patronage, and for your future entertainment; and as the most of you have already acted your particular parts of it, both comic and tragic, in reality at Lexington, Bunker's-Hill, the Great-Bridge, &c., &c., &c., to the very great applause of yourselves, tho' not of the whole house, no doubt you will preserve the marks, or memory of it, as long as you live, as it is wrote in capital American characters and letters of blood on your posteriors: And however some Whigs may censure you for your affected mirth (as they term it, in the deplorable situation you are now in, like hogs in a pen, and in want of elbow room), yet I can by no means agree with them, but think it a proof of true heroism and philosophy, to endeavour to make the best of a bad bargain, and laugh at yourselves, to prevent others from laughing at you; and tho' you are deprived of the use of your teeth, it is no reason you should be bereaved of the use of your tongues, your eyes, your ears, and your risible faculties and powers. That would be cruel indeed! after the glorious and fatiguing campaign you have made, and the many signal victories obtained over whole herds of cattle and swine, routing flocks of sheep, lambs and geese, storming hen-roosts, and taking them prisoners, and thereby raising the glory of Old England to a pitch she never knew before. And ye Macs, and ye Donalds upon Donalds, go on, and may our gallows-hills and liberty poles be honour'd and adorn'd with some of your heads: Why should Tyburn and Temple-bar make a monopoly of so valuable a commodity?

Wishing you abundance of entertainment in the re-acting this Tragi-Comedy, and of which I should be proud to take a part with you, tho' I have reason to think you would not of choice let me come within three hundred yards of your stage, lest I should rob you of your laurels, receive the clap of the whole house, and pass for a second Garrick among you, as you know I always act with applause, speak bold—point blank—off hand—and without prompter.

I am, My Lords and Gentlemen Buffoons,

Your always ready humble servant,

DICK RIFLE.

THE PREFACE

Solomon said, "Oppression makes a wise man mad:" but what would he have said, had he lived in these days, and seen the oppression of the people of Boston, and the distressed situation of the inhabitants of Charlestown, Falmouth, Stonnington, Bristol, Norfolk, &c.? Would he not have said, "The tongue of the sucking child cleaveth to the roof of his mouth for thirst; the young children ask for bread, but no man breaketh it unto them?" "They that did feed delicately, perish in the streets; they that were brought up in scarlet, embrace the dung." What would he have said of rejected petitions, disregarded supplications, and contemned remonstrances? Would he not have said, "From hardness of heart, good Lord, deliver us?" What would he have said of a freeborn people butchered— their towns desolated, and become an heap of ashes—their inhabitants become beggars, wanderers and vagabonds—by the cruel orders of an unrelenting tyrant, wallowing in luxury, and wantonly wasting the people's wealth, to oppress them the more? Would he not have said, it was oppression and ingratitude in the highest degree, exceeding the oppression of the children of Israel? and, like Moses, have cried out, let the people go? Would he not have wondered at our patience and long-suffering, and have said, " 'Tis time to change our master!—'Tis time to part!"—And had he been an American born, would he not have shewed his wisdom by adopting the language of independency? Happy then for America in these fluctuating times, she is not without her Solomons, who see the necessity of heark'ning to reason, and listening to the voice of COMMON SENSE.

THE GODDESS OF LIBERTY

Hail! Patriots,[1] hail! by me inspired be!
Speak boldly, think and act for Liberty,
United sons, America's choice band,
Ye Patriots firm, ye sav'ours of the land.
Hail! Patriots, hail! rise with the rising sun,
Nor quit your labour, till the work is done.
Ye early risers in your country's cause,
Shine forth at noon, for Liberty and Laws.
Build a strong tow'r, whose fabric may endure
Firm as a rock, from tyranny secure.
Yet would you build my fabric to endure,
Be your hearts warm—but let your hands be pure.
Never to shine, yourselves, your country sell;
But think you nobly, while in place act well.
Let no self-server general trust betray,
No picque, no party, bar the public way.
Front an arm'd world, with union on your side:
No foe shall shake you—if no friends divide.
At night repose, and sweetly take your rest;
None sleeps so sound as those by conscience blest;
May martyr'd patriots whisper in your ear,
To tread the paths of virtue without fear;
May pleasing visions charm your patriot eyes;
While Freedom's sons shall hail you blest and wise,
Hail! my last hope, she cries, inspired by me,
Wish, talk, write, fight, and die—for LIBERTY.

[1] The Congress

THE PROLOGUE

Spoken by Mr. Peter Buckstail.

Since 'tis the fashion, preface, prologue next,
Else what's a play?—like sermon without text!
Since 'tis the fashion then, I'll not oppose;
For what's a man if he's without a nose?
The curtain's up—the music's now begun,
What is 't?—Why murder, fire, and sword, and gun.
What scene?—Why blood!—What act?—Fight and be free!
Or be ye slaves—and give up liberty!
Blest Continent, while groaning nations round
Bend to the servile yoke, ignobly bound,
May ye be free—nor ever be opprest
By murd'ring tyrants, but a land of rest!
What say ye to 't? what says the audience?
Methinks I hear some whisper COMMON SENSE.
Hark! what say them Tories?—Silence—let 'em speak,
Poor fools! dumb—they hav'n't spoke a word this week,
Dumb let 'em be, at full end of their tethers,
'Twill save the expense of tar and of feathers:
Since old Pluto's lurch'd 'em, and swears he does not know
If more these Tory puppy curs will bark or no.
Now ring the bell—Come forth, ye actors, come,
The Tragedy's begun, beat, beat the drum,
Let's all advance, equipt like volunteers,
Oppose the foe, and banish all our fears.
We will be free—or bravely we will die, ⎫
And leave to Tories tyrants' legacy,   ⎬
And all our share of its dependency.   ⎭

DRAMATIS PERSONÆ

LORD PARAMOUNT,	Mr. Bute.
LORD MOCKLAW,	Mr. Mansfield.
LORD HYPOCRITE,	Mr. Dartmouth.
LORD POLTRON,	Mr. Sandwich.
LORD CATSPAW,	Mr. North.
LORD WISDOM,	Mr. Chatham.
LORD RELIGION,	Bishop of St. Asaph.
LORD JUSTICE,	Mr. Camden.
LORD PATRIOT,	Mr. Wilkes.
BOLD IRISHMAN,	Mr. Burke.
JUDAS	Mr. Hutchinson.
CHARLEY,	Mr. Jenkinson.
BRAZEN,	Mr. Wedderburne.
COLONEL,	Mr. Barre.
LORD BOSTON,	Mr. Gage.
ADMIRAL TOMBSTONE,	Mr. Graves.
ELBOW ROOM,[1]	Mr. Howe.
MR. CAPER,	Mr. Burgoyne.
LORD KIDNAPPER,	Mr. Dunmore.
GENERAL WASHINGTON.	
GENERAL LEE.	
GENERAL PUTNAM.	

Officers, Soldiers, Sailors, Citizens, Negroes, &c., &c., &c.

[1] It seems to be generally thought that the expression of "Elbow Room" is to be attributed to General Howe, and not to General Burgoyne.

THE FALL

OF

BRITISH TYRANNY, &c.

ACT I.

Scene I. *At St. James's.*

Lord Paramount [*solus, strutting about*].

Many long years have rolled delightfully on, whilst I have been basking in the sunshine of grandeur and power, whilst I have imperceptibly (tho' not unsuspected) guided the chariot of state, and greased with the nation's gold the imperial wheels.

'Tis I that move the mighty engine of royalty, and with the tincture of my somniferous opiate or (in the language of a courtier) by the virtue of my secret influence, I have lulled the axletree to sleep, and brought on a pleasing insensibility.

Let their champion, Lord Wisdom, groan, he is now become feeble and impotent, a mere cripple in politics; their Lord Patriot's squint has lost its basilisk effect: and the bold Irishman may bellow the *Keenew* till he's hoarse, he's no more when compar'd to me than an Irish salmon to a Scotch herring: I care not a bawbee for them all. I'll reign in Britain, I'll be king of their counsels, and chief among the princes.

Oh! ambition, thou darling of my soul! stop not till I rise superior to all superlative, till I mount triumphantly the pinnacle of glory, or at least open the way for one of my own family and name to enter without opposition.

The work is now cut out, and must be finish'd, I have ventur'd too far to recede, my honour's at stake, my importance, nay my life, depends upon it!

Last night's three hours' closeting has effectually done the business; then I spoke my mind in such terms as to make a lasting impression, never to be eradicated—all—all was given up to me, and now since I hold the reins of government, since I am possessed of supreme power, every thing shall be subservient to my royal will and pleasure.

SCENE II.

Enter MOCKLAW.

MOCKLAW. I am your Lordship's most obedient humble servant.

PARAMOUNT. Be seated,—I sent for you to have a small conference with you—and to let you know, your advice respecting certain points of law, I have found succeeded to admiration; even beyond my most sanguine expectations.

MOCKLAW. I am heartily glad of it, altho' the advice I gave your Lordship, I cannot say, was law; yet, your Lordship can easily pass it as such by a royal proclamation: and should it ever be disputed, I have quirks and quibbles enough at your service, with Mr. Brazen and Mr. Attorney-General's assistance, to render it so doubtful, obscure and ambiguous, as to puzzle Lord Justice, perplex Dunning, and confound Glynn.

PARAMOUNT. Can you show me an instance of a royal proclamation passing for a law? or advise me how to make it such, if you can, I shall make it well worth your study.

MOCKLAW. My Lord, as you have now got a parliament exactly to your mind, ev'ry thing you propose will be granted; but in order that you may see precedents are not wanting—there is a statute in the reign of Henry the 8th that expressly shews the then parliament passed a law that the king's proclamation should be the law of the land—

PARAMOUNT. Are you sure of that?

MOCKLAW. My Lord, here it is—this is real law: *Luce meridiana clariora.* When we find any thing of this kind, ready made to our hands, it's a treasure we should never part with.

[PARAMOUNT *reads.*

PARAMOUNT. I see it plain! this, this alone is worth a ton of gold.—Now, by St. Andrew! I'll strike a stroke that shall surprise all Europe, and make the boldest of the adverse party turn pale and tremble —Scotch politics, Scotch intrigues, Scotch influence, and Scotch impudence (as they have termed it), they shall see ere long shine with unheard of splendour, and the name of Lord Paramount the mighty, shall blaze in the annals of the world with far greater lustre (as a consummate politician) than the name of Alexander the Great, as an hero!

MOCKLAW. That day I much wish for,—but, with your Lordship's permission, I would just mention, that secrecy and dissimulation are the soul of enterprise; your Lordship hath many enemies, who watch ev'ry movement of state with a jealous and wary eye.

PARAMOUNT. I know it, but the futile attempts of my timid adversaries have hitherto proved abortive—so far I have borne down all opposition, and those (even some of the greatest of them) who not long since were my most open, as well as secret enemies, I now behold with the most princely pleasure, the earliest to attend, to congratulate me on my birthday, tho' uninvited, bow down, and make the most submissive congees. Have you not seen this, Mocklaw? and how I keep them in expectation of something, by now and then bestowing part of a gracious smile amongst a dozen of them?

MOCKLAW. I have, my Lord, and no doubt they interpret that as a favourable omen;—however, policy, my Lord, would dictate that to you, if there were no other consideration.

PARAMOUNT. True, and yet they are cursedly mistaken—and now, Mocklaw, as I have ever found you to be well dispos'd towards me, and the cause I espouse, and as I trust you continue satisfy'd with my former bounty, and my promise now of granting you a pension for life, with liberty to retire, I shall make you my confident, and disclose to you a secret no man except myself yet knows, which I expect you have so much honour to let it remain a secret to all the world (I mean as to the main point I have in view).

MOCKLAW. Depend upon it, my Lord, I am sincerely devoted to your Lordship, command me, I care not what it is, I'll screw, twist and strain the law as tight as a drumhead, to serve you.

PARAMOUNT. I shall at this time but just give you a hint of the plan I've drawn up in my own mind. You must have perceived in me a secret hankering for majesty for some time past, notwithstanding my age;—but as I have considered the great dislike the nation in general have, as to my person, I'll wave my own pretensions, and bend my power and assiduity to it in favour of one, the nearest a kin to me, you know who I mean, and a particular friend of yours, provided I continue to be dictator,

as at present; and further, I intend America shall submit.—
What think you of it so far?

MOCKLAW. A day I've long wish'd to see! but you stagger
me, my Lord, not as to my honour, secrecy, or resolution to
serve you, but as to the accomplishment of such grand designs.

PARAMOUNT. 'Tis true, I have undertaken a mighty task, a
task that would have perplexed the Council of Nice, and stagger'd even Julius Cæsar—but—

MOCKLAW. You have need, my Lord, of all your wisdom,
fortitude and power, when you consider with whom you have
to contend—Let me see—Lord Wisdom—Lord Religion—Lord
Justice—Lord Patriot—the bold Irishman, &c., &c., &c., and
the wisdom of the United Colonies of America in Congress to
cope with; as individuals they are trifling, but in league combined may become potent enemies.

PARAMOUNT. Granted—But are you so little of a lawyer as not
to know the virtue of a certain specific I'm possess'd of, that will
accomplish any thing, even to performing miracles? Don't you
know there's such sweet music in the shaking of the treasury keys,
that they will instantly lock the most babbling patriot's tongue?
transform a Tory into a Whig, and a Whig into a Tory? make a
superannuated old miser dance, and an old Cynic philosopher
smile. How many thousand times has your tongue danc'd at
Westminster Hall to the sound of such music?

MOCKLAW. Enchanting sounds, powerful magic, there's no
withstanding the charms of such music, their potency and influence are irresistible—that is a point of law I can by no means
give up, of more force than all the acts of parliament since
the days of King Alfred.

PARAMOUNT. I'm glad you acknowledge that—Now then for
a line of politics—I propose to begin first by taxing America, as a
blind—that will create an eternal animosity between us, and by
sending over continually ships and troops, this will, of course, produce a civil war—weaken Britain by leaving her coasts defense-
less, and impoverish America; so that we need not fear any thing
from that quarter. Then the united fleets of France and Spain
with troops to appear in the channel, and make a descent, while
my kinsman with thirty thousand men lands in Scotland, marches
to London, and joins the others: What then can prevent the
scheme from having the wish'd for effect? This is the main
point, which keep to yourself.

MOCKLAW. If it has failed heretofore, 'tis impossible it should fail now; nothing within the reach of human wisdom was ever planned so judiciously; had Solomon been alive, and a politician, I would have sworn your Lordship had consulted him.—But I would beg leave to hint to your Lordship the opposition to be apprehended from the militia of England, and the German forces that may be sent for according to treaty.

PARAMOUNT. As to the militia, they are half of them my friends, witness Lancaster, Manchester, Liverpool, &c., &c., &c., the other half scarce ever fired a gun in their lives, especially those of London; and I shall take care by shaking the keys a little to have such officers appointed over them, who are well known to be in my interest. As to the German forces, I have nothing to apprehend from them; the parliament can soon pass an act against the introduction of foreign troops, except the French or Spaniards, who can't be called foreign, they are our friends and nearest neighbours. Have you any thing further to object against the probability of this plan?

MOCKLAW. Nothing, my Lord, but the people of Ireland, who must be cajoled or humbugg'd.

PARAMOUNT. As to that, let me alone, I shall grant the Roman Catholics, who are by far the most numerous, the free exercise of their religion, with the liberty of bearing arms, so long unjustly deprived of, and disarm in due time all the Protestants in their turn.

MOCKLAW. That will be a noble stroke, the more I consider it, the more I'm surpris'd at your Lordship's profound wisdom and foresight: I think success is certain.

PARAMOUNT. Then this is the favourable crisis to attempt it; 'tis not the thought of a day, a month, or a year. Have you any more objections?

MOCKLAW. I have one more, my Lord—

PARAMOUNT. Well, pray let's hear it; these lawyers will be heard.

MOCKLAW. The Bishops and Clergy are a powerful, numerous body; it would be necessary, my Lord, to gain them over, or keep them silent—A religious war is the worst of wars.

PARAMOUNT. You are very right, I have 'em fast enough— Mammon will work powerfully on them—The keys—the keys— His Grace my Lord of Suffolk is managing this business for me, and feeding them with the hopes of being all created Archbishops here, and each to have a diocese, and Bishops of their own appointment in America; not a city or town there but must be provided with a Bishop: There let religion erect her holy altars, by which means their revenues will be augmented beyond that of a Cardinal. All this we must make 'em believe.

MOCKLAW. True, my Lord, what is a Bishop without faith? This is the grandest stroke of religious circumvention that ever was struck.—I've done, my Lord.

PARAMOUNT. Very well, you'll not fail to meet the privy council here this evening; in the mean time you'll go and search the statutes for other precedents to strengthen the cause; and remember I have enjoin'd you to secrecy.

MOCKLAW. Depend upon it, my Lord, I cannot prove ungrateful to your Lordship, nor such an enemy to myself.

[*Exit* MOCKLAW.

SCENE III. LORD PARAMOUNT [*solus*].

This Mocklaw is a cursed knowing dog, and I believe the father of Brazen; how readily he found an old act of parliament to my purpose, as soon as I told him I would make it worth his study; and the thoughts of a pension will make him search his old worm-eaten statute books from the reign of King Arthur down to this present time; how he raises objections too to make me think his mind is ever bent on study to serve me. The shaking of the treasury keys is a fine bait. [*Rings the bell.*] Charters, magna chartas, bill of rights, acts of assembly, resolves of congresses, trials by juries (and acts of parliament too) when they make against us, must all be annihilated; a suspending power I approve of, and of royal proclamations.   [*Enter* CHARLEY.

CHARLEY. I wait your Lordship's orders.

PARAMOUNT. Write a number of cards, and see that the Lords of the privy council, and Mr. Judas, be summoned to give their attendance this evening at six o'clock, at my Pandemonium.

CHARLEY. I'm gone, my Lord.   [*Exit* CHARLEY.

PARAMOUNT [*solus*].

How do we shew our authority? how do we maintain the royal prerogative? keep in awe the knowing ones of the opposite party, and blind the eyes of the ignorant multitude in Britain? Why, by spirited measures, by an accumulation of power, of deception, and the shaking of the keys, we may hope to succeed, should that fail, I'll enforce them with the pointed bayonet; the Americans from one end to the other shall submit, in spite of all opposition; I'll listen to no overtures of reconciliation from any petty self-constituted congress, they shall submit implicitly to such terms as I of my royal indulgence please to grant. I'll shew them the impudence and weakness of their resolves, and the strength of mine; I will never soften; my inflexibility shall stand firm, and convince them the second Pharaoh is at least equal to the first. I am unalterably determined at every hazard and at the risk of every consequence to compel the colonies to absolute submission. I'll draw in treasure from every quarter, and, Solomon-like, wallow in riches; and Scotland, my dear Scotland, shall be the paradise of the world. Rejoice in the name of Paramount, and the sound of a bawbee shall be no more heard in the land of my nativity.—

SCENE IV.

Enter CHARLEY *in haste.*

CHARLEY. My Lord, the notices are all served.

PARAMOUNT. It's very well, Charley.

CHARLEY. My Lord, be pleased to turn your eyes, and look out of the window, and see the Lord Mayor, Aldermen, Common Council and Liverymen going to St. James's with the address.

PARAMOUNT. Where? Sure enough—Curse their impudence; how that squinting scoundrel swells with importance—Mind, Charley, how fond he is of bowing to the gaping multitude, and ev'ry upstart he sees at a window—I hope he'll not turn his blear eyes t'wards me—I want none of his bows, not I—Stand before me, Charley—

CHARLEY. I will, my Lord, and if he looks this way, I'll give him such a devilish grin as best suits such fellows as him, and make him remember it as long as he lives.

PARAMOUNT. Do so, Charley; I hate the dog mortally, I religiously hate him, and hope ere long to have satisfaction for his insolence and the freedoms he has taken with me and my connections; I shall never forget the many scandalous verses, lampoons and pasquinades he made upon us.

CHARLEY. Indeed, he has used your Lordship too ill ever to be forgotten or forgiven.

PARAMOUNT. Damn him, I never intend to do either—See again how he bows—there again—how the mob throw up their hats, split their throats; how they huzza too; they make a mere god of the fellow; how they idolize him—Ignorant brutes!

CHARLEY. A scoundrel; he has climb'd up the stilts of preferment strangely, my Lord.

PARAMOUNT. Strangely, indeed; but it's our own faults.

CHARLEY. He has had better luck than honester folks; I'm surpris'd to think he has ever rose to the honour of presenting a remonstrance, or rather, that he could ever have the impudence to think of remonstrating.

PARAMOUNT. Aye, Charley, you see how unaccountably things turn out; his audacity is unparalleled—a Newgate dog.

CHARLEY. My Lord, I believe the fellow was never known to blush; and, indeed, it's an observation I made some time ago, and I believe a just one, without an exception, that those who squint never blush.

PARAMOUNT. You must be mistaken, Charley.

CHARLEY. No, my Lord, it's a fact, I had an uncle squinted exactly like him, who was guilty of many scandalous things, and yet all the parish, with the parson at their head, could not make him blush, so that at last he became a by-word—Here comes old shame-the-devil; this dog is the very spawn of him.

PARAMOUNT. Hoot, mon, ye give your uncle a shocking character.

CHARLEY. I only mention it, my Lord, for the similarity's sake.

PARAMOUNT. For the spawn of him, and the similarity's sake, I'm apt to think you've been abusing your own cousin all this while.

CHARLEY. God forbid, my Lord, I should be any how allied to him.

PARAMOUNT. I fancy, Charley, if the truth was known, your uncle did not mention you in his will, and forgot to leave you the mansion-house and farm at Gallows-hill. Am I right, Charley?

CHARLEY. You're right, my Lord, upon my honour—but—

PARAMOUNT. I thought so— Well, never mind— Ha, ha, ha, who are those two fat fellows there, that go in such state?

CHARLEY. I suppose them to be a couple of Livery Tallow-chandlers, my Lord, by their big bellies.

PARAMOUNT. Ha, ha,—what work the guards would make amongst them—but they must not be called yet.—And who are those other two behind 'em?

CHARLEY. This is Mr. Hone, and the other Mr. Strap, a couple of the Corporation Barbers, forsooth.

PARAMOUNT. Ha, ha, ha, I thought they had been a couple of Dukes;—and that one—who is he with the monstrous wig?

CHARLEY. That is Mr. Alderman Pipeshank, in Newgate-street.

PARAMOUNT. A parcel of Newgate dogs altogether— Well it is a good deal of satisfaction to me to think how this fellow will be received at St. James's; he'll not return back so pleas'd as he seems to be now, I warrant you—I have taken care he shall meet with a d——d cold reception there; he will have to make his appearance before Lord Frostyface, Lord Scarecrow, Lord Sneerwell, Lord Firebrand, Lord Mawmouth, Lord Waggon-jaws, Lord Gripe, Lord Brass, Lord Surly and Lord Tribu-lation, as hard-fac'd fellows as himself; and the beauty of it is, not one of them loves him a whit more than I do.

CHARLEY. That will be rare diversion for them that are present; he'll look then, my Lord, like Sampson making sport for the Philistines.

PARAMOUNT. Aye, but I wish he was as blind too, as Sampson was.—Well Charley, we have been dispos'd to be a little merry with this ridiculous parade, this high life below stairs. I wish you had begun your description a little sooner, before they were all gone; the looks of these wiseacres afford us some mirth, tho' we despise them and their politics, and it's not unlikely it may end in blood—Be it so, I'm prepar'd for the worst.

CHARLEY. Rather so, my Lord, than submit to such rascals.

PARAMOUNT. I'll give up my life first for a sacrifice.

[*Exit* CHARLEY.

SCENE V.

Enter MOCKLAW, POLTRON, HYPOCRITE, CATSPAW, BRAZEN, JUDAS. [*All seated.*]

PARAMOUNT. My Lords and Gentlemen, it seems opposition to our measures are making hasty strides; the discontented faction, the supporters and encouragers of rebellion, and whole hearts are tainted therewith, seem bent, if possible, on the destruction of Britain, and their own aggrandisement. Are not the daily papers filled with treasonable resolves of American congresses and committees, extracts of letters, and other infamous pieces and scurrilous pamphlets, circulating with unusual industry throughout the kingdom, by the enemies of Britain, thereby poisoning the minds of our liege subjects with their detestable tenets?—And did you not this day see the procession, and that vile miscreant Lord Patriot at their head, going to St. James's with their remonstrance, in such state and parade as manifestly tended to provoke, challenge and defy majesty itself, and the powers of government? and yet nothing done to stop their pernicious effects.—Surely, my Lords and Gentlemen, you must agree with me, that it is now become highly expedient that an immediate stop should be put to such unwarrantable and dangerous proceedings, by the most vigorous and coercive measures.

MOCKLAW. I entirely agree with your Lordship, and was ever firmly of opinion, that licentiousness of every kind (particularly that of the Press) is dangerous to the state; the rabble should be kept in awe by examples of severity, and a proper respect should be enforced to superiors. I have sufficiently shewn my dislike to the freedom of the Press, by the examples I have frequently made (tho' too favourable) of several Printers, and others, who had greatly trespassed, and if they still persist, other measures should be taken with them, which the laws will point out; and as to Lord Patriot, he's a fellow that has been outlaw'd, scandal-proof, little to be got by meddling with him; I would advise to let him alone for the present, and humble America first.

MR. BRAZEN. I am very clear in it, please your Lordship; there are numbers of men in this country who are ever studying how to perplex and entangle the state, constantly thwarting government, in ev'ry laudable undertaking; this clamorous faction must be curbed, must be subdued and crush'd—our thunder must go forth, America must be conquered. I am for blood and fire to crush the rising glories of America—They boast of her strength; she must be conquered, if half of Germany is called to our assistance.

MR. POLTRON. I entirely agree with you, Mr. Brazen; my advice is, that Lord Boston and Admiral Tombstone be immediately despatch'd to Boston, with two or three regiments (tho' one would be more than sufficient) and a few ships to shut up their ports, disannul their charter, stop their trade, and the pusillanimous beggars, those scoundrel rascals, whose predominant passion is fear, would immediately give up, on the first landing of the regulars, and fly before 'em like a hare before the hounds; that this would be the case, I pawn my honour to your Lordships, nay, I'll sacrifice my life: My Lords, I have moreover the testimony of General Amherst and Colonel Grant to back my assertion; besides, here's Mr. Judas, let him speak.

LORD HYPOCRITE. If this is the same Colonel Grant that was at Fort Duquesne, the same that ran away from the French and Indians, the same that was rescued by Colonel Washington, I have no idea of his honour or testimony.

LORD POLTRON. He's a Gentleman, my Lord Hypocrite, of undoubted veracity.

LORD HYPOCRITE. You might as well have said courage too, I have exceptions against both; and as to General Amherst's assertion that he could drive all America with five thousand men, he must have been joking, as he is quite of a diff'rent opinion now.

LORD CATSPAW. What is your opinion of your countrymen, Mr. Judas, with respect to their courage?

JUDAS. The same that I have ever told you, my Lord: as to true courage they have none, I know 'em well—they have a plenty of a kind of enthusiastic zeal, which they substitute in the room of it; I am very certain they would never face the regulars, tho' with the advantage of ten to one.

LORD HYPOCRITE. All this, and a great deal more, would never convince me of the general cowardice of the Americans— but of the cowardice of Grant I've been long convinced, by numbers of letters formerly from America—I'm for doing the business effectually; don't let us be too sanguine, trust to stories told by every sycophant, and hurry heels over head to be laugh'd at; the Americans are bold, stubborn, and sour; it will require foreign assistance to subdue 'em.

LORD CATSPAW. These four Americans, ignorant brutes, un- broke and wild, must be tamed; they'll soon be humble if punish'd; but if disregarded, grow fierce.—Barbarous nations must be held by fear, rein'd and spurr'd hard, chain'd to the oar, and bow'd to due control, till they look grim with blood; let's first humble America, and bring them under our feet; the olive-branch has been held out, and they have rejected it; it now becomes us to use the iron rod to break their disobedience; and should we lack it, foreign assistance is at hand.

LORD HYPOCRITE. All this I grant, but I'm for sending a force sufficient to crush 'em at once, and not with too much precipitation; I am first for giving it a colour of impartiality, forbearance and religion.—Lay it before parliament; we have then law on our side, and endeavour to gain over some or all of the Methodist Teachers, and in particular my very good friend Mr. Wesley, their Bishop, and the worthy Mr. Clapum, which task I would undertake; it will then have the sanction of religion, make it less suspected, and give it a better grace.

LORD CATSPAW. I should choose it to be done by consent of parliament; we stand then on firmer ground; there's no doubt they'll grant ev'ry thing your Lordship proposes upon my motion: but to tell the truth, I'd rather be in Purgatory so long, than to run the gauntlet of the Bold Irishman's tongue.

MOCKLAW. Aye, aye, don't part with the law while it's in our favour, or we can have it by asking for—and as to the Bold Irishman, don't be brow-beaten, you must summon all your brass, and put on a rugged highwayman's face like his; I expect some work of that kind too, but the devil himself sha'n't browbeat me.

PARAMOUNT. I am glad to find, my Lords and Gentlemen, you all see the necessity of sending over troops and ships; I intend my Lord Catspaw shall lay it before parliament, and am very certain they'll pass any acts I can desire. I thank you, Lord Hypocrite, for your kind offer, and accept of it; my Lord of Suffolk is negotiating the same business with the rest of my Lords the Bishops, and will succeed; so that it will carry the appearance of law, of religion, and will be sufficiently grac'd; I'll warrant you no one shall have cause to complain of its wanting grace. And now, my Lords and Gentlemen, as it's so late, and we have gone through all the business at this time proposed, you are at your liberty to withdraw. [*Exeunt.*

PARAMOUNT [*solus*].

The fate of England and America is now fixed, irrevocably fixed; the storm is ready to burst; the low'ring clouds portend their fate my glory, their fall my triumph—But |I must haste to be gone, the ceremonies await my presence; deeds of darkness must be done by night, and, like the silent mole's work, under ground:

Now rushing forth in sober twilight gray,
Like prowling wolf, who ranges for his prey.

[*Exit.*

ACT II.

SCENE I.

LORD WISDOM, LORD RELIGION, LORD JUSTICE.

LORD WISDOM.

I much lament, my Lords, the present unhappy situation of my country; where e'er I turn mine eyes, to Europe, Asia, Africa, or America, the prospect appears the same—Look up to the throne, and behold your king, if I may now call him by that soft title—Where is the wisdom, the justice, the religion, that once adorn'd that throne, and shed the benign influence of their bright rays thro' the four quarters of the globe? Alas! they're flown!

Mark his forlorn looks—his countenance dejected, a sullen greatness fixed on his brow, as if it veil'd in blood some awful purpose, his eyes flaming and sanguinary; how I bewail you, for your predecessor's sake! Long, long have I been an old, and I trust a faithful, servant in the family—Can I then restrain one tear? No, 'tis impossible! View that arch-dragon, that old fiend, Paramount, that rebel in grain, whispering in his ear. View his wretched ministers hovering round him, to accomplish their accursed purpose, and accelerate his destruction. View the whole herd of administration (I know 'em well) and tell me if the world can furnish a viler set of miscreants? View both houses of parliament, and count the number of Tyrants, Jacobites, Tories, Placemen, Pensioners, Sycophants, and Panders. View the constitution, is she not disrob'd and dismantled? is she not become like a virgin deflower'd? View our fleets and armies commanded by bloody, murdering butchers! View Britain herself as a sheep without a shepherd! And lastly view America, for her virtue bleeding and for her liberty weltering in her blood!

LORD RELIGION. Such hath, and ever will be the fate of kings, who only listen to the voice of pleasure, thrown in their way by the sirens of administration, which never fail to swallow them up like quicksand—like a serpent, who charms and fascinates, bewitches and enchants with his eye the unwary bird; witness the fatal catastrophe of Rehoboam, who rejected the counsel of the wise and experienced, and gave up all to the advice and guidance of young, unskilful and wicked counsellors. Had he listen'd to you, my Lord, had he followed your advice, all, all would have gone well—Under your auspicious administration Britain flourished, but ever since has been on the decline, and patriotism, like religion, scarcely now more than a sounding brass or a tinkling cymbal.

LORD WISDOM. My counsel has been rejected—my conciliatory plan thrown under the table, and treated with contempt; the experience of gray hairs called the superannuated notions of old age—my bodily infirmities—my tottering frame—my crazy carcase, worn out in the service of my country, and even my very crutches, have been made the subject of their ridicule.

LORD JUSTICE. Gratitude, like religion and patriotism, are about taking their flight, and the law of the land stands on tiptoe; the constitution, that admirable fabric, that work of ages, the envy of the world, is deflower'd indeed, and made to commit a rape upon her own body, by the avaricious frowns of her own father, who is bound to protect her, not to destroy.—Her pillars are thrown down, her capitals broke, her pedestals demolish'd, and her foundation nearly destroy'd.—Lord Paramount and his wretched adviser Mocklaw baffle all our efforts.—The statutes of the land superseded by royal proclamations and dispensing powers, &c., &c., the bloody knife to be held to the throats of the Americans, and force them to submit to slav'ry.—Administration have commenced bloody tyrants, and those that should protect the subject are become their executioners; yet will I dispute with them inch by inch, while there's a statute book left in the land. Come forth, thou grand deceiver! I challenge thee to come forth!

LORD WISDOM. Our friends must bestir themselves once more, perhaps we may yet turn the scale.—If the voice of religion, wisdom and justice should fail, let us sound the trumpet of liberty and patriotism, that will conquer them in America, I know; let us try to storm them here with the united whole, and if by a base majority they still carry their point, we can nevertheless wash our hands and be clean.

LORD RELIGION. [From the pulpit, in the house of God, have I spoken aloud, I have lifted up my voice like a trumpet. O Britain, how art thou fallen! Hear now, O house of Britain, is it a small thing for you to weary man, but will you weary your God also? In the house of Lords have I borne my testimony: Hear now, O ye Princes, and I will yet declare in Britain, and shew forth in America, I will not cease till I bring about (if possible) unity, peace and concord.

LORD WISDOM. Much to be wished for; but alas! I fear it's now too late; I foresee the tendency and consequence of those diabolical measures that have been pursued with unrelenting fury. Britain will ruin her trade, waste her wealth, her strength, her credit and her importance in the scale of Europe. When a British king proves ungrateful and haughty, and strives to be independent of his people (who are his sole support), the people will in their turn likewise strive to be independent of him and his myrmidons, and will be free; they will erect the anfractuous standard of independency, and thousands and tens of thousands will flock to it, and solace themselves under its shade.—They has often been told of this, but affected to despise it; they know not America's strength, they are ignorant of it; fed by the flatt'ry of every sycophant tale, imagine themselves almighty, and able to subdue the whole world. America will be lost to Britain forever, and will prove her downfall. America is wise, and will shake off the galling yoke before it be rivetted on them; they will be drove to it, and who can blame them? Who can blame a galley-slave for making his escape?—Britain will miscarry in her vile projects, her knight errant, her Don Quixote schemes in America: America will resist; they are not easily to be subdued (nay, 'tis impossible); Britain will find it a harder task than to conquer France and Spain united, and will cost 'em more blood and treasure than a twice Seven Years' War with those European powers; they will stand out till Britons are tired. Britain will invite her with kind promises and open arms; America will reject them; America will triumph, rejoice and flourish, and become the glory of the earth; Britain will languidly hold down her head, and become first a prey to a vile Pretender, and then be subject to the ravagers of Europe. I love the Americans, because they love liberty. Liberty flourishes in the wilds of America. I honour the plant, I revere the tree, and would cherish its branches. Let us, my friends, join hands with them, follow their example, and endeavour to support expiring liberty in Britain; whilst I have a tongue to speak, I will support her wherever found; while I have crutches to crawl with, I will try to find her out, and with the voice of an archangel will demand for a sacrifice to the nation those miscreants who have wickedly and wantonly been the ruin of their country. O Liberty! O my Country!

LORD RELIGION. O Religion! O Virtue! whither art thou fleeing? O thou Defender of the Faith? O ye mighty Lords and Commons! O ye deluded Bishops, ye learned props of our unerring church, who preach up vengeance, force and fire, instead of peace! be wise in time, lest the Americans be driven to work out their own salvation without fear or trembling.   [*Exeunt.*

SCENE II.

LORD PATRIOT, BOLD IRISHMAN, COLONEL.

BOLD IRISHMAN.

That Brazen Lawyer,[1] that Lord Chancellor, that wou'd be, held forth surprisingly last night, he beat the drum in your ears, brother soldier.

COLONEL. I think he did; he beat a Tatoo for us all.

LORD PATRIOT. No politicians, but lawyer politicians, it seems will go down; if we believe him, we must all turn lawyers now, and prate away the liberties of the nation.

COLONEL. Aye, first we must learn to rail at the clamourous faction, disappointed politicians—ever restless—ever plotting—constantly thwarting government, in laudable and blameable purposes.—Inconsiderable party—inconsistent in their own politics—hostile to all government, soured by disappointment, and urged by want—proceeding to unjustifiable lengths—and then sound the magnanimity of a British senate, animated by the sacred fire caught from a high-spirited people—

BOLD IRISHMAN. And the devil knows what beside—Magnanimity and sacred fire, indeed!—Very magnanimous sounds, but pompous nothings! Why did he not tell us where was the magnanimity of the British senate at the time of the dispute about Falkland's Island? What sort of fire animated them then?—Where was the high spirit of the people?—Strange sort of fire, and strange sort of spirit, to give up to our inveterate enemies, the Spaniards, our property unasked for, and cut our best friends and brethren, the Americans' throats, for defending theirs against lawless tyranny; their sacred fire became then all fume, and the strength of their boasted spirits evaporated into invisible effluvium; the giant then sunk sure enough spontaneously into a dwarf; and now, it seems, the dwarf having been feeding upon smoky fire and evaporated spirits, is endeavouring to swell himself into a giant again, like the frog in the fable, till he bursts himself in silent thunder—But let the mighty Philistine, the Goliath Paramount, and his oracle Mocklaw,

[1] See Wedderburne's Speech.

with their thunder bellowed from the brazen mortar-piece of a turn-coat lawyer, have a care of the little American David!

LORD PATRIOT. Aye, indeed! America will prove a second Sampson to 'em; they may put out his eyes for a while, but he'll pull their house down about their ears for all that. Mr. Brazen seem'd surpris'd at the thought of relinquishing America, and bawl'd out with the vociferation of an old miser that had been robb'd—Relinquish America! relinquish America! forbid it heavens! But let him and his masters take great care, or America will save 'em the trouble, and relinquish Britain.

COLONEL. Or I'm much mistaken, Brazen says, establish first your superiority, and then talk of negotiating.

LORD PATRIOT. That doctrine suits 'em best; just like a cowardly pickpocket, or a bloody highwayman, knock a man down first, and then tell him stand and deliver.

COLONEL. A just comparison, and excellent simile, by my soul! But I'm surpris'd he did not include the Clergy among the number of professions unfit (as he said) to be politicians.

BOLD IRISHMAN. Did you ever know a lawyer to be concerned with religion, unless he got a fee by it? he'll take care and steer clear of that; if it don't come in his way, he'll never break his neck over a church bible, I warrant you—Mammon is his god —Judge Jeffereys is his priest—Star-chamber doctrine is his creed—fire, flames and faggot, blood, murder, halters and thund'ring cannon are the ceremonies of his church—and lies, misrepresentations, deceit, hypocrisy and dissimulation are the articles of his religion.

LORD PATRIOT. You make him a monster, indeed.

BOLD IRISHMAN. Not half so bad as he is, my Lord; he's following close to the heels of that profound sage, that oracle, Mocklaw, his tutor: I can compare the whole herd of them to nothing else but to the swine we read of running headlong down the hill, Paramount their devil, Mocklaw the evil spirit, and Brazen their driver.

COLONEL. And thus they'll drive liberty from out the land; but when a brave people, like the Americans, from their infancy us'd to liberty (not as a gift, but who inherit it as a birth-right, but not as a mess of pottage, to be bought by, or sold to, ev'ry hungry glutton of a minister) find attempts made to reduce them to slavery, they generally take some desperate successful measure for their deliverance. I should not be at all surpris'd to hear of independency proclaim'd throughout their land, of Britain's armies beat, their fleets burnt, sunk, or otherwise destroy'd. The same principle which Mr. Brazen speaks of, that inspires British soldiers to fight, namely the ferment of youthful blood, the high spirit of the people, a love of glory, and a sense of national honour, will inspire the Americans to withstand them; to which I may add, liberty and property.—But what is national honour? Why, national pride.—What is national glory? Why, national nonsense, when put in competition with liberty and property.

LORD PATRIOT. Of Britain I fear liberty has taken its farewell, the aspiring wings of tyranny hath long hovered over, and the over-shadowing influence of bribery hath eclips'd its rays and dark'ned its lustre; the huge Paramount, that temporal deity, that golden calf, finds servile wretches enough so base as to bow down, worship and adore his gilded horns;—let 'em e'en if they will:—But as for me, tho' I should stand alone, I would spurn the brute, were he forty-five [1] times greater than he is; I'll administer, ere long, such an emetic to him, as shall make the monster disgorge the forty millions yet unaccounted for, and never shall it be said, that Patriot ever feared or truckled to him, or kept a silent tongue when it should speak.

BOLD IRISHMAN. There I'll shake hands with you, and my tongue shall echo in their ears, make their arched ceiling speak, the treasury bench crack, and the great chair of their great speaker tremble, and never will I cease lashing them, while lashing is good, or hope remains; and when the voice of poor liberty can no longer be heard in Britain or Hibernia, let's give Caledonia a kick with our heels, and away with the goddess to the American shore, crown her, and defy the grim king of tyranny, at his peril, to set his foot there.—Here let him stay, and wallow in sackcloth and ashes, like a beast as he is, and, Nebuchadnezzar-like, eat grass and thistles.   [*Exeunt.*

> *See Paramount, upon his awful throne,*
> *Striving to make each freeman's purse his own!*
> *While Lords and Commons most as one agree,*
> *To grace his head with crown of tyranny.*
> *They spurn the laws,—force constitution locks,*
> *To seize each subject's coffer, chest and box;*
> *Send justice packing, as tho' too pure unmix'd,*
> *And hug the tyrant, as if by law he's fix'd.*

[1] Alluding to North-Briton, Number forty-five.

ACT III.

SCENE I. *In Boston.*

SELECTMAN, CITIZEN.

SELECTMAN.

At length, it seems, the bloody flag is hung out, the ministry and parliament, ever studious in mischief, and bent on our destruction, have ordered troops and ships of war to shut our ports, and starve us into submission.

CITIZEN. And compel us to be slaves; I have heard so. It is a fashionable way to requite us for our loyalty, for the present we made them of Louisburg, for our protection at Duquesne, for the assistance we gave them at Quebec, Martinico, Guadaloupe and the Havannah. Blast their councils, spurn their ingratitude! Soul of Pepperel! whither art thou fled?

SELECTMAN. They seem to be guided by some secret demon; this stopping our ports and depriving us of all trade is cruel, calculated to starve and beggar thousands of families, more spiteful than politic, more to their own disadvantage than ours: But we can resolve to do without trade; it will be the means of banishing luxury, which has ting'd the simplicity and spotless innocence of our once happy asylum.

CITIZEN. We thank heaven, we have the necessaries of life in abundance, even to an exuberant plenty; and how oft have our hospitable tables fed numbers of those ungrateful monsters, who would now, if they could, famish us?

SELECTMAN. No doubt, as we abound in those temporal blessings, it has tempted them to pick our pockets by violence, in hopes of treasures more to their minds.

CITIZEN. In that these thirsters after gold and human blood will be disappointed. No Perus or Mexicos here they'll find; but the demon you speak of, tho' he acts in secret, is notoriously known. Lord Paramount is that demon, that bird of prey, that ministerial cormorant, that waits to devour, and who first thought to disturb the repose of America; a wretch, no friend to mankind, who acts thro' envy and avarice, like Satan, who 'scap'd from hell to disturb the regions of paradise; after ransacking Britain and Hibernia for gold, the growth of hell, to feed his luxury, now waits to rifle the bowels of America.

SELECTMAN. May he prove more unsuccessful than Satan; blind politics, rank infatuation, madness detestable, the concomitants of arbitrary power! They can never think to succeed; but should they conquer, they'll find that he who overcometh by force and blood, hath overcome but half his foe. Capt. Preston's massacre is too recent in our memories; and if a few troops dar'd to commit such hellish unprovok'd barbarities, what may we not expect from legions arm'd with vengeance, whose leaders harbour principles repugnant to freedom, and possess'd with more than diabolical notions? Surely our friends will oppose them with all the power heaven has given them.

CITIZEN. Nothing more certain; each citizen and each individual inhabitant of America are bound by the ties of nature; the laws of God and man justify such a procedure; passive obedience for passive slaves, and non-resistance for servile wretches who know not, neither deserve, the sweets of liberty. As for me and my house, thank God, such detestable doctrine never did, nor ever shall, enter over my threshold.

SELECTMAN. Would all America were so zealous as you.— The appointment of a general Continental Congress was a judicious measure, and will prove the salvation of this new world, where counsel mature, wisdom and strength united; it will prove a barrier, a bulwark, against the encroachments of arbitrary power.

CITIZEN. I much approve of the choice of a congress; America is young, she will be to it like a tender nursing mother, she will give it the paps of virtue to suck, cherish it with the milk of liberty, and fatten it on the cream of patriotism; she will train it up in its youth, and teach it to shun the poison of British voluptuousness, and instruct it to keep better company. Let us, my friend, support her all in our power, and set on foot an immediate association; they will form an intrenchment, too strong for ministerial tyranny to o'erleap.

SELECTMAN. I am determined so to do, it may prevent the farther effusion of blood.

SCENE II.

Enter a MINISTER.

MINISTER.

My friends, I yet will hail you good morrow, tho' I know not how long we may be indulg'd that liberty to each other; doleful tidings I have to tell.

SELECTMAN. With sorrow we have heard it, good morrow, sir.

MINISTER. Wou'd to God it may prove false, and that it may vanish like the dew of the morning.

CITIZEN. Beyond a doubt, sir, it's too true.

MINISTER. Perhaps, my friends, you have not heard all.

SELECTMAN. We have heard too much, of the troops and ships coming over, we suppose you mean; we have not heard more, if more there be.

MINISTER. Then worse I have to tell, tidings which will raise the blood of the patriot, and put your virtue to the proof, will kindle such an ardent love of liberty in your breasts, as time will not be able to exterminate—

CITIZEN. Pray, let us hear it, I'm all on fire.

SELECTMAN. I'm impatient to know it, welcome or unwelcome.

MINISTER. Such as it is, take it; your charter is annihilated; you are all, all declared rebels; your estates are to be confiscated; your patrimony to be given to those who never labour'd for it; popery to be established in the room of the true catholic faith; the Old South, and other houses of our God, converted perhaps into nunneries, inquisitions, barracks and common jails, where you will perish with want and famine, or suffer an ignominious death; your wives, children, dearest relations and friends forever separated from you in this world, without the prospect of receiving any comfort or consolation from them, or the least hope of affording any to them.

SELECTMAN. Perish the thought!

CITIZEN. I've heard enough!—To arms! my dear friends, to arms! and death or freedom be our motto!

MINISTER. A noble resolution! Posterity will crown the urn of the patriot who consecrates his talents to virtue and freedom; his name shall not be forgot; his reputation shall bloom with unfading verdure, while the name of the tyrant, like his vile body, shall moulder in the dust. Put your trust in the Lord of hosts, he is your strong tower, he is your helper and defense, he will guide and strengthen the arm of flesh, and scatter your enemies like chaff.

SELECTMAN. Let us not hesitate.

CITIZEN. Not a single moment;—'tis like to prove a mortal strife, a never-ending contest.

MINISTER. Delays may be dangerous.—Go and awake your brethren that sleep;—rouse them up from their lethargy and supineness, and join, with confidence, temporal with spiritual weapons. Perhaps they be now landing, and this moment, this very moment, may be the last of your liberty. Prepare yourselves—be ready—stand fast—ye know not the day nor the hour. May the Ruler of all send us liberty and life. Adieu! my friends. [*Exeunt.*

SCENE III. *In a street in Boston.*

*Frequent town-meetings and consultations amongst the inhabitants; —*LORD BOSTON *arrives with the forces and ships;—lands and fortifies Boston.*

WHIG *and* TORY.

WHIG. I have said and done all that man could say or do.— 'Tis wrong, I insist upon it, and time will show it, to suffer them to take possession of Castle William and fortify Boston Neck.

TORY. I cannot see, good sir, of what advantage it will be to them;—they've only a mind, I suppose, to keep their soldiers from being inactive, which may prejudice their health.

WHIG. I wish it may prove so, I would very gladly confess your superior knowledge in military manœuvres; but till then, suffer me to tell you, it's a stroke the most fatal to us,—no less, sir, but to cut off the communication between the town and country, making prisoners of us all by degrees, and give 'em an opportunity of making excursions, and in a short time subdue us without resistance.

TORY. I think your fears are groundless.

WHIG. Sir, my reason is not to be trifled with. Do you not see or hear ev'ry day of insults and provocations to the peaceable inhabitants? This is only a prelude. Can men of spirit bear forever with such usage? I know not what business they have here at all.

TORY. I suppose they're come to protect us.

WHIG. Damn such protectors, such cut-throat villains; protect us? from what? from whom?—

TORY. Nay, sir, I know not their business;—let us yet bear with them till we know the success of the petition from the Congress;—if unfavourable, then it will be our time.

WHIG. Then, I fear, it will be too late; all that time we lose, and they gain ground; I have no notion of trusting to the success of petitions, waiting twelve months for no answer at all. Our assemblies have petitioned often, and as often in vain; 't would be a miracle in these days to hear of an American petition being granted; their omnipotences, their demi-godships (as they think themselves) no doubt think it too great a favour done us to throw our petitions under their table, much less vouchsafe to read them.

TORY. You go too far;—the power of King, Lords and Commons is uncontroulable.

WHIG. With respect to tyrannising they would make it so, if they could, I know, but there's a good deal to be said and done first; we have more than half the bargain to make.

TORY. Sure you would not go to dispute by arms with Great-Britain.

WHIG. Sure I would not suffer you to pick my pocket, sir.

TORY. If I did, the law is open for you—

WHIG. I have but a poor opinion of law, when the devil sits judge.

TORY. What would you do then, sir, if I was to pick your pocket?

WHIG. Break your head, sir—

TORY. Sure you don't mean as you say, sir—

WHIG. I surely do—try me, sir—

TORY. Excuse me, sir, I am not of your mind, I would avoid every thing that has the appearance of rashness.—Great-Britain's power, sir—

WHIG. Great-Britain's power, sir, is too much magnified, 't will soon grow weak, by endeavouring to make slaves of American freemen; we are not Africans yet, neither bond-slaves. —You would avoid and discourage every thing that has the appearance of patriotism, you mean.—

TORY. Who? me, sir?

WHIG. Yes, you, sir;—you go slyly pimping, spying and sneaking about, cajoling the ignorant, and insinuating bugbear notions of Great-Britain's mighty power into weak people's ears, that we may tamely give all up, and you be rewarded, perhaps, with the office of judge of the admiralty, or continental hangman, for ought I know.

TORY. Who? me, sir?

WHIG. Aye, you, sir;—and let me tell you, sir, you've been long suspected—

TORY. Of what, sir?

WHIG. For a rank Tory, sir.

TORY. What mean you, sir?

WHIG. I repeat it again—suspected to be an enemy to your country.

TORY. By whom, sir? Can you show me an instance?

WHIG. From your present discourse I suspect you—and from your connections and artful behaviour all suspect you.

TORY. Can you give me a proof?

WHIG. Not a point blank proof, as to my own knowledge; you're so much of a Jesuit, you have put it out of my power;—but strong circumstances by information, such as amount to a proof in the present case, sir, I can furnish you with.

TORY. Sir, you may be mistaken.

WHIG. 'Tis not possible, my informant knows you too well.

TORY. Who is your informant, sir?

WHIG. A gentleman, sir; and if you'll give yourself the trouble to walk with me, I'll soon produce him.

TORY. Another time; I cannot stay now;—'tis dinner time.

WHIG. That's the time to find him

TORY. I cannot stay now.

WHIG. We'll call at your house then.

TORY. I dine abroad, sir.

WHIG. Be gone, you scoundrel! I'll watch your waters; 'tis time to clear the land of such infernal vermin.

[*Exeunt both different ways.*

SCENE IV. *In Boston, while the Regulars were flying from Lexington.*

LORD BOSTON *surrounded by his guards and a few officers.*

LORD BOSTON. If Colonel Smith succeeds in his embassy, and I think there's no doubt of it, I shall have the pleasure this ev'ning, I expect, of having my friends Hancock and Adams's good company; I'll make each of them a present of a pair of handsome iron ruffles, and Major Provost shall provide a suitable entertainment for them in his apartment.

OFFICER. Sure they'll not be so unpolite as to refuse your Excellency's kind invitation.

LORD BOSTON. Shou'd they, Colonel Smith and Major Pitcairn have my orders to make use of all their rhetoric and the persuasive eloquence of British thunder.

Enter a MESSENGER *in haste.*

MESSENGER. I bring your Excellency unwelcome tidings—

LORD BOSTON. For heaven's sake! from what quarter?

MESSENGER. From Lexington plains.

LORD BOSTON. 'Tis impossible!

MESSENGER. Too true, sir.

LORD BOSTON. Say—what is it? Speak what you know.

MESSENGER. Colonel Smith is defeated, and fast retreating.

LORD BOSTON. Good God!—What does he say? Mercy on me!

MESSENGER. They're flying before the enemy.

LORD BOSTON. Britons turn their backs before the Rebels!— The Rebels put Britons to flight?—Said you not so?

MESSENGER. They are routed, sir;—they are flying this instant;—the Provincials are numerous, and hourly gaining strength;—they have nearly surrounded our troops. A rein-forcement, sir—a timely succour may save the shatter'd remnant Speedily! speedily, sir! or they're irretrievably lost!

LORD BOSTON. Good God! What does he say? Can it be possible?

MESSENGER. Lose no time, sir.

LORD BOSTON. What can I do?—Oh dear!

OFFICER. Draw off a detachment—form a brigade; prepare part of the train; send for Lord Percy; let the drums beat to arms.

LORD BOSTON. Aye, do, Captain; you know how, better than I. (*Exit* OFFICER.) Did the Rebels dare to fire on the king's troops? Had they the courage? Guards, keep round me.

MESSENGER. They're like lions; they have killed many of our bravest officers and men; and if not checked instantly, will totally surround them, and make the whole prisoners. This is no time to parley, sir.

LORD BOSTON. No, indeed; what will become of me?

Enter EARL PERCY.

EARL PERCY. Your orders, sir.

LORD BOSTON. Haste, my good Percy, immediately take command of the brigade of reinforcement, and fly to the assis-tance of poor Smith!—Lose no time, lest they be all cut off, and the Rebels improve their advantage, and be upon us; and God knows what quarter they'll give.—Haste, my noble Earl!— Speedily!—Speedily!—Where's my guard?

EARL PERCY. I'm gone, sir.

[*Exeunt* PERCY *and* OFFICERS—*drums beating to arms.*

LORD BOSTON. What means this flutt'ring round my heart? this unusual chilness? Is it fear? No, it cannot be, it must proceed from my great anxiety, my perturbation of mind for the fate of my countrymen. A drowsiness hangs o'er my eyelids;—fain would I repose myself a short time;—but I must not;—I must wait;—I'll to the top of yon eminence,—there I shall be safer. Here I cannot stay;—there I may behold something favourable to calm this tumult in my breast.—But, alas! I fear—Guards, attend me. [*Exeunt* LORD BOSTON *and* GUARDS.

SCENE V. LORD BOSTON *and* GUARDS *on a hill in Boston, that overlooks Charlestown.*

LORD BOSTON. Clouds of dust and smoke intercept my sight; I cannot see; I hear the noise of cannon—Percy's cannon—Grant him success!

OFFICER OF GUARD. Methinks, sir, I see British colours waving.

LORD BOSTON. Some ray of hope.—Have they got so near?—Captain, keep a good lookout; tell me every thing you see. My eyes are wondrous dim.

OFFICER. The two brigades have join'd—Now Admiral Tombstone bellows his lower tier on the Provincials. How does your Excellency?

LORD BOSTON. Right;—more hope still.—I'm bravely to what I was. Which way do our forces tend?

OFFICER. I can distinguish nothing for a certainty now; such smoke and dust!

LORD BOSTON. God grant Percy courage!

OFFICER. His ancestors were brave, sir.

LORD BOSTON. Aye, that's no rule—no rule, Captain; so were mine.—A heavy firing now.—The Rebels must be very numerous—

OFFICER. They're like caterpillars; as numerous as the locusts of Egypt.

LORD BOSTON. Look out, Captain, God help you, look out.

OFFICER. I do, sir.

LORD BOSTON. What do you see now? Hark! what dreadful noise!

ONE OF THE GUARD. [*Aside.*] How damn'd afraid he is.

ANOTHER OF THE GUARD. [*Aside.*] He's one of your chimney corner Generals—an old granny.

OFFICER. If I mistake not, our troops are fast retreating; their fire slackens; the noise increases.

LORD BOSTON. Oh, Captain, don't say so!

OFFICER. 'Tis true, sir, they're running—the enemy shout victory.

LORD BOSTON. Upon your honour?—say—

OFFICER. Upon my honour, sir, they're flying t'wards Charlestown. Percy's beat;—I'm afraid he's lost his artillery.

LORD BOSTON. Then 'tis all over—the day is lost—what more can we do?

OFFICER. We may, with the few troops left in Boston, yet afford them some succour, and cover their retreat across the water; 'tis impossible to do more.

LORD BOSTON. Go instantly; I'll wait your return. Try your utmost to prevent the Rebels from crossing. Success attend you, my dear Captain, God prosper you! [*Exit* OFFICER.] Alas! alas! my glory's gone; my honour's stain'd. My dear guards, don't leave me, and you shall have plenty of porter and sourcrout.

SCENE VI. ROGER *and* DICK, *two shepherds near Lexington, after the defeat and flight of the Regulars.*

ROGER. Whilst early looking, Dick, ere the sun was seen to tinge the brow of the mountain, for my flock of sheep, nor dreaming of approaching evil, suddenly mine eyes beheld from yon hill a cloud of dust arise at a small distance; the intermediate space were thick set with laurels, willows, evergreens, and bushes of various kinds, the growth of wild nature, and which hid the danger from my eyes, thinking perchance my flock had thither stray'd; I descended, and straight onward went; but, Dick, judge you my thoughts at such a disappointment: Instead of my innocent flock of sheep, I found myself almost encircled by a herd of ravenous British wolves.

DICK. Dangerous must have been your situation, Roger, whatever were your thoughts.

ROGER. I soon discovered my mistake; finding a hostile appearance, I instantly turn'd myself about, and fled to alarm the shepherds.

DICK. Did they pursue you?

ROGER. They did; but having the start, and being acquainted with the by-ways, I presently got clear of their voracious jaws.

DICK. A lucky escape, indeed, Roger; and what route did they take after that?

ROGER. Onwards, t'wards Lexington, devouring geese, cattle and swine, with fury and rage, which, no doubt, was increased by their disappointment; and what may appear strange to you, Dick (tho' no more strange than true), is, they seem'd to be possessed of a kind of brutish music, growling something like our favourite tune Yankee Doodle (perhaps in ridicule), till it were almost threadbare, seeming vastly pleased (monkey-like) with their mimickry, as tho' it provoked us much.

DICK. Nature, Roger, has furnish'd some brute animals with voices, or, more properly speaking, with organs of sound that nearly resemble the human. I have heard of crocodiles weeping like a child, to decoy the unwary traveller, who is no sooner within their reach, but they seize and devour instantly.

ROGER. Very true, Dick, I have read of the same; and these wolves, being of the canine breed, and having the properties of blood-hounds, no doubt are possess'd of a more acute sense of smelling, more reason, instinct, sagacity, or what shall I call it? than all other brutes. It might have been a piece of cunning of theirs, peculiar to them, to make themselves pass for shepherds, and decoy our flocks; for, as you know, Dick, all our shepherds both play and sing Yankee Doodle, our sheep and lambs are as well acquainted with that tune as ourselves, and always make up to us whene'er they hear the sound.

DICK. Yes, Roger; and now you put me in mind of it I'll tell you of something surprising in my turn: I have an old ram and an old ewe, that, whenever they sing Yankee Doodle together, a skilful musician can scarcely distinguish it from the bass and tenor of an organ.

ROGER. Surprising indeed, Dick, nor do I in the least doubt it; and why not, as well as Balaam's ass, speak? and I might add, many other asses, now-a-days; and yet, how might that music be improved by a judicious disposition of its various parts, by the addition of a proper number of sheep and young lambs; 't would then likewise resemble the counter, counter tenor, treble, and finest pipes of an organ, and might be truly called nature's organ; methinks, Dick, I could forever sit and hear such music,

Where all the parts in complication roll,
And with its charming music feast the soul!

DICK. Delightful, indeed; I'll attempt it with what little skill
I have in music; we may then defy these wolves to imitate it,
and thereby save our flocks: I am well convinced, Roger, these
wolves intended it rather as a decoy than by way of ridicule,
because they live by cunning and deception; besides, they could
never mean to ridicule a piece of music, a tune, of which such
brutes cannot be supposed to be judges, and, which is allowed
by the best masters of music to be a composition of the most sublime kind, and would have done honour to a Handel or a Correl-
lius. Well, go on, Roger, I long to hear the whole.

ROGER. When they came to Lexington, where a flock of our
innocent sheep and young lambs, as usual, were feeding and
sporting on the plain, these dogs of violence and rapine with
haughty stride advanc'd, and berated them in a new and unheard
of language to us.

DICK. I suppose learn'd at their own fam'd universities—

ROGER. No doubt; they had teachers among them—two old
wolves their leaders, not unlike in features to Smith and Pitcairn,
as striving to outvie each other in the very dregs of brutal eloquence, and more than Billingsgate jargon, howl'd in their ears
such a peal of new-fangled execrations, and hell-invented oratory,
till that day unheard in New-England, as struck the whole flock
with horror, and made them for a while stand aghast, as tho'
all the wolves in the forest had broke loose upon them.

DICK. Oh, shocking!—Roger, go on.

ROGER. Not content with this, their murdering leaders, with
premeditated malice, keen appetite, and without provocation,
gave the howl for the onset, when instantly the whole herd, as if
the devil had entered into them, ran violently down the hill, and
fixed their talons and jaws upon them, and as quick as lightning
eight innocent young lambs fell a sacrifice to their fury, and victims to their rapacity; the very houses of our God were no longer
a sanctuary; many they tore to pieces, and some at the very foot
of the altar; others were dragged out as in a wanton, gamesome
mood.

DICK. Barbarity inexpressible! more than savage cruelty! I
hope you'll make their master pay for 'em; there is a law of this
province, Roger, which obliges the owner of such dogs to pay for
the mischief they do.

ROGER. I know it, Dick; he shall pay, never fear, and that handsomely too; he has paid part of it already.

DICK. Who is their master, Roger?

ROGER. One Lord Paramount; they call him a free-booter; a fellow who pretends to be proprietor of all America, and says he has a deed for it, and chief ranger of all the flocks, and pretends to have a patent for it; has been a long time in the practice of killing and stealing sheep in England and Ireland, and had like to have been hang'd for it there, but was reprieved by the means of his friend *George*—I forgot his other name—not Grenville—not George the Second—but another George—

DICK. It's no matter, he'll be hang'd yet; he has sent his dogs to a wrong place, and lugg'd the wrong sow by the ear; he should have sent them to Newfoundland, or Kamchatka, there's no sheep there—But never mind, go on, Roger.

ROGER. Nor was their voracious appetites satiated there; they rush'd into the town of Concord, and proceeded to devour every thing that lay in their way; and those brute devils, like Sampson's foxes (and as tho' they were men), thrice attempted with firebrands to destroy our corn, our town-house and habitations.

DICK. Heavens! Could not all this provoke you?

ROGER. It did; rage prompted us at length, and found us arms 'gainst such hellish mischief to oppose.

DICK. Oh, would I had been there!

ROGER. Our numbers increasing, and arm'd with revenge, we in our turn play'd the man; they, unus'd to wounds, with hideous yelling soon betook themselves to a precipitate and confused flight, nor did we give o'er the chase, till Phœbus grew drowsy, bade us desist, and wished us a good night.

DICK. Of some part of their hasty retreat I was a joyful spectator, I saw their tongues lolling out of their mouths, and heard them pant like hunted wolves indeed.

ROGER. Did you not hear how their mirth was turn'd into mourning? their fury into astonishment? how soon they quitted their howling Yankee Doodle, and chang'd their notes to bellowing? how nimbly (yet against their will) they betook themselves to dancing? And he was then the bravest dog that beat time the swiftest, and footed Yankee Doodle the nimblest.

DICK. Well pleased, Roger, was I with the chase, and glorious sport it was: I oft perceiv'd them tumbling o'er each other heels over head; nor did one dare stay to help his brother—but, with bloody breech, made the best of his way—nor ever stopped till they were got safe within their lurking-holes—

ROGER. From whence they have not the courage to peep out, unless four to one, except (like a skunk) forc'd by famine.

DICK. May this be the fate of all those prowling sheep-stealers, it behooves the shepherds to double the watch, to take uncommon precaution and care of their tender flocks, more especially as this is like to be an uncommon severe winter, by the appearance of wolves, so early in the season—but, hark!—Roger, methinks I hear the sound of melody warbling thro' the grove—Let's sit a while, and partake of it unseen.

ROGER. With all my heart.—Most delightful harmony! This is the First of May; our shepherds and nymphs are celebrating our glorious St. Tammany's day; we'll hear the song out, and then join in the frolic, and chorus it o'er and o'er again—This day shall be devoted to joy and festivity.

SONG.

[TUNE. *The hounds are all out, &c.*]

1.

Of *St. George*, or *St. Bute*, let the poet Laureat sing,
Of *Pharaoh* or *Pluto* of old,
While he rhymes forth their praise, in false, flattering lays,
I'll sing of St. Tamm'ny the bold, my brave boys.

2.

Let Hibernia's sons boast, make Patrick their toast;
And Scots Andrew's fame spread abroad.
Potatoes and oats, and Welch leeks for Welch goats,
Was never St. Tammany's food, my brave boys.

3.

In freedom's bright cause, Tamm'ny pled with applause,
And reason'd most justly from nature;
For this, this was his song, all, all the day long:
Liberty's the right of each creature, brave boys.

4.

Whilst under an oak his great parliament sat,
His throne was the crotch of the tree;
With Solomon's look, without statutes or book,
He wisely sent forth his decree, my brave boys.

5.

His subjects stood round, not the least noise or sound,
Whilst freedom blaz'd full in each face:
So plain were the laws, and each pleaded his cause;
That might *Bute*, *North* and *Mansfield* disgrace, my brave
boys.

6.

No duties, nor stamps, their blest liberty cramps,
A king, tho' no *tyrant*, was he;
He did oft'times declare, nay, sometimes wou'd swear,
The least of his subjects were free, my brave boys.

7.

He, as king of the woods, of the rivers and floods,
Had a right all beasts to controul;
Yet, content with a few, to give nature her due:
So gen'rous was Tammany's soul! my brave boys.

8.

In the morn he arose, and a-hunting he goes,
Bold Nimrod his second was he.
For his breakfast he'd take a large venison steak,
And despis'd your slip-slops and tea, my brave boys.

9.

While all in a row, with squaw, dog and bow,
Vermilion adorning his face,
With feathery head he rang'd the woods wide:
St. George sure had never such grace, my brave boys?

10.

His jetty black hair, such as Buckskin saints wear,
Perfumed with bear's grease well smear'd,
Which illum'd the saint's face, and ran down apace,
Like the oil from Aaron's old beard, my brave boys.

11.

The strong nervous deer, with amazing career,
In swiftness he'd fairly run down;
And, like Sampson, wou'd tear wolf, lion or bear.
Ne'er was such a saint as our own, my brave boys.

12.

When he'd run down a stag, he behind him wou'd lag;
For, so noble a soul had he!
He'd stop, tho' he lost it, tradition reports it,
To give him fresh chance to get free, my brave boys.

13.

With a mighty strong arm, and a masculine bow,
His arrow he drew to the head,
And as sure as he shot, it was ever his lot,
His prey it fell instantly dead, my brave boys.

14.

His table he spread where the venison bled,
Be thankful, he used to say;
He'd laugh and he'd sing, tho' a saint and a king,
And sumptuously dine on his prey, my brave boys.

15.

Then over the hills, o'er the mountains and rills
He'd caper, such was his delight;
And ne'er in his days, Indian history says,
Did lack a good supper at night, my brave boys.

16.

On an old stump he sat, without cap or hat.
When supper was ready to eat,
Snap, his dog, he stood by, and cast a sheep's eye
For ven'son, the king of all meat, my brave boys.

17.

Like Isaac of old, and both cast in one mould,
Tho' a wigwam was Tamm'ny's cottage,
He lov'd sav'ry meat, such that patriarchs eat,
Of ven'son and squirrel made pottage, brave boys.

18.

When fourscore years old, as I've oft'times been told,
To doubt it, sure, would not be right,
With a pipe in his jaw, he'd buss his old squaw,
And get a young saint ev'ry night, my brave boys.

19.

As old age came on, he grew blind, deaf and dumb,
Tho' his sport, 'twere hard to keep from it,
Quite tired of life, bid adieu to his wife,
And blazed like the tail of a comet, brave boys.

20.

What country on earth, then, did ever give birth
To such a magnanimous saint?
His acts far excel all that history tell,
And language too feeble to paint, my brave boys.

21.

Now, to finish my song, a full flowing bowl
I'll quaff, and sing all the long day,
And with punch and wine paint my cheeks for my saint,
And hail ev'ry First of sweet *May*, my brave boys.

DICK. What a seraphic voice! how it enlivens my soul! Come
away, away, Roger, the moments are precious.

[*Exeunt* DICK *and* ROGER.

SCENE VII. *In a chamber, near Boston, the morning after the
battle of Bunkers-Hill.*

CLARISSA. How lovely is this new-born day!—The sun rises
with uncommon radiance after the most gloomy night my wearied
eyes ever knew.—The voice of slumber was not heard—the angel
of sleep was fled—and the awful whispers of solemnity and
silence prevented my eye-lids from closing.—No wonder—the
terrors and ideas of yesterday—such a scene of war—of tumult—
hurry and hubbub—of horror and destruction—the direful noise
of conflict—the dismal hissing of iron shot in volleys flying—
such bellowing of mortars—such thund'ring of cannon—such
roaring of musketry—and such clashing of swords and bayonets
—such cries of the wounded—and such streams of blood—such a
noise and crush of houses, steeples, and whole streets of desolate
Charlestown falling—pillars of fire, and the convulsed vortex
of fiery flakes, rolling in flaming wreaths in the air, in dreadful
combustion, seemed as tho' the elements and whole earth were
envelop'd in one general, eternal conflagration and total ruin,
and intermingled with black smoke, ascending, on the wings of
mourning, up to Heaven, seemed piteously to implore the Al-

mighty interposition to put a stop to such devastation, lest the whole earth should be unpeopled in the unnatural conflict—Too, too much for female heroism to dwell upon—But what are all those to the terrors that filled my affrighted imagination the last night?—Dreams—fancies—evil bodings—shadows, phantoms and ghastly visions continually hovering around my pillow, goading and harrowing my soul with the most terrific appearances, not imaginary, but real—Am I awake?—Where are the British murderers?—where's my husband?—my son?—my brother?—Something more than human tells me all is not well: If they are among the slain, 'tis impossible.—I—Oh! [*She cries.*]

Enter a NEIGHBOUR [*a spectator of the battle*].

NEIGHBOUR. Madam, grieve not so much.

CLARISSA. Am I wont to grieve without a cause? Wou'd to God I did;—mock me not—What voice is that? methinks I know it—some angel sent to comfort me?—welcome then. [*She turns about.*] Oh, my Neighbour, is it you? My friend, I have need of comfort. Hast thou any for me?—say—will you not speak? Where's my husband?—my son?—my brother? Hast thou seen them since the battle? Oh! bring me not unwelcome tidings! [*Cries.*]

NEIGHBOUR. [*Aside. What shall I say?*] Madam, I beheld them yesterday from an eminence.

CLARISSA. Upon that very eminence was I. What then?—

NEIGHBOUR. I saw the brave man Warren, your son and brother.

CLARISSA. What? O ye gods!—Speak on friend—stop—what saw ye?

NEIGHBOUR. In the midst of the tempest of war—

CLARISSA. Where are they now?—That I saw too—What is all this?

NEIGHBOUR. Madam, hear me—

CLARISSA. Then say on—yet—Oh, his looks!—I fear!

NEIGHBOUR. When General Putnam bid the vanguard open their front to the—

CLARISSA. Oh, trifle not with me—dear Neighbour!—where shall I find them?—say—

NEIGHBOUR. [*Aside. Heavens! must I tell her!*] Madam, be patient—right and left, that all may see who hate us, we are prepar'd for them—

CLARISSA. What then?—Can you find 'em?—

NEIGHBOUR. I saw Warren and the other two heroes firm as Roxbury stand the shock of the enemy's fiercest attacks, and twice put to flight their boasted phalanx.—

CLARISSA. All that I saw, and more; say—wou'd they not come to me, were they well?—

NEIGHBOUR. Madam, hear me—

CLARISSA. Oh! he will not speak.

NEIGHBOUR. The enemy return'd to the charge, and stumbling o'er the dead and wounded bodies of their friends, Warren received them with indissoluble firmness, and notwithstanding their battalious aspect, in the midst of the battle, tho' surrounded with foes on ev'ry side—

CLARISSA. Oh, my Neighbour!—

NEIGHBOUR. Madam—his nervous arm, like a giant refresh'd with wine, hurl'd destruction where'er he came, breathing heroic ardour to advent'rous deeds, and long time in even scale the battle hung, till at last death turn'd pale and affrighted at the carnage—they ran—

CLARISSA. Who ran?

NEIGHBOUR. The enemy, Madam, gave way—

CLARISSA. Warren never ran—yet—oh! I wou'd he had—I fear—[Cries.]

NEIGHBOUR. I say not so, Madam.

CLARISSA. What say ye then? he was no coward, Neighbour—

NEIGHBOUR. Brave to the last. [Aside. I forgot myself.]

CLARISSA. What said you? O Heavens! brave to the last! those words—why do you keep me thus?—cruel—

NEIGHBOUR. [Aside. She will know it.] I say, Madam, by some mistaken orders on our side, the enemy rallied and return'd to the charge with fresh numbers, and your husband, son, and brother—Madam—

CLARISSA. Stop!—O ye powers!—What?—say no more—yet let me hear—keep me not thus—tell me, I charge thee—

NEIGHBOUR. [Aside. I can hold no longer, she must know it.] Forgive me, Madam—I saw them fall—and Michael, the arch-angel, who vanquish'd Satan, is not more immortal than they. [Aside. Who can relate such woes without a tear?]

CLARISSA. Oh! I've heard enough—too—too much [Cries.] yet—if thou hast worse to tell—say on—nought worse can be —O ye gods!—cruel—cruel—thrice cruel—cou'd ye not leave me one—[*She faints, and is caught by her friend, and placed in a chair; he rings the bell, the family come in, and endeavour to bring her to.*]

NEIGHBOUR. With surprising fortitude she heard the melancholy relation, until I came to the last close—she then gave me a mournful look, lifted up her eyes, and immediately sunk motionless into my arms.

WOMAN. Poor soul!—no wonder—how I sympathize with her in her distress—my tender bosom can scarcely bear the sight! A dreadful loss! a most shocking scene it was, that brothers should with brothers war, and in intestine fierce opposition meet, to seek the blood of each other, like dogs for a bare bone, who so oft in generous friendship and commerce join'd, in festivals of love and joy unanimous as the sons of one kind and indulgent father, and separately would freely in a good cause spend their blood and sacrifice their lives for him.

NEIGHBOUR. A terrible black day it was, and ever will be remembered by New-England, when that vile Briton (unworthy the name of a Briton), Lord Boston (curse the name!), whose horrid murders stain American soil with blood; perish his name! a fratricide! 'twas he who fir'd Charlestown, and spread desolation, fire, flames and smoke in ev'ry corner—he was the wretch, that waster of the world, that licens'd robber, that blood-stain'd insulter of a free people, who bears the name of Lord Boston, but from henceforth shall be called Cain, that pillag'd the ruins, and dragg'd and murder'd the infant, the aged and infirm— (But look, she recovers.)

CLARISSA. O ye angels! ye cherubims and seraphims! waft their souls to bliss, bathe their wounds with angelic balsam, and crown them with immortality. A faithful, loving and beloved husband, a promising and filial son, a tender and affectionate brother: Alas! what a loss!—Whom have I now to comfort me? —What have I left, but the voice of lamentation: [*She weeps.*] Ill-fated bullets—these tears shall sustain me—yes, ye dear friends! how gladly wou'd I follow you—but alas! I must still endure tribulation and inquietudes, from which you are now exempt; I cannot cease to weep, ye brave men, I will mourn your fall—weep on—flow, mine eyes, and wash away their blood, till the fountain of sorrow is dried up—but, oh! it never— never will—my sympathetic soul shall dwell on your bosoms, and floods of tears shall water your graves; and since all other comfort is deny'd me, deprive me not of the only consolation left me of meditating on your virtues and dear memories, who fell in defense of liberty and your country—ye brave men—ye more than friends—ye martyrs to liberty!—This, this is all I ask, till sorrow overwhelms me.—I breathe my last; and ye yourselves, your own bright spirits, come and waft me to your peaceful abode, where the voice of lamentation is not heard, neither shall we know any more what it is to separate.

> *Eager the patriot meets his desperate foe*
> *With full intent to give the fatal blow;*
> *The cause he fights for animates him high,*
> *His wife, his children and his liberty:*
> *For these he conquers, or more bravely dies,*
> *And yields himself a willing sacrifice.*   [*Exeunt.*

ACT IV.

SCENE I. *Near Norfolk, in Virginia, on board a man-of-war,* LORD KIDNAPPER, *in the state-room; a boat appears rowing towards the ship.*

SAILOR *and* BOATSWAIN.

SAILOR. Boatswain!

BOATSWAIN. Holla.

SAILOR. Damn my eyes, Mr. Boatswain, but here's a black flag of truce coming on board.

BOATSWAIN. Sure enough—where are they from?

SAILOR. From hell, I suppose—for they're as black as so many devils.

BOATSWAIN. Very well—no matter—they're recruits for the Kidnapper.

SAILOR. We shall be all of a colour by and by—damn me—

BOATSWAIN. I'll go and inform his Lordship and his pair of doxies of it; I suppose by this time they have trim'd their sails, and he's done heaving the log.   [*Exit* BOATSWAIN.

SCENE II. *Near the state-room.*

BOATSWAIN. Where's his Lordship?

SERVANT. He's in the state-room.

BOATSWAIN. It's time for him to turn out; tell him I want to speak to him.

SERVANT. I dare not do it, Boatswain; it's more than my life is worth.

BOATSWAIN. Damn your squeamish stomach, go directly, or I'll go myself.

SERVANT. For God's sake! Boatswain—

BOATSWAIN. Damn your eyes, you pimping son of a bitch, go this instant, or I'll stick my knife in your gammons.

SERVANT. O Lord! Boatswain. [SERVANT goes.]

BOATSWAIN [solus]. What the devil—keep a pimp guard here, better station the son of a bitch at the mast head, to keep a look out there, lest Admiral Hopkins be upon us.

Enter KIDNAPPER.

KIDNAPPER. What's your will, Boatswain?

BOATSWAIN. I beg your Lordship's pardon [*Aside. But you can soon fetch up Leeway, and spread the water sail again.*], please your honour, here's a boat full of fine recruits along side for you.

KIDNAPPER. Recruits, Boatswain? you mean soldiers from Augustine, I imagine; what reg'mentals have they on?

BOATSWAIN. Mourning, please your honour, and as black as our tarpawling.

KIDNAPPER. Ha, ha, well, well, take 'em on board, Boatswain, I'll be on deck presently.

BOATSWAIN. With submission to your honour, d' ye see, [*Scratching his head.*] I think we have gallows-looking dogs enough on board already—the scrapings of Newgate, and the refuse of Tyburn, and when the wind blows aft, damn 'em, they stink like polecats—but d' ye see, as your honour pleases, with submission, if it's Lord Paramount's orders, why it must be so, I suppose—but I've done my duty, d' ye see—

KIDNAPPER. Ha, ha, the work must be done, Boatswain, no matter by whom.

BOATSWAIN. Why, aye, that's true, please your honour, any port in a storm—if a man is to be hang'd, or have his throat cut, d' ye see—who are so fit to do it as his own slaves? especially as they're to have their freedoms for it; nobody can blame 'em, nor your honour neither, for you get them for half price, or nothing at all, d' ye see me, and that will help to lessen poor Owld England's taxes, and when you have done with 'em here, and they get their brains knock'd out, d' ye see, your honour can sell them in the West-Indies, and that will be something in your honour's pocket, d' ye see—well, ev'ry man to his trade—but, damn my impudence for all, I see your honour knows all about it—d' ye see. [*Exit* BOATSWAIN.

SCENE III. LORD KIDNAPPER *returns to his state-room; the* BOATSWAIN *comes on deck and pipes.*

All hands ahoy—hand a rope, some of you Tories, forward there, for his worship's reg'ment of black guards to come aboard.

Enter NEGROES.

BOATSWAIN. Your humble servant, Gentlemen, I suppose you want to see Lord Kidnapper?—Clear the gangway there of them Tyburn tulips. Please to walk aft, brother soldiers, that's the fittest birth for you, the Kidnapper's in the state-room, he'll hoist his sheet-anchor presently, he'll be up in a jiffin—as soon as he has made fast the end of his small rope athwart Jenny Bluegarter and Kate Common's stern posts.

FIRST SAILOR. Damn my eyes, but I suppose, messmate, we must bundle out of our hammocks this cold weather, to make room for these black regulars to stow in, tumble upon deck, and choose a soft berth among the snow?

SECOND SAILOR. Blast 'em, if they come within a cable's length of my hammock, I'll kick 'em to hell through one of the gun ports.

BOATSWAIN. Come, come, brothers, don't be angry, I suppose we shall soon be in a warmer latitude—the Kidnapper seems as fond of these black regulars (as you call 'em, Jack) as he is of the brace of whores below; but as they come in so damn'd slow, I'll put him in the humour of sending part of the fleet this winter to the coast of Guinea, and beat up for volunteers, there he'll get recruits enough for a hogshead or two of New-England rum, and a few owld pipe-shanks, and save poor Owld-England the trouble and expense of clothing them in the bargain.

FIRST SAILOR. Aye, Boatswain, any voyage, so it's a warm one—if it's to hell itself—for I'm sure the devil must be better off than we, if we are to stay here this winter.

SECOND SAILOR. Any voyage, so it's to the southward, rather than stay here at lazy anchor—no fire, nothing to eat or drink, but suck our frosty fists like bears, unless we turn sheep-stealers again, and get our brains knock'd out. Eigh, master cook, you're a gentleman now—nothing to do—grown so proud, you won't speak to poor folks, I suppose?

COOK. The devil may cook for 'em for me—if I had any thing to cook—a parcel of frozen half-starv'd dogs. I should never be able to keep 'em out of the cook room, or their noses out of the slush-tub.

BOATSWAIN. Damn your old smoky jaws, you're better off than any man aboard, your trouble will be nothing,—for I suppose they'll be disbursted in different messes among the Tories, and it's only putting on the big pot, cockey. Ha, ha, ha.

COOK. What signifies, Mr. Boatswain, the big pot or the little pot, if there's nothing to cook? no fire, coal or wood to cook with? Blast my eyes, Mr. Boatswain, if I disgrease myself so much, I have had the honour, damn me (tho' I say it that shou'dn't say it) to be chief cook of a seventy-four gun ship, on board of which was Lord Abel-Marl and Admiral Poke-Cock.

BOATSWAIN. Damn the liars—old singe-the-devil—you chief cook of a seventy-four gun ship, eigh? you the devil, you're as proud as hell, for all you look as old as Matheg'lum, hand a pair of silk stockings for our cook here, d' ye see—lash a handspike athwart his arse, get a ladle full of slush and a handful of brimstone for his hair, and step one of you Tories there for the devil's barber to come and shave and dress him. Ha, ha, ha.

COOK. No, Mr. Boatswain, it's not pride—but look 'e (as I said before), I'll not disgrease my station, I'll throw up my commission, before I'll stand cook for a parcel of scape gallows, convict Tory dogs and run-away Negroes.

BOATSWAIN. What's that you say? Take care, old frosty face—What? do you accuse his worship of turning kidnapper, and harbouring run-away Negroes?—Softly, or you'll be taken up for a Whig, and get a handsome coat of slush and hog's feathers for a christmas-box, cockey: Throw up your commission, eigh? throw up the pot-halliards, you mean, old piss-to-windward? Ha, ha, ha.

COOK. I tell you, Mr. Boatswain—I——

BOATSWAIN. Come, come, give us a chaw of tobacco, Cook— blast your eyes, don't take any pride in what I say—I'm only joking, d' ye see——

COOK. Well, but Mr. Boatswain——

BOATSWAIN. Come, avast, belay the lanyards of your jaws, and let's have no more of it, d' ye see. [BOATSWAIN *pipes*.] Make fast that boat along side there. [*Exeunt ev'ry man to his station.*

SCENE IV. LORD KIDNAPPER *comes up on the quarter-deck.*

KIDNAPPER. Well, my brave blacks, are you come to list?

CUDJO. Eas, massa Lord, you preazee.

KIDNAPPER. How many are there of you?

CUDJO. Twenty-two, massa.

KIDNAPPER. Very well, did you all run away from your masters?

CUDJO. Eas, massa Lord, eb'ry one, me too.

KIDNAPPER. That's clever; they have no right to make you slaves, I wish all the Negroes wou'd do the same, I'll make 'em free—what part did you come from?

CUDJO. Disse brack man, disse one, disse one, disse one, disse one, come from Hamton, disse one, disse one, disse one, come from Nawfok, me come from Nawfok too.

KIDNAPPER. Very well, what was your master s name?

CUDJO. Me massa name Cunney Tomsee.

KIDNAPPER. Colonel Thompson—eigh?

CUDJO. Eas, massa, Cunney Tomsee.

KIDNAPPER. Well then I'll make you a major—and wha.'s your name?

CUDJO. Me massa cawra me Cudjo.

KIDNAPPER. Cudjo?—very good—was you ever christened, Cudjo?

CUDJO. No massa, me no crissen.

KIDNAPPER. Well, then I'll christen you—you shall be called Major Cudjo Thompson, and if you behave well, I'll soon make you a greater man than your master, and if I find the rest of you behave well, I'll make you all officers, and after you have serv'd Lord Paramount a while, you shall have money in your pockets, good clothes on your backs, and be as free as them white men there. [*Pointing forward to a parcel of Tories.*]

CUDJO. Tankee, massa, gaw bresse, massa Kidnap.

SAILOR. [*Aside.*] What a damn'd big mouth that Cudjo has—as large as our main hatch-way——

COOK. [*Aside.*] Aye, he's come to a wrong place to make a good use of it—it might stand some little chance at a Lord Mayor's feast.

KIDNAPPER. Now go forward, give 'em something to eat and drink there. [*Aside.*] Poor devils, they look half starved and naked like ourselves.

COOK. [*Aside.*] I don't know where the devil they'll get it; the sight of that fellow's mouth is enough to breed a famine on board, if there was not one already.

SAILOR. Aye, he'd tumble plenty down his damn'd guts and swallow it, like Jones swallow'd the whale.

KIDNAPPER. To-morrow you shall have guns like them white men—Can you shoot some of them rebels ashore, Major Cudjo?

CUDJO. Eas, massa, me try.

KIDNAPPER. Wou'd you shoot your old master, the Colonel, if you could see him?

CUDJO. Eas, massa, you terra me, me shoot him down dead.

KIDNAPPER. That's a brave fellow—damn 'em—down with them all—shoot all the damn'd rebels.

SERJEANT. [*Aside.*] Brave fellows indeed!

KIDNAPPER. Serjeant!

SERJEANT. I wait your Lordship's commands.

KIDNAPPER. Serjeant, to-morrow begin to teach those black recruits the exercise, and when they have learn'd sufficiently well to load and fire, then incorporate them among the regulars and the other Whites on board; we shall in a few days have some work for 'em, I expect—be as expeditious as possible. [*Aside to him.*] Set a guard over them every night, and take their arms from them, for who knows but they may cut our throats.

SERJEANT. Very true, My Lord, I shall take particular care.

[*Exit* KIDNAPPER; SERJEANT *and* NEGROES *walk forward.*

SCENE V.

SERJEANT. Damn 'em, I'd rather see half their weight in beef.

BOATSWAIN. Aye, curse their stomachs, or mutton either; then our Cook wou'dn't be so damn'd lazy as he is, strutting about the deck like a nobleman, receiving Paramount's pay for nothing.

SERJEANT. Walk faster, damn your black heads. I suppose, Boatswain, when this hell-cat reg'ment's complete, they'll be reviewed in Hyde park?——

BOATSWAIN. Aye, blast my eyes, and our Chaplain with his dirty black gown, or our Cook, shall be their general, and review 'em, for he talks of throwing up his pot-halliards commission, in hopes of it.

SERJEANT. Ha, ha, ha.——

COOK. I 'd see the devil have 'em first.——

[*Exeunt* SERJEANT, &c.

SCENE VI. *In the cabin.*

LORD KIDNAPPER, CAPTAIN SQUIRES, *and* CHAPLAIN.

KIDNAPPER. These blacks are no small acquisition, them and the Tories we have on board will strengthen us vastly; the thoughts of emancipation will make 'em brave, and the encouragement given them by my proclamation, will greatly intimidate the rebels—internal enemies are worse than open foes.——

CHAPLAIN. Very true, My Lord; David prayed that he might be preserved from secret enemies.

KIDNAPPER. Aye, so I've heard, but I look upon this to be a grand manœuvre in politics; this is making dog eat dog—thief catch thief—the servant against his master—rebel against rebel—what think you of that, parson?

CHAPLAIN. A house divided thus against itself cannot stand, according to scripture—My Lord, your observation is truly scriptural.

KIDNAPPER. Scripture? poh, poh—I've nothing to do with scripture—I mean politically, parson.

CHAPLAIN. I know it very well; sure, My Lord, I understand you perfectly.

KIDNAPPER. Faith that's all I care for; if we can stand our ground this winter, and burn all their towns that are accessible to our ships, and Colonel Connolly succeeds in his plan, there's not the least doubt but we shall have supplies from England very early in the spring, which I have wrote for; then, in conjunction with Connolly, we shall be able to make a descent where we please, and drive the rebels like hogs into a pen.

CHAPLAIN. And then gather them (as the scriptures say) as a hen gathereth her chickens.

KIDNAPPER. True, Mr. Scripture.

CAPTAIN SQUIRES. Very good, but you must take care of the hawks.

KIDNAPPER. What do you mean by the hawks, Captain?

CAPTAIN SQUIRES. I mean the shirt-men, the rifle-men, My Lord.

KIDNAPPER. Aye, damn 'em, hawks indeed; they are cursed dogs; a man is never safe where they are, but I'll take care to be out of their reach, let others take their chance, for I see they have no respect to persons—I suppose they wou'd shoot at me, if I were within their reach.

CHAPLAIN. Undoubtedly, they would be more fond of you than of a wild turkey; a parcel of ignorant, unmannerly rascals, they pay no more respect to a Lord than they wou'd to a devil.

KIDNAPPER. The scoundrels are grown so damn'd impudent too, that one can scarcely get a roasting pig now-a-days, but I'll be even with some of 'em by and by.

CHAPLAIN. I hope we shall get something good for our Christmas dinner—so much abstinence and involuntary mortification, cannot be good for the soul—a war in the body corporal is of more dangerous consequence than a civil war to the state, or heresy and schism to the church.

KIDNAPPER. Very true, parson—very true—now I like your doctrine—a full belly is better than an empty sermon; preach that doctrine;—stick to that text, and you'll not fail of making converts.

CHAPLAIN. The wisest of men said, there is nothing better, than that a man should enjoy that which he hath, namely, eat, drink, and be merry, if he can.

KIDNAPPER. You're very right—Solomon was no fool, they say—[*He sings.*]

> *Give me a charming lass, Twangdillo cries,*
> *I know no pleasure, but love's sweet joys.*

CHAPLAIN. [*Sings.*]

> *Give me the bottle, says the red face sot,*
> *For a whore I'd not give six-pence, not a groat.*

Yet two is better than one, my Lord, for the scriptures further say, if one be alone, how can there be heat? You seem to be converted to that belief, for you have a brace of them, as the Boatswain says.

KIDNAPPER. Ha, ha. It's a pity but you were a bishop, you have the scriptures so pat—now I'll go and take a short nap, meanwhile; Captain, if any thing new happens, pray order my servant to wake me.

CAPTAIN SQUIRES. I will, my Lord.   [*Exit* KIDNAPPER.

CHAPLAIN. And you and I'll crack a bottle, Captain; (bring a bottle, boy!) 'tis bad enough to perish by famine, but ten thousand times worse to be chok'd for want of moisture. His Lordship and two more make three; and you and I and the bottle make three more, and a three-fold cord is not easily broken; so we're even with him.

CAPTAIN SQUIRES. With all my heart.—Boy, bear a hand!

TOM. Coming, sir.

CHAPLAIN. Tom, Tom!—make haste, you scoundrel!—fetch two bottles. I think we can manage it.

Enter TOM *with the bottles.*

CHAPLAIN. That's right, Tom.—Now bring the glasses, and shut the door after you. [*Exit* TOM.

SCENE VII. *In Boston. A council of war after the battle of Bunker's-Hill.*

LORD BOSTON, ADMIRAL TOMBSTONE, ELBOW ROOM, MR. CAPER, GENERAL CLINTON, EARL PERCY.

LORD BOSTON. I fully expected, with the help of the last reinforcement you brought me over, and the advice and assistance of three accomplish'd and experienc'd Generals, I should have been able to have subdued the rebels, and gain'd immortal laurels to myself—have return'd to Old England like a Roman Consul, with a score or two of the rebel Generals, Colonels and Majors, to have grac'd my triumph.

ELBOW ROOM. You have been vastly disappointed, sir—you must not look for laurels (unless wild ones) nor expect triumphs (unless sham ones) from your own victories or conquests in America.

LORD BOSTON. And yet, not more disappointed than you, sir— witness your thrasonical speeches on your first landing, provided you had but elbow room—and Mr. Caper too, to bring over Monsieur Rigadoon, the dancing-master, and Signor Rosin, the fiddler forsooth; he thought, no doubt, to have country danc'd the rebels out of their liberty with some of his new cuts— with his soft music to have fascinated their wives and daughters, and with some of 'em, no doubt, to have taken the tour of America, with his reg'ment of fine, sleek, prancing horses, that have been feeding this six months on codfish tails; he thought to have grown fat with feasting, dancing, and drinking tea with the Ladies, instead of being the skeleton he now appears to be— not to mention any thing of his letter, wherein he laments Tom's absence; for[1] "had Tom been with him (he says) he wou'd have been out of danger, and quite secure from the enemy's shot."

PERCY. I think, Gentlemen, we're even with you now; you have had your mirth and frolic with us, for dancing "Yankee Doodle," as you called it, from Lexington.—I find you have had a severer dance, a brave sweat at Bunker's Hill, and have been obliged to pay the fiddler in the bargain.

[1] See Burgoyne's letter.

CLINTON. However, Gentlemen, I approve (at proper seasons) of a little joking, yet I can by no means think (as we have had such bad success with our crackers) that this is a proper time to throw your squibs.

LORD BOSTON. I grant you, sir, this is a very improper time for joking; for my part, I was only speaking as to my own thoughts, when Mr. Elbow Room made remarks, which he might as well have spared.

ELBOW ROOM. I took you, sir, as meaning a reflection upon us for our late great loss, and particularly to myself, for expressing some surprise on our first landing, that you should suffer a parcel of ignorant peasants to drive you before 'em like sheep from Lexington; and I must own I was a little chagrin'd at your seeming so unconcern'd at such an affair as this (which had nearly prov'd our ruin), by your innuendoes and ironical talk of accomplish'd Generals, Roman Consuls and triumphs.

LORD BOSTON. My mentioning accomplish'd Generals, surely, sir, was rather a compliment to you.

ELBOW ROOM. When irony pass current for compliments, and we take it so, I shall have no objection to it.

MR. CAPER. The affair of Lexington, My Lord Boston, at which you were so much affrighted (if I am rightly inform'd), was because you then stood on your own bottom, this of Bunker's Hill you seem secretly to rejoice at, only because you have three accomplish'd and experienc'd Generals to share the disgrace with you, besides the brave Admiral Tombstone—you talk of dancing and fiddling, and yet you do neither, as I see.

LORD BOSTON. And pray, sir, what did you do with the commission, the post, the Duke of Grafton gave you, in lieu of your losses at Preston election, and the expenses of your trial at the king's bench for a riot, which had emptied your pockets?—Why you sold it—you sold it, sir—to raise cash to gamble with.——

ADMIRAL TOMBSTONE. Damn it, don't let us kick up a dust among ourselves, to be laugh'd at fore and aft—this is a hell of a council of war—though I believe it will turn out one before we've done—a scolding and quarrelling like a parcel of damn'd butter whores—I never heard two whores yet scold and quarrel, but they got to fighting at last.

CLINTON. Pray, Gentlemen, drop this discourse, consider the honour of England is at stake, and our own safety depends upon this day's consultation.

LORD BOSTON. 'Tis not for argument's sake—but the dignity of my station requires others should give up first.

ELBOW ROOM. Sir, I have done, lest you should also accuse me of obstructing the proceedings of the council of war.

MR. CAPER. For the same reason I drop it now.

LORD BOSTON. Well, Gentlemen, what are we met here for?

ADMIRAL TOMBSTONE. Who the devil shou'd know, if you don't?—damn it, didn't you send for us?

LORD BOSTON. Our late great loss of men has tore up the foundation of our plan, and render'd all further attempts impracticable—'t will be a long time ere we can expect any more reinforcements—and if they should arrive, I'm doubtful of their success.

CLINTON. The provincials are vastly strong, and seem no novices in the art of war; 'tis true we gain'd the hill at last, but of what advantage is it to us?—none—the loss of 1400 as brave men as Britain can boast of, is a melancholy consideration, and must make our most sanguinary friends in England abate of their vigour.

ELBOW ROOM. I never saw or read of any battle equal to it—never was more martial courage display'd, and the provincials, to do the dogs justice, fought like heroes, fought indeed more like devils than men; such carnage and destruction not exceeded by Blenheim, Minden, Fontenoy, Ramillies, Dettingen, the battle of the Boyne, and the late affair of the Spaniards and Algerines—a mere cock-fight to it—no laurels there.

MR. CAPER. No, nor triumphs neither—I regret in particular the number of brave officers that fell that day, many of whom were of the first families in England.

ADMIRAL TOMBSTONE. Aye, a damn'd affair indeed—many powder'd beaus—petit maitres—fops—fribbles—skip jacks—macaronies—jack puddings—noblemen's bastards and whores' sons fell that day—and my poor marines stood no more chance with 'em than a cat in hell without claws.

LORD BOSTON. It can't be help'd, Admiral; what is to be done next?

ADMIRAL TOMBSTONE. Done?—why, what the devil have you done? nothing yet, but eat Paramount's beef, and steal a few Yankee sheep—and that, it seems, is now become a damn'd lousy, beggarly trade too, for you hav'n't left yourselves a mouthful to eat.

[*Aside.*] "*Bold at the council board,*
But cautious in the field, he shunn'd the sword."

LORD BOSTON. But what can we do, Admiral?

ADMIRAL TOMBSTONE. Do?—why, suck your paws—that's all you're like to get. [*Aside.*] But avast, I must bowse taught there, or we shall get to loggerheads soon, we're such damn'd fighting fellows.

LORD BOSTON. We must act on the defensive this winter, till reinforcements arrive.

ADMIRAL TOMBSTONE. Defensive? aye, aye—if we can defend our bellies from hunger, and prevent a mutiny and civil war among the small guts there this winter, we shall make a glorious campaign of it, indeed—it will read well in the American Chronicles.

LORD BOSTON. I expect to be recalled this winter, when I shall lay the case before Lord Paramount, and let him know your deplorable situation.

ADMIRAL TOMBSTONE. Aye, do—and lay it behind him too; you've got the weather-gage of us this tack, messmate; but I wish you a good voyage for all—and don't forget to tell him, the poor worms are starving too, having nothing to eat, but half starv'd dead soldiers and the ships' bottoms. [*Aside.*] A cunning old fox, he's gnaw'd his way handsomely out of the Boston cage—but he'll never be a *wolf*, for all that.

MR. CAPER. I shall desire to be recalled too—I've not been us'd to such fare—and not the least diversion or entertainment of any sort going forward here—I neither can nor will put up with it.

ADMIRAL TOMBSTONE. I think we're all a parcel of damn'd boobies for coming three thousand miles upon a wild-goose chase —to perish with cold—starve with hunger—get our brains knock'd out, or be hang'd for sheep-stealing and robbing hen-roosts.

LORD BOSTON. I think, Admiral, you're always grumbling— never satisfied.

ADMIRAL TOMBSTONE. Satisfied? I see no appearance of it— we have been here these twelve hours, scolding upon empty stomachs—you may call it a council of war (and so it is indeed, a war with the guts) or what you will—but I call it a council of famine.

LORD BOSTON. As it's so late, Gentlemen, we'll adjourn the council of war till to-morrow at nine o'clock—I hope you'll all attend, and come to a conclusion.

ADMIRAL TOMBSTONE. And I hope you'll then conclude to favour us with one of them fine turkeys you're keeping for your sea store [*Aside.*] or that fine, fat, black pig you or some of your guard stole out of the poor Negroe's pen. As it's near Christmas, and you're going to make your exit—you know the old custom among the sailors—pave your way first—let us have one good dinner before we part, and leave us half a dozen pipes of Mr. Hancock's wine to drink your health, and a good voyage, and don't let us part with dry lips.

> *Such foolish councils, with no wisdom fraught,*
> *Must end in wordy words, and come to nought;*
> *Just like St. James's, where they bluster, scold,*
> *They nothing know—yet they despise being told.*

[*Exeunt.*

ACT V.

SCENE I. *At Montreal.*

GENERAL PRESCOT *and* OFFICER.

GENERAL PRESCOT.

So it seems indeed, one misfortune seldom comes alone.—The rebels, after the taking of Ticonderoga and Chamblee, as I just now learn by a Savage, marched immediately to besiege St. John's, and are now before that place, closely investing it, and no doubt intend paying us a visit soon.

OFFICER. Say you so? then 'tis time to look about us.

GEN. PRESCOT. They'll find us prepar'd, I'll warrant 'em, to give 'em such a reception as they little dream of—a parcel of Yankee dogs.

OFFICER. Their success, no doubt, has elated them, and given 'em hopes of conquering all Canada soon, if that's their intent.

GEN. PRESCOT. No doubt it is—but I'll check their career a little.——

Enter SCOUTING OFFICER, *with* COLONEL ALLEN,
and other prisoners.

SCOUTING OFFICER. Sir, I make bold to present you with a few prisoners—they are a scouting detachment from the army besieging St. John's.

GEN. PRESCOT. Prisoners? Rebels, I suppose, and scarcely worth hanging.

COL. ALLEN. Sir, you suppose wrong—you mean scarcely worth your while to attempt.

GEN. PRESCOT. Pray, who are you, sir?

COL. ALLEN. A man, sir, and who had the honour, till now, to command those brave men, whom you call rebels.

GEN. PRESCOT. What is your name? If I may be so bold?

COL. ALLEN. Allen.

GEN. PRESCOT. Allen?

COL. ALLEN. Yes, Allen.

GEN. PRESCOT. Are you that Allen, that Colonel Allen (as they call him) that dar'd to take Ticonderoga?

COL. ALLEN. The same—the very man.

GEN. PRESCOT. Then rebels you are, and as such I shall treat you, for daring to oppose Lord Paramount's troops, and the laws of the land.

COL. ALLEN. Prisoners we are, 'tis true—but we despise the name of a rebel—With more propriety that name is applicable to your master—'tis he who attempts to destroy the laws of the land, not us—we mean to support them, and defend our property against Paramount's and parliamentary tyranny.

GEN. PRESCOT. To answer you were a poorness of spirit I despise; when rebels dare accuse, power that replies, forgets to punish; I am not to argue that point with you: And let me tell you, sir, whoever you are, it now ill becomes you thus to talk —You're my prisoner—your life is in my hands, and you shall suffer immediately—Guards! take them away.

COL. ALLEN. Cruel insult!—pardon these brave men!—what they have done has been by my orders—I am the only guilty person (if guilt there be), let me alone suffer for them all. [*Opening his breast.*] Here! take your revenge—Why do you hesitate?—Will you not strike a breast that ne'er will flinch from your pointed bayonet?

GEN. PRESCOT. Provoke me not—Remember you're my prisoners.

COL. ALLEN. Our souls are free!—Strike, cowards, strike!—I scorn to beg my life.

GEN. PRESCOT. Guards! away with them—I'll reserve you for a more ignominious death—your fate is fix'd—away with them.

COL. ALLEN. [*Going off.*] Be glutted, ye thirsters after human blood—Come, see me suffer—mark my eye, and scorn me, if my expiring soul confesses fear—Come, see and be taught virtue, and to die as a patriot for the wrongs of my country.

[*Exeunt* PRISONERS *and* GUARDS.

SCENE II. *A Dungeon.*

COL. ALLEN. What! ye infernal monsters! murder us in the dark?—What place is this?—Who reigns king of these gloomy mansions?—You might favour us at least with one spark of light—Ye cannot see to do your business here.

OFFICER. 'Tis our orders.

COL. ALLEN. Ye dear, ye brave, wretched friends!—now would I die for ye all—ye share a death I wou'd gladly excuse you from—'Tis not death I fear—this is only bodily death—but to die noteless in the silent dark, is to die scorn'd, and shame our suff'ring country—we fall undignify'd by villains' hands—a sacrifice to Britain's outcast blood-hounds—This, this shakes the soul!—Come then, ye murderers, since it must be so—do your business speedily—Farewell, my friends! to die with you is now my noblest claim since to die for you was a choice deny'd—What are ye about?—Stand off, ye wretches!

OFFICER. I am order'd to lay you in irons. [*They seize him.*] You must submit.

COL. ALLEN. What, do you mean to torture us to death with chains, racks and gibbets? rather despatch us immediately—Ye executioners, ye inquisitors, does this cruelty proceed from the lenity I shewed to the prisoners I took?—Did it offend you that I treated them with friendship, generosity, honour and humanity? —If it did, our suff'rings will redound more to our honour, and our fall be the more glorious—But remember, this fall will prove your own one day—Wretches! I fear you not, do your worst; and while I here lay suff'ring and chain'd on my back to the damp floor, I'll yet pray for your conversion.

OFFICER. Excuse us, we have only obey'd our order.

COL. ALLEN. Then I forgive you; but pray execute them.

> *Oh! my lost friends! 'tis liberty, not breath,*
> *Gives the brave life. Shun slav'ry more than death.*
> *He who spurns fear, and dares disdain to be,*
> *Mocks chains and wrongs—and is forever free;*
> *While the base coward, never safe, tho' low,*
> *Creeps but to suff'rings, and lives on for woe!*

[*Exeunt* GUARDS.

SCENE III. *In the Camp at Cambridge.*

GENERAL WASHINGTON, GENERAL LEE, *and* GENERAL PUTNAM.

GENERAL WASHINGTON.

Our accounts from the Northward, so far, are very favourable; Ticonderoga, Chamblee, St. John's and Montreal our troops are already in possession of—and Colonel Arnold, having penetrated Canada, after suff'ring much thro' cold, fatigue and want of provisions, is now before Quebec, and General Montgomery, I understand, is in full march to join him; see these letters. [*They read.*

GEN. LEE. The brave, the intrepid Arnold, with his handful of fearless troops, have dar'd beyond the strength of mortals— Their courage smil'd at doubts, and resolutely march'd on, clamb'ring (to all but themselves) insurmountable precipices, whose tops, covered with ice and snow, lay hid in the clouds, and dragging baggage, provisions, ammunition and artillery along with them, by main strength, in the dead of winter, over such stupendous and amazing heights, seems almost unparallelled in history!—'Tis true, Hannibal's march over the Alps comes the nearest to it—it was a surprising undertaking, but when compar'd to this, appears but as a party of pleasure, an agreeable walk, a sabbath day's journey.

GEN. PUTNAM. Posterity will stand amazed, and be astonish'd at the heroes of this new world, that the spirit of patriotism should blaze to such a height, and eclipse all others, should outbrave fatigue, danger, pain, peril, famine and even death itself, to serve their country; that they should march, at this inclement season, thro' long and dreary deserts, thro' the remotest wilds, covered with swamps and standing lakes, beset with trees, bushes and briars, impervious to the cheering rays of the sun, where are no traces or vestiges of human footsteps, wild, untrodden paths, that strike terror into the fiercest of the brute creation.

No bird of song to cheer the gloomy desert!
No animals of gentle love's enliven!

GEN. LEE. Let Britons do the like—no—they dare not attempt it—let 'em call forth the Hanoverian, the Hessian, the hardy Ruffian, or, if they will, the wild Cossacks and Kalmucks of Tartary, and they would tremble at the thought! And who but Americans dare undertake it? The wond'ring moon and stars stood aloof, and turn'd pale at the sight!

GEN. WASHINGTON. I rejoice to hear the Canadians received them kindly, after their fatigue furnish'd them with the necessaries of life, and otherways treated them very humanely—And the savages, whose hair stood on end, and look'd and listen'd with horror and astonishment at the relation of the fatigues and perils they underwent, commiserated them, and afforded all the succour in their power.

GEN. LEE. The friendship of the Canadians and Savages, or even their neutrality alone, are favourable circumstances that cannot fail to hearten our men; and the junction of General Montgomery will inspire 'em with fresh ardour.

GEN. PUTNAM. Heavens prosper 'em!

Enter OFFICER *and* EXPRESS.

OFFICER. Sir, here's an Express.

EXPRESS. I have letters to your Excellency.

GEN. WASHINGTON. From whence?

EXPRESS. From Canada, sir.

GEN. WASHINGTON. From the army?

EXPRESS. From the headquarters, sir.

GEN. WASHINGTON. I hope matters go well there.—Had General Montgomery join'd Colonel Arnold when you left it?

EXPRESS. He had, sir—these letters are from both those gentlemen.   [*Gives him the letters.*

GEN. WASHINGTON. Very well. You may now withdraw and refresh yourself, unless you've further to say—I'll dispatch you shortly.

EXPRESS. Nothing further, sir.

[*Exeunt* OFFICER *and* EXPRESS.

GEN. WASHINGTON. [*Opens and reads the letter to* GENERALS LEE *and* PUTNAM.] I am well pleased with their contents—all but the behaviour of the haughty Carleton—to fire upon a flag of truce, hitherto unprecedented, even amongst Savages or Algerines—his cruelty to the prisoners is cowardly, and personal ill treatment of General Montgomery is unbecoming a General—a soldier—and beneath a Gentleman—and leaves an indelible mark of brutality—I hope General Montgomery, however, will not follow his example.

GEN. LEE. I hope so too, sir—if it can be avoided; it's a disgrace to the soldier, and a scandal to the Gentleman—so long as I've been a soldier, my experience has not furnish'd me with a like instance.

GEN. PUTNAM. I see no reason why he shou'dn't be paid in his own coin.—If a man bruises my heel, I'll break his head—I cannot see the reason or propriety of bearing with their insults—does he not know it's in our power to retaliate fourfold?

GEN. LEE. Let's be good natur'd, General—let us see a little more of it first——

GEN. PUTNAM. I think we have seen enough of it already for this twelve-months past. Methinks the behaviour of Lord Boston, the ill treatment of poor Allen, to be thrown into a loathsome dungeon like a murderer, be loaded with irons, and transported like a convict, would sufficiently rouse us to a just retaliation—that imperious red coat, Carleton, should be taught good manners—I hope to see him ere long in our College at Cambridge——

GEN. LEE. I doubt; he'll be too cunning, and play truant—he has no notion of learning American manners; ev'ry dog must have his day (as the saying is); it may be our time by and by—the event of war is uncertain——

GEN. PUTNAM. Very true, sir; but don't let us be laugh'd at forever.

Enter an OFFICER *in haste.*

OFFICER. Sir, a messenger this moment from Quebec waits to be admitted.

GEN. WASHINGTON. Let him enter. [*Exit* OFFICER.

Enter MESSENGER.

GEN. WASHINGTON. What news bring you?

MESSENGER. I am sorry, sir, to be the bearer of an unpleasing tale——

GEN. WASHINGTON. Bad news have you?—have you letters?

MESSENGER. None, sir—I came off at a moment's warning—my message is verbal.

GEN. WASHINGTON. Then relate what you know.

MESSENGER. After the arrival and junction of General Montgomery's troops with Colonel Arnold's, Carleton was summoned to surrender; he disdaining any answer, fir'd on the flag of truce——

GEN. WASHINGTON. That we have heard—go on.

MESSENGER. The General finding no breach could be effected in any reasonable time, their walls being vastly strong, and his cannon rather light, determined to attempt it by storm—The enemy were apprized of it—however, he passed the first barrier, and was attempting the second, where he was unfortunately killed, with several other brave officers——

GEN. WASHINGTON. Is General Montgomery killed?

MESSENGER. He is certainly, sir.

GEN. WASHINGTON. I am sorry for it—a brave man—I could wish him a better fate!——

GEN. LEE. I lament the loss of him—a resolute soldier——

GEN. PUTNAM. Pity such bravery should prove unsuccessful; such merit unrewarded;—but the irreversible decree of Providence!——who can gainsay?—we may lament the loss of a friend, but 'tis irreligious to murmur at pre-ordination. What happ'ned afterwards?

MESSENGER. The officer next in command, finding their attacks at that time unsuccessful, retired in good order.

GEN. WASHINGTON. What became of Colonel Arnold?

MESSENGER. Colonel Arnold, at the head of about three hundred and fifty brave troops, and Captain Lamb's company of artillery, having in the mean time passed through St. Rocques, attacked a battery, and carried it, tho' well defended, with the loss of some men—

GEN. PUTNAM. I hope they proved more successful.

GEN. LEE. Aye, let us hear.

MESSENGER. The Colonel about this time received a wound in his leg, and was obliged to crawl as well as he cou'd to the hospital, thro' the fire of the enemy, and within fifty yards of the walls, but, thro' Providence, escap'd any further damage.——

GEN. PUTNAM. Aye, providential indeed!

GEN. WASHINGTON. Is he dangerously wounded?

MESSENGER. I am told not, sir.

GEN. WASHINGTON. I am glad of it.—What follow'd?

MESSENGER. His brave troops pushed on to the second barrier, and took possession of it.

GEN. WASHINGTON. Very good—proceed.

MESSENGER. A party of the enemy then sallying out from the palace-gate, attacked them in the rear, whom they fought with incredible bravery for three hours, and deeds of eternal fame were done; but being surrounded on all sides, and overpowered by numbers, were at last obliged to submit themselves as prisoners of war.

GEN. PUTNAM. Heav'ns! could any thing prove more unlucky? such brave fellows deserve better treatment than they'll get (I'm afraid) from the inhuman Carleton.

GEN. LEE. Such is the fortune of war, and the vicissitudes attending a military life; to-day conquerors, to-morrow prisoners.

GEN. WASHINGTON. He dares not treat them ill—only as prisoners. Did you learn how those brave fellows were treated?

MESSENGER. It was currently reported in the camp they were treated very humanely.

GEN. WASHINGTON. A change for the better.

GEN. PUTNAM. Produc'd by fear, no doubt from General Montgomery's letter—but no matter from what cause.

GEN. LEE. How far did the remainder of the army retire?

MESSENGER. About two miles from the city, where they are posted very advantageously, continuing the blockade, and waiting for reinforcements.

GEN. LEE. Did the enemy shew any peculiar marks of distinction to the corpse of General Montgomery?

MESSENGER. He was interred in Quebec, with ev'ry possible mark of distinction.

GEN. WASHINGTON. What day did the affair happen on?

MESSENGER. On the last day of the year.

GEN. WASHINGTON. A remarkable day! When was the General interred?

MESSENGER. The second of January.

GEN. LEE. What number of men in the whole attack was killed? did you learn?

MESSENGER. About sixty killed and wounded.

GEN. WASHINGTON. Have you any thing further to communicate?

MESSENGER. Nothing, sir, but to inform you they are all in good spirits, and desire reinforcements, and heavy artillery may be sent them as soon as possible.

GEN. WASHINGTON. That be our business—with all despatch. You may for the present withdraw. Serjeant!

Enter SERJEANT.

SERJEANT. I wait your order, sir.

GEN. WASHINGTON. See that the Messenger and his horse want for nothing.

SERJEANT. I shall, sir.   [*Exeunt* SERJEANT *and* MESSENGER.

SCENE IV.

GEN. WASHINGTON. I'll despatch an Express to the Congress. This repulse, if I mistake not (or victory, as Carleton may call it), will stand 'em but in little stead—'t will be only a temporary reprieve—we'll reinforce our friends, let the consequence be what it may—Quebec must fall, and the lofty strong walls and brazen gates (the shield of cowards) must tumble by an artificial earthquake; should they continue in their obstinacy, we'll arm our friends with missive thunders in their hands, and stream death on them swifter than the winds.

GEN. LEE. I lament the loss of the valiant Montgomery and his brave officers and soldiers (at this time more especially) 'tis the fortune of war, 'tis unavoidable; yet, I doubt not, out of their ashes will arise new heroes.

GEN. PUTNAM. Who can die a more glorious, a more honourable death than in their country's cause?—let it redouble our ardour, and kindle a noble emulation in our breasts—let each American be determined to conquer or die in a righteous cause.

GEN. WASHINGTON. I have drawn my sword, and never will I sheathe it, till America is free, or I'm no more.

GEN. LEE. Peace is despaired of, and who can think of submission? The last petition from the Congress, like the former, has been disregarded; they prayed but for liberty, peace and safety, and their omnipotent authoritative supreme-ships will grant them neither: War, then, war open and understood, must be resolved on; this, this will humble their pride, will bring their tyrant noses to the ground, teach 'em humility, and force them to hearken to reason when 'tis too late. My noble General, I join you. [*Drawing his sword.*] I'll away with the scabbard, and sheathe my sword in the bosom of tyranny.

GEN. PUTNAM. Have you not read the speech, where frowning revenge and sounds of awful dread for disgrace at Lexington and loss at Bunker's Hill echo forth? Not smiling peace, or pity, tame his sullen soul; but, Pharaoh-like, on the wings of tyranny he rides and forfeits happiness to feast revenge, till the waters of the red sea of blood deluge the tyrant, with his mixed host of vile cut-throats, murderers, and bloody butchers.

GEN. WASHINGTON. Yet, finding they cannot conquer us, gladly would they make it up by a voluntary free-will offering of a million of money in bribes, rather than be obliged to relish the thoughts of sacrificing their cursed pride and false honour, they sending over to amuse us (to put us off our guard) a score or two of commissioners with sham negotiations in great state, to endeavour to effect, by bribery, deception and chicanery, what they cannot accomplish by force. Perish such wretches!— detested be their schemes!—Perish such monsters!—a reproach to human understanding—their vaunted boasts and threats will vanish like smoke, and be no more than like snow falling on the moist ground, melt in silence, and waste away—Blasted, forever blasted be the hand of the villainous traitor that receives their gold upon such terms—may he become leprous, like Naaman, the Syrian, yea, rather like Gehazi, the servant of Elisha, that it may stick to him for ever.

GEN. PUTNAM. I join you both, and swear by all the heroes of New-England, that this arm, tho' fourscore and four [*Drawing his sword.*], still nervous and strong, shall wield this sword to the last in the support of liberty and my country, revenge the insult offer'd to the immortal Montgomery, and brutal treatment of the brave Allen.

> *O Liberty! thou sunshine of the heart!*
> *Thou smile of nature, and thou soul of art!*
> *Without thy aid no human hope cou'd grow,*
> *And all we cou'd enjoy were turn'd to woe.*

                         [*Exeunt.*

THE EPILOGUE.

SPOKEN BY MR. FREEMAN.

Since tyrants reign, and lust and lux'ry rule;
Since kings turn Neroes—statesmen play the fool;
Since parli'ment in cursed league combine,
To sport with rights that's sacred and divine;
Destroying towns with direful conflagration,
And murder subjects without provocation!
These are but part of evils we could name,
Not to their glory, but eternal shame.
Petitions—waste paper—great Pharaoh cries,
Nor care a rush for your remonstrances.
Each Jacobite, and ev'ry pimping Tory,
Waits for your wealth, to raise his future glory:
Or pensions sure, must ev'ry rascal have,
Who strove his might, to make FREEMAN a slave.
Since this the case, to whom for succour cry?
To God, our swords, and sons of liberty!
Cast off the idol god!—kings are but vain!
Let justice rule, and independence reign.
Are ye not men? Pray who made men, but God?
Yet men make kings—to tremble at their nod!
What nonsense this—let's wrong with right oppose,
Since nought will do, but sound, impartial blows.
Let's act in earnest, not with vain pretence,
Adopt the language of sound COMMON SENSE,
And with one voice proclaim INDEPENDENCE.
Convince your foes you will defend your right,
That blows and knocks is all they will get by 't.
Let tyrants see that you are well prepar'd,
By proclamations, sword, nor speeches scar'd;
That liberty freeborn breathe in each soul!
One god-like union animate the whole!

End of the First Campaign.

THE
POLITICIAN OUT-WITTED

By Samuel Low

SAMUEL LOW

(b. December 12, 1765)

Very little is known about the author of "The Politician Out-witted,[1] a play which I have selected as representative of the efforts of the American drama, as early as 1789, to reflect the political spirit of the time. Assiduous search on the part of the present editor has failed to bring to light any information from any of the historical societies regarding Mr. Low, except that he was born on December 12, 1765, and that he must have been, in his political sympathies, an anti-federalist. The reader who is interested in literary comparisons might take this play of Low's and read it in connection with Dunlap's "The Father," in which a prologue gives a very excellent example of the American spirit. Dunlap's "Darby's Return" might likewise be read in connection with "The Politican Out-witted," inasmuch as it refers to the Federal Constitution, and to Washington's inauguration.

The present play, which was opposed to the Federal union, was, according to some authorities, offered to the actors, Hallam and Henry, and was promptly rejected by them. There is no record of the piece having thereafter succeeded in reaching the theatre. It is mentioned both in Dunlap and in Seilhamer in a casual manner.

In the New York Directory, of 1794, we find Samuel Low mentioned as a clerk in the Treasury Department, and, in a later Directory of 1797–1798, he is referred to as the first bookkeeper in the Bank of New York.[2]

[1] The/Politician Out-witted,/a/Comedy,/In Five Acts./Written in the Year 1788./ By an American./"Then let not Censure, with malignant joy,/"The harvest of his humble hope destroy!"/Falconer's Shipwreck. [Colophon.]/New-York:/Printed for the Author, by W. Ross, in Broad-Street,/and Sold by the Different Booksellers./ M. DCC. LXXXIX./

[2] Through the assiduous researches of a member of the staff of the Americana Division of the New York Public Library, who has generously given me permission to use the results of this investigation, there is brought to light, in the New York Directory for 1803, the name of Widow Ann Low, keeper of a boarding-house. There is a plausible theory framed by this investigator that, maybe, Samuel Low died during the New York yellow fever epidemic of 1803, although his name does not occur in the New York *Evening Post* death lists for that year. It may be that our Samuel, as revealed in the annals of the Dutch Reform Church, v. 1, p. 273; v. 32, p. 23 (New York Geneological and Biographical Society), married Anne Creiger, as recorded on April 20, 1797, and that she may be the "Widow Ann" referred to above. The Nicholas Low mentioned in the Directories of the time as President of

In the preface to his published poems, after the diffident manner of the time, Low says: "Many of the pieces were written at a very early age, and most of them under singular disadvantages; among which, application to public business, for many years past, was not the least; not only because it allowed little leisure for literary pursuits, but because it is of a nature peculiarly inimical to the cultivation of poetic talent. For his own amusement and improvement he has written—at the request of his friends he publishes."

We know that he was a writer of odes, exhibiting some grace in his handling of this poetic form. He is also credited with having written a long poem entitled "Winter Displayed," in 1794. In 1800, two volumes of poems appeared in New York, and among the subscribers listed were John Jacob Astor, William Dunlap, Philip Hone, Dr. Peter Irving, and members of the Beekman and Schermerhorn families.[1] Examining the contents of these volumes, one discovers that Samuel Low, in a social and fraternal way, must have been a very active member of New York society. On January 8, 1800, his "Ode on the Death of Washington" was recited by Hodgkinson at the New York Theatre.

At St. Paul's Church, and at Trinity Church, his anthems and odes were ever to the fore. He must have been a member of the Tammany Society, or Columbian Order, because a "Hymn to Liberty" was penned by him, and sung in church on the anniversary of that organization, May 12, 1790.

His Masonic interests are indicated throughout the volume by poems written especially for such orders as the Holland Lodge, and the Washington Chapter of Royal Arch Masons. He was also asked to write an epitaph on John Frederick Roorbach.

His interest in politics may likewise be seen in several poems written about the Constitution of the United States; while his literary taste may be measured by his tribute to Kotzebue, the "second Shakespeare," in which occur the lines:

> "*The purest, sweetest among modern bards*
> *Who tread the difficult dramatic path.*"

the Bank of New York, and who was well-to-do, must have been the brother, or some near relation. There are many Samuel Lows of this period; one (1739–1807) mentioned in the D. A. R. Lineage, v. 15; another who married Margaret Kip. The nearest we get to our Low's parentage is a reference, in the Reports of the New York Geneological and Biographical Society, v. 29, p. 36, to John and Súsanna Low, whose son, Samuel, was born December 22, 1765. Identification has yet to be established.

[1] Poems. By Samuel Low. In two volumes. New York: Printed by T. & J. Swords. 1800.

Except for this, as one of the biographical sources says, nothing is known of Low's history, "and he is only saved from absolute oblivion by his two small volumes of poems."

Yet "The Politician Out-witted" has historical value, and, in its dialogue, exhibits how well Low had studied the artificial comedy of Sheridan. The construction of the plot is mechanical, but the convictions of the two opposing fathers, on the subject of the Constitution, give the play an interest in character and in viewpoint which is marked. It is not a piece adapted to the theatre, there being slight action of a cumulative kind; but, as an example of early closet drama, it cannot be ignored.

THE

POLITICIAN OUT-WITTED,

A

C O M E D Y,

IN FIVE ACTS.

Written in the YEAR 1788.

BY AN AMERICAN.

" Then let not Cenſure, with malignant joy,
" The harveſt of his humble hope deſtroy!"

Falconer's Shipwreck.

N E W - Y O R K:

PRINTED FOR THE AUTHOR, BY W. ROSS, IN BROAD-STREET,
AND SOLD BY THE DIFFERENT BOOKSELLERS.

M.DCC.LXXXIX.

FAC-SIMILE TITLE-PAGE TO THE 1789 EDITION

DRAMATIS PERSONÆ

MEN.

TRUEMAN.

OLD LOVEYET.

CHARLES LOVEYET, *engaged to* HARRIET.

FRANKTON, *his Friend.*

WORTHNOUGHT.
HUMPHRY.

TOUPEE.

THOMAS.

WOMEN.

HARRIET, *Daughter to* TRUEMAN.

MARIA, *her Friend.*

TABITHA CANTWELL.

HERALD.

DOLLY.

SCENE—The city of New-York. Time of four acts is one day, and the fifth act commences the second day.

THE
POLITICIAN OUT-WITTED
ACT I.

Scene I. Old Loveyet's *House.*

Enter Old Loveyet.

Ugh, ugh, ugh,—what a sad rage for novelty there is in this foolish world! How eagerly all your inspectors in the *Daily Advertiser*, the *New-York Packet*, and all the long catalogue of advertisers and intelligencers, catch'd at the news of the day just now at the Coffee-House; though a wise man and a king has told them, there's nothing new under the sun. Ugh, ugh, ugh.

Enter Thomas.

Well, Thomas, what's the news?   [*Eagerly.*

Thomas. Nothing strange, sir.

Loveyet. That's more than I can say, Thomas, for I'm sure 'tis strange to hear so many people praise this same new Constitution, as it is call'd. — Has the *New-York Journal* been brought to-day?

Thomas. Yes, sir.   [*Fetches the newspaper.*

Loveyet. Look if it contains anything worth reading, Thomas; anything in behalf of the good old cause.

Thomas. Yes, sir, here's something will suit your honour's notion to a hair.   [*Offers it to* Loveyet.

Loveyet. No, Thomas, do you read it,—I'm afraid I shall cast my eyes upon something that's on the other side of the question; some wicked consolidation scheme or another.

Thomas. Why, you know, sir, there's never anything in this paper but what's on your side of the question.

Loveyet. True, true; by my body, you're right enough, Tom.—I forgot that; but never mind; since you've got the paper, do you read it.

Thomas. He only wants me to read, because he can't see to do it himself,—he's almost as blind as a bat, and yet he won't use spectacles for fear of being thought old.   [*Aside.*

LOVEYET. Come, Thomas, let's have it,—I'm all ears to hear you.

THOMAS. 'Tis a pity you have not a little more eyesight and brains along with your ears. [*Aside.*] [*Reads.*] "Extract of a letter from a gentleman in Boston, dated February the third, 1788.—Our convention will pass the federal government by a considerable majority: The more it is examined, the more converts are made for its adoption. This you may rely on."

LOVEYET. 'Tis a cursed lie.—Why, why, you confounded scoundrel, do you mean to ridicule your master?

THOMAS. I ask pardon, sir; I thought it was the *New-York Journal;* but I see it is Mr. Child's *Daily Advertiser.*

LOVEYET. A plague on his aristocratic intelligence!—Begone, you vile foe to American Liberty, or I'll—

[*Exit* THOMAS.

Enter TRUEMAN.

What, my friend Trueman! well, what's the news, eigh?

TRUEMAN. I have not learn'd a single monosyllable, sir.

LOVEYET. Nothing concerning this same Constitution there is so much talk about, friend Horace? A miserable Constitution, by the bye. If mine was no better,—ugh, ugh, ugh,—I say, if— ugh, ugh, if my constitution was no better than this same political one, I solemnly swear, as true as I am this day, man and boy, two score and three years, five months, eleven days, six hours, and, and,— [*Pulling out his watch.*] fifty-nine minutes old; why, I —I—I would,—I don't know what I wou'd not do. Ugh, ugh.

TRUEMAN. Mr. Loveyet, you run on in such a surprising manner with your narrations, imprecations, admirations, and interrogations, that, upon my education, sir, I believe you are approaching to insanity, frenzy, lunacy, madness, distraction,—a man of your age—

LOVEYET. Age, sir, age!—And what then, sir, eigh! what then? I'd have you to know, sir, that I shall not have lived forty years till next spring twelvemonth, old as I am; and if my countenance seems to belie me a little or so, why—trouble, concern for the good of my country, sir, and this tyrannical, villainous Constitution have made me look so; but my health is sound, sir; my lungs are good, sir, [*Raising his voice.*]—ugh, ugh, ugh,—I am neither spindle-shank'd nor crook-back'd, and I can kiss a pretty girl with as good a relish as—ugh, ugh,—ha, ha, ha. A man of five and forty, old, forsooth! ha, ha. My age, truly!—ugh, ugh, ugh.

TRUEMAN. You talk very valiantly, Mr. Loveyet; very valiantly indeed; I dare say now you have temerity and enterprise enough, even at this time of day, to take a *wife*.

LOVEYET. To be sure I have. Let me see,—I shou'd like a woman an inch or two less than six feet high now, and thick in proportion: By my body, such a woman wou'd look noble by the side of me when she was entient.

TRUEMAN. Oh, monstrous! Entient! an entient woman by the side of an antient husband! Most preposterous, unnatural, and altogether incongruous!

LOVEYET. Poh, a fig for your high-flown nonsense. I suppose you think it would cost me a great deal of trouble.

TRUEMAN. No, no; some clever young blade will save you the trouble.

LOVEYET. By my body, I should love dearly to have such a partner; she would be a credit to me when she had me under the arm.

TRUEMAN. Under the *thumb*, you mean.

LOVEYET. Under the *Devil, you* mean.

TRUEMAN. You're right; you might as well be under the Devil's government as petticoat government; you're perfectly right there.

LOVEYET. I'm not perfectly right;—I—I—I mean *you* are not perfectly right; and as for her age, why I should like her to be—let me see—about ten years younger than myself: a man shou'd be at least ten years older than his wife.

TRUEMAN. Ten years; fifty-three and ten are sixty-three. Then you mean your wife shall be fifty-three years of age.

LOVEYET. S'death, sir! I tell you I am but two and forty years old: She sha'n't be more than thirty odd, sir, and she shall be ten years younger than I am too.

TRUEMAN. Yes, thirty odd years younger than *you* are; ha, ha. The exiguity of those legs is a most promising earnest of your future exploits, and demonstrate your agility, virility, salubrity, and amorosity; ha, ha, ha. I can't help laughing to think what a blessed union there will be between August and December; a jolly, buxom, wanton, wishful, plethoric female of thirty odd, to an infirm, decrepit, consumptive, gouty, rheumatic, asthmatic, phlegmatic mortal of near seventy; ha, ha. Exquisitely droll and humourous, upon my erudition. It puts me in mind of a hot bed in a hard winter, surrounded with ice, and made verdant and flourishing only by artificial means.

LOVEYET. Pshaw, you're a fool!

Enter TOUPEE.

TOUPEE. Pardonnez moy, monsieur. I hope it not be any intrusion; par dieu, I will not frize dat Jantemon à la mode Paris no more, becase he vas fronte me.

TRUEMAN. What's the matter, Mr. Toupee?

TOUPEE. I vill tella your honare of the fracas. I vas vait on monsieur a—choses, and make ma compliment avec beaucoup de grace, ven monsieur vas read de news papier; so I say, is your honare ready for be dress? De great man say, "No—, d—n de barbare." [*In a low voice.*] I tell de parsone, sare, I have promise 'pon honare for dress one great man vat is belong to de Congress, 'bout dis time, sans manquer: De ansare vas (excuse moy, monsieur), "go to h-ll, if you be please; I must read 'bout de Constitution." Dis is de ole affair, monsieur, en verité.

LOVEYET. Sixty-three, indeed! Heaven forbid! But if I was so old, my constitution is good; age is nothing, the constitution is all,—ugh, ugh, ugh.

TOUPEE. Sare, you vill give me leaf, vat is dat Constitution?

LOVEYET. Hold your prating, you booby.

TOUPEE. You booby,—Vat is dat booby, I vonder!

TRUEMAN. Ha, ha, a good constitution! With great propriety did the man ask you what constitution you meant. Ha, ha, ha.

TOUPEE. Par Dieu, monsieur de Schoolmastare sall larn a me vat is de booby! oui, an de Constitution,—foy d'Homme d'Honneur.

TRUEMAN. What a figure for a sound constitution! ha, ha.

LOVEYET. Ugh, hang you for an old simpleton! Talk of *my* age and constitution.—Ugh, ugh, ugh. [*Exit.*

TRUEMAN. Fractious old blockhead!

TOUPEE. Blockhead! Pourquoi you call a mine head von block, sare?

TRUEMAN. I mean that old curmudgeon who goes hobbling along there, like a man of forty.

TOUPEE. Pardonnez moy, monsieur; S'il vous plaît, ve make de éclaircissement, if you tell me vat is de interpretation—you booby.

TRUEMAN. What! have you the effrontery to call me a booby? S'death, you scoundrel, what do you mean?

TOUPEE. Vous ne m'entendez pas.   [*Hastily*.

TRUEMAN. Do you threaten me, you insignificant thing? Do you call me names?

TOUPEE. Diable! me no stand under your names.

TRUEMAN. Zounds and fury! I am raving. Must I bear to be abus'd in this manner, by a vile Tonsor?

TOUPEE. Yes, you Schoolmastare; you tell me vat be you booby.

TRUEMAN. Pertinacious, audacious reptile! [*Canes* TOUPEE.

TOUPEE. Ah, mon dieu! mon dieu!   [*Runs off*.

TRUEMAN. To insult a professor of Orthography, Analogy, Syntax, and Prosody!

SCENE II. *A Street.*

Enter YOUNG LOVEYET.

In compliance with the commands of a father, here I am, once more in the place of my nativity. Duty to him, and curiosity to know, why he has enjoined my sudden departure so peremptorily, as well as a desire to see New-York (perhaps never to leave it more) have all conspir'd to bring me here sooner than I am expected,—let me see—yes, I must try to find out Frankton first. [HUMPHRY *crosses the stage*.] Here, friend, honest man, prithee stop.

HUMPHRY. What's your will?

LOVEYET. Can you inform me, friend, where one Mr. Frankton lives?

HUMPHRY. No, I don't know where anybody lives in this big city, not I; for my part, I believe how they all lives in the street, there's such a monstrous sight of people a scrouging backards and forards, as the old saying is. If I was home now——

LOVEYET. Where is your home, if I may make so free?

HUMPHRY. Oh, you may make free and welcome, for the more freer the more welcomer, as the old saying is; I never thinks myself too good to discourse my superiors: There's some of our townsfolks now, why some of 'um isn't so good as I, to be sure. There's Tom Forge, the blacksmith, and little Daniel Snip, the tailor, and Roger Peg, the cobbler, and Tim Frize, the barber, and Landlord Tipple, that keeps the ale-house at the sign of the

Turk's Head, and Jeremy Stave, the clerk of the meeting-house, why, there an't one of 'um that's a single copper before a beggar, as the old saying is; but what o' that? We isn't all born alike, as father says; for my part, I likes to be friendly, so give us your hand. You mus'n't think how I casts any reflections on you; no, no, I scorn the action. [*They shake hands.*] That's hearty now—Friendship is a fine thing, and, a friend indeed is a friend in need, as the saying is.

LOVEYET. What an insufferable fool it is!   [*Half aside.*

HUMPHRY. Yes, it is insufferable cool, that's sartin; but it's time to expect it.

LOVEYET. Worse and worse!

HUMPHRY. Yes, I warrant you it will be worser and worser before long; so I must e'en go home soon, and look after the corn and the wheat, or else old father will bring his pigs to a fine market, as the old proverb goes.

LOVEYET. You're quite right; you mean your father wou'd bring his corn to a fine market: You mean it as a figurative expression, I presume.

HUMPHRY. Not I, I isn't for none of your figure expressions, d' ye see, becase why, I never larnt to cipher;—every grain of corn a pig! Ha, ha, ha. That's pleasant, ecod; why the Jews wou'dn't dare for to shew their noses out o'doors, everything wou'd smell so woundily of pork! Ha, ha, ha.

LOVEYET. A comical countryman of mine this. [*Aside.*] What is your name, my honest lad?

HUMPHRY. Why, if you'll tell me your name, I'll tell you mine, d' ye see; for, one good turn desarves another, as the old saying is, and, evil be to them that evil thinks, every tub must stand upon its own bottom, and, when the steed is stolen, shut the stable door, and, while the grass grows, the mare starves—the horse I mean; it don't make no odds, a horse is a mare, but a mare an't a horse, as father says, d' ye see—and——

LOVEYET. What a monstrous combination of nonsense!

HUMPHRY. Don't tell me what I am, but tell me what I have been——

LOVEYET. Prithee, Mr. Sancho, let's have no more of those insipid proverbs. You was going to tell me your name.

HUMPHRY. My name is Cubb,—Humphry Cubb, at your sarvice, as the saying is.

LOVEYET. Hah! my worthy friend Frankton——

Enter FRANKTON.

FRANKTON. My best, my long expected Charles! your arrival has made me the happiest man alive.   [*They embrace.*

LOVEYET. I am heartily glad to see you, George, and to meet you so opportunely; 'tis not fifteen minutes since I landed on my native soil, and you are the very person, above every other in the city, whom I wish'd first to see.

FRANKTON. Then you have not forgot your friend.

LOVEYET. Far from it, Frankton; be assured that the joy I now feel at meeting with *you,* is by no means the least I expect to experience.

FRANKTON. Our satisfaction is then mutual—your friends are all happy and well, and I know your arrival will not a little contribute to *their* felicity, as well as mine—but who have you here, Loveyet? Landed not fifteen minutes ago, and in close confab with one of our Boors already?

HUMPHRY. A boar! why you're worser than he there—he only took father's *corn* for *pigs,* but do you take *me* for a *boar,* eigh? Do I look like a *hog,* as the saying is?

FRANKTON. Begone, you illiterate lubber!—My dear Charles, I have a thousand things to say to you, and this is an unfit place for conversation.

LOVEYET. We will adjourn to the Coffee-House.

FRANKTON. No, you shall go with me to my lodgings.

HUMPHRY. Why, what a cruel-minded young dog he is! See how he swaggers and struts—he looks very like the Pharisee's head, on old *Coming Sir,* honest Dick Tipple's sign, I think—No, now I look at him good, he's the very moral of our Tory.

LOVEYET. I wait your pleasure, Frankton.

FRANKTON. Then allons! [*Exeunt* FRANKTON *and* LOVEYET.

HUMPHRY. [*Burlesquing them.*] Forward, march—as our Captain says—[*Struts after them.*]—Literary lubber, eigh! But I'll be up with the foutre.

FRANKTON *and* LOVEYET *return.*

FRANKTON. Do you call me a foutre, you rascal?

HUMPHRY. Call you a future! ha, ha, ha. I was a talking about something that I was a going for to do some other time, sir.—Doesn't future magnify some other time, eigh?

FRANKTON. The future signifies the time to come, to be sure.

HUMPHRY. Well, then, isn't I right? What argufies your signifies, or your magnifies? There an't the toss up of a copper between 'um—I wou'dn't give a leather button for the choice, as the old proverb goes.

FRANKTON. Harkee, Mr. Talkative, if you ever——

HUMPHRY. No, sir, never,—that I won't—no, no, you may be sure of that.

FRANKTON. Sure of what?

HUMPHRY. Nothing, sir; we can be sartin of nothing in this world, as Mr. Thumpum says.

LOVEYET. Ha, ha, ha.

FRANKTON. Oh, what a precious numskull it is!

LOVEYET. [To FRANKTON.] I have a letter here, which announces to my father, my intention to leave the West-Indies the beginning of March, but I miss'd of the expected conveyance— I have half a mind to send it yet. I would not have him apprized of my arrival; for I wish to try if he would know me;—and yet I long to embrace my aged and venerable parent.—Will you do me the favour to take this letter to my father, Mr. Cubb? He lives at number two hundred and fifty, in Queen-Street, in a three-story red brick house.—I'll reward you for it.

HUMPHRY. As for your rewards, I'm above it, d' ye see: If I do it, I'll do it without fear or reward, as the saying is; but if you think fit, you may treat a body to the valuation of a mug or so. Don't you love ale? for they says how the Yorkers is cursed fellows for strong beer.

LOVEYET. What a digression!

HUMPHRY. I scorn your words—'tis no transgression at all to drink ale—Why, Parson Thumpum himself drinks ale.

LOVEYET. Well, will you carry the letter? You shall have as much strong beer when you come back as you can stagger under.

HUMPHRY. Why, if I was for to have my beer a-board before I go, I shou'dn't get top-heavy, as the saying is; for I can carry as much weight in my head as e'er a he that wears a head, without staggering.

FRANKTON. I dare say you can; you have always plenty of that.

HUMPHRY. Yes, you're right—I know what you mean; I've got it here a little, as old Mr. Scourge says. [Exeunt FRANKTON and LOVEYET.] But as for what you said just now—no, no, sir; I'll never foutre you, I warrant you—I always curses and swears in plain English, d' ye see—I—what's he gone? I hope he won't come back again for the sixth time; three times has he been in and out within the circumference of a minute. But I won't stay here no longer—I'll go and try if I can't find out where Doll lives, my old sweetheart; I an't so poor, but what I can buy her a ribbon or so; and, if all comes to all, I can get a new pair o' breeches too; for, to be sure, this one doesn't look quite so decent, and if that doesn't fetch her, the devil shall, as the old saying is. I'm cursedly afraid, I sha'n't be able to find out her quarters. [*Exit.*

SCENE III. MR. FRIENDLY'S *House.*

Enter HARRIET *and* MARIA.

HARRIET. Pray, Maria, how were you entertained at the Assembly last night?

MARIA. Very indifferently, I assure you, my dear: You know, Harriet, I do most cordially hate dancing at any time; but what must one do with one's self these irksome, heavy, dreary Winters? If it were not for cards, visits to and from, and——

HARRIET. Assemblies.

MARIA. Yes, as my last resource, Assemblies, I should absolutely be in a state of despair before Spring.—Then one may take an excursion on York or Long-Island—an agreeable sail on the East-River—a walk in the Broadway, Pharisee-like, to be seen of men, and—to see them—and then how refreshing to take a negligent stroll on the Battery, the Fort, the Mall, and from thence to Miss Such-a-one, then to Mrs. Such-a-one, then to Lady What's-her-name, and then home;—but now I am half of my time as motionless as Pitt's statue; as petrified and inanimate as an Egyptian mummy, or rather frozen snake, who crawls out of his hole now and then in this season to bask in the rays of the sun.

HARRIET. And whenever the sunshine of Mr. Frankton's eyes breaks upon you, you revive.

MARIA. Pshaw—I wish you had Mr. Frankton yourself, since you are so full of his sweet image.

HARRIET. I'm sure you did not wish so last night: Your eyes seem'd to say,—I wish I could secure the good-for-nothing, agreeable rake.

MARIA. Oh, you *heard* my *eyes* say so, did you? I ask pardon of your penetration.

HARRIET. But do you really think the Winter is so destitute of comforts?

MARIA. Ha, ha, comforts! by comforts I suppose you mean the sweets of domestic life—the large portion of comfort arising from a large winter fire, and the very pleasing tittle-tattle of an antiquated maiden aunt, or the equally pleasing (tho' less loquacious) society of a husband, who, with a complaisance peculiar to husbands, responds—sometimes by a doubtful shrug, sometimes a stupid yawn, a lazy stretch, an unthinking stare, a clownish nod, a surly no, or interrogates you with a—humph? till bed time, when, heaven defend us! you are doom'd to be snor'd out of your wits till day-break, when——

HARRIET. Hold, Maria—what a catalogue of uncomfortable comforts have you run over.—Pleasure and Comfort are words which imply the same thing with me; but in this enlighten'd age, when words are so curiously refin'd and defin'd, modern critics and fashionable word-mongers have, in the abundance of their wisdom, made a very nice distinction between them—for my part, I always endeavour to reconcile modish pleasure with real comfort, and custom with reason, as much as is in any way consistent with the obligation one is under to conform a little to the perverse notions of mankind.

MARIA. There now!—you know I can't abide to hear you moralize—prithee, my dear Harriet, leave that to grey beards and long-ear'd caps—everything is beautiful in its season, you know.

HARRIET. Common sense and propriety are ever in season, Maria, and I was going to mention a *sentimental* pleasure, a *rational* enjoyment, which is peculiar to the present *season*, tho' beautiful in every one, if you had not got frightened at the idea of being *comforted*.

MARIA. Well, my dear comfortable, rational, sentimental Harriet! Let me hear what this rational enjoyment of yours is?

HARRIET. Hearing a good play, my dear.

MARIA. Hearing a good play! why not seeing it, pray?

HARRIET. Because I believe plays are frequently seen, and not heard; at least, not as they ought to be.

MARIA. I protest you are quite a critic, Harriet.

HARRIET. If you desire amusement, what so likely to beguile the heavy hours as Comedy? If your spirits are depress'd, what so replete with that which can revive them as the laughter-loving Thalia? If the foibles and vices of human nature ought to suffer correction, in what way can they be satiriz'd so happily and successfully as on the stage;—or if elegance of language, and refinement of sentiment——

MARIA. Humph—there's sentiment again.

HARRIET. You dislike every good thing I have mentioned this morning, Maria,—except one.

MARIA. What's that, my dear?

HARRIET. Mr. Frankton.

MARIA. Ha, ha. Why, to be sure, the good things of this life are not to be despis'd, and men are not the worst creatures belonging to this life, nor Mr. Frankton the worst of men, but—apropos, about plays—did you observe how much I was affected the other night at the tragedy of Zara?

HARRIET. I really did not—I wish I had seen such a pleasing proof of your sensibility.

MARIA. Oh, you cruel creature!—wish to see your friend in tears?

HARRIET. 'Tis rather unusual to see a lady of your taste and spirit, either weep at a pathetic incident in tragedy, or laugh at a comic scene; and as for the gentlemen, your lads of spirit, such as are falsely called *ladies' men*, they are not so masculine as to understand, and, therefore, not so effeminate as to weep; tho' one would conclude, from their effeminacy in appearance and behaviour, that they would cry if you were to look at them.

MARIA. To be sure, a little matter will draw tears from the feminine part of mankind.

HARRIET. For your part, you seem'd to be neither laughing nor crying, but rather displeas'd and uneasy.

MARIA. Oh, you mistake the matter entirely, my dear; your skill in physiognomy is but indifferent, I find—why, after the tragedy was over, I laugh'd most inordinately for a considerable time.

HARRIET. On what account, pray?

MARIA. Why, you must know, my dear, Mr. Frankton sat in the box opposite to the one I was in.

HARRIET. Yes, I know your dear Mr. Frankton was in the opposite box.

MARIA. My dear Mr. Frankton! Did I say so? Why I could not say more of him, were he my husband.

HARRIET. If you conform to custom, you would not say so much of a husband.

MARIA. But I did not say any such thing. Says I, you must know, my dear Harriet——

HARRIET. No, no, there was no Harriet mentioned.

MARIA. But I say there was—so, as I was going to tell you, you must know, my dear Harriet, that Mr. Frankton sat opposite to me at the theatre; and as he seem'd to be very much chagrin'd at the attention which was paid me by a couple of beaux, I took some pains to mortify him a little; for, tho' he strove to hide his uneasiness by chattering, and whispering, and tittering, and shewing his white teeth, his embarrassment was very visible under his affected unconcern.

HARRIET. How exactly she has described her own situation and feelings! [*Aside.*]—I find that you acquire *your skill in physiognomy* from sympathy; or from making suitable comparisons, and drawing natural inferences from them; but now for the remainder of your pleasant anecdote, Maria.

MARIA. So, I was extremely civil to my two worshipping votaries, grinn'd when they did, and talk'd as much nonsense as either of them. During this scene of mock-gallantry, one of my love-sick swains elevated his eyes in a most languishing manner; and, clasping his sweet, unlucky hands together rather eagerly, my little dog Muff happen'd to be in the way, by which means my pet was squeez'd rather more than it lik'd, and my Adonis's finger bit by it so feelingly, that it would have delighted you to see how he twisted his soft features about, with the excruciating anguish. Ha, ha, ha.

HARRIET. Ha, ha, ha. Exceeding ludicrous indeed!—But pray, my dear careless, sprightly Maria, was you not a little nettled to see Mr. Frankton and his nymphs so great? And are you not deeply in love with each other, notwithstanding your coquetry at the theatre, and his levity at the Assembly?—Yes, yes,—your aversion to the dancing last night was only pretence. I hope when your hearts are cemented by wedlock, you will both do better.

MARIA. It will be well if I do no worse; but, to hear you talk, one would swear you were not in love yourself.

HARRIET. Love is an amiable weakness, of which our sex are peculiarly susceptible.

MARIA. Ha, ha, ha; *of which our sex are peculiarly susceptible* —what an evasion!—and so my dear lovelorn, pensive, sentimental, romantic Harriet has never experienced that same *amiable weakness* which, it seems, the weaker sex is so susceptible of. But I won't tease you about Mr. Loveyet any more; adieu.

[*Going.*

HARRIET. Ha, ha; why in such sudden haste, my dear?

MARIA. I have already made my visit longer than I intended, and I have plagu'd you enough now; adieu.

HARRIET. Ha, ha, ha; that is laughable enough.

[*Exeunt, separately.*

End of the First Act.

ACT II.

SCENE I   FRANKTON'S *Lodgings.*

FRANKTON *and* YOUNG LOVEYET *sitting.*

LOVEYET. When did you say you saw her?

FRANKTON. Last night, in company with several other belles of no small note, who did not look a tittle the handsomer for appearing at the same time with her, I assure you.

LOVEYET. Then she's as charming as ever.

FRANKTON. Charming as ever! By all that's beautiful, a Seraphim is nothing to her! And as for Cherubims, when they compete with her,

> *Conscious of her superior charms they stand,*
> *And rival'd quite by such a beauteous piece*
> *Of mortal composition; they, reluctant,*
> *Hide their diminish'd heads.*

LOVEYET. You extol her in very rapturous strains, George—I hope you have not been smitten by her vast perfections, like the Cherubims.

FRANKTON. I am really enraptur'd with the bewitching little Goddess!

LOVEYET. Do you positively think her so much superior to the generality of women?

FRANKTON. Most indubitably I do—don't you, pray?

LOVEYET. I thought her handsome once—but—but—but you certainly are not in love with her.

FRANKTON. Not I, faith. Ha, ha, ha. My enamorata and yours are two distinct persons, I assure you—and two such beauties!—By all that's desirable, if there was only one more in the city who could vie with the lovely girls, and boast of the same elegantly proportioned forms; the same beauty, delicacy and symmetry of features; the same celestial complexion, in which the lily and carnation are equally excell'd; the same——

LOVEYET. Oh, monstrous! Why, they exceed all the Goddesses I ever heard of, by your account.

FRANKTON. Well, if you had let me proceed, I should have told you that if one more like them could be found in town, they would make a more beautiful triple than the three renowned goddesses who were candidates for beauty and a golden apple long ago; but no matter now.—The account you have given of the lovely Harriet, has rekindled the flame she so early inspir'd me with, and I already feel myself all the lover; how then shall I feel, when I once more behold the dear maid, like the mother of mankind—"with grace in all her steps, heaven in her eye; in every gesture, dignity and love!"

FRANKTON. Aye—and what do you think of your father's sending for you to marry you to this same beautiful piece of mortality?

LOVEYET. Is it possible? Then I am happy indeed! But this surpasses my most sanguine hopes!

FRANKTON. Did you suppose he would object to the alliance then?

LOVEYET. I did not know,—my hope was only founded on the *probability* of his approving it.

FRANKTON. Well, I can now inform you that your hope has a better basis to rest on, and that there is as fair a prospect of its being shortly swallowed up in fruition as ever Cupid and Hymen presented to a happy mortal's view.—For your farther comfort, I have the pleasure to acquaint you, that Mr. Trueman is equally fond of the match.

LOVEYET. Better and better—my dear George! You are the best of friends,—my happy genius! My very guardian angel!

FRANKTON. Well said, Heroics—come, spout away.

LOVEYET. Yes, I *am* happy, very happy, indeed: Moralists disparage this world too much,—there *is* such a thing as happiness under the sun,—I *feel* it now most irrefragably,—*here* it vibrates in a most extatic manner.

FRANKTON. Why, you are positively the arrantest love-sick swain that ever had recourse to a philter.

LOVEYET. Profane heretic in love! Did not you extol the two Seraphims just now in the same generous language? But you have never experienced the blissful transition from doubt and solicitude to certainty and peace, as I do now.

FRANKTON. How do you know that?

LOVEYET. I only conjecture so—Did you ever feel the same transports I do?

FRANKTON. How, in the name of sense, should I know how you feel?

LOVEYET. Feel!—I feel that kind heaven, my friend, my father, and my dearest girl, all conspire to bless me!

FRANKTON. There he rides his hobby-horse again.

LOVEYET. Aye, and a generous horse he is—he carries me very pleasantly, I assure you.

FRANKTON. Yes, and, I dare say, could convey you more agreeably and speedily to Paradise than the Ass did Mahomet.

LOVEYET. Ha, ha. I think you have improved my idea.

FRANKTON. To improve your reason, and check your strange delirium, I have.

LOVEYET. I will talk more dispassionately;—but my heart *will* palpitate at the thought of meeting the lovely source of its joy, and the ultimatum of all its wishes!

FRANKTON. I suppose you know she lives with Mr. Friendly.

LOVEYET. With Mr. Friendly!

FRANKTON. Yes, she is nearly related to his family, and as the style in which they live, corresponds with her former prosperity better than the present ineligible situation of her father does, he has granted them her valuable company, after their repeated solicitations had prov'd the sincerity of their regard.

LOVEYET. But how do you account for Mr. Trueman's poverty, since fortune has lately put it so much in Harriet's power to relieve him from it? I dare not think it arises from her want of filial regard; I do not know anything so likely to abate the ardour of my attachment as a knowledge of that; but it is an ungenerous suggestion, unworthy the benignity and tenderness of the gentle Harriet.

FRANKTON. It is so.—Two things, on the part of the old gentleman, are the cause: his pride will not suffer him to be the subject of a daughter's bounty; and his regard for that daughter's welfare, makes him fearful of being instrumental in impairing her fortune.

LOVEYET. I thought the angelic girl could not be ungrateful to the parent of her being; but don't let us tarry—I am already on the wing.

FRANKTON. You are too sanguine; you must not expect to succeed without a little opposition.

LOVEYET. How! what say you? pray be explicit.

FRANKTON. I will remove your suspense.—There is a Mr. Worthnought, a thing by some people call'd a man, a beau, a fine gentleman, a smart fellow; and by others a coxcomb, a puppy, a baboon and an ass.

LOVEYET. And what of him?

FRANKTON. Nothing; only he visits Miss Harriet frequently.

LOVEYET. Hah!—and does she countenance his addresses?

FRANKTON. I'll explain.—He imagines she is fond of him, because she does not actually discard him; upon which presumption he titters, capers, vows, bows, talks scraps of French, and sings an amorous lay—with such an irresistibly languishing air, that she cannot do less than compliment him—on the fineness of his voice, for instance; the smartness of his repartees, the brilliancy of his wit, the gaiety and vivacity of his temper, his genteel carriage, his handsome person, his winning address, his——

LOVEYET. Hah! you surely cannot be in earnest, Frankton.

FRANKTON. To be serious then,—the sum total of the affair, I take to be this.—In order to kill a heavy hour, she sometimes suffers the fool to be in her company, because the extravagance of his behaviour, and the emptiness of his upper region furnish her with a good subject for ridicule; but *your* presence will soon make him dwindle into his primitive insignificance.

LOVEYET. If your prediction proves false, Harriet will be false indeed;—but I must see her straightway.

FRANKTON. I think you go pretty well fraught with the fruits of our united deliberations.

LOVEYET. Deliberations!—away with the musty term—
No caution need my willing footsteps guide;—
When Love impels—what evil can betide?
Patriots may fear, their rulers lack more zeal,
And nobly tremble for the public weal;
To front the battle, and to fear no harm,
The shield *must glitter on the warrior's arm:*
Let such dull prudence their *designs attend,*
But Love, *unaided,* shall *obtain its end!* [*Exeunt.*

SCENE II. OLD LOVEYET'S *House.*

Enter OLD LOVEYET *and* TRUEMAN.

LOVEYET. I tell you it is the most infernal scheme that ever was devis'd.

TRUEMAN. And I tell you, sir, that your argument is heterodox, sophistical, and most preposterously illogical.

LOVEYET. I insist upon it, sir, you know nothing at all about the matter; and, give me leave to tell you, sir—

TRUEMAN. What—give you leave to tell me I know nothing at all about the matter! I shall do no such thing, sir—I'm not to be govern'd by your *ipse dixit.*

LOVEYET. I desire none of your musty Latin, sir, for I don't understand it, not I.

TRUEMAN. Oh, the ignorance of the age! To oppose a plan of government like the new Constitution. Like it, did I say? —There never was one like it:—neither Minos, Solon, Lycurgus nor Romulus, ever fabricated so wise a system;—why it is a political phenomenon, a prodigy of legislative wisdom, the fame of which will soon extend almost *ultramundane,* and astonish the nations of the world with its transcendent excellence.—To what a sublime height will the superb edifice attain!

LOVEYET. Your aspiring edifice shall never be erected in *this* State, sir.

TRUEMAN. Mr. Loveyet, you will not listen to reason: only attend calmly one moment—[*Reads.*]—"We the people of the United States, in order to form a more perfect union, establish justice, insure domestic tranquillity, provide—"

LOVEYET. I tell you I won't hear it.

TRUEMAN. Mark all that. [*Reads again.*] "Section the first. —All legislative powers herein granted shall be vested in a Congress of the United States, which shall consist of a Senate and House of Representatives." Very judicious and salutary, upon my erudition.—"Section the second——"

LOVEYET. I'll hear no more of your sections.

TRUEMAN. "Section the second.—The House of Representatives——"

LOVEYET. They never shall represent me, I promise them.

TRUEMAN. Why, you won't hear me out.

LOVEYET. I have heard enough to set me against it.

TRUEMAN. You have not heard a *quantum sufficit* to render you competent to give a decisive opinion; besides, you hear with passion and prejudice.

LOVEYET. I don't care for that; I say it is a devilish design upon our liberty and property; by my body, it is;—it would reduce us to poverty and slavery.

Enter HUMPHRY, *listening.*

HUMPHRY. What's that about liberty, and property, and slavery, and popery, and the devil? I hope the pope and the devil an't come to town for to play the devil, and make nigers of us!

TRUEMAN. You will have it your own way.

LOVEYET. To be sure I will—in short, sir, the old Constitution is good enough for me.

HUMPHRY. I wonder what Constitution magnifies.

TRUEMAN. The old Constitution!—ha, ha, ha, ha. Superlatively ludicrous and facetious, upon my erudition; and highly productive of risibility—ha, ha, ha. The old Constitution! A very shadow of a government—a perfect *caput mortuum;*— why, one of my schoolboys would make a better: 'tis grown as superannuated, embecilitated, valetudinarianated, invalidated, enervated and dislocated as an old man of sixty odd.

LOVEYET. Ah, that's me—that's me—sixty odd, eigh— [*Aside.*] I—I—ugh, ugh, I know what you want:—a consolidation and annihilation of the States.

TRUEMAN. A consolidation and annihilation!—You certainly have bid defiance to the first rudiments of grammar, and sworn war against the whole body of lexicographers. Mercy on me! If words are to be thus abus'd and perverted, there is an end of the four grand divisions of grammar at once: If consolidation and annihilation are to be us'd synonymously, there is a total annihilation of all the moods, tenses, genders, persons, nouns, pronouns, verbs, adverbs, substantives, conjunctions, interjections, prepositions, participles,——   [*Coughs.*

HUMPHRY. Oh dear, oh dear,—what a wise man a Schoolmaster is!

TRUEMAN. How can the States be consolidated and annihilated too? If they are consolidated or compounded into one national mass, surely the individual States cannot be annihilated, for, if they were annihilated, where would be the States to compose a consolidation?—Did you ever study Logic, sir?

LOVEYET. No, but I've studied common sense tho', and that tells me I am right, and consequently you are wrong; there, that's as good logic as yours.

TRUEMAN. You mean Paine's *Common Sense*, I suppose—yes, yes, there you manifest something like common sense, Mr. Loveyet.

LOVEYET. 'Tis no such thing, sir; it lately took three speakers, and much better ones than Paine, no less than three whole days, to prove that consolidation and annihilation are one and the same thing.

TRUEMAN. An execrable Triumvirate—a *scandalum magnatum* to all public bodies: I suppose they and their adherents are now sitting in Pandemonium, excogitating their diabolical machinations against us.

LOVEYET. A pack of nonsensical stuff!

TRUEMAN. Harkee, Mr. Loveyet, I will propound a problem to you. We will suppose there are two parallel lines drawn on this floor, which, notwithstanding they may be very contiguous to each other, and advance *ad infinitum*, can never approximate so near as to effect a junction, in which fundamental axiom all mathematicians profess a perfect congruity and acquiescence:—now, to elucidate the hypothesis a little, we will suppose here is one line; and we will further suppose here is another line. [*Draws his cane over* LOVEYET'S *feet, which makes him jump.*] Now we will suppose that line is you, and this line is compos'd, form'd, constituted, made up of discernment, political knowledge, public spirit, and true republicanism,—but, as I predicated antecedently, *that* line is you—[*Striking his cane on* LOVEYET'S *feet.*] You must not forget *that*.

LOVEYET. S'death, sir, do you mean to make a mathematical instrument of me, to try experiments with?

TRUEMAN. Now take notice—as the East is to the West, the North Pole to the South ditto, the Georgium Sidus to this terraqueous globe, or the Aborigines of America to the Columbians of this generation, so is that line to this line, or Mr. Loveyet to true wisdom and judgment; sometimes appearing to verge towards a coalition with them, but never to effect it. There, sir,—in this argument, you have a major, a minor and a conclusion, consonant to the received principles of logic.

LOVEYET. Confound your senseless comparisons; your problems, your mathematics, and your Georgium Sidus.

HUMPHRY. Aye, confound your gorgon hydras, I say too.

LOVEYET. Here you have been spending your breath to prove —what?—that I am not a rational human being, but a mathematical line.

TRUEMAN. I know you are not a mathematical line; you are not the twentieth part so straight and well made;—I only wish to convince you that the present government is an *ignis fatuus* that is leading you and thousands more to ruin.

LOVEYET. But I don't choose to be convinc'd by you.

TRUEMAN. No more than you'll be convinc'd you are sixty years old, I suppose.

LOVEYET. Now see there again, see there! isn't this enough to try Job's patience? I'll let you know that my bodily and political Constitutions are both good, sir, both sound alike.

TRUEMAN. I know they are. Ha, ha, ha.

HUMPHRY. Pray, old gentleman, what sort of things may them same constitutions be?

TRUEMAN. Avaunt, thou plebeian, thou ignoramus!

HUMPHRY. Why, I lay now I can say that as good as you, for all you're such a fine scholard.—I won't be plain, thou ignorant mouse.

TRUEMAN. *"Monstrum horrendum, cui lumen ademptum!"*

HUMPHRY. Monstrous memorandums, cu—no, I can't say that; that's too hard for me. Well, what a glorious thing it is for to have good larning.

LOVEYET. Sixty odd years indeed! provoking wretch!

HUMPHRY. What a bloody passion he's in!

TRUEMAN. Pray, Mr. Loveyet, do not anathematize me so; —if you do not civilize your phraseology a little, I must have recourse to a little castigation, for, *necessitas non habet legem*, you know, Mr. Loveyet.

LOVEYET. I know nothing about such nonsense, not I.

TRUEMAN. You are the most unenlightened, contumacious, litigious, petulant, opprobrious, proditorious, misanthropic mortal I ever confabulated a colloquy with; by the dignity of my profession you are.

HUMPHRY. What monstrous queer words he discourses the old fellow with!

LOVEYET. Mighty pleasant and witty, by my body; sixty years, forsooth!—But I'll be aveng'd of you.—Your daughter sha'n't have my son—there, sir,—how do you like that? Sixty years, indeed! Ugh, ugh.

HUMPHRY. What an old reprobate it is! He swears till he sweats again.

TRUEMAN. What an unlucky affair! [*Aside.*

LOVEYET. And give me leave to tell you, Mr. Schoolmaster, I was an old—I—I mean—I was a *great* fool to disparage him so much as to think of the match.

TRUEMAN. Illiberal aspersion! But were I as contemptible as you think me, a disastrous war has rendered me so; and as for my child, Providence has placed her above dependence on an unfortunate father: the bequest of a worthy relation has made her, what the world calls, rich; but her mind—is far richer; the most amiable temper, improved by a virtuous and refined education (not to mention her beauty) deservedly makes her the object of general love and respect, and renders your present resolution a matter of perfect indifference to me.

LOVEYET. Well, well, so be it; but you never shall be Charles's father-in-law, for all that—that's as fix'd as fate,—you may beg my forgiveness for your faults by and by, but your daughter shall never be mine, I promise you.

TRUEMAN. Conceited old sot! [*Exit.*

HUMPHRY. He's gone at last.

LOVEYET. What brought *you* here, pray?

HUMPHRY. Why, my legs, to be sure.—Here, old gentleman, if you'll promise you won't get in such a passion as you did just now, I've got some news to tell you.

LOVEYET. I in a passion? 'tis no such thing—I didn't mind anything he said, because he's old and fretful;—but what news, eigh—what news?

HUMPHRY. Here's a letter for you. [*Gives it to* LOVEYET.

LOVEYET. [*Opens the letter and reads.*] I am heartily glad, 'faith! [*Reads again.*]—'Od's my life, I'm as happy as the Great Mogul, and as good-natur'd—

HUMPHRY. That's clever; I likes to see people good-natur'd, —it makes me as happy as the Great Pogul.

LOVEYET. I'll go tell old Trueman's daughter, Charles is coming, but not for her—I know she'll be mortify'd, poor girl, but I can't help that. Who gave you this letter?

HUMPHRY. Why your son, to be sure.

LOVEYET. When did you leave the *Havanna,* pray?

HUMPHRY. The *Havanna?*

LOVEYET. Yes, are you not from the West-Indies?

HUMPHRY. Who—me?—not I.

LOVEYET. Why, what the plague makes you think he was my son, then?

HUMPHRY. Because he said you was his father—that's a good reason, an't it? But it's a wise son knows his own father, as the old saying is.

LOVEYET. How can that be, when the letter is dated in the Island of Cuba, the twentieth day of January, and he says he don't expect to leave it till the beginning of March, and this is only February, so it is impossible he shou'd be here yet.

HUMPHRY. May be you an't the old gentleman, then.

LOVEYET. To be sure I an't an *old* gentleman. Did he say I was old, eigh?

HUMPHRY. Yes, I believe he did.

LOVEYET. I believe you lie—and I'll let you know that I an't old enough to be his father, you—

HUMPHRY. Well, if the case lies there, that settles the harsh, d' ye see; but, for my part, I think how you look old enough and ugly enough to be his great-grandfather, as the old saying is.

LOVEYET. Sirrah, get out of my house, or I'll break your bones for you.

HUMPHRY. I'm a going—howsomever, give me the letter again; you've got no business with it—you an't his father.

LOVEYET. You lie! I am his father—if he was here, he wou'dn't deny it.

HUMPHRY. Why, he is here, I tell you—here in New-York. I suppose how he's made a small mistake about the day of the month, and says he's just arrived from the East-Indies, for he's cursed apt for to make blunders;—that about the corn and the pigs; ha, ha, ha.

LOVEYET. Do you laugh at me, you vagabond?

HUMPHRY. Not I, old gentleman; I've got too much respect for old age, I'll insure you.

LOVEYET. I shall go distracted!

HUMPHRY. Put on your spectacles and look again—I'm sure your eyes must perceive you, for I'll give my corporal oath he an't in the East-Indies.

LOVEYET. It is not the East-Indies, you great calf; you mean the West-Indies.

HUMPHRY. No matter if it's East or West; the odds an't much for the matter o' that.

LOVEYET. What an abominable fool!

HUMPHRY. I'm no more a fool than you are—

LOVEYET. Be gone, you scoundrel! Here, Thomas—[*Enter* THOMAS.], lug this fellow out of doors.

THOMAS. Yes, sir.

HUMPHRY. No, you sha'n't tho', d' ye see.

THOMAS. I'm cursedly afraid of the great two-handed fellow too. [*Aside, and exit with* HUMPHRY.

LOVEYET [*manet*].

Abusive rascal! But I won't put myself in a passion with such a vile animal.—I—I'll read the letter again.

"Honour'd Sir,

"I have just time enough to acquaint you by the *Oceanus*, Captain Seaborn, who is now preparing to sail, that I have at length adjusted my business so as to be able to leave this place for New-York, the beginning of March; in which case you may look for me before the first of April next; when I promise myself the happiness of seeing you once more, and enjoying the society of the best of parents: till then I shall continue to be, with truly filial attachment, and anxious expectation of the happy event, your obliged and dutiful son,—CHARLES LOVEYET."

I wonder he don't say anything of the coffee and madeira I wrote to him about;—egad, I must mind the main chance; a penny sav'd, is a penny got; and charity begins at home. By strictly attending to these excellent maxims, I am worth about five and twenty per cent. more than any other merchant in the city; and as for that stupid proverb, money is the root of all evil, 'tis well enough for those to say so, who have none; for my part, I know that much of the good things of this world is better than not enough—that a man can live longer upon a hundred thousand pounds than one thousand pounds—that if, the more we have the more we want, the more we have the more we make— and that it is better to make hay while the sun shines *against* a rainy day, when I shall be upon my last legs, than to work and toil like an ass *in* the rain; so it plainly appears that money is the root of all good;—that's my logic.—I long to see the young rogue tho' —I dare say he looks very like his father;—but, had I thought old Trueman wou'd have us'd me so ill, I wou'd not have wrote for him yet; for he shall not have his old sweetheart:—if he offers to disobey me in this respect, by my body, I'll disinherit the ungracious dog immediately. [*Exit.*

SCENE III. *Another part of* LOVEYET'S *House.*

DOLLY *and* THOMAS.

THOMAS. I've set a bowl of grog before him, pretty much to the northward, and a luncheon of bread and beef almost as big as his head; for he said he was consumed hungry.

DOLLY. I language to behold him;—but I'm afraid he'll be rude to a body. [*Enter* HUMPHRY, *with a large luncheon of bread and butter.*] Oh, as I'm alive, it is Humphry; old Cubb, the miller's son! Now will the great bear be for rumpling and hugging a body, as he us'd to do. [*Aside.*

HUMPHRY. How d' ye do again, as the saying is? You're a devilish honest fellow, as I'm a gentleman; and thank 'e for your frugality, with all my heart: I've eaten up all the beef and grog, so I thought I wou'd go to the cupboard, and cut a small slice of bread and butter, d' ye see.

THOMAS. Why didn't you cut yourself a larger slice, while you was about it?

HUMPHRY. Oh, it's big enough, thank 'e; I never eat much at a meal; but if I crave more, I'll speak. [*Sees* DOLLY.] Wha—what—Doll! is that you? Oh, the wonderful works of nature! Who 'd ha' thought to ha' found you here. What, don't you know me? not know your old sweetheart? By Job, I want to buss you, most lasciviously. [*Crams all the bread in his mouth in haste, and offers to kiss her.*—THOMAS *hinders him.*

DOLLY. Oh, oh!

THOMAS. What, do you dare to do such a thing before me, you country brute?

HUMPHRY. Aye, no ooner said than done; that's my way.

THOMAS. But you sha'n't say nor do your lascivious tricks before me, I warrant you.

DOLLY. Oh, the filthy beast! he has frightened me out of my seventy-seven senses; he has given me a fever.

HUMPHRY. I don't care if you'll give me a favour, or not; for I don't value it an old horse-shoe, not I; I can get favours enough in New-York, if I go to the expense.—I know what—I suppose you forget when Jack Wrestle, the country mack-marony—

DOLLY. Oh, oh!

HUMPHRY. Why, in the country you us'd for to kiss me without axing.

DOLLY. I scorn your words, you worthless blackguard; so I do.   [*Cries.*

THOMAS. Sir, I'd have you to know, sir, that I won't suffer you, sir, to abuse this young lady, sir, in this manner, sir; and, sir—in short, sir, you're a dirty fellow, for your pains, sir.

HUMPHRY. And you're a great litterly lubber, as the saying is; and if you'll be so friendly as for to fetch the mug of ale you promis'd me, I'll lick you out of pure gratitude: have a care— grog makes me fight like a tyger.

THOMAS. It's a bargain,—I shou'd be sorry to try you; but I'll go lace you ale a little, and that will spoil your fighting, I warrant you.   [*Aside, and exit.*

DOLLY. You sha'n't fight him.—Oh, law, I wou'dn't trust myself with him alone, for the riches of the Indians! [*Exit, after him.*

HUMPHRY. [*Mimicking her.*] What an unfaithless trollop! She's got to be very vartuous since she's liv'd in town, but vartue is but skin deep, as the saying is:—wou'dn't even let me kiss her;—I meant nothing but the genteel thing neither,—all in an honest way. I wonder what she can see in that clumsy booby's face, for to take his part, sooner than I!—but I'll go buy a new coat and breeches, and get my head fricaseed, and my beard comb'd a little, and then I'll cut a dash with the best on 'em. I'll go see where that ill-looking fellow stays with the ale.   [*Exit.*

End of the Second Act.

ACT III.

SCENE I. *A Barber's Shop.*

HUMPHRY *in new clothes, reading a newspaper.*—
TOUPEE *shaving him.*

HUMPHRY. Pray now, master barber, what does Constitution mean? I hears so many people a quarrelling about it,—I wish I cou'd get somebody to give me the exclamation of it; here it is among the news too. It's spelt C, O, N, con—S, T, I, sti—consti —T, U, tu—constitu—T, I, ti—constituti—O, N, on—con-sti-tu-ti-on,—but your city folks calls it Constitushon; they've got such a queer pronouncication.

TOUPEE. Vat you please, sare?

HUMPHRY. Yes, it pleases me well enough; I only want to know what it magnifies.

TOUPEE. Je ne vous entens pas, monsieur.

HUMPHRY. Why, what outlandish dialogue is that you're a talking? I can't understand your lingo as well as the School-master's, with his monstrous memorandums, and his ignorant mouses.

TOUPEE. You be 'quainted with monsieur de Schoolmastare, monsieur?

HUMPHRY. Yes, mounsieur; he and the consumptive old gentleman, old what's his name, was a wrangling about that confounded name that I was axing you about;—caw-con-[*Looks at the paper.*] aye, Constitution.

TOUPEE. Dat Constitution is no bon;—de Schoolmastare vas strike me for dat. By gar, I get de satisfaction!

HUMPHRY. He talks as crooked as a Guinea niger. [*Aside.*

TOUPEE. He vas call me—ah, le diable!—block; dis—[*Points to his head.*] blockhead, oui, blockhead.

HUMPHRY. If you've got a mind, I'll lather him for you.

TOUPEE. Yes; den I vill lader you for nothing.

HUMPHRY. You lather me for nothing?—I'll lather you for less yet, you barber-looking—

TOUPEE. No, no; me lader you so. [*Lathers* HUMPHRY's *face.*

HUMPHRY. Oh, with soap-suds, you mean:—I ax pardon, mounsieur; I thought how you was a going for to lather me without soap-suds or razor, as the old proverb is.

TOUPEE. Dat is no possible, monsieur.

HUMPHRY. I believe not; you shou'd be shav'd as clean as a whistle, if you was; 'faith should you.

TOUPEE. Yes, I will shave you very clean;—here is de bon razor for shave de beard. [*Draws the razor over the back of* HUMPHRY's *hand, to shew him it can cut a hair.*]

HUMPHRY. [*Bellowing out.*] You ill-looking, lousy, beard-combing, head-shaving rascal! Did you ever know any body for to have a beard upon their hand?

TOUPEE. You be von big 'merican brute, sur mon âme!

HUMPHRY. You lie, as the saying is. What a mouth he makes whenever he goes for to talk his gibberage!—He screws it up for all the world like a pickled oyster. I must have a care I don't get some of that snuff out of his nose.

TOUPEE. You please for taste de snuff?

HUMPHRY. I don't care if I *smell* some. [*Takes a pinch of snuff, which makes him sneeze, while* TOUPEE *is shaving him; by which he gets his face cut.*]

TOUPEE. Prenez garde à vous!

HUMPHRY. The devil take the snuff and you! [*Going.*

TOUPEE. S'il vous plaît, monsieur, you vill please for take de —de—vat is dat—de lettre—de shallange to monsieur de School-mastare, for fight me?

HUMPHRY. Yes, that I will, with the most carefullest manner; —he shall have it in the greatest pleasure.

[TOUPEE *gives a paper to* HUMPHRY.

TOUPEE. Dat is de bon civility,—I vill be your—a—very good friend.

HUMPHRY. Thank 'e kindly, Mounsieur. [*Exeunt, severally.*

SCENE II. *A Street.*

Enter YOUNG LOVEYET *and* HUMPHRY.

LOVEYET. Not find where he lives?

HUMPHRY. No;—you're the most unluckiest gentleman for making of blunders,—didn't you tell me how your father liv'd in number two hundred and fifty, in Queen-Street, in the three-story brick house?

LOVEYET. I did; is not that the house?

HUMPHRY. No—why, your father don't live there.

LOVEYET. Did you enquire for Mr. Loveyet?

HUMPHRY. Yes, I saw Mr. Loveyet.

LOVEYET. The devil is in the fellow, I believe. Did you give him my letter?

HUMPHRY. Yes, but I didn't want to.

LOVEYET. Why not?

HUMPHRY. Becase I wanted for to carry it to your father.

LOVEYET. What makes you think Mr. Loveyet is not my father?

HUMPHRY. Somebody told me so that's got a good right to know; I've his own words for it.

LOVEYET. My father tell you so?

HUMPHRY. The young man is crazy, I believe.—I say Mr. Loveyet said you wasn't his son; so I suppose he can't be your father by that.

LOVEYET. I forgot that the letter would probably produce this misunderstanding. [*Aside.*]—He is the only one I know, whom I have a right to call my father.

HUMPHRY. May be you're the old fellow's bastard, and if you're a bastard, you can't be a son, you know: aye, that's the catch, I suppose.

LOVEYET. Your new clothes make you quite smart, Mr. Cubb.

HUMPHRY. Yes, don't I look quite smart, with these here new clothes? they're all new, I'll insure you—only a little the worse for wear; I bought 'em at the vandue option, at the Fly-Market.

LOVEYET. But how came you by that patch on one side of your face, and that large crop of beard on the other?

HUMPHRY. Mounsieur, the outlandish barber, give me a small cut across the whiskers; but the best of all you ha'n't seen yet;—see here. [*Pulls off his hat.*

LOVEYET. Aye, now you look something like—quite fierce—entirely the fine gentleman, upon my falsehood. A genteel dress is the very soul of a man, Mr. Cubb.

HUMPHRY. Like enough, for I've got more soul to shew myself, now I cut such a dash; I've got a soul to see the shews at the play-house; and, I think, I've got a great deal more soul to spend a few shillings at the ale-house.

LOVEYET. That's true; I'm glad you remind me of my promise.

HUMPHRY. Not I, I didn't remind you,—I scorn it.

LOVEYET. I dare say you do. [*Gives him money.*] There, drink my health with that.

HUMPHRY. With all my heart—soul, I mean;—aye, here's soul enough—[*Jingling the money.*]—to buy the matter o' twenty mugs;—come, let's go at once.

LOVEYET. I?—excuse me, sir; I have particular business elsewhere.—Sir, your most humble servant.

HUMPHRY. Sir, I am your most humble sarvint too. [*Bows awkwardly.*) [*Exeunt, severally.*

SCENE III. MR. FRIENDLY'S *House.*

Enter HARRIET.

[*Knocking at the door.*] What an incessant knocking! Mr. Friendly's family are out, and between their company and my own, I expect to be engaged all day: I am fairly tired of these morning visits;—they are fashionable, and, therefore, agreeable, to those who can make propriety and happiness subservient to custom and false politeness; but, for my part—

Enter SERVANT.

SERVANT. Miss Airy is waiting in her carriage, madam.

HARRIET. Admit her. [*Exit* SERVANT.] She is the only one I wish to see this morning.

Enter MARIA.

MARIA. My dear Harriet, I am rejoic'd to find you at home; —I this minute heard something, which I knew would make you happy; and that, I trust, is a good excuse for troubling you twice a day with my company.

HARRIET. You wrong my friendship, Maria, if you think you can oblige me too often with your desirable company; 'tis true I was wishing for a little cessation of that torrent of formal visitors which is pouring in from morning till night; but far be it from Harriet to reckon her Maria among that number.

MARIA. You are very good, my dear; but you must give me leave to be a little jealous that I am not the only one who is favoured with such a preference.

HARRIET. Indeed, I do not know any one I have a particular desire to see this morning, except yourself.

MARIA. You forget Mr. Loveyet, when you say so.

HARRIET. Poh! I am not talking of men.

MARIA. No; but it is very probable you are *thinking* of *a man*.

HARRIET. And pray what reason have you to think, that my thoughts run upon such an improper subject?

MARIA. *Improper subject*, —ha, ha, ha. So my very discreet, prudish little Harriet never lets man enter into her head; tho' it is pretty notorious somebody has enter'd into her heart long ago.

HARRIET. Your discernment must be very subtle, if you know all that is in my heart.

MARIA. I only judge of your heart, by your tongue; and the abundance of the former is generally inferred from the speech of the latter.—Yes, yes—that constant, hypocritical heart of yours is now throbbing with love, hope, curiosity, and—a thousand speechless sensations, the improper subject of which, I do not hesitate to declare, is odious man; and that man, the accomplished Mr. Loveyet.

HARRIET. Pshaw,—how can you tantalize one so?

MARIA. Well, well, it shall not be serv'd like Tantalus any more: *he* was doom'd to behold; and, beholding, to wish and languish for the tempting draught, in vain: but a better doom awaits the happy Harriet;—what she desires is not thus interdicted, but will soon be obtain'd, and—

HARRIET. How strangely you talk, Maria.

MARIA. Well, I will not keep you in suspense any longer. Old Mr. Loveyet has received a letter from his son, signifying his intention to leave the West-Indies shortly after its date, so you may expect to see him very soon. Then hey for a wedding, &c.

HARRIET. Ha, ha; you are a droll girl.

MARIA. But my time is precious; I am just going to the widow Affable's:—about twelve months ago she paid me a visit, when, agreeably to the form in such cases made and provided, she beg'd I would be more sociable, and she would take it so kindly of me: —accordingly I shall step in *en passant*, to shew her my sociability and kindness, which I shall, perhaps, repeat at the end of another year.

HARRIET. How can you be so cruel? The pleasure I experience in your society, makes me regret that any one should be deprived of it.

MARIA. That is very strange:—I should imagine, if you priz'd my company so much, you would wish me to withhold it from others; because, the more I bless them with my presence, the less will come to your share, you know, my dear;—nor is it easy to conceive how you could be so fond of my sweet person, without being jealous at the partiality of others;—but, after all, good people, they say, are scarce; and my humble admirers shall find the saying verified in me; because they are not fully sensible of my superior value; but, since you prove the contrary, by extolling my conversation and friendship so much, I likewise shall observe a contrary conduct, and indulge you with a *tête-à-tête* frequently, my dear.—But I have fifty places to call at yet:—I am to wait on Miss Nancy Startup, Miss Biddy Dresswise, Miss Gaudy, Miss Titterwell, Mrs. Furbelow, Mrs. Neverhome, Mrs— *et cætera, et cætera;* which visits I mean to pay with all the formality and fashionable shortness in my power: from thence I shall proceed to Mademoiselle Mincit, the milliner; from thence to two or three score of shops in William-Street, to buy a prodigious number of important—

HARRIET. Trifles.

MARIA. You are right, my dear;—as I live, I would not be one of those officious "Nothing else, Ma'ms?" for all the goods from the North Church to Maiden-Lane.—Adieu,—I leave you to meditate on what I have told you.

HARRIET. Farewell. [*Exit* MARIA.] Now Maria is gone, I will see no more company.—If anything can be an excuse for a falsehood, the present occasion offers a very good one:—I feel my mind pretty much at ease, and I do not choose to have it disturbed by the impertinence of pretended friends.—Who is there?

Enter SERVANT.

SERVANT. Madam.

HARRIET. Whoever calls to see me to-day, remember I am not at home.

SERVANT. Mr. Worthnought is here now, Madam; must I deny you to him?

HARRIET. Undoubtedly. [*Exit* SERVANT.] I am disgusted with the repetition of that coxcomb's nonsense.—[*Sighs.*]—I wish Charles was here:—In spite of the false delicacy of that tyrant, Custom, which forbids us to speak the exquisite effusions of a susceptible heart, I can now speak boldly, while that heart dictates to the willing tongue what complacence it feels at the prospect of its Charles's return. [*Exit.*

SCENE IV. *Another part of* MR. FRIENDLY'S *House.*
WORTHNOUGHT, *discovered solus.*

WORTHNOUGHT. Who comes here! He sha'n't see her, if I don't, 'foregad—Curse me, but he shall go away with a flea in his ear.

Enter YOUNG LOVEYET, *followed by* HUMPHRY.

HUMPHRY. Mr. Lovit—Mr. Lovit.—[*Takes him aside.*] As I was a going along, d' ye see, I see you pop in here, and so I follow'd you, to tell you, how old Mr. Lovit said he was intend for to go for to see the old fellow's daughter, to tell her something about the letter. Don't Mrs. Harriet live here?

LOVEYET. I'll make haste, and supersede the design of his errand, if possible;—it would be a pity he should come before I had appriz'd Harriet I was not in the West-Indies. [*Aside.*] —I am obliged to you for your information. [*To* HUMPHRY.

HUMPHRY. Thank 'e, as the saying is. [*Going,—*WORTHNOUGHT *whispers with him.*]—What's that to you?—How clumsy moun-sieur has dress'd his calabash!—Powder'd over the face and eyes. [*Exit.*

WORTHNOUGHT. I wish I knew what he wanted with him;—perhaps it is something about me. [*Aside.*

LOVEYET. What Butterfly is this we have here!—I suppose it is the fop, Frankton mentioned. [*Aside.*

WORTHNOUGHT. Sir, I have the honour to be, with the pro-foundest respect and esteem, your most obedient, most devoted, and most obliged humble slave, *foy d'Homme d'Honneur*—Tol lol, &c. [*Sings.*

LOVEYET. A very pompous salutation, truly. [*Aside.*]—Your polite address does me too much honour, sir;—I cannot conceive how you can be my obliged slave, as I do not recollect I ever saw you before.

WORTHNOUGHT. Why, sir, I'll tell you:—Your appearance, sir, bespeaks the gentleman of distinction, sir,—

LOVEYET. My *appearance;*—superficial coxcomb! [*Aside.*

WORTHNOUGHT. 'Tis true, my words were words of course; but I meant every word, sir, 'pon hanor.—"Cupid, Gad of saft persuasion, &c." [*Sings affectedly, and takes snuff.*

LOVEYET. Humph,—To whom, sir, am I indebted, for so much civility?

WORTHNOUGHT. Dick Worthnought, esquire, at your service, sir.

LOVEYET. The very fool. [*Aside.*

WORTHNOUGHT. And give me leave to add, sir, that I feel the highest felicity, that you have given me so good an opportunity of asking you, in my turn, for the favour of your name, sir.

LOVEYET. My name is Loveyet, sir.—With what solemnity the coxcomb talks! [*Aside.*

WORTHNOUGHT. A native of this city, I presume, Mr. Loveyet.

LOVEYET. I am, sir; but I have been absent for some years, and, as I was a youth when I left the city, I cannot be supposed to have retained much of the Yorker.

WORTHNOUGHT. Pardon me, sir;—to a person of penetration, the Yorker is still conspicuous under the disguise of the foreigner; and I am proud to have the hanor of being your countryman, sir.

LOVEYET. I fancy the honour is by no means reciprocal. [*Aside.*

WORTHNOUGHT. You are acquainted with Miss Harriet Trueman, I presume, Mr. Loveyet.

LOVEYET. I was formerly acquainted with the lady.

WORTHNOUGHT. You must know, sir, that your humble servant has the hanor and felicity of being that lady's very humble admirer.

LOVEYET. I dare say she is admired by all who have the pleasure of knowing her.

WORTHNOUGHT. Give me leave, sir,—I mean her lover.

LOVEYET. Conceited ape! [Aside.

WORTHNOUGHT. *You* have no pretensions, sir, I presume.

LOVEYET. Pretensions?

WORTHNOUGHT. Aye, sir; I thought you might have a small *penchant*, as the French call it;—you apprehend me; but she don't intend to see company to-day. I am monstrously chagrin'd, sir, 'foregad, that I have it not in my power to introduce you to the divine mistress of my heart; but, as matters are circumstanc'd, I think it is not worth our while to stay.

LOVEYET. I mean to see Miss Trueman before I shall think so.

WORTHNOUGHT. Oh, fie, sir;—you wou'd not force a lady to give you her company against her inclination:—perhaps, indeed, she may appear to receive you with some warmth, and you may flatter yourself you have fairly made a canquest of her, and think Dick Worthnought esquire, is out-rival'd; but if so, you are most demnably bit, 'foregad, for she's as slippery as ice, tho' not quite so cold;—she is the very standard of true modern coquetry, the quintessence of the *beau-monde*, and the completest example of New-York levity, that New-York has the hanor to call its beautiful inhabitant: ha, ha,—she'll jilt you; —however, the dear creature, with all her amiable foibles, has been so profuse of her attention to me, that I should be ungrateful not to acknowledge the various favours she has hanor'd me with.

LOVEYET. Consummate impudence! [*Aside.*]—Miss Trueman's character is well known, sir.

WORTHNOUGHT. Miss Trueman's character! Demme, sir, do you mean to say anything against her character?

LOVEYET. No;—and I will take care you shall not, with impunity.

WORTHNOUGHT. You are the most unmannerly fellow I ever convers'd with, 'pan hanor.

LOVEYET. And you the most contemptible puppy; or that fellow would be unmannerly enough to chastise you for your insolence.

WORTHNOUGHT. That's a demnable rub, demme;—curse him, I'm afraid he isn't afraid of me, after all. [*Aside.*]—You wou'd find me as brave as yourself then; demme, but you wou'd.

LOVEYET. I'll try you. [*Offers to cane him, which makes him cry out.—Then enter* HARRIET, *hastily.*]

HARRIET. Oh, dear!—what's the matter?
[*Seeing* CHARLES, *she shrieks.*

LOVEYET. My dearest,—my adorable Harriet!

HARRIET. Is it possible? I did not dream that Mr. Loveyet was the person who wanted to see me.

LOVEYET. And am I again blest with a sight of the dear object of all my wishes and affections!—I thank you, heaven; you have been bountiful, indeed! The rolling billows, under your propitious guidance, have at length wafted me to my native land, to love and my dear Harriet.

WORTHNOUGHT. What the devil does he mean! [*Aside.*

HARRIET. Your unexpected appearance, and the unaccountable circumstance which attends it, have discomposed me in such a manner, that I cannot express, as I wish, how happy I am in your safe arrival.

WORTHNOUGHT. Hah,—happy in his arrival! If so, she will not be very happy in his rival, I'm afraid. [*Aside.*

LOVEYET. I will explain the occasion of my charmer's fright immediately;—at present I can only tell you that your wou'd-be lover, here—

HARRIET. My lover!

LOVEYET. So he confidently call'd himself, and took such other insufferably vain and impudent freedoms with your name, that I attempted to give him a little wholesome admonition with this, if his effeminate cries had not brought my lovely Harriet in to prevent me; but the very attempt has proved him to be the basest of dastards. [*While he is saying this,* WORTHNOUGHT *makes several attempts to interrupt him.*]

HARRIET. [*To* WORTHNOUGHT.] I am equally surpriz'd and incens'd, sir, that you would dare to take such freedoms with my name.

LOVEYET. Be assured, Miss Harriet, if you condescend to grant your valuable company to such superficial gentry, they will ever prove themselves as unworthy of it as he has; but your goodness does not let you suspect the use which such characters make of the intimacy they are honour'd with, or you would spurn their unmeaning flattery, and ridiculous fopperies, with indignation.

HARRIET. I ever till now consider'd him as a respectful, well-meaning person, as far as regarded myself; and as such, gave him a prudent share of my civilities; but I never thought either his intellects or his person sufficient to entitle him to a partial intimacy.

WORTHNOUGHT. You cannot deny, madam, that I have repeatedly experienced the most flattering proofs of your partiality, that a lady (who values her reputation) can ever bestow on her admirer.

HARRIET. Contemptible thing! An admirer, forsooth! Of what?—Your ideas are too mean and frothy to let you admire anything but my dress, or some other trifle as empty and superficial as the trifler I am speaking to. My demeanour towards you was nothing but the effect of cheerfulness and politeness; qualities which, I believe, are inherent in me, and of which, therefore, all with whom I am acquainted are the objects; but your present unmanly and insupportably impudent discourse, makes me despise myself almost as much as you, for allowing such a wretch even that small degree of attention which he so illy deserved.

WORTHNOUGHT. You are very insulting, madam, 'pan hanor.—

LOVEYET. How apt such fellows are to have *honour* in their mouths.   [*Aside.*

WORTHNOUGHT. This is only a trick to conceal your inconstancy during his absence; but it is the nature of the sex to deceive us.

HARRIET. 'Tis the nature of a fool to say so; and if that fool does not instantly quit the subject and the house together, I must request the favour of Mr. Loveyet to make him.

LOVEYET. "As matters are circumstanced, Mr. Worthnought, I think it is not worth your while to stay."

WORTHNOUGHT. Her unparallel'd rudeness shall not compel me to leave the house, till I please.

LOVEYET. "Oh, fie, sir,—you would not force a lady to give you her company against her inclination."

WORTHNOUGHT. You are very fond of echoing my words, it seems.

LOVEYET. Yes, when I can apply them to your disappointment and disgrace.—"I am monstrously chagrin'd, sir, 'foregad, that I have it not in my power to introduce you to the divine mistress of my heart." Ha, ha, ha.

WORTHNOUGHT. 'Tis very well,—I will have revenge;—if the laws of politeness (which I would rather die than infringe) did not forbid swearing before a *lady* [*In a contemptuous tone.*], curse me, but I would d——n you for a—

LOVEYET. [*Interrupting him.*]—"You must know, sir, I have the hanor and felicity of being this lady's very humble admirer." —You have failed in your predictions, I think, sir.

WORTHNOUGHT. Yes, and she shall soon pay for her duplicity; tho' I would not have you think that her ill usage mortifies me in the least: I never was in love with her, nor did I ever intend marriage, which is more than *she* can say; and, I believe, it is fortunate for us both, that you arriv'd when you did, or something might have happened, which would have obliged me to marry her, merely to prevent her from being miserable.—Ha, ha, ha. Tol lol, &c. [*Exit.*

HARRIET. What a superlative wretch!

LOVEYET. He is too contemptible to cost you a thought, Harriet:—none but the puppy tribe, and a few splenetic old maids, will pay any attention to his slander; they, no doubt, will spread it with avidity;—but to be traduced by such, is to be praised.—Hah!—there comes my father;—I forgot to tell you I expected him here: I will try if he knows me.

Enter OLD LOVEYET.

OLD LOVEYET. Madam, your most obedient;—Sir, your servant.

LOVEYET. [*Bows.*] I find he does not know me:—Nature, be still: for now I feel he is indeed my father.

HARRIET. Mr. Loveyet, I am happy to see you.

OLD LOVEYET. She would not be quite so happy, if she knew my errand. [*Aside.*]—I have waited on you, madam, upon disagreeable business.

HARRIET. How, sir?—I beg you will not leave me in suspense: What is it?

OLD LOVEYET. It is a matter of a delicate nature, madam, and therefore, must not be spoken at random.

LOVEYET. Heaven avert any unfavourable event! [*Aside.*

HARRIET. Mr. Loveyet, your cautious innuendoes give me sensible uneasiness.

LOVEYET. I will withdraw, Miss Trueman;—My love—friendship, I would say, though it wishes to afford you happiness, and participate in your troubles, does not presume to intrude on the private conversation Mr. Loveyet wishes.

HARRIET. I dare say your presence is no restraint, sir.

OLD LOVEYET. I don't know that, madam: pray, who is the gentleman?

HARRIET. The gentleman is my very particular friend, sir.·

OLD LOVEYET. By my body, here is rare work going on.—[*Aside.*]—Well, madam, as the gentleman is your *very particular friend*; and as his *love*—friendship, I mean, is so great, that you dare to entrust all your secrets with him; I shall acquaint you, that, as you and my son have long entertained a partiality for each other, and being desirous to fulfill all my engagements, as well as to make him happy, I have wrote for him to come and conclude the marriage; but, for very good reasons, I have this day determined to forbid the bans; and Mr. Trueman says, he is very willing too.

LOVEYET. Hah!—what can all this mean? [*Aside.*

OLD LOVEYET. You must know, madam, your father has us'd me very ill; and—to be plain with you, madam, your familiarity with this person, convinces me you wou'd have play'd the fool with my son, without my breaking the match. Ugh, ugh.

LOVEYET. The old gentleman imagines I am going to cut myself out, it seems. [*Aside to* HARRIET.

HARRIET. You do not know who this is, sir, or you would not put any improper constructions on the friendly freedom you have observ'd between us.

LOVEYET. True; and, therefore, you need not be concerned at what he says.—Since he has made this unlucky resolution, he must not know who I am. [*Aside to* HARRIET.

OLD LOVEYET. How well she dissembles!—*Friendly freedom,*—a pretty term that, for the wanton hussy. [*Aside.*] —I wish Charles was here now; he wou'd acknowledge his father's kindness in preventing a match, which, I am sure, would end in sorrow and disappointment.

LOVEYET. I doubt that much.—This parent of mine is a singular character.   [*Aside to* HARRIET.

HARRIET. It is necessary you should be made acquainted with some of his oddities: his most striking peculiarity is a desire to be thought younger than he is; and, I dare say, some remark of my father, respecting his age, is the only cause of his present ill humour.

OLD LOVEYET. Look how they whisper!—well, she is the most brazen coquette I ever knew!—Yes, yes, now her scandalous conduct is glaring enough. [*Aside.*] —I wish you and your *very particular friend*, a good day, madam.   [*Exit.*

HARRIET. I think our troubles increase fast: how unlucky, that this dispute should happen at the very crisis of your arrival;—an event which we fondly expected would be attended with the most pleasing circumstances.

LOVEYET. Those fond expectations, my lovely partner in trouble, shall soon be realized;—this is only the momentary caprice of old age.

HARRIET. You must take care not to talk of *age*, before him.

LOVEYET. Yes, my fair monitor; I shall think of that: and now permit me, in my turn, to give you a little advice.—In the first place, I would have you go to your father—fall at his feet—clasp your fair hands, thus—beseeching him in such terms as that gentle heart is so well form'd to dictate, and persuading him with the all-prevailing music of that tuneful voice, to recall his rigourous intention, nor doom such angelic goodness and beauty to despair, by persisting to oppose an alliance which alone can make you blest: and without which, the most faithful of lovers will be rendered the most wretched one on earth. I shall take a similar method with my old gentleman, and I think I can insure myself success.

HARRIET. This is all very fine; but—to have the voluntary consent of the parent one loves,—how infinitely more agreeable! I would not offend mine, for the world: and yet—

LOVEYET. And yet you will be obliged to offend him, by having me, eigh?

HARRIET. Pshaw;—how strangely you misconstrue my meaning: I was going to observe, that I expect his obstinacy and pride will prove invincible, in spite of all the rhetoric you are pleased to ascribe to me.

LOVEYET. Then we will employ a little rhetoric, against which another class of fathers are not quite so invincible.—Parsons are plenty, you know; and Gold and Silver are persuasive little words. *Love* inspires me with the spirit of prophecy, and tells me I shall soon with propriety call the loveliest of her sex, mine.

HARRIET. You are very eloquent, Mr. Loveyet: I do not think the subject merits so many florid speeches.

LOVEYET. Not merit them!—

> *'Tis not in human language, to define*
> *Merit so rare, and beauty—so divine!*
> *Then what avails this little praise of mine?*

HARRIET. *Harriet deserves not praise so great as thine.*

[*Exeunt.*

End of the Third Act.

ACT IV.

SCENE I. TRUEMAN'S *House.*

TRUEMAN [*solus*].

I sincerely lament this unfortunate dispute.—I know Harriet loves that young fellow, though he has been so long absent; and, therefore, I regret it; for, to what end do I live but to see her happy!—But I will not give way to his father;—perhaps he may think better of the matter, for I know him to be of a placable nature, though passionate;—and yet he seems to be inflexible in his resolution.

Enter HUMPHRY.

HUMPHRY. Sarvint, Mr. Schoolmaster;—here's a challenge for you. [*Gives* TRUEMAN *the barber's note.*

TRUEMAN. A challenge! Surely the old blockhead would not make himself so ridiculous.

HUMPHRY. Yes, it's for that;—I remember he said you call'd him a blockhead.

TRUEMAN. You may go and tell him I advise him to relinquish his knight-errant project, or I will expose his absurdity by taking the advantage which the law offers in such cases.

HUMPHRY. That is, you'll take the law of him, if he goes for to fight you.

TRUEMAN. Fight me!—Oh, grovelling idea! Wit-forsaken progeny of a more than soporific pericranium! Fight me!—Hear and be astonished, O Cicero, Demosthenes, Socrates, Plato, Seneca, Aristotle,—

HUMPHRY. Oh, for shame!—Do you read Haristotle?

TRUEMAN. Be it known to thee, thou monstrous mass of ignorance, if such an uninformed clod, dull and heavy as that element to which it must trace its origin, can comprehend these very obvious and palpable truths, expressed in the most plain, simple, easy, unscholastic diction.—I repeat again, that you may apprehend me with the greater perspicuity and facility,—be it known to thee, that those immaculate sages would have died rather than have used such an expression; by the dignity of my profession, they would:—'tis true that the ancients had such things as single combats among the Olympic games, and they were always performed by the populace; but such a fight, alias a tilt, a tournament, a wrestle, could not, according to the rule of right, and the eternal fitness and aptitude of things, be properly denominated a *bona fide* fight; for, as I before observed, it was *ipso facto*, a game, an Olympic game.—Olympic, from Olympus.

HUMPHRY. Pray now, Mr. Schoolmaster, if a body mought be so bold, what do you think of the last war? Does your Schoolmastership think how that was a fona bide fight?

TRUEMAN. You are immensely illiterate; but I will reply to your interrogatory.—My opinion of the late war, is as follows, to wit.—*Imprimis.* The Americans were wise, brave and virtuous to struggle for that liberty, independence and happiness, which the new government will now render secure. *Item.* The Americans were prodigious fortunate to obtain the said liberty, independence and happiness. A war, encounter, combat, or, if you please, fight like this, is great and glorious; it will immortalize the name of the renowned WASHINGTON,—more than that of Cincinnatus, Achilles, Æneas, Alexander the Great, Scipio, Gustavus Vasa, Mark Anthony, Kouli Khan, Cæsar or Pompey.

HUMPHRY. Cæsar and Pompey! Why them is nigers' names.

TRUEMAN. *O tempora! O mores!*

HUMPHRY. He talks Greek like a Trojan.—Tempora mores; —I suppose how that's as much as to say, it was the temper of the Moors, that's the nigers, for to be call'd Cæsar and Pompey. —I guess how he can give me the exclamation of that plaguy word.—Con—let me see [*Spells it in the manner he did before.*]—

Please your worshipful reverence, Mr. Schoolmaster, what's Latin for Constitution?

TRUEMAN. To tell you what is Latin for Constitution, will not make you a particle the wiser; I will, therefore, explain it in the vernacular tongue.—Constitution then, in its primary, abstract, and true signification, is a concatenation or coacervation of simple, distinct parts, of various qualities or properties, united, compounded, or constituted in such a manner, as to form or compose a system or body, when viewed in its aggregate or general nature. In its common, or generally received, acceptation, it implies two things.—First, the nature, habit, disposition, organization or construction of the natural, corporeal, or animal system.—Secondly, a political system, or plan of government. This last definition, I apprehend, explains the Constitution you mean.

HUMPHRY. Like enough, but I don't understand a single word you've been a talking about.

TRUEMAN. No! 'Tis not my fault then:—If plainness of language, clearness of description, and a grammatical arrangement of words will not suffice, I can do no more.

Enter OLD LOVEYET *listening.*

HUMPHRY. I mean the Constitution that you read in the newspapers about; that that your worship was a going to get at loggerheads with old Mr. What's-his-name, about.

LOVEYET. I'll old you, you rascal!

TRUEMAN. Did you never hear your friends in the country talk of the new Constitution?

HUMPHRY. Not I, I never heard anybody talk about it, at the Pharisee's Head;—I don't believe Jeremy Stave, the clark of the meeting-house, no, nor Parson Thumpum himself ever heard of such a word—No, not even old Mr. Scourge, the Schoolmaster.

TRUEMAN. A hopeful genius, for a Schoolmaster, upon my education. Do you send him to me,—I'll qualify him for that important station.

HUMPHRY. And I'll be qualify'd I never larnt such a word when I went to his school.

TRUEMAN. Nor any other one, I believe, properly speaking.

HUMPHRY. Oh yes, I'll say that for him;—he us'd to take a great deal of pains for to larn us proper speaking.

TRUEMAN. The Constitution you hear so much noise about, is a new government, which some great and good men have lately contrived, and now recommend for the welfare and happiness of the American nation.

LOVEYET. Oh, the traitor!

HUMPHRY. But didn't old Mr. What's-his-name say, how they wanted for to make slaves of us?

LOVEYET. There's *old* Mr. What's-his-name, again.

TRUEMAN. Mr. Loveyet is a weak man;—you must not mind what he says.

LOVEYET. Oh, I shall burst!

TRUEMAN. Only think now of his sending me a challenge, because I told him he was sixty odd years of—

LOVEYET. [*Running towards them.*] Death and the devil! Have I sent you a challenge?

HUMPHRY. No, not you, old gentleman.

LOVEYET. I'll give you *old* gentleman.—Take that, for calling me old again. [*Offers to strike him; but missing his blow, he falls down.*] Oh, what an unlucky dog I am! My evil genius is certainly let loose today.

TRUEMAN. Let us coolly enquire into this enigmatical affair, Mr. Loveyet. [*Breaks open the note, and reads.*] What is all this? — Booby — blockhead — satisfaction — challenge — courage — honour—gentleman—honour'd per Monsieur Cubb.

HUMPHRY. Aye, that's I.

TRUEMAN. And pray, Mr. Cubb, who gave you this pretty epistle?

HUMPHRY. Why, mounsieur, the barber.

TRUEMAN. By the dignity of my profession, it must be so:—Now there's a solution to the enigma.—Mr. Loveyet, you will excuse my mistaking this business so much;—the paltry Frisieur never enter'd my head;—you recollect I gave him a little flagellation this morning.

LOVEYET. Yes, and I recollect the occasion too;—this confounded upstart Constitution (that cause of all my crosses and troubles) is at the bottom of every mischief.

TRUEMAN. Yes, your wou'd-be Constitution, has indeed done a deal of mischief.

LOVEYET. I deny it;—it is perfectly inoffensive and mild.

TRUEMAN. Mild, indeed:—happy would it be for America, if her government was more coercive and energetic!—I suppose you have heard that Massachusetts has ratified this upstart Constitution;—this is the sixth grand column in the federal edifice; we only want three more to make up the lucky nine; and then the nine Muses will make our western world their permanent abode; and *he* who is at once their Favourite and Patron, will preside over the whole: then we shall see another Golden Age; arts will then flourish, and literature be properly encouraged. That's the grand *desideratum* of *my* wishes.

LOVEYET. A fig for your Latin and your literature!—That's the way your unconstitutional Constitutionalists take the advantage of our weak side, and—

TRUEMAN. And the said weak side being easily discovered, as you have but one side,—go on, sir.

LOVEYET. And cram their unconstitutional bolus down our throats, with Latin;—you and your vile junto of perfidious politicians want to *Latin* us out of our liberties.

HUMPHRY. Well, why don't they take the law of the polli-kitchens then, eigh?

TRUEMAN. Mr. Loveyet, I never knew a man of your age and wisdom—

LOVEYET. Age, sir!—Wisdom!—Yes, wisdom, sir.—Age again, eigh? Ugh, ugh.

TRUEMAN. Was there ever such preposterous behaviour!— You are getting as crazy as your favorite Constitution.

LOVEYET. You are crazier than either, you old blockhead, or you would not make such a crazy speech: I say my constitution is a thousand per cent. better than yours. Ugh, ugh, ugh.

TRUEMAN. A pretty figure for a good constitution! What a striking instance of health, youth, and beauty! How emblematically grotesque! The very image of deformity and infirmity! A perfect mirror for Milton's description of Sin and Death.

> *Not Yorick's skull, nor Hamlet's ghost,*
> *Nor all the tragic, stage-made host;*
> *With saucer eyes, and looks aghast,*
> *Would make me run away so fast:*
> *Not all who Milton's head inspire,—*
> *"Gorgons and Hydras and Chimæras dire!"*
> *Nor haggard Death, nor snake-torn Sin,*
> *Look half so ugly, old and thin;*
> *No—all his hell-born, monstrous crew,*
> *Are not so dire a sight as you!*

[*While* TRUEMAN *is saying this,* LOVEYET *appears to be in a violent rage, and makes several attempts to interrupt the former, who shuns* LOVEYET, *as if afraid.*]

LOVEYET. Fire and murder!—Must I bear to be held up for such a monster? Perdition!—What shall I do? What shall I say?—Oh! oh! oh!—Oh! liberty! Oh, my country! Look how he ridicules me!—Did ever any poor man suffer so much for the good of his country!—But I won't give up the glorious cause yet;—sir,—Mr. Trueman—I insist upon it, the new Constitution, sir, —I say, that the old—the new—that—that—'Zounds and fury! — [*Running towards him, and making an attempt to strike him.*

TRUEMAN. My dear Mr. Loveyet, compose yourself a little; —for heaven's sake, sir, consider;—your animal Constitution is not able to withstand the formidable opposition of my political one;—the shock is too great;—let me persuade you, sir; and as soon as nine States accede to the adoption of the new Constitution, we will investigate the merits of the old. Ha, ha, ha.

[*This speech and the preceding one, are to be spoken at the same time; during which,* TRUEMAN *and* LOVEYET *run about the stage, and* HUMPHRY *retreats from them as they approach him.*]

Enter HARRIET *alarmed.*

HARRIET. Oh, Papa,—my dear Papa, what's the matter!

LOVEYET. And, sir, as sure as—as—eight times nine is sixty-three, your new government is not bottom, not sound; and—

TRUEMAN. And as sure as you are sixty-three, your head is not sound.

LOVEYET. Here is your incomparable daughter;—I came here to acquaint you of her scandalous conduct; but now she can save me that trouble.

TRUEMAN. How, sir! My daughter's scandalous conduct?

LOVEYET. I was going to tell you. I caught her with a strange gallant,—a "very particular friend;" whose "love,—friendship, I would say," was so sincere, that she was kind enough to grant him a little "friendly freedom," in my presence.

TRUEMAN. Heaven protect me! There certainly must be something in this.   [*Aside.*

LOVEYET. And that I have received a letter from my son.

HUMPHRY. Aye, now he's his son again.   [*Aside.*

LOVEYET. And that he will be here soon, and that when he comes, I am going to marry him to Miss Maria Airy.

HUMPHRY. I must go tell Mr. Lovit of that, at once.

[*Aside, and exit.*

LOVEYET. And—but it is no matter now:—I suppose she will tell you a fine story of a cock and a bull.

HARRIET. I shall not be base enough to deceive a father, I give you my honour, sir.

LOVEYET. I am very much mistaken if you have not given *that* to somebody already:—A woman's honour is a very perishable commodity; a little thing often spoils it.

HARRIET. By what a feeble tenure does poor woman hold her character and peace of mind!—It is true, sir, that a woman's *reputation* is too frequently, with ruffian cruelty, blasted in the bud, without a cause; and that so effectually, that it seldom or never flourishes again; but let me remind you, sir, in the words of the poet, that—

"*Honour's a sacred tie, the law of kings;—*
It ought not to be sported with."

LOVEYET. I say it ought to be sported with; and, by my body, tis capital sport, too;—eigh, Horace?—[*Sings.*]—"Then hoity toity, whisky frisky, &c."

TRUEMAN. A truce to your insipid, hard-labour'd wit: the honour you are pleased to call in question, is not an empty name which can be purchased with gold; it is too inestimable to be counterpoised by that imaginary good; otherwise the titles of Honourable and Excellent would be always significant of his Honour's or his Excellency's intrinsic worth;—a thing "devoutly to be wish'd," but unfortunately too seldom exemplified; for, as the dramatic muse elegantly says of money,—"Who steals my purse, steals trash."

LOVEYET. I deny it;—the dramatic muse, as you call him, was a fool:—trash indeed! Ha, ha, ha. Money trash! Ready Rhino trash! Golden, glittering, jingling money!—I'm sure he cou'dn't mean the hard stuff.

TRUEMAN. Very sublime conceptions, upon my erudition; and expressed by some truly elegant epithets; but your ideas, like your conscience, are of the fashionable, elastic kind;—self-interest can stretch them like Indian-rubber.

LOVEYET. What a stupid old gudgeon!—Well, you'll believe what I tell you, sooner or later, Mr. Schoolmaster; so your servant:—as for you, Miss Hypocrite, I wish your Honour farewell, and I guess you may do the same. [*Exit.*

TRUEMAN. These insinuations, Harriet, have put my anxiety to the rack.

HARRIET. I am happy I can so soon relieve you from it, sir. Young Mr. Loveyet arrived this morning; but, it seems, the old gentleman has entirely forgot him, during his long absence; and when he heard his father's resolution, in consequence of the dispute he had with you, he did not think proper to make himself known. It was this which made him think me so culpable, that you hear he talks of marrying him to my friend Maria.

TRUEMAN. I see into the mistake; but the worst construction the affair will admit, does not justify his using you so indecently; and, if it were not for the more powerful consideration of a daughter's happiness, I would make him repent it.

HARRIET. I have ever found my honoured, my only parent both wise in concerting plans for that daughter's happiness, and good in executing them to the utmost of his ability; and, I dare say, he does not think her alliance with Mr. Loveyet's son will prove unfavourable to her happiness.

TRUEMAN. Far from it, my child:—Your unusual good sense makes a common-place lecture unnecessary, Harriet; but beware of flattery and dissimulation; for the manners of the present age are so dissolute, that the young fellows of these degenerate days think they cannot be fine gentlemen without being rakes, and— in short, rascals; for they make a merit even of debauching innocence:—indeed, that is scarcely to be wondered at, when so many of those who are called ladies of taste and fashion, strange as it may seem, like them the better for it;—but I hope, you and Mr. Loveyet are exceptions to such depravity.

HARRIET. I think I can venture to assure you, we *are*, sir;— and now, if my father has nothing more to impart, I will take my leave of him; and be assured, sir, your advice shall be treasured here, as a sacred pledge of paternal love.—Adieu, Papa.

TRUEMAN. Farewell, Harriet;—Heaven prosper your designs.
[*Exeunt severally.*

SCENE II. *A Street.*

Enter HUMPHRY *and* WORTHNOUGHT *meeting.*

WORTHNOUGHT. Sir, your most obedient.

HUMPHRY. Here's that mackmarony again. [*Aside.*

WORTHNOUGHT. I have not the honour to know your name, sir, but if you will inform me what you were whispering with Mr.

Loveyet about, you will make me the most obsequious and devoted of your slaves.

HUMPHRY. My slave!—Why, I wou'dn't have you for a slave,
if you was to pay me for it;—with your silk sattin breeches, and
your lily white gloves, and your crimp'd up toes, and your fine
powder'd calabash, that's so smart outside.

WORTHNOUGHT. You entirely mistake my meaning, friend;—
I'm a man of quality.—Do I look like a servant, a hireling, a vile
menial?

HUMPHRY. No, you look more like a dancing-master, a fight-
ing-master, or a play-actor, or some such flashy folks; but looks
is nothing, for everybody dresses alike nowadays; like master,
like man, as the old saying is; ecod, you can't tell a Congressman
from a marchant's 'prentice, everybody dresses so fine.

WORTHNOUGHT. Ha, ha, ha,—he is pasitively a very eccentric
bady, and there is a small tincture of a barbarous sart of wit in
what he says; but it wants an immensity of correction, an infini-
tude of polishing; he is a mere son of nature, everything he says
is express'd in such a Gathic, uncouth, Anti-Chesterfieldian style;
and as for his dress, it is pasitively most prepasterously clownish
and original.

HUMPHRY. Why he talks as many long-winded, old-fashioned
words, as the Schoolmaster.

WORTHNOUGHT. Mr.—Mr.—Pray what is your proper name,
besides Humphry? Your sirname, I mean.

HUMPHRY. My proper sirname is Humphry Cubb; why our
family is the most largest family within the circumroundibus of
fifty miles, and the most grandest too, tho' I say it that shou'dn't
say it; for my father's father's great-grandfather was a just-ass
of the peace, when King George the third was a sucking baby,
and, therefore, as father says, a greater *man* then, than he was,
ha, ha, ha. And his great aunt, by his mother's side, had the
honour to be chief waiting woman to Mynheer Van Hardspraken-
crampdejawmetlongname, the Dutch governor's public scratche-
tary; but I needn't go so far back neither, for I've got, at this
present time, no less than two second cousins; one of 'em is
soup-provider for the county, and t' other belongs to the liglisla-
ture, and both belonging to our family too;—both Cubbs.

WORTHNOUGHT. Yes, the world abounds with Cubbs, just
such unlick'd ones as you are;—there is a profusion of them in

this city.—You must know, *I* am Dick Worthnought, esquire; a gentleman, a buck of the blood, and a—you understand me.

HUMPHRY. Why, your family must be as big as mine, then; for I've seen hundreds of such Worth-nothing bloody bucks as you, since I've been in town.

WORTHNOUGHT. Your criticisms are perfectly barbarous and disagreeable, 'foregad; but,—will you let me know what you and the West-India young gentleman were whispering about, at Miss Trueman's?

HUMPHRY. Yes.—You can have Miss Trueman now, if you've a mind.

WORTHNOUGHT. Can I? Only prove your words, and enroll me your everlasting, your indissoluble friend, demme.

HUMPHRY. Friend me none of your friends; I don't want such everlasting friends as you, d' ye see, becase why, if you never make a beginning with your friendship, I'm sure it can't be everlasting; and if you've got a mind to shew your friendliness, I'm sure you cou'dn't have a more fitter time than now.

WORTHNOUGHT. What wou'd the addity have me say, I wonder.

HUMPHRY. I wou'dn't have you say anything,—you talk too much already, for the matter o' that; I like for to see people do things, not talk 'em.

WORTHNOUGHT. There [*Gives him money.*]—is that what you want?

HUMPHRY. Aye, I thought you understood me well enough.— Your friendship wants as much spurring and kicking and coaxing as our lazy old gelding at home;—I wou'dn't trust such a friend as far as I cou'd fling a cow by the tail.

WORTHNOUGHT. Poh, poh,—to the point, to the point.

HUMPHRY. Why, then you must know, how old Mr. Lovit is a going for to marry the West-Indian young gentleman to young Mistress Airy, I think he call'd her; and so you can go try Mistress Harriet yourself, for I'm sure she won't have him now.

WORTHNOUGHT. Why, pray?

HUMPHRY. Why if she gets him, she'll get a bastard, for old Mr. Lovit isn't his father.

WORTHNOUGHT. No?

HUMPHRY. No;—and then he and the Schoolmaster kick'd up a proper rumpus about a challenge I fetch'd him; and that's all the news you'll get for your money.—A poor shilling that won't buy ale to my oysters to-night. [*Exit.*

WORTHNOUGHT [*manet*].

This is a lucky meeting, 'foregad;—I'll go immediately and report, that young Loveyet has of late seen my quondam charmer carry a copy of him in miniature about her, which (strange to tell) is continually growing nearer to the life; and that he refuses to have her, on that account.—"If she gets him, she will get a bastard."—By which I choose to understand,—matters have gone so far, that she cannot save herself from that disgrace, even if she marries him.—Now, in order that this tale of mine may transpire briskly, I must first see some of my tattling female friends;—they will set it a going like wild-fire.—Split me, but it is an excellent thought;—ha, ha, ha. Poor Loveyet [*Exit.*

SCENE III. HERALD's *House.*

Enter CANTWELL *and* HERALD.

CANTWELL. I am very happy to find you home;—I was almost eat up with the vapours before I saw you. [*Sighs.*]—Well, what's the news, Miss Herald?

HERALD. Nothing strange, Miss Tabitha; I am as barren of anything new, as an old Almanack.

CANTWELL. Oh shocking!—"as barren of anything new."— What an odious expression!—The most vulgarest comparison in nature.

HERALD. Umph.—I suppose, if Mr. Gracely was here, you would not be so much in the dumps.

CANTWELL. Ah, Miss Herald!—If you felt the corruptions of your wicked heart, you would be in the dumps too, as you call it. [*Sighs.*

HERALD. I believe there is a certain corruption in your heart, which our sex are apt to feel very sensibly, and that is the want of a husband.

CANTWELL. The want of a husband!—I vow, you are monstrous indelicate, Miss Herald; I am afraid you are wandering from the paths of vartue, as dear good Mr. Gracely says.

HERALD. There comes his very reverse,—Mr. Worthnought.

CANTWELL. Ah, he is a profane rake; he is lighter than vanity, as Mr. Gracely says;—a mere painted sepulchre.

HERALD. That ancient sepulchre of yours is pretty much daub'd, I think. [*Aside.*

Enter WORTHNOUGHT.

WORTHNOUGHT. Ladies, *J'ay bien de la joye de vous voir.* I have the supernal and superlative hanor and felicity, of being most respectfully yours.

CANTWELL. I hope I have the pleasure to see Mr. Worthnought well.

WORTHNOUGHT. *Là, Là, Mademoiselle; assez bien: Je vous suis obligé.*—She has reviv'd her wither'd chaps with rouge in a very nasty manner, 'pan hanor. [*Aside.*]—Have you heard the news, respecting Miss Harriet Trueman, ladies?

CANTWELL. Yes, now I think on 't, there is a report about town, that old Mr. Loveyet saw her and another rather familiar together.

WORTHNOUGHT. Oh, you have not heard half, madam.

CANTWELL. Do, let us hear, Mr. Worthnought.

HERALD. Aye, do; but do not say anything that will hurt Miss Tabitha's delicacy; for, before you came in, I was complaining that I was *barren* of anything new, and she was almost ready to swoon at the expression.

WORTHNOUGHT. If Miss Tabitha has such an antipathy to barrenness, she will not be offended at my subject, which is a very prolific one, I assure you; for Miss Trueman is on the verge of *bearing* a son.

CANTWELL. Oh, horrid! What will this wicked world come to at last!—A good-for-nothing, wanton hussy.

WORTHNOUGHT. Very true, madam:—by persons of easy notions of virtue, indeed, it would be considered a trifling *faux pas*, as the French call it; a perfect *bagatelle;* or, at most, a superficial act of incontinency; but to those who have such rigid notions of virtue as Miss Cantwell, for example, or Miss Herald, or their humble servant; it appears quite another thing, quite another thing, ladies:—though it is one of my foibles;—I own it is a fault to be so intalerably nice about the affairs of women; but it is a laudable imperfection, if I may be allowed the phrase;—it is erring on the safe side, for women's affairs are delicate things to meddle with, ladies.

CANTWELL. You are perfectly in the right, Mr. Worthnought; but one can't help speaking up for the honour of one's sex, you know.

WORTHNOUGHT. Very true, madam:—to make the matter still worse, ladies, Mr. Loveyet is just arrived from abroad to be married to her; and the old gentleman is going to ally him immediately to Miss Maria Airy in consequence of it.

HERALD. I am glad of that, however;—I will forgive Miss Trueman her failing, if that is the case, for then I shall have a better chance to gain Frankton. [*Aside.*

WORTHNOUGHT. But this is *entre nous*, ladies.—[*Looks at his watch.*] Hah,—the *tête-à-tête!*—Ladies, I have the hanor to be your slave. [*Going.*

CANTWELL. You are positively the greatest lady's man, Mr. Worthnought,—

WORTHNOUGHT. I am proud of your compliment, madam; and I wish Miss Tabitha could consider me such, from her own experience; it would be conferring the highest hanor on her slave, 'pan hanor.

CANTWELL. Oh, sir,—your politeness quite confuses me. [*Curtsying.*

WORTHNOUGHT. Miss Herald, your thrice devoted.—*Mademoiselle, je suis votre Serviteur très humble.*

CANTWELL. Mr. Worthnought, your servant.—[*Exit* WORTHNOUGHT.]—Don't you think he is a very pretty fellow, Miss Herald?—He's the very pattern of true politeness; his address is so winning and agreeable,—and then, he talks French, with the greatest felicity imaginable.

HERALD. I cannot say I see many perfections in him; but you talk'd very differently just now;—Mr. Worthnought then was lighter than vanity; and now, it seems, he has more weight with you, than good Mr. Gracely.

CANTWELL. You are only mortify'd that Mr. Worthnought took so little notice of you, ma'am; you see he prefers me to you, though you value yourself so much upon being a little young, ma'am; you see men of sense don't mind a few years, ma'am; so your servant, ma'am. [*Exit.*

HERALD [*manet*].

What a vain old fool! Now will she make this story of her swain spread like a contagion: as for me, I must circulate it pretty briskly too; perhaps, it may make me succeed better with Frankton; otherwise the poor girl might lie in peaceably, for me. [*Exit.*

SCENE IV. OLD LOVEYET'S *House.*

OLD LOVEYET *discovered solus.*

Enter CHARLES LOVEYET.

CHARLES. Mr. Loveyet, your most obedient.

LOVEYET. Sir, your servant.

CHARLES. Don't you know me, sir?

LOVEYET. Yes, I think I have seen you before.

CHARLES. You really have, sir.

LOVEYET. Oh, yes, I recollect now;—you are the person who have supplanted my son.

CHARLES. Indeed, sir, I am not that person.

LOVEYET. How!—Was you not with Harriet Trueman, this morning?

CHARLES. Yes, sir; but I have no intention to supplant your son, I assure you; on the contrary, it is the supreme wish of my heart, that his love may be rewarded with so rich a treasure as the amiable Harriet.

LOVEYET. He shall be rewarded with a much richer one, if he is wise enough to think so.

CHARLES. If it be wisdom to prefer another to Harriet, then may I ever remain a fool!   [*Aside.*

LOVEYET. But pray, sir, what is your business with me?

CHARLES. My business is first to know if you have any objection to my marrying Miss Trueman, sir.

LOVEYET. What a paradoxical fellow this is! [*Aside.*]—Did not you this minute say, you did not intend to have her?

CHARLES. I did not, sir; I mean to have her if possible, and that without disappointing your son; but I shall explain myself better, by telling you who I am. Look at me well, sir—did you never see such a face before?

LOVEYET. I hope I am not talking to a lunatic! [*Aside.*]—Yes, I saw you this morning.

CHARLES. Did you never see me before that, sir?

LOVEYET. [*Looks at him steadfastly.*] Yes,—I'm sure I have; and I'm very much mistaken, if—yes, that reconciles all his strange conduct;—it must be so;—it is Charles himself.

CHARLES. My father!   [*Embracing him.*

LOVEYET. And are you indeed my son?

CHARLES. I hope I am, sir; and as such, I thus kneel to obtain forgiveness for deceiving you so.   [*Kneels.*

LOVEYET. Rise up my lad;—by my body, I am rejoic'd to see you;—you did take your father in a little, to be sure; but never mind it;—I'll take you in another way, perhaps.

CHARLES. I wish you would take me in the matrimonial way, sir;—that would be a most agreeable take in.

LOVEYET. Well, well, we shall not disagree about that:—I am very happy this affair clears up Harriet's conduct so well; she is a fine girl, that's certain; and, if you love her as much as you formerly did, why—I don't know what I may not do.

CHARLES. Oh, sir, you make me unspeakably happy! If my Love is to be the condition of the welcome Bond, I do not care if it is executed to-morrow; for, were the penalty an age of love, I am sure I could pay it.

LOVEYET. By my body, I'll have a wedding soon, and a merry one too:—I'll go and make it up with old Trueman;—but then he must not talk of the Constitution.—That's true, Charles, what government are you for, eigh?—The old or the new?

CHARLES. Sir?

LOVEYET. I say, which Constitution do you like best?

CHARLES. What the mischief shall I say!—Now Love befriend me. [Aside.] Since you seem desirous of knowing my opinion on this subject, sir; I must candidly tell you, I am decidedly in favour of the new Constitution.

LOVEYET. Hah—the new Constitution!—A good-for-nothing, corrupted, aristocratic profligate!—But you shall not have her now; that is as fixed as fate.

CHARLES. Oh, cruel event! How soon all my towering hopes fall prostrate in the dust!—Do, sir, try and think better of the matter;—I will promise to make myself think or do anything you please, rather than have the double misfortune to offend my father, and lose my Harriet.

LOVEYET. Base foe to the liberties of his country!

CHARLES. It is very strange, sir, that you should be so violent about such matters, at your time of life.

LOVEYET. Hah! do you dare?—Yes, he wants to provoke me still more;—to talk to me about my time of life! Why, I'm not old enough for your father, you great whelp you:—Ungracious young bastard,—to have the assurance to ridicule his father!—Out of my house, you 'scape-grace!

CHARLES. Unnatural usage for so trivial an offense!—But I obey you, sir: I'll remain no longer in the house of a father, who is so destitute of a father's feelings; and since I see you value my happiness so little, sir, I shall not think myself undutiful, if I take some necessary steps to promote it myself.

LOVEYET. Out of my house, I say!—Promote your own happiness, forsooth; did you ever know any one to be happy without money, you fool?—And what will you do, if I don't choose to give you any, eigh?

CHARLES. As well as I can:—I have a few of your unnecessary thousands in my hands, thank fortune;—I'll try if *they* will not befriend me, if their avaricious owner, and my unnatural parent will not.   [*Aside, and exit.*

LOVEYET. My time of life, indeed.—Provoking profligate!— I'll give Miss Airy all I'm worth, if she'll consent to have him;— the graceless fellow has us'd me so ill, that he shall be punish'd for it.   [*Exit.*

End of the Fourth Act.

ACT V.

SCENE I. *A Street.*

Enter YOUNG LOVEYET, HUMPHRY, *and a* NEGRO *with a trunk on his head.*

LOVEYET. Did you hear him say so?

HUMPHRY. Yes; he said how he was intend you should have Miss Mary Airy, or Airy Mary, or some such a name.

LOVEYET. Say you so, father?—I believe I shall do myself the pleasure to baulk you. I want you to go a little way with my man; but you will be sure to make no mistake.

HUMPHRY. No, no, never fear me; I an't so apt for to make blunders as you.

LOVEYET. [*Looking at his watch.*] 'Sdeath! I should have been with her half an hour ago.—I know I can depend on you. Here, Cuffy, go with this gentleman.

HUMPHRY. Why, if I *am* a gentleman, Mr. Cuffy needn't give himself the trouble;—I can carry it myself.

CUFFY. Tankee, massa buckaraw; you gi me lilly lif, me bery glad;—disa ting damma heby. [*Puts down the trunk.*]—An de debelis crooka tone in a treet more worsa naw pricka pear for poor son a bitch foot; an de cole pinch um so too!—

LOVEYET. No, no, you shall carry it;—your head is harder than his.

HUMPHRY. To be sure, my head *is* a little soft.

LOVEYET. You must let him take it to number two hundred and twenty-one, Broadway;—will you remember the direction?

HUMPHRY. Yes, number two hundred and twenty-one, Broadway.

LOVEYET. Right;—and enquire for Mr. Frankton, and tell him who it is from.

HUMPHRY. Aye, aye, let me alone for that. [*Exit, with* NEGRO.

LOVEYET [*manet*].

I think I am even with the old gentleman now;—but I lament the necessity of this conduct; and, if a man could eat and digest matrimony, without a little matter of money, I would forgive my unreasonable father, with all my heart; and he might eat his gold himself; though, by the bye, this sum of money, in equity and good conscience, is mine.—Now he wants to cross my inclination, by making me the rival of my friend;—what a strange whim! But if I don't trick him out of his project and his money too, it shall not be my fault. [*Exit.*

SCENE II. MR. FRIENDLY'S *House.*

HARRIET [*solus*].

Notwithstanding the arrival of Charles, and the happy result of the interview with my father, my mind is not at ease;—these strange rumours must have some foundation;—one says he is married to Maria; another says, he is discovered to be illegitimate; a third reports, he was found in company with a woman of ill fame; and to conclude the catalogue of evil tidings, a fourth says, that old Mr. Loveyet is going to disinherit him, in consequence of his having made him a grandfather, since his arrival.—But here he comes.

Enter YOUNG LOVEYET.

LOVEYET. She seems very thoughtful;—perhaps, she too has been unfortunate in her suit to her father;—or, what is far worse, perhaps,—but I will not cherish such gloomy apprehensions.—Your servant, madam.

HARRIET. Good day, Mr. Loveyet.—"Your servant, madam!" —What a stoical salutation! I fear there is too much truth in what I have heard. [*Aside.*

LOVEYET. You seem unusually serious, Miss Harriet: I hope Mr. Trueman has not proved relentless as you expected.

HARRIET. No sir; it gives me pleasure to acquaint you, my father was all kindness and forgiveness.

LOVEYET. I wish I could say so of mine;—he indeed was kind and forgiving too at first; but no sooner had I begun to anticipate approaching happiness, than one luckless circumstance deprived me of all that love and hope had inspired.

HARRIET. An unlucky circumstance, indeed; but would the disappointment really be so great, if you were obliged to give up the thought of an alliance with me?

LOVEYET. How, Miss Harriet! Give up the thought of having you!—By heaven, it must be so!—Yes, the beau would never have presumed to say so much if it were not so;—and Frankton's ambiguous account of them both, confirms the suspicion;—and then the extravagant encomiums he bestowed on her yesterday. —Confusion! my fears were just, though he ridicul'd me for exposing them.—But she must not see my anxiety. [Aside.

HARRIET. If my doubts are well founded, he must be an adept in the art of dissimulation. I will try him a little farther.— [Aside.] What think you, Mr. Loveyet, of our New-York beauties? Have not the superior charms of so many fine women, been able to overcome such old-fashioned notions as constancy and priority of affection?

LOVEYET. I have beheld their beauty with equal pleasure and astonishment; and the understanding, the affability, and vivacity, by which strangers, with so much propriety, characterize my fair countrywomen, give them a pre-eminence over the ladies of most other countries, that is highly gratifying to a mind already so much attached to its native city, by the most endearing of all human ties;—they are all that the warmest, the most luxuriant fancy can wish; beautiful—almost beyond the possibility of an increase of charms; and—I had almost said, they furnish room for love and warm conceptions, "even to madness!"

HARRIET. I am in doubt no longer;—such passionate expressions must have Love for their prompter. [Aside.

LOVEYET. My friend Frankton extolled them highly; but his description derogates from their desert;—you, too, he praised;— I listened to him—with unspeakable delight, and believed him with all the ardour of faith and expectation; for I could readily believe that, which I had so often, so sweetly experienced;—but when you last blest my eyes with that enchanting form, how was the idea exceeded by the reality!—To do justice to *such* perfection, the praises I this minute bestowed on the ladies I have seen, would be spiritless and insufficient!—To charms like Miss Harriet's, what hermit could remain insensible!—*I* was not insensible; —the tender passion, I began so early to entertain; a passion, which length of absence, and a succession of objects and events, had rendered too dormant, was then excited to sensations the most exquisitely sensible;—was then taught to glow with a flame, too fervent to be now suppressed!

HARRIET. Were I but sure of his sincerity! [*Aside.*

LOVEYET. With what indifference she hears me!—If she is so insensible to the genuine effusions of a heart like mine, I am lost indeed! But I will try a little deception to discover the truth. [*Aside.*] —What a lovely picture Mr. Frankton drew of Miss Airy! But it was not too highly finished; for a thousand Loves and Graces have conspired, to make her the most accomplished of her sex.

HARRIET. My pride shall not let him triumph over my chagrin. [*Aside.*] —I know Miss Airy to be as accomplished as you represent her, sir: and Mr. Frankton gave such a lovely description of her, you say;—I dare say he did;—oh,—yes—yes [*Appears disconcerted, by striving to hide her concern.*]—he loves her to distraction;—Mr. Frankton has doubtless made a wise choice.

LOVEYET. By all that's false, she is concerned at Frankton's having praised his mistress! She absolutely loves him! [*Aside.*

HARRIET. And you have seen the amiable Miss Airy, sir.

LOVEYET. Forgive me, honour and veracity. [*Aside.*] —Yes, Miss Trueman; and not without a deep sense of her uncommon worth and beauty.

HARRIET. I admire your discernment, sir;—Mr. Frankton, too, is a very nice judge of female merit; and he cannot evince his judgment better, than by praising my friend Maria.

LOVEYET. Pardon me, madam: with submission to your friend's merit, I think his panegyric would better apply to you.

HARRIET. That compliment is too great, to be meant, I fancy.

LOVEYET. I rather think, you value the author of it so little, that you would as soon he should withhold it, madam.

HARRIET. Certainly, sir, when I have reason to think there is another who has a better right to it, and for whom it is secretly intended.

LOVEYET. You wrong me much, madam:—some tattling gossip or designing knave, has whispered some falsehood to my prejudice;—probably my *rival*,—Mr. Worthnought.

HARRIET. If you have come here with a design to use me ill, sir, I beg you will tell me so, and then I shall act accordingly.

LOVEYET. Your actions accord very illy with your *professions*, I think, madam.

HARRIET. *Your* duplicity, sir, both in word and action, justifies my retorting that ungenerous accusation.

LOVEYET. I entreat you to believe me, Miss Harriet, when I say, I am unconscious of having done anything I ought to be ashamed of, since my arrival: I am so confident of this, that the circulation of a malicious rumour, however dishonourable to me, would give me little disquiet, did I not reflect, that it is the object of Harriet's credulity;—a reflection, that is the source of real unhappiness to me:—be kind then, Harriet, and tell me wherein I am guilty;—obscurity in a matter so interesting, gives more torture to the mind, than the most unwelcome truth.

HARRIET. He must be sincere. [*Aside.*] —Your request shall be comply'd with, sir.—The principal offence you are charged with, is your having been smitten by the lady, on whom you have bestowed such liberal commendation;—be that as it may, I heard Mr. Loveyet talk of such a match:—I believe it will require a more able advocate than yourself, to defend *this* cause.

LOVEYET. Suppose I assure you, on the sacred honour of a gentleman, that what you have heard is false;—suppose I add the more important sanction of an oath, to seal the truth.

HARRIET. I will save you that trouble:—you have an advocate *here*, which has already gained your cause.

LOVEYET. Oh, Harriet, you are too good!—Conscious as I am of the rectitude of my conduct, as it respects my Harriet;—sure as I am of not deserving your displeasure, I still feel myself unworthy of such matchless goodness.

HARRIET. You say too much; and compel me to tell you that you merit my highest esteem.

LOVEYET. Esteem! What a cold epithet!—And am not I entitled to something more than *esteem?*

HARRIET. Excuse the poverty of the expression; and be assured, my heart dictated a more exalted word;—let this confession atone for the fault.

LOVEYET. And yet I would fain attract your esteem too; for, I have heard connoisseurs in the science of Love say, it is possible to *love* an object, and that to distraction, without having a particle of *esteem* for it.

HARRIET. I have assured you that *my* esteem is at least equalled by a more passionate affection:—but how strangely you talk!—First you acknowledge yourself unworthy of my favour;—then you are alarmed that I should only esteem you; and when I talk of a passion, superior to mere *Platonic* love, you are afraid, on the other hand, it is a blind, enthusiastic impulse, not founded on *esteem.*—How inconsistent are lovers!

LOVEYET. Your reasoning, like your person, surprises, charms and subdues:—I will be more consistent;—but our contention is only for pre-eminence in love;—delightful emulation! Agreeable inconsistency!

HARRIET. I am now ashamed of my childish suspicions; but I should not have been so credulous, had it not been for an affection, which rendered my better judgment blind to the fallacy, and made me more apprehensive of your inconstancy, than satisfied of your innocence; and this disposed me to misinterpret every thing you said.

LOVEYET. And your apparent indifference, in consequence of that misinterpretation, excited similar suspicions in me; and thus, mutual distrust produced mutual misapprehension.

HARRIET. But you have not told me the particulars of your interview with old Mr. Loveyet.

LOVEYET. Were you to hear those particulars, they would only afford you pain;—'tis sufficient for me to tell you, he has turned me out of his house, only because I told him, I was a friend to the new Constitution, forsooth.

HARRIET. He is a strange character:—when I call'd on my father, I was alarmed to find them at high words;—and he abus'd *me* most unmercifully.

LOVEYET. He did? 'Tis well for him he has call'd himself my father;—but if my Harriet consents, I will immediately put myself in a situation that will justify my preventing his future ill usage:—Fortune has enabled me to act independent either of his frown or his favour;—I have taken such measures, in consequence of his base usage, as will guard us against the effects of the one, without obliging us to cringe for the other.

HARRIET. I am happy to hear it; but affluence is not my object, nor poverty my dread; and I am happy I can convince you how little I desire an alliance for interest, by now tendering you the whole of my trifling fortune, in case your father should deprive you of yours.

LOVEYET. Charming Harriet! Miracle of disinterested love! Thus let me evince my gratitude. [Kneels, and kisses her hand.

HARRIET. Pray do not worship me, Mr. Loveyet; I am less generous than you imagine;—self-love is at the bottom of this noble declaration; for if I did not suppose you capable of making me happier than any other man, I would keep both my fortune and my person, to myself.

LOVEYET. Better and better!—Your explanation gives me new reason to adore such uncommon worth, and makes me blest beyond measure! By heaven, New-York does not contain such a fortunate fellow!

Enter FRANKTON.

HARRIET. [Seeing FRANKTON.]—Ha, ha. You could not say more, if you were addressing my friend Maria.

LOVEYET. Talk not of your friend Maria,—

HARRIET. *You* talked enough of her perfections just now, for both of us.

FRANKTON. He did, eigh? [Aside.

LOVEYET. I spoke of her as I thought she deserv'd; she is a lovely creature, but—but [Sees FRANKTON.]—Frankton!

FRANKTON. I hope Miss Trueman will excuse my coming in so abruptly:—I have been looking for Mr. Loveyet, all over the city; at last I concluded, I might find him here.

HARRIET. Really sir; and pray, what made you conclude so?

FRANKTON. I thought it was within the compass of probability, madam.

LOVEYET. Perhaps it was the lady you wanted to see so much, Frankton;—that *she* might be here, was certainly within the compass of probability.

FRANKTON. Had I then known what I have discovered since, I should have looked for you at some place not very distant from the lady, whose perfections you have been contemplating with so much admiration; for by Miss Harriet's account, you have seen her, perhaps, more than once.

LOVEYET. I saw her yesterday, and was charmed with her beauty.—Whenever I am betrayed into one falsehood, I am obliged to support it with twenty more.   [*Aside.*

HARRIET. It is really so, sir;—he was enraptured with her idea just now.—I fear your friend is your rival, sir.

LOVEYET. And I fear my friend is my rival, madam.

HARRIET. Nay, what cause have you for *such* a fear?

LOVEYET. About as good as you have, my dear.—I am glad you came in when you did, Frankton; for you must know, we have had certain mutual doubts and jealousies; in consequence of which, a little ill-natured altercation, otherwise called love, ensued: a small foretaste of conjugal felicity; but the short-liv'd storm soon subsided, and a reconciliation made all calm again.

FRANKTON. I have something to say to you in private, Loveyet. [*Aside to* LOVEYET.] —I am sorry to deprive you of Mr. Loveyet's company, madam; but I trust you will excuse me, when I tell you I have particular business with him.

HARRIET. By all means, sir.

FRANKTON. Your most obedient, madam.

LOVEYET. [*Goes up to* HARRIET.]—Adieu;—expect me soon, and be assured of my unalterable fidelity. [*Exit with* FRANKTON.

HARRIET. Farewell.—I wish he had look'd for you a little farther, before he had taken you away.—There are so many captivating objects in the city (as he has already seen and declared), and dissipation abounds so much among us, that who knows, if he is now sincere, how long he will remain so;—and how long after marriage:—"Ah, there's the rub."—Well, matrimony will put his constancy to the test, that's one comfort;—it is a hazardous expedient, but it is a certain one.

SCENE III. *A Street.*

Enter FRANKTON *and* YOUNG LOVEYET.

LOVEYET. He denounces perpetual enmity against me; threatens me with beggary, and (what is worse) resolves to prevent my union with Harriet, and thus blast all my hopes; but I shall take care to disappoint his views;—I have just sent the most valuable part of my property to—

FRANKTON. Hah! There goes Miss Airy, I believe:—pray excuse me, Charles; perhaps she has observed me. You have eased my mind of its doubts, and your resolution has made your friend happy.—Adieu.   [*Exit in haste.*

LOVEYET [*manet*].

A plague take your hurry, I say:—In the very moment of my telling him about sending the money to his house, he must conceit he saw Miss Airy;—but he has not received it yet, or he would have told me.—I hope Humphry has made no mistake;—I must see about it immediately. [*Exit*.

SCENE IV. *The Street before* MARIA'S *House.*

Enter HUMPHRY *and* NEGRO *with a trunk.*

HUMPHRY. This here is the house, I warrant you;—these crooked figures is enough for to puzzle a lawyer.—He said number two hundred and twenty-one:—two two's and a one stands for that, and there it is. [*Knocks,—Servant comes out.*] Does one Mr. Frankton live here, pray?

SERVANT. No;—he is here pretty often though, and I expect he will live here altogether, by and by.

HUMPHRY. Aye, I suppose he's only a lodger;—yes, this must be the place.

SERVANT. 'Tis not the place you want, I believe.—Mr. Airy lives here.

HUMPHRY. Mr. Airy! Aye, aye, now I've got it.—Here, Mr. What-d'ye-call'um, will you please to tell Miss Mary, somebody wants for to speak to her. [*Exit* SERVANT.] Now I've found out the mistake;—since I told him how the old man was a going for to marry him to Miss Mary, he thought he must obey the old fellow, for fear he shou'dn't let him have any of his money, and she's got a swinging fortune, they say; so he sent the trunk to her.— But what shou'd he tell me to take it to Mr. Frankton's for?— Why I suppose he thought I should find him here, for the man says he's here very often:—and then the number on the door; why, that settles the matter at once,—there can't be two numbers alike, in the same street, sartainly:—Yes, he's made one of his old blunders.

SERVANT *returns.*

SERVANT. Please to walk in, sir.

HUMPHRY. Aye, aye;—here, master Cuffy, this way.

[*They go in*.

SCENE V. *A Room in* MARIA'S *House.*

MARIA *and* OLD LOVEYET *discovered sitting.*

LOVEYET. It certainly is a mistake, madam; I have sent nothing out of my house to-day.

MARIA. He said it was from Mr. Loveyet, sir.—I confess I could not conceive what could induce you to send me a trunk of money.

LOVEYET. Who brought it, madam?

MARIA. A clownish kind of person, sir,—a countryman, I believe.

LOVEYET. Ah, now I begin to suspect something.—What a sad rascal!—want to cheat his father! But this lucky mistake will spoil his project.   [*Aside.*

MARIA. You are striving to unravel the mystery, sir.—I am afraid the man has made some serious mistake.

LOVEYET. No matter,—it could not have come to a more suitable place; for, now it is here, it shall be yours, if you will consent to a proposal I have to make to you; for I have discovered it to be my property, after all.

MARIA. If I can with propriety consent to anything you may propose, I will, sir;—but I hope you do not think either your or your son's *money* will tempt me.

LOVEYET. No, madam,—that is to say, I dare say it will not tempt you to do anything that is wrong;—but money is a tempting thing too,—though not quite so tempting as Miss Maria.— Hem, hem.—There was a delicate compliment for her! [*Aside.*

MARIA. Mercy on me! What can the ugly old mortal mean! It cannot be possible he would have the vanity to propose his odious self.   [*Aside.*

LOVEYET. You must know, madam, my son has lately arrived from the West-Indies—

MARIA. Really?—You rejoice me, sir.—Happy, happy Harriet!

LOVEYET. Not so happy as you imagine, madam; for she is not to have my son, I assure you; I intend a lady of greater beauty and merit for him, who is not very far from me now,— provided she and her father have no objection.—There I put it home to her [*Aside.*]. Ugh, ugh.

MARIA. I fear there is something in this rumour about Harriet.
                                             [*Aside.*

LOVEYET. Come, shall it be so, eigh?—Well, silence gives consent.—I know you can't have any particular objection. I must have you for a—Ugh, ugh, uh.

MARIA. I must humour this joke a little. [*Aside.*] —The honour you wish to confer on me, is so great, Mr. Loveyet, that I want words to express a suitable acknowledgment;—but what will the world say, when a gentleman of Mr. Loveyet's sedateness and experience stoops to a giddy girl like me?

LOVEYET. By my body, she thinks I want to have her myself. —Why, what a lucky young dog I am! I wish old Trueman was here now;—'ods my heart, and my life, and my—ugh, ugh,—but I must talk the matter over coolly with her. Hem, hem. [*Aside.*] —Oh, you dear little charming, angelic creature;—I love you so much, I cou'd find in my heart to—'Zounds! I cou'd eat you up. —By my body, but you must give me a sweet kiss. [*Offers to kiss her.*] 'Sblood! I can't bear it any longer. [*Snatches a kiss.*]— Ugh, ugh.

MARIA. What a preposterous old dotard! [*Aside.*] —You will excuse me, Mr. Loveyet; I have company waiting for me.

LOVEYET. By all means, my blossom;—it goes to my very heart to part with you, though;—but go to your company, my love, go, go.—I wou'dn't disoblige you, nor put the least thing in your way, for the seraglio—of the Grand Seignior. You may give up the trunk to my son now, if he calls for it, my love. [*Exit* MARIA.] Oh, what a dear creature! Such sweet lips,—such panting, precious, plump, little—oh, I cou'd jump out of my skin at the thoughts of it!—By my body, I must have her, and poor Charles may have Harriet, for all.—A fig for both the Constitutions now, I say; I wou'dn't give my dear little Maria for a score of them. [*Exit.*

SCENE VI. *A Street.*

Enter YOUNG LOVEYET.

I wish I could find that fellow;—I cannot think he has been treacherous;—but it is very strange, neither he nor my man have returned yet:—I am tired of seeking Frankton too;—since he made free to call at Harriet's for me, I think I will go to Miss Airy's for him: they say she lives near by. [*Enter* HUMPHRY.]— Well, sir, what have you done with the trunk?

HUMPHRY. Why, what you told me, to be sure. I've been a making your man Cuffy drunk, with some of the money you give me; but he's 'most sober now.

LOVEYET. Did you see Mr. Frankton?

HUMPHRY. No; but I carried the trunk to his lodgings though: I was just a going to Mr. Airy's, to see if I cou'dn't find you there.

LOVEYET. Mr. Airy's?

HUMPHRY. Aye,—where Mr. Frankton lodges; number two hundred and twenty-one;—there it is before your eyes.

LOVEYET. That is number one hundred and twenty-two;— you did not carry it there, I hope.

HUMPHRY. Yes I did.—Why isn't that the place?

LOVEYET. Confound your dull brains!—Did you not enquire who liv'd there?

HUMPHRY. Yes, Mr. Airy lives there.

LOVEYET. What a strange circumstance!—You are sure Mr. Airy lives there.

HUMPHRY. Sure and sartin;—why I see the young lady you're a going to be married to, and I give her the trunk; for I think the sarvint said how Mr. Frankton lodg'd there.—I hope there's no harm done.

LOVEYET. I hope so too;—I must step in, and see; but this is the last time I shall send you with a message.   [Goes in.

HUMPHRY. Like enough, for I'm a going home in the country to-morrow.   [Exit.

SCENE VII. TRUEMAN'S *House.*

Enter TRUEMAN [*reading a letter*].

This is very unaccountable;—Richard Worthnought, eigh:— I wish, Mr. Worthnought, you had been at my school a while, before you scrawl'd this wretched epistle:—but the subject is still more unintelligible.

Enter WORTHNOUGHT.

WORTHNOUGHT. Mr. Trueman, I am yours.

TRUEMAN. I deny it.—Heaven forbid, such a thing as you should be either mine or my daughter's!

WORTHNOUGHT. I should not gain much credit by the alliance, I believe.—You have received my letter, sir, I presume.

TRUEMAN. I think you *presume*—rather more than becomes you, sir.

WORTHNOUGHT. I find, the foolish old Put don't like me. [*Aside.*] —I am sorry you do not approve of my offer; but, but— a—rat me, but I must have her, for all that. Ha, ha, ha;—'foregad, I must, old gentleman.

Enter OLD LOVEYET.

LOVEYET. But I say you shall not have her, sir;—there, I suppose you will have the impudence to call *me old* gentleman next.

WORTHNOUGHT. Demme, sir; what have *you* to do with his daughter?

LOVEYET. Nothing; but my son has something to do with her: ha'n't he, friend Horace?

TRUEMAN. Heyday! what does all this mean?—Has any State rejected the new Constitution?

WORTHNOUGHT. Come, let's have no palitics, for gad's sake;— rat the canstitution;—I wou'dn't give *une Fille de joye*, for all the musty canstitutions in christendom.

TRUEMAN. By the dignity of my profession, you never read Publius then; or you would have liked *one* constitution.

WORTHNOUGHT. Publius! ha, ha, ha.—I read Publius! Not I, sir, I assure you:—an *outré* fellow,—a dull, mysterious, mechanical writer, as ever I refused to read, split me.

LOVEYET. So he is, so he is, sir: by my body, I am glad to find *somebody* of my mind.

[TRUEMAN *and* LOVEYET *retire to the back of the stage.*

Enter FRANKTON *and* HUMPHRY.

FRANKTON. You saw him go into Miss Airy's house, this morning, you say.

HUMPHRY. Yes.   [*Walks thoughtlessly about the stage.*

FRANKTON. I think, this is a tolerable confirmation of the matter.   [*Aside.*

WORTHNOUGHT. Hah,—Frankton;—'foregad, I am yours, superlatively.

FRANKTON. Are you, positively? Hah,—she is here. [*Enter* MARIA, *on the opposite side.*] Your humble servant, Miss Airy.

MARIA. [*Pretends to take no notice of* FRANKTON.] Mr. Trueman, I hope I have the pleasure to see you well.

TRUEMAN. I thank you, madam. [*Resumes his discourse with*
LOVEYET, *who does not yet observe* MARIA.]

MARIA. I hoped to have found Miss Harriet here, sir.

TRUEMAN. Madam?— [*Turns to* LOVEYET *again.*

LOVEYET. Therefore, sir, as I was telling you, I am determined
to have her. [*To* TRUEMAN.

TRUEMAN. [*Leaving* LOVEYET.] How is this, madam?—Mr.
Loveyet tells me, he is determined to have you.

FRANKTON. Who! How!—Have who, sir?
[*Loud and earnestly.*

LOVEYET. [*Seeing* MARIA.] By my body, there she is herself.
—Have who, sir?—Why, have this lady, sir; who do you think?
—My sweet Miss Airy, I have the transcendent pleasure to kiss
your hand, ugh, ugh.

MARIA. Oh, fie, Mr. Loveyet.—I will have the pleasure to
tease Frankton, now. [*Retires with* OLD LOVEYET, *whispering,
and looking tenderly at him.*]

FRANKTON. Amazement!—The *old* fellow! [*Aside.*

WORTHNOUGHT. This is all very· astanishing, 'foregad:—
demme, but she deserves to die an old maid, if she has *him*.
[*Aside.*

MARIA. [*Pretends to observe* FRANKTON, *for the first time.*]—Mr.
Frankton!—I did not observe you before: I give you joy of your
friend's arrival, sir;—I suppose you have seen him;—he is very
agreeable.

FRANKTON. Then I need not ask you, if you have seen him,
madam.

MARIA. He was at my house not two hours ago.

FRANKTON. Did not you see him before that, madam?

MARIA. I did not, sir.

FRANKTON. Detested falsehood! [*Aside.*

MARIA. The old gentleman acquainted me of his arrival, only
a few minutes before.

LOVEYET. Eigh, how,—old gentleman!—she did not mean
me, I hope. [*Aside.*

FRANKTON. And you think Mr. Loveyet is so agreeable then.

LOVEYET. Aye, that's me;—by my body, he is jealous of me.
Ha, ha; poor young fool! [*Aside.*

FRANKTON. He thinks very highly of *you*, I assure you,
madam; he speaks of you with admiration.

MARIA. And what of that, sir?—You speak as if you thought him my *only* admirer. [*Affectedly.*

FRANKTON. Disgusting vanity! [*Aside.*] —No, madam,—the number of your admirers is at least equal to that of your acquaintance;—but there is only one, who sincerely *loves*, as well as admires you.

LOVEYET. Come, come, sir; none of your airs, sir:—*love* her indeed;—why—why, she don't love *you*.

[*Ogling and winking at her, &c.*

WORTHNOUGHT. Ha, ha, gudgeons all, demme;—old square toes is cursedly bit; I see that. [*Aside.*

MARIA. Mr. Loveyet, I return'd the trunk to your son.

HUMPHRY. His son.—Ha, ha.

LOVEYET. Yes, yes, he told me so just now:—the poor dog was ready to jump out of his skin, when I told him he should have Harriet.

Enter CANTWELL *and* HERALD.

WORTHNOUGHT. Oh, the devil!—Now shall I be blown up, like a barrel of gun-powder. [*Aside.*

CANTWELL. Servant, gentlemen and ladies.—How is your daughter, Mr. Trueman? I hope she is likely to do well.

TRUEMAN. I hope she is, madam; it is a match which we all approve.

CANTWELL. No, no, sir; I mean concerning her late affair.

HERALD. Why, young Loveyet certainly would not stoop so low, as to have her now.

TRUEMAN. 'Zounds! Why not, pray?

LOVEYET. What, in the name of ill luck, can they mean!— I hope, I—oh, there they come.

Enter HARRIET *and* CHARLES LOVEYET.

CANTWELL. Oh, dear, here they are;—why she don't look as if that was the case. [*To* HERALD.

TRUEMAN. I desire, ladies, to know what you mean, by these mysterious whispers.

CANTWELL. La! sir; you only want to put a body to the blush; but if you want an explanation, that gentleman [*Pointing to* WORTHNOUGHT.] can give it to you.

CHARLES. The villain! [*Aside.*] —I fancy *I* could explain it as well.

WORTHNOUGHT. Hem, hem,—now comes on my trial. [*Aside.*

CHARLES. But first,—your blessing, sir. [*Kneels to his father.*

HARRIET. And yours, sir. [*Kneels to* TRUEMAN.

LOVEYET. What,—married already!

CHARLES. This ten minutes, sir. [*Rising.*

CANTWELL
AND } Married!
HERALD

WORTHNOUGHT. Then my ill-star'd fortune is decided. [*Aside.*

TRUEMAN. Upon my erudition, you have been too precipitate, Harriet; but I have no reason to think, you will repent it; you, therefore, have my sincerest benediction. [*Raising her.*

MARIA. I give you joy, my dear. [*To* HARRIET.

FRANKTON. Now all my fears have vanished.

[*Aside, and goes to* YOUNG LOVEYET.

LOVEYET. By my body, you have made quick work of it, Charles.

CHARLES. For fear of the worst, I have. [*Aside.*

LOVEYET. But—but are you in favour of the new Constitution yet?

CHARLES. At present I can think of no Constitution but that of Love and Matrimony, sir.

LOVEYET. And I shall be sorry if your matrimonial Constitution does not prove the better one of the two.—Eigh, Maria?

WORTHNOUGHT. Dick Worthnought, esquire, thou art an ass and a liar; and, what is worse than both,—as poor as poverty. Oh, Fortune, thou blind disposer of human events, when wilt thou make a man of me? [*Going angrily.*

CHARLES. Stay a little, if you please, sir.—My happiness is too great at present, to let me take that revenge, which the baseness of your conduct deserves: but justice bids me accuse you of having wickedly, and without cause, endeavoured to injure the reputation of this lady, whom it is my highest boast and felicity now to call my wife; my making her such, however, at the very time when the baneful tongue of Slander is so diligent to damn her spotless fame,—[*Looking significantly at* CANTWELL *and* HERALD.]—will at once convince the public of her innocence, and the cruelty of her enemies. With her, you have also injured her connexions; but I, for my own part, am fully satisfied with those symptoms of shame and repentance, which you now evince.

TRUEMAN. Upon my education, I did not think him susceptible of either.—A few minutes ago, I received this audacious epistle from him.

"Sir, I have the honour to—acquaint you—that I have an inclination—to marry your daughter,—notwithstanding—the late scandalous—reports that are transpiring to her disadvantage, and (what is still worse) the—comparative meanness—of her fortune to mine."—The comparative meanness of her fortune to mine.

HARRIET,
MARIA,
LOVEYET, } Ha, ha, ha.
CHARLES,
FRANKTON,

WORTHNOUGHT. Never was put so much to my trumps, 'foregad.   [*Exit.*

HERALD. Unmannerly wretches!   [*Scornfully, and exit.*

CANTWELL. Oh, the wickedness of this wicked world!
     [*Exit after her.*

LOVEYET. Why, this is just as it should be now;—I think business goes on finely.

MARIA. You will not think so, much longer.   [*Aside.*

LOVEYET. By my body, I am as merry as a cricket;—an't you, Maria? For my part, I feel so well pleased, I could find in my heart to—to do as you have done;—[*To* CHARLES.] cou'dn't you, my love?   [*To* MARIA.

MARIA. Yes, sir.

LOVEYET. Oh, you dear little rogue! With whom, eigh, with whom?—Don't be bashful,—tell them.—I know she means me.
     [*Aside.*

MARIA. I beg to be excused from telling that, sir; but I will tell you who it is I would *not* have.

LOVEYET. Aye, that's him.—[*Aside, looking at* FRANKTON.] —Well, who is it you won't have, Maria, who is it?

MARIA. You, sir.   [*Emphatically.*

LOVEYET. Me, eigh?—me—me, Maria?

CHARLES. Preposterous infatuation!

LOVEYET. D——'d, wanton, treacherous jilt!
     [*Walks about discomposed.*

MARIA. You have jilted yourself, sir;—nothing but excess of dotage and self-conceit could have let you impose on yourself in such a manner.

FRANKTON. And may I then hope—

MARIA. Hope?—Oh, yes, sir;—you have my permission to *hope* for anything you please.

CHARLES. And you, madam, the disposition to gratify his hopes, I fancy.

LOVEYET. I fancy you lie, sir; and you sha'n't have Harriet, for your impertinence.

CHARLES. Excuse me, father;—it is not in your power to prevent that;—the happy deed is already executed.

LOVEYET. 'Zounds! that's true!—and, what is still worse, the other deed is executed too.—Fire and fury! All is lost, for the sake of that inveigling, perfidious young Syren. Ugh, ugh, ugh.

TRUEMAN. [*Burlesquing what* LOVEYET *has said in a former scene.*] " 'Sdeath, sir! I tell you I am but two and forty years old: she sha'n't be more than thirty odd, sir; and she shall be ten years younger than I am too.—A man of five and forty, old, forsooth!" Ha, ha, ha.

LOVEYET. Perdition! Is this what I have come to at last?—Despis'd,—betray'd,—laugh'd at,—supplanted by a puppy,—[*Pointing to* FRANKTON]—trick'd out of my money by a graceless, aristocratic son,—I—I'll—I'll go hang myself.

[*Exit in a passion.*

HUMPHRY. This is, for all the world, like the show I see t'other night, at the Play-house.

CHARLES. His agitation of mind distresses me: my happiness is not complete, while it is enjoyed at the expense of a father's:—painful reflection!—We will go immediately, Harriet, and endeavour to pacify him.

> *His conduct shall instruct the hoary Sage,*
> *That youth and beauty were not meant for age;*
> *His rage, resentment, av'rice, dotage, pride,*
> *(Sad view of human nature's frailest side!)*
> *Shall mend us all;—but chiefly I shall prove,*
> *That all his Politics, can never match my* LOVE.

The End.

THE CONTRAST

By

ROYALL TYLER

Royall Tyler

ROYALL TYLER
(1757–1826)

William Dunlap is considered the father of the American Theatre, and anyone who reads his history of the American Theatre will see how firmly founded are his claims to this title. But the first American play to be written by a native, and to gain the distinction of anything like a "run" is "The Contrast," [1] by Royall Tyler. Unfortunately for us, the three hundred page manuscript of Tyler's "Life," which is in possession of one of his descendants, has never been published. Were that document available, it would throw much valuable light on the social history of New England. For Tyler was deep-dyed in New England traditions, and, strange to say, his playwriting began as a reaction against a Puritanical attitude toward the theatre.

When Tyler came to New York on a very momentous occasion, as an official in the suppression of Shays's Rebellion, he had little thought of ever putting his pen to paper as a playwright, although he was noted from earliest days as a man of literary ambition, his tongue being sharp in its wit, and his disposition being brilliant in the parlour. It was while in what was even then considered to be the very gay and wicked city of New York, that Royall Tyler went to the theatre for the first time, and, on that auspicious occasion, witnessed Sheridan's "The School for Scandal." We can imagine what the brilliancy of that moment must have been to the parched New England soul of our first American dramatist.

Two days afterwards, inspiration began to burn, and he dashed off, in a period of a few weeks, the comedy called "The Contrast," not so great a "contrast," however, that the literary student would fail to recognize "The School for Scandal" as its chief inspiration.

[1] The/Contrast,/a/Comedy;/In Five Acts:/Written By a/Citizen of the United States;/Performed with Applause at the Theatres in New-York,/Philadelphia, and Maryland;/and published (under an Assignment of the Copy-Right) by/Thomas Wignell./*Primus ego in patriam/Aonio—deduxi vertice Musas.*/Virgil./(Imitated.)/First on our shores I try Thalia's powers,/And bid the *laughing, useful* Maid be ours./Philadelphia:/From the Press of Prichard & Hall, in Market Street:/Between Second and Front Streets./M. DCC. XC. [See Frontispiece.]

Our young dramatist, whose original name, William Clark Tyler, was changed, by act of Court, to Royall, was born in Boston on July 18, 1757, near the historic ground of Faneuil Hall. His father was one of the King's Councillors, and figured in the Stamp Act controversy. From him, young Tyler inherited much of his ability. The family was wealthy and influential. Naturally, the father being a graduate of Harvard, his son likewise went to that institution. His early boyhood, when he was at the grammar school, was passed amidst the tumult of the Stamp Act, and the quartering of troops in Boston. When he entered Harvard as a freshman, on July 15, 1772, three days before he was fifteen years old, he was thoroughly accustomed to the strenuous atmosphere of the coming Revolution.

There were many students in his class, who afterwards won distinction as chief justices, governors and United States senators, but at that time none of them were so sedate as to ignore the usual pranks of the college boy. Tyler's temperament is well exhibited by the fact that he was one of the foremost instigators in a fishing party from his room window, when the students hooked the wig of the reverend president from his head one morning as that potentate was going to chapel.

Tyler graduated with a B.A. degree from Harvard in July, 1776, the Valedictorian of his class; and was similarly honoured with a B.A. by Yale (1776). Three years after, he received an M.A. from Harvard and, in later life (1811), from the University of Vermont. He read law for three years with the Hon. Francis Dana, of Cambridge, and the Hon. Benjamin Hichbourne, of Boston, during that time being a member of a club which used to meet at the rooms of Colonel John Trumbull, well known to all students as a soldier and painter. Unfortunate for us that the life-size canvas of Royall Tyler, painted by Trumbull, was destroyed by fire. We are assured by Trumbull, in his "Reminiscences," that during those long evenings, they "regaled themselves with a cup of tea instead of wine, and discussed subjects of literature, politics and war." In 1778, Tyler found himself by the side of Trumbull, fighting against the British and serving a short while under General Sullivan.

In 1779, he was admitted to the bar, and there followed a long succession of activities, in which he moved from place to place, finally associating himself definitely with the early history of Vermont, and Brattleboro in particular.

There is much interesting data in existence relating to Royall Tyler's literary activities, as a writer of witty articles, sprightly verse and autobiographical experiences—in a style which, while lacking in distinction, is none the less a measure of the sprightliness of the author's disposition. It is not my purpose to enter into a discussion of anything but Royall Tyler as the author of "The Contrast." He wrote several other plays besides,[1] one dealing with the wild-cat land speculation in Georgia. But the play under discussion is fully representative of his dramatic ability, an ability which would scarcely be worthy of too much commendation were it not for the fact that Tyler may be regarded as the creator of the Yankee type in American drama.

In 1787, Shays's Rebellion brought Tyler once more under the command of Major-General Benjamin Lincoln, with whom he had served in the Revolutionary War. As an aide, he was required to go into the State of New York, and arrange for the pursuit and capture of Shays. It was, as I have said, while on this mission in New York City that he went to the theatre for the first time. He witnessed Sheridan's "The School for Scandal," and in the audience on the occasion there very probably sat George Washington. The latter was a constant frequenter of the little John Street Theatre, where Wignell was the chief comedian. Apart from *Jonathan's* description of this "Colonial" Playhouse, as it looked after the Revolution, we have Seilhamer's impression (i, 212), as follows:

" . . . the theatre in John Street . . . for a quarter of a century was to New York what the Southwark Theatre was to Philadelphia. Both houses were alike in appearance, but the New York Theatre stood back about sixty feet from the street, with a covered way of rough wooden materials from the sidewalk to the doors. It was principally of wood and was painted red. It had two rows of boxes, and a pit and gallery, the capacity of the house when full being about eight hundred dollars. The stage was sufficiently large for all the requirements of that theatrical era, and the dressing-rooms and green room were in a shed adjacent to the theatre."

This was, it seems, the first time Tyler had ever left New England. His manuscript was finished in three weeks, and

[1] For example, "The Duelists," a Farce in three acts; "The Georgia Spec; or, Land in the Moon" (1797); "The Doctor in Spite of Himself," an imitation of Molière; and "Baritaria; or, The Governor of a Day," being adventures of Sancho Panza. He also wrote a libretto, "May-day in Town; or, New York in an Uproar." (See Sonneck: "Early Opera in America.")

shortly after handed over to the American Company for production. So loath was he to have his name connected with it, that, when he gave the manuscript to Wignell, he consigned also to that actor the copyright, with the instruction that, when the play was published, on the title-page, the piece should be credited to the authorship of "a citizen of the United States." Of all the productions which came from his pen, the very prosaic and doubtfully authoritative Vermont Law Reports is the only publication bearing his name on the title-page.

"The Contrast" was produced on April 16, 1787, at the John Street Theatre, in New York, by the American Company, the original cast including Mr. Henry and Mr. Hallam as the rival lovers, and Mr. Wignell in the part of *Jonathan*, the first stage Yankee. Anyone who has read the play will quite understand why it is that the honours so easily fell to Mr. Wignell rather than to Mr. Henry or to Mr. Hallam, and it is no surprise, therefore, to find, after the initial performance, that jealousy began to manifest itself between these three gentlemen,—so much so, indeed, that, when the time arrived for the Company to go to Philadelphia, in December, 1787, Mr. Wignell was unable to present "The Contrast" in the theatre, and had to content himself with a reading, because it was "impracticable at this time to entertain the public with a dramatic representation." The Notice continued: Mr. Wignell, "in compliance with the wishes of many respectable citizens of Philadelphia, proposes to read that celebrated performance at the City Tavern on Monday evening, the 10th inst. The curiosity which has everywhere been expressed respecting this first dramatic production of American genius, and the pleasure which it has already afforded in the theatres of New York and Maryland, persuade Mr. Wignell that his excuses on this occasion will be acceptable to the public and that even in so imperfect a dress, the intrinsic merit of the comedy will contribute to the amusement and command the approbation of the audience." Of Wignell and his associates, an excellent impression may be had from a first hand description by W. B. Wood, in his "Personal Recollections."

Whether the intrinsic merits of the play would contribute to the amusement of audiences to-day is to be doubted, although it is a striking dramatic curio. The play in the reading is scarcely exciting. It is surprisingly devoid of situation. Its chief characteristic is "talk," but that talk, reflective in its spirit of "The

School for Scandal," is interesting to the social student. When the ladies discuss the manners of the times and the fashions of the day, they discuss them in terms of the Battery, in New York, but in the spirit of London. The only native product, as I have said, is *Jonathan,* and his surprise over the play-house, into which he is inveigled, measures the surprise which must have overwhelmed the staid New England conscience of Royall Tyler, when he found himself actually in that den of iniquity,—the theatre. For the first time in the American Drama, we get New England dialogue and some attempt at American characterization. Wignell, being himself a character actor of much ability, and the son of a player who had been a member of Garrick's Company in London, it is small wonder that he should have painted the stage Yankee in an agreeable and entertaining and novel manner.

But, undoubtedly, the only interest that could attach itself to this comedy for the theatre-going audience of to-day would be in its presentment according to the customs and manners of the time. In fact, one would be very much entertained were it possible to make *Letitia* and *Charlotte* discuss their social schemes and ambitions in a parlour which reflected the atmosphere of New York in 1787. As a matter of fact, however, the audience that crowded into the little John Street Theatre, on the opening night of "The Contrast," was treated to an interior room, which was more closely akin to a London drawing-room than to a parlour in Manhattan. According to the very badly drawn frontispiece, which Wignell used in the printed edition of the play, and which William Dunlap executed, we see a very poor imitation of the customs, costumes, and situations which Tyler intended to suggest.

Indeed, we wonder whether Dunlap, when he drew this picture, did not have a little malice in his heart; for there is no doubt that he showed jealousy over the success of "The Contrast," when, after a three years' stay in London, under the tutelage of Benjamin West, he returned to America to find "The Contrast" the talk of the town. Both he and Seilhamer who, however prejudiced they may be in some of their judgments and in some of their dates, are nevertheless the authorities for the early history of the American Theatre, try their best to take away from the credit due Tyler as an American dramatist. They both contend that "The Contrast," though it was repeated several times in succession—and this repetition of a native drama before audiences more accustomed to the English product must have been a sign of its acceptance,—was scarcely what they would consider a success. As evidence, Seilhamer claims that, just as soon as Royall Tyler handed over the copyright of his play to Wignell, the latter advertised the printed edition whenever the subscribers' list was sufficiently large to warrant the publication. It was not, however, until several years after this advertisement, that the play was actually published, the subscribers being headed by the name of President George Washington, and including many of Washington's first cabinet, four signers of the Declaration of Independence, and several Revolutionary soldiers. According to Seilhamer, the American dramatists of those days were very eager to follow the work of their contemporary craftsmen, and, in the list of subscribers, we find the names of Dunlap, Peter Markoe, who wrote "The Patriot Chief" (1783), Samuel Low, author of "The Politician Out-witted" (1789), and Colonel David Humphreys, who translated from the French "The Widow of Malabar; or, The Tyranny of Custom" (1790).

We are told by some authorities that Royall Tyler was on friendly terms with the actors of this period, a fact accentuated all the more because his brother, Col. John S. Tyler, had become manager of the Boston Theatre. In many ways he was a great innovator, if, on one hand, he broke through the New England prejudices against the theatre, and if, on the other hand, during his long career as lawyer and as judge of the Supreme Court of Vermont, he broke through the traditional manner of conducting trials, as is evidenced by many human, amusing anecdotes, illustrative of his wit and quick repartee. He was married to Mary Palmer, in 1794, and brought up a family of eleven children, a number of whom won distinction in the ministry, but none of whom followed their father's taste for playwriting. He mingled with the most intellectual society of the time, being on intimate terms with the Adams family, the Quincys and Cranchs, and identifying himself very closely with the literary history of the country.

In a record of New England periodicals, his name will figure constantly as contributing editor. We have letters of his, descriptive of his home life in Brattleboro, Vermont, filled with a kindly benevolence and with a keen sense of humour. It was there that he died on August 16, 1826. But, all told, we fear that even though Royall Tyler has the distinction of being one of the first American dramatists, he came into the theatre purely by accident. "The Contrast" is not, strictly speaking, a very dramatic representation.

When, in June, 1912, Brattleboro celebrated its local history with a pageant, a production of "The Contrast" was rehearsed and given in a little hall, fitted up to represent the old John Street Theatre. A scene from the play was given at an American Drama Matinée, produced by the American Drama Committee of the Drama League of America, New York Centre, on January 22 and 23, 1917,—the conversation between *Jonathan* and *Jenny*. In Philadelphia, under the auspices of the Drama League Centre, and in coöperation with the University of Pennsylvania, the play, in its entirety, was presented on January 18, 1917, by the "Plays and Players" organization. A revival was also given in Boston, produced in the old manner, "and the first rows of seats were reserved for those of the audience who appeared in the costume of the time."

The play in its first edition is rare, but, in 1887, it was reprinted by the Dunlap Society. The general reader is given an opportunity of judging how far *Jonathan* is the typical Yankee, and how far Royall Tyler cut the pattern which later was followed by other playwrights in a long series of American dramas, in which the Yankee was the chief attraction.[1]

[1] The song which occurs in the play under the title, "Alknomook," had great popularity in the eighteenth century. Its authorship was attributed to Philip Freneau, in whose collected poems it does not appear. It is also credited to a Mrs. Hunter, and is contained in her volume of verse, published in 1806. It appears likewise in a Dublin play of 1740, "New Spain; or, Love in Mexico." See also, the *American Museum*, vol. 1, page 77. The singing of "Yankee Doodle" is likewise to be noted (See Sonneck's interesting essay on the origin of "Yankee Doodle," General Bibliography), not the first time it appears in early American Drama, as readers of Barton's "Disappointment" (1767) will recognize.

AS A JUST ACKNOWLEDGMENT OF THE LIBERAL EXERTIONS
BY WHICH THE *STAGE* HAS BEEN RESCUED FROM
AN IGNOMINIOUS PROSCRIPTION,

THE CONTRAST,

(BEING THE FIRST ESSAY OF *AMERICAN* GENIUS IN THE
DRAMATIC ART)

IS MOST RESPECTFULLY DEDICATED

TO

THE PRESIDENT AND MEMBERS OF THE

Dramatic Affociation,

BY

THEIR MOST OBLIGED

AND

MOST GRATEFUL SERVANT,

THOMAS WIGNELL.

PHILADELPHIA,
1 January, 1790.

DEDICATION PAGE IN THE FIRST EDITION OF "THE CONTRAST"

ADVERTISEMENT

The Subscribers (to whom the Editor thankfully professes his obligations) may reasonably expect an apology for the delay which has attended the appearance of "The Contrast;" but, as the true cause cannot be declared without leading to a discussion, which the Editor wishes to avoid, he hopes that the care and expence which have been bestowed upon this work will be accepted, without further scrutiny, as an atonement for his seeming negligence.

In justice to the Author, however, it may be proper to observe that this Comedy has many claims to the public indulgence, independent of its intrinsic merits: It is the first essay of American genius in a difficult species of composition; it was written by one who never critically studied the rules of the drama, and, indeed, had seen but few of the exhibitions of the stage; it was undertaken and finished in the course of three weeks; and the profits of one night's performance were appropriated to the benefit of the sufferers by the fire at *Boston.*

These considerations will, therefore, it is hoped, supply in the closet the advantages that are derived from representation, and dispose the reader to join in the applause which has been bestowed on this Comedy by numerous and judicious audiences, in the Theatres of *Philadelphia, New-York,* and *Maryland.*

PROLOGUE

Written by a young gentleman of New-York, and spoken by Mr. Wignell.

Exult, each patriot heart!—this night is shewn
A piece, which we may fairly call our own;
Where the proud titles of "My Lord! Your Grace!"
To humble *Mr.* and plain *Sir* give place.
Our Author pictures not from foreign climes
The fashions or the follies of the times;
But has confin'd the subject of his work
To the gay scenes—the circles of New-York.
On native themes his Muse displays her pow'rs;
If ours the faults, the virtues too are ours.
Why should our thoughts to distant countries roam,
When each refinement may be found at home?
Who travels now to ape the rich or great,
To deck an equipage and roll in state;
To court the graces, or to dance with ease,
Or by hypocrisy to strive to please?
Our free-born ancestors such arts despis'd;
Genuine sincerity alone they priz'd;
Their minds, with honest emulation fir'd,
To solid good—not ornament—aspir'd;
Or, if ambition rous'd a bolder flame,
Stern virtue throve, where indolence was shame.

But modern youths, with imitative sense,
Deem taste in dress the proof of excellence;
And spurn the meanness of your homespun arts,
Since homespun habits would obscure their parts;
Whilst all, which aims at splendour and parade,
Must come from Europe, *and be ready made.*
Strange! we should thus our native worth disclaim,
And check the progress of our rising fame.
Yet *one*, whilst imitation bears the sway,
Aspires to nobler heights, and points the way.

Be rous'd, my friends! his bold example view;
Let your own Bards be proud to copy *you!*
Should rigid critics reprobate our play,
At least the patriotic heart will say,
"Glorious our fall, since in a noble cause.
"The bold *attempt alone* demands applause."
Still may the wisdom of the Comic Muse
Exalt your merits, or your faults accuse.
But think not, 'tis her aim to be severe;—
We all are mortals, and as mortals err.
If candour pleases, we are truly blest;
Vice trembles, when compell'd to stand confess'd.
Let not light Censure on your faults offend,
Which aims not to expose them, but amend.
Thus does our Author to your candour trust;
Conscious, the *free* are generous, as just.

CHARACTERS

	New-York.	*Maryland.*
COL. MANLY,	Mr. Henry.	Mr. Hallam.
DIMPLE,	Mr. Hallam.	Mr. Harper.
VAN ROUGH,	Mr. Morris.	Mr. Morris.
JESSAMY,	Mr. Harper.	Mr. Biddle.
JONATHAN,	Mr. Wignell.	Mr. Wignell.
CHARLOTTE,	Mrs. Morris.	Mrs. Morris.
MARIA,	Mrs. Harper.	Mrs. Harper.
LETITIA,	Mrs. Kenna.	Mrs. Williamson.
JENNY,	Miss Tuke.	Miss W. Tuke.

SERVANTS.

SCENE, New-York.

N.B. The lines marked with inverted commas, "thus", are omitted in the representation.

THE CONTRAST

ACT I.

Scene I. *An Apartment at* Charlotte's.

Charlotte *and* Letitia *discovered.*

Letitia. And so, Charlotte, you really think the pocket-hoop unbecoming.

Charlotte. No, I don't say so: It may be very becoming to saunter round the house of a rainy day; to visit my grand-mamma, or to go to Quakers' meeting: but to swim in a minuet, with the eyes of fifty well-dressed beaux upon me, to trip it in the Mall, or walk on the Battery, give me the luxurious, jaunty, flowing bell-hoop. It would have delighted you to have seen me the last evening, my charming girl! I was dangling o'er the battery with Billy Dimple; a knot of young fellows were upon the platform; as I passed them I faltered with one of the most bewitching false steps you ever saw, and then recovered myself with such a pretty confusion, flirting my hoop to discover a jet black shoe and brilliant buckle. Gad! how my little heart thrilled to hear the confused raptures of—"*Demme, Jack, what a delicate foot!*" "*Ha! General, what a well-turned*—"

Letitia. Fie! fie! Charlotte [*Stopping her mouth.*]. I protest you are quite a libertine.

Charlotte. Why, my dear little prude, are we not all such libertines? Do you think, when I sat tortured two hours under the hands of my friseur, and an hour more at my toilet, that I had any thoughts of my aunt Susan, or my cousin Betsey? though they are both allowed to be critical judges of dress.

Letitia. Why, who should we dress to please, but those who are judges of its merits?

Charlotte. Why, a creature who does not know *Buffon* from *Souflè*—Man!—my Letitia—Man! for whom we dress, walk, dance, talk, lisp, languish, and smile. Does not the grave Spectator assure us that even our much bepraised diffidence, modesty, and blushes are all directed to make ourselves good wives and mothers as fast as we can? Why, I'll undertake with one flirt of this hoop to bring more beaux to my feet in one week than the grave Maria, and her sentimental circle, can do, by sighing sentiment till their hairs are grey.

LETITIA. Well, I won't argue with you; you always out-talk me; let us change the subject. I hear that Mr. Dimple and Maria are soon to be married.

CHARLOTTE. You hear true. I was consulted in the choice of the wedding clothes. She is to be married in a delicate white satin, and has a monstrous pretty brocaded lutestring for the second day. It would have done you good to have seen with what an affected indifference the dear sentimentalist [turned over a thousand pretty things, just as if her heart did not palpitate with her approaching happiness, and at last made her choice and] [1] arranged her dress with such apathy as if she did not know that plain white satin and a simple blond lace would shew her clear skin and dark hair to the greatest advantage.

LETITIA. But they say her indifference to dress, and even to the gentleman himself, is not entirely affected.

CHARLOTTE. How?

LETITIA. It is whispered that if Maria gives her hand to Mr. Dimple, it will be without her heart.

CHARLOTTE. Though the giving the heart is one of the last of all laughable considerations in the marriage of a girl of spirit, yet I should like to hear what antiquated notions the dear little piece of old-fashioned prudery has got in her head.

LETITIA. Why, you know that old Mr. John-Richard-Robert-Jacob-Isaac-Abraham-Cornelius Van Dumpling, Billy Dimple's father (for he has thought fit to soften his name, as well as manners, during his English tour) was the most intimate friend of Maria's father. The old folks, about a year before Mr. Van Dumpling's death, proposed this match: the young folks were accordingly introduced, and told they must love one another. Billy was then a good-natured, decent-dressing young fellow, with a little dash of the coxcomb, such as our young fellows of fortune usually have. At this time, I really believe she thought she loved him; and had they then been married, I doubt not they might have jogged on, to the end of the chapter, a good kind of a sing-song, lack-a-daysaical life, as other honest married folks do.

---

[1] The omitted passages in the First Edition, indicated by inverted commas, are here enclosed in heavy brackets.

CHARLOTTE. Why did they not then marry?

LETITIA. Upon the death of his father, Billy went to England to see the world and rub off a little of the patroon rust. During his absence, Maria, like a good girl, to keep herself constant to her *nown true-love*, avoided company, and betook herself, for her amusement, to her books, and her dear Billy's letters. But, alas! how many ways has the mischievous demon of inconstancy of stealing into a woman's heart! Her love was destroyed by the very means she took to support it.

CHARLOTTE. How?—Oh! I have it—some likely young beau found the way to her study.

LETITIA. Be patient, Charlotte; your head so runs upon beaux. Why, she read *Sir Charles Grandison, Clarissa Harlow, Shenstone,* and the *Sentimental Journey;* and between whiles, as I said, Billy's letters. But, as her taste improved, her love declined. The contrast was so striking betwixt the good sense of her books and the flimsiness of her love-letters, that she discovered she had unthinkingly engaged her hand without her heart; and then the whole transaction, managed by the old folks, now appeared so unsentimental, and looked so like bargaining for a bale of goods, that she found she ought to have rejected, according to every rule of romance, even the man of her choice, if imposed upon her in that manner. Clary Harlow would have scorned such a match.

CHARLOTTE. Well, how was it on Mr. Dimple's return? Did he meet a more favourable reception than his letters?

LETITIA. Much the same. She spoke of him with respect abroad, and with contempt in her closet. She watched his conduct and conversation, and found that he had by travelling acquired the wickedness of Lovelace without his wit, and the politeness of Sir Charles Grandison without his generosity. The ruddy youth, who washed his face at the cistern every morning, and swore and looked eternal love and constancy, was now metamorphosed into a flippant, palid, polite beau, who devotes the morning to his toilet, reads a few pages of Chesterfield's letters, and then minces out, to put the infamous principles in practice upon every woman he meets.

CHARLOTTE. But, if she is so apt at conjuring up these sentimental bugbears, why does she not discard him at once?

LETITIA. Why, she thinks her word too sacred to be trifled with. Besides, her father, who has a great respect for the memory of his deceased friend, is ever telling her how he shall renew his years in their union, and repeating the dying injunctions of old Van Dumpling.

CHARLOTTE. A mighty pretty story! And so you would make me believe that the sensible Maria would give up Dumpling Manor, and the all-accomplished Dimple as a husband, for the absurd, ridiculous reason, forsooth, because she despises and abhors him. Just as if a lady could not be privileged to spend a man's fortune, ride in his carriage, be called after his name, and call him her *nown dear lovee* when she wants money, without loving and respecting the great he-creature. Oh! my dear girl, you are a monstrous prude.

LETITIA. I don't say what I would do; I only intimate how I suppose she wishes to act.

CHARLOTTE. No, no, no! A fig for sentiment. If she breaks, or wishes to break, with Mr. Dimple, depend upon it, she has some other man in her eye. A woman rarely discards one lover until she is sure of another. Letitia little thinks what a clue I have to Dimple's conduct. The generous man submits to render himself disgusting to Maria, in order that she may leave him at liberty to address me. I must change the subject.

[*Aside, and rings a bell.*

Enter SERVANT.

Frank, order the horses to.——Talking of marriage, did you hear that Sally Bloomsbury is going to be married next week to Mr. Indigo, the rich Carolinian?

LETITIA. Sally Bloomsbury married!—why, she is not yet in her teens.

CHARLOTTE. I do not know how that is, but you may depend upon it, 'tis a done affair. I have it from the best authority. There is my aunt Wyerly's Hannah (you know Hannah; though a black, she is a wench that was never caught in a lie in her life); now, Hannah has a brother who courts Sarah, Mrs. Catgut the milliner's girl, and she told Hannah's brother, and Hannah, who, as I said before, is a girl of undoubted veracity, told it directly to me, that Mrs. Catgut was making a new cap for Miss Bloomsbury, which, as it was very dressy, it is very probable is designed for a wedding cap. Now, as she is to be married, who can it be to, but to Mr. Indigo? Why, there is no other gentleman that visits at her papa's.

LETITIA. Say not a word more, Charlotte. Your intelligence is so direct and well grounded, it is almost a pity that it is not a piece of scandal.

CHARLOTTE. Oh! I am the pink of prudence. Though I cannot charge myself with ever having discredited a tea-party by my silence, yet I take care never to report any thing of my acquaintance, especially if it is to their credit,—*discredit*, I mean, —until I have searched to the bottom of it. It is true, there is infinite pleasure in this charitable pursuit. Oh! how delicious to go and condole with the friends of some backsliding sister, or to retire with some old dowager or maiden aunt of the family, who love scandal so well that they cannot forbear gratifying their appetite at the expence of the reputation of their nearest relations! And then to return full fraught with a rich collection of circumstances, to retail to the next circle of our acquaintance under the strongest injunctions of secrecy,—ha, ha, ha!—interlarding the melancholy tale with so many doleful shakes of the head, and more doleful "Ah! who would have thought it! so amiable, so prudent a young lady, as we all thought her, what a monstrous pity! well, I have nothing to charge myself with; I acted the part of a friend, I warned her of the principles of that rake, I told her what would be the consequence; I told her so, I told her so."— Ha, ha, ha!

LETITIA. Ha, ha, ha! Well, but, Charlotte, you don't tell me what you think of Miss Bloomsbury's match.

CHARLOTTE. Think! why I think it is probable she cried for a plaything, and they have given her a husband. Well, well, well, the puling chit shall not be deprived of her plaything: 'tis only exchanging London dolls for American babies.—Apropos, of babies, have you heard what Mrs. Affable's high-flying notions of delicacy have come to?

LETITIA. Who, she that was Miss Lovely?

CHARLOTTE. The same; she married Bob Affable of Schenectady. Don't you remember?

Enter SERVANT.

SERVANT. Madam, the carriage is ready.

LETITIA. Shall we go to the stores first, or visiting?

CHARLOTTE. I should think it rather too early to visit, especially Mrs. Prim; you know she is so particular.

LETITIA. Well, but what of Mrs. Affable?

CHARLOTTE. Oh, I'll tell you as we go; come, come, let us hasten. I hear Mrs. Catgut has some of the prettiest caps arrived you ever saw. I shall die if I have not the first sight of them. [*Exeunt.*

SCENE II. *A Room in* VAN ROUGH'S *House.*

MARIA [*sitting disconsolate at a table, with books, &c.*].

SONG.[1]

I.

The sun sets in night, and the stars shun the day;
But glory remains when their lights fade away!
Begin, ye tormentors! your threats are in vain,
For the son of Alknomook shall never complain.

II.

Remember the arrows he shot from his bow;
Remember your chiefs by his hatchet laid low:
Why so slow?—do you wait till I shrink from the pain?
No—the son of Alknomook will never complain.

III.

Remember the wood where in ambush we lay;
And the scalps which we bore from your nation away:
Now the flame rises fast, you exult in my pain;
But the son of Alknomook can never complain.

IV.

I go to the land where my father is gone;
His ghost shall rejoice in the fame of his son:
Death comes like a friend, he relieves me from pain;
And thy son, O Alknomook! has scorn'd to complain.

There is something in this song which ever calls forth my affections. The manly virtue of courage, that fortitude which steels the heart against the keenest misfortunes, which interweaves the laurel of glory amidst the instruments of torture and death, displays something so noble, so exalted, that in despite of the prejudices of education, I cannot but admire it, even in a

[1] A page reproduction of the original music is given in the Dunlap reprint of this play.

savage. The prepossession which our sex is supposed to entertain for the character of a soldier is, I know, a standing piece of
raillery among the wits. A cockade, a lapell'd coat, and a feather,
they will tell you, are irresistible by a female heart. Let it be
so. Who is it that considers the helpless situation of our sex,
that does not see that we each moment stand in need of a protector, and that a brave one too? [Formed of the more delicate
materials of nature, endowed only with the softer passions,
incapable, from our ignorance of the world, to guard against the
wiles of mankind, our security for happiness often depends upon
their generosity and courage:—Alas! how little of the former do
we find!] How inconsistent! that man should be leagued to
destroy that honour upon which solely rests his respect and
esteem. Ten thousand temptations allure us, ten thousand passions betray us; yet the smallest deviation from the path of
rectitude is followed by the contempt and insult of man, and
the more remorseless pity of woman; years of penitence and
tears cannot wash away the stain, nor a life of virtue obliterate
its remembrance. [Reputation is the life of woman; yet courage
to protect it is masculine and disgusting; and the only safe
asylum a woman of delicacy can find is in the arms of a man of
honour. How naturally, then, should we love the brave and the
generous; how gratefully should we bless the arm raised for our
protection, when nerv'd by virtue and directed by honour!]
Heaven grant that the man with whom I may be connected—
may be connected!—Whither has my imagination transported
me—whither does it now lead me? Am I not indissolubly engaged, [by every obligation of honour which my own consent
and my father's approbation can give,] to a man who can never
share my affections, and whom a few days hence it will be
criminal for me to disapprove—to disapprove! would to heaven
that were all—to despise. For, can the most frivolous manners,
actuated by the most depraved heart, meet, or merit, anything
but contempt from every woman of delicacy and sentiment?

[VAN ROUGH *without*: Mary!]

Ha! my father's voice—Sir!—

Enter VAN ROUGH.

VAN ROUGH. What, Mary, always singing doleful ditties, and
moping over these plaguy books.

MARIA. I hope, sir, that it is not criminal to improve my mind with books; or to divert my melancholy with singing, at my leisure hours.

VAN ROUGH. Why, I don't know that, child; I don't know that. They us'd to say, when I was a young man, that if a woman knew how to make a pudding, and to keep herself out of fire and water, she knew enough for a wife. Now, what good have these books done you? have they not made you melancholy? as you call it. Pray, what right has a girl of your age to be in the dumps? hav'n't you every thing your heart can wish; an't you going to be married to a young man of great fortune; an't you going to have the quit-rent of twenty miles square?

MARIA. One hundredth part of the land, and a lease for life of the heart of a man I could love, would satisfy me.

VAN ROUGH. Pho, pho, pho! child; nonsense, downright nonsense, child. This comes of your reading your story-books; your Charles Grandisons, your Sentimental Journals, and your Robinson Crusoes, and such other trumpery. No, no, no! child, it is money makes the mare go; keep your eye upon the main chance, Mary.

MARIA. Marriage, sir, is, indeed, a very serious affair.

VAN ROUGH. You are right, child; you are right. I am sure I found it so, to my cost.

MARIA. I mean, sir, that as marriage is a portion for life, and so intimately involves our happiness, we cannot be too considerate in the choice of our companion.

VAN ROUGH. Right, child; very right. A young woman should be very sober when she is making her choice, but when she has once made it, as you have done, I don't see why she should not be as merry as a grig; I am sure she has reason enough to be so. Solomon says that "there is a time to laugh, and a time to weep." Now, a time for a young woman to laugh is when she has made sure of a good rich husband. Now, a time to cry, according to you, Mary, is when she is making choice of him; but *I* should think that a young woman's time to cry was when she despaired of *getting* one. Why, there was your mother, now: to be sure, when I popp'd the question to her she did look a little silly; but when she had once looked down on her apron-strings, as all modest young women us'd to do, and drawled out ye-s, she was as brisk and as merry as a bee.

MARIA. My honoured mother, sir, had no motive to melancholy; she married the man of her choice.

VAN ROUGH. The man of her choice! And pray, Mary, an't you going to marry the man of your choice—what trumpery notion is this? It is these vile books [*Throwing them away.*]. I'd have you to know, Mary, if you won't make young Van Dumpling the man of *your* choice, you shall marry him as the man of *my* choice.

MARIA. You terrify me, sir. Indeed, sir, I am all submission. My will is yours.

VAN ROUGH. Why, that is the way your mother us'd to talk. "My will is yours, my dear Mr. Van Rough, my will is yours;" but she took special care to have her own way, though, for all that.

MARIA. Do not reflect upon my mother's memory, sir—

VAN ROUGH. Why not, Mary, why not? She kept me from speaking my mind all her *life*, and do you think she shall henpeck me now she is *dead* too? Come, come; don't go to sniveling; be a good girl, and mind the main chance. I'll see you well settled in the world.

MARIA. I do not doubt your love, sir, and it is my duty to obey you. I will endeavour to make my duty and inclination go hand in hand.

VAN ROUGH. Well, well, Mary; do you be a good girl, mind the main chance, and never mind inclination. Why, do you know that I have been down in the cellar this very morning to examine a pipe of Madeira which I purchased the week you were born, and mean to tap on your wedding day?—That pipe cost me fifty pounds sterling. It was well worth sixty pounds; but I over-reach'd Ben Bulkhead, the supercargo: I'll tell you the whole story. You must know that—

Enter SERVANT.

SERVANT. Sir, Mr. Transfer, the broker, is below. [*Exit.*

VAN ROUGH. Well, Mary, I must go. Remember, and be a good girl, and mind the main chance. [*Exit.*

MARIA [*alone*].

How deplorable is my situation! How distressing for a daughter to find her heart militating with her filial duty! I know my father loves me tenderly; why then do I reluctantly obey him?

[Heaven knows! with what reluctance I should oppose the will of a parent, or set an example of filial disobedience;] at a parent's command, I could wed awkwardness and deformity. [Were the heart of my husband good, I would so magnify his good qualities with the eye of conjugal affection, that the defects of his person and manners should be lost in the emanation of his virtues.] At a father's command, I could embrace poverty. Were the poor man my husband, I would learn resignation to my lot; I would enliven our frugal meal with good humour, and chase away misfortune from our cottage with a smile. At a father's command, I could almost submit to what every female heart knows to be the most mortifying, to marry a weak man, and blush at my husband's folly in every company I visited. But to marry a depraved wretch, whose only virtue is a polished exterior; [who is actuated by the unmanly ambition of conquering the defenceless; whose heart, insensible to the emotions of patriotism, dilates at the plaudits of every unthinking girl;] whose laurels are the sighs and tears of the miserable victims of his specious behaviour—Can he, who has no regard for the peace and happiness of other families, ever have a due regard for the peace and happiness of his own? Would to heaven that my father were not so hasty in his temper! Surely, if I were to state my reasons for declining this match, he would not compel me to marry a man,—whom, though my lips may solemnly promise to honour, I find my heart must ever despise. [*Exit.*

End of the First Act.

ACT II.

SCENE I.

Enter CHARLOTTE *and* LETITIA.

CHARLOTTE [*at entering*].

Betty, take those things out of the carriage and carry them to my chamber; see that you don't tumble them. My dear, I protest, I think it was the homeliest of the whole. I declare I was almost tempted to return and change it.

LETITIA. Why would you take it?

CHARLOTTE. [Didn't Mrs. Catgut say it was the most fashionable?

LETITIA. But, my dear, it will never fit becomingly on you.

CHARLOTTE. I know that; but did not you hear Mrs. Catgut say it was fashionable?

LETITIA. Did you see that sweet airy cap with the white sprig?

CHARLOTTE. Yes, and I longed to take it; but,] my dear, what could I do? Did not Mrs. Catgut say it was the most fashionable; and if I had not taken it, was not that awkward, gawky Sally Slender ready to purchase it immediately?

LETITIA. [Did you observe how she tumbled over the things at the next shop, and then went off without purchasing any thing, nor even thanking the poor man for his trouble? But, of all the awkward creatures, did you see Miss Blouze endeavouring to thrust her unmerciful arm into those small kid gloves?

CHARLOTTE. Ha, ha, ha, ha!]

LETITIA. Then did you take notice with what an affected warmth of friendship she and Miss Wasp met? when all their acquaintance know how much pleasure they take in abusing each other in every company.

CHARLOTTE. Lud! Letitia, is that so extraordinary? Why, my dear, I hope you are not going to turn sentimentalist. Scandal, you know, is but amusing ourselves with the faults, foibles, follies, and reputations of our friends; indeed, I don't know why we should have friends, if we are not at liberty to make use of them. But no person is so ignorant of the world as to suppose, because I amuse myself with a lady's faults, that I am obliged to quarrel with her person every time we meet: believe me, my dear, we should have very few acquaintances at that rate.

SERVANT *enters and delivers a letter to* CHARLOTTE, *and*—[*Exit.*

CHARLOTTE. You'll excuse me, my dear.

[*Opens and reads to herself.*

LETITIA. Oh, quite excusable.

CHARLOTTE. As I hope to be married, my brother Henry is in the city.

LETITIA. What, your brother, Colonel Manly?

CHARLOTTE. Yes, my dear; the only brother I have in the world.

LETITIA. Was he never in this city?

CHARLOTTE. Never nearer than Harlem Heights, where he lay with his regiment.

LETITIA. What sort of a being is this brother of yours? If he is as chatty, as pretty, as sprightly as you, half the belles in the city will be pulling caps for him.

CHARLOTTE. My brother is the very counterpart and reverse of me: I am gay, he is grave; I am airy, he is solid; I am ever selecting the most pleasing objects for my laughter, he has a tear for every pitiful one. And thus, whilst he is plucking the briars and thorns from the path of the unfortunate, I am strewing my own path with roses.

LETITIA. My sweet friend, not quite so poetical, and a little more particular.

CHARLOTTE. Hands off, Letitia. I feel the rage of simile upon me; I can't talk to you in any other way. My brother has a heart replete with the noblest sentiments, but then, it is like—it is like—Oh! you provoking girl, you have deranged all my ideas—it is like—Oh! I have it—his heart is like an old maiden lady's band-box; it contains many costly things, arranged with the most scrupulous nicety, yet the misfortune is that they are too delicate, costly, and antiquated for common use.

LETITIA. By what I can pick out of your flowery description, your brother is no beau.

CHARLOTTE. No, indeed; he makes no pretension to the character. He'd ride, or rather fly, an hundred miles to relieve a distressed object, or to do a gallant act in the service of his country; but, should you drop your fan or bouquet in his presence, it is ten to one that some beau at the farther end of the room would have the honour of presenting it to you before he had observed that it fell. I'll tell you one of his antiquated, anti-gallant notions. He said once in my presence, in a room full of company, —would you believe it?—in a large circle of ladies, that the best evidence a gentleman could give a young lady of his respect and affection was to endeavour in a friendly manner to rectify her foibles. I protest I was crimson to the eyes, upon reflecting that I was known as his sister.

LETITIA. Insupportable creature! tell a lady of her faults! If he is so grave, I fear I have no chance of captivating him.

CHARLOTTE. [His conversation is like a rich, old-fashioned brocade,—it will stand alone; every sentence is a sentiment. Now you may judge what a time I had with him, in my twelve months' visit to my father. He read me such lectures, out of pure brotherly affection, against the extremes of fashion, dress, flirting, and coquetry, and all the other dear things which he knows I dote upon, that I protest his conversation made me as melancholy as if I had been at church; and, heaven knows, though I never prayed to go there but on one occasion, yet I would have exchanged his conversation for a psalm and a sermon. Church is rather melancholy, to be sure; but then I can ogle the beaux, and be regaled with "here endeth the first lesson," but his brotherly *here*, you would think had no end.] You captivate him! Why, my dear, he would as soon fall in love with a box of Italian flowers. There is Maria, now, if she were not engaged, she might do something. Oh! how I should like to see that pair of pensorosos together, looking as grave as two sailors' wives of a stormy night, with a flow of sentiment meandering through their conversation like purling streams in modern poetry.

LETITIA. Oh! my dear fanciful—

CHARLOTTE. Hush! I hear some person coming through the entry.

Enter SERVANT.

SERVANT. Madam, there's a gentleman below who calls himself Colonel Manly; do you choose to be at home?

CHARLOTTE. Shew him in. [*Exit* SERVANT.] Now for a sober face.

Enter COLONEL MANLY.

MANLY. My dear Charlotte, I am happy that I once more enfold you within the arms of fraternal affection. I know you are going to ask (amiable impatience!) how our parents do,—the venerable pair transmit you their blessing by me—they totter on the verge of a well-spent life, and wish only to see their children settled in the world, to depart in peace.

CHARLOTTE. I am very happy to hear that they are well. [*Coolly.*] Brother, will you give me leave to introduce you to our uncle's ward, one of my most intimate friends?

MANLY [*Saluting* LETITIA.]. I ought to regard your friends as my own.

CHARLOTTE. Come, Letitia, do give us a little dash of your vivacity; my brother is so sentimental and so grave, that I protest he'll give us the vapours.

MANLY. Though sentiment and gravity, I know, are banished the polite world, yet I hoped they might find some countenance in the meeting of such near connections as brother and sister.

CHARLOTTE. Positively, brother, if you go one step further in this strain, you will set me crying, and that, you know, would spoil my eyes; and then I should never get the husband which our good papa and mamma have so kindly wished me—never be established in the world.

MANLY. Forgive me, my sister,—I am no enemy to mirth; I love your sprightliness; and I hope it will one day enliven the hours of some worthy man; but when I mention the respectable authors of my existence,—the cherishers and protectors of my helpless infancy, whose hearts glow with such fondness and attachment that they would willingly lay down their lives for my welfare,—you will excuse me if I am so unfashionable as to speak of them with some degree of respect and reverence.

CHARLOTTE. Well, well, brother; if you won't be gay, we'll not differ; I will be as grave as you wish. [Affects gravity.] And so, brother, you have come to the city to exchange some of your commutation notes for a little pleasure.

MANLY. Indeed you are mistaken; my errand is not of amusement, but business; and as I neither drink nor game, my expences will be so trivial, I shall have no occasion to sell my notes.

CHARLOTTE. Then you won't haye occasion to do a very good thing. Why, here was the Vermont General—he came down some time since, sold all his musty notes at one stroke, and then laid the cash out in trinkets for his dear Fanny. I want a dozen pretty things myself; have you got the notes with you?

MANLY. I shall be ever willing to contribute, as far as it is in my power, to adorn or in any way to please my sister; yet I hope I shall never be obliged for this to sell my notes. I may be romantic, but I preserve them as a sacred deposit. Their full amount is justly due to me, but as embarrassments, the natural consequences of a long war, disable my country from supporting its credit, I shall wait with patience until it is rich enough to discharge them. If that is not in my day, they shall be transmitted as an honourable certificate to posterity, that I have humbly imitated our illustrious WASHINGTON, in having exposed my health and life in the service of my country, without reaping any other reward than the glory of conquering in so arduous a contest.

CHARLOTTE. Well said heroics. Why, my dear Henry, you have such a lofty way of saying things, that I protest I almost tremble at the thought of introducing you to the polite circles in the city. The belles would think you were a player run mad, with your head filled with old scraps of tragedy; and, as to the beaux, they might admire, because they would not understand you. But, however, I must, I believe, venture to introduce you to two or three ladies of my acquaintance.

LETITIA. And that will make him acquainted with thirty or forty beaux.

CHARLOTTE. Oh! brother, you don't know what a fund of happiness you have in store.

MANLY. I fear, sister, I have not refinement sufficient to enjoy it.

CHARLOTTE. Oh! you cannot fail being pleased.

LETITIA. Our ladies are so delicate and dressy.

CHARLOTTE. And our beaux so dressy and delicate.

LETITIA. Our ladies chat and flirt so agreeably.

CHARLOTTE. And our beaux simper and bow so gracefully.

LETITIA. With their hair so trim and neat.

CHARLOTTE. And their faces so soft and sleek.

LETITIA. Their buckles so tonish and bright.

CHARLOTTE. And their hands so slender and white.

LETITIA. I vow, Charlotte, we are quite poetical.

CHARLOTTE. And then, brother, the faces of the beaux are of such a lily-white hue! None of that horrid robustness of constitution, that vulgar corn-fed glow of health, which can only serve to alarm an unmarried lady with apprehensions, and prove a melancholy memento to a married one, that she can never hope for the happiness of being a widow. I will say this to the credit of our city beaux, that such is the delicacy of their complexion, dress, and address, that, even had I no reliance upon the honour of the dear Adonises, I would trust myself in any possible situation with them, without the least apprehensions of rudeness.

MANLY. Sister Charlotte!

CHARLOTTE. Now, now, now, brother [*Interrupting him.*], now don't go to spoil my mirth with a dash of your gravity, I am so glad to see you, I am in tiptop spirits. Oh! that you could be with us at a little snug party. There is Billy Simper, Jack Chaffé, and Colonel Van Titter, Miss Promonade, and the two Miss Tambours, sometimes make a party, with some other ladies, in a side-box, at the play. Everything is conducted with such decorum,—first we bow round to the company in general, then to each one in particular, then we have so many inquiries after each other's health, and we are so happy to meet each other, and it is so many ages since we last had that pleasure, [and if a married lady is in company, we have such a sweet dissertation upon her son Bobby's chin-cough;] then the curtain rises, then our sensibility is all awake, and then, by the mere force of apprehension, we torture some harmless expression into a double meaning, which the poor author never dreamt of, and then we have recourse to our fans, and then we blush, and then the gentlemen jog one another, peep under the fan, and make the prettiest remarks; and then we giggle and they simper, and they giggle and we simper, and then the curtain drops, and then for nuts and oranges, and then we bow, and it's Pray, ma'am, take it, and Pray, sir, keep it, and, Oh! not for the world, sir; and then the curtain rises again, and then we blush and giggle and simper and bow all over again. Oh! the sentimental charms of a side-box conversation! [*All laugh.*]

MANLY. Well, sister, I join heartily with you in the laugh; for, in my opinion, it is as justifiable to laugh at folly as it is reprehensible to ridicule misfortune.

CHARLOTTE. Well, but, brother, positively I can't introduce you in these clothes: why, your coat looks as if it were calculated for the vulgar purpose of keeping yourself comfortable.

MANLY. This coat was my regimental coat in the late war. The public tumults of our state have induced me to buckle on the sword in support of that government which I once fought to establish. I can only say, sister, that there was a time when this coat was respectable, and some people even thought that those men who had endured so many winter campaigns in the service of their country, without bread, clothing, or pay, at least deserved that the poverty of their appearance should not be ridiculed.

CHARLOTTE. We agree in opinion entirely, brother, though it would not have done for me to have said it: it is the coat makes the man respectable. In the time of the war, when we were almost frightened to death, why, your coat was respectable, that is, fashionable; now another kind of coat is fashionable, that is, respectable. And, pray, direct the tailor to make yours the height of the fashion.

MANLY. Though it is of little consequence to me of what shape my coat is, yet, as to the height of the fashion, there you will please to excuse me, sister. You know my sentiments on that subject. I have often lamented the advantage which the French have over us in that particular. In Paris, the fashions have their dawnings, their routine, and declensions, and depend as much upon the caprice of the day as in other countries; but there every lady assumes a right to deviate from the general *ton* as far as will be of advantage to her own appearance. In America, the cry is, What is the fashion? and we follow it indiscriminately, because it is so.

CHARLOTTE. Therefore it is, that when large hoops are in fashion, we often see many a plump girl lost in the immensity of a hoop-petticoat, whose want of height and *en-bon-point* would never have been remarked in any other dress. When the high head-dress is the mode, how then do we see a lofty cushion, with a profusion of gauze, feathers, and ribband, supported by a face no bigger than an apple; whilst a broad, full-faced lady, who really would have appeared tolerably handsome in a large head-dress, looks with her smart chapeau as masculine as a soldier.

MANLY. But remember, my dear sister, and I wish all my fair countrywomen would recollect, that the only excuse a young lady can have for going extravagantly into a fashion is because it makes her look extravagantly handsome.—Ladies, I must wish you a good morning.

CHARLOTTE. But, brother, you are going to make home with us.

MANLY. Indeed I cannot. I have seen my uncle and explained that matter.

CHARLOTTE. Come and dine with us, then. We have a family dinner about half-past four o'clock.

MANLY. I am engaged to dine with the Spanish ambassador. I was introduced to him by an old brother officer; and instead of freezing me with a cold card of compliment to dine with him ten days hence, he, with the true old Castilian frankness, in a friendly manner, asked me to dine with him to-day—an honour I could not refuse. Sister, adieu—madam, your most obedient—

[*Exit.*

CHARLOTTE. I will wait upon you to the door, brother; I have something particular to say to you.   [*Exit.*

LETITIA [*alone*]. What a pair!—She the pink of flirtation, he the essence of everything that is *outré* and gloomy.—I think I have completely deceived Charlotte by my manner of speaking of Mr. Dimple; she's too much the friend of Maria to be confided in. He is certainly rendering himself disagreeable to Maria, in order to break with her and proffer his hand to me. This is what the delicate fellow hinted in our last conversation. [*Exit.*

SCENE II. *The Mall.*

Enter JESSAMY.

Positively this Mall is a very pretty place. I hope the cits won't ruin it by repairs. To be sure, it won't do to speak of in the same day with Ranelagh or Vauxhall; however, it's a fine place for a young fellow to display his person to advantage. Indeed, nothing is lost here; the girls have taste, and I am very happy to find they have adopted the elegant London fashion of looking back, after a genteel fellow like me has passed them. —Ah! who comes here? This, by his awkwardness, must be the Yankee colonel's servant. I'll accost him.

Enter JONATHAN.

JESSAMY. *Votre très-humble serviteur, Monsieur.* I understand Colonel Manly, the Yankee officer, has the honour of your services.

JONATHAN. Sir!—

JESSAMY. I say, sir, I understand that Colonel Manly has the honour of having you for a servant.

JONATHAN. Servant! Sir, do you take me for a neger,—I am Colonel Manly's waiter.

JESSAMY. A true Yankee distinction, egad, without a difference. Why, sir, do you not perform all the offices of a servant? do you not even blacken his boots?

JONATHAN. Yes; I do grease them a bit sometimes; but I am a true blue son of liberty, for all that. Father said I should come as Colonel Manly's waiter, to see the world, and all that; but no man shall master me: my father has as good a farm as the Colonel.

JESSAMY. Well, sir, we will not quarrel about terms upon the eve of an acquaintance from which I promise myself so much satisfaction;—therefore, *sans cérémonie*—

JONATHAN. What?—

JESSAMY. I say I am extremely happy to see Colonel Manly's waiter.

JONATHAN. Well, and I vow, too, I am pretty considerably glad to see you; but what the dogs need of all this outlandish lingo? Who may you be, sir, if I may be so bold?

JESSAMY. I have the honour to be Mr. Dimple's servant, or, if you please, waiter. We lodge under the same roof, and should be glad of the honour of your acquaintance.

JONATHAN. You a waiter! by the living jingo, you look so topping, I took you for one of the agents to Congress.

JESSAMY. The brute has discernment, notwithstanding his appearance.—Give me leave to say I wonder then at your familiarity.

JONATHAN. Why, as to the matter of that, Mr.——; pray, what's your name?

JESSAMY. Jessamy, at your service.

JONATHAN. Why, I swear we don't make any great matter of distinction in our state between quality and other folks.

JESSAMY. This is, indeed, a levelling principle.—I hope, Mr. Jonathan, you have not taken part with the insurgents.

JONATHAN. Why, since General Shays has sneaked off and given us the bag to hold, I don't care to give my opinion; but you'll promise not to tell—put your ear this way—you won't tell?—I vow I did think the sturgeons were right.

JESSAMY. I thought, Mr. Jonathan, you Massachusetts-men always argued with a gun in your hand. Why didn't you join them?

JONATHAN. Why, the Colonel is one of those folks called the Shin—Shin—dang it all, I can't speak them *lignum vitæ* words— you know who I mean—there is a company of them—they wear a China goose at their button-hole—a kind of gilt thing.—Now the Colonel told father and brother,—you must know there are, let me see—there is Elnathan, Silas, and Barnabas, Tabitha— no, no, she's a she—tarnation, now I have it—there's Elnathan, Silas, Barnabas, Jonathan, that's I—seven of us, six went into the wars, and I stayed at home to take care of mother. Colonel said that it was a burning shame for the true blue Bunker-Hill sons of liberty, who had fought Governor Hutchinson, Lord North, and the Devil, to have any hand in kicking up a cursed dust against a government which we had, every mother's son of us, a hand in making.

JESSAMY. Bravo!—Well, have you been abroad in the city since your arrival? What have you seen that is curious and entertaining?

JONATHAN. Oh! I have seen a power of fine sights. I went to see two marble-stone men and a leaden horse that stands out in doors in all weathers; and when I came where they was, one had got no head, and t' other wer'n't there. They said as how the leaden man was a damn'd tory, and that he took wit in his anger and rode off in the time of the troubles.

JESSAMY. But this was not the end of your excursion.

JONATHAN. Oh, no; I went to a place they call Holy Ground. Now I counted this was a place where folks go to meeting; so I put my hymn-book in my pocket, and walked softly and grave as a minister; and when I came there, the dogs a bit of a meeting-house could I see. At last I spied a young gentlewoman standing by one of the seats which they have here at the doors. I took her to be the deacon's daughter, and she looked so kind, and so obliging, that I thought I would go and ask her the way to lecture, and—would you think it?—she called me dear, and sweeting, and honey, just as if we were married: by the living jingo, I had a month's mind to buss her.

JESSAMY. Well, but how did it end?

JONATHAN. Why, as I was standing talking with her, a parcel of sailor men and boys got round me, the snarl-headed curs fell a-kicking and cursing of me at such a tarnal rate, that I vow I was glad to take to my heels and split home, right off, tail on end, like a stream of chalk.

JESSAMY. Why, my dear friend, you are not acquainted with the city; that girl you saw was a—[Whispers.]

JONATHAN. Mercy on my soul! was that young woman a harlot!—Well! if this is New-York Holy Ground, what must the Holy-day Ground be!

JESSAMY. Well, you should not judge of the city too rashly. We have a number of elegant fine girls here that make a man's leisure hours pass very agreeably. I would esteem it an honour to announce you to some of them.—Gad! that announce is a select word; I wonder where I picked it up.

JONATHAN. I don't want to know them.

JESSAMY. Come, come, my dear friend, I see that I must assume the honour of being the director of your amusements. Nature has given us passions, and youth and opportunity stimulate to gratify them. It is no shame, my dear Blueskin, for a man to amuse himself with a little gallantry.

JONATHAN. Girl huntry! I don't altogether understand. I never played at that game. I know how to play hunt the squirrel, but I can't play anything with the girls; I am as good as married.

JESSAMY. Vulgar, horrid brute! Married, and above a hundred miles from his wife, and think that an objection to his making love to every woman he meets! He never can have read, no, he never can have been in a room with a volume of the divine Chesterfield.—So you are married?

JONATHAN. No, I don't say so; I said I was as good as married, a kind of promise.

JESSAMY. As good as married!—

JONATHAN. Why, yes; there's Tabitha Wymen, the deacon's daughter, at home; she and I have been courting a great while, and folks say as how we are to be married; and so I broke a piece of money with her when we parted, and she promised not to spark it with Solomon Dyer while I am gone. You wou'dn't have me false to my true-love, would you?

JESSAMY. Maybe you have another reason for constancy; possibly the young lady has a fortune? Ha! Mr. Jonathan, the solid charms: the chains of love are never so binding as when the links are made of gold.

JONATHAN. Why, as to fortune, I must needs say her father is pretty dumb rich; he went representative for our town last year. He will give her—let me see—four times seven is—seven times four—nought and carry one,—he will give her twenty acres of land—somewhat rocky though—a Bible, and a cow.

JESSAMY. Twenty acres of rock, a Bible, and a cow! Why, my dear Mr. Jonathan, we have servant-maids, or, as you would more elegantly express it, waitresses, in this city, who collect more in one year from their mistresses' cast clothes.

JONATHAN. You don't say so!—

JESSAMY. Yes, and I'll introduce you to one of them. There is a little lump of flesh and delicacy that lives at next door, waitress to Miss Maria; we often see her on the stoop.

JONATHAN. But are you sure she would be courted by me?

JESSAMY. Never doubt it; remember a faint heart never— blisters on my tongue—I was going to be guilty of a vile proverb; flat against the authority of Chesterfield. I say there can be no doubt that the brilliancy of your merit will secure you a favourable reception.

JONATHAN. Well, but what must I say to her?

JESSAMY. Say to her! why, my dear friend, though I admire your profound knowledge on every other subject, yet, you will pardon my saying that your want of opportunity has made the female heart escape the poignancy of your penetration. Say to her! Why, when a man goes a-courting, and hopes for success, he must begin with doing, and not saying.

JONATHAN. Well, what must I do?

JESSAMY. Why, when you are introduced you must make five or six elegant bows.

JONATHAN. Six elegant bows! I understand that; six, you say? Well—

JESSAMY. Then you must press and kiss her hand; then press and kiss, and so on to her lips and cheeks; then talk as much as you can about hearts, darts, flames, nectar, and ambrosia— the more incoherent the better.

JONATHAN. Well, but suppose she should be angry with I?

JESSAMY. Why, if she should pretend—please to observe, Mr. Jonathan—if she should pretend to be offended, you must—But I'll tell you how my master acted in such a case: He was seated by a young lady of eighteen upon a sofa, plucking with a wanton hand the blooming sweets of youth and beauty. When the lady thought it necessary to check his ardour, she called up a frown upon her lovely face, so irresistibly alluring, that it would have warmed the frozen bosom of age; remember, said she, putting her delicate arm upon his, remember your character and my honour. My master instantly dropped upon his knees, with eyes swimming with love, cheeks glowing with desire, and in the gentlest modulation of voice he said: My dear Caroline, in a few months our hands will be indissolubly united at the altar; our hearts I feel are already so; the favours you now grant as evidence of your affection are favours indeed; yet, when the ceremony is once past, what will now be received with rapture will then be attributed to duty.

JONATHAN. Well, and what was the consequence?

JESSAMY. The consequence!—Ah! forgive me, my dear friend, but you New-England gentlemen have such a laudable curiosity of seeing the bottom of everything;—why, to be honest, I confess I saw the blooming cherub of a consequence smiling in its angelic mother's arms, about ten months afterwards.

JONATHAN. Well, if I follow all your plans, make them six bows, and all that, shall I have such little cherubim consequences?

JESSAMY. Undoubtedly.—What are you musing upon?

JONATHAN. You say you'll certainly make me acquainted?— Why, I was thinking then how I should contrive to pass this broken piece of silver—won't it buy a sugar-dram?

JESSAMY. What is that, the love-token from the deacon's daughter?—You come on bravely. But I must hasten to my master. Adieu, my dear friend.

JONATHAN. Stay, Mr. Jessamy—must I buss her when I am introduced to her?

JESSAMY. I told you, you must kiss her.

JONATHAN. Well, but must I buss her?

JESSAMY. Why kiss and buss, and buss and kiss, is all one.

JONATHAN. Oh! my dear friend, though you have a profound knowledge of all, a pugnency of tribulation, you don't know everything.   [*Exit.*

JESSAMY [*alone*].

Well, certainly I improve; my master could not have insinuated himself with more address into the heart of a man he despised. Now will this blundering dog sicken Jenny with his nauseous pawings, until she flies into my arms for very ease. How sweet will the contrast be between the blundering Jonathan and the courtly and accomplished Jessamy!

End of the Second Act.

ACT III.

SCENE I. DIMPLE'S *Room*.

DIMPLE [*discovered at a toilet, reading*].

"Women have in general but one object, which is their beauty." Very true, my lord; positively very true. "Nature has hardly formed a woman ugly enough to be insensible to flattery upon her person." Extremely just, my lord; every day's delightful experience confirms this. "If her face is so shocking that she must, in some degree, be conscious of it, her figure and air, she thinks, make ample amends for it." The sallow Miss Wan is a proof of this. Upon my telling the distasteful wretch, the other day, that her countenance spoke the pensive language of sentiment, and that Lady Wortley Montague declared that, if the ladies were arrayed in the garb of innocence, the face would be the last part which would be admired, as Monsieur Milton expresses it, she grin'd horribly a ghastly smile. "If her figure is deformed, she thinks her face counterbalances it."

Enter JESSAMY *with letters.*

DIMPLE. Where got you these, Jessamy?
JESSAMY. Sir, the English packet is arrived.

DIMPLE [*opens and reads a letter enclosing notes*].
"Sir,

"I have drawn bills on you in favour of Messrs. Van Cash and Co. as per margin. I have taken up your note to Col. Piquet, and discharged your debts to my Lord Lurcher and Sir Harry Rook. I herewith enclose you copies of the bills, which I have no doubt will be immediately honoured. On failure, I shall empower some lawyer in your country to recover the amounts.
"I am, sir,

"Your most humble servant,
"JOHN HAZARD."

Now, did not my lord expressly say that it was unbecoming a well-bred man to be in a passion, I confess I should be ruffled. [*Reads.*] "There is no accident so unfortunate, which a wise man may not turn to his advantage; nor any accident so fortunate, which a fool will not turn to his disadvantage." True, my lord; but how advantage can be derived from this I can't see. Chesterfield himself, who made, however, the worst practice of the most excellent precepts, was never in so embarrassing a situation. I love the person of Charlotte, and it is necessary I should command the fortune of Letitia. As to Maria!—I doubt not by my *sang-froid* behaviour I shall compel her to decline the match; but the blame must not fall upon me. A prudent man, as my lord says, should take all the credit of a good action to himself, and throw the discredit of a bad one upon others. I must break with Maria, marry Letitia, and as for Charlotte—why, Charlotte must be a companion to my wife. —Here, Jessamy!

Enter JESSAMY.

DIMPLE *folds and seals two letters.*

DIMPLE. Here, Jessamy, take this letter to my love. [*Gives one.*
JESSAMY. To which of your honour's loves?—Oh! [*Reading.*]
to Miss Letitia, your honour's rich love.

DIMPLE. And this [*Delivers another.*] to Miss Charlotte
Manly. See that you deliver them privately.

JESSAMY. Yes, your honour. [*Going.*

DIMPLE. Jessamy, who are these strange lodgers that came
to the house last night?

JESSAMY. Why, the master is a Yankee colonel; I have not
seen much of him; but the man is the most unpolished animal
your honour ever disgraced your eyes by looking upon. I have
had one of the most *outré* conversations with him!—He really
has a most prodigious effect upon my risibility.

DIMPLE. I ought, according to every rule of Chesterfield, to
wait on him and insinuate myself into his good graces.—Jessamy, wait on the Colonel with my compliments, and if he is
disengaged I will do myself the honour of paying him my respects.—Some ignorant, unpolished boor—

JESSAMY *goes off and returns.*

JESSAMY. Sir, the Colonel is gone out, and Jonathan his servant says that he is gone to stretch his legs upon the Mall.—
Stretch his legs! what an indelicacy of diction!

DIMPLE. Very well. Reach me my hat and sword. I'll
accost him there, in my way to Letitia's, as by accident;
pretend to be struck with his person and address, and endeavour to steal into his confidence. Jessamy, I have no business
for you at present. [*Exit.*

JESSAMY [*taking up the book*].

My master and I obtain our knowledge from the same source;
—though, gad! I think myself much the prettier fellow of the
two. [*Surveying himself in the glass.*] That was a brilliant
thought, to insinuate that I folded my master's letters for him;
the folding is so neat, that it does honour to the operator. I
once intended to have insinuated that I wrote his letters too;
but that was before I saw them; it won't do now: no honour
there, positively.—"Nothing looks more vulgar [*Reading*

affectedly.], ordinary, and illiberal than ugly, uneven, and ragged nails; the ends of which should be kept even and clean, not tipped with black, and cut in small segments of circles."—Segments of circles! surely my lord did not consider that he wrote for the beaux. Segments of circles! what a crabbed term! Now I dare answer that my master, with all his learning, does not know that this means, according to the present mode, to let the nails grow long, and then cut them off even at top. [*Laughing without.*] Ha! that's Jenny's titter. I protest I despair of ever teaching that girl to laugh; she has something so execrably natural in her laugh, that I declare it absolutely discomposes my nerves. How came she into our house! [*Calls.*] Jenny!

Enter JENNY.

JESSAMY. Prythee, Jenny, don't spoil your fine face with laughing.

JENNY. Why, mustn't I laugh, Mr. Jessamy?

JESSAMY. You may smile; but, as my lord says, nothing can authorize a laugh.

JENNY. Well, but I can't help laughing.—Have you seen him, Mr. Jessamy? ha, ha, ha!

JESSAMY. Seen whom?

JENNY. Why Jonathan, the New-England colonel's servant. Do you know he was at the play last night, and the stupid creature don't know where he has been. He would not go to a play for the world; he thinks it was a show, as he calls it.

JESSAMY. As ignorant and unpolished as he is, do you know, Miss Jenny, that I propose to introduce him to the honour of your acquaintance?

JENNY. Introduce him to me! for what?

JESSAMY. Why, my lovely girl, that you may take him under your protection, as Madame Ramboulliet did young Stanhope; that you may, by your plastic hand, mould this uncouth cub into a gentleman. He is to make love to you.

JENNY. Make love to me!—

JESSAMY. Yes, Mistress Jenny, make love to you; and, I doubt not, when he shall become *domesticated* in your kitchen, that this boor, under your auspices, will soon become *un amiable petit Jonathan.*

JENNY. I must say, Mr. Jessamy, if he copies after me, he will be vastly, monstrously polite.

JESSAMY. Stay here one moment, and I will call him.—
Jonathan!—Mr. Jonathan! [*Calls.*]

JONATHAN [*Within.*]. Holla! there.—[*Enters.*] You promise
to stand by me—six bows you say. [*Bows.*]

JESSAMY. Mrs. Jenny, I have the honour of presenting Mr.
Jonathan, Colonel Manly's waiter, to you. I am extremely happy
that I have it in my power to make two worthy people acquainted
with each other's merits.

JENNY. So, Mr. Jonathan, I hear you were at the play last
night.

JONATHAN. At the play! why, did you think I went to the
devil's drawing-room?

JENNY. The devil's drawing-room!

JONATHAN. Yes; why an't cards and dice the devil's device,
and the play-house the shop where the devil hangs out the vanities of the world upon the tenter-hooks of temptation. I believe
you have not heard how they were acting the old boy one night,
and the wicked one came among them sure enough, and went
right off in a storm, and carried one quarter of the play-house with
him. Oh! no, no, no! you won't catch me at a play-house, I
warrant you.

JENNY. Well, Mr. Jonathan, though I don't scruple your
veracity, I have some reasons for believing you were there; pray,
where were you about six o'clock?

JONATHAN. Why, I went to see one Mr. Morrison, the *hocus-
pocus* man; they said as how he could eat a case knife.

JENNY. Well, and how did you find the place?

JONATHAN. As I was going about here and there, to and again,
to find it, I saw a great crowd of folks going into a long entry that
had lanterns over the door; so I asked a man whether that was
not the place where they played *hocus-pocus?* He was a very civil,
kind man, though he did speak like the Hessians; he lifted up
his eyes and said, "They play *hocus-pocus* tricks enough there,
Got knows, mine friend."

JENNY. Well—

JONATHAN. So I went right in, and they shewed me away, clean
up to the garret, just like meeting-house gallery. And so I saw
a power of topping folks, all sitting round in little cabins, "just
like father's corn-cribs;" and then there was such a squeaking
with the fiddles, and such a tarnal blaze with the lights, my head
was near turned. At last the people that sat near me set up such

a hissing—hiss—like so many mad cats; and then they went thump, thump, thump, just like our Peleg threshing wheat, and stampt away, just like the nation; and called out for one Mr. Langolee,—I suppose he helps act[s] the tricks.

JENNY. Well, and what did you do all this time?

JONATHAN. Gor, I—I liked the fun, and so I thumpt away, and hiss'd as lustily as the best of 'em. One sailor-looking man that sat by me, seeing me stamp, and knowing I was a cute fellow, because I could make a roaring noise, clapt me on the shoulder and said, "You are a d——d hearty cock, smite my timbers!" I told him so I was, but I thought he need not swear so, and make use of such naughty words.

JESSAMY. The savage!—Well, and did you see the man with his tricks?

JONATHAN. Why, I vow, as I was looking out for him, they lifted up a great green cloth and let us look right into the next neighbour's house. Have you a good many houses in New-York made so in that 'ere way?

JENNY. Not many; but did you see the family?

JONATHAN. Yes, swamp it; I see'd the family.

JENNY. Well, and how did you like them?

JONATHAN. Why, I vow they were pretty much like other families;—there was a poor, good-natured curse of a husband, and a sad rantipole of a wife.

JENNY. But did you see no other folks?

JONATHAN. Yes. There was one youngster; they called him Mr. Joseph; he talked as sober and as pious as a minister; but, like some ministers that I know, he was a sly tike in his heart for all that: He was going to ask a young woman to spark it with him, and—the Lord have mercy on my soul!—she was another man's wife.

JESSAMY. The Wabash!

JENNY. And did you see any more folks?

JONATHAN. Why, they came on as thick as mustard. For my part, I thought the house was haunted. There was a soldier fellow, who talked about his row de dow, dow, and courted a young woman; but, of all the cute folk I saw, I liked one little fellow—

JENNY. Aye! who was he?

JONATHAN. Why, he had red hair, and a little round plump face like mine, only not altogether so handsome. His name was

—Darby;—that was his baptizing name; his other name I forgot. Oh! it was Wig—Wag—Wag-all, Darby Wag-all,—pray, do you know him? —I should like to take a sling with him, or a drap of cyder with a pepper-pod in it, to make it warm and comfortable.

JENNY. I can't say I have that pleasure.

JONATHAN. I wish you did; he is a cute fellow. But there was one thing I didn't like in that Mr. Darby; and that was, he was afraid of some of them 'ere shooting irons, such as your troopers wear on training days. Now, I'm a true born Yankee American son of liberty, and I never was afraid of a gun yet in all my life.

JENNY. Well, Mr. Jonathan, you were certainly at the play-house.

JONATHAN. I at the play-house!—Why didn't I see the play then?

JENNY. Why, the people you saw were players.

JONATHAN. Mercy on my soul! did I see the wicked players?—Mayhap that 'ere Darby that I liked so was the old serpent himself, and had his cloven foot in his pocket. Why, I vow, now I come to think on't, the candles seemed to burn blue, and I am sure where I sat it smelt tarnally of brimstone.

JESSAMY. Well, Mr. Jonathan, from your account, which I confess is very accurate, you must have been at the play-house.

JONATHAN. Why, I vow, I began to smell a rat. When I came away, I went to the man for my money again; you want your money? says he; yes, says I; for what? says he; why, says I, no man shall jocky me out of my money; I paid my money to see sights, and the dogs a bit of a sight have I seen, unless you call listening to people's private business a sight. Why, says he, it is the School for Scandalization.—The School for Scandalization!—Oh! ho! no wonder you New-York folks are so cute at it, when you go to school to learn it; and so I jogged off.

JESSAMY. My dear Jenny, my master's business drags me from you; would to heaven I knew no other servitude than to your charms.

JONATHAN. Well, but don't go; you won't leave me so.—

JESSAMY. Excuse me.—Remember the cash. [*Aside to him, and—Exit.*]

JENNY. Mr. Jonathan, won't you please to sit down. Mr.

Jessamy tells me you wanted to have some conversation with me.
[*Having brought forward two chairs, they sit.*]

JONATHAN. Ma'am!—

JENNY. Sir!—

JONATHAN. Ma'am!—

JENNY. Pray, how do you like the city, sir?

JONATHAN. Ma'am!—

JENNY. I say, sir, how do you like New-York?

JONATHAN. Ma'am!—

JENNY. The stupid creature! but I must pass some little time with him, if it is only to endeavour to learn whether it was his master that made such an abrupt entrance into our house, and my young mistress' heart, this morning. [*Aside.*] As you don't seem to like to talk, Mr. Jonathan—do you sing?

JONATHAN. Gor, I—I am glad she asked that, for I forgot what Mr. Jessamy bid me say, and I dare as well be hanged as act what he bid me do, I'm so ashamed. [*Aside.*] Yes, ma'am, I can sing —I can sing Mear, Old Hundred, and Bangor.

JENNY. Oh! I don't mean psalm tunes. Have you no little song to please the ladies, such as Roslin Castle, or the Maid of the Mill?

JONATHAN. Why, all my tunes go to meeting tunes, save one, and I count you won't altogether like that 'ere.

JENNY. What is it called?

JONATHAN. I am sure you have heard folks talk about it; it is called Yankee Doodle.

JENNY. Oh! it is the tune I am fond of; and, if I know anything of my mistress, she would be glad to dance to it. Pray, sing!

JONATHAN [*sings*].

Father and I went up to camp,
    Along with Captain Goodwin;
And there we saw the men and boys,
    As thick as hasty-pudding.
            Yankee doodle do, &c.

And there we saw a swamping gun,
    Big as log of maple,
On a little deuced cart,
    A load for father's cattle.
            Yankee doodle do, &c.

And every time they fired it off
It took a horn of powder,
It made a noise—like father's gun,
Only a nation louder.
　　　　　Yankee doodle do, &c.

There was a man in our town,
His name was—

No, no, that won't do. Now, if I was with Tabitha Wymen and Jemima Cawley down at father Chase's, I shouldn't mind singing this all out before them—you would be affronted if I was to sing that, though that's a lucky thought; if you should be affronted, I have something dang'd cute, which Jessamy told me to say to you.

JENNY. Is that all! I assure you I like it of all things.

JONATHAN. No, no; I can sing more; some other time, when you and I are better acquainted, I'll sing the whole of it—no, no—that's a fib—I can't sing but a hundred and ninety verses: our Tabitha at home can sing it all.—[Sings.]

Marblehead's a rocky place,
And Cape-Cod is sandy;
Charlestown is burnt down,
Boston is the dandy.
　　　　　Yankee doodle, doodle do, &c.

I vow, my own town song has put me into such topping spirits that I believe I'll begin to do a little, as Jessamy says we must when we go a-courting.—[Runs and kisses her.] Burning rivers! cooling flames! red-hot roses! pig-nuts! hasty-pudding and ambrosia!

JENNY. What means this freedom? you insulting wretch. [Strikes him.]

JONATHAN. Are you affronted?

JENNY. Affronted! with what looks shall I express my anger?

JONATHAN. Looks! why as to the matter of looks, you look as cross as a witch.

JENNY. Have you no feeling for the delicacy of my sex?

JONATHAN. Feeling! Gor, I—I feel the delicacy of your sex pretty smartly [Rubbing his cheek.], though, I vow, I thought when you city ladies courted and married, and all that, you put feeling out of the question. But I want to know whether you are really affronted, or only pretend to be so? 'Cause, if you are certainly right down affronted, I am at the end of my tether; Jessamy didn't tell me what to say to you.

JENNY. Pretend to be affronted!

JONATHAN. Aye, aye, if you only pretend, you shall hear how I'll go to work to make cherubim consequences. [*Runs up to her.*]

JENNY. Begone, you brute!

JONATHAN. That looks like mad; but I won't lose my speech. My dearest Jenny—your name is Jenny, I think?—My dearest Jenny, though I have the highest esteem for the sweet favours you have just now granted me—Gor, that's a fib, though; but Jessamy says it is not wicked to tell lies to the women. [*Aside.*] I say, though I have the highest esteem for the favours you have just now granted me, yet you will consider that, as soon as the dissolvable knot is tied, they will no longer be favours, but only matters of duty and matters of course.

JENNY.   Marry you! you audacious monster! get out of my sight, or, rather, let me fly from you.   [*Exit hastily.*

JONATHAN. Gor! she's gone off in a swinging passion, before I had time to think of consequences. If this is the way with your city ladies, give me the twenty acres of rock, the bible, the cow, and Tabitha, and a little peaceable bundling.

SCENE II. *The Mall.*

Enter MANLY.

It must be so, Montague! and it is not all the tribe of Mandevilles that shall convince me that a nation, to become great, must first become dissipated. Luxury is surely the bane of a nation: Luxury! which enervates both soul and body, by opening a thousand new sources of enjoyment, opens, also, a thousand new sources of contention and want: Luxury! which renders a people weak at home, and accessible to bribery, corruption, and force from abroad. When the Grecian states knew no other tools than the axe and the saw, the Grecians were a great, a free, and a happy people. The kings of Greece devoted their lives to the service of their country, and her senators knew no other superiority over their fellow-citizens than a glorious pre-eminence in danger and virtue. They exhibited to the world a noble spectacle,—a number of independent states united by a similarity of language, sentiment, manners, common interest, and common consent, in one grand mutual league of protection. And, thus united, long might they have continued the cherishers of arts and sciences, the protectors of the oppressed, the scourge of tyrants, and the safe asylum of liberty. But when foreign gold, and still more pernicious, foreign luxury had crept among them, they sapped the vitals of their virtue. The virtues of their ancestors were only found in their writings. Envy and suspicion, the vices of little minds, possessed them. The various states engendered jealousies of each other; and, more unfortunately, growing jealous of their great federal council, the Amphictyons, they forgot that their common safety had existed, and would exist, in giving them an honourable extensive prerogative. The common good was lost in the pursuit of private interest; and that people who, by uniting, might have stood against the world in arms, by dividing, crumbled into ruin;—their name is now only known in the page of the historian, and what they once were is all we have left to admire. Oh! that America! Oh! that my country, would, in this her day, learn the things which belong to her peace!

Enter DIMPLE.

DIMPLE. You are Colonel Manly, I presume?

MANLY. At your service, sir.

DIMPLE. My name is Dimple, sir. I have the honour to be a lodger in the same house with you, and, hearing you were in the Mall, came hither to take the liberty of joining you.

MANLY. You are very obliging, sir.

DIMPLE. As I understand you are a stranger here, sir, I have taken the liberty to introduce myself to your acquaintance, as possibly I may have it in my power to point out some things in this city worthy your notice.

MANLY. An attention to strangers is worthy a liberal mind, and must ever be gratefully received. But to a soldier, who has no fixed abode, such attentions are particularly pleasing.

DIMPLE. Sir, there is no character so respectable as that of a soldier. And, indeed, when we reflect how much we owe to those brave men who have suffered so much in the service of their country, and secured to us those inestimable blessings that we now enjoy, our liberty and independence, they demand every attention which gratitude can pay. For my own part, I never meet an officer, but I embrace him as my friend, nor a private in distress, but I insensibly extend my charity to him.—I have hit the Bumkin off very tolerably. [Aside.

MANLY. Give me your hand, sir! I do not proffer this hand to everybody; but you steal into my heart. I hope I am as insensible to flattery as most men; but I declare (it may be my weak side) that I never hear the name of soldier mentioned with respect, but I experience a thrill of pleasure which I never feel on any other occasion.

DIMPLE. Will you give me leave, my dear Colonel, to confer an obligation on myself, by shewing you some civilities during your stay here, and giving a similar opportunity to some of my friends?

MANLY. Sir, I thank you; but I believe my stay in this city will be very short.

DIMPLE. I can introduce you to some men of excellent sense, in whose company you will esteem yourself happy; and, by way of amusement, to some fine girls, who will listen to your soft things with pleasure.

MANLY. Sir, I should be proud of the honour of being acquainted with those gentlemen;—but, as for the ladies, I don't understand you.

DIMPLE. Why, sir, I need not tell you, that when a young gentleman is alone with a young lady he must say some soft things to her fair cheek—indeed, the lady will expect it. To be sure, there is not much pleasure when a man of the world and a finished coquette meet, who perfectly know each other; but how delicious is it to excite the emotions of joy, hope, expectation, and delight in the bosom of a lovely girl who believes every tittle of what you say to be serious!

MANLY. Serious, sir! In my opinion, the man who, under pretensions of marriage, can plant thorns in the bosom of an innocent, unsuspecting girl is more detestable than a common robber, in the same proportion as private violence is more despicable than open force, and money of less value than happiness.

DIMPLE. How he awes me by the superiority of his sentiments. [Aside.] As you say, sir, a gentlemen should be cautious how he mentions marriage.

MANLY. Cautious, sir! [No person more approves of an intercourse between the sexes than I do. Female conversation softens our manners, whilst our discourse, from the superiority of our literary advantages, improves their minds. But, in our young country, where there is no such thing as gallantry, when a gentleman speaks of love to a lady, whether he mentions marriage or not, she ought to conclude either that he meant to insult her or that his intentions are the most serious and honourable.] How mean, how cruel, is it, by a thousand tender assiduities, to win the affections of an amiable girl, and, though you leave her virtue unspotted, to betray her into the appearance of so many tender partialities, that every man of delicacy would suppress his inclination towards her, by supposing her heart engaged! Can any man, for the trivial gratification of his leisure-hours, affect the happiness of a whole life! His not having spoken of marriage may add to his perfidy, but can be no excuse for his conduct.

DIMPLE. Sir, I admire your sentiments;—they are mine. The light observations that fell from me were only a principle of the tongue; they came not from the heart; my practice has ever disapproved these principles.

MANLY. I believe you, sir. I should with reluctance suppose that those pernicious sentiments could find admittance into the heart of a gentleman.

DIMPLE. I am now, sir, going to visit a family, where, if you please, I will have the honour of introducing you. Mr. Manly's ward, Miss Letitia, is a young lady of immense fortune; and his niece, Miss Charlotte Manly, is a young lady of great sprightliness and beauty.

MANLY. That gentleman, sir, is my uncle, and Miss Manly my sister.

DIMPLE. The devil she is! [*Aside.*] Miss Manly your sister, sir? I rejoice to hear it, and feel a double pleasure in being known to you.—Plague on him! I wish he was at Boston again, with all my soul. [*Aside.*]

MANLY. Come, sir, will you go?

DIMPLE. I will follow you in a moment, sir. [*Exit* MANLY.] Plague on it! this is unlucky. A fighting brother is a cursed appendage to a fine girl. Egad! I just stopped in time; had he not discovered himself, in two minutes more I should have told him how well I was with his sister. Indeed, I cannot see the satisfaction of an intrigue, if one can't have the pleasure of communicating it to our friends. [*Exit.*

End of the Third Act.

ACT IV.

SCENE I. CHARLOTTE'S *Apartment.*

CHARLOTTE *leading in* MARIA.

CHARLOTTE. This is so kind, my sweet friend, to come to see me at this moment. I declare, if I were going to be married in a few days, as you are, I should scarce have found time to visit my friends.

MARIA. Do you think, then, that there is an impropriety in it? —How should you dispose of your time?

CHARLOTTE. Why, I should be shut up in my chamber; and my head would so run upon—upon—upon the solemn ceremony that I was to pass through!—I declare, it would take me above two hours merely to learn that little monosyllable—*Yes.*—Ah! my dear, your sentimental imagination does not conceive what that little tiny word implies.

MARIA. Spare me your raillery, my sweet friend; I should love your agreeable vivacity at any other time.

CHARLOTTE. Why, this is the very time to amuse you. You grieve me to see you look so unhappy.

MARIA. Have I not reason to look so?

CHARLOTTE. [What new grief distresses you?

MARIA. Oh! how sweet it is, when the heart is borne down with misfortune, to recline and repose on the bosom of friendship! Heaven knows that, although it is improper for a young lady to praise a gentleman, yet I have ever concealed Mr. Dimple's foibles, and spoke of him as of one whose reputation I expected would be linked with mine: but his late conduct towards me has turned my coolness into contempt. He behaves as if he meant to insult and disgust me; whilst my father, in the last conversation on the subject of our marriage, spoke of it as a matter which laid near his heart, and in which he would not bear contradiction.

CHARLOTTE. This works well: oh! the generous Dimple. I'll endeavour to excite her to discharge him. [*Aside.*] But, my dear friend, your happiness depends on yourself. Why don't you discard him? Though the match has been of long standing, I would not be forced to make myself miserable: no parent in the world should oblige me to marry the man I did not like.

MARIA. Oh! my dear, you never lived with your parents, and do not know what influence a father's frowns have upon a daughter's heart. Besides, what have I to allege against Mr. Dimple, to justify myself to the world? He carries himself so smoothly, that every one would impute the blame to me, and call me capricious.

CHARLOTTE. And call her capricious! Did ever such an objection start into the heart of woman? for my part, I wish I had fifty lovers to discard, for no other reason than because I did not fancy them.] My dear Maria, you will forgive me; I know your candour and confidence in me; but I have at times, I confess, been led to suppose that some other gentleman was the cause of your aversion to Mr. Dimple.

MARIA. No, my sweet friend, you may be assured, that though I have seen many gentlemen I could prefer to Mr. Dimple, yet I never saw one that I thought I could give my hand to, until this morning.

CHARLOTTE. This morning!

MARIA. Yes; one of the strangest accidents in the world. The odious Dimple, after disgusting me with his conversation, had just left me, when a gentleman, who, it seems, boards in the same house with him, saw him coming out of our door, and, the houses looking very much alike, he came into our house instead of his lodgings; nor did he discover his mistake until he got into the parlour, where I was: he then bowed so gracefully, made such a genteel apology, and looked so manly and noble!—

CHARLOTTE. I see some folks, though it is so great an impropriety, can praise a gentleman, when he happens to be the man of their fancy. [*Aside*.]

MARIA. I don't know how it was,—I hope he did not think me indelicate,—but I asked him, I believe, to sit down, or pointed to a chair. He sat down, and, instead of having recourse to observations upon the weather, or hackneyed criticisms upon the theatre, he entered readily into a conversation worthy a man of sense to speak, and a lady of delicacy and sentiment to hear. He was not strictly handsome, but he spoke the language of sentiment, and his eyes looked tenderness and honour.

CHARLOTTE. Oh! [*Eagerly*.] you sentimental, grave girls, when your hearts are once touched, beat us rattles a bar's length. And so you are quite in love with this he-angel?

MARIA. In love with him! How can you rattle so, Charlotte? Am I not going to be miserable? [*Sighs*.] In love with a gentleman I never saw but one hour in my life, and don't know his name!

No; I only wished that the man I shall marry may look, and talk, and act, just like him. Besides, my dear, he is a married man.

CHARLOTTE. Why, that was good-natured.—He told you so, I suppose, in mere charity, to prevent you falling in love with him?

MARIA. He didn't tell me so; [*Peevishly.*] he looked as if he was married.

CHARLOTTE. How, my dear; did he look sheepish?

MARIA. I am sure he has a susceptible heart, and the ladies of his acquaintance must be very stupid not to—

CHARLOTTE. Hush! I hear some person coming.

[*Enter* LETITIA.

LETITIA. My dear Maria, I am happy to see you. Lud! what a pity it is that you have purchased your wedding clothes.

MARIA. I think so. [*Sighing.*]

LETITIA. Why, my dear, there is the sweetest parcel of silks come over you ever saw! Nancy Brilliant has a full suit come; she sent over her measure, and it fits her to a hair; it is immensely dressy, and made for a court-hoop. I thought they said the large hoops were going out of fashion.

CHARLOTTE. Did you see the hat? Is it a fact that the deep laces round the border is still the fashion?]

DIMPLE [*within*]. Upon my honour, sir.

MARIA. Ha! Dimple's voice! My dear, I must take leave of you. There are some things necessary to be done at our house. Can't I go through the other room?

Enter DIMPLE *and* MANLY.

DIMPLE. Ladies, your most obedient.

CHARLOTTE. Miss Van Rough, shall I present my brother Henry to you? Colonel Manly, Maria—Miss Van Rough, brother.

MARIA. Her brother! [*Turns and sees* MANLY.] Oh! my heart! the very gentleman I have been praising.

MANLY. The same amiable girl I saw this morning!

CHARLOTTE. Why, you look as if you were acquainted.

MANLY. I unintentionally intruded into this lady's presence this morning, for which she was so good as to promise me her forgiveness.

CHARLOTTE. Oh! ho! is that the case! Have these two penso-rosos been together? Were they Henry's eyes that looked so tender-ly? [*Aside.*] And so you promised to pardon him? and could you be so good-natured?—have you really forgiven him? I beg you would do it for my sake [*Whispering loud to* MARIA.]. But, my dear, as you are in such haste, it would be cruel to detain you; I can show you the way through the other room.

MARIA. Spare me, my sprightly friend.

MANLY. The lady does not, I hope, intend to deprive us of the pleasure of her company so soon.

CHARLOTTE. She has only a mantua-maker who waits for her at home. But, as I am to give my opinion of the dress, I think she cannot go yet. We were talking of the fashions when you came in, but I suppose the subject must be changed to something of more importance now.—Mr. Dimple, will you favour us with an account of the public entertainments?

DIMPLE. Why, really, Miss Manly, you could not have asked me a question more *mal-apropos*. For my part, I must confess that, to a man who has traveled, there is nothing that is worthy the name of amusement to be found in this city.

CHARLOTTE. Except visiting the ladies.

DIMPLE. Pardon me, madam; that is the avocation of a man of taste. But for amusement, I positively know of nothing that can be called so, unless you dignify with that title the hopping once a fortnight to the sound of two or three squeaking fiddles, and the clattering of the old tavern windows, or sitting to see the miser-able mummers, whom you call actors, murder comedy and make a farce of tragedy.

MANLY. Do you never attend the theatre, sir?

DIMPLE. I was tortured there once.

CHARLOTTE. Pray, Mr. Dimple, was it a tragedy or a comedy?

DIMPLE. Faith, madam, I cannot tell; for I sat with my back to the stage all the time, admiring a much better actress than any there—a lady who played the fine woman to perfection; though, by the laugh of the horrid creatures round me, I suppose it was comedy. Yet, on second thoughts, it might be some hero in a tragedy, dying so comically as to set the whole house in an uproar.—Colonel, I presume you have been in Europe?

MANLY. Indeed, sir, I was never ten leagues from the continent.

DIMPLE. Believe me, Colonel, you have an immense pleasure to come; and when you shall have seen the brilliant exhibitions of

Europe, you will learn to despise the amusements of this country as much as I do.

MANLY. Therefore I do not wish to see them; for I can never esteem that knowledge valuable which tends to give me a distaste for my native country.

DIMPLE. Well, Colonel, though you have not travelled, you have read.

MANLY. I have, a little, and by it have discovered that there is a laudable partiality which ignorant, untravelled men entertain for everything that belongs to their native country. I call it laudable; it injures no one; adds to their own happiness; and, when extended, becomes the noble principle of patriotism. Travelled gentlemen rise superior, in their own opinion, to this: but if the contempt which they contract for their country is the most valuable acquisition of their travels, I am far from thinking that their time and money are well spent.

MARIA. What noble sentiments!

CHARLOTTE. Let my brother set out from where he will in the fields of conversation, he is sure to end his tour in the temple of gravity.

MANLY. Forgive me, my sister. I love my country; it has its foibles undoubtedly;—some foreigners will with pleasure remark them—but such remarks fall very ungracefully from the lips of her citizens.

DIMPLE. You are perfectly in the right, Colonel—America has her faults.

MANLY. Yes, sir; and we, her children, should blush for them in private, and endeavour, as individuals, to reform them. But, if our country has its errors in common with other countries, I am proud to say America—I mean the United States—have displayed virtues and achievements which modern nations may admire, but of which they have seldom set us the example.

CHARLOTTE. But, brother, we must introduce you to some of our gay folks, and let you see the city, such as it is. Mr. Dimple is known to almost every family in town; he will doubtless take a pleasure in introducing you.

DIMPLE. I shall esteem every service I can render your brother an honour.

MANLY. I fear the business I am upon will take up all my time, and my family will be anxious to hear from me.

MARIA. His family! But what is it to me that he is married! [*Aside.*] Pray, how did you leave your lady, sir?

CHARLOTTE. My brother is not married [*Observing her anxiety.*]; it is only an odd way he has of expressing himself. Pray, brother, is this business, which you make your continual excuse, a secret?

MANLY. No, sister; I came hither to solicit the honourable Congress, that a number of my brave old soldiers may be put upon the pension-list, who were, at first, not judged to be so materially wounded as to need the public assistance. My sister says true [*To* MARIA.]: I call my late soldiers my family. Those who were not in the field in the late glorious contest, and those who were, have their respective merits; but, I confess, my old brother-soldiers are dearer to me than the former description. Friendships made in adversity are lasting; our countrymen may forget us, but that is no reason why we should forget one another. But I must leave you; my time of engagement approaches.

CHARLOTTE. Well, but, brother, if you will go, will you please to conduct my fair friend home? You live in the same street—I was to have gone with her myself—[*Aside.*] A lucky thought.

MARIA. I am obliged to your sister, sir, and was just intending to go. [*Going.*

MANLY. I shall attend her with pleasure. [*Exit with* MARIA, *followed by* DIMPLE *and* CHARLOTTE.]

MARIA. Now, pray, don't betray me to your brother.

[CHARLOTTE. [*Just as she sees him make a motion to take his leave.*] One word with you, brother, if you please.

[*Follows them out.*

Manent DIMPLE *and* LETITIA.

DIMPLE. You received the billet I sent you, I presume?
LETITIA. Hush!—Yes.
DIMPLE. When shall I pay my respects to you?
LETITIA. At eight I shall be unengaged.

Re-enter CHARLOTTE.

DIMPLE. Did my lovely angel receive my billet?
[*To* CHARLOTTE.

CHARLOTTE. Yes.
DIMPLE. What hour shall I expect with impatience?
CHARLOTTE. At eight I shall be at home unengaged.

DIMPLE. Unfortunately! I have a horrid engagement of business at that hour. Can't you finish your visit earlier, and let six be the happy hour?

CHARLOTTE. You know your influence over me.]

[*Exeunt severally.*

SCENE II. VAN ROUGH'S *House.*

VAN ROUGH [*alone*].

It cannot possibly be true! The son of my old friend can't have acted so unadvisedly. Seventeen thousand pounds! in bills! Mr. Transfer must have been mistaken. He always appeared so prudent, and talked so well upon money-matters, and even assured me that he intended to change his dress for a suit of clothes which would not cost so much, and look more substantial, as soon as he married. No, no, no! it can't be; it cannot be. But, however, I must look out sharp. I did not care what his principles or his actions were, so long as he minded the main chance. Seventeen thousand pounds! If he had lost it in trade, why the best men may have ill-luck; but to game it away, as Transfer says—why, at this rate, his whole estate may go in one night, and, what is ten times worse, mine into the bargain. No, no; Mary is right. Leave women to look out in these matters; for all they look as if they didn't know a journal from a ledger, when their interest is concerned they know what's what; they mind the main chance as well as the best of us—I wonder Mary did not tell me she knew of his spending his money so foolishly. Seventeen thousand pounds! Why, if my daughter was standing up to be married, I would forbid the banns, if I found it was to a man who did not mind the main chance.— Hush! I hear somebody coming. 'Tis Mary's voice: a man with her too! I shou'dn't be surprised if this should be the other string to her bow. Aye, aye, let them alone; women understand the main chance.—Though, i' faith, I'll listen a little.

[*Retires into a closet.*

MANLY *leading in* MARIA.

MANLY. I hope you will excuse my speaking upon so important a subject so abruptly; but, the moment I entered your room, you struck me as the lady whom I had long loved in imagination, and never hoped to see.

MARIA. Indeed, sir, I have been led to hear more upon this subject than I ought.

MANLY. Do you, then, disapprove my suit, madam, or the abruptness of my introducing it? If the latter, my peculiar situation, being obliged to leave the city in a few days, will, I hope, be my excuse; if the former, I will retire, for I am sure I would not give a moment's inquietude to her whom I could devote my life to please. I am not so indelicate as to seek your immediate approbation; permit me only to be near you, and by a thousand tender assiduities to endeavour to excite a grateful return.

MARIA. I have a father, whom I would die to make happy; he will disapprove—

MANLY. Do you think me so ungenerous as to seek a place in your esteem without his consent? You must—you ever ought to consider that man as unworthy of you who seeks an interest in your heart, contrary to a father's approbation. A young lady should reflect that the loss of a lover may be supplied, but nothing can compensate for the loss of a parent's affection. Yet, why do you suppose your father would disapprove? In our country, the affections are not sacrificed to riches or family-aggrandizement: should you approve, my family is decent, and my rank honourable.

MARIA. You distress me, sir.

MANLY. Then I will sincerely beg your excuse for obtruding so disagreeable a subject, and retire.   [*Going.*

MARIA. Stay, sir! your generosity and good opinion of me deserve a return; but why must I declare what, for these few hours, I have scarce suffered myself to think?—I am—

MANLY. What?

MARIA. Engaged, sir; and, in a few days, to be married to the gentleman you saw at your sister's.

MANLY. Engaged to be married! And have I been basely invading the rights of another? Why have you permitted this? Is this the return for the partiality I declared for you?

MARIA. You distress me, sir. What would you have me say? You are too generous to wish the truth. Ought I to say that I dared not suffer myself to think of my engagement, and that I am going to give my hand without my heart? Would you have me confess a partiality for you? If so, your triumph is complete, and can be only more so when days of misery with the man I cannot love will make me think of him whom I prefer.

MANLY. [*After a pause.*]. We are both unhappy; but it is your duty to obey your parent—mine to obey my honour. Let us, therefore, both follow the path of rectitude; and of this we may be assured, that if we are not happy, we shall, at least, deserve to be so. Adieu! I dare not trust myself longer with you.   [*Exeunt severally.*

End of the Fourth Act.

ACT V.

SCENE I. DIMPLE'S *Lodgings.*

JESSAMY [*meeting* JONATHAN].

Well, Mr. Jonathan, what success with the fair?

JONATHAN. Why, such a tarnal cross tike you never saw! You would have counted she had lived upon crab-apples and vinegar for a fortnight. But what the rattle makes you look so tarnation glum?

JESSAMY. I was thinking, Mr. Jonathan, what could be the reason of her carrying herself so coolly to you.

JONATHAN. Coolly, do you call it? Why, I vow, she was fire-hot angry: may be it was because I buss'd her.

JESSAMY. No, no, Mr. Jonathan; there must be some other cause: I never yet knew a lady angry at being kissed.

JONATHAN. Well, if it is not the young woman's bashfulness, I vow I can't conceive why she shou'dn't like me.

JESSAMY. May be it is because you have not the graces, Mr. Jonathan.

JONATHAN. Grace! Why, does the young woman expect I must be converted before I court her?

JESSAMY. I mean graces of person: for instance, my lord tells us that we must cut off our nails even at top, in small segments of circles—though you won't understand that—In the next place, you must regulate your laugh.

JONATHAN. Maple-log seize it! don't I laugh natural?

JESSAMY. That's the very fault, Mr. Jonathan. Besides, you absolutely misplace it. I was told by a friend of mine that you laughed outright at the play the other night, when you ought only to have tittered.

JONATHAN. Gor! I—what does one go to see fun for if they can't laugh?

JESSAMY. You may laugh; but you must laugh by rule.

JONATHAN. Swamp it—laugh by rule! Well, I should like that tarnally.

JESSAMY. Why, you know, Mr. Jonathan, that to dance, a lady to play with her fan, or a gentleman with his cane, and all other natural motions, are regulated by art. My master has composed an immensely pretty gamut, by which any lady or gentleman, with a few years' close application, may learn to laugh as gracefully as if they were born and bred to it.

JONATHAN. Mercy on my soul! A gamut for laughing—just like fa, la, sol?

JESSAMY. Yes. It comprises every possible display of jocularity, from an *affettuoso* smile to a *piano* titter, or full chorus *fortissimo* ha, ha, ha! My master employs his leisure-hours in marking out the plays, like a cathedral chanting-book, that the ignorant may know where to laugh; and that pit, box, and gallery may keep time together, and not have a snigger in one part of the house, a broad grin in the other, and a d——d grum look in the third. How delightful to see the audience all smile together, then look on their books, then twist their mouths into an agreeable simper, then altogether shake the house with a general ha, ha, ha! loud as a full chorus of Handel's at an Abbey-commemoration.

JONATHAN. Ha, ha, ha! that's dang'd cute, I swear.

JESSAMY. The gentlemen, you see, will laugh the tenor; the ladies will play the counter-tenor; the beaux will squeak the treble; and our jolly friends in the gallery a thorough bass, ho, ho, ho!

JONATHAN. Well, can't you let me see that gamut?

JESSAMY. Oh! yes, Mr. Jonathan; here it is. [*Takes out a book.*] Oh! no, this is only a titter with its variations. Ah, here it is. [*Takes out another.*] Now, you must know, Mr. Jonathan, this is a piece written by Ben Johnson [*sic*], which I have set to my master's gamut. The places where you must smile, look grave, or laugh outright, are marked below the line. Now look over me. "There was a certain man"—now you must smile.

JONATHAN. Well, read it again; I warrant I'll mind my eye.

JESSAMY. "There was a certain man, who had a sad scolding wife,"—now you must laugh.

JONATHAN. Tarnation! That's no laughing matter though.

JESSAMY. "And she lay sick a-dying;"—now you must titter.

JONATHAN. What, snigger when the good woman's a-dying!
Gor, I—

JESSAMY. Yes, the notes say you must—"And she asked her
husband leave to make a will,"—now you must begin to look
grave;—"and her husband said"—

JONATHAN. Aye, what did her husband say?—Something dang'd
cute, I reckon.

JESSAMY. "And her husband said, you have had your will all
your life-time, and would you have it after you are dead, too?"

JONATHAN. Ho, ho, ho! There the old man was even with her;
he was up to the notch—ha, ha, ha!

JESSAMY. But, Mr. Jonathan, you must not laugh so. Why,
you ought to have tittered *piano*, and you have laughed *fortissimo*.
Look here; you see these marks, A, B, C, and so on; these are the
references to the other part of the book. Let us turn to it, and
you will see the directions how to manage the muscles. This
[*Turns over.*] was note D you blundered at.—"You must purse
the mouth into a smile, then titter, discovering the lower part
of the three front upper teeth."

JONATHAN. How? read it again.

JESSAMY. "There was a certain man"—very well!—"who had
a sad scolding wife,"—why don't you laugh?

JONATHAN. Now, that scolding wife sticks in my gizzard so
pluckily that I can't laugh for the blood and nowns of me. Let
me look grave here, and I'll laugh your belly full, where the old
creature's a-dying.

JESSAMY. "And she asked her husband"—[*Bell rings.*] My
master's bell! he's returned, I fear.—Here, Mr. Jonathan, take
this gamut; and I make no doubt but with a few years' close application, you may be able to smile gracefully. [*Exeunt severally.*

SCENE II. CHARLOTTE'S *Apartment.*

Enter MANLY.

MANLY. What, no one at home? How unfortunate to meet the
only lady my heart was ever moved by, to-find her engaged to another, and confessing her partiality for me! Yet engaged to a man
who, by her intimation, and his libertine conversation with me,

I fear, does not merit her. Aye! there's the sting; for, were I assured that Maria was happy, my heart is not so selfish but that it would dilate in knowing it, even though it were with another. But to know she is unhappy!—I must drive these thoughts from me. Charlotte has some books; and this is what I believe she calls her little library. [*Enters a closet.*

Enter DIMPLE *leading* LETITIA.

LETITIA. And will you pretend to say now, Mr. Dimple, that you propose to break with Maria? Are not the banns published? Are not the clothes purchased? Are not the friends invited? In short, is it not a done affair?

DIMPLE. Believe me, my dear Letitia, I would not marry her.

LETITIA. Why have you not broke with her before this, as you all along deluded me by saying you would?

DIMPLE. Because I was in hopes she would, ere this, have broke with me.

LETITIA. You could not expect it.

DIMPLE. Nay, but be calm a moment; 'twas from my regard to you that I did not discard her.

LETITIA. Regard to me!

DIMPLE. Yes; I have done everything in my power to break with her, but the foolish girl is so fond of me that nothing can accomplish it. Besides, how can I offer her my hand when my heart is indissolubly engaged to you?

LETITIA. There may be reason in this; but why so attentive to Miss Manly?

DIMPLE. Attentive to Miss Manly! For heaven's sake, if you have no better opinion of my constancy, pay not so ill a compliment to my taste.

[LETITIA. Did I not see you whisper to her to-day?

DIMPLE. Possibly I might—but something of so very trifling a nature that I have already forgot what it was.

LETITIA. I believe she has not forgot it.

DIMPLE. My dear creature,] how can you for a moment suppose I should have any serious thoughts of that trifling, gay, flighty coquette, that disagreeable—

Enter CHARLOTTE.

DIMPLE. My dear Miss Manly, I rejoice to see you; there is a charm in your conversation that always marks your entrance into company as fortunate.

LETITIA. Where have you been, my dear?

CHARLOTTE. Why, I have been about to twenty shops, turning over pretty things, and so have left twenty visits unpaid. I wish you would step into the carriage and whisk round, make my apology, and leave my cards where our friends are not at home; that, you know, will serve as a visit. Come, do go.

LETITIA. So anxious to get me out! but I'll watch you. [*Aside.*] Oh! yes, I'll go; I want a little exercise. Positively [DIMPLE *offering to accompany her.*], Mr. Dimple, you shall not go; why, half my visits are cake and caudle visits; it won't do, you know, for you to go. [*Exit, but returns to the door in the back scene and listens.*]

DIMPLE. This attachment of your brother to Maria is fortunate.

CHARLOTTE. How did you come to the knowledge of it?

DIMPLE. I read it in their eyes.

CHARLOTTE. And I had it from her mouth. It would have amused you to have seen her! She, that thought it so great an impropriety to praise a gentleman that she could not bring out one word in your favour, found a redundancy to praise him.

DIMPLE. I have done everything in my power to assist his passion there: your delicacy, my dearest girl, would be shocked at half the instances of neglect and misbehaviour.

CHARLOTTE. I don't know how I should bear neglect; but Mr. Dimple must misbehave himself indeed, to forfeit my good opinion.

DIMPLE. Your good opinion, my angel, is the pride and pleasure of my heart; and if the most respectful tenderness for you, and an utter indifference for all your sex besides, can make me worthy of your esteem, I shall richly merit it.

CHARLOTTE. All my sex besides, Mr. Dimple!—you forgot your *tête-à-tête* with Letitia.

DIMPLE. How can you, my lovely angel, cast a thought on that insipid, wry-mouthed, ugly creature!

CHARLOTTE. But her fortune may have charms?

DIMPLE. Not to a heart like mine. The man, who has been blessed with the good opinion of my Charlotte, must despise the allurements of fortune.

CHARLOTTE. I am satisfied.

DIMPLE. Let us think no more on the odious subject, but devote the present hour to happiness.

CHARLOTTE. Can I be happy when I see the man I prefer going to be married to another?

DIMPLE. Have I not already satisfied my charming angel that I can never think of marrying the puling Maria? But, even if it were so, could that be any bar to our happiness? for, as the poet sings,

> *Love, free as air, at sight of human ties,*
> *Spreads his light wings, and in a moment flies.*

Come, then, my charming angel! why delay our bliss? The present moment is ours; the next is in the hand of fate.

[*Kissing her.*

CHARLOTTE. Begone, sir! By your delusions you had almost lulled my honour asleep.

DIMPLE. Let me lull the demon to sleep again with kisses. [*He struggles with her; she screams.*]

Enter MANLY.

MANLY. Turn, villain! and defend yourself. [*Draws.*]

VAN ROUGH *enters and beats down their swords.*

VAN ROUGH. Is the devil in you? are you going to murder one another? [*Holding* DIMPLE.

DIMPLE. Hold him, hold him,—I can command my passion.

Enter JONATHAN.

JONATHAN. What the rattle ails you? Is the old one in you? let the Colonel alone, can't you? I feel chock full of fight,—do you want to kill the Colonel?—

MANLY. Be still, Jonathan; the gentleman does not want to hurt me.

JONATHAN. Gor! I—I wish he did; I'd shew him yankee boys play, pretty quick.—Don't you see you have frightened the young woman into the *hystrikes*?

VAN ROUGH. Pray, some of you explain this; what has been the occasion of all this racket?

MANLY. That gentleman can explain it to you; it will be a very diverting story for an intended father-in-law to hear.

VAN ROUGH. How was this matter, Mr. Van Dumpling?

DIMPLE. Sir,—upon my honour,—all I know is, that I was talking to this young lady, and this gentleman broke in on us in a very extraordinary manner.

VAN ROUGH. Why, all this is nothing to the purpose; can you explain it, Miss? [*To* CHARLOTTE.]

Enter LETITIA [*through the back scene*].

LETITIA. I can explain it to that gentleman's confusion. Though long betrothed to your daughter [*To* VAN ROUGH.], yet, allured by my fortune, it seems (with shame do I speak it) he has privately paid his addresses to me. I was drawn in to listen to him by his assuring me that the match was made by his father without his consent, and that he proposed to break with Maria, whether he married me or not. But, whatever were his intentions respecting your daughter, sir, even to me he was false; for he has repeated the same story, with some cruel reflections upon my person, to Miss Manly.

JONATHAN. What a tarnal curse!

LETITIA. Nor is this all, Miss Manly. When he was with me this very morning, he made the same ungenerous reflections upon the weakness of your mind as he has so recently done upon the defects of my person.

JONATHAN. What a tarnal curse and damn, too!

DIMPLE. Ha! since I have lost Letitia, I believe I had as good make it up with Maria. Mr. Van Rough, at present I cannot enter into particulars; but, I believe, I can explain everything to your satisfaction in private.

VAN ROUGH. There is another matter, Mr. Van Dumpling, which I would have you explain:—pray, sir, have Messrs. Van Cash & Co. presented you those bills for acceptance?

DIMPLE. The deuce! Has he heard of those bills! Nay, then, all's up with Maria, too; but an affair of this sort can never prejudice me among the ladies; they will rather long to know what the dear creature possesses to make him so agreeable. [*Aside.*] Sir, you'll hear from me. [*To* MANLY.]

MANLY. And you from me, sir.—

DIMPLE. Sir, you wear a sword.—

MANLY. Yes, sir. This sword was presented to me by that brave Gallic hero, the Marquis DE LA FAYETTE. I have drawn it in the service of my country, and in private life, on the only occasion where a man is justified in drawing his sword, in defence of a lady's honour. I have fought too many battles in the service of my country to dread the imputation of cowardice. Death from a man of honour would be a glory you do not merit;

you shall live to bear the insult of man and the contempt of that sex whose general smiles afforded you all your happiness.

DIMPLE. You won't meet me, sir? Then I'll post you for a coward.

MANLY. I'll venture that, sir. The reputation of my life does not depend upon the breath of a Mr. Dimple. I would have you to know, however, sir, that I have a cane to chastise the insolence of a scoundrel, and a sword and the good laws of my country to protect me from the attempts of an assassin.—

DIMPLE. Mighty well! Very fine, indeed! Ladies and gentlemen, I take my leave; and you will please to observe, in the case of my deportment, the contrast between a gentleman who has read Chesterfield and received the polish of Europe, and an unpolished, untravelled American.   [*Exit.*

Enter MARIA.

MARIA. Is he indeed gone?—

LETITIA. I hope, never to return.

VAN ROUGH. I am glad I heard of those bills; though it's plaguy unlucky; I hoped to see Mary married before I died.

MANLY. Will you permit a gentleman, sir, to offer himself as a suitor to your daughter? Though a stranger to you, he is not altogether so to her, or unknown in the city. You may find a son-in-law of more fortune, but you can never meet with one who is richer in love for her, or respect for you.

VAN ROUGH. Why, Mary, you have not let this gentleman make love to you without my leave?

MANLY. I did not say, sir—

MARIA. Say, sir!—I—the gentleman, to be sure, met me accidentally.

VAN ROUGH. Ha, ha, ha! Mark me, Mary; young folks think old folks to be fools; but old folks know young folks to be fools. Why, I knew all about this affair:—This was only a cunning way I had to bring it about. Hark ye! I was in the closet when you and he were at our house. [*Turns to the company.*] I heard that little baggage say she loved her old father, and would die to make him happy! Oh! how I loved the little baggage!—And you talked very prudently, young man. I have inquired into your character, and find you to be a man of punctuality and mind the main chance. And so, as you love Mary, and Mary loves you, you shall have my consent immediately to be married. I'll settle my fortune on you, and go and live with you the remainder of my life.

MANLY. Sir, I hope—

VAN ROUGH. Come, come, no fine speeches; mind the main chance, young man, and you and I shall always agree.

LETITIA. I sincerely wish you joy [*Advancing to* MARIA.]; and hope your pardon for my conduct.

MARIA. I thank you for your congratulations, and hope we shall at once forget the wretch who has given us so much disquiet, and the trouble that he has occasioned.

CHARLOTTE. And I, my dear Maria,—how shall I look up to you for forgiveness? I, who, in the practice of the meanest arts, have violated the most sacred rights of friendship? I can never forgive myself, or hope charity from the world; but, I confess, I have much to hope from such a brother; and I am happy that I may soon say, such a sister.

MARIA. My dear, you distress me; you have all my love.

MANLY. And mine.

CHARLOTTE. If repentance can entitle me to forgiveness, I have already much merit: for I despise the littleness of my past conduct. I now find that the heart of any worthy man cannot be gained by invidious attacks upon the rights and characters of others;—by countenancing the addresses of a thousand;—or that the finest assemblage of features, the greatest taste in dress, the genteelest address, or the most brilliant wit, cannot eventually secure a coquette from contempt and ridicule.

MANLY. And I have learned that probity, virtue, honour, though they should not have received the polish of Europe, will secure to an honest American the good graces of his fair countrywomen, and, I hope, the applause of THE PUBLIC.

The End.

ANDRÉ

By

WILLIAM DUNLAP

WILLIAM DUNLAP

WILLIAM DUNLAP:
FATHER OF THE AMERICAN THEATRE
(1766–1839)

The life of William Dunlap is full of colour and variety. Upon his shoulders very largely rests the responsibility for whatever knowledge we have of the atmosphere of the early theatre in America, and of the personalities of the players. For, as a boy, his father being a Loyalist, there is no doubt that young William used to frequent the play-house of the Red Coats, and we would like to believe actually saw some of the performances with which Major André was connected.

He was born at Perth Amboy, then the seat of government for the Province of New Jersey, on February 10, 1766 (where he died September 28, 1839), and, therefore, as an historian of the theatre, he was able to glean his information from first hand sources. Yet, his monumental work on the "History of the American Theatre" was written in late years, when memory was beginning to be overclouded, and, in recent times, it has been shown that Dunlap was not always careful in his dates or in his statements. George Seilhamer, whose three volumes, dealing with the American Theatre before the year 1800, are invaluable, is particularly acrimonious in his strictures against Dunlap. Nevertheless, he has to confess his indebtedness to the Father of the American Theatre.

Dunlap was many-sided in his tastes and activities. There is small reason to doubt that from his earliest years the theatre proved his most attractive pleasure. But, when he was scarcely in the flush of youth, he went to Europe, and studied art under Benjamin West. Throughout his life he was ever producing canvases, and designing, and his interest in the art activity of the country, which connects his name with the establishment of the New York Academy of Design, together with his writing on the subject, make him an important figure in that line of work.

On his return from Europe, as we have already noted, he was fired to write plays through the success of Royall Tyler, and he began his long career as dramatist, which threw him upon his own inventive resourcefulness, and so closely identified him with the name of the German, Kotzebue, whose plays he used to translate and adapt by the wholesale, as did also Charles Smith.

The pictures of William Dunlap are very careful to indicate in realistic fashion the fact that he had but one eye. When a boy, one of his playmates at school threw a stone, which hit his right eye. But though he was thus early made single-visioned, he saw more than his contemporaries; for he was a man who mingled much in the social life of the time, and he had a variety of friends, among them Charles Brockden Brown, the novelist, and George Frederick Cooke, the tragedian. He was the biographer for both of them, and these volumes are filled with anecdote, which throws light, not only on the subjects, but upon the observational taste of the writer. There are those who claim that he was unjust to Cooke, making him more of a drunkard than he really was. And the effect the book had on some of its readers may excellently well be seen by Lord Byron's exclamation, after having finished it. As quoted by Miss Crawford, in her "Romance of the American Theatre," he said: "Such a book! I believe, since 'Drunken Barnaby's Journal,' nothing like it has drenched the press. All green-room and tap-room, drams and the drama. Brandy, whiskey-punch, and, latterly, toddy, overflow every page. Two things are rather marvelous; first, that a man should live so long drunk, and next that he should have found a sober biographer."

Dunlap's first play was called "The Modest Soldier; or, Love in New York" (1787). We shall let him be his own chronicler:

As a medium of communication between the playwriter and the manager, a man was pointed out, who had for a time been of some consequence on the London boards, and now resided under another name in New York. This was the Dubellamy of the English stage, a first singer and *walking-gentleman*. He was now past his meridian, but still a handsome man, and was found sufficiently easy of access and full of the courtesy of the old school. A meeting was arranged at the City Tavern, and a bottle of Madeira discussed with the merits of this first-born of a would-be author. The wine was praised, and the play was praised—the first, perhaps, made the second tolerable—that must be good which can repay a man of the world for listening to an author who reads his own play.

In due course of time, the youthful playwright reached the presence of the then all-powerful actors, Hallam and Henry, and, after some conference with them, the play was accepted. But though accepted, it was not produced, that auspicious occasion being deferred whenever the subject was broached. At this time, young Dunlap was introduced to the stony paths of playwriting. He had to alter his manuscript in many ways, only to see it laid upon the shelf until some future occasion. And, according to his confession, the reason the piece did not receive immediate production was because there was no part which Henry, the six-foot, handsome idol of the day, could see himself in to his own satisfaction.

Dunlap's next play was "The Father; or, American Shandy-ism,[1] which was produced on September 7, 1789. It was published almost immediately, and was later reprinted, under the title of "The Father of an Only Child."

Most historians call attention to the fact that to Dunlap belongs the credit of having first introduced to the American stage the German dialect of the later Comedian. Even as we look to Tyler's "The Contrast" for the first Yankee, to Samuel Low's "Politician Out-witted" for an early example of Negro dialect, so may we trace other veins of American characteristics as they appeared in early American dramas.

But it is to "Darby's Return,"[2] the musical piece, that our interest points, because it was produced for the benefit of Thomas Wignell, at the New-York Theatre (November 24, 1789), and probably boasted among its first-nighters George Washington. Writes Dunlap:

> The eyes of the audience were frequently bent on his countenance, and to watch the emotions produced by any particular passage upon him was the simultaneous employment of all. When Wignell, as *Darby*, recounts what had befallen him in America, in New York, at the adoption of the Federal Constitution, and the inauguration of the President, the interest expressed by the audience in the looks and the changes of countenance of this great man became intense.

And then there follows an indication by Dunlap of where Washington smiled, and where he showed displeasure. And,

[1] The/Father;/or,/American Shandy-ism./A Comedy,/As performed at the New-York Theatre,/By the/Old American Company./Written in the year 1788./With what fond hope, through many a blissful hour,/We give the soul to Fancy's pleasing pow'r./Conquest of Canaan./New-York:/Printed by Hodge, Allen & Campbell./M, DCC, LXXXIX./

[2] Darby's Return:/A Comic Sketch,/As Performed at the New-York Theatre,/November 24, 1789,/For the Benefit of Mr. Wignell. Written by William Dunlap./New-York:/Printed by Hodge, Allen and Campbell./And Sold at their respective Bookstores,/and by Berry and Rogers./M, DCC, LXXXIX./

altogether, there was much perturbation of mind over every quiver of his eye-lash. The fact of the matter is, as a playgoer, the Father of our Country figured quite as constantly as the Father of our Theatre. When the seat of Government changed from New York to Philadelphia, President Washington's love of the theatre prompted many theatrical enterprises to follow in his wake, and we have an interesting picture, painted in words by Seilhamer (ii, 316), of the scene at the old Southwark on such an occasion. He says:

[The President] frequently occupied the east stage-box, which was fitted up expressly for his reception. Over the front of the box was the United States coat-of-arms and the interior was gracefully festooned with red drapery. The front of the box and the seats were cushioned. According to John [*sic*] Durang, Washington's reception at the theatre was always exceedingly formal and ceremonious. A soldier was generally posted at each stage-door; four soldiers were placed in the gallery; a military guard attended. Mr. Wignell, in a full dress of black, with his hair elaborately powdered in the fashion of the time, and holding two wax candles in silver candle-sticks, was accustomed to receive the President at the box-door and conduct Washington and his party to their seats. Even the newspapers began to take notice of the President's contemplated visits to the theatre.

This is the atmosphere which must have attended the performance of Dunlap's "Darby's Return."

The play which probably is best known to-day, as by William Dunlap, is his "André,[1] in which Washington figures as the General, later to appear under his full name, when Dunlap utilized the old drama in a manuscript libretto, entitled "The Glory of Columbia—Her Yeomanry" (1817). The play was produced on March 30, 1798, after Dunlap had become manager of the New Park Theatre, within whose proscenium it was given. Professor Matthews, editing the piece for the Dunlap Society (No. 4, 1887), claims that this was the first drama acted in the United States during Washington's life, in which he was made to appear on the stage of a theatre. But it must not be forgotten that in "The Fall of British Tyranny," written in 1776, by Leacock, Washington appears for the first time in any piece of American

[1] André;/A Tragedy, in Five Acts:/As Performed by the Old American Company,/ New-York, March 30, 1798./To which are added,/Authentic Documents/respecting/ Major André;/Consisting of/Letters to Miss Seward,/The/Cow Chace,/Proceedings of the Court Martial, &c./Copy Right Secured./New-York:/Printed by T. & J. Swords, No. 99 Pearl-street./1798./

fiction. Dunlap writes of the performance (American Theatre, ii, 20):

The receipts were 817 dollars, a temporary relief. The play was received with warm applause, until Mr. Cooper, in the character of a young American officer, who had been treated as a brother by André when a prisoner with the British, in his zeal and gratitude, having pleaded for the life of the spy in vain, tears the American cockade from his casque, and throws it from him. This was not, perhaps could not be, understood by a mixed assembly; they thought the country and its defenders insulted, and a hiss ensued—it was soon quieted, and the play ended with applause. But the feeling excited by the incident was propagated out of doors. Cooper's friends wished the play withdrawn, on his account, fearing for his popularity. However, the author made an alteration in the incident, and subsequently all went on to the end with applause.

A scene from the last act of "André"[1] was produced at an American Drama Matinée, under the auspices of the American Drama Committee of the Drama League of America, New York Centre, on January 22nd and 23rd, 1917. There are many Arnold and André plays, some of which have been noted by Professor Matthews.[2] Another interesting historical study is the stage popularity of Nathan Hale.

We might go on indefinitely, narrating incidents connected with Dunlap as citizen, painter, playwright, author, and theatrical manager, for within a very short time he managed the John Street and New Park Theatres, retiring for a while in 1805.

But this is sufficient to illustrate the pioneer character of his work and influence. Inaccurate he may have been in his "History of the American Theatre," but the atmosphere is there, and he never failed to recognize merit, and to give touches of character to the actors, without which our impression of the early theatre in this country would be the poorer. The name of William Dunlap is intimately associated with the beginnings of American painting, American literary life and the American Theatre. It is for these he will ever remain distinguished.

As a playwright, he wrote so rapidly, and so constantly utilized over and over again, not only his own material, but the materials of others, that it is not surprising to find him often in dispute with

[1] One of Dunlap's best-known tragedies was "Leicester," published by David Longworth in 1807.
[2] Freneau began a play, "The Spy" (Pattee, "Poems of Philip Freneau"), in which André was a character.

dramatic authors of the time. A typical disagreement occurred in the case of the actor John Hodgkinson (1767–1805), whose drama, "The Man of Fortitude; or, the Knight's Adventure," given at the John Street Theatre, on June 7, 1797, was, according to Dunlap, based on his own one-act verse play, "The Knight's Adventure," submitted to the actor some years before.

Only the play, based on the 1798 edition, is here reproduced. The authentic documents are omitted.

ANDRE;

A *TRAGEDY*, IN FIVE ACTS:

AS PERFORMED BY THE OLD AMERICAN COMPANY,
NEW-YORK, MARCH 30, 1798.

TO WHICH ARE ADDED

AUTHENTIC DOCUMENTS

RESPECTING

MAJOR ANDRE;

CONSISTING OF

LETTERS TO MISS SEWARD,

THE

COW CHACE,

PROCEEDINGS OF THE **COURT MARTIAL,** &c.

COPY RIGHT SECURED.

NEW-YORK:
Printed by T. & J. SWORDS, No. 99 Pearl-street.
—1798.—

FAC-SIMILE TITLE-PAGE OF THE FIRST EDITION

PREFACE

More than nine years ago the Author made choice of the death of Major André as the Subject of a Tragedy, and part of what is now offered to the public was written at that time. Many circumstances discouraged him from finishing his Play, and among them must be reckoned a prevailing opinion that recent events are unfit subjects for tragedy. These discouragements have at length all given way to his desire of bringing a story on the Stage so eminently fitted, in his opinion, to excite interest in the breasts of an American audience.

In exhibiting a stage representation of a real transaction, the particulars of which are fresh in the minds of many of the audience, an author has this peculiar difficulty to struggle with, that those who know the events expect to see them *all* recorded; and any deviation from what they remember to be fact, appears to them as a fault in the poet; they are disappointed, their expectations are not fulfilled, and the writer is more or less condemned, not considering the difference between the poet and the historian, or not knowing that what is intended to be exhibited is a free poetical picture, not an exact historical portrait.

Still further difficulties has the Tragedy of André to surmount, difficulties independent of its own demerits, in its way to public favour. The subject necessarily involves political questions; but the Author presumes that he owes no apology to any one for having shewn himself an American. The friends of Major André (and it appears that all who knew him were his friends) will look with a jealous eye on the Poem, whose principal incident is the sad catastrophe which his misconduct, in submitting to be an instrument in a transaction of treachery and deceit, justly brought upon him: but these friends have no cause of offence; the Author has adorned the poetical character of André with every virtue; he has made him his Hero; to do which, he was under the necessity of making him condemn his own conduct, in the one dreadfully unfortunate action of his life. To shew the effects which Major André's excellent qualities had upon the minds of men, the Author has drawn a generous and amiable youth, so blinded by his love for the accomplished Briton, as to consider his country, and the great commander of her armies, as in the commission of such horrid injustice, that he, in the anguish of his soul, disclaims the service. In this it appears, since the first representation, that the Author has gone near to offend the veterans of the American army who were present on the first night, and who not knowing the sequel of the action, felt much disposed to condemn him: but surely they must remember the diversity of opinion which agitated the minds of men at that time, on the question of the propriety of putting André to death; and when they add the circumstances of André's having saved the life of this youth, and gained his ardent friendship, they will be inclined to mingle with their disapprobation, a sentiment of pity, and excuse, perhaps commend the Poet, who has represented the action without sanctioning it by his approbation.

As a sequel to the affair of the cockade, the Author has added the following lines, which the reader is requested to insert, page 55, between the 5th and 15th lines, instead of the lines he will find there, which were printed before the piece was represented.*—

BLAND.

Noble M'Donald, truth and honour's champion!
Yet think not strange that my intemperance wrong'd thee:
Good as thou art! for, would'st thou, canst thou, think it?
My tongue, unbridled, hath the same offence,
With action violent, and boisterous tone,
Hurl'd on that glorious man, whose pious labours
Shield from every ill his grateful country!
That man, whom friends to adoration love,
And enemies revere.—Yes, M'Donald,
Even in the presence of the first of men
Did I abjure the service of my country,
And reft my helmet of that glorious badge
Which graces even the brow of Washington.
How shall I see him more!—

M'DONALD.

Alive himself to every generous impulse,
He hath excus'd the impetuous warmth of youth,
In expectation that thy fiery soul,

* See p. 557.

Chasten'd by time and reason, will receive
The stamp indelible of godlike virtue.
To me, in trust, he gave this badge disclaim'd,
With power, when thou shouldst see thy wrongful error,
From him, to reinstate it in thy helm,
And thee in his high favour. [*Gives the cockade.*

BLAND [*takes the cockade and replaces it*].

Shall I speak my thoughts of thee and him?
No:—let my actions henceforth shew what thou
And he have made me. Ne'er shall my helmet
Lack again its proudest, noblest ornament,
Until my country knows the rest of peace,
Or Bland the peace of death! [*Exit.*

This alteration, as well as the whole performance, on the second night, met the warm approbation of the audience.

To the performers the Author takes this opportunity of returning his thanks for their exertions in his behalf; perfectly convinced, that on this, as on former occasions, the members of the Old American Company have anxiously striven to oblige him.

If this Play is successful, it will be a proof that recent events may be so managed in tragedy as to command popular attention; if it is unsuccessful, the question must remain undetermined until some more powerful writer shall again make the experiment. The Poem is now submitted to the ordeal of closet examination, with the Author's respectful assurance to every reader, that as it is not his interest, so it has not been his intention, to offend any; but, on the contrary, to impress, through the medium of a pleasing stage exhibition, the sublime lessons of Truth and Justice upon the minds of his countrymen.

W. DUNLAP.

New-York, April 4th, 1798.

PROLOGUE

SPOKEN BY MR. MARTIN.

A native Bard, a native scene displays,
And claims your candour for his daring lays:
Daring, so soon, in mimic scenes to shew,
What each remembers as a real woe.
Who has forgot when gallant ANDRÉ died?
A name by Fate to Sorrow's self allied.
Who has forgot, when o'er the untimely bier,
Contending armies paus'd, to drop a tear.

Our Poet builds upon a fact tonight;
Yet claims, in building, every Poet's right;
To choose, embellish, lop, or add, or blend,
Fiction with truth, as best may suit his end;
Which, he avows, is pleasure to impart,
And move the passions but to mend the heart.

Oh, may no party-spirit blast his views,
Or turn to ill the meanings of the Muse:
She sings of wrongs long past, Men as they were,
To instruct, without reproach, the Men that are;
Then judge the Story by the genius shewn,
And praise, or damn, it, for its worth alone.

CHARACTERS

GENERAL, *dress, American staff uniform, blue, faced with buff, large gold epaulets, cocked hat, with the black and white cockade, indicating the union with France, buff waistcoat and breeches, boots,*   Mr. Hallam.

M'DONALD, *a man of forty years of age, uniform nearly the same of the first,*   Mr. Tyler.

SEWARD, *a man of thirty years of age, staff uniform,*   Mr. Martin.

ANDRÉ, *a man of twenty-nine years of age, full British uniform after the first scene,*   Mr. Hodgkinson.

BLAND, *a youthful but military figure, in the uniform of a Captain of horse—dress, a short blue coat, faced with red, and trimmed with gold lace, two small epaulets, a white waistcoat, leather breeches, boots and spurs; over the coat, crossing the chest from the right shoulder, a broad buff belt, to which is suspended a manageable hussar sword; a horseman's helmet on the head, decorated as usual, and the union cockade affixed,*   Mr. Cooper.

MELVILLE, *a man of middle age, and grave deportment; his dress a Captain's uniform when on duty; a blue coat, with red facings, gold epaulet, white waistcoat and breeches, boots and cocked hat, with the union cockade,*   Mr. Williamson.

BRITISH OFFICER,   Mr. Hogg.

AMERICAN OFFICER,   Mr. Miller.

CHILDREN,   Master Stockwell and Miss Hogg.

AMERICAN SERGEANT,   Mr. Seymour.

AMERICAN OFFICERS AND SOLDIERS, &c.

MRS. BLAND,   Mrs. Melmoth.

HONORA,   Mrs. Johnson.

SCENE, the Village of Tappan, Encampment, and adjoining Country. Time, ten hours.

ANDRÉ

ACT I.

SCENE I. *A Wood seen by starlight; an Encampment at a distance appearing between the trees.*

Enter MELVILLE.

MELVILLE.

The solemn hour, "when night and morning meet,"
Mysterious time, to superstition dear,
And superstition's guides, now passes by;
Deathlike in solitude. The sentinels,
In drowsy tones, from post to post, send on
The signal of the passing hour. "All's well,"
Sounds through the camp. Alas! all is not well;
Else, why stand I, a man, the friend of man,
At midnight's depth, deck'd in this murderous guise,
The habiliment of death, the badge of dire,
Necessitous coercion. 'T is not well.
—In vain the enlighten'd friends of suffering man
Point out, of war, the folly, guilt, and madness.
Still, age succeeds to age, and war to war;
And man, the murderer, marshalls out his hosts
In all the gaiety of festive pomp,
To spread around him death and desolation.
How long! how long!——
—Methinks I hear the tread of feet this way.
My meditating mood may work me woe.   [*Draws.*
Stand, whoso'er thou art. Answer. Who's there?

Enter BLAND.

BLAND.

A friend.

MELVILLE.

Advance and give the countersign.

BLAND.

Hudson.

MELVILLE.

What, Bland!

BLAND.

Melville, my friend, you *here*?

MELVILLE.

And *well*, my brave young friend. But why do you,
At this dead hour of night, approach the camp,
On foot, and thus alone?

BLAND.

        I have but now
Dismounted; and, from yon sequester'd cot,
Whose lonely taper through the crannied wall
Sheds its faint beams, and twinkles midst the trees,
Have I, adventurous, grop'd my darksome way.
My servant, and my horses, spent with toil,
There wait till morn.

MELVILLE.

        Why waited not yourself?

BLAND.

Anxious to know the truth of those reports
Which, from the many mouths of busy Fame,
Still, as I pass'd, struck varying on my ear,
Each making th' other void. Nor does delay
The colour of my hasteful business suit.
I bring dispatches for our great Commander;
And hasted hither with design to wait
His rising, or awake him with the sun.

MELVILLE.

You will not need the last, for the blest sun
Ne'er rises on his slumbers; by the dawn
We see him mounted gaily in the field,
Or find him wrapt in meditation deep,
Planning the welfare of our war-worn land.

BLAND.

Prosper, kind heaven! and recompense his cares.

MELVILLE.

You're from the South, if I presume aright?

BLAND.

I am; and, Melville, I am fraught with news?
The South teems with events; convulsing ones:
The Briton, there, plays at no mimic war;
With gallant face he moves, and gallantly is met.
Brave spirits, rous'd by glory, throng our camp;
The hardy hunter, skill'd to fell the deer,
Or start the sluggish bear from covert rude;
And not a clown that comes, but from his youth
Is trained to pour from far the leaden death,
To climb the steep, to struggle with the stream,
To labour firmly under scorching skies,
And bear, unshrinking, winter's roughest blast.
This, and that heaven-inspir'd enthusiasm
Which ever animates the patriot's breast,
Shall far outweigh the lack of discipline.

MELVILLE.

Justice is ours; what shall prevail against her?

BLAND.

But as I past along, many strange tales,
And monstrous rumours, have my ears assail'd:
That Arnold had prov'd false; but he was ta'en,
And hung, or to be hung—I know not what.
Another told, that all our army, with their
Much lov'd Chief, sold and betray'd, were captur'd.
But, as I nearer drew, at yonder cot,
'T was said, that Arnold, traitor like, had fled;
And that a Briton, tried and prov'd a spy,
Was, on this day, as such, to suffer death.

MELVILLE.

As you drew near, plain truth advanced to meet you.
'T is even as you heard, my brave young friend.
Never had people on a single throw
More interest at stake; when he, who held
For us the die, prov'd false, and play'd us foul.
But for a circumstance of that nice kind,

Of cause so microscopic, that the tongues
Of inattentive men call it the effect
Of chance, we must have lost the glorious game.

BLAND.

Blest, blest be heaven! whatever was the cause!

MELVILLE.

The blow ere this had fallen that would have bruis'd
The tender plant which we have striven to rear,
Crush'd to the dust, no more to bless this soil.

BLAND.

What warded off the blow?

MELVILLE.

The brave young man, who this day dies, was seiz'd
Within our bounds, in rustic garb disguis'd.
He offer'd bribes to tempt the band that seiz'd him;
But the rough farmer, for his country arm'd,
That soil defending which his ploughshare turn'd,
Those laws, his father chose, and he approv'd,
Cannot, as mercenary soldiers may,
Be brib'd to sell the public-weal for gold.

BLAND.

'T is well. Just heaven! O, grant that thus may fall
All those who seek to bring this land to woe!
All those, who, or by open force, or dark
And secret machinations, seek to shake
The Tree of Liberty, or stop its growth,
In any soil where thou hast pleas'd to plant it.

MELVILLE.

Yet not a heart but pities and would save him;
For all confirm that he is brave and virtuous;
Known, but till now, the darling child of Honour.

BLAND [*contemptuously*].

And how is call'd this—honourable spy?

MELVILLE.

André's his name.

BLAND [*much agitated*].

André!

MELVILLE.

Aye, Major André.

BLAND.

André! Oh no, my friend, you're sure deceiv'd—
I'll pawn my life, my ever sacred fame,
My General's favour, or a soldier's honour,
That gallant André never yet put on
The guise of falsehood. Oh, it cannot be!

MELVILLE.

How might I be deceiv'd? I've heard him, seen him,
And what I tell, I tell from well-prov'd knowledge;
No second tale-bearer, who heard the news.

BLAND.

Pardon me, Melville. Oh, that well-known name,
So link'd with circumstances infamous!—
My friend must pardon me. Thou wilt not blame
When I shall tell what cause I have to love him:
What cause to think him nothing more the pupil
Of Honour stern, than sweet Humanity.
Rememberest thou, when cover'd o'er with wounds,
And left upon the field, I fell the prey
Of Britain? To a loathsome prison-ship
Confin'd, soon had I sunk, victim of death,
A death of aggravated miseries;
But, by benevolence urg'd, this best of men,
This gallant youth, then favour'd, high in power,
Sought out the pit obscene of foul disease,
Where I, and many a suffering soldier lay,
And, like an angel, seeking good for man,
Restor'd us light, and partial liberty.
Me he mark'd out his own. He nurst and cur'd,
He lov'd and made his friend. I liv'd by him,
And in my heart he liv'd, till, when exchang'd,
Duty and honour call'd me from my friend.—
Judge how my heart is tortur'd.—Gracious heaven!
Thus, thus to meet him on the brink of death—

A death so infamous! Heav'n grant my prayer.   *[Kneels.*
That I may save him, O, inspire my heart
With thoughts, my tongue with words that move to pity!

    [Rises.

Quick, Melville, shew me where my André lies.

MELVILLE.

Good wishes go with you.

BLAND.

I'll save my friend.   *[Exeunt.*

SCENE, *the Encampment, by starlight.*

Enter the GENERAL, M'DONALD *and* SEWARD.

GENERAL.

'T is well. Each sentinel upon his post
Stands firm, and meets me at the bayonet's point;
While in his tent the weary soldier lies,
The sweet reward of wholesome toil enjoying;
Resting secure as erst within his cot
He careless slept, his rural labour o'er;
Ere Britons dar'd to violate those laws,
Those boasted laws by which themselves are govern'd,
And strove to make their fellow-subjects slaves.

SEWARD.

They know to whom they owe their present safety.

GENERAL.

I hope they know that to themselves they owe it:
To that good discipline which they observe,
The discipline of men to order train'd,
Who know its value, and in whom 't is virtue:
To that prompt hardihood with which they meet
Or toil or danger, poverty or death.
Mankind who know not whence that spirit springs,
Which holds at bay all Britain's boasted power,
Gaze on their deeds astonish'd. See the youth
Start from his plough, and straightway play the hero;
Unmurmuring bear such toils as veterans shun;

Rest all content upon the dampsome earth;
Follow undaunted to the deathful charge;
Or, when occasion asks, lead to the breach,
Fearless of all the unusual din of war,
His former peaceful mates. O patriotism!
Thou wond'rous principle of god-like action!
Wherever liberty is found, there reigns
The love of country. Now the self-same spirit
Which fill'd the breast of great Leonidas,
Swells in the hearts of thousands on these plains,
Thousands who never heard the hero's tale.
'T is this alone which saves thee, O my country!
And, till that spirit flies these western shores,
No power on earth shall crush thee!

SEWARD.

'T is wond'rous!
The men of other climes from this shall see
How easy 't is to shake oppression off;
How all resistless is an union'd people:
And hence, from our success (which, by my soul,
I feel as much secur'd, as though our foes
Were now within their floating prisons hous'd,
And their proud prows all pointing to the east),
Shall other nations break their galling fetters,
And re-assume the dignity of man.

M'DONALD.

Are other nations in that happy state,
That, having broke Coercion's iron yoke,
They can submit to Order's gentle voice,
And walk on earth self-ruled? I much do fear it.
As to ourselves, in truth, I nothing see,
In all the wond'rous deeds which we perform,
But plain effects from causes full as plain.
Rises not man for ever 'gainst oppression?
It is the law of life; he can't avoid it.
But when the love of property unites
With sense of injuries past, and dread of future,
Is it then wonderful, that he should brave
A lesser evil to avoid a greater?

GENERAL [*sportively*].

'T is hard, quite hard, we may not please ourselves,
By our great deeds ascribing to our virtue.

SEWARD.

M'Donald never spares to lash our pride.

M'DONALD.

In truth I know of nought to make you proud.
I think there's none within the camp that draws
With better will his sword than does M'Donald.
I have a home to guard.   My son is—butcher'd—

SEWARD.

Hast thou no nobler motives for thy arms
Than love of property and thirst of vengeance?

M'DONALD.

Yes, my good Seward, and yet nothing wond'rous.
I love this country for the sake of man.
My parents, and I thank them, cross'd the seas,
And made me native of fair Nature's world,
With room to grow and thrive in.   I have thriven;
And feel my mind unshackled, free, expanding,
Grasping, with ken unbounded, mighty thoughts,
At which, if chance my mother had, good dame,
In Scotia, our revered parent soil,
Given me to see the day, I should have shrunk
Affrighted.   Now, I see in this new world
A resting spot for man, if he can stand
Firm in his place, while Europe howls around him,
And all unsettled as the thoughts of vice,
Each nation in its turn threats him with feeble malice.
One trial, now, we prove; and I have met it.

GENERAL.

And met it like a man, my brave M'Donald.

M'DONALD.

I hope so; and I hope my every act
Has been the offspring of deliberate judgment;
Yet, feeling second's reason's cool resolves.

Oh! I could hate, if I did not more pity,
These bands of mercenary Europeans,
So wanting in the common sense of nature,
As, without shame, to sell themselves for pelf,
To aid the cause of darkness, murder man—
Without inquiry murder, and yet call
Their trade the trade of honour—high-soul'd honour—
Yet honour shall accord in act with falsehood.
Oh, that proud man should e'er descend to play
The tempter's part, and lure men to their ruin!
Deceit and honour badly pair together.

SEWARD.

You have much shew of reason; yet, methinks
What you suggest of one, whom fickle Fortune,
In her changeling mood, hath hurl'd, unpitying,
From her topmost height to lowest misery,
Tastes not of charity. André, I mean.

M'DONALD.

I mean him, too; sunk by misdeed, not fortune.
Fortune and chance, Oh, most convenient words!
Man runs the wild career of blind ambition,
Plunges in vice, takes falsehood for his buoy,
And when he feels the waves of ruin o'er him,
Curses, in "good set terms," poor Lady Fortune.

GENERAL [*sportively to* SEWARD].

His mood is all untoward; let us leave him.
Tho' he may think that he is bound to rail,
We are not bound to hear him.   [*To* M'DONALD.
Grant you that?

M'DONALD.

Oh, freely, freely! you I never rail on.

GENERAL.

No thanks for that; you've courtesy for office.

M'DONALD.

You slander me.

GENERAL.

          Slander that would not wound.
Worthy M'Donald, though it suits full well

The virtuous man to frown on all misdeeds;
Yet ever keep in mind that man is frail;
His tide of passion struggling still with Reason's
Fair and favourable gale, and adverse
Driving his unstable Bark upon the
Rocks of error. Should he sink thus shipwreck'd,
Sure it is not Virtue's voice that triumphs
In his ruin. I must seek rest. Adieu!

[*Exeunt* GENERAL *and* SEWARD.

M'DONALD.

Both good and great thou art: first among men:
By nature, or by early habit, grac'd
With that blest quality which gives due force
To every faculty, and keeps the mind
In healthful equipoise, ready for action;
Invaluable temperance—by all
To be acquired, yet scarcely known to any.   [*Exit.*

End of the First Act.

ACT II.

SCENE, *a Prison.*

ANDRÉ, *discovered in a pensive posture, sitting at a table; a book
by him and candles: his dress neglected, his hair dishevelled:
he rises and comes forward.*

ANDRÉ.

Kind heaven be thank'd for that I stand alone
In this sad hour of life's brief pilgrimage!
Single in misery; no one else involving,
In grief, in shame, and ruin. 'T is my comfort.
Thou, my thrice honour'd sire, in peace went'st down
Unto the tomb, nor knew to blush, nor knew
A pang for me! And thou, revered matron,
Couldst bless thy child, and yield thy breath in peace!
No wife shall weep, no child lament, my loss.
Thus may I consolation find in what
Was once my woe. I little thought to joy
In not possessing, as I erst possest,

Thy love, Honora! André's death, perhaps,
May cause a cloud pass o'er thy lovely face;
The pearly tear may steal from either eye;
For thou mayest feel a transient pang, nor wrong
A husband's rights: more than a transient pang
O mayest thou never feel! The morn draws nigh
To light me to my shame. Frail nature shrinks.—
And *is* death then so fearful? I have brav'd
Him, fearless, in the field, and steel'd my breast
Against his thousand horrors; but his cool,
His sure approach, requires a fortitude
Which nought but conscious rectitude can give.

[*Retires, and sits leaning.*

Enter BLAND *unperceived by* ANDRÉ.

BLAND.

And is that André! Oh, how chang'd! Alas!
Where is that martial fire, that generous warmth,
Which glow'd his manly countenance throughout,
And gave to every look, to every act,
The tone of high chivalrous animation?—
André, my friend! look up.

ANDRÉ.
Who calls *me* friend?

BLAND.

Young Arthur Bland.

ANDRÉ [*rising*].
That name sounds like a friend's. [*With emotion.*
I have inquir'd for thee—wish'd much to see thee—
I prithee take no note of these fool's tears—
My heart was full—and seeing thee—

BLAND [*embracing him*].
O André!—
I have but now arrived from the south—
Nor heard—till now—of this—I cannot speak.
Is this a place?—Oh, thus to find my friend!

ANDRÉ.
Still dost thou call me friend? I, who dared act
Against my reason, my declared opinion;

Against my conscience, and a soldier's fame?
Oft in the generous heat of glowing youth,
Oft have I said how fully I despis'd
All bribery base, all treacherous tricks in war:
Rather my blood should bathe these hostile shores,
And have it said, "he died a gallant soldier,"
Than with my country's gold encourage treason,
And thereby purchase gratitude and fame.

BLAND.

Still mayest thou say it, for thy heart's the same.

ANDRÉ.

Still is my heart the same: still may I say it:
But now my deeds will rise against my words;
And should I dare to talk of honest truth,
Frank undissembling probity and faith,
Memory would crimson o'er my burning cheek,
And actions retrospected choke the tale.
Still is my heart the same.   But there has past
A day, an hour— which ne'er can be recall'd!
Unhappy man! tho' all thy life pass pure;
Mark'd by benevolence thy every deed;
The out-spread map, which shews the way thou'st trod,
Without one devious track, or doubtful line;
It all avails thee nought, if in one hour,
One hapless hour, thy feet are led astray;—
Thy happy deeds, all blotted from remembrance;
Cancel'd the record of thy former good.
Is it not hard, my friend?   Is 't not unjust?

BLAND.

Not every record cancel'd—Oh, there are hearts,
Where Virtue's image, when 't is once engrav'd,
Can never know erasure.

ANDRÉ.

Generous Bland!   [*Takes his hand.*
The hour draws nigh which ends my life's sad story.
I should be firm—

BLAND.

By heaven thou shalt not die!
Thou dost not sure deserve it. Betray'd, perhaps—

Condemn'd without due circumstance made known?
Thou didst not mean to tempt our officers?
Betray our yeoman soldiers to destruction?
Silent. Nay, then 't was from a duteous wish
To serve the cause thou wast in honour bound—

ANDRÉ.

Kind is my Bland, who to his generous heart,
Still finds excuses for his erring friend.
Attentive hear and judge me.—
Pleas'd with the honours daily shower'd upon me,
I glow'd with martial heat, my name to raise
Above the vulgar herd, who live to die,
And die to be forgotten. Thus I stood,
When, avarice or ambition Arnold tempted,
His country, fame, and honour to betray;
Linking his name to infamy eternal.
In confidence it was to be propos'd,
To plan with him the means which should ensure
Thy country's downfall. Nothing then I saw
But confidential favour in the service,
My country's glory, and my mounting fame;
Forgot my former purity of thought,
And high-ton'd honour's scruples disregarded.

BLAND.

It was thy duty so to serve thy country.

ANDRÉ.

Nay, nay; be cautious ever to admit
That duty can beget dissimulation.
On ground, unoccupied by either part,
Neutral esteem'd, I landed, and was met.
But ere my conference was with Arnold clos'd,
The day began to dawn: I then was told
That till the night I must my safety seek
In close concealment. Within your posts convey'd,
I found myself involv'd in unthought dangers.
Night came. I sought the vessel which had borne
Me to the fatal spot; but she was gone.
Retreat that way cut off, again I sought
Concealment with the traitors of your army.

Arnold now granted passes, and I doff'd
My martial garb, and put on curs'd disguise!
Thus in a peasant's form I pass'd your posts;
And when, as I conceiv'd, my danger o'er,
Was stopt and seiz'd by some returning scouts.
So did ambition lead me, step by step,
To treat with traitors, and encourage treason;
And then, bewilder'd in the guilty scene,
To quit my martial designating badges,
Deny my name, and sink into the spy.

BLAND.

Thou didst no more than was a soldier's duty,
To serve the part on which he drew his sword.
Thou shalt not die for this. Straight will I fly—
I surely shall prevail—

ANDRÉ.

It is in vain.
All has been tried. Each friendly argument—

BLAND.

All has not yet been tried. The powerful voice
Of friendship in thy cause, has not been heard.
My General favours *me*, and loves my father—
My gallant father! would that he were here!
But he, perhaps, now wants an André's care,
To cheer his hours—perhaps, now languishes
Amidst those horrors whence thou sav'd'st his son!
The present moment claims my thought. André—
I fly to save thee!—

ANDRÉ.

Bland, it is in vain.
But, hold—there is a service thou may'st do me.

BLAND.

Speak it.

ANDRÉ.

Oh, think, and as a soldier think,
How I must die—The *manner* of my death—
Like the base ruffian, or the midnight thief,
Ta'en in the act of stealing from the poor,

To be turn'd off the felon's—murderer's cart,
A mid-air spectacle to gaping clowns:—
To run a short, an envied course of glory,
And end it on a gibbet.——

BLAND.

Damnation!!

ANDRÉ.

Such is my doom. Oh! have the manner changed,
And of mere death I'll think not. Dost thou think—?
Perhaps thou canst gain *that*——?

BLAND [*almost in a frenzy*].
Thou shalt not die!

ANDRÉ.

Let me, Oh! let me die a soldier's death,
While friendly clouds of smoke shroud from all eyes
My last convulsive pangs, and I'm content.

BLAND [*with increasing emotion*].
Thou shalt not die! Curse on the laws of war!—
If worth like thine must thus be sacrificed,
To policy so cruel and unjust,
I will forswear my country and her service:
I'll hie me to the Briton, and with fire,
And sword, and every instrument of death
Or devastation, join in the work of war!
What, shall worth weigh for nought? I will avenge thee!

ANDRÉ.

Hold, hold, my friend; thy country's woes are full.
What! wouldst thou make me cause another traitor?
No more of this; and, if I die, believe me,
Thy country for my death incurs no blame.
Restrain thy ardour—but ceaselessly intreat,
That André may at least die as he lived,
A soldier.

BLAND.

By heaven thou shalt not die!—
[BLAND *rushes off:* ANDRÉ *looks after him with an expression
of love and gratitude, then retires up the stage. Scene closes.*]

SCENE, *the* GENERAL'S *Quarters.*

Enter M'DONALD *and* SEWARD, *in conversation.*

M'DONALD [*coming forward*].

Three thousand miles the Atlantic wave rolls on,
Which bathed Columbia's shores, ere, on the strand
Of Europe, or of Afric, their continents,
Or sea-girt isles, it chafes.—

SEWARD.

Oh! would to heaven
That in mid-way between these sever'd worlds,
Rose barriers, all impassable to man,
Cutting off intercourse, till either side
Had lost all memory of the other!

M'DONALD.

What spur now goads thy warm imagination?

SEWARD.

Then might, perhaps, one land on earth be found,
Free from th' extremes of poverty and riches;
Where ne'er a scepter'd tyrant should be known,
Or tyrant lordling, curses of creation;—
Where the faint shrieks of woe-exhausted age,
Raving, in feeble madness, o'er the corse
Of a polluted daughter, stained by lust
Of viand-pamper'd luxury, might ne'er be heard;—
Where the blasted form of much abused
Beauty, by villainy seduced, by knowledge
All unguarded, might ne'er be view'd, flitting
Obscene, 'tween lamp and lamp, i' th' midnight street
Of all defiling city; where the child——

M'DONALD.

Hold! Shroud thy raven imagination!
Torture not me with images so curst!

SEWARD.

Soon shall our foes, inglorious, fly these shores.
Peace shall again return. Then Europe's ports
Shall pour a herd upon us, far more fell

Than those, her mercenary sons, who, now,
Threaten our sore chastisement.

M'DONALD.

Prophet of ill,

From Europe shall enriching commerce flow,
And many an ill attendant; but from thence
Shall likewise flow blest Science. Europe's knowledge,
By sharp experience bought, we should appropriate;
Striving thus to leap from that simplicity,
With ignorance curst, to that simplicity,
By knowledge blest; unknown the gulf between.

SEWARD.

Mere theoretic dreaming!

M'DONALD

Blest wisdom

Seems, from out the chaos of the social world,
Where good and ill, in strange commixture, float,
To rise, by strong necessity, impell'd;
Starting, like Love divine, from womb of Night,
Illuming all, to order all reducing;
And shewing, by its bright and noontide blaze,
That happiness alone proceeds from justice.

SEWARD.

Dreams, dreams! Man can know nought but ill on earth

M'DONALD.

I'll to my bed, for I have watch'd all night;
And may my sleep give pleasing repetition
Of these my waking dreams! Virtue's incentives.   [*Exit.*

SEWARD.

Folly's chimeras rather: guides to error.

Enter BLAND, *preceded by a* SERGEANT.

SERGEANT.

Pacquets for the General.   [*Exit.*

BLAND.

Seward, my friend!

SEWARD.

Captain! I'm glad to see the hue of health
Sit on a visage from the sallow south.

BLAND.

The lustihood of youth hath yet defied
The parching sun, and chilling dew of even.
The General—Seward—?

SEWARD.

I will lead you to him.

BLAND.

Seward, I must make bold.   Leave us together,
When occasion offers.   'T will be friendly.

SEWARD.

I will not cross your purpose.   [*Exeunt.*

SCENE, *A Chamber.*

Enter MRS. BLAND.

MRS. BLAND.

Yes, ever be this day a festival
In my domestic calendar.   This morn
Will see my husband free.   Even now, perhaps,
Ere yet Aurora flies the eastern hills,
Shunning the sultry sun, my Bland embarks.
Already, on the Hudson's dancing wave,
He chides the sluggish rowers, or supplicates
For gales propitious; that his eager arms
May clasp his wife, may bless his little ones.
Oh! how the tide of joy makes my heart bound,
Glowing with high and ardent expectation!

Enter two CHILDREN.

1st CHILD.

Here we are, Mama, up, and dress'd already.

MRS. BLAND.

And why were ye so early?

1st CHILD.

Why, did not you tell us that Papa was to be home to-day?

MRS. BLAND.

I said, perhaps.

2nd CHILD [*disappointed*].

Perhaps!

1st CHILD.

I don't like perhaps's.

2nd CHILD.

No, nor I neither; nor "may be so's."

MRS. BLAND.

We make not certainties, my pretty loves;
I do not like "perhaps's" more than you do.

2nd CHILD.

Oh! don't say so, Mama! for I'm sure I hardly ever ask you anything but you answer me with "may be so," "perhaps," —or "very likely." "Mama, shall I go to the camp to-morrow, and see the General?" "May be so, my dear." Hang "may be so," say I.

MRS. BLAND.

Well said, Sir Pertness.

1st CHILD.

But I am sure, Mama, you said, that, to-day, Papa would have his liberty.

MRS. BLAND.

So, your dear father, by his letters, told me.

2nd CHILD.

Why, then, I *am sure* he will be here to-day. When he can come *to us*, I'm sure he will not stay among those strange Englishmen and Hessians. I often wish'd that I had wings to fly, for then I would soon be with him.

MRS. BLAND.

Dear boy!

Enter SERVANT *and gives a letter to* MRS. BLAND.

SERVANT.

An express, madam, from New-York to Headquarters, in passing, delivered this.

2nd CHILD.

Papa's coming home to-day, John.

[*Exeunt* SERVANT *and* CHILDREN.

MRS. BLAND.

What fears assail me! Oh! I did not want
A letter now! [*She reads in great agitation, exclaiming, while her
   eyes are fixed on the paper.*]
My husband! doom'd to die! Retaliation!
   [*She looks forward with wildness, consternation and horror.*
To die, if André dies! He dies to-day!—
My husband to be murdered! And to-day!
To-day, if André dies! Retaliation!
O curst contrivance!—Madness relieve me!
Burst, burst, my brain!—Yet—André is not dead:
My husband lives. [*Looks at the letter.*] "One man has power."
I fly to save the father of my children!

[*Rushes out.*

End of the Second Act.

ACT III.

SCENE, *the* GENERAL'S *Quarters.*

The GENERAL *and* BLAND *come forward.*

GENERAL [*papers in his hand*].

Captain, you are noted here with honourable
Praises. Depend upon that countenance
From me, which you have prov'd yourself so richly
Meriting. Both for your father's virtues,
And your own, your country owes you honour—
The sole return the poor can make for service.

BLAND.

If from my country ought I've merited,
Or gain'd the approbation of her champion,

At any other time, I should not dare,
Presumptuously, to shew my sense of it;
But now, my tongue, all shameless, dares to name
The boon, the precious recompense, I wish,
Which, granted, pays all service, past or future,
O'erpays the utmost I can e'er achieve.

GENERAL.

Brief, my young friend, briefly, your purpose.

BLAND.

If I have done my duty as a soldier;
If I have brav'd all dangers for my country;
If my brave father has deserved ought;
Call all to mind—and cancel all—but grant
My one request—mine, and humanity's.

GENERAL.

Be less profuse of words, and name your wish;
If fit, its fitness is the best assurance
That not in vain you sue; but, if unjust,
Thy merits, nor the merits of thy race,
Cannot its nature alter, nor my mind,
From its determined opposition change.

BLAND.

You hold the fate of my most lov'd of friends;
As gallant soldier as e'er faced a foe,
Bless'd with each polish'd gift of social life,
And every virtue of humanity.
To me, a saviour from the pit of death,
To me, and many more my countrymen.
Oh! could my words portray him what he is;
Bring to your mind the blessings of his deeds,
While thro' the fever-heated, loathsome holds,
Of floating hulks, dungeons obscene, where ne'er
The dewy breeze of morn, or evening's coolness,
Breath'd on our parching skins, he pass'd along,
Diffusing blessings; still his power exerting,
To alleviate the woes which ruthless war,
Perhaps, thro' dire necessity, heap'd on us;
Surely, the scene would move you to forget

His late intent—(tho' only serving then,
As duty prompted)—and turn the rigour
Of War's iron law from him, the best of men,
Meant only for the worst.

GENERAL.

Captain, no more.

BLAND.

If André lives, the prisoner finds a friend;
Else helpless and forlorn—
All men will bless the act, and bless thee for it.

GENERAL.

Think'st thou thy country would not curse the man,
Who, by a clemency ill-tim'd, ill-judg'd,
Encourag'd treason? That *pride* encourag'd,
Which, by denying us the rights of nations,
Hath caus'd those ills which thou hast now portray'd?
Our prisoners, brave and generous peasantry,
As rebels have been treated, not as men.
'T is mine, brave yeomen, to assert your rights;
'T is mine to teach the foe, that, though array'd
In rude simplicity, ye, yet, are men,
And rank among the foremost. Oft their scouts,
The very refuse of the English arms,
Unquestion'd, have our countrymen consign'd
To death, when captur'd, mocking their agonies.

BLAND.

Curse them! [*Checking himself.*] Yet let not censure fall on
    André.
Oh, there are Englishmen as brave, as good,
As ever land on earth might call its own;
And gallant André is among the best!

GENERAL.

Since they have hurl'd war on us, we must shew
That by the laws of war we will abide;
And have the power to bring their acts for trial,
To that tribunal, eminent 'mongst men,
Erected by the policy of nations,
To stem the flood of ills, which else fell war

Would pour, uncheck'd, upon the sickening world,
Sweeping away all trace of civil life.

BLAND.

To pardon him would not encourage ill.
His case is singular; his station high;
His qualities admired; his virtues lov'd.

GENERAL.

No more, my good young friend: it is in vain.
The men entrusted with thy country's rights
Have weigh'd, attentive, every circumstance.
An individual's virtue is, by them,
As highly prized as it can be by thee.
I know the virtues of this man, and love them.
But the destiny of millions, millions
Yet unborn, depends upon the rigour
Of this moment. The haughty Briton laughs
To scorn our armies and our councils. Mercy,
Humanity, call loudly, that we make
Our now despised power be felt, vindictive.
Millions demand the death of this young man.
My injur'd country, he his forfeit life
Must yield, to shield thy lacerated breast
From torture. [*To* BLAND.] Thy merits are not overlook'd.
Promotion shall immediately attend thee.

BLAND [*with contemptuous irony*].

Pardon me, sir, I never shall deserve it.
[*With increasing heat.*] The country that forgets to reverence
          virtue;
That makes no difference 'twixt the sordid wretch,
Who, for reward, risks treason's penalty,
And him unfortunate, whose duteous service
Is, by mere accident, so chang'd in form,
As to assume guilt's semblance, I serve not:
Scorn to serve. I have a soldier's honour,
But 't is in union with a freeman's judgment,
And when I act, both prompt. Thus from my helm
I tear, what once I proudly thought, the badge
Of virtuous fellowship. [*Tears the cockade from his helmet.*] My
          sword I keep. [*Puts on his helmet.*]

Would, André, thou hadst never put thine off!
Then hadst thou through opposers' hearts made way
To liberty, or bravely pierc'd thine own! [*Exit.*

GENERAL.

Rash, headstrong, maddening boy!
Had not this action past without a witness,
Duty would ask that thou shouldst rue thy folly—
But, for the motive, be the deed forgotten. [*Exit.*

SCENE, *a Village.*

At a distance some tents. In front muskets, drums, and other indications of soldiers' quarters.

Enter MRS. BLAND *and* CHILDREN, *attended by* MELVILLE.

MELVILLE.

The General's doors to you are ever open.
But why, my worthy friend, this agitation?
Our Colonel, your husband——

MRS. BLAND [*in tears, gives him the letter*].

Read, Melville

1st CHILD.

Do not cry, Mama, for I'm sure if Papa said he would come
home to-day he will come yet: for he always does what he says
he will.

MRS. BLAND.

He cannot come, dear love; they will not let him.

2nd CHILD.

Why, then, they told him lies. Oh, fie upon them!

MELVILLE [*returning the letter*].

Fear nothing, Madam, 't is an empty threat:
A trick of policy. They dare not do it.

MRS. BLAND.

Alas! alas! what dares not power to do?
What art of reasoning, or what magic words,
Can still the storm of fears these lines have rais'd?
The wife's, the mother's fears? Ye innocents,

Unconscious on the brink of what a perilous
Precipice ye stand, unknowing that to-day
Ye are cast down the gulf, poor babes, ye weep
From sympathy. Children of sorrow, nurst,
Nurtur'd, midst camps and arms; unknowing man,
But as man's fell destroyer; must ye now,
To crown your piteous fate, be fatherless?
O, lead me, lead me to him! Let me kneel,
Let these, my children, kneel, till André, pardon'd,
Ensures to me a husband, them a father.

MELVILLE.

Madam, duty forbids further attendance.
I am on guard to-day. But see your son;
To him I leave your guidance. Good wishes
Prosper you!   *[Exit* MELVILLE.

Enter BLAND.

MRS. BLAND.

My Arthur, O my Arthur!

BLAND.

My mother!   *[Embracing her.*

MRS. BLAND.

My son, I have been wishing
For you——   *[Bursts into tears, unable to proceed.*

BLAND.

But whence this grief, these tears, my mother?
Why are these little cheeks bedew'd with sorrow?
          [He kisses the children, who exclaim, Brother, brother!
Have I done ought to cause a mother's sadness?

MRS. BLAND.

No, my brave boy! I oft have fear'd, but never
Sorrow'd for thee.

BLAND.

High praise!—Then bless me, Madam;
For I have pass'd through many a bustling scene
Since I have seen a father or a mother.

MRS. BLAND.

Bless thee, my boy! O bless him, bless him, Heaven!
Render him worthy to support these babes!
So soon, perhaps, all fatherless—dependent.—

BLAND.

What mean'st thou, madam? Why these tears?

MRS. BLAND.

Thy father——

BLAND.

A prisoner of war—I long have known it—
But made so without blemish to his honour,
And soon exchang'd, returns unto his friends,
To guard these little ones, and point and lead,
To virtue and to glory.

MRS. BLAND.

Never, never!
His life, a sacrifice to André's *manes*,[1]
Must soon be offer'd. Even now, endungeon'd,
Like a vile felon, on the earth he lies,
His death expecting. André's execution
Gives signal for the murder of thy father—
André now dies!—

BLAND [*despairingly*].

My father and my friend!!

MRS. BLAND.

There is but one on earth can save my husband—
But one can pardon André.

BLAND.

Haste, my mother!
Thou wilt prevail. Take with thee in each hand
An unoffending child of him thou weep'st.
Save—save them both! This way—haste—lean on me.
                                              [*Exeunt.*

---

[1] Spirit of the dead; shade.

SCENE, *the* GENERAL'S *Quarters.*

Enter the GENERAL *and* M'DONALD.

GENERAL.

Here have I intimation from the foe,
That still they deem the spy we have condemn'd,
Merely a captive; by the laws of arms
From death protected; and retaliation,
As they term it, threaten, if we our purpose hold.
Bland is the victim they have singled out,
Hoping his threaten'd death will André save.

M'DONALD.

If I were Bland I boldly might advise
My General how to act. Free, and in safety,
I will now suppose my counsel needless.

Enter an AMERICAN OFFICER.

OFFICER.

Another flag hath from the foe arriv'd,
And craves admittance.

GENERAL.

        Conduct it hither.   [*Exit* OFFICER.
Let us, unwearied hear, unbias'd judge,
Whate'er against our martial court's decision,
Our enemies can bring.

Enter BRITISH OFFICER, *conducted by the* AMERICAN OFFICER.

GENERAL.

        You are welcome, sir.
What further says Sir Henry?

BRITISH OFFICER.

        This from him.
He calls on you to think what weighty woes
You now are busy bringing on your country.
He bids me say, that, if your sentence reach
The prisoner's life (prisoner of arms he deems him,
And no spy), on him alone it falls not.
He bids me loud proclaim it, and declare,

If this brave officer, by cruel mockery
Of war's stern law, and justice's feign'd pretence,
Be murder'd; the sequel of our strife, bloody,
Unsparing and remorseless, *you* will make.
Think of the many captives in our power.
Already one is mark'd; for André mark'd;—
And when his death, unparallel'd in war,
The signal gives, then Colonel Bland must die.

GENERAL.

'T is well, sir; bear this message in return.
Sir Henry Clinton knows the laws of arms:
He is a soldier, and, I think, a brave one.
The prisoners he retains he must account for.
Perhaps the reckoning's near. I, likewise, am
A soldier; entrusted by my country.
What I shall judge most for that country's good,
That shall I do. When doubtful, I consult
My country's friends; never her enemies.
In André's case there are no doubts: 't is clear:
Sir Henry Clinton knows it.

BRITISH OFFICER.
Weigh consequences.

GENERAL.

In strict regard to consequence I act;
And much should doubt to call that action right,
However specious, whose apparent end
Was misery to man. That brave officer
Whose death you threaten, for himself drew not
His sword—his country's wrongs arous'd his mind;
Her good alone his aim; and if his fall
Can further fire that country to resistance,
He will, with smiles, yield up his glorious life,
And count his death a gain; and tho' Columbians
Will lament his fall, they will lament in blood.

[GENERAL *walks up the stage.*

M'DONALD.
Hear this! hear this, mankind!

BRITISH OFFICER.

Thus am I answered?

Enter a SERGEANT *with a letter.*

SERGEANT.

Express from Colonel Bland.   [*Delivers it and exit.*

GENERAL.

With your permission.   [*Opens it.*

BRITISH OFFICER.

Your pleasure, sir. It may my mission further.

M'DONALD.

O, Bland! my countryman, surely I know thee!

GENERAL.

'T is short: I will put form aside, and read it.
   [*Reads.*] "Excuse me, my Commander, for having a moment
doubted your virtue: but you love me.   If you waver, let this
confirm you.   My wife and children, to you and my country.
Do *your* duty."   Report this to your General.

BRITISH OFFICER.

I shall, sir.
   [*Bows, and exit with* AMERICAN OFFICER.

GENERAL.

O, Bland! my countryman!   [*Exit with emotion.*

M'DONALD.

Triumph of virtue!
Like him and thee, still be Americans.
Then, tho' all-powerful Europe league against us,
And pour in arms her legions on our shores;
Who is so dull would doubt their shameful flight?
Who doubt our safety, and our glorious triumph?

SCENE, *the Prison.*

Enter BLAND.

BLAND.

Lingering, I come to crush the bud of hope
My breath has, flattering, to existence warm'd.

Hard is the task to friendship! hard to say,
To the lov'd object there remains no hope,
No consolation for thee; thou *must* die;
The worst of deaths; no circumstance abated.

Enter ANDRÉ *in his uniform, and dress'd.*

ANDRÉ.

Is there that state on earth which friendship cannot cheer?

BLAND.

Little *I* bring to cheer thee, André.

ANDRÉ.

I understand. 'T is well. 'T will soon be past.
Yet, 't was not much I ask'd. A soldier's death.
A trifling change of form.

BLAND.

         Of that I spoke not.
By vehemence of passion hurried on,
I pleaded for thy precious life alone;
The which denied, my indignation barr'd
All further parley. But strong solicitation
Now is urg'd to gain the wish'd-for favour.

ANDRÉ.

What is 't o'clock?

BLAND.

         'T is past the stroke of nine.

ANDRÉ.

Why, then, 't is almost o'er. But to be hung—
Is there no way to escape that infamy?
What then *is* infamy?—no matter—no matter.

BLAND.

Our General hath received another flag.

ANDRÉ.

Soliciting for me?

BLAND.

         On thy behalf.

ANDRÉ.

I have been ever favour'd.

BLAND.

Threat'nings, now;
No more solicitations. Harsh, indeed,
The import of the message: harsh, indeed.

ANDRÉ.

I am sorry for it. Would that I were dead,
And all was well with those I leave behind.

BLAND.

Such a threat! Is it not enough, just heaven,
That I must lose this man?   Yet there was left
One for my soul to rest on.   But, to know
That the same blow deprives them both of life—

ANDRÉ.

What mean'st thou, Bland? Surely my General
Threats not retaliation.   In vengeance,
Dooms not some better man to die for me?

BLAND.

The best of men.

ANDRÉ.

Thou hast a father, captive—

I dare not ask—

BLAND.

That father dies for thee.

ANDRÉ.

Gracious heaven! how woes are heap'd upon me!
What! cannot one, so trifling in life's scene,
Fall, without drawing such a ponderous ruin?
Leave me, my friend, awhile—I yet have life—
A little space of life—let me exert it
To prevent injustice:—From death to save
Thy father, thee to save from utter desolation.

BLAND.

What mean'st thou, André?

ANDRÉ.

Seek thou the messenger
Who brought this threat. I will my last entreaty
Send by him. My General, sure, will grant it.

BLAND.

To the last thyself!   [*Exit.*

ANDRÉ.

If, at this moment,
When the pangs of death already touch me,
Firmly my mind against injustice strives,
And the last impulse to my vital powers
Is given by anxious wishes to redeem
My fellowmen from pain; surely my end,
Howe'er accomplish'd, is not infamous.   [*Exit.*

End of the Third Act.

ACT IV.

SCENE, *the Encampment.*

Enter M'DONALD *and* BLAND.

BLAND.

It doth in truth appear, that as a—spy—
Detested word!—brave André must be view'd.
His sentence he confesses strictly just.
Yet sure a deed of mercy, from *thy* hand,
Could never lead to ill. By such an act,
The stern and blood-stain'd brow of War
Would be disarm'd of half its gorgon horrors;
More humanized customs be induced;
And all the race of civilized man
Be blest in the example. Be it thy suit:
'T will well become thy character and station.

M'DONALD.

Trust me, young friend, I am alone the judge
Of what becomes my character and station:
And having judg'd that this young Briton's death,
Even 'though attended by thy father's murder,
Is necessary, in these times accurs'd,

When every thought of man is ting'd with blood,
I will not stir my finger to redeem them.
Nay, much I wonder, Bland, having so oft
The reasons for this necessary rigour
Enforced upon thee, thou wilt still persist
In vain solicitations. Imitate
Thy father!

BLAND.

    My father knew not André.
I know his value; owe to him my life;
And, gratitude, that first, that best of virtues,—
Without the which man sinks beneath the brute,—
Binds me in ties indissoluble to him.

M'DONALD.

That man-created virtue blinds thy reason.
Man owes to man all love; when exercised,
He does no more than duty. Gratitude,
That selfish rule of action, which commands
That we our preference make of men,
Not for their worth, but that they did *us* service,
Misleading reason, casting in the way
Of justice stumbling-blocks, cannot be virtue.

BLAND.

Detested sophistry!—'T was André sav'd me!

M'DONALD.

He sav'd thy life, and thou art grateful for it.
How self intrudes, delusive, on man's thoughts!
He sav'd thy life, yet strove to damn thy country;
Doom'd millions to the haughty Briton's yoke;
The best, and foremost in the cause of virtue,
To death, by sword, by prison, or the halter:
His sacrifice now stands the only bar
Between the wanton cruelties of war,
And our much-suffering soldiers: yet, when weigh'd
With gratitude, for that he sav'd *thy* life,
These things prove gossamer, and balance air:—
Perversion monstrous of man's moral sense!

BLAND.

Rather perversion monstrous of all good,
Is thy accurs'd, detestable opinion.
Cold-blooded reasoners, such as thee, would blast
All warm affection; asunder sever
Every social tie of humanized man.
Curst be thy sophisms! cunningly contriv'd
The callous coldness of thy heart to cover,
And screen thee from the brave man's detestation.

M'DONALD.

Boy, boy!

BLAND.

Thou knowest that André's not a spy.

M'DONALD.

I know him one. Thou hast acknowledg'd it.

BLAND.

Thou liest!

M'DONALD.

Shame on thy ruffian tongue! how passion
Mars thee! I pity thee! Thou canst not harm,
By words intemperate, a virtuous man.
I pity thee! for passion sometimes sways
My older frame, through former uncheck'd habit:
But when I see the havoc which it makes
In others, I can shun the snare accurst,
And nothing feel but pity.

BLAND [*indignantly*].

Pity me! [*Approaches him, and speaks in an under voice.*
Thou canst be cool, yet, trust me, *passion* sways thee.
Fear does not *warm* the blood, yet 't is a *passion*.
Hast thou no feeling? I have call'd thee liar!

M'DONALD.

If thou could'st make me one, I then might grieve.

BLAND.

Thy coolness goes to freezing: thou'rt a coward.

M'DONALD.

Thou knowest thou tell'st a falsehood.

BLAND.

Thou shalt know
None with impunity speaks thus of me.
That to rouse thy courage. [*Touches him gently, with his open
hand, in crossing him.* M'DONALD *looks at him unmoved.*]
Dost thou not yet feel?

M'DONALD.

For *thee* I feel. And tho' another's acts
Cast no dishonour on the worthy man,
I still feel for thy father. Yet, remember,
I may not, haply, ever be thus guarded;
I may not always the distinction make,
However just, between the blow intended
To provoke, and one that's meant to injure.

BLAND.

Hast thou no sense of honour?

M'DONALD.

Truly, yes:
For I am honour's votary. Honour, with me,
Is worth: 't is truth; 't is virtue; 't is a thing,
So high pre-eminent, that a boy's breath,
Or brute's, or madman's blow, can never reach it.
My honour is so much, so truly mine,
That none hath power to wound it, save myself.

BLAND.

I will proclaim thee through the camp a coward.

M'DONALD.

Think better of it! Proclaim not thine own shame.

BLAND.

I'll brand thee—Damnation! [*Exit.*

M'DONALD.

O, passion, passion!
A man who values fame, far more than life;
A brave young man; in many things a good;
Utters vile falsehood; adds injury to insult;
Striving with blood to seal such foul injustice;

And all from impulse of unbridled feeling.—   [*Pause.*
Here comes the mother of this headstrong boy,
Severely rack'd—What shall allay her torture?
For common consolation, *here*, is insult.

Enter Mrs. Bland *and* Children.

MRS. BLAND.

O my good friend!

M'DONALD [*taking her hand*].

        I know thy cause of sorrow.
Art thou now from our Commander?

MRS. BLAND [*drying her tears, and assuming dignity*].

        I am.
But vain is my entreaty. All unmov'd
He hears my words, he sees my desperate sorrow.
Fain would I blame his conduct—but I cannot.
Strictly examin'd, with intent to mark
The error which so fatal proves to *me*,
My scrutiny but ends in admiration.
Thus when the prophet from the Hills of Moab,
Look'd down upon the chosen race of heaven,
With fell intent to curse; ere yet he spake,
Truth all resistless, emanation bright
From great Adonai, fill'd his froward mind,
And chang'd the curses of his heart to blessings.

M'DONALD.

Thou payest high praise to virtue. Whither now?—

MRS. BLAND.

I still must hover round this spot until
My doom is known.

M'DONALD.

        Then to my quarters, lady,
There shall my mate give comfort and refreshment:
One of your sex can best your sorrows soothe.   [*Exeunt.*

SCENE, *the Prison.*

Enter BLAND.

BLAND.

Where'er I look cold desolation meets me.
My father—André—and self-condemnation!
Why seek I André now? Am *I* a man,
To soothe the sorrows of a suffering friend?
The weather-cock of passion! fool inebriate!
Who could with ruffian hand strive to provoke
Hoar wisdom to intemperance! who could lie!
Aye, swagger, lie, and brag!—Liar! Damnation!!
O, let me steal away and hide my head,
Nor view a man, condemn'd to harshest death,
Whose words and actions, when by mine compar'd,
Shew white as innocence, and bright as truth.
I now would shun him; but that his shorten'd
Thread of life, gives me no line to play with.
He comes, with smiles, and all the air of triumph;
While I am sinking with remorse and shame:
Yet *he* is doom'd to death, and *I* am free!

Enter ANDRÉ.

ANDRÉ.

Welcome, my Bland! Cheerly, a welcome hither!
I feel assurance that my last request
Will not be slighted. Safely thy father
Shall return to thee. [*Holding out a paper.*] See what employ-
    ment
For a dying man. Take thou these verses;
And, after my decease, send them to her
Whose name is woven in them; whose image
Hath controul'd my destiny. Such tokens
Are rather out of date. Fashions
There are in love as in all else; they change
As variously. A gallant Knight, erewhile,
Of Cœur de Lion's day, would, dying, send
His heart home to its mistress; degenerate
Soldier I, send but some blotted paper.

BLAND.

If 't would not damp thy present cheerfulness,
I would require the meaning of thy words.
I ne'er till now did hear of André's mistress.

ANDRÉ.

Mine is a story of that common kind,
So often told, with scanty variation,
That the pall'd ear loaths the repeated tale.
Each young romancer chooses for his theme
The woes of youthful hearts, by the cold hand
Of frosty Age, arm'd with parental power,
Asunder torn.   But I long since have ceas'd
To mourn; well satisfied that she I love,
Happy in holy union with another,
Shares not my wayward fortunes.   Nor would I
Now these tokens send, remembrance to awaken,
But that I know her happy: and the happy
Can think on misery and share it not.

BLAND [agitated].

Some one approaches.

ANDRÉ.

Why, 't is near the time.
But tell me, Bland, say—is the manner chang'd?

BLAND.

I hope it—but I yet have no assurance.

ANDRÉ.

Well, well!

HONORA [without].

I must see him.

ANDRÉ.

Whose voice was that?
My senses!—Do I dream—?   [Leans on BLAND.

Enter HONORA.

HONORA.

Where is he?

ANDRÉ.

'T is she!!   [*Starts from* BLAND
and advances towards HONORA; *she rushes into his arms.*]

HONORA.

It is enough! He lives, and *I* shall save him.
          [*She faints in the arms of* ANDRÉ.

ANDRÉ.

She sinks—assist me, Bland! O, save her, save her!
       [*Places her in a chair, and looks tenderly on her.*
Yet, why should she awake from that sweet sleep!
Why should she open her eyes—[*Wildly.*]—to see me hung!
What does she here? Stand off—[*Tenderly.*]—and let her die.
How pale she looks! how worn that tender frame!—
She has known sorrow! Who could injure her?

BLAND.

She revives—André—soft, bend her forward.
         [ANDRÉ *kneels and supports her.*

HONORA.

André—!

ANDRÉ.

Lov'd excellence!

HONORA.

  Yes, it is André!   [*Rises and looks at him.*
No more deceived by visionary forms,
By him supported—   [*Leans on him.*

ANDRÉ.

        Why is this?
Thou dost look pale, Honora—sick and wan—
Languid thy fainting limbs—

HONORA.

        All will be well.
But was it kind to leave me as thou didst—?
So rashly to desert thy vow-link'd wife?—

ANDRÉ.

When made another's both by vows and laws—

HONORA [*quitting his support*].

What meanest thou?

ANDRÉ.

Didst thou not marry him?

HONORA.

Marry!

ANDRÉ.

Didst thou not give thy hand away
From me?

HONORA.

O, never, never!

ANDRÉ.

Not married?

HONORA.

To none but thee, and but in will to thee.

ANDRÉ.

O blind, blind wretch!—Thy father told me——

HONORA.

Thou wast deceived. They hurried me away,
Spreading false rumours to remove thy love—
[*Tenderly.*] Thou didst too soon believe them.

ANDRÉ.

Thy father—
How could I but believe Honora's father?
And he did tell me so. I reverenced age,
Yet knew, age was not virtue. I believed
His snowy locks, and yet they did deceive me!
I have destroy'd myself and thee!—Alas!
Ill-fated maid! why didst thou not forget me?
Hast thou rude seas and hostile shores explor'd
For this? To see my death? Witness my shame?

HONORA.

I come to bless thee, André; and shall do it.
I bear such offers from thy kind Commander,
As must prevail to save thee. Thus the daughter
May repair the ills her cruel sire inflicted.
My father, dying, gave me cause to think

That arts were us'd to drive thee from thy home;
But what those arts I knew not. An heiress left,
Of years mature, with power and liberty,
I straight resolv'd to seek thee o'er the seas.
A long-known friend who came to join her lord,
Yielded protection and lov'd fellowship.—
Indeed, when I did hear of thy estate
It almost kill'd me:—I was weak before—

ANDRÉ.

'T is I have murder'd thee!—

HONORA.

All shall be well.
Thy General heard of me, and instant form'd
The plan of this my visit. I am strong,
Compar'd with what I was. Hope strengthens me;
Nay, even solicitude supports me now;
And when thou shalt be safe, *thou* wilt support me.

ANDRÉ.

Support thee!—O heaven! What!—And must I die?
Die!—and leave her *thus*—suffering—unprotected!—

Enter MELVILLE *and* GUARD.

MELVILLE.

I am sorry that my duty should require
Service, at which my heart revolts; but, sir,
Our soldiers wait in arms. All is prepar'd——

HONORA.

To death!—Impossible! Has my delay,
Then, murder'd him?—A momentary respite—

MELVILLE.

Lady, I have no power.

BLAND.

Melville, my friend,
This lady bears dispatches of high import,
Touching this business:—should they arrive too late——

HONORA.

For pity's sake, and heaven's, conduct me to him;
And wait the issue of our conference.
Oh, 't would be murder of the blackest dye,
Sin execrable, not to break thy orders—
Inhuman, thou art not.

MELVILLE.

Lady, thou say'st true;
For rather would I lose my rank in arms,
And stand cashier'd for lack of discipline,
Than, gain 'mongst military men all praise,
Wanting the touch of sweet humanity.

HONORA.

Thou grantest my request?

MELVILLE.

Lady, I do.

Retire! [SOLDIERS *go out.*

BLAND.

I know not what excuse, to martial men,
Thou canst advance for this; but to thy heart
Thou wilt need none, good Melville.

ANDRÉ.

O, Honora!

HONORA.

Cheer up, I feel assur'd. Hope wings my flight,
To bring thee tidings of much joy to come.
[*Exit* HONORA, *with* BLAND *and* MELVILLE.

ANDRÉ.

Eternal blessings on thee, matchless woman!—
If death now comes, he finds the veriest coward
That e'er he dealt withal. I cannot think
Of dying. Void of fortitude, each thought
Clings to the world—the world that holds Honora!
[*Exit.*

End of the Fourth Act.

ACT V.

SCENE, *the Encampment.*

Enter BLAND.

BLAND.

Suspense—uncertainty—man's bane and solace!
How racking now to me! My mother comes.
Forgive me, O my father! if in this war,
This wasting conflict of my wildering passions,
Memory of thee holds here a second place!
M'Donald comes with her. I would not meet him:
Yet I will do it. Summon up some courage—
Confess my fault, and gain, if not *his* love,
At least the approbation of *my* judgment.

Enter MRS. BLAND *and* CHILDREN *with* M'DONALD.

BLAND.

Say, madam, is there no change of counsel,
Or new determination?

MRS. BLAND.

> *Nought new*, my son.
The tale of misery is told unheard.
The widow's and the orphans' sighs
Fly up, unnoted by the eye of man,
And mingle, undistinguish'd, with the winds.
My friend [*To* M'DONALD.], attend thy duties. I must away.

2nd CHILD.

You need not cry, Mama, the General will do it, I am sure;
for I saw him cry. He turn'd away his head from you, but I
saw it.

MRS. BLAND.

Poor thing! come let us home and weep. Alas!
I can no more, for war hath made men rocks.

[*Exeunt* MRS. BLAND *and* CHILDREN.

BLAND.

Colonel, I used thee ill this morning.

M'DONALD.

No!
Thyself thou used'st most vilely, I remember.

BLAND.

Myself sustained the injury, most true;
But the intent of what I said and did
Was ill to thee alone: I'm sorry for it.
Seest thou these blushes?   They proceed from warmth
As honest as the heart of man e'er felt;—
But not with shame unmingled, while I force
This tongue, debased, to own, it slander'd thee,
And utter'd—I could curse it—utter'd falsehood.
Howe'er misled by passion, still my mind
Retains that sense of honest rectitude
Which makes the memory of an evil deed
A troublesome companion.   I was wrong.

M'DONALD.

Why, now this glads me; for thou *now* art right.
Oh, may thy tongue, henceforward, utter nought
But Truth's sweet precepts, in fair Virtue's cause!
Give me thy hand.   [*Takes his hand.*]   Ne'er may it grasp a
          sword
But in defense of justice.

BLAND.

                    Yet, erewhile,
A few short hours scarce past, when this vile hand
Attempted on *thee* insult;   and was raised
Against thy honour;   ready to be raised
Against thy life.   If this my deep remorse—

M'DONALD.

No more, no more.   'T is past.   Remember it
But as thou would'st the action of another,
By thy enlighten'd judgment much condemn'd;
And serving as a beacon in the storms
Thy passions yet may raise.   Remorse is vice:
Guard thee against its influence debasing.
Say to thyself, "I am not what I was;
I am not *now* the instrument of vice;

I'm changed; I am a man; Virtue's firm friend;
Sever'd for ever from my former self;
No link, but in remembrance salutary."

BLAND.

[How¹ all men tower above me!

M'DONALD.

Nay, not so.
Above what once thou wast, some few do rise;
None above what thou art.

BLAND.

It shall be so.

M'DONALD.

It is so.

BLAND.

Then to prove it.
For I must yet a trial undergo,
That will require a consciousness of virtue.   [*Exit.*

M'DONALD.

Oh, what a temper doth in man reside!
How capable of yet unthought perfection!]   [*Exit.*

SCENE, *the* GENERAL'S *Quarters.*

Enter GENERAL *and* SEWARD.

GENERAL.

Ask her, my friend, to send by thee her pacquets.
                                        [*Exit* SEWARD.

Oh, what keen struggles must I undergo!
Unbless'd estate! to have the power to pardon;
The court's stern sentence to remit;—give life;—
Feel the strong wish to use such blessed power;
Yet know that circumstances strong as fate
Forbid to obey the impulse. Oh, I feel
That man should never shed the blood of man!

¹ Insert the lines which were substituted after the first night for the lines here put in brackets. They are given in the Preface, page 509.

Enter SEWARD.

SEWARD.

Nought can the lovely suitor satisfy,
But conference with thee, and much I fear
Refusal would cause madness.

GENERAL.
Yet to admit,
To hear, be tortur'd, and refuse at last—

SEWARD.

Sure never man such spectacle of sorrow
Saw before. Motionless the rough-hewn soldiers
Silent view her, or walk aside and weep.

GENERAL [*after a pause*].

Admit her. [SEWARD *goes out.*] Oh, for the art, the precious art,
To reconcile the sufferer to his sorrows!
[HONORA *rushes in, and throws herself wildly on her knees before
him; he endeavours to raise her.*

HONORA.

Nay, nay, here is my place, or here, or lower,
Unless thou grant'st his life. All forms away!
Thus will I clasp thy knees, thus cling to thee.—
I am his wife—'tis I have ruin'd him—
Oh, save him! Give him to me! Let us cross
The mighty seas, far, far—ne'er to offend again.—
        [*The* GENERAL *turns away, and hides his eyes with his hand.*

Enter SEWARD *and an* OFFICER.

GENERAL.

Seward, support her—my heart is torn in twain.
[HONORA *as if exhausted, suffers herself to be raised, and leans on*
SEWARD.

OFFICER.

This moment, sir, a messenger arrived
With well confirm'd and mournful information,
That gallant Hastings, by the lawless scouts
Of Britain taken, after cruel mockery
With shew of trial and condemnation,
On the next tree was hung.

HONORA [*wildly*].
Oh, it is false!

GENERAL.
Why, why, my country, did I hesitate?   [*Exit.*
[HONORA *sinks, faints, and is borne off by* SEWARD *and* OFFICER.

SCENE, *the Prison.*

ANDRÉ *meeting* BLAND.

ANDRÉ.
How speeds Honora? [*Pause.*] Art thou silent, Bland?
Why, then I know my task. The mind of man,
If not by vice debas'd, debilitated,
Or by disease of body quite unton'd,
Hath o'er its thoughts a power—energy divine!
Of fortitude the source and every virtue—
A godlike power, which e'en o'er circumstance
Its sov'reignty exerts. Now, from my thoughts,
Honora! Yet she is left alone—expos'd—

BLAND.
O, André, spurn me, strike me to the earth;
For what a wretch am I, in André's mind,
That he can think he leaves his love alone,
And I retaining life!

ANDRÉ.
             Forgive me, Bland,
My thoughts glanc'd not on thee. Imagination
Pictur'd only, then, her orphan state, helpless;
Her weak and grief-exhausted frame. Alas!
This blow will kill her!

BLAND [*kneeling*].
             Here do I myself
Devote, my fortune consecrate, to thee,
To thy remembrance, and Honora's service!—

ANDRÉ.
Enough! Let me not see her more—nor think of her—
Farewell! farewell, sweet image! Now for death.

BLAND.

Yet that you shouldst the felon's fate fulfill—
Damnation! my blood boils. Indignation
Makes the current of my life course wildly
Through its round, and maddens each emotion.

ANDRÉ.

Come, come, it matters not.

BLAND.

I do remember,
When a boy, at school, in our allotted tasks,
We, by our puny acts, strove to portray
The giant thoughts of Otway. I was Pierre.—
O, thou art Pierre's reality! a soldier,
On whose manly brow sits fortitude enamour'd!
A Mars, abhorring vice, yet doom'd to die
A death of infamy; thy corse expos'd
To vulgar gaze—halter'd—distorted—Oh!!
      [Pauses, and then adds in a low, hollow voice.
Pierre had a friend to save him from such shame—
And so hast thou.

ANDRÉ.

No more, as thou dost love me.

BLAND.

I have a sword, and arm, that never fail'd me.

ANDRÉ.

Bland, such an act would justly thee involve,
And leave that helpless one thou sworest to guard,
Expos'd to every ill. Oh! think not of it.

BLAND.

If thou wilt not my aid—take it thyself.
      [Draws and offers his sword.

ANDRÉ.

No, men will say that cowardice did urge me.
In my mind's weakness, I did wish to shun
That mode of death which error represented
Infamous: Now let me rise superior;
And with a fortitude too true to start
From mere appearances, shew your country,

That she, in me, destroys a man who might
Have liv'd to virtue.

BLAND [*sheathing his sword*].

        I will not think more of it;
I was again the sport of erring passion.

ANDRÉ.

Go thou and guide Honora from this spot.

HONORA [*entering*].

Who shall oppose his wife? I will have way!
They, cruel, would have kept me from thee, André.
Say, am I not thy wife? *Wilt* thou deny me?
Indeed I am not dress'd in bridal trim.
But I have travel'd far:—rough was the road—
Rugged and rough—that must excuse my dress.
[*Seeing* ANDRÉ'S *distress.*] Thou art not glad to see me.

ANDRÉ.

Break my heart!

HONORA.

Indeed, I feel not much in spirits. I wept but now.

Enter MELVILLE *and* GUARD.

BLAND [*to* MELVILLE].

Say nothing.

ANDRÉ.

I am ready.

HONORA [*seeing the* GUARD].

        Are *they* here?
Here again!—The *same*—but they shall not harm me—
I am with *thee*, my André—I am safe—
And *thou* art safe with me. Is it not so?

                    [*Clinging to him.*

Enter MRS. BLAND.

MRS. BLAND.

Where is this lovely victim?

BLAND.

Thanks, my mother.

MRS. BLAND.

M'Donald sent me hither. My woes are past.
Thy father, by the foe releas'd, already
Is in safety. This be forgotten now;
And every thought be turn'd to this sad scene.
Come, lady, home with me.

HONORA.

Go home with thee?
Art thou my André's mother? We will home
And rest, for thou art weary—very weary.
[*Leans on* MRS. BLAND.
[ANDRÉ *retires to the* GUARD, *and goes off with them, looking on her to the last, and with an action of extreme tenderness takes leave of her.* MELVILLE *and* BLAND *accompany him.*

HONORA.

Now we will go. Come, love! Where is he?
All gone!—I do remember—I awake—
They have him. Murder! Help! Oh, save him! save him!
[HONORA *attempts to follow, but falls.* MRS. BLAND *kneels to assist her. Scene closes.*

SCENE, *the Encampment.*

Procession to the execution of ANDRÉ. *First enter Pioneers— Detachment of Infantry—Military Band of Music—Infantry. The Music having passed off, enter* ANDRÉ *between* MELVILLE *and* AMERICAN OFFICER; *they sorrowful, he cheerfully conversing as he passes over the stage.*

ANDRÉ.

It may in me be merely prejudice,
The effect of young-opinion deep engraved
Upon the tender mind by care parental;
But I must think your country has mistook
Her interests. Believe me, but for this I should

Not willingly have drawn a sword against her.

[They bow their heads in silence.

Opinion must, nay ought, to sway our actions;
Therefore—

*Having crossed the stage, he goes out as still conversing with them.
Another detachment of Infantry, with muffled and craped drums,
close the procession: as soon as they are off—*
*Scene draws and discovers the distant view of the Encampment.
Procession enters in same order as before, proceeds up the stage,
and goes off on the opposite side.*

Enter M'DONALD, *leading* BLAND, *who looks wildly back.*

BLAND.

I dare not *thee* resist. Yet why, O, why
Thus hurry me away—?—

M'DONALD.

Would'st thou behold——

BLAND.

Oh, name it not!

M'DONALD.

Or would'st thou, by thy looks
And gestures wild, o'erthrow that manly calmness
Which, or assum'd or felt, so well becomes thy friend?

BLAND.

What means that cannon's sound?

M'DONALD [*after a pause*].

Signal of death
Appointed. André, thy friend, is now no more!

BLAND.

Farewell, farewell, brave spirit! O, let my countrymen,
Henceforward, when the cruelties of war
Arise in their remembrance; when their ready
Speech would pour forth torrents in their foe's dispraise,
Think on this act accurst, and lock complaint in silence.

*[*BLAND *throws himself on the earth.*

M'DONALD.

Such are the dictates of the heart, not head.
Oh, may the children of Columbia still
Be taught by every teacher of mankind,
Each circumstance of calculative gain,
Or wounded pride, which prompted our oppressors:
May every child be taught to lisp the tale:
And may, in times to come, no foreign force,
No European influence, tempt to misstate,
Or awe the tongue of eloquence to silence.
Still may our children's children deep abhor
The motives, doubly deep detest the actors;
Ever remembering, that the race who plan'd,
Who acquiesced, or did the deeds abhor'd,
Has pass'd from off the earth; and, in its stead,
Stand men who challenge love or detestation
But from their proper, individual deeds.
Never let memory of the sire's offence
Descend upon the son.

Curtain drops.

THE INDIAN PRINCESS

By J. N. BARKER

JAMES NELSON BARKER
(1784–1858)

In a letter written to William Dunlap, from Philadelphia, on June 10, 1832, James Nelson Barker very naïvely and very fully outlined his career, inasmuch as he had been informed by Manager Wood that Mr. Dunlap wished such an account for his "History of the American Stage."

From this account, we learn that whatever dramatic ability Mr. Barker possessed came from the enthusiasm created within him as a reader of wide range. For example, in 1804, he became the author of a one-act piece, entitled "Spanish Rover," furnished in plot by Cervantes. In 1805, he wrote what he describes as a Masque, entitled "America," in which poetic dialogue afforded America, Science and Liberty the opportunity of singing in unison. He confesses that this Masque was "to close a drama I had projected on the adventures of Smith in Virginia, in the olden time." Then followed a tragedy suggested by Gibbon, entitled "Attila," but Mr. Barker had advanced only two acts when news came to him that John Augustus Stone was at work on a play of the same kind.

In his letter to Dunlap, Mr. Barker deplored this coincidence, which put a stop to "Attila." "But have you never yourself been the victim of these odd coincidences, and, just as you had fixed upon a subject or a title, found yourself superseded—a thing next in atrocity to the ancients' stealing all one's fine thoughts. My comedy of 'Tears and Smiles' was to be called 'Name it Yourself,' when out comes a 'Name it Yourself,' in England, and out comes too a 'Smiles and Tears,' with a widow, an Irishman, and almost all my *dramat. pers.* I wrote the 'Indian Princess,' and an 'Indian Princess' appears in England. Looking over the old English dramatists, I am struck with the 'Damon and Pythias' of Edwards as a subject, but am scarcely set down to it, when lo, the modern play in London; and what is worse, with the fine part of Pythias absolutely transformed into a snivelling fellow, who bellows like a calf at the prospect of dying for his friend. 'Wallace' was purloined from me in like manner, and several other heroes: at length I fix upon 'Epaminondas', as a 'learned Theban' of so philosophical a cast of character, that even the French had not thought of him for the boards. I form my plot, and begin *con amore*, when I am told that Dr. Bird has written a 'Pelopidas' and an 'Epaminondas,' comprehending the whole life of the latter."

Then, having finished with his diatribe against coincidence— a diatribe which excellently well shows the channels in which Barker's literary mind ran, and likewise the closeness with which he followed the literary activity of the period among his associates, he continued in his narrative to Dunlap:

" 'Tears and Smiles' was written between May 1 and June 12, of 1806, with the character of a Yankee intended for Jefferson. By the way, such a Yankee as I drew!" he writes. "I wonder what Hackett would say to it! The truth is, I had never even seen a Yankee at the time."

Then, in view of Barker's political tastes which, in consideration of the dramatists of those days, one must always take into account, he wrote a piece called "The Embargo; or, What News?" borrowed from Murphy's "Upholsterer," and produced on March 16, 1808.

Between this play and 1809, "The Indian Princess" was written, and what Barker has to say about it will be quoted in its proper place.

Right now, we are letting him enumerate his own literary activities, which were many and continuous.

In 1809, he Americanized Cherry's "Travellers," a dramatic method which has long been in vogue between America and England, and has, in many respects, spoiled many American comedies for English consumption.

In 1812, at the request of Manager Wood, Mr. Barker made a dramatization of Scott's "Marmion," and, strange to say, it was announced as being written by Thomas Morton, Esq.

"This was audacious enough in all conscience," says Mr. Barker, "but the finesse was successful, and a play most probably otherwise destined to neglect, ran like wild fire through all our theatres." On March 24, 1817, there was acted in Philadelphia, Barker's "The Armourer's Escape; or, Three Years at Nootka Sound," described by Mr. Barker as a melodramatic sketch, founded on the adventures of John Jewett, the armourer of the ship *Boston*, in which Jewett himself assumed the hero's rôle.

This same year he likewise wrote "How to Try a Lover," suggested by Le Brun's novel. Finally, in 1824, on March 12, there was performed "Superstition," a five-act drama. This closed the account that Barker sent to Dunlap.

We see from it a number of things relative to placing Barker as a literary personage. First, his interest in literature made him draw from all sources, combining Scott with Holinshed, and turning, as was the wont of the cultivated American of that day, to the romantic literatures of the past. Secondly, Barker's interest in Colonial History was manifest by his return, time and time again, to Colonial records for dramatic material. Furthermore, as a participant in the political disputes of his day, it would have been a surprise had Barker not directed his pen to some reflection of the discussions of the period.

James Nelson Barker was the son of the Honourable John Barker, one-time Mayor of Philadelphia, and ex-Revolutionary soldier. He was born in that city on June 17, 1784.

His education was received in Philadelphia, and he must have entered the literary and political arenas at an early age. After the fashion of the day, he was trained in the old-time courtesy and in the old-time manner of defending one's honour with the sword, for it is recorded that he was once severely wounded in a duel.

At the outbreak of the War of 1812, he received a commission, fighting mostly on the Canadian frontier, and winning distinction as a Captain of Artillery. After the close of the War, he was supported by the Democratic Party, and elected Mayor of the City of Philadelphia. Later, he upheld "Old Hickory" for the Presidency, and, after filling the position of the Collector of the Port of Philadelphia from 1829–1838, on the election of Van Buren to the presidency, he was appointed First Controller of the Treasury, and moved to Washington. From that time on, he was connected with the highest offices in the department. His pen was continually dedicated to the support of Democracy, and, during the years from 1832–1836, he figured as a contributor to many papers of the time on political topics. He lived until March 9, 1858.

I have selected his play, "The Indian Princess,"[1] as an example

---

[1] The/Indian Princess;/or,/La Belle Sauvage./An Operatic Melo-Drame./In Three Acts./Performed at the Theatres Philadelphia and/Baltimore./By J. N. Barker./ First Acted April 6, 1808./Philadelphia,/Printed by T. & G. Palmer,/For G. E. Blake, No. 1, South Third-Street./1808./

of the numberless dramas that grew up around the character of
Pocahontas. The reader will find it particularly of interest to
contrast with this piece G. W. P. Custis's "Pocahontas; or, The
Settlers of Virginia" (1830), and John Brougham's burlesque,
"Po-ca-hon-tas; or, The Gentle Savage."

The Indian Drama, in America, is a subject well worth careful
attention. There are numberless plays mentioned by Laurence
Hutton in his "Curiosities of the American Stage" which, though
interesting as titles, have not been located as far as manuscripts
are concerned.

Barker's "The Indian Princess" is one of the earliest that deal
with the character of Pocahontas. The subject has been interestingly treated in an article by Mr. E. J. Streubel (*The Colon-
nade*, New York University, September, 1915).

Barker had originally intended his play, "The Indian Princess,"
to be a legitimate drama, instead of which, when it was first
produced, it formed the libretto for the music by a man named
John Bray, of the New Theatre. In his letter to Dunlap, he says:

" 'The Indian Princess,' in three acts .   . begun some time
before, was taken up in 1808, at the request of Bray, and worked
up into an opera, the music to which he composed. It was first
performed for his benefit on the 6th of April, 1808, to a crowded
house; but Webster, particularly obnoxious, at that period, to
a large party, having a part in it, a tremendous tumult took
place, and it was scarcely heard. I was on the stage, and directed
the curtain to be dropped. It has since been frequently acted in,
I believe, all the theatres of the United States. A few years
since, I observed, in an English magazine, a critique on a drama
called 'Pocahontas; or, the Indian Princess,' produced at Drury
Lane. From the sketch given, this piece differs essentially from
mine in the plan and arrangement; and yet, according to the
critic, they were indebted for this very stupid production 'to
America, where it is a great favourite, and is to be found in all
the printed collections of stock plays.' The copyright of the
'Indian Princess' was also given to Blake, and transferred to
Longworth. It was printed in 1808 or 1809. George Washington
Custis, of Arlington, has, I am told, written a drama on the same
subject."

An account of the riot is to be found in Durang's "History of
the Philadelphia Stage," and the reader, in order to gain some
knowledge of the popularity of "The Indian Princess," may

likewise obtain interesting material in Manager Wood's "Diary," the manuscript of which is now in possession of the University of Pennsylvania. When the play was given in Philadelphia, the advertisement announced, "The principal materials forming this dramatic trifle are extracted from the General History of Virginia, written by Captain Smith, and printed London, folio, 1624; and as close an adherence to historic truth has been preserved as dramatic rules would allow of."

It was given its first New York production at the Park Theatre on June 14, 1808.

THE

INDIAN PRINCESS

OR,

LA BELLE SAUVAGE.

AN OPERATIC MELO-DRAME.

IN THREE ACTS.

PERFORMED AT THE THEATRES PHILADELPHIA AND
BALTIMORE.

BY J. N. BARKER.

FIRST ACTED APRIL 6, 1808.

PHILADELPHIA,

PRINTED BY T. & G. PALMER,
FOR G. E. BLAKE, NO. 1, SOUTH THIRD-STREET.

....

1808.

FAC-SIMILE TITLE-PAGE TO THE 1808 EDITION

PREFACE

While I am proud to acknowledge my grateful sense of those flattering marks of liberal kindness with which my dramatic entrée has been greeted by an indulgent audience, I feel so fully conscious of the very humble merit of this little piece, that perhaps nothing but the peculiar circumstances under which it was acted should have induced me to publish it. In sending it to the press I am perfectly apprized of the probability that it goes only to add one more to the list of those unfortunate children of the American drama, who, in the brief space that lies between their birth and death, are doomed to wander, without house or home, unknown and unregarded, or who, if heeded at all, are only picked up by some critic beadle to receive the usual treatment of vagrants. Indeed, were I disposed to draw comfort from the misfortunes of others, I might make myself happy with the reflection, that however my vagabond might deserve the lash, it would receive no more punishment than those who deserved none at all; for the gentlemen castigators seldom take the pains to distinguish Innocence from Guilt, but most liberally bestow their stripes on all poor wanderers who are unhappily of American parentage. Far, however, from rejoicing at this circumstance, I sincerely deplore it. In all ages, and in every country, even the sturdiest offspring of genius have felt the necessity and received the aid of a protecting hand of favour to support and guide their first trembling and devious footsteps; it is not, therefore, wonderful, that here, where every art is yet but in its infancy, the youthful exertions of dramatic poetry, unaided and unsupported, should fail, and that its imbecile efforts should for ever cease with the failure; that chilled by total neglect, or chid with undeserved severity; depressed by ridicule, starved by envy, and stricken to the earth by malevolence, the poor orphan, heartless and spirit-broken, should pine away a short and sickly life. I am not, I believe, quite coxcomb enough to advance the most distant hint that the child of my brain deserves a better fate; that it may meet with it I might, however, be indulged in hoping, under the profession that the hope proceeds from considerations distinct from either it or myself. Dramatic genius, with genius of every other kind, is assuredly native of our soil, and there wants but the wholesome and kindly breath of favour to invigourate its delicate frame, and bid it rapidly arise from its cradle to blooming maturity. But alas! poor weak ones! what a climate are ye doomed to draw your first breath in! the teeming press has scarcely ceased groaning at your delivery, ere you are suffocated with the stagnant atmosphere of entire apathy, or swept out of existence by the hurricane of unsparing, indiscriminating censure!

Good reader, I begin to suspect that I have held you long enough by the button. Yet, maugre my terror of being tiresome, and in despite of my clear anticipation of the severe puns which will be made in this punning city, on my *childish* preface, I must push my allusion a little further, to deprecate the wrath of the critics, and arouse the sympathies of the ladies. Then, O ye sage censors! ye goody gossips at poetic births! I vehemently importune ye to be convinced, that for my bantling I desire neither rattle nor bells; neither the lullaby of praise, nor the pap of patronage, nor the hobby-horse of honour. 'Tis a plain-palated, home-bred, and I may add independent urchin, who laughs at sugar plums, and from its little heart disdains gilded gingerbread. If you like it—so; if not—why so; yet, without being mischievous, it would fain be amusing; therefore, if its gambols be pleasant, and your gravities permit, laugh; if not, e'en turn aside your heads, and let the wanton youngling laugh by itself. If it speak like a sensible child, prithee, pat its cheek, and say so; but if it be ridiculous when it would be serious, smile, and permit the foolish attempt to pass. But do not, O goody critic, apply the birch, because its unpractised tongue cannot lisp the language of Shakspeare, nor be very much enraged, if you find it has to creep before it can possibly walk.

To your bosoms, ladies, sweet ladies! the little stranger flies with confidence for protection; shield it, I pray you, from the iron rod of rigour, and scold it yourselves, as much as you will, for on *your* smooth and polished brows it can never read wrinkled cruelty; the mild anger of *your* eyes will not blast it like the fierce scowl of the critic; the chidings of *your* voice will be soothing music to it, and it will discover the dimple of kindness in your very frowns. Caresses it does not ask; its modesty would shrink from that it thought it deserved not; but if its faults be infantile, its punishment should be gentle, and from you, dear ladies, correction would be as thrillingly sweet as that the little *Jean Jacques* received from the fair hand of Mademoiselle Lambercier.

THE AUTHOR.

ADVERTISEMENT

The principal materials that form this dramatic trifle are extracted from the General History of Virginia, written by Captain Smith, and printed London, folio, 1624; and as close an adherence to historic truth has been preserved as dramatic rules would allow of. The music [1] was furnished by Mr. John Bray, of the New Theatre.

DRAMATIS PERSONÆ

EUROPEANS.

DELAWAR,	Mr. Warren.
CAPTAIN SMITH,	Mr. Rutherford.
LIEUTENANT ROLFE,	Mr. Wood.
PERCY,	Mr. Charnock.
WALTER,	Mr. Bray.
LARRY,	Mr. Webster.
ROBIN,	Mr. Jefferson.
TALMAN,	Mr. Durang.
GERALDINE,	Mrs. Francis.
KATE,	Miss Hunt.
ALICE,	Mrs. Mills.

SOLDIERS *and* ADVENTURERS.

VIRGINIANS.

POWHATAN, *king,*	Mr. Serson.
NANTAQUAS, *his son,*	Mr. Cone.
MIAMI, *a prince,*	Mr. Mills.
GRIMOSCO, *a priest,*	Mr. Cross.
POCAHONTAS, *the princess,*	Mrs. Wilmot.
NIMA, *her attendant,*	Miss Mullen.

WARRIORS *and* INDIAN GIRLS.

SCENE, Virginia.

[1] The music is now published and sold by Mr. G. E. Blake, No. 1, South Third-street, Philadelphia.

THE INDIAN PRINCESS

ACT I.

SCENE I. *Powhatan River; wild and picturesque. Ships appear. Barges approach the shore, from which land* SMITH, ROLFE, PERCY, WALTER, LARRY, ROBIN, ALICE, &c.

Chorus.

Jolly comrades, raise the glee,
Chorus it right cheerily;
For the tempest's roar is heard no more,
And gaily we tread the wish'd-for shore:
 Then raise the glee merrily,
 Chorus it cheerily,
For past are the perils of the blust'ring sea.

SMITH. Once more, my bold associates, welcome. Mark
What cheery aspects look upon our landing:
The face of Nature dimples o'er with smiles,
The heav'ns are cloudless, whiles the princely sun,
As glad to greet us in his fair domain,
Gives us gay salutation—
 LARRY. [*To* WALTER.]   By St. Patrick
His fiery majesty does give warm welcome.
Arrah! his gracious smiles are melting—
 WALTER.   Plague!
He burthens us with favours till we sweat.
 SMITH. What think ye, Percy, Rolfe, have we not found
Sir Walter Raleigh faithful in his tale?
Is 't not a goodly land? Along the bay,
How gay and lovely lie its skirting shores,
Fring'd with the summer's rich embroidery!
 PERCY. Believe me, sir, I ne'er beheld that spot
Where Nature holds more sweet varieties.
 SMITH. The gale was kind that blew us hitherward.
This noble bay were undiscover'd still,
Had not that storm arose propitious,

And, like the ever kindly breath of heav'n,
Which sometimes rides upon the tempest's wing,
Driv'n us to happiest destinies, e'en then
When most we fear'd destruction from the blast.

ROLFE. Let our dull, sluggish countrymen at home
Still creep around their little isle of fogs,
Drink its dank vapours, and then hang themselves.
In this free atmosphere and ample range
The bosom can dilate, the pulses play,
And man, erect, can walk a manly round.

ROBIN. [*Aside.*] Aye, and be scalp'd and roasted by the Indians.

SMITH. Now, gallant cavalier adventurers,
On this our landing spot we'll rear a town
Shall bear our good king's name to after-time,
And yours along with it; for ye are men
Well worth the handing down; whose paged names
Will not disgrace posterity to read:
Men born for acts of hardihood and valour,
Whose stirring spirits scorn'd to lie inert,
Base atoms in the mass of population
That rots in stagnant Europe. Ye are men
Who a high wealth and fame will bravely win,
And wear full worthily. I still shall be
The foremost in all troubles, toil, and danger,
Your leader and your captain, nought exacting
Save strict obedience to the watchful care
Which points to your own good: be wary then,
And let not any mutinous hand unravel
Our close knit compact. Union is its strength:
Be that remember'd ever. Gallant gentlemen,
We have a noble stage, on which to act
A noble drama; let us then sustain
Our sev'ral parts with credit and with honour.
Now, sturdy comrades, cheerly to our tasks!

                 [*Exeunt* SMITH, ROLFE, &c.

SCENE II. *A grove.*

Enter WALTER *and* LARRY.

LARRY. Now by the black eyes of my Katy, but that master
of yours and captain of mine is a prince!

WALTER. Tut, you hav'n't seen an inch yet of the whole hero. Had you followed him as I have, from a knee-high urchin, you'd confess that there never was soldier fit to cry comrade to him. O! 'twould have made your blood frisk in your veins to have seen him in Turkey and Tartary, when he made the clumsy infidels dance to the music of his broad sword!

LARRY. Troth now, the mussulmans may have been mightily amused by the caper; but for my part I should modestly prefer skipping to the simple jig of an Irish bag-pipe.

WALTER. Then he had the prettiest mode of forming their manners—

LARRY. Arrah, how might that be?

WALTER. For example: whenever they were so ill-bred as to appear with their turbans on before him, he uses me this keen argument to convince them they shewed discourtesy. He whips me out his sword, and knocks their turbans off—

LARRY. Knocks their turbans off?

WALTER. Aye, egad, and their heads to boot.

LARRY. A dev'lish cutting way of reasoning indeed; that argument cou'dn't be answered asily.

WALTER. Devil a tongue ever wagg'd in replication, Larry. —Ah! my fairy of felicity—my mouthful of melody—my wife—

Enter ALICE.

Well, Alice, we are now in the wilds of Virginia, and, tell me truly, doesn't repent following me over the ocean, wench? wilt be content in these wild woods, with only a little husband, and a great deal of love, pretty Alice?

ALICE. Can you ask that? are not all places alike if you are with me, Walter?

Song.—ALICE.

In this wild wood will I range;
    Listen, listen, dear!
Nor sigh for towns so fine, to change
    This forest drear.
Toils and dangers I'll despise,
    Never, never weary;
And be, while love is in thine eyes,
    Ever cheery.

Ah! what to me were cities gay;
Listen, listen, dear!
If from me thou wert away,
Alas! how drear!
Oh! still o'er sea, o'er land I'll rove,
Never, never weary;
And follow on where leads my love,
Ever cheery.

LARRY. Och! the creature!

WALTER. Let my lips tell thee what my tongue cannot. [*Kiss.*

LARRY. Aye, do, do stop her mellifluous mouth; for the little nightingale warbles so like my Kate, she makes me sigh for Ballinamoné; ah! just so would the constant creature carol all day about, roving through the seas and over the woods.

Enter ROBIN.

ROBIN. Master Walter, the captain is a going to explore the country, and you must along.

WALTER. That's our fine captain, always stirring.

ROBIN. Plague on his industry! would you think it, we are all incontinently to fall a chopping down trees, and building our own houses, like the beavers.

LARRY. Well, sure, that's the fashionable mode of paying rent in this country.

ALICE. O, Walter, these merciless savages! I sha'n't be merry till you return—

ROBIN. I warrant ye, mistress Alice—Lord love you I shall be here.

WALTER. Cheerly, girl; our captain will make the red rogues scamper like so many dun deer. Savages, quotha! at sight of him, their copper skins will turn pale as silver, with the very alchemy of fear. Come, a few kisses, *en passant*, and then away! cheerly, my dainty Alice.   [*Exeunt* WALTER *and* ALICE.

ROBIN. Aye, go your ways, master Walter, and when you are gone—

LARRY. What then! I suppose you'll be after talking nonsense to his wife. But if ever I catch you saying your silly things—

ROBIN. Mum, Lord love you, how can you think it? But hark ye, master Larry, in this same drama that our captain spoke of, you and I act parts, do we not?

LARRY. Arrah, to be sure, we are men of parts.

ROBIN. Shall I tell you in earnest what we play in this merry comedy?

LARRY. Be doing it.

ROBIN. Then we play the parts of two fools, look you, to part with all at home, and come to these savage parts, where, Heaven shield us, our heads may be parted from our bodies. Think what a catastrophe, master Larry!

LARRY. So the merry comedy ends a doleful tragedy, and exit fool in the character of a hero! That's glory, sirrah, a very feather in our cap.

ROBIN. A light gain to weigh against the heavy loss of one's head. Feather quotha! what use of a plumed hat without a head to wear it withal?

LARRY. Tut, man, our captain will lead us through all dangers.

ROBIN. Will he? an' he catch me following him through these same dangers—

LARRY. Och, you spalpeen! I mean he'll lead us out of peril.

ROBIN. Thank him for nothing; for I've predetermined, look you, not to be led into peril. Oh, master Larry, what a plague had I to do to leave my snug cot and my brown lass, to follow master Rolfe to this devil of a country, where there's never a girl nor a house!

LARRY. Out, you driveller! didn't I leave as neat a black-ey'd girl, and as pretty a prolific potato-patch all in tears—

ROBIN. Your potato-patch in tears! that's a bull, master Larry—

LARRY. You're a calf, master Robin. Wasn't it raining? Och, I shall never forget it; the thunder rolling, and her tongue a-going, and her tears and |the rain; och, bother, but it was a dismal morning!

Song—LARRY.

I.

Och! dismal and dark was the day, to be sure,
When Larry took leave of sweet Katy Maclure;
And clouds dark as pitch hung just like a black lace
O'er the sweet face of Heav'n and my Katy's sweet face.
Then, while the wind blow'd, and she sigh'd might and main,
   Drops from the black skies
   Fell—and from her black eyes;
Och! how I was soak'd with her tears—and the rain.

[*Speaks.*] And then she gave me this beautiful keep-sake [*Shows a pair of scissors.*], which if ever I part with, may a tailor clip me in two with his big shears. Och! when Katy took you in hand, how nicely did you snip and snap my bushy, carroty locks; and now you're cutting the hairs of my heart to pieces, you tieves you—

[*Sings.*] Och! Hubbaboo—Gramachree—Hone!

II.

When I went in the garden, each bush seem'd to sigh
Because I was going—and nod me good-bye;
Each stem hung its head, drooping bent like a bow,
With the weight of the water—or else of its woe;
And while sorrow, or wind, laid some flat on the ground,
    Drops of rain, or of grief,
    Fell from every leaf,
Till I thought in a big show'r of tears I was drown'd.

[*Speaks.*] And then each bush and leaf seem'd to sigh, and say, "don't forget us, Larry." I won't, said I.—"But arrah, take something for remembrance," said they; and then I dug up this neat jewel [*Shows a potato.*]; you're a little withered to be sure, but if ever I forget your respectable family, or your delightful dwelling place—may I never again see any of your beautiful brothers and plump sisters!—Och! my darling, if you had come hot from the hand of Katy, how my mouth would have watered at ye; now, you divil, you bring the water into my eyes.

[*Sings.*] Och! Hubbaboo—Gramachree—Hone!   [*Exeunt.*

SCENE III. *Werocomoco, the royal village of* POWHATAN. INDIAN GIRLS *arranging ornaments for a bridal dress. Music.*

NIMA. Let us make haste, my companions, to finish the dress of the bride; to-day the prince Miami returns with our hunters from the chase; to-morrow he will bear away our princess to his own nation.

Enter POCAHONTAS *from the wood, with bow and arrow, and a flamingo (red bird). Music as she enters.*
PRINCESS. See, Nima, a flamingo.

INDIAN GIRLS *crowd around, and admire the bird.*

PRINCESS. O Nima! I will use my bow no longer; I go out to the wood, and my heart is light; but while my arrow flies, I sorrow; and when the bird drops through the branches, tears come into mine eyes. I will no longer use my bow.

Distant hunting-horn. Music. They place themselves in attitudes of listening. Hunting-horn nearer.

NIMA. 'Tis Miami and our hunters. Princess, why are your looks sad?

PRINCESS. O Nima! the prince comes to bear me far from my father and my brother. I must quit for ever the companions and the woods that are dear to me. Nima, the Susquehannocks are a powerful nation, and my father would have them for his friends. He gives his daughter to their prince, but his daughter trembles to look upon the fierce Miami.

Music. HUNTERS *seen winding down the hills; they are met by the women of the village;* MIAMI *approaches* POCAHONTAS, *and his attendants lay skins at her feet.*

MIAMI. Princess, behold the spoils I bring thee. Our hunters are laden with the deer and the soft furred beaver. But Miami scorned such prey: I watched for the mighty buffalo and the shaggy bear; my club felled them to the ground, and I tore their skins from their backs. The fierce carcajou had wound himself around the tree, ready to dart upon the hunter; but the hunter's eyes were not closed, and the carcajou quivered on the point of my spear. I heard the wolf howl as he looked at the moon, and the beams that feel upon his upturned face shewed my tomahawk the spot it was to enter. I marked where the panther had crouched, and, before he could spring, my arrow went into his heart. Behold the spoil the Susquehannock brings thee!

PRINCESS. Susquehannock, thou'rt a mighty hunter. Powhatan shall praise thee for his daughter. But why returns not my brother with thee?

MIAMI. Nantaquas still finds pleasure in the hunt, but the soul of Miami grew weary of being away from Werocomoco, for there dwelt the daughter of Powhatan.

PRINCESS. Let us go to my father.

Music. Exeunt PRINCESS *and* MIAMI *into palace, followea by* NIMA *and train; the others into their several cabins.*

SCENE IV. *A Forest.* SMITH *enters, bewildered in its mazes. Music, expressive of his situation.*

SMITH. 'Tis all in vain! no clue to guide my steps.   [*Music.*
By this the explorers have return'd despairing,
And left their forward leader to his fate.
The rashness is well punish'd, that, alone,
Would brave the entangling mazes of these wilds.
The night comes on, and soon these gloomy woods
Will echo to the yell of savage beasts,
And savage men more merciless. Alas!
And am I, after all my golden dreams
Of laurel'd glory, doom'd in wilds to fall,
Ignobly and obscure, the prey of brutes?   [*Music.*
Fie on these coward thoughts! this trusty sword,
That made the Turk and Tartar crouch beneath me,
Will stead me well, e'en in this wilderness.

[*Music.*

O glory! thou who led'st me fearless on,
Where death stalk'd grimly over slaughter'd heaps,
Or drank the drowning shrieks of shipwreck'd wretches,
Swell high the bosom of thy votary!   [*Music. Exit* SMITH

Music. A party of INDIANS *enter, as following* SMITH, *and steal cautiously after him. The Indian yell within. Music, hurried. Re-enter* SMITH, *engaged with the* INDIANS; *several fall. Exeunt, fighting, and enter from the opposite side the Prince* NANTAQUAS, *who views with wonder the prowess of* SMITH; *when the music has ceased he speaks.*

Sure 'tis our war-god, Aresqui himself, who lays our chiefs low! Now they stop; he fights no longer; he stands terrible as the panther, which the fearful hunter dares not approach. Stranger, brave stranger, Nantaquas must know thee!   [*Music.*

He rushes out, and re-enters with SMITH.

PRINCE. Art thou not then a God?
SMITH. As thou art, warrior, but a man.
PRINCE. Then art thou a man like a God; thou shalt be the brother of Nantaquas. Stranger, my father is king of the country, and many nations obey him: will thou be the friend of the great Powhatan?

SMITH. Freely, prince; I left my own country to be the red man's friend.

PRINCE. Wonderful man, where is thy country?

SMITH. It lies far beyond the wide water.

PRINCE. Is there then a world beyond the wide water? I thought only the sun had been there: thou comest then from behind the sun?

SMITH. Not so, prince.

PRINCE. Listen to me. Thy country lies beyond the wide water, and from it do mine eyes behold the sun rise each morning.

SMITH. Prince, to your sight he seems to rise from thence, but your eyes are deceived, they reach not over the wilderness of waters.

PRINCE. Where sleeps the sun then?

SMITH. The sun never sleeps. When you see him sink behind the mountains, he goes to give light to other countries, where darkness flies before him, as it does here, when you behold him rise in the east: thus he chases Night for ever round the world.

PRINCE. Tell me, wise stranger, how came you from your country across the wide water? when our canoes venture but a little from the shore, the waves never fail to swallow them up.

SMITH. Prince, the Great Spirit is the friend of the white men, and they have arts which the red men know not.

PRINCE. My brother, will you teach the red men?

SMITH. I come to do it. My king is a king of a mighty nation; he is great and good: go, said he, go and make the red men wise and happy.

During the latter part of the dialogue, the INDIANS *had crept in, still approaching till they had almost surrounded* SMITH. *A burst of savage music. They seize and bear him off, the* PRINCE *in vain endeavouring to prevent it.*

PRINCE. Hold! the white man is the brother of your prince; hold, coward warriors! [*He rushes out.*

SCENE V. *Powhatan River, as the first scene.*

Enter LARRY.

Now do I begin to suspect, what, to be sure, I've been certain of a long time, that master Robin's a little bit of a big rogue. I just now observed him with my friend Walter's wife. Arrah! here they come. By your leave, fair dealing, I'll play the eavesdropper behind this tree. [*Retires behind a tree.*

Enter ALICE, *followed by* ROBIN.

ROBIN. But, mistress Alice, pretty Alice.

ALICE. Ugly Robin, I'll not hear a syllable.

ROBIN. But plague, prithee, Alice, why so coy?

Enter WALTER [*observing them, stops*].

ALICE. Master Robin, if you follow me about any longer with your fooleries, my Walter shall know of it.

ROBIN. A fig for Walter! is he to be mentioned the same day with the dapper Robin? can Walter make sonnets and madrigals, and set them, and sing them? besides, the Indians have eat him by this, I hope.

WALTER. Oh, the rascal!

ROBIN. Come, pretty one, quite alone, no one near, even that blundering Irishman away.

LARRY. O you spalpeen! I'll blunder on you anon.

ROBIN. Shall we, Alice, shall we?

Quartetto.

ROBIN.	Mistress Alice, say, Walter's far away, 　　　Pretty Alice! Nay, now—prithee, pray, Shall we, Alice? hey! 　　　Mistress Alice?
ALICE.	Master Robin, nay— Prithee, go your way, 　　　Saucy Robin! If you longer stay, You may rue the day, 　　　Master Robin.

WALTER. [*Aside.*] True my Alice is.

LARRY. [*Aside.*] Wat shall know of this.

ROBIN. [*Struggling.*] Pretty Alice!

WALTER. [*Aside.*] What a rascal 'tis!

LARRY. [*Aside.*] He'll kill poor Rob, I wis!

ROBIN. [*Struggling.*]　　　Mistress Alice,
　　　　　Let me taste the bliss—
　　　　　　　　　　　　[*Attempts to kiss her.*
ALICE.　　　　　Taste the bliss of this,　　[*Slaps his face.*
　　　　　Saucy Robin!
WALTER. [*Advancing.*] Oh, ·vhat wond'rous bliss!
LARRY. [*Advancing.*] How d'ye like the kiss?
ALICE.　　⎫
WALTER.　⎬　　　　　Master Robin?
LARRY.　　⎭

　　　　　　　　　　　　[ROBIN *steals off.*
WALTER. Jackanapes!
LARRY. Aye, hop off, cock robin! Blood and thunder now, that such a sparrow should try to turn hawk, and pounce on your little pullet here.
ALICE. Welcome, my bonny Walter.
WALTER. A sweet kiss, Alice, to season my bitter tidings. Our captain's lost.
LARRY.　⎫
　　　　　⎬ Lost!
ALICE.　 ⎭

WALTER. You shall hear. A league or two below this, we entered a charming stream, that seemed to glide through a fairy land of fertility. I must know more of this, said our captain. Await my return here. So bidding us moor the pinnace in a broad basin, where the Indian's arrows could reach us from neither side, away he went, alone in his boat, to explore the river to its head.
LARRY. Gallant soul!
WALTER. What devil prompted us to disobey his command I know not, but scarce was he out of sight, when we landed; and mark the end on't: up from their ambuscado started full three hundred black fiends, with a yell that might have appalled Lucifer, and whiz came a cloud of arrows about our ears. Three tall fellows of ours fell: Cassen, Emery, and Robinson. Our lieutenant, with Percy and myself, fought our way to the water side, where, leaving our canoe as a trophy to the victors, we plunged in, ducks, and, after swimming, dodging, and diving like regained the pinnace that we had left like geese.
ALICE. Heaven be praised, you are safe; but our poor captain—

WALTER. Aye; the day passed and he returned not; we came back for a reinforcement, and to-morrow we find him, or perish.

ALICE. Perish!—

WALTER. Aye; shame seize the poltroon who wou'dn't perish in such a cause; wou'dn't you, Larry?

LARRY. By Saint Patrick, it's the thing I would do, and hould my head the higher for it all the days of my life after.

WALTER. But see, our lieutenant and master Percy.

Enter ROLFE *and* PERCY.

ROLFE. Good Walter look to the barge, see it be ready
By earliest dawn.

WALTER.   I shall, sir.

ROLFE.   And be careful,
This misadventure be not buzz'd abroad,
Where 't may breed mutiny and mischief. Say
We've left the captain waiting our return,
Safe with the other three; meantime, choose out
Some certain trusty fellows, who will swear
Bravely to find their captain or their death.

WALTER. I'll hasten, sir, about it.

LARRY.   Good lieutenant,
Shall I along?

ROLFE.   In truth, brave Irishman,
We cannot have a better. Pretty Alice,
Will you again lose Walter for a time?

ALICE. I would I were a man, sir, then, most willingly I'd lose myself to do our captain service.

ROLFE. An Amazon!

WALTER.   Oh, 'tis a valiant dove.

LARRY. But come; Heaven and St. Patrick prosper us.

                  [*Exeunt* WALTER, LARRY, ALICE.

ROLFE. Now, my sad friend, cannot e'en this arouse you?
Still bending with the weight of shoulder'd Cupid?
Fie! throw away that bauble, love, my friend:
That glist'ning toy of listless laziness,
Fit only for green girls and growing boys
T' amuse themselves withal. Can an inconstant,
A fickle changeling, move a man like Percy?

PERCY. Cold youth, how can you speak of that you feel not?
You never lov'd.

ROLFE.   Hum! yes, in mine own way;
Marry, 'twas not with sighs and folded arms;
For mirth I sought in it, not misery.
Sir, I have ambled through all love's gradations
Most jollily, and seriously the whilst.
I have sworn oaths of love on my knee, yet laugh'd not;
Complaints and chidings heard, but heeded not;
Kiss'd the cheek clear from tear-drops, and yet wept not;
Listen'd to vows of truth, which I believed not;
And after have been jilted—

PERCY.   Well!

ROLFE.   And car'd not.

PERCY. Call you this loving?

ROLFE.   Aye, and wisely loving.
Not, sir, to have the current of one's blood
Froz'n with a frown, and molten with a smile;
Make ebb and flood under a lady Luna,
Liker the moon in changing than in chasteness.
'Tis not to be a courier, posting up
To the seventh heav'n, or down to the gloomy centre,
On the fool's errand of a wanton—pshaw!
Women! they're made of whimsies and caprice,
So variant and so wild, that, ty'd to a God,
They'd dally with the devil for a change.—
Rather than wed a European dame,
I'd take a squaw o' the woods, and get papooses.

PERCY. If Cupid burn thee not for heresy,
Love is no longer catholic religion.

ROLFE. An' if he do, I'll die a sturdy martyr.
And to the last preach to thee, pagan Percy,
Till I have made a convert. Answer me,
Is not this idol of thy heathen worship
That sent thee hither a despairing pilgrim;
Thy goddess, Geraldine, is she not false?

PERCY. Most false!

ROLFE.   For shame, then; cease adoring her;
Untwine the twisted cable of your arms,
Heave from your freighted bosom all its charge,
In one full sigh, and puff it strongly from you;
Then, raising your earth-reading eyes to Heaven,

Laud your kind stars you were not married to her,
And so forget her.
　　PERCY. Ah! my worthy Rolfe,
'Tis not the hand of infant Resolution
Can pluck this rooted passion from my heart:
Yet what I can I will; by heaven! I will.
　　ROLFE. Why, cheerly said; the baby Resolution
Will grow apace; time will work wonders in him.
　　PERCY. Did she not, after interchange of vows—
But let the false one go, I will forget her.
Your hand, my friend; now will I act the man.
　　ROLFE. Faith, I have seen thee do 't, and burn'd with shame,
That he who so could fight should ever sigh.
　　PERCY. Think'st thou our captain lives?
　　ROLFE. 　　　　　　　　　　Tush! he must live;
He was not born to perish so.　Believe 't,
He'll hold these dingy devils at the bay,
Till we come up and succour him.
　　PERCY. 　　　　　　　　And yet
A single arm against a host—alas!
I fear me he has fallen.
　　ROLFE. 　　　　　　Then never fell
A nobler soul, more valiant, or more worthy,
Or fit to govern men.　If he be gone,
Heaven save our tottering colony from falling!
But see, th' adventurers from their daily toil.

Enter adventurers, WALTER, LARRY, ROBIN, ALICE, &c.

WALTER. Now, gentlemen labourers, a lusty roundelay after
the toils of the day; and then to a sound sleep, in houses of our
own building.

Roundelay Chorus.

Now crimson sinks the setting sun,
And our tasks are fairly done.
Jolly comrades, home to bed,
Taste the sweets by labour shed;
Let his poppy seal your eyes,
Till another day arise,
For our tasks are fairly done,
As crimson sinks the setting sun.

ACT II.

SCENE I. *Inside the palace at Werocomoco.* POWHATAN *in state,* GRIMOSCO, &c., *his wives, and warriors, ranged on each side. Music.*

POWHATAN. My people, strange beings have appeared among us; they come from the bosom of the waters, amid fire and thunder; one of them has our war-god delivered into our hands: behold the white being!

Music. SMITH *is brought in; his appearance excites universal wonder;* POCAHONTAS *expresses peculiar admiration.*

POCAHONTAS. O Nima! is it not a God!

POWHATAN. Miami, though thy years are few, thou art experienced as age; give us thy voice of counsel.

MIAMI. Brothers, this stranger is of a fearful race of beings; their barren hunting grounds lie beneath the world, and they have risen, in monstrous canoes, through the great water, to spoil and ravish from us our fruitful inheritance. Brothers, this stranger must die; six of our brethren have fall'n by his hand. Before we lay their bones in the narrow house, we must avenge them: their unappeased spirits will not go to rest beyond the mountains; they cry out for the stranger's blood.

NANTAQUAS. Warriors, listen to my words; listen, my father, while your son tells the deeds of the brave white man. I saw him when 300 of our fiercest chiefs formed the warring around him. But he defied their arms; he held lightning in his hand. Wherever his arm fell, there sunk a warrior: as the tall tree falls, blasted and riven, to the earth, when the angry Spirit darts his fires through the forest. I thought him a God; my feet grew to the ground; I could not move!

POCAHONTAS. Nima, dost thou hear the words of my brother.

NANTAQUAS. The battle ceased, for courage left the bosom of our warriors; their arrows rested in their quivers; their bowstrings no longer sounded; the tired chieftains leaned on their war-clubs, and gazed at the terrible stranger, whom they dared not approach. Give an ear to me, king: 't was then I held out the hand of peace to him, and he became my brother; he forgot his arms, for he trusted to his brother: he was discoursing wonders to his friend, when our chiefs rushed upon him, and bore him away. But oh! my father, he must not die; for he is not a war captive; I promised that the chain of friendship should be bright between us. Chieftains, your prince must not falsify his word; father, your son must not be a liar!

POCAHONTAS. Listen, warriors; listen, father; the white man is my brother's brother!

GRIMOSCO. King! when last night our village shook with the loud noise, it was the Great Spirit who talk'd to his priest; my mouth shall speak his commands: King, we must destroy the strangers, for they are not our God's children; we must take their scalps, and wash our hands in the white man's blood, for he is an enemy to the Great Spirit.

NANTAQUAS. O priest, thou hast dreamed a false dream; Miami, thou tellest the tale that is not. Hearken, my father, to my true words! the white man is beloved by the Great Spirit; his king is like you, my father, good and great; and he comes from a land beyond the wide water, to make us wise and happy!

POWHATAN *deliberates. Music.*

POWHATAN. Stranger, thou must prepare for death. Six of our brethren fell by thy hand. Thou must die.

POCAHONTAS. Father, O father!

SMITH. Had not your people first beset me, king,
I would have prov'd a friend and brother to them;
Arts I'd have taught, that should have made them gods,
And gifts would I have given to your people,
Richer than red men ever yet beheld.
Think not I fear to die. Lead to the block.
The soul of the white warrior shall shrink not.
Prepare the stake! amidst your fiercest tortures,
You'll find its fiery pains as nobly scorned,
As when the red man sings aloud his death-song.

POCAHONTAS. Oh! shall that brave man die!

Music. The KING *motions with his hand, and* SMITH *is led to the block.*

MIAMI. [*To executioners.*] Warriors, when the third signal strikes, sink your tomahawks in his head.

POCAHONTAS. Oh, do not, warriors, do not! Father, incline your heart to mercy; he will win your battles, he will vanquish your enemies! [*First signal.*] Brother, speak! save your brother! Warriors, are you brave? preserve the brave man! [*Second signal.*]

Miami, priest, sing the song of peace; ah! strike not, hold! mercy!

Music. The third signal is struck, the hatchets are lifted up: when the Princess, *shrieking, runs distractedly to the block, and presses* Smith's *head to her bosom.*

White man, thou shalt not die; or I will die with thee!

Music. She leads Smith *to the throne, and kneels.*

My father, dost thou love thy daughter? listen to her voice; look upon her tears: they ask for mercy to the captive. Is thy child dear to thee, my father? Thy child will die with the white man.

Plaintive music. She bows her head to his feet. Powhatan, *after some deliberation, looking on his daughter with tenderness, presents her with a string of white wampum.* Pocahontas, *with the wildest expression of joy, rushes forward with* Smith, *presenting the beads of peace.*

Captive! thou art free!—

*Music. General joy is diffused—*Miami *and* Grimosco *only appear discontented. The prince* Nantaquas *congratulates* Smith. *The* Princess *shows the most extravagant emotions of rapture.*

Smith. O woman! angel sex! where'er thou art,
Still art thou heavenly. The rudest clime
Robs not thy glowing bosom of its nature.
Thrice blessed lady, take a captive's thanks!
         [He bows upon her hand.
Pocahontas. My brother!—
       [Music. Smith *expresses his gratitude.*
Nantaquas. Father, hear the design that fills my breast. I will go among the white men; I will learn their arts; and my people shall be made wise and happy.
Pocahontas. I too will accompany my brother.
Miami. Princess!—
Pocahontas. Away, cruel Miami; you would have murdered my brother!—

POWHATAN. Go, my son; take thy warriors, and go with the white men. Daughter, I cannot lose thee from mine eyes; accompany thy brother but a little on his way. Stranger, depart in peace; I entrust my son to thy friendship.

SMITH. Gracious sir,
He shall return with honours and with wonders;
My beauteous sister! noble brother, come!

Music. Exeunt, on one side, SMITH, PRINCESS, NANTAQUAS, NIMA, *and train. On the other,* KING, PRIEST, MIAMI, &c. *The two latter express angry discontent.*

SCENE II. *A forest.*

Enter PERCY, ROLFE.

ROLFE. So far indeed 'tis fruitless, yet we'll on.
PERCY. Aye, to the death.
ROLFE. Brave Percy, come, confess
You have forgot your love.
PERCY. Why, faith, not quite;
Despite of me, it sometimes through my mind
Flits like a dark cloud o'er a summer sky;
But passes off like that, and leaves me cloudless.
I can't forget that she was sweet as spring;
Fair as the day.
ROLFE. Aye, aye, like April weather;
Sweet, fair, and faithless.
PERCY. True alas! like April!

Song—PERCY.

Fair Geraldine each charm of spring possest,
  Her cheek glow'd with the rose and lily's strife;
Her breath was perfume, and each winter'd breast
  Felt that her sunny eyes beam'd light and life.

Alas! that in a form of blooming May,
  The mind should April's changeful liv'ry wear!
Yet ah! like April, smiling to betray,
  Is Geraldine, as false as she is fair!

ROLFE. Beshrew the little gipsy! let us on.

[*Exeunt* PERCY, ROLFE.

Enter LARRY, WALTER, ROBIN, &c.

LARRY. Go no further? Och! you hen-hearted cock robin!

ROBIN. But, master Larry—

WALTER. Prithee, thou evergreen aspen leaf, thou non-intermittent ague! why didst along with us?

ROBIN. Why, you know, my master Rolfe desired it; and then you were always railing out on me for chicken-heartedness. I came to shew ye I had valour.

WALTER. But forgetting to bring it with thee, thou wouldst now back for it; well, in the name of Mars, go; return for thy valour, Robin.

ROBIN. What! alone?

LARRY. Arrah! then stay here till it comes to you, and then follow us.

ROBIN. Stay here! O Lord, methinks I feel an arrow sticking in my gizzard already! Hark ye, my sweet master, let us sing.

LARRY. Sing?

ROBIN. Sing; I'm always valiant when I sing. Beseech you, let us chaunt the glee that I dish'd up for us three.

LARRY. It has a spice of your cowardly cookery in it.

WALTER. But since 'tis a provocative to Robin's valour—

LARRY. Go to: give a lusty hem, and fall on.

Glee.

We three, adventurers be,
Just come from our own country;
We have cross'd thrice a thousand ma,
Without a penny of money.

We three, good fellows be,
Who wou'd run like the devil from Indians three;
We never admir'd their bowmandry;
Oh, give us whole skins for our money.

We three, merry men be,
Who gaily will chaunt our ancient glee,
Though a lass or a glass, in this wild country,
Can't be had, or for love, or for money.

LARRY. Well, how do you feel?

ROBIN. As courageous as, as a—

LARRY. As a wren, little Robin. Are you sure, now, you won't be after fancying every deer that skips by you a divil, and every bush a bear?

ROBIN. I defy the devil; but hav'n't you heard, my masters, how the savages go a hunting, drest out in deer-skin? How could you put one in mind, master Larry? O Lord! that I should come a captain-hunting! the only game we put up is deer that carry scalping knives! or if we beat the bush to start a bold commander, up bolts a bloody bear!

[WALTER *and* LARRY *exchange significant nods.*

LARRY. To be sure we're in a parlous case. The forest laws are dev'lish severe here: an they catch us trespassing upon their hunting ground, we shall pay a neat poll-tax: nothing less than our heads will serve.

ROBIN. Our heads?

WALTER. Yes, faith! they'll soon collect their capitation.
They wear men's heads, sir, hanging at the breast,
Instead of jewels; and at either ear,
Most commonly, a child's, by way of ear-drop.

ROBIN. Oh! curse their finery! jewels, heads, O Lord!

LARRY. Pshaw man! don't fear. Perhaps they'll only burn us.
What a delicate roasted Robin you wou'd make!
Troth! they'd so lick their lips!

ROBIN.   A roasted robin!—

WALTER. Tut! if they only burn us, 'twill be brave.
Robin shall make our death-songs.

ROBIN.   Death-songs, oh!
[ROBIN *stands motionless with fear.*

LARRY. By the good looking right eye of Saint Patrick,
There's Rolfe and Percy, with a tribe of Indians.   [*Looking out.*

ROBIN. Indians! they're pris'ners, and we—we're dead men!

[*While* WALTER *and* LARRY *exeunt,* ROBIN *gets up into a tree.*]

O Walter, Larry! ha! what gone, all gone!
Poor Robin, what is to become of thee?

Enter SMITH, POCAHONTAS, NANTAQUAS, PERCY, ROLFE, NIMA *and* INDIANS, LARRY *and* WALTER.

SMITH. At hazard of her own dear life she saved me.
E'en the warm friendship of the prince had fail'd,
And death, inevitable death, hung over me.
Oh, had you seen her fly, like Pity's herald,
To stay the uplifted hatchet in its flight;
Or heard her, as with cherub voice she pled,
Like Heav'n's own angel-advocate, for mercy.
POCAHONTAS. My brother, speak not so.   [*Bashfully.*
ROLFE.   What gentleness!
What sweet simplicity! what angel softness!

ROLFE *goes to her. She, timidly, but with evident pleasure, receives his attentions. During this scene the* PRINCESS *discovers the first advances of love in a heart of perfect simplicity.* SMITH, &c., *converse apart.*

ROBIN. [*In the tree.*] Egad! there's never a head hanging to their ears; and their ears hang to their heads, for all the world as if they were christians; I'll venture down among them.
                                             [*Getting down.*
NIMA. Ah!   [*Bends her bow, and is about to shoot at him.*
LARRY. Arrah! my little dark Diana, choose noble game, that's only little Robin.
ROBIN. Aye, bless you, I'm only little Robin.   [*Jumps down.*

NIMA *examines him curiously, but fearfully.*

ROBIN. Gad, she's taken with my figure; ah! there it is now; a personable fellow shall have his wench any where. Yes, she's admiring my figure. Well, my dusky dear, how could you like such a man as I am?
NIMA. Are you a man?
ROBIN. I'll convince you of it some day. Hark ye, my dear.
                                             [*Attempts to whisper.*
NIMA. Ah! don't bite.
ROBIN. Bite! what do you take me for?
NIMA. A racoon.
ROBIN. A racoon! Why so?
NIMA. You run up the tree.   [*Motions as if climbing.*
LARRY. Well said, my little pagan Pythagoras!—
Ha! ha!

ROBIN. Hum! [*Retires disconcerted.*

ROLFE *and* PERCY *come forward.*

ROLFE. Tell me, in sooth, didst ever mark such sweetness!
Such winning—such bewitching gentleness!

PERCY. What, caught, my flighty friend, love-lim'd at last?
O Cupid, Cupid! thou'rt a skilful birder.
Although thou spread thy net, i' the wilderness,
Or shoot thy bird-bolt from an Indian bow,
Or place thy light in savage ladies' eyes,
Or pipe thy call in savage ladies' voices,
Alas! each tow'ring tenant of the air
Must fall heart pierc'd—or stoop, at thy command,
To sigh his sad notes in thy cage, O Cupid!

ROLFE. A truce; a truce! O friend, her guiltless breast
Seems Love's pavilion, where, in gentle sleep,
The unrous'd boy has rested. O my Percy!
Could I but wake the slumb'rer—

PERCY. Nay, i' faith,
Take courage; thou hast given the alarm:
Methinks the drowsy god gets up apace.

ROLFE. Say'st thou?

SMITH. Come, gentlemen, we'll toward the town.

NANTAQUAS. My sister, you will now return to our father.

PRINCESS. Return, my brother?

NANTAQUAS. Our father lives but while you are near him.
Go, my sister, make him happy with the knowledge of his
son's happiness. Farewell, my sister!

[*The* PRINCESS *appears dejected.*

SMITH. Once more, my guardian angel, let me thank thee.

[*Kissing her hand.*

Ere long we will return to thee, with presents
Well worth a princess' and a king's acceptance.
Meantime, dear lady, tell the good Powhatan
We'll show the prince such grace and entertainment,
As shall befit our brother and his son.
Adieu, sweet sister.

Music. They take leave of the PRINCESS; *she remains silently
dejected; her eyes anxiously follow* ROLFE, *who lingers behind,
and is the last to take leave.*

PRINCESS. Stranger, wilt thou too come to Werocomoco?

ROLFE. Dost thou wish it, lady?

PRINCESS. [*Eagerly.*] O yes!

ROLFE. And why, lovely lady?

PRINCESS. My eyes are pleased to see thee, and my ears to hear thee, stranger.

ROLFE. And did not the others who were here also please thy sight and hearing?

PRINCESS. Oh! they were all goodly; but—their eyes looked not like thine; their voices sounded not like thine; and their speeches were not like thy speeches, stranger.

ROLFE. Enchanting simplicity! But why call me stranger? Captain Smith thou callest brother. Call me so too.

PRINCESS. Ah, no!

ROLFE. Then thou thinkest not of me as thou dost of him? [*She shakes her head and sighs.*] Is Captain Smith dear to thee?

PRINCESS. Oh yes! very dear; [ROLFE *is uneasy.*] and Nantaquas too: they are my brothers;—but—that name is not thine—thou art—

ROLFE. What, lovely lady?

PRINCESS. I know not; I feel the name thou art, but I cannot speak it.

ROLFE. I am thy lover, dear princess.

PRINCESS. . Yes, thou art my lover. But why call me princess?

ROLFE. Dear lady, thou art a king's daughter.

PRINCESS. And if I were not, what wouldst thou call me?

ROLFE. Oh! if thou wert a beggar's, I would call thee love!

PRINCESS. I know not what a beggar is; but oh! I would I were a beggar's daughter, so thou wouldst call me love. Ah! do not longer call me king's daughter. If thou feelest the name as I do, call me as I call thee: thou shalt be *my* lover; I will be *thy* lover.

ROLFE. Enchanting, lovely creature! [*Kisses her ardently.*

PRINCESS. Lover, thou hast made my cheek to burn, and my heart to beat! Mark it.

ROLFE. Dear innocence! [*Putting his hand to her heart.*

PRINCESS. Lover, why is it so? To-day before my heart beat, and mine eyes were full of tears; but then my white brother was in danger. Thou art not in danger, and yet behold—[*Wipes a tear from her eye.*] Besides, then, my heart hurt me, but now! Oh, now!—Lover, why is it so?

[*Leaning on him with innocent confidence.*

ROLFE. Angel of purity! thou didst to-day feel pity; and now —Oh, rapturous task to teach thee the difference!—now, thou dost feel love.

PRINCESS. Love!

ROLFE. Love: the noblest, the sweetest passion that could swell thy angel bosom.

PRINCESS. Oh! I feel that 'tis very sweet. Lover, with thy lips thou didst make me feel it. My lips shall teach thee sweet love. [*Kisses him, and artlessly looks up in his face; placing her hand upon his heart.*] Does thy heart beat?

ROLFE. Beat! O heaven!—

[ROBIN, *who had been with* NIMA, *comes forward.*

ROBIN. Gad! we must end our amours, or we shall be left. Sir, my master, hadn't we better—

ROLFE. Booby! idiot!

Enter WALTER.

WALTER. Sir, lieutenant, the captain awaits your coming up.

ROLFE. I'll follow on the instant.

PRINCESS. Thou wilt not go?

ROLFE. But for a time, love.

PRINCESS. I do not wish thee to leave me.

ROLFE. I must, love; but I will return.

PRINCESS. Soon—very soon?

ROLFE. Very—very soon.

PRINCESS. I am not pleased now—and yet my heart beats. Oh, lover!

ROLFE. My angel! there shall not a sun rise and set, ere I am with thee. Adieu! thy own heavenly innocence be thy safe-guard. Farewell, sweet love!

Music. He embraces her and exit, followed by ROBIN *and* WALTER. PRINCESS *looks after him. A pause.*

PRINCESS. O Nima!

NIMA. Princess, white men are pow-wows. The white man put his lips here, and I felt something—here—

[*Putting her hand to her heart.*

PRINCESS. O lover!

She runs to the place whence ROLFE *went out, and gazes after him.*

Music. Enter from opposite side, MIAMI.

MIAMI. [*Sternly.*] Princess!

PRINCESS. [*Turning.*] Ah!

MIAMI. Miami has followed thy steps. Thou art the friend of the white men.

PRINCESS. Yes, for they are good and godlike.

MIAMI. Mine eyes beheld the pale youth part from you; your arms were entwined, your lips were together!

[*Struggling with jealousy.*

PRINCESS. He is my lover; I am his lover.

[*Still looking after* ROLFE.

MIAMI. [*Stamps with anger.*] Hear me! In what do the red yield to the white men? and who among the red men is like Miami? While I was yet a child, did the dart which my breath blew through my sarbacan ever fail to pierce the eye of the bird? What youth dared, like Miami, to leap from the precipice, and drag the struggling bear from the foaming torrent? Is there a hunter—is there a warrior—skilful and brave as Miami? Come to my cabin, and see the scalps and the skins that adorn it. They are the trophies of the Susquehannock!

PRINCESS. Man, mine eyes will never behold thy trophies. They are not pleased to look on thee.

[*Averting her eyes with disgust.*

MIAMI. Ha! [*Pause—he resumes in a softened tone.*] Princess, I have crossed many woods and waters, that I might bear the daughter of Powhatan to my nation. Shall my people cry out, with scorn, "behold! our prince returns without his bride?" In what is the pale youth above the red Miami?

PRINCESS. Thine eyes are as the panther's; thy voice like the voice of the wolf. Thou shouldst make my heart beat with joy; and I tremble before thee. Oh no! Powhatan shall give me to my lover. I will be my lover's bride!

Music. MIAMI *stamps furiously; his actions betray the most savage rage of jealousy; he rushes to seize the* PRINCESS, *but, recollecting that her attendants are by, he goes out in an agony, by his gestures menacing revenge. The* PRINCESS *exit on the opposite side, followed by train.*

SCENE III. *Werocomoco.*

Music. Enter from the palace POWHATAN *and* GRIMOSCO; *met by the* PRINCESS, *who runs to her father.*

POWHATAN. My daughter!
PRINCESS. O father! the furious Miami!
POWHATAN. What of the prince?
PRINCESS. Father, my father! do not let the fierce prince bear me to his cruel nation!
POWHATAN. How!
PRINCESS. By the spirit of my mother, I implore my father. Oh! if thou deliver me to the Susquehannock, think not thine eyes shall ever again behold me; the first kind stream that crosses our path shall be the end of my journey; my soul shall seek the soul of the mother that loved me, far beyond the mountains.
POWHATAN. Daughter, mention not thy mother!
PRINCESS. Her shade will pity her unhappy child, and I shall be at rest in her bosom.   [*Weeping.*
POWHATAN. Rest in my bosom, my child! [*She starts with joyful emotion.*] Thou shalt not go from thy father.
PRINCESS. Father; dear father!   [*Seizing his hand.*

Music. An INDIAN *enters, bearing a red hatchet.*

INDIAN. King!
POWHATAN. Thou art of the train of the Susquehannock: speak.
INDIAN. My prince demands his bride.
                    [*The* PRINCESS *clings fearfully to the* KING.
POWHATAN. Tell thy prince, my daughter will not leave her father.
INDIAN. Will Powhatan forget his promise to Miami?
POWHATAN. Powhatan will not forget his promise to her mother; and he vowed, while the angel of death hovered over her, that the eye of tender care should never be averted from her darling daughter.
INDIAN. Shall not then my prince receive his bride?
POWHATAN. The daughter of Powhatan—never.
INDIAN. Take then his defiance.
                    [*Music. He presents the red hatchet.*

POWHATAN. The red hatchet! 'Tis well. Grimosco, summon our warriors.

GRIMOSCO. O king! might I—

POWHATAN. Speak not. Tell our chiefs to assemble; and show them the war-signal [*Exit* GRIMOSCO.]. Go, tell your master, the great Powhatan will soon meet him, terrible as the minister of vengeance. [*Exit* INDIAN.] The chiefs approach. My child, retire from this war scene.

PRINCESS. O dear parent! thine age should have been passed in the shade of peace; and do I bring my father to the bloody war-path?

POWHATAN. Not so; the young prince has often dared my power, and merited my vengeance; he shall now feel both.

PRINCESS. Alas! his nation is numerous and warlike.

POWHATAN. Fear not, my child; we will call the valiant Nantaquas from his brothers; the brave English too will join us.

PRINCESS. Ah! then is thy safety and success certain.

[*Exit into palace, followed by* NIMA, &c.

Music. Enter GRIMOSCO *and* WARRIORS.

POWHATAN. Brave chieftains! need I remind you of the victories you have gained; the scalps you have borne from your enemies? Chieftains, another victory must be won; more trophies from your foes must deck your cabins; the insolent Miami has braved your king, and defied him with the crimson tomahawk. Warriors! we will not bury it till his nation is extinct. Ere we tread the war-path, raise to our god Aresqui the song of battle, then march to triumph and to glory.

SONG TO ARESQUI.

Aresqui! Aresqui!
Lo! thy sons for war prepare!
Snakes adorn each painted head,
While the cheek of flaming red
Gives the eye its ghastly glare.
Aresqui! Aresqui!
Through the war-path lead aright,
Lo! we're ready for the fight.

War Song.

FIRST INDIAN.   See the cautious warrior creeping!
SECOND INDIAN.   See the tree-hid warrior peeping!
FIRST INDIAN.   Mark! Mark!
          Their track is here; now breathless go!
SECOND INDIAN.   Hark! Hark!
          The branches rustle—'tis the foe!
CHORUS.   Now we bid the arrow fly—
          Now we raise the hatchet high.
          Where is urg'd the deadly dart,
          There is pierced a chieftain's heart;
          Where the war-club swift descends,
          A hero's race of glory ends!
FIRST INDIAN.   In vain the warrior flies—
          From his brow the scalp we tear.
SECOND INDIAN.   Or home the captiv'd prize,
          A stake-devoted victim, bear.
FIRST AND SECOND INDIAN.   The victors advance—
          And while amidst the curling blaze,
          Our foe his death-song tries to raise—
          Dance the warriors' dance.
                              [*War-dance.*
GRAND CHORUS.   Aresqui! Aresqui!
          Through the war-path lead aright—
          Lo! we're ready for the fight.
                              [*March to battle.*

ACT III.

SCENE I.   *Jamestown—built.*

WALTER *and* ALICE.

WALTER.   One mouthful more. [*Kiss.*]   Oh! after a long lent
of absence, what a charming relish is a kiss, served from the lips
of a pretty wife, to a hungry husband.

ALICE.   And, believe me, I banquet at the high festival of
return with equal pleasure.   But what has made your absence
so tedious, prithee?

WALTER.   Marry, girl, thus it was: when we had given the
enemies of our ally, Powhatan, defeature, and sent the rough

Miami in chains to Werocomoco, our captain dispatches his
lieutenant, Rolfe, to supply his place, here, in the town; and
leading us to the water's edge, and leaping into the pinnace,
away went we on a voyage of discovery. Some thousand miles
we sailed, and many strange nations discovered; and for our
exploits, if posterity reward us not, there is no faith in history.

ALICE. And what were your exploits?

WALTER.   Rare ones, egad!
We took the devil, Okee, prisoner.

ALICE. And have you brought him hither?

WALTER.   No: his vot'ries
Redeem'd him with some score or two of deer-skins.
Then we've made thirty kings our tributaries:
Such sturdy rogues, that each could easily
Fillip a buffalo to death with 's finger.

ALICE. But have you got their treasures?

WALTER.   All, my girl.
Imperial robes of raccoon, crowns of feather;
Besides the riches of their sev'ral kingdoms—
A full boat load of corn.

ALICE.   Oh, wonderful!

WALTER. Aye, is it not? But, best of all, I've kiss'd
The little finger of a mighty queen.
Sweet soul! among the court'sies of her court,
She gave us a Virginian mascarado.

ALICE. Dost recollect the fashion of it?

WALTER.   Oh!
Were I to live till Time were in his dotage,
'Twould never from mine eyes. Imagine first,
The scene, a gloomy wood; the time, midnight;
Her squawship's maids of honour were the masquers;
Their masks were wolves' heads curiously set on,
And, bating a small difference of hue,
Their dress e'en such as madam Eve had on
Or ere she eat the apple.

ALICE.   Pshaw!

WALTER.   These dresses,
All o'er perfum'd with the self-same pomado
Which our fine dames at home buy of old Bruin,
Glisten'd most gorgeously unto the moon.
Thus, each a firebrand brandishing aloft,

Rush'd they all forth, with shouts and frantic yells,
In dance grotesque and diabolical,
Madder than mad Bacchantes.
    ALICE.   O the powers!
    WALTER. When they had finished the divertisement
A beauteous Wolf-head came to me—
    ALICE.   To you?
    WALTER. And lit me with her pine-knot torch to bedward,
Where, as the custom of the court it was,
The beauteous Wolf-head blew the flambeau out,
And then—
    ALICE. Well!
    WALTER.   Then, the light being out, you know,
To all that follow'd I was in the dark.
Now you look grave. In faith I went to sleep.
Could a grim wolf rival my gentle lamb?
No, truly, girl: though in this wilderness
The trees hang full of divers colour'd fruit,
From orange-tawny to sloe-black, egad,
They'll hang until they rot or ere I pluck them,
While I've my melting, rosy nonpareil.   [*Kiss.*
    ALICE. Oh! you're a Judas!
    WALTER.   Then am I a Jew!

Enter SMITH, PERCY, NANTAQUAS, LARRY, &c.

    SMITH. Yet, prince, accept at least my ardent thanks:
A thousand times told over, they would fail
To pay what you and your dear sister claim.
Through my long absence from my people here,
You have sustain'd their feebleness.
    NANTAQUAS.   O brother,
To you, the conqueror of our father's foes;
To you, the sun which from our darken'd minds
Has chas'd the clouds of error, what can we
Not to remain your debtors?
    SMITH.   Gen'rous soul!
Your friendship is my pride. But who knows aught
Of our young Rolfe?
    PERCY.   This morning, sir, I hear,
An hour ere our arrival, the lieutenant
Accompanied the princess to her father's.

SMITH. Methinks our laughing friend has found at last
The power of sparkling eyes. What say you, prince,
To a brave, worthy soldier for your brother?
  NANTAQUAS. Were I to choose, I'd put all other by
To make his path-way clear unto my sister.
But come, sir, shall we to my father's banquet?
One of my train I've sent to give him tidings
Of your long-wish'd for coming.
  SMITH.   Gentle prince,
You greet my fresh return with welcome summons,
And I obey it cheerfully. Good Walter,
And, worthy sir [*To* LARRY.], be it your care
To play the queen bee here, and keep the swarm
Still gathering busily. Look to it well:
Our new-raised hive must hold no drones within it.
Now, forward, sirs, to Werocomoco.
                    [*Exeunt* SMITH, PRINCE, PERCY, &c.

Manent WALTER *and* LARRY.

  WALTER. So, my compeer in honour, we must hold
The staff of sway between us.
  LARRY.   Arrah, man,
If we hould it between us, any rogue
Shall run clean off before it knocks him down,
While at each end we tug for mastery.
  WALTER. Tush, man! we'll strike in unison.
  LARRY.   Go to—
  WALTER. And first, let's to the forest—the young sparks
In silken doublets there are felling trees,
Poor, gentle masters, with their soft palms blister'd;
And, while they chop and chop, they swear and swear,
Drowning with oaths the echo of their axe.
  LARRY. Are they so hot in choler?
  WALTER.   Aye.
  LARRY.   We'll cool 'em;
And pour cold patience down their silken sleeves.
  WALTER. Cold patience!
  LARRY.   In the shape of water, honey.
  WALTER. A notable discovery; come away!
  LARRY. Ha! isn't that a sail?
  WALTER.   A sail! a fleet! [*Looking toward the river.*

Enter TALMAN.

TALMAN. We have discovered nine tall ships.
LARRY.   Discovered!
Away, you rogue, we have discovered them,
With nature's telescopes. Run—scud—begone—
Down to the river! Och, St. Pat, I thank you!

Go toward river. Huzza within. Music expresses joyful bustle.
Scene closes.

SCENE II. *A grove.*

Enter ROBIN *and* NIMA.

ROBIN. Aye, bless you, I knew I should creep into your heart
at last, my little dusky divinity.
NIMA. Divinity! what's that?
ROBIN. Divinity—it's a—Oh, it's a pretty title that we lords of
the creation bestow upon our playthings. But hist! here they
come. Now is it a knotty point to be argued, whether this
parting doth most affect the mistress and master, or the maid
and man. Let Cupid be umpire, and steal the scales of Justice to
weigh our heavy sighs.   [*Retire.*

Enter ROLFE *and* POCAHONTAS.

PRINCESS. Nay, let me on—
ROLFE.   No further, gentle love;
The rugged way has wearied you already.
PRINCESS. Feels the wood pigeon weariness, who flies,
Mated with her beloved? Ah! lover, no.
ROLFE. Sweet! in this grove we will exchange adieus;
My steps should point straight onward; were thou with me,
Thy voice would bid me quit the forward path
At every pace, or fix my side-long look,
Spell-bound, upon thy beauties.
PRINCESS.   Ah! you love not
The wild-wood prattle of the Indian maid,
As once you did.
ROLFE.   By heaven! my thirsty ear,
Could ever drink its liquid melody.

Oh! I could talk with thee, till hasty night,
Ere yet the sentinel day had done his watch;
Veil'd like a spy, should steal on printless feet,
To listen to our parley! Dearest love!
My captain has arrived, and I do know,
When honour and when duty call upon me,
Thou wouldst not have me chid for tardiness.
But, ere the matin of to-morrow's lark,
Do echo from the roof of nature's temple,
Sweetest, expect me.

    PRINCESS.   Wilt thou surely come?

    ROLFE. To win thee from thy father will I come;
And my commander's voice shall join with mine,
To woo Powhatan to resign his treasure.

    PRINCESS. Go then, but ah! forget not—

    ROLFE.   I'll forget
All else, to think on thee!

    PRINCESS.   Thou art my life!
I lived not till I saw thee, love; and now,
I live not in thine absence. Long, Oh! long
I was the savage child of savage Nature;
And when her flowers sprang up, while each green bough
Sang with the passing west wind's rustling breath;
When her warm visitor, flush'd Summer, came,
Or Autumn strew'd her yellow leaves around,
Or the shrill north wind pip'd his mournful music,
I saw the changing brow of my wild mother
With neither love nor dread. But now, Oh! now,
I could entreat her for eternal smiles,
So thou might'st range through groves of loveliest flowers,
Where never Winter, with his icy lip,
Should dare to press thy cheek.

    ROLFE.   My sweet enthusiast!

    PRINCESS. O! 'tis from thee that I have drawn my being:
Thou'st ta'en me from the path of savage error,
Blood-stain'd and rude, where rove my countrymen,
And taught me heavenly truths, and fill'd my heart
With sentiments sublime, and sweet, and social.
Oft has my winged spirit, following thine,
Cours'd the bright day-beam, and the star of night,
And every rolling planet of the sky,

Around their circling orbits. O my love!
Guided by thee, has not my daring soul,
O'ertopt the far-off mountains of the east,
Where, as our fathers' fable, shad'wy hunters
Pursue the deer, or clasp the melting maid,
'Mid ever blooming spring? Thence, soaring high
From the deep vale of legendary fiction,
Hast thou not heaven-ward turn'd my dazzled sight,
Where sing the spirits of the blessed good
Around the bright throne of the Holy One?
This thou hast done; and ah! what couldst thou more,
Belov'd preceptor, but direct that ray,
Which beams from Heaven to animate existence,
And bid my swelling bosom beat with love!

    ROLFE. O, my dear scholar!
    PRINCESS.   Prithee, chide me, love:
My idle prattle holds thee from thy purpose.
    ROLFE. O! speak more music! and I'll listen to it,
Like stilly midnight to sweet Philomel.
    PRINCESS. Nay, now begone; for thou must go: ah! fly,
The sooner to return—
    ROLFE.   Thus, then, adieu!   [*Embrace.*
But, ere the face of morn blush rosy red,
To see the dew-besprent, cold virgin ground
Stain'd by licentious step; Oh, long before
The foot of th' earliest furred forrester,
Do mark its imprint on morn's misty sheet,
With sweet good morrow will I wake my love.
    PRINCESS. To bliss thou'lt wake me, for I sleep till then
Only with sorrow's poppy on my lids.

Music. Embrace; and exit ROLFE, *followed by* ROBIN; PRINCESS
looks around despondingly.

But now, how gay and beauteous was this grove!
Sure ev'ning's shadows have enshrouded it,
And 'tis the screaming bird of night I hear,
Not the melodious mock-bird. Ah! fond girl!
'Tis o'er thy soul the gloomy curtain hangs;
'Tis in thy heart the rough-toned raven sings.
O lover! haste to my benighted breast;
Come like the glorious sun, and bring me day!

Song.

When the midnight of absence the day-scene pervading
    Distils its chill dew o'er the bosom of love,
Oh, how fast then the gay tints of nature are fading!
    How harsh seems the music of joy in the grove!
While the tender flow'r droops till return of the light,
Steep'd in tear drops that fall from the eye of the night.

    But Oh! when the lov'd-one appears,
      Like the sun a bright day to impart,
    To kiss off those envious tears,
        To give a new warmth to the heart;
          Soon the flow'ret seeming dead
          Raises up its blushing head,
          Glows again the breast of love,
          Laughs again the joyful grove;
          While once more the mock-bird's throat
          Trolls the sweetly various note.
But ah! when dark absence the day-scene pervading
    Distils its chill dew o'er the bosom of love,
Oh! fast then the gay tints of nature are fading!
    Oh! harsh seems the music of joy in the grove!
And the tender flow'r droops till return of the light,
Steep'd in tear drops that fall from the eye of the night.

PRINCESS. Look, Nima, surely I behold our captive,
The prince Miami, and our cruel priest.
    NIMA. Lady, 'tis they; and now they move this way.
    PRINCESS. How earnest are their gestures; ah! my Nima,
When souls like theirs mingle in secret council,
Stern murder's voice alone is listen'd to.
Miami too at large—O trembling heart,
Most sad are thy forebodings; they are here—
Haste, Nima; let us veil us from their view.

                            [*They retire.*

Enter MIAMI *and* GRIMOSCO.

GRIMOSCO. Be satisfied; I cannot fail—hither the king will soon come. This deep shade have I chosen for our place of meeting. Hush! he comes. Retire, and judge if Grimosco have vainly boasted—away!   [MIAMI *retires.*

Enter POWHATAN.

POWHATAN. Now, priest, I attend the summons of thy voice.

GRIMOSCO. So you consult your safety, for 'tis the voice of warning.

POWHATAN. Of what would you warn me?

GRIMOSCO. Danger.

POWHATAN. From whom?

GRIMOSCO. Your enemies.

POWHATAN. Old man, these have I conquered.

GRIMOSCO. The English still exist.

POWHATAN. The English!

GRIMOSCO. The nobler beast of the forest issues boldly from his den, and the spear of the powerful pierces his heart. The deadly adder lurks in his covert till the unwary footstep approach him.

POWHATAN. I see no adder near me.

GRIMOSCO. No, for thine eyes rest only on the flowers under which he glides.

POWHATAN. Away, thy sight is dimmed by the shadows of age.

GRIMOSCO. King, for forty winters hast thou heard the voice of counsel from my lips, and never did its sound deceive thee; never did my tongue raise the war cry, and the foe appeared not. Be warned then to beware the white man. He has fixed his serpent eye upon you, and, like the charmed bird, you flutter each moment nearer to the jaw of death.

POWHATAN. How, Grimosco?

GRIMOSCO. Do you want proof of the white man's hatred to the red? Follow him àlong the bay; count the kings he has conquered, and the nations that his sword has made extinct.

POWHATAN. Like a warrior he subdued them, for the chain of friendship bound them not to each other. The white man is brave as Aresqui; and can the brave be treacherous?

GRIMOSCO. Like the red feathers of the flamingo is craft, the brightest plume that graces the warrior's brow. Are not your people brave? Yet does the friendly tree shield them while the hatchet is thrown. Who doubts the courage of Powhatan? Yet has the eye of darkness seen Powhatan steal to the surprise of the foe.

POWHATAN. Ha! priest, thy words are true. I will be satisfied. Even now I received a swift messenger from my son:

to-day he will conduct the English to my banquet. I will demand of him if he be the friend of Powhatan.

GRIMOSCO. Yes; but demand it of him as thou drawest thy reeking hatchet from his cleft head. [KING *starts*.] The despoilers of our land must die!

POWHATAN. What red man can give his eye-ball the glare of defiance when the white chief is nigh? He who stood alone amidst seven hundred foes, and, while he spurned their king to the ground, dared them to shoot their arrows; who will say to him, "White man, I am thine enemy?" No one. My chiefs would be children before him.

GRIMOSCO. The valour of thy chiefs may slumber, but the craft of thy priest shall watch. When the English sit at that banquet from which they shall never rise; when their eyes read nothing but friendship in thy looks, there shall hang a hatchet over each victim head, which, at the silent signal of Grimosco—

POWHATAN. Forbear, counsellor of death! Powhatan cannot betray those who have vanquished his enemies; who are his friends, his brothers.

GRIMOSCO. Impious! Can the enemies of your God be your friends? Can the children of another parent be your brethren? You are deaf to the counsellor: 'tis your priest now speaks. I have heard the angry voice of the Spirit you have offended; offended by your mercy to his enemies. Dreadful was his voice; fearful were his words. Avert his wrath, or thou art condemned; and the white men are the ministers of his vengeance.

POWHATAN. Priest!

GRIMOSCO. From the face of the waters will he send them, in mighty tribes, and our shores will scarce give space for their footsteps. Powhatan will fly before them; his beloved child, his wives, all that is dear to him, he will leave behind. Powhatan will fly; but whither? which of his tributary kings will shelter him? Not one. Already they cry, "Powhatan is ruled by the white; we will no longer be the slaves of a slave!"

POWHATAN. Ha!

GRIMOSCO. Despoiled of his crown, Powhatan will be hunted from the land of his ancestors. To strange woods will the fugitive be pursued by the Spirit whom he has angered—

POWHATAN. Oh, dreadful!

GRIMOSCO. And at last, when the angel of death obeys his call of anguish, whither will go his condemned soul? Not to the fair forests, where his brave fathers are. Oh! never will Powhatan clasp the dear ones who have gone before him. His exiled, solitary spirit will forever houl on the barren heath where the wings of darkness rest. No ray of hope shall visit him; eternal will be his night of despair.

POWHATAN. Forbear, forbear! O priest, teach me to avert the dreadful doom.

GRIMOSCO. Let the white men be slaughtered.

POWHATAN. The angry Spirit shall be appeased. Come.

[*Exit.*

GRIMOSCO. Thy priest will follow thee.

Enter MIAMI.

MIAMI. Excellent Grimosco! Thy breath, priest, is a deadly pestilence, and hosts fall before it. Yet—still is Miami a captive.

GRIMOSCO. Fear not. Before Powhatan reach Werocomoco thou shalt be free. Come.

MIAMI. Oh, my soul hungers for the banquet; for then shall Miami feast on the heart of his rival!

[*Exeunt with savage triumph.*

Music. The PRINCESS *rushes forward, terror depicted in her face. After running alternately to each side, and stopping undetermined and bewildered, speaks.*

PRINCESS. O whither shall I fly? what course pursue?
At Werocomoco, my frenzied looks
Would sure betray me. What if hence I haste?
I may o'ertake my lover, or encounter
My brother and his friends. Away, my Nima!

[*Exit* NIMA.

O holy Spirit! thou whom my dear lover
Has taught me to adore and think most merciful,
Wing with thy lightning's speed my flying feet!

[*Music. Exit* PRINCESS.

SCENE III. *Near Jamestown.*

Enter LARRY, *and* KATE *as a page.*

LARRY. Nine ships, five hundred men, and a lord governor! Och! St. Patrick's blessing be upon them; they'll make this land flow with buttermilk like green Erin. What say you, master page, isn't this a nice neat patch to plant potatoes—I mean, to plant a nation in?

KATE. There's but one better.

LARRY. And which might that be?

KATE. E'en little green Erin that you spoke of.

LARRY. And were you ever—och, give me your fist—were you ever in Ireland?

KATE. It's there I was born—

LARRY. I saw its bloom on your cheek.

KATE. And bred.

LARRY. I saw it in your manners.

KATE. Oh, your servant, sir. [*Bows.*] And there, too, I fell in love.

LARRY. And, by the powers, so did I; and if a man don't fall into one of the beautiful bogs that Cupid has digged there, faith he may stand without tumbling, though he runs over all the world beside. Och, the creatures, I can see them now—

KATE. Such sparkling eyes—

LARRY. Rosy cheeks—

KATE. Pouting lips—

LARRY. Tinder hearts! Och, sweet Ireland!

KATE. Aye, it was there that I fixed my affections after all my wanderings.

*Song.—*KATE.

Young Edward, through many a distant place,
　　Had wandering pass'd, a thoughtless ranger;
And, cheer'd by a smile from beauty's face,
　　Had laugh'd at the frowning face of danger.
　　　　Fearless Ned,
　　　　Careless Ned,
　　Never with foreign dames was a stranger;
　　　　And huff,
　　　　Bluff,
He laugh'd at the frowning face of danger.

But journeying on to his native place,
     Through Ballinamoné pass'd the stranger;
Where, fix'd by the charms of Katy's face,
     He swore he'd no longer be a ranger,
         Pretty Kate,
         Witty Kate,
Vow'd that no time could ever change her;
         And kiss,
         Bliss—
O, she hugg'd to her heart the welcome stranger.

LARRY. How's that? Ballinamoné, Kate, did you say, Kate?

KATE. Aye, Katy Maclure; as neat a little wanton tit—

LARRY. My wife a wanton tit!—Hark ye, master Whipper-snapper, do you pretend—

KATE. Pretend! no, faith, sir, I scorn to *pretend*, sir; I am above boasting of ladies' favours, unless I receive 'em. Pretend, quotha!

LARRY. Fire and faggots! Favours!—

KATE. You seem to know the girl, mister—a—

LARRY. Know her! she's my wife.

KATE. Your wife! Ridiculous! I thought, by your pother, that she had been *your friend's wife*, or your mistress. Hark ye, mister—a—cuckoo—

LARRY. Cuckoo!

KATE. Your ear. Your wife loved me as she did herself.

LARRY. She did?

KATE. Couldn't live without me; all day we were together.

LARRY. You were!

KATE. As I'm a cavalier; and all night—we lay——

LARRY. How?

KATE. How! why, close as two twin potatoes; in the same bed, egad!

LARRY. Tunder and turf! I'll split you from the coxcomb to the——

KATE. Ay, do split the twin potato asunder, do.

                            [*Discovers herself.*

LARRY. It is—no—what! Och, is it nobody but yourself? O my darling!—[*Catches her in his arms.*] And so—But how did you?—And where—and what—O boderation! [*Kisses.*]

And how d' ye do? and how's your mother? and the pigs and praties, and—kiss me, Kate.   [*Kiss.*

KATE. So; now may I speak?

LARRY. Aye, do be telling me—but stop every now and then, that I may point your story with a grammatical kiss.

KATE. Oh, hang it! you'll be for putting nothing but periods to my discourse.

LARRY. Faith, and I should be for counting—[*Kisses.*]—four. —Arrah! there, then; I've done with that sentence.

KATE. You remember what caused me to stay behind, when you embarked for America?

LARRY. Aye, 'twas because of your old sick mother. And how does the good lady? [KATE *weeps.*] Ah! well, Heaven rest her soul.—Cheerly, cheerly. To be sure, I can't give *you* a mother; but I tell you what I'll do, I'll give your children one; and that's the same thing, you know. So, kiss me, Kate. Cheerly.

KATE. One day, as I sat desolate in my cottage, a carriage broke down near it, from which a young lady was thrown with great violence. My humble cabin received her, and I attended her till she was able to resume her journey.

LARRY. My kind Kate!

·KATE. The sweet young lady promised me her protection, and pressed me to go with her. So, having no mother—nor Larry to take care of——

LARRY. You let the pigs and praties take care of themselves.

KATE. I placed an honest, poor neighbour in my cottage, and followed the fortunes of my mistress—and—O Larry, such an angel!

LARRY. But where is she?

KATE. Here, in Virginia.

LARRY. Here?

KATE. Aye, but that's a secret.

LARRY. Oh! is it so? that's the reason then you won't tell it me.

GERALDINE, *as a page, and* WALTER *appear behind.*

KATE. That's she.

LARRY. Where?

KATE. There.

LARRY. Bother! I see no one but a silken cloaked spark, and our Wat; devil a petticoat!

KATE. That spark is my mistress.

LARRY. Be asy. Are you sure you ar'n't his mistress?

KATE. Tut, now you've got the twin potatoes in your head.

LARRY. Twins they must be, if any, for faith I hav'n't had a *single* potato in my head this many a long day. But come, my Kate, tell me how you and your mistress happened to jump into—

KATE. Step aside then.

LARRY. Have with you, my dapper page. [*They retire.*

GERALDINE *and* WALTER *advance.*

GERALDINE. You know this Percy, then?

WALTER. Know him! Oh, yes!
He makes this wild wood, here, a past'ral grove.
He is a love-lorn shepherd; an Orlando,
Carving love-rhymes and ciphers on the trees,
And warbling dying ditties of a lady
He calls false Geraldine.

GERALDINE. O my dear Percy!
How has one sad mistake marr'd both our joys! [*Aside.*

WALTER. Yet though a shepherd, he can wield a sword
As easy as a crook.

GERALDINE. Oh! he is brave.

WALTER. As Julius Cæsar, sir, or Hercules;
Or any other hero that you will,
Except our captain.

GERALDINE. Is your captain, then,
Without his peer?

WALTER. Aye, marry is he, sir,
Sans equal in this world. I've follow'd him
Half o'er the globe, and seen him do such deeds!
His shield is blazon'd with three Turkish heads.

GERALDINE. Well, sir.

WALTER. And I, boy, saw him win the arms;
Oh, 'twas the bravest act!

GERALDINE. Prithee, recount it.

WALTER. It was at Regal, close beleaguer'd then
By the duke Sigismund of Transylvania,
Our captain's general. One day, from the gate
There issued a gigantic mussulman,
And threw his gauntlet down upon the ground,

Daring our christian knights to single combat.
It was our captain, sir, pick'd up the glove,
And scarce the trump had sounded to the onset,
When the Turk Turbisha had lost his head.
His brother, fierce Grualdo, enter'd next,
But left the lists sans life or turban too.
Last came black Bonamolgro, and he paid
The same dear forfeit for the same attempt.
And now my master, like a gallant knight,
His sabre studied o'er with ruby gems,
Prick'd on his prancing courser round the field,
In vain inviting fresh assailants; while
The beauteous dames of Regal, who, in throngs
Lean'd o'er the rampart to behold the tourney,
Threw show'rs of scarfs and favours from the wall,
And wav'd their hands, and bid swift Mercuries
Post from their eyes with messages of love;
While manly modesty and graceful duty
Wav'd on his snowy plume, and, as he rode,
Bow'd down his casque unto the saddle bow.

GERALDINE. It was a deed of valour, and you've dress'd it
In well-beseeming terms. And yet, methinks,
I wonder at the ladies' strange delight;
And think the spectacle might better suit
An audience of warriors than of women.
I'm sure I should have shudder'd—that is, sir,
If I were woman.

WALTER.   Cry your mercy, page;
Were you a woman, you would love the brave.
You're yet but boy; you'll know the truth of this,
When father Time writes man upon your chin.

GERALDINE. No doubt I shall, sir, when I get a beard.

WALTER. My master, boy, has made it crystal clear:
Be but a Mars, and you shall have your Venus.

Song—WALTER.

Captain Smith is a man of might,
In Venus' soft wars or in Mars' bloody fight:
For of widow, or wife, or of damsel bright,
    A bold blade, you know, is all the dandy.

One day his sword he drew,
And a score of Turks he slew;
　　When done his toil,
　　He snatch'd the spoil,
　　And, as a part,
　　The gentle heart
Of the lovely lady Tragabizandy.

Captain Smith trod the Tartar land;
While before him, in terror, fled the turban'd band,
With his good broad-sword, that he whirl'd in his hand,
　　To a three-tail'd bashaw he gave a pat-a.

　　The bashaw, in alarm,
　　Turn'd tails, and fled his arm.
　　　　But face to face,
　　　　With lovely grace,
　　　　In all her charms,
　　　　Rush'd to his arms
The beautiful lady Calamata.

Captain Smith, from the foaming seas,
From pirates, and shipwreck, and miseries,
In a French lady's arms found a haven of ease;
　　Her name—pshaw! from memory quite gone 't has.

　　And on this savage shore,
　　Where his faulchion stream'd with gore,
　　　　His noble heart
　　　　The savage dart
　　　　Had quiver'd through;
　　　　But swifter flew
To his heart the pretty princess Pocahontas.　　[*Exit* WALTER.

Enter KATE.

GERALDINE. Now, brother page—

KATE.　　　　　　　Dear mistress, I have found
My faithful Larry.

GERALDINE.　　　　Happy girl! and I
Hope soon to meet my heart's dear lord, my Percy.
Hist! the lord governor—

KATE. He little thinks
Who is the page he loves so—
GERALDINE. Silence.
KATE. Mum.

Enter DELAWAR, WALTER, LARRY, &c.

DELAWAR. Each noble act of his that you recite
Challenge all my wonder and applause.
Your captain is a brave one; and I long
To press the hero's hand. But look, my friends,
What female's this, who, like the swift Camilla,
On airy step flies hitherward?
WALTER. My lord,
This is the lovely princess you have heard of;
Our infant colony's best patroness;
Nay, sir, its foster-mother.
DELAWAR. Mark how wild—

Music. The PRINCESS *enters, with wild anxiety in her looks;
searches eagerly around for* SMITH *and* ROLFE.

DELAWAR. Whom do you look for, lady?
PRINCESS. They are gone!
Gone to be slaughter'd!
WALTER. If you seek our captain,
He has departed for your father's banquet.
PRINCESS. Then they have met, and they will both be lost,
My lover and my friend. O! faithless path,
That led me from my lover! Strangers, fly!
If you're the white man's friends—
DELAWAR. Lady, we are.
PRINCESS. Then fly to save them from destruction!
DELAWAR. How?
PRINCESS. Inquire not; speak not; treachery and death
Await them at the banquet.
DELAWAR. Haste, my friends,
Give order for immediate departure.
PRINCESS. E'en now, perhaps, they bleed! O lover! brother!
Fly, strangers, fly!

Music. Drum beats; a bustle; scene closes.

SCENE IV. *At Werocomoco; banquet.* SMITH, ROLFE, PERCY, NANTAQUAS, POWHATAN, &c., *seated.* GRIMOSCO, MIAMI *and a number of* INDIANS *attending.*

POWHATAN. White warriors, this is the feast of peace, and yet you wear your arms. Will not my friends lay by their warlike weapons? They fright our fearful people.

SMITH. Our swords are part of our apparel, king;
Nor need your people fear them. They shall rest
Peaceful within their scabbards, if Powhatan
Call them not forth, with voice of enmity.

POWHATAN. Oh, that can never be! feast then in peace,
Children and friends—

Leaves his place and comes forward to GRIMOSCO.

O priest! my soul is afraid it will be stained with dishonour.

GRIMOSCO. Away! the Great Spirit commands you. Resume your seat; hold the white men in discourse; I will but thrice wave my hand, and your foes are dead. [KING *resumes his seat.*] [*To* MIAMI.] Now, prince, has the hour of vengeance arrived.

POWHATAN. [*With a faltering voice.*] Think not, white men, that Powhatan wants the knowledge to prize your friendship. Powhatan has seen three generations pass away; and his locks of age do not float upon the temples of folly.

GRIMOSCO *waves his hand: the* INDIANS *steal behind the* ENGLISH, MIAMI *behind* ROLFE. KING *proceeds.*

If a leaf but fall in the forest, my people cry out with terror, "hark! the white warrior comes!" Chief, thou art terrible as an enemy, and Powhatan knows the value of thy friendship.

GRIMOSCO *waves his hand again; the* INDIANS *seize their tomahawks, and prepare to strike.* KING *goes on.*

Think not, therefore, Powhatan can attempt to deceive thee—

The KING'S *voice trembles; he stops, unable to proceed. The* INDIANS' *eyes are fixed on* GRIMOSCO, *waiting for the last signal. At this moment the* PRINCESS *rushes in.*

PRINCESS. Treachery to the white men!

At the same instant, drum and trumpet without. Music. The ENGLISH *seize the uplifted arms of the* INDIANS, *and form a tableau, as enter* DELAWAR *and his party. After the music, the* SOLDIERS *take charge of the* INDIANS. POCAHONTAS *flies to the arms of* ROLFE.

NANTAQUAS. O father!

[POWHATAN *is transfixed with confusion.*

SMITH. Wretched king! what fiend could urge you?

POWHATAN. Shame ties the tongue of Powhatan. Ask of that fiend-like priest, how, to please the angry Spirit, I was to massacre my friends.

SMITH. Holy Religion! still beneath the veil
Of sacred piety what crimes lie hid!
Bear hence that monster. Thou ferocious prince—

MIAMI. Miami's tortures shall not feast your eyes!

[*Stabbing himself.*

SMITH. Rash youth, thou mightst have liv'd—

MIAMI. Liv'd! man, look there!

[*Pointing to* ROLFE *and* PRINCESS. *He is borne off.*

POWHATAN. Oh, if the false Powhatan might—

SMITH.   No more.
Wiser than thou have been the dupes of priesthood.
Your hand. The father of this gen'rous pair
I cannot choose but love. My noble lord,
I pray you pardon my scant courtesy
And sluggish duty, which so tardy-paced
Do greet your new arrival—

DELAWAR.   Valiant captain!
Virtue-ennobled sir, a hero's heart
Will make mine proud by its most near acquaintance.

[*Embrace.*

SMITH. Your coming was most opportune, my lord.
One moment more—

DELAWAR.   Nay, not to us the praise.
Behold the brilliant star that led us on.

SMITH. Oh! blest is still its kindly influence!
Could a rough soldier play the courtier, lady,
His practis'd tongue might grace thy various goodness,
With proper phrase of thanks; but oh! reward thee!
Heaven only can—

PRINCESS.   And has, my brother. See!
I have its richest gift.   [*Turning to* ROLFE.
ROLFE.   My dearest love!
SMITH. Her brother, sir, and worthy of that name.

Introduces NANTAQUAS *to* DELAWAR; PERCY *and* GERALDINE, *who had been conversing, advance.*

PERCY. You tell me wonders.
GERALDINE.   But not miracles.
Being near the uncle, sir, I knew the lady.
    PERCY. And was I then deceived?
    GERALDINE.   What, gentle Percy!
Young man, 'twas not well done, in idle pique,
To wound the heart that lov'd you.
    PERCY.   O sir! speak!
My Geraldine, your niece, is she not married?
    DELAWAR. Nor like to be, poor wench, but to her grave,
If mourning for false lovers break maids' hearts.
    PERCY. Was she then true? O madman! idiot!
To let the feeble breath of empty rumour
Drive me from heavenly happiness!
    DELAWAR.   Poor girl!
She fain would have embark'd with me.
    PERCY.   Ah, sir!
Why did she not?
    DELAWAR.   Marry, sir, I forbade her:
The rough voyage would have shook her slender health
To dissolution.
    GERALDINE.   Pardon, sir; not so—
    DELAWAR. How now, pert page?
    GERALDINE.   For here she is, my lord.
And the rough voyage has giv'n her a new life.
    PERCY. My Geraldine!
    DELAWAR.   My niece! O brazenface!
Approach me not; fly from your uncle's anger;
Fly to your husband's arms for shelter, hussy!
                   [GERALDINE *flies to* PERCY'S *embrace.*
    PERCY. Oh! speechless transport! mute let me infold thee!
    DELAWAR. [*To* KATE.] And you, my little spark, perhaps,
        your cloak

Covers another duteous niece—or daughter.
Speak, lady: for I see that title writ
In crimson characters upon your cheek.
Art of my blood?

LARRY. No, sir, she's of my flesh;
Flesh of my flesh, my lord. Now, arrah, Kate,
Don't blush. This goodly company all knows
My flesh may wear the breeches, without scandal.

WALTER. Listen not, Alice, to his sophistry.
Sir, if our good wives learn this argument,
They'll logically pluck away our—

ALICE. Tut:
Fear ye not that; for when a woman would,
She'll draw them on without a rule of reason.

DELAWAR. Methinks 'tis pairing time among the turtles.
Who have we here?

ROBIN and NIMA come forward.

ROBIN. A pair of pigeons, sir; or rather a robin and a dove.
A wild thing, sir, that I caught in the wood here. But when I
have clipt her wings, and tamed her, I hope (without offence to
this good company) that we shall bill without biting more than
our neighbours.

SMITH. Joy to ye, gentle lovers; joy to all;
A goodly circle, and a fair. Methinks
Wild Nature smooths apace her savage frown,
Moulding her features to a social smile.
Now flies my hope-wing'd fancy o'er the gulf
That lies between us and the aftertime,
When this fine portion of the globe shall teem
With civiliz'd society; when arts,
And industry, and elegance shall reign,
As the shrill war-cry of the savage man
Yields to the jocund shepherd's roundelay.
Oh, enviable country! thus disjoin'd
From old licentious Europe! may'st thou rise,
Free from those bonds which fraud and superstition
In barbarous ages have enchain'd *her* with;—
Bidding the antique world with wonder view
A great, yet virtuous empire in the west!

Finale.

Freedom, on the western shore
  Float thy banner o'er the brave;
Plenty, here thy blessings pour;
  Peace, thy olive sceptre wave!

PERCY, WALTER, &c.

Fire-eyed Valour, guard the land;
  Here uprear thy fearless crest;

PRINCESS, KATE, ALICE, &c.

Love, diffuse thy influence bland
  O'er the regions of the west.
CHORUS, *Freedom, &c.*

LARRY.

Hither, lassie, frank and pretty,
  Come and live without formality.
Thou, in English christen'd Pity,
  But call'd, in Irish, Hospitality.
CHORUS, *Freedom, &c.*

The End.

SHE WOULD BE A SOLDIER

By M. M. NOAH

M. M. NOAH

MORDECAI MANUEL NOAH
(1785–1851)

Mr. Noah was born in Philadelphia, July 19, 1785, the son of Portuguese Jewish descent, it being stated by some sources that his father not only fought in the Revolutionary Army, but was a sufficient friend of George Washington to have the latter attend his wedding. In his early years, he was apprenticed, according to the custom of the day, to a carver and gilder, but he spent most of his evenings in the Franklin Library and at the theatre, likewise attending school in his spare time, where, among the pupils, he met John and Steven Decatur, famed afterwards in the history of the American Navy. He filled a minor position in the Auditor's office in Philadelphia, but his tastes inclined more to journalistic than they did to desk work, and, in 1800, he travelled to Harrisburg as a political reporter.

Several years after this, he went to Charleston, and studied law, but before he had had a chance to practise, he became the editor of the Charleston *City Gazette*, and, advocating those principles which resulted in the War of 1812, he used his pen, under the pseudonym of *Muley Molack*, to disseminate those ideas in editorials. The consequence is he encouraged much hatred, and was forced into many duels to support his opinions. In 1811, he was offered the position of Consul at Riga by President Madison, but declined. In 1813, he was sent by Mr. Monroe, as Consul, to Tunis, at a time when the United States was having trouble with Algerian piracy.

During all this period, his pen was actively busy, and while he was abroad he did much travelling which resulted, in 1819, in his publishing a book of travels.

In 1816, he returned to New York, and settled there as a journalist. Being a Tammanyite in politics, we find him filling the position of Sheriff, Judge and Surveyor of the Port at various periods. He was, likewise, an editor of some skill, and his name is associated with the columns of the *New York Enquirer*, the *Evening Star*, the *Commercial Advertiser*, the *Union*, and the *Times and Messenger*.

His political career may be measured in the following manner: In 1821 he became Sheriff. In 1823, he was admitted to the bar of New York, and in 1829 to the bar of the Supreme Court of the United States. This same year he was appointed Surveyor of the Port of New York.

Entering very prominently in politics, he opposed the election of Van Buren, and gave his vote to General Harrison. Governor Seward appointed him, in 1841, Judge of the Court of Sessions. The same year he was made a Supreme Court Commissioner.

It was in 1825 that, as one of the early Zionists of America, he entered into negotiations for the purchase of nearly three thousand acres of land on Grand Island, in New York State, where it was his dream to establish the City of Ararat, a haven of Judaism in this country. This venture became the basis for a story by Israel Zangwill, called "Noah's Ark." He died in New York on March 22, 1851, having lived in that city since 1813.

Any full Bibliography will give a sufficient idea of the scope of Major Noah's pen. He lived at a time when American Letters were beginning to develop, himself a friend of most of the literary figures of the day—Cooper, Irving, Fitz-Green Halleck and others. And we have an excellent impression of the manner in which the younger literary men regarded the authority of Noah in the "Reminiscences" of J. T. Trowbridge:

"Come with me," he [Mr. Noah] said, putting on his hat; and we went out together, I with my roll of manuscript, he with his stout cane. Even if I had been unaware of the fact, I should very soon have discovered that I was in company with an important personage. Everybody observed him, and it seemed as if every third or fourth man we met gave him a respectful salute. He continued his friendly talk with me in a way that relieved me of all sense of my own insignificance in the shadow of his celebrity and august proportions.

As far as his theatrical association is concerned, we can have no better source of information than a letter written by Noah to William Dunlap, and published in the latter's "History of the American Theatre." It is quoted in full:

New-York, July 11, 1832.

To William Dunlap, Esq.,
Dear Sir:

I am happy to hear that your work on the American Drama is in press, and trust that you may realize from it that harvest of fame and money to which your untiring industry and diversified labours give you an eminent claim. You desire me to furnish you a list of my dramatic productions; it will, my dear sir, constitute a sorry link in the chain of American writers—my plays have all been *ad captandum:* a kind of *amateur* performance, with no claim to the character of a settled, regular, or domiciliated writer for the green-room—a sort of volunteer supernumerary—a dramatic writer by "particular desire, and for this night only," as they say in the bills of the play; my "line," as you well know, has been in the more rugged paths of politics, a line in which there is more fact than poetry, more feeling than fiction; in which, to be sure, there are "exits and entrances"—where the "prompter's whistle" is constantly heard in the voice of the people; but which, in our popular government, almost disqualifies us for the more soft and agreeable translation to the lofty conceptions of tragedy, the pure diction of genteel comedy, or the wit, gaiety, and humour of broad farce.

I had an early hankering for the national drama, a kind of juvenile patriotism, which burst forth, for the first time, in a few sorry doggerels in the form of a prologue to a play, which a Thespian company, of which I was a member, produced in the South-Street Theatre—the old American Theatre in Philadelphia. The idea was probably suggested by the sign of the Federal Convention at the tavern opposite the theatre. You, no doubt, remember the picture and the motto: an excellent piece of painting of the kind, representing a group of venerable personages engaged in public discussions, with the following distich:

"These thirty-eight great men have signed a powerful deed,
    That better times, to us, shall very soon succeed."

The sign must have been painted soon after the adoption of the Federation Constitution, and I remember to have stood "many a time and oft," gazing, when a boy, at the assembled patriots, particularly the venerable head and spectacles of Dr. Franklin, always in conspicuous relief. In our Thespian corps, the honour of cutting the plays, substituting new passages, casting parts, and writing couplets at the exits, was divided between myself and a fellow of infinite wit and humour, by the name of Helmbold; who subsequently became the editor of a scandalous little paper, called *The Tickler:* He was a rare rascal, perpetrated all kind of calumnies, was constantly mulcted in fines, sometimes imprisoned, was full of faults, which were forgotten in his conversational qualities and dry sallies of genuine wit, particularly his Dutch stories. After years of singular vicissitudes, Helmbold joined the army as a common soldier, fought bravely during the late war, obtained a commission, and died. Our little company soon dwindled away; the expenses were too heavy for our pockets; our writings and performances were sufficiently wretched, but as the audience was admitted without cost, they were too polite to express any disapprobation. We recorded all our doings in a little weekly paper, published, I believe, by Jemmy Riddle, at the corner of Chestnut and Third-Street, opposite the tavern kept by that sturdy old democrat, Israel Israel.

From a boy, I was a regular attendant of the Chestnut-Street Theatre, during the management of Wignell and Reinagle, and made great efforts to compass the purchase of a season ticket, which I obtained generally of the treasurer, George Davis, for eighteen dollars. Our habits through life are frequently governed and directed by our early steps. I seldom missed a night; and always retired to bed, after witnessing a good play, gratified and improved: and thus, probably, escaped the haunts of taverns, and the pursuits of depraved pleasures, which too frequently allure and destroy our young men; hence I was always the firm friend of the drama, and had an undoubted right to oppose my example through life to the horror and hostility expressed by sectarians to plays and play-houses generally. Independent of several of your plays which had obtained possession of the stage, and were duly incorporated in the legitimate drama, the first call to support the productions of a fellow townsman, was, I think, Barker's opera of *The Indian Princess.* Charles Inger-soll had previously written a tragedy, a very able production for a very young man, which was supported by all the "good society;" but Barker, who was "one of us," an amiable and intelligent young fellow, who owed nothing to hereditary rank, though his father was a Whig, and a soldier of the Revolution, was in reality a fine spirited poet, a patriotic ode writer, and finally a gallant soldier of the late war. The managers gave Barker an excellent chance with all his plays, and he had merit and popularity to give them in return full houses.

About this time, I ventured to attempt a little melo-drama, under the title of "The Fortress of Sorrento" [1808], which, not having money enough to pay for printing, nor sufficient influence to have acted, I thrust the manuscript in my pocket, and, having occasion to visit New-York, I called in at David Longworth's Dramatic Repository one day, spoke of the little piece, and struck a bargain with him, by giving him the manuscript in return for a copy of every play he had published, which at once furnished me with a tolerably large dramatic collection. I believe the play never was performed, and I was almost ashamed to own it; but it was my first regular attempt at dramatic composition.

In the year 1812, while in Charleston, Mr. Young requested me to write a piece for his wife's benefit. You remember her, no doubt; remarkable as she was for her personal beauty and amiable deport-ment, it would have been very ungallant to have refused, particularly as he requested that it should be a *"breeches part,"* to use a green-room term, though she was equally attractive in every character. Poor Mrs. Young! she died last year in Philadelphia. When she first arrived in New-York, from London, it was difficult to conceive a more perfect beauty; her complexion was of dazzling whiteness, her golden hair and ruddy complexion, figure somewhat *embonpoint*, and graceful carriage, made her a great favourite. I soon produced the little piece, which was called "Paul and Alexis; or, the Orphans of the Rhine." I was, at that period, a very active politician, and my political opponents did me the honour to go to the theatre the night it was performed, for the purpose of hissing it, which was not attempted until the curtain fell, and the piece was successful. After three years' absence in Europe and Africa, I saw the same piece performed at the Park, under the title of "The Wandering Boys,"[1] which even now holds possession of the stage. It seems Mr. Young sent the manuscript to London, where the title was changed, and the bantling cut up, altered, and considerably improved.

About this time, John Miller, the American bookseller in London, paid us a visit. Among the passengers in the same ship was a fine English girl of great talent and promise, Miss Leesugg, afterwards Mrs. Hackett. She was engaged at the Park as a singer, and Phillips, who was here about the same period fulfilling a most successful engagement, was decided and unqualified in his admiration of her talent. Every one took an interest in her success: she was gay, kind-hearted, and popular, always in excellent spirits, and always perfect. Anxious for her success, I ventured to write a play for her benefit, and in three days finished the patriotic piece of "She Would be a Soldier; or, the Battle of Chippewa,"[2] which, I was happy to find, produced her an excellent house. Mrs. Hackett retired from the stage after her marriage, and lost six or seven years of profitable and unrivalled engagement.[3]

After this play, I became in a manner domiciliated in the green-room. My friends, Price and Simpson, who had always been exceedingly kind and liberal, allowed me to stray about the premises like one of the family, and, always anxious for their success, I ven-

---

[1] John Kerr wrote "The Wandering Boys; or, The Castle of Olival" (1823), which Dr. Atkinson believes was taken from the same French source as Noah's piece.

[2] She Would Be A Soldier,/or the/Plains of Chippewa;/An Historical Drama,/In Three Acts./By M. M. Noah./Performed for the first time on the 21st/of June, 1819./ New-York:/Published at Longworth's Dramatic Repository,/Shakspeare Gallery./ G. L. Birch & Co. Printers./1819./[At one time, Edwin Forrest played the Indian in this piece.]

[3] Catherine Leesugg married James H. Hackett, the American actor, in 1819. As early as 1805, some critics in England spoke of her as the Infant Roscius. Of her, the newspaper versifier proclaimed:
"There's sweet Miss Leesugg—by-the-by, she's not pretty,
She's a little too large, and has not too much grace,
Yet there's something about her so witching and witty,
'Tis pleasure to gaze on her good-humoured face."

tured upon another attempt for a holy-day occasion, and produced
"Marion; or, the Hero of Lake George." It was played on the 25th
of November, Evacuation day [1821], and I bustled about among
my military friends, to raise a party in support of a military play,
and what with generals, staff-officers, rank and file, the Park Theatre
was so crammed, that not a word of the play was heard, which was
a very fortunate affair for the author. The managers presented me
with a pair of handsome silver pitchers, which I still retain as a
memento of their good-will and friendly consideration. You must
bear in mind that while I was thus employed in occasional attempts
at play-writing, I was engaged in editing a daily journal, and in all
the fierce contests of political strife: I had, therefore, but little time
to devote to all that study and reflection so essential to the success
of dramatic composition.

My next piece, I believe, was written for the benefit of a relative
and friend, who wanted something to bring a house; and as the
struggle for liberty in Greece was at that period the prevailing excite-
ment, I finished the melodrama of the *Grecian Captive*, which was
brought out with all the advantages of good scenery and music
[June 17, 1822]. As a "good house" was of more consequence to
the actor than fame to the author, it was resolved that the hero of
the piece should make his appearance on an elephant, and the
heroine on a camel, which were procured from a neighbouring
menagerie, and the *tout ensemble* was sufficiently imposing, only it
happened that the huge elephant, in shaking his skin, so rocked the
castle on his back, that the Grecian general nearly lost his balance,
and was in imminent danger of coming down from his "high estate,"
to the infinite merriment of the audience. On this occasion, to use
another significant phrase, a "gag" was hit upon of a new character
altogether. The play was printed, and each auditor was presented
with a copy gratis, as he entered the house. Figure to yourself a
thousand people in a theatre, each with a book of the play in hand—
imagine the turning over a thousand leaves simultaneously, the buzz
and fluttering it produced, and you will readily believe that the
actors entirely forgot their parts, and even the equanimity of the
elephant and camel were essentially disturbed.

My last appearance, as a dramatic writer, was in another national
piece, called "The Siege of Tripoli," which the managers persuaded
me to bring out for my own benefit, being my first attempt to derive
any profit from dramatic efforts. The piece was elegantly got up—
the house crowded with beauty and fashion—everything went off
in the happiest manner; when, a short time after the audience had
retired, the Park Theatre was discovered to be on fire, and in a short
time was a heap of ruins. This conflagration burnt out all my
dramatic fire and energy, since which I have been, as you well know,

peaceably employed in settling the affairs of the nations, and mildly engaged in the political differences and disagreements which are so fruitful in our great state.

I still, however, retain a warm interest for the success of the drama, and all who are entitled to success engaged in sustaining it, and to none greater than to yourself, who have done more, in actual labour and successful efforts, than any man in America. That you may realize all you have promised yourself, and all that you are richly entitled to, is the sincere wish of

Dear sir,
Your friend and servant,
M. M. NOAH.

Wm. Dunlap, Esq.

SHE WOULD BE A SOLDIER,

OR THE

PLAINS OF CHIPPEWA;

AN HISTORICAL DRAMA,

IN THREE ACTS.

BY M. M. NOAH.

PERFORMED FOR THE FIRST TIME ON THE 21ST OF JUNE, 1819.

NEW-YORK :

Published at Longworth's Dramatic Repository,
Shakspeare Gallery.

G. L. Birch & Co. Printers.

1819.

FAC-SIMILE TITLE-PAGE TO 1819 EDITION

PREFACE

The following dramatic *bagatelle* was written in a few days, and its reception, under every circumstance, far exceeded its merits. I had no idea of printing it, until urged to do so by some friends connected with theatres, who, probably, were desirous of using it without incurring the expense of transcribing from the original manuscript. Writing plays is not my "vocation;" and even if the mania was to seize me, I should have to contend with powerful obstacles, and very stubborn prejudices; to be sure, these, in time, might be removed, but I have no idea of being the first to descend into the arena, and become a gladiator for the American Drama. These prejudices against native productions, however they may be deplored as impugning native genius, are nevertheless very natural. An American audience, I have no doubt, would be highly pleased with an American play, if the performance afforded as much gratification as a good English one; but they pay their money to be pleased, and if we cannot afford pleasure, we have no prescriptive right to ask for approbation. In England, writing of plays is a profession, by which much money is made if the plays succeed; hence a dramatic author goes to work, *secundum artem.*—He employs all his faculties, exhausts all his resources, devotes his whole time, capacity and ingenuity to the work in hand; the hope of reward stimulates him —the love of fame urges him on—the opposition of rivals animates his exertions—and the expectation of applause sweetens his labours—and yet, nine times out of ten, he fails. Mr. Dunlap, of this city, has written volumes of plays, and written well, "excellent well," but he made nothing; nay, he hardly obtained that civic wreath which he fairly earned. Barker, of Philadelphia, whose muse is the most delicate and enticing, has hung up his harp, which, I dare say, is covered with dust and cobwebs; and even Harby, of Charleston, whose talents are of the finest order, and who is a bold yet chaste poet, gained but little profit and applause from his labours. We must not expect, therefore, more encouragement for the American Drama than may be sufficient to urge us on. We will succeed in time, as well as the

English, because we have the same language, and equal intellect; but there must be system and discipline in writing plays—a knowledge of stage effect—of sound, cadences, fitness of time and place, interest of plot, spirit of delineation, nature, poetry, and a hundred *et ceteras*, which are required, to constitute a good dramatic poet, who cannot, in this country, and while occupied in other pursuits, spring up over night like asparagus, or be watered and put in the sun, like a geranium in a flower pot.

I wrote this play in order to promote the benefit of a performer who possesses talent, and I have no objections to write another for any deserving object. New plays, in this country, are generally performed, for the first time, as anonymous productions: I did not withhold my name from this, because I knew that my friends would go and see it performed, with the hope of being pleased, and my opponents would go with other motives, so that between the two parties a good house would be the result. This was actually the case, and two performances produced nearly $2,400; I hope this may encourage Americans of more talent to attempt something.

National plays should be encouraged. They have done everything for the British nation, and can do much for us; they keep alive the recollection of important events, by representing them in a manner at once natural and alluring. We have a fine scope, and abundant materials to work with, and a noble country to justify the attempt. The "Battle of Chippewa" was selected, because it was the most neat and spirited battle fought during the late war, and I wish I was able to do it more justice.

N.

New-York, July, 1819.

DRAMATIS PERSONÆ [1]

GENERAL,	Mr. Graham.
JASPER,	Mr. Robertson.
LENOX,	Mr. Pritchard.
HON. CAPTAIN PENDRAGON,	Mr. Simpson.
JERRY,	Mr. Barnes.
LAROLE,	Mr. Spiller.
JENKINS,	Mr. Johnson.
INDIAN CHIEF,	Mr. Maywood.
1ST OFFICER,	Mr. Bancker.
SOLDIER,	Mr. Nexsen.
WAITER,	Mr. Oliff.
JAILOR,	Mr. Baldwin.

Soldiers, Peasants, Indians, &c.

CHRISTINE,	Miss Leesugg.
ADELA,	Miss Johnson.
MAID,	Mrs. Wheatley.

Peasant Women, &c.

---

[1] In **Dr.** Atkinson's copy of this play, the following cast is given: as a note, in the handwriting of Henry Wallack:

PHILADELPHIA, 1819.

GENERAL,	Hughes.
JASPER,	
LENOX,	Darley, John, Jr.
PENDRAGON,	Wood, William.
JERRY,	Jefferson, Joseph.
LAROLE,	Blissett, Francis.
CHIEF,	Wallack, Henry.
CHRISTINE,	Darley, Mrs. John (Miss E. Westray).
ADELA,	Wood, Mrs. Wm. (Miss J. Westray).

SHE WOULD BE A SOLDIER,
or; the
PLAINS OF CHIPPEWA

ACT I.

SCENE I. *A Valley with a neat Cottage on the right, an Arbour on the left, and picturesque Mountains at a distance.*

Enter from the cottage, JASPER *and* JENKINS.

JENKINS. And so, neighbour, you are not then a native of this village?

JASPER. I am not, my friend; my story is short, and you shall hear it. It was my luck, call it bad or good, to be born in France, in the town of Castlenaudary, where my parents, good honest peasants, cultivated a small farm on the borders of the canal of Midi. I was useful, though young; we were well enough to live, and I received from the parish school a good education, was taught to love my country, my parents, and my friends; a happy temper, a common advantage in my country, made all things easy to me; I never looked for to-morrow to bring me more joy than I experienced to-day.

JENKINS. Pardon my curiosity, friend Jasper: how came you to leave your country, when neither want nor misfortune visited your humble dwelling?

JASPER. Novelty, a desire for change, an ardent disposition to visit foreign countries. Passing through the streets of Toulouse one bright morning in spring, the lively drum and fife broke on my ear, as I was counting my gains from a day's marketing. A company of soldiers neatly dressed, with white cockades, passed me with a brisk step; I followed them through instinct— the sergeant informed me that they were on their way to Bordeaux, from thence to embark for America, to aid the cause of liberty in the new world, and were commanded by the Marquis de la Fayette. That name was familiar to me; La Fayette was a patriot—I felt like a patriot, and joined the ranks immediately.

JENKINS. Well, you enlisted and left your country?

JASPER. I did. We had a boisterous passage to America, and endured many hardships during the revolution. I was wounded at Yorktown, which long disabled me, but what then? I served under great men, and for a great cause; I saw the independence of the thirteen states acknowledged, I was promoted to a sergeancy by the great Washington, and I sheathed my sword, with the honest pride of knowing, that I had aided in establishing a powerful and happy republic.

JENKINS. You did well, honest Jasper, you did well; and now you have the satisfaction of seeing your country still free and happy.

JASPER. I have, indeed. When the army was disbanded, I travelled on foot to explore the uncultivated territory which I had assisted in liberating. I purchased a piece of land near the great lakes, and with my axe levelled the mighty oaks, cleared my meadows, burnt out the wolves and bears, and then built that cottage there.

JENKINS. And thus became a settler and my neighbour; thanks to the drum and fife and the white cockade, that lured you from your home.

JASPER. In a short time, Jenkins, everything flourished; my cottage was neat, my cattle thriving, still I wanted something— it was a wife. I was tired of a solitary life, and married Kate, the miller's daughter; you knew her.

JENKINS. Ay, that I did; she was a pretty lass.

JASPER. She was a good wife—ever cheerful and industrious, and made me happy: poor Kate! I was without children for several years; at length my Christine was born, and I have endeavoured, in cultivating her mind, and advancing her happiness, to console myself for the loss of her mother.

JENKINS. Where is Christine? where is your daughter, neighbour Jasper?

JASPER. She left the cottage early this morning with Lenox, to climb the mountains and see the sun rise; it is time for them to return to breakfast.

JENKINS. Who is this Mr. Lenox?

JASPER. An honest lieutenant of infantry, with a gallant spirit and a warm heart. He was wounded at Niagara, and one stormy night, he presented himself at our cottage door, pale and haggard. His arm had been shattered by a ball, and he had received a flesh wound from a bayonet: we took him in—for an old soldier never closes his door on a wounded comrade—Christine nursed him, and he soon recovered. But I wish they were here—it is growing late: besides, this is a busy day, friend Jenkins.

JENKINS. Ah, how so?

JASPER. You know Jerry Mayflower, the wealthy farmer; he has offered to marry my Christine. Girls must not remain single if they can get husbands, and I have consented to the match, and he will be here to-day to claim her hand.

JENKINS. But will Christine marry Jerry? She has been too well educated for the honest farmer.

JASPER. Oh, she may make a few wry faces, as she does when swallowing magnesia, but the dose will go down. There is some credit due to a wife who improves the intellect of her husband; aye, and there is some pride in it also. Girls should marry. Matrimony is like an old oak; age gives durability to the trunk, skill trims the branches, and affection keeps the foliage ever green. But come, let us in. [JASPER *and* JENKINS *enter the cottage.*

Pastoral Music.—LENOX *and* CHRISTINE *are seen winding down the mountains—his left arm is in a sling.*

CHRISTINE. At last we are at home.—O my breath is nearly gone. You soldiers are so accustomed to marching and counter-marching, that you drag me over hedge and briar, like an empty baggage-wagon. Look at my arm, young Mars, you've made it as red as pink, and as rough as—then my hand—don't attempt to kiss it, you—wild man of the woods.

LENOX. Nay, dear Christine, be not offended; if I have passed rapidly over rocks and mountains, it is because you were with me. My heart ever feels light and happy when I am permitted to walk with you; even the air seems newly perfumed, and the birds chaunt more melodiously; and see, I can take my arm out of confinement—your care has done this; your voice administered comfort, and your eyes affection. What do I not owe you?

CHRISTINE. Owe me? Nothing, only one of your best bows, and your prettiest compliments. But I do suspect, my serious cavalier, that your wounds were never as bad as you would have me think. Of late you have taken your recipes with so much grace, have swallowed so many bitter tinctures with a playful smile, that I believe you've been playing the invalid, and would make me your nurse for life—O sinner as you are, what have you to say for yourself?

LENOX. Why, I confess, dear Christine, that my time has passed with so much delight, that even the call of duty will find me reluctant to quit these scenes, so dear to memory, hospitality, and, let me add, to love. Be serious, then, dear Christine, and tell me what I have to hope; even now I expect orders from my commanding officer, requiring my immediate presence at the camp; we are on the eve of a battle—Speak!

CHRISTINE. Why, you soldiers are such fickle game, that if we once entangle you in the net, 'tis ten to one but the sight of a new face will be sufficiently tempting to break the mesh—you're just as true as the smoke of your cannon, and you fly off at the sight of novelty in petticoats, like one of your Congreve rockets—No, I won't love a soldier—that's certain.

LENOX. Nay, where is our reward then for deserving well of our country? Gratitude may wreath a chaplet of laurel, but trust me, Christine, it withers unless consecrated by beauty.

CHRISTINE. Well, that's a very pretty speech, and deserves one of my best courtesies. Now suppose I should marry you, my "dear ally Croaker," I shall expect to see myself placed on the summit of a baggage-wagon, with soldiers' wives and a few dear squalling brats, whose musical tones drown e'en the "squeaking of the wry-neck'd fife;" and if I should escape from the enemy at the close of a battle, I should be compelled to be ever ready, and "pack up my tatters and follow the drum."—No, no, I can't think of it.

LENOX. Prithee, be serious, dear Christine, your gaiety alarms me. Can you permit me to leave you without a sigh? Can I depart from that dear cottage and rush to battle without having the assurance that there is a heart within which beats in unison with mine? a heart which can participate in my glory, and sympathize in my misfortunes?

CHRISTINE. No—not so, Lenox; your glory is dear to me, your happiness my anxious wish. I have seen you bear pain like a soldier, and misfortune like a man. I am myself a soldier's daughter, and believe me, when I tell you, that under the appearance of gaiety, my spirits are deeply depressed at your approaching departure. I have been taught, by a brave father, to love glory when combined with virtue. There is my hand;—be constant, and I am ever your friend; be true, and you shall find me ever faithful.

LENOX. Thanks—a thousand thanks, beloved Christine; you have removed a mountain of doubts and anxious wishes from my heart: I did hope for this reward, though it was a daring one. Love and honour must now inspire me, and should we again be triumphant in battle, I shall return to claim the reward of constancy—a reward dearer than thrones—the heart of a lovely and virtuous woman.

CHRISTINE. Enough, dear Lenox; I shall never doubt your faith. But come, let us in to breakfast—stay—my knight of the rueful countenance, where is the portrait which you have been sketching of me? Let me look at your progress.

LENOX. 'Tis here. *[Gives a small drawing book.*

CHRISTINE. [*Opening it.*] Heavens, how unlike! Why Lenox, you were dreaming of the *Venus de Medici* when you drew this— Oh, you flatterer!

LENOX. Nay, 'tis not finished; now stand there, while I sketch the drapery.—[*Places her at a distance, takes out a pencil, and works at the drawing.*]

CHRISTINE. Why, what a statue you are making of me. Pray, why not make a picture of it at once? Place me in that bower, with a lute and a lap dog, sighing for your return; then draw a soldier disguised as a pilgrim, leaning on his staff, and his cowl thrown back; let that pilgrim resemble thee, and then let the little dog bark, and I fainting, and there's a subject for the pencil and pallet.

LENOX. Sing, dear Christine, while I finish the drawing—it may be the last time I shall ever hear you.

CHRISTINE. Oh, do not say so, my gloomy cavalier; a soldier, and despair?

THE KNIGHT ERRANT.
Written by the late Queen of Holland.

It was Dunois, the young and brave, was bound to Palestine,
But first he made his orisons before St. Mary's shrine:
And grant, immortal Queen of Heav'n, was still the soldier's
   prayer,
That I may prove the bravest knight, and love the fairest fair.

His oath of honour on the snrine he grav'd it with his sword,
And follow'd to the Holy Land the banner of his Lord;
Where, faithful to his noble vow, his war-cry fill'd the air—
Be honour'd, aye, the bravest knight, beloved the fairest fair.

They ow'd the conquest to his arm, and then his liege lord said,
The heart that has for honour beat must be by bliss repaid:
My daughter Isabel and thou shall be a wedded pair,
For thou art bravest of the brave, she fairest of the fair.

And then they bound the holy knot before St. Mary's shrine,
Which makes a paradise on earth when hearts and hands combine;
And every lord and lady bright that was in chapel there,
Cry'd, Honour'd be the bravest knight, belov'd the fairest fair.

LENOX. There, 'tis finished—how do you like it?

CHRISTINE. Why, so, so—if you wish something to remind you of me, it will do.

LENOX. No, not so; your image is too forcibly impressed here to need so dull a monitor. But I ask it to reciprocate—wear this for my sake [*Gives a miniature.*], and think of him who, even in the battle's rage, will not forget thee. [*Bugle sounds at a distance.*] Hark! 'tis a bugle of our army. [*Enter a* SOLDIER, *who delivers a letter to* LENOX *and retires—*LENOX *opens and reads it.*]

"The enemy, in force, has thrown up entrenchments near Chippewa; if your wounds will permit, join your corps without delay—a battle is unavoidable, and I wish you to share the glory of a victory. You have been promoted as an aid to the general for your gallantry in the last affair. It gives me pleasure to be the first who announces this grateful reward—lose not a moment.
                              Your friend,
                                        MANDEVILLE."

I must be gone immediately.

Enter JASPER *and* JENKINS *from the cottage.*

JASPER. Ah! Lenox, my boy, good morning to you. Why Christine, you have had a long ramble with the invalid.

CHRISTINE. Lenox leaves us immediately, dear father; the army is on the march.

JASPER. Well, he goes in good time, and may success attend him. Ods my life, when I was young, the sound of the drum and fife was like the music of the spheres, and the noise and bustle of a battle was more cheering to me, than "the hunter's horn in the morning." You will not forget us, Lenox, will you?

LENOX. Forget ye? Never—I should be the most ungrateful of men, could I forget that endearing attention which poured oil into my wounds, and comforted the heart of a desponding and mutilated soldier. No, Jasper, no; while life remains, yourself and daughter shall never cease to live in my grateful remembrance. [CHRISTINE *and* LENOX *enter the cottage.*

Pastoral Music.—Peasants are seen winding down the mountains, headed by JERRY, *dressed for a festive occasion, with white favours, nosegays, &c.*

JERRY. Here I am, farmer Jasper—come to claim Miss Crissy as my wife, according to your promise, and have brought all my neighbours. How do you do?

JASPER. Well—quite well—and these are all your neighbours?

JERRY. Yes—there's Bob Short, the tanner; Nick Anvil, the blacksmith; Patty, the weaver's daughter—and the rest of 'em; come here, Patty, make a curtchey to the old soger—[PATTY *comes forward.*]—a pretty girl! I could have had her, but she wanted edication—she wanted the airs and graces, as our schoolmaster says.

JASPER. Well, farmer, you are an honest man, but I fear my Christine will not approve this match, commenced without her advice, and concluded without her consent. Then her education has been so different from—

JERRY. O, fiddle-de-dee, I don't mind how larned she is, so much the better—she can teach me to parlyvoo, and dance solos and duets, and such elegant things, when I've done ploughing.

JASPER. But I'm not sure that she will like you.

JERRY. Not like me? Come, that's a good one; only look at my movements—why she can't resist me. I'm the boy for a race, for an apple-paring or quilting frolic—fight a cock, hunt an opossum, or snare a partridge with any one.—Then I'm a squire, and a county judge, and a *brevet* ossifer in the militia besides; and a devil of a fellow at an election to boot. Not have me? damme, that's an insult. Besides, sergeant Jasper, I've been to the wars since I've seen ye—got experience, laurels and lilies, and all them there things.

JASPER. Indeed!

JERRY. Yes—sarved a campaign, and was at the battle of Queenstown. What do you think of that?

JASPER. And did you share in the glory of that spirited battle?

JERRY. O yes, I shared in all the glory—that is—I didn't fight. I'll tell you how it was: I marched at the head of my village sogers, straight as the peacock in my farm yard, and I had some of the finest lads in our county, with rifles—well, we march'd and camp'd, and camp'd and march'd, and were as merry as grigs until we arrived at the river: half the troops had cross'd and were fighting away like young devils: ods life, what a smoke! what a popping of small arms, and roaring of big ones! and what a power of red coats!

JASPER. Well, and you panted to be at them? clubb'd your rifles, and dashed over?

JERRY. Oh no, I didn't—I was afear'd that in such a crowd, nobody would see how I fought, so I didn't cross at all. Besides, some one said, it were contrary to law and the constitution, to go into the enemy's country, but if they com'd into our country, it were perfectly lawful to flog 'em.

JASPER. And you did not cross?

JERRY. Oh no, I stood still and look'd on; it were contrary to the constitution of my country, and my own constitution to boot —so I took my post out of good gun shot, and felt no more fear nor you do now.

JASPER. No doubt. Admirable sophistry, that can shield cowards and traitors, under a mistaken principle of civil government! I've heard of those scruples, which your division felt when in sight of the enemy. Was that a time to talk of constitutions— when part of our gallant army was engaged with unequal numbers? Could you calmly behold your fellow citizens falling on all sides, and not avenge their death? Could you, with arms in your hands, the enemy in view, with the roar of cannon thundering on your ear, and the flag of your country waving amidst fire and smoke—could you find a moment to think of constitutions? Was that a time to pause and suffer coward scruples to unnerve the arm of freemen?

JERRY. Bravo! bravo! sergeant Jasper; that's a very fine speech—I'll vote for you for our assemblyman; now just go that over again, that I may get it by heart for our next town meeting —blazing flags—fiery cannon—smoking constitutions—

JASPER. I pray you pardon me. I am an old soldier, and fought for the liberty which you enjoy, and, therefore, claim some privilege in expressing my opinion. But come, your friends are idle, let us have breakfast before our cottage door.—Ah, Jerry, my Crissy would make a fine soldier's wife: do you know that I have given her a military education?

JERRY. No, surely—

JASPER. Aye, she can crack a bottle at twelve paces with a pistol.

JERRY. Crack a bottle! Come, that's a good one; I can crack a bottle too, but not so far off.

JASPER. And then she can bring down a buck, at any distance.

JERRY. Bring down a buck? I don't like that—can't say as how I like my wife to meddle with bucks. Can she milk—knit garters—make apple butter and maple sugar—dance a reel after midnight, and ride behind her husband on a pony, to see the trainings of our sogers—that's the wife for my money. Oh, here she comes.

Enter CHRISTINE *and* LENOX *from the cottage.*

JASPER. Christine, here is farmer Mayflower and his friends, who have come to visit our cottage, and you in particular.

CHRISTINE. They are all welcome. Good morning, Jerry— how is it with you?

JERRY. Purely, Miss Crissy, I'm stout and hearty, and you look as pretty and as rosy as a field of pinks on a sunshiny morning.

JASPER. Come here, farmer—give me your hand—Christine, yours—[*Joins them.*]—there; may you live long and happy, and my blessings ever go with you.

CHRISTINE. [*Aside in amazement.*] Heavens! what can this mean? [LENOX *is agitated—pause—*JASPER *and group retire—* LENOX *remains at a distance.*]

JERRY. Why, Miss Crissy, your father has consented that I shall marry you, and I've come with my neighbours to have a little frolic, and carry you home with me.

CHRISTINE. And am I of so little moment as not to be consulted? Am I thus to be given away by my father without one anxious question? [*With decision.*] Farmer, pardon my frankness; on this occasion, sincerity alone is required—I do not like you, I will not marry you—nay, do not look surprised. I am a stranger to falsehood and dissimulation, and thus end at once all hopes of ever becoming my husband.

JERRY. Why, now, Miss Crissy, that's very cruel of you—I always had a sneaking kindness for you, and when your father gave his consent, I didn't dream as how you could refuse me.

CHRISTINE. My father has ever found me dutiful and obedient, but when he bestows my hand, without knowing whether my heart or inclinations accompany it, I feel myself bound to consult my own happiness. I cannot marry you, farmer.

LENOX. [*Advancing.*] All things are prepared, and I am now about to depart. Christine, farewell! Friends, good fortune await you! [*Aside.*] Dear Christine, remember me. [*Exit hastily.*

JERRY. Lack-a-daisy! What a disappointment to me, when I had put my house in such nice order—painted my walls—got a new chest upon chest—two new bed quilts, and a pair of pumps, and had the pig-sty and dairy whitewashed.—Hang me, after all, I believe, she is only a little shy. Oh, I see it now, she only wants a little coaxing—a little sparking or so—I've a great mind to kiss her. I will, too. [*Approaches* CHRISTINE, *who stands at a distance, buried in deep thought.*

CHRISTINE. Begone—dare not touch me! Heavens, am I reserved for this humiliation? Could my father be so cruel?

JERRY. Now, Crissy, don't be so shy—you know you like me—you know you said t' other day, when I were out training, that I held up my head more like a soger than anybody in the ranks; come now, let's make up; you'll always find me a dutiful husband, and if I ever flog you, then my name's not Jerry.

Enter JASPER *from the cottage, with a basket*; PEASANTS *following with fruit.*

JASPER. Come, let us have breakfast in the open air—help me to arrange the table.

JERRY. Breakfast! Oh, true, I've a powerful appetite. [*Assists.*

CHRISTINE. [*Aside.*] What is to be done? I have not a moment to lose; my father is stern and unyielding—I know his temper too well, to hope that my entreaties will prevail with him—the farmer is rich, and gold is a powerful tempter. I must be gone—follow Lenox, and in disguise, to avoid this hateful match. I'll in, whilst unobserved. [*Enters the cottage.*

JASPER. Come, sit down, farmer and neighbours; and you, my pretty lads and lasses, let's have a dance. Ah, here is a foraging party. [*Enter* SOLDIERS.

Party dance—several pastoral and fancy dances—and as the whole company retires, CHRISTINE *comes from the cottage with cautious steps—she is dressed in a frock coat, pantaloons and hat.*

CHRISTINE. They are gone—now to escape. Scenes of my infancy—of many a happy hour, farewell! Oh, farewell, forever! [*Exit.*

JASPER *and* JERRY *return.*

JERRY. She refused me plumply.

JASPER. Impossible!

JERRY. No, it's quite possible. Farmer, said she, I will *not* marry you—and hang me if there's any joke in that.

JASPER. Refuse an honest man? A wealthy one, too? And one whom her father gives to her? Trifling girl! Insensible to her happiness and interest. What objections had she to you, farmer?

JERRY. Objections! Oh, none in the world, only she wouldn't marry me; she didn't seem struck at all with my person.

JASPER. Mere coyness—maiden bashfulness.

JERRY. So I thought, sergeant Jasper, and was going to give her a little kiss, when she gave me such a look, and such a push, as quite astounded me.

JASPER. I will seek and expostulate with the stubborn girl. Ah, Jerry, times have strangely altered, when young women choose husbands for themselves, with as much ease and indifference, as a ribbon for their bonnet. [*Enters the cottage.*

JERRY. So they do—the little independent creatures as they are—but what Miss Crissy could see in me to refuse, hang me if I can tell. I'm call'd as sprightly a fellow as any in our county, and up to everything—always ready for fun, and perfectly good-natured. [*Enter* JASPER *from the cottage, agitated.*

JASPER. She is nowhere to be found—she has gone off and left her poor old father. In her room, I found these lines scrawled with a pencil: "You have driven your daughter from you, by urging a match that was hateful to her. Was her happiness not worth consulting?" What's to be done? Where has she gone? Ah, a light breaks in upon me—to the camp—to the camp!

JERRY. Oho! I smell a rat too—she's gone after Mr. Lenox, the infantry ossifer. Oh, the young jade! But come along, old soger—get your hat and cane, and we'll go arter her—I'm a magistrate, and will bring her back by a habes corpus. [*They enter the cottage.*

SCENE II. *A Wood.*

Enter CHRISTINE *in haste, looking back with fear.*

CHRISTINE. On, on, or I shall be pursued and o'ertaken—I

have lost my way. Ah, yonder is the camp—I see the flags and tents—a short time and I shall be with you, dear Lenox. [*Exit.*

Enter JASPER, JERRY *and* PEASANTS.

JERRY. We're on the right track, farmer; I know all tracks—used to 'em when I hunt 'possums.

JASPER. Cruel girl! to desert her old father, who has ever been kind and affectionate.

JERRY. Cruel girl! to desert me, who intended to be so very affectionate, if he had given me a chance.

JASPER. We cannot be far from the outposts, let us continue our search.   [*Exeunt.*

SCENE III. *A Camp. A row of tents in the rear with camp flags at equal distances; on the right wing is a neat marquee, and directly opposite to it another. Sentinels on duty at each marquee.*

Enter from the marquee, LENOX *and* ADELA.

LENOX. I never was more surprised! just when I had brush'd up my arms, and prepared to meet the enemy, who should I find in camp but you, my old hoyden scholar. Why Adela, you have grown nearly as tall as a grenadier, and as pretty—zounds, I would kiss you, if I dare.

ADELA. I am delighted to see you, dear Lenox; you are still as gay and amiable as when you taught your little Adela to conjugate verbs, and murder French; I heard of your gallantry and wounds, and imagined I should see you limping on crutches, with a green patch over one eye, and a wreath of laurel around your head, a kind of limping, one-eyed cupid; but I find you recovered from your wounds, and ready for new ones, my soldier.

LENOX. Bravo! the little skipping girl, who was once so full of mischief, has grown a tall and beautiful woman. But what brings you to camp, Adela? What have you to do with "guns and drums? heaven save the mark!"

ADELA. Why, my father wrote for me, expecting that the campaign was drawing to a close; but scarcely had I arrived here, when intelligence reached us that the enemy, in force, had occupied a position near Chippewa; it was too late to return, so I remained to see a little skirmishing.

LENOX. And are you prepared to endure the privations of a camp?

ADELA. Oh, it is delightful! it is something out of the common order of things, something new—such echoing of bugles—glistening of fire-arms, and nodding of plumes—such marchings and countermarchings—and such pretty officers too, Lenox; but then a terrible accident happened to me the other day.

LENOX. Aye, what was it?

ADELA. Why you must know, that I accompanied my father, who with his suite, and a small detachment, went out on a reconnoitering project.—Just as we *debouched* from the wood, according to the military phrase, we came suddenly and unexpectedly on a foraging party of the enemy, who began to fight and retreat at the same time.

LENOX. Well?

ADELA. My horse happening to be an old trooper, the moment the bugles sounded, and he heard the prattle of the small arms, he dashed in amongst them, and there was I screaming in a most delightful style, which, by some, must have been mistaken for a war-whoop, and to mend the matter, a very polite and accomplished Indian took aim at me with his rifle, and actually shot away the plume from my hat, which, I dare say, was as valuable a prize to him as I should have been.

LENOX. And how did you escape from your perilous situation?

ADELA. Oh, I soon recovered my fright, and reined in my old horse; my father and a few soldiers cut in before me, and covered my retreat, so that in the conclusion of this little affair, I gained a feather in my cap, though the enemy carried off the plume; and I found myself at last on the field of battle, as cool as any hero in the army.

LENOX. And so, my lively Adela, you have been fairly introduced to Mars and Bellona; how do you like them?

ADELA. Prodigiously. I find, after all, that courage is something like a cold bath; take the first plunge, and all is over. Lord, Lenox, how delightful it would have been, had I been armed and fought gallantly in that affair; my name would have been immortalized like Joan of Arc's. Congress would have voted me a medal, I should have had a public dinner at Tammany-Hall, and his honour the mayor would have made me one of his prettiest speeches, in presenting me with the freedom of the great city in a gold box.

LENOX. And so, then, you admire a military life?

ADELA. Oh, I'm in raptures with it! I am a perfect female Quixote, and would relinquish a thousand dandy beaux for one brave fellow; and, therefore, Lenox, don't be surprised, if you should see me going about from tent to tent, chaunting the old songs of

> "*Soldier, soldier, marry me,*
> *With your fife and drum.*"

CHRISTINE *suddenly appears in the background and surveys the party with astonishment.*

CHRISTINE. Heavens! what do I see? Lenox, and with a female so affectionately?

LENOX. Your spirits charm me, dear Adela, and revive those feelings for you, that time has impaired, but not destroyed. But come, let us in and see your worthy father.

[*Leads her into the tent to the left.*

CHRISTINE. Cruel, unkind, false Lenox! Are these your vows of constancy? are these your protestations of love? Scarcely are you free from our cottage, when your vows and pledges are but air. Wretched Christine! what will become of you? I have deserted my father's house to avoid a hateful match, and seek the protection of the man I love; he is false, and I am lost. What's to be done? Return home a penitent, and meet the frowns of my father, and be wedded to the man I hate? Never. Seek out Lenox, and upbraid him with his falsehood? No, pride and wounded honour will not permit me. Let him go—he is a wretch who trifles with the affections of a woman. I care not what becomes of me, despair is all that I have left. Ha! a thought strikes me with the lightning's force—the army—I will enlist—this disguise is favourable, and in the battle's rage, seek that death which quickly awaits me—'tis resolved. [CORPORAL *passes over the stage.*] Hist, corporal.

CORPORAL. Well, my lad, what would ye?

CHRISTINE. I would enlist, good corporal, and serve my country.

CORPORAL. Enlist! As a drummer or fifer, I suppose.

CHRISTINE. No; in the ranks—and though small, you will find me capable. Give me your musket. [CHRISTINE *takes the musket, shoulders, presents, and goes through a few motions.*]

CORPORAL. Well done, my little fellow; you'll do, if it's only for a fugelman; come along to our sergeant, and receive the bounty. [*Exit.*

CHRISTINE. Now, Lenox, now am I fully revenged for your cruel desertion. [*Follows.*

End of the First Act.

ACT II.

SCENE I. *York, in Upper Canada; a Tavern meanly furnished.*

Enter LaROLE, *in pursuit of the chambermaid.*

LaROLE. Come here, you littel demoiselle—you bootiful sauvage, vy you run vay from me—hay?

MAID. I wish you would let me alone, mounsure, you officers' gentlemen are very disagreeable things.

LaROLE. Disagreeable? ma foi! I am one joli garçon, one pretti batchelor; disagreeable? I vill tell you, ma belle grizette, I am maître de mode, I give de leçons for dance, to speake de English, and de Française aussi; I can fence, aha! or fight de duel, or de enemi, je suis un soldat.

MAID. Well, if you're a soldier, you have no business to be following me up and down the house like a pet lamb. Why don't you go to camp?

LaROLE. Camp? vat is de camp? Oho, le champ de bataille; I shall tell you, mademoiselle, I did fight at the bataille de Vittoria, com un diable, like littel devil. I did kill beaucoup d'Anglais. Mai my maître, le capitain, he did give me a dam tump on my head wis his rapier, and did knock me down from on top of my horse, and make a me von prisonier.

MAID. Poor fellow! And so, mounsure, you were made prisoner?

LaROLE. Oui, ven I could not run avay, begar I surrender like von brave homme, and now I am jentiman to capitain Pendragoon; I do brus his coat, poudre his hair, and pull his corset tight, and ven he was order to come to Amérique, and fight wis de Yankee Doodel, begar me come too. I arrive ici, I am here, to make a littel de love to you.

MAID. Well now, once for all, I tell you not to be following me; I don't like Frenchmen—I can't parlyvoo.

LaROLE. You no like de Frenchiman? O quell barbare! vy you ave von abominable goût, mademoiselle, von shockin taste.

I shall tell you, mademoiselle, en my contree, en France, de ladies are ver fond of me. O beaucoup, I am so charmant—so aimable, and so jentee, I have three five sweetheart, ami de cœur, mai for all dat I do love you ver mush, par example.

MAID. Let me go! [*Bell rings.*] There, your master calls you.

[*Exit.*

LAROLE. Dam de littel bell, I vill not come; mon maître he always interrupt me ven I make de love to the pretti ladi, he be jealous, begar I vill not come.   [*Exit opposite side.*

Enter CAPTAIN PENDRAGON, *dressed in the British uniform, but in the extreme of fashion—throws himself into a chair.*

PENDRAGON. Oh, curse such roads! My bones are making their way out of their sockets—such vile, abominable, detestable— Waiter!—If my friends at Castle Joram only knew the excruciating fatigues which I am undergoing in this barbarous land—Why, waiter!—or if his highness the commander-in-chief was only sensible of my great sacrifices to—Why, waiter! where the devil are you?

Enter WAITER.

WAITER. Here I be, sir.

PENDRAGON. Why didn't you come when I first called? Do you think I've got lungs like a hunter? I'm fatigued and hungry. Get me an anchovy, a toast, and a bottle of old port.

WAITER. A what, sir? an ancho—

PENDRAGON. Yes, sir, an anchovy—small ones—delicate.

WAITER. Why, sir, we don't know what these are in this country.

PENDRAGON. The devil you don't! Then pray, sir, what have you to eat in this damn'd house fit for a gentleman?

WAITER. Why, sir, not much—the army eats us out of house and home. We have some very excellent fresh bear meat, sir.

PENDRAGON. Bear meat! Why, what the devil, fellow, do you take me for a Chickasaw, or an Esquimau? Bear meat! the honourable captain Pendragon, who never ate anything more gross than a cutlet at Molly's chop-house, and who lived on pigeons' livers at Very's, in Paris, offered bear meat in North America! I'll put that down in my travels.

WAITER. Why, sir, it is considered here a great delicacy.

PENDRAGON. The devil it is! Then pray, sir, what are your ordinary fares, if bear's meat is considered a delicacy?

WAITER. Why, truly, sir, this is but a young country, and we have to live upon what we can catch. Pray, would you fancy some 'possum fat and hominy?

PENDRAGON. Oh, shocking! begone, fellow—you'll throw me into a fever with your vile bill of fare. Get me a cup of tea—mix it, hyson and souchong, with cream and muffins.

WAITER. We can't give you any of those things, sir.—However, you can have an excellent cup of sage tea, sweetened with honey.

PENDRAGON. Sage tea! Why, you rascal, do you intend to throw me into a perspiration by way of curing my hunger? or do you take me for a goose or a duck, that you intend stuffing me with sage? Begone, get out, you little deformed fellow! [*Exit* WAITER.] I shall perish in this barbarous land—bear meat, 'possum fat, and sage tea! O dear St. James! I wish I was snug in my old quarters. LaRole! [*Enter* LAROLE.] Where the devil do you hide yourself in this damn'd house? Why, I shall starve—there's nothing to eat, fit for a gentleman.

LAROLE. Oui, monsieur, dis is von damn contree, I can find nosing to eat. I did look into all de pantri, mai parbleu, I find only a ver pretti demoiselle, mai, I could not eat her.

PENDRAGON. We must be off to the camp, LaRole, my quarters there will be infinitely more agreeable. I shall get the blue devils in this cursed place.

LAROLE. Vell, sair, I have all de devils ventre bleu, das you can imagine; dere is no politesse, no respect, nosing paid to me.

PENDRAGON. My fit of the blues is coming on me; sing me a song, LaRole.

LAROLE. A chanson? Vell, sair, I shall sing to frighten avay de littel blue devil; vill you I shall sing de English or de Française?

PENDRAGON. Oh, English, by all means—curse your foreign lingo.

LAROLE. Ahem! Ahem! you shall understand.

> *Vat is dis dull town to me,*
> *Robin Hadair?*
> *Vere is all de joys on earth, dat*
> *Make dis town—*
>
> [*A bugle sounds without.*

Ha! what is dat? who de devil intrup me in my chanson?

INDIAN CHIEF. [*Speaks without.*] Have them all ready, with their rifles and tomahawks in order; [*Enters with another* INDIAN.] and you, Coosewatchie, tell our priests to take their stand on yonder hill, and as my warriors pass them, examine whether they have fire in their eyes. [*Exit* INDIAN.] How now, who have we here?

PENDRAGON. [*Examining him with his glass.*] Where the devil did this character come from? he's one of the fancy, I suppose.

INDIAN. Who and what are you?

PENDRAGON. Who am I? Why, sir, I am the honourable captain Pendragon, of his majesty's guards, formerly of the buffs.

INDIAN. [*Aside.*] The officer who is to be under my command. Well sir, you have lately arrived from across the great waters: How did you leave my father, the King of England?

PENDRAGON. How! call my most gracious sovereign your father? Why, sir, you are the most familiar—impertinent— 'sdeath! I shall choke—What the devil do you mean?

INDIAN. [*Coolly.*] What should I mean, young man, but to inquire after the health of my father, who commands my respect, who has honoured me with his favours, and in whose cause I am now fighting.

PENDRAGON. Well, sir, if you have the honour to hold a commission from his majesty, I desire that you will speak of him with proper awe, and not call him your father, but your gracious master.

INDIAN. Young man, the Indian warrior knows no master but the Great Spirit, whose voice is heard in thunder, and whose eye is seen in the lightning's flash; free as air, we bow the knee to no man; our forests are our home, our defence is our arms, our sustenance the deer and the elk, which we run down. White men encroach upon our borders, and drive us into war; we raise the tomahawk against your enemies, because your king has promised us protection and supplies. We fight for freedom, and in that cause, the great king and the poor Indian start upon equal terms.

PENDRAGON. A very clever spoken fellow, pon honour; I'll patronise him.

LaROLE. Parbleu, he is von very sensible sauvage; vill you take von pinch snuff?

INDIAN. Pshaw!

LaROLE. He say pshaw, I see he is born in de voods.

PENDRAGON. And are you prepared to fan these Yankees? We shall flog them without much fatigue, I understand.

INDIAN. Not so fast, young soldier; these pale-faced enemies of ours fight with obstinacy; accustomed to a hardy life, to liberty and laws, they are not willing to relinquish those blessings on easy terms; if we conquer them, it must be by no moderate exertions: it will demand force and cunning.

PENDRAGON. Oh, dry dogs, I suppose, not to be caught napping; well, I'm up to them, we'll fan them in high style; the ragged nabobs, I understand, are not far off, and our troops are in fine preservation.

INDIAN. True, preparation must be made to meet them. You are under my orders.

PENDRAGON. The devil I am!

INDIAN. Aye, sir; your general, at my request, has ordered you here to take command of a company of my warriors; but you must not appear in that dress: change it quickly, or they will not be commanded by you; they are men, and fight under the orders of men.

PENDRAGON. Change my dress! why what the devil do you mean, sir?

INDIAN. Mean? that you should appear in the ranks like a warrior, and not like a rabbit trussed for dressing—off with these garments, which give neither pleasure to the eye nor ease to the limbs—put on moccasins, wrap a blanket around you, put rings through your nose and ears, feathers in your head, and paint yourself like a soldier, with vermilion.

PENDRAGON. Why, this is the most impertinent and presuming savage in the wilds of North America. Harkee, sir, I'd have you to know, that I am a man of fashion, and one of the fancy—formerly of the buffs, nephew of a peer of the realm, and will be a member of parliament, in time; an officer of great merit and great services, Mr.—Red Jacket. Paint my face, and fight without clothes? I desire, sir, that you will please to take notice, that I fought at Badahoz with the immortal Wellington, and had the honour to be wounded, and promoted, and had a medal for my services in that affair, Mr.—Split-log. Put rings in my nose? a man of taste, and the *ne plus ultra* of Bond-street, the very mirror of fashion and elegance? Sir, I beg you to observe, that I am not to be treated in this manner—I shall resent this insult. Damme, I shall report you to the commander-in-chief at the

Horse Guards, and have you courtmartialled for unfashionable deportment—Mr.—Walk-in-the-Water.

INDIAN. Come, come, sir, enough of this trifling; I do not understand it; you have heard my orders—obey them, or, after the battle, I'll roast you before a slow fire!   [*Exit.*

LaROLE. O le barbare! O de dam sauvage! dis is de most impertinent dog in de vorld. Roast before de fire! Parbleu, mon maître, ve are not de littel pig.

PENDRAGON. I'm horrified! lost in amazement! but I'll resent it. Damme, I'll caricature him.

LaROLE. Oh, I vish I vas fight encore at Saragossa, vis mi lor Villainton; par example, I did get some hard tumps, mai I did get plenti to eat; but ici I ave nosing but de little bear to mange.

PENDRAGON. Come along—courage, LaRole. We'll fan the Yankee Doodles in our best style, and then get a furlough, and be off to White-Hall, and the rings in our noses will afford anecdotes for the bon-ton for a whole year. Allons.   [*Exeunt.*

SCENE II. *The American Camp at daybreak. The drum and fife plays the reveille. Sentinels on duty before the tents.*

LENOX *enters from the tent on the right,* GENERAL *and* ADELA *from the left.*

LENOX. Good morning, general; you are "stirring with the lark"—and you also, Adela.

GENERAL. The times require the utmost vigilance, Lenox; the enemy cannot escape a battle now, and we must be prepared at all points to meet him. Decision and energy cannot fail to promote success.

ADELA. And what is to become of me, father, in the battle? Am I to ride the old trooper again, and run the risk of having the tip of my nose carried away by a musket ball, and left on the field of battle in all my glory?

GENERAL. You shall be taken care of, dear Adela; we will place you in the rear, among the baggage-wagons.

ADELA. And if they should be captured, I become also a prisoner, and probably a prize to some gallant Indian chief, who will make me his squaw, and teach me to kill deer. O delightful thought!   [*Bugles sound.*

GENERAL. The troops are under arms, and approaching.

[*Quick march—the* GENERAL, LENOX *and* ADELA *pass to the left,
and stand near the tent; the troops advance;* CHRISTINE
*is among them, dressed in uniform; they pass round the
stage in regular order, then form the line two deep;* CHRIS-
TINE *is in front on the right, and keeps her eye fixed anxiously
on* LENOX; *drum beats the roll; the troops come to an order,
and then proceed through the manual by the tap of drum, and
finally to a present; the* GENERAL, LENOX, *and other officers
advance, and pass through the line in review; the flags wave,
and the band strikes up "Hail Columbia."*]

GENERAL. Well—everything is right.   And now, soldiers, to
your posts;   remember, discipline, subordination, courage, and
country, and victory will be ours.   [GENERAL, LENOX *and* ADELA,
enter the tent to the left.   The troops march off. CHRISTINE
and a SOLDIER, *headed by a* CORPORAL, *return to relieve
guard at each tent.   Port arms and whisper the countersign.*
CHRISTINE *is placed before the tent on the right, her comrade
on the left.* CORPORAL *retires with the two relieved sentries.
After a pause, she beckons to her comrade.*]
CHRISTINE. Hist—comrade!
SOLDIER. Well, what is it?
CHRISTINE. Will you exchange places?   There is no difference
—and the sun will be too powerful for me presently.   Look, here
is a dollar.
SOLDIER. With all my heart.   [*They cross quickly, the* SOLDIER
*receives the money—*CHRISTINE *now paces before the tent
into which* LENOX, ADELA *and the* GENERAL *have retired.*]
CHRISTINE. Could I but see the false, perfidious LENOX, and
upbraid him with his cruelty!   [*She is in great uneasiness, pauses
occasionally, and looks into the tent—her comrade is watching her.*
LENOX *sings within.*]

Shall the pleasures of life unknown fade away,
In viewing those charms so lovely and gay?
Shall the heart which has breath'd forth rapturous flame,
Be hid from the world and unsought for by fame?

Thus spoke the fond Roscoe to Scylla the fair,
As he gaz'd on her charms, with a love-soothing care:
Hear now the last wish, that fondly I sigh,
I'll conquer in love, or in battle I'll die.

He girded his armour and flew to the field,
Determin'd while life flow'd never to yield;
The foe was subdued, but death's cruel dart
Was aim'd at the valiant and fond Roscoe's heart:

But the blow was defeated—he lived to enjoy
The sight of his Scylla, no longer so coy,
And his laurels fresh bloom'd, as she smil'd on the youth,
And gave her fair hand in reward for his truth.

CHRISTINE. Ha, that false voice! I can no longer bear it!
[*Throws down her gun, and is about entering the tent, when her comrade, who has been attentively regarding her movements, rushes over and seizes her.*]
SOLDIER. Where are you going?
CHRISTINE. Unhand me this instant!　　　[*Struggles.*
SOLDIER. Guards, there!

Enter an OFFICER *with* SOLDIERS, *who attempts to seize* CHRISTINE *—she draws her sword and stands on the defensive, and after some resistance, escapes.*

OFFICER. Pursue him quickly!　　　[SOLDIERS *pursue.*
SOLDIER. He crosses the bridge.
OFFICER. The sentinels will reach him with their guns.
　　　　　　　　　　　　　　　　[*Muskets discharged.*
SOLDIER. They have him—he is not hurt.

GENERAL, ADELA *and* LENOX *rush from the tent.*

GENERAL. What means this confusion?
2ND OFFICER. The sentinel who was placed here on duty, attempted, for some desperate purpose, to enter your tent; but being discovered, he refused to surrender, drew his sword on me and the guard, and, after some resistance, has been disarmed and secured.
LENOX. Good heavens! What object could he have had?
2ND OFFICER. I know not—but he is a new recruit, probably a spy from the enemy.
GENERAL. It must be so—see that a court martial be called to try him, and bring the result to me without delay. If he is guilty, a dreadful example shall be made of him. Begone.
　　　　　　　　　　　　　[*Exeunt* GENERAL, SOLDIERS, &c.

SCENE III. *Another Part of the Camp.*

ENTER JASPER, JERRY *and* PEASANTS.

JASPER. Nowhere to be found. I have asked everybody in the camp in vain—she is lost to me. Unhappy, cruel girl! to quit her old and fond father thus.

JERRY. Unhappy girl! to leave me in such an ungenteel manner too, run away from me on my wedding day! but I'll find her out.

JASPER. Impossible! we must return, dejected and disappointed.

JERRY. I'll peep into every tent, bribe the sogers—I've got a little money left. [JASPER *and* PEASANTS *retire.* CORPORAL *crosses the stage.*] Hist, corporal!

CORPORAL. Well, what would you?

JERRY. Why no, sure—it isn't—yes, it is—why Corporal Flash, how do you do? Don't you know me?

CORPORAL. Can't say I do, sir.

JERRY. Why, not know Jerry Mayflower? Don't you remember me at the battle of Queenstown, when you were in the boat and I on land, and you were crossing to fight Johnny Bull, and I didn't cross at all?

CORPORAL. Oh, I remember you now—I remember calling you a cowardly rascal at the time.

JERRY. So you did—how have you been? I am very glad to see you—you're not killed, I take it?

CORPORAL. No, not exactly killed—but I was wounded—an honour which you didn't seem to care much about.

JERRY. No, not much; I'm not very ambitious that way.

CORPORAL. What brings you to the camp, just when we are about having another brush with the enemy—do you want to run away again? Zounds! you deserve a round hundred at the halberts.

JERRY. Yes, I deserve many things that I don't get—but pray, corporal, mout you have seen a young woman in this here camp lately?

CORPORAL. Oh, plenty, among the suttlers.

JERRY. No, a kind of a pretty girl, a little lady-like, parlyvoos, and carries her head up straight.

CORPORAL. No—I've seen no such person.

JERRY. Well, Corporal Flash, I've a little cash, and what say you to a jug of whiskey punch? Brave men, you know, like you and I, should drink with one another.

CORPORAL. With all my heart; you're good for nothing else but to drink with.

JERRY. Then come along, my boy; we'll drown care, raise our spirits, and swallow the enemy in a bumper.   [*Exeunt.*

SCENE IV. *A Prison.*

Enter two OFFICERS, GUARDS *and* CHRISTINE. OFFICERS *seat themselves at a table, with pens and ink.*

1ST OFFICER. Young man, come forward. You have been charged with an act of mutiny, and with an attempt, for some unknown cause, to force your way, with arms in your hand, into the tent of the commanding general. We are convened for your trial—we have examined the testimony; and as you are a stranger in our ranks, no feelings of prejudice could have given a false colouring to that testimony. What have you to say?

CHRISTINE. Nothing.

OFFICER. Nothing?

CHRISTINE. Nothing! [*With firmness.*] I am guilty!

OFFICER. Have a care, pause before you make this avowal of your guilt.

CHRISTINE. [*With settled firmness.*] I have considered it well, and am ready to meet the consequences. I am guilty. [*With a burst of anguish.*] Oh, most guilty!

OFFICER. Unhappy young man, what could have tempted you to this act? Who set you on?

CHRISTINE. Seek not to know the cause, 'tis buried here. Do your duty—I am prepared for the result.

OFFICER. [*To the Board.*] The charge is fully admitted, and the rules of war prescribe the punishment. The object he had in view must yet be discovered; 'tis plain, however, that he is a spy, and has no hope of pardon. Record the verdict and sentence, for the inspection and concurrence of the general. [OFFICER *writes. The company rise from the table, and one approaches* CHRISTINE, *who appears buried in thought.*]

OFFICER. Young man, I deeply commiserate your unhappy situation, but the rules of war are rigid, and must be enforced. You must prepare to die!

CHRISTINE. [*Starts, but recovers herself quickly.*] I am ready.

OFFICER. I would offer you hope, but acts of mutiny, and when covering such suspicious motives as yours, cannot be pardoned. You have but a day to live. I deeply regret it, for you appear to have qualities which, in time, would have made you a valuable citizen. You are cut off in youth, probably from the hopes of a fond parent.

CHRISTINE. [*In agony.*] Oh, no more—no more!

OFFICER. All the sympathy and indulgence which can be offered you shall be yours! Farewell.

[*Exit* OFFICERS, GUARDS, &c.

CHRISTINE. At length 'tis concluded, and an ignominious death terminates my unmerited sufferings. Cruel father! and still more cruel Lenox! thus to have wounded the heart that loved you. Oh, what a situation is mine! separated from all I hold dear, sentenced to die, and in this disguise; to leave my poor father, and to know that death, alone, can tell my sad story. What's to be done? Discover all? No, no. Expose my weakness and folly—to see the false Lenox wedded to another, and I forced to accept the hand I loathe—to be pointed at for one who, lost to the delicacy of her sex, followed a perfidious lover in disguise, and, tortured by jealousy, enlisted, was mutinous, and sentenced to die; but who, to save a miserable life, avowed her situation, and recorded her disgrace at once? Never, never! let me die, and forever be forgotten—'tis but a blow, and it will end the pangs which torment me here. [*Enter a* SOLDIER, *who beckons.*] I am ready, lead the way. [*Exit.*

SCENE V. *Another part of the Prison.*

Enter the JAILOR, *driving* JERRY *before him.*

JAILOR. In, in, you mutinous dog! do you come here to breed a riot in our camp?

JERRY. Now, my dear good-natured jailor, only have pity on me, and I'll tell you all about it.

JAILOR. I won't hear you—didn't you breed a riot?

JERRY. Why no, it was not me. I am as innocent as a young lamb. I'll tell you how it was—come, sit down on this bench with me. [*They sit.*] You must know that I'm a farmer, pretty well off, as a body mout say, and I wanted a wife; hard by our village, there lived an old soger with a pretty daughter, so I courted the old man for his daughter, and he consented to the match.

JAILOR. Well?

JERRY. And so I got together all my neighbours, and, with music, went to the old soger's to get my sweetheart, when, lo and behold! after all my trouble, she refused me plump.

JAILOR. No, did she?

JERRY. Ay, indeed; she didn't seem stricken with the proposal—and for fear her father would force her to marry me, egad, she run away.

JAILOR. And where did she go?

JERRY. I can't say, but her father and a whole *posse comitatus*, as we justices call 'em, went in search of her to the camp, and when I came here, I found some of my old comrades who fought with me at Queenstown; and so having a little money, we went to take a comfortable pitcher of whiskey punch together, and so, while over our cups, they doubted my valour, and hinted that I run away before the battle.

JAILOR. Well, and what did you do?

JERRY. Why, I offered to fight 'em single-handed all round, and we got into a dispute, and so when my money was all gone, they tweaked my nose, boxed my ears, and kick'd me out of the tent. So I then kick'd up a row, and—that's all.

JAILOR. A very pretty story, indeed! You look like a mutinous dog—so come, get into the black hole.

JERRY. Now, my dear jailor, do let me escape, and I'll give you the prettiest little pig in my farmyard.

JAILOR. What! bribe an honest and humane jailor, and with a pig? In with you.

JERRY. Well, but I've nothing to eat—I shall be half starved.

JAILOR. Oh no, you shall have something to employ your grinders on. [*Goes out, and returns with a black loaf, and a pitcher of water.*] There!

JERRY. O dear, nothing else but black bread and cold water? Can't you get me a pickle?

JAILOR. I think you're in a devil of a pickle already—come, get in! [*Removes a board from the scene, which discovers a small dark hole.* JERRY *supplicates.*]

JERRY. How long am I to be here, Mr. Jailor, in company with myself?

JAILOR. That depends on your good behaviour. [*Cannon are heard.*] There! the battle has commenced.

JERRY. [*Putting his head out of the hole.*] O dear, what's that? The great guns are going off. Are you sure, my dear jailor, that this prison is bomb proof?

JAILOR. Take your head in, you great land turtle.

JERRY. Oh, what will become of me?

End of the Second Act.

ACT III.

Scene in front of a pavilion tent; trumpets and drums sounding.

Enter GENERAL, LENOX, SOLDIERS, OFFICERS, &c.

GENERAL. At length victory has crown'd our arms, and the result of this action will keep alive the spirits of our troops, and the hopes of our country. Hark! the bugles are sounding a retreat, and the enemy has abandoned the field and taken to his entrenchments. Lenox, your hand—your conduct this day has confirmed our hopes—allow me in the name of our country to thank you.

LENOX. Not a word, dear general, not a word; I have merely done my duty, and done no more than every soldier in our ranks.

GENERAL. What is the result of this day's action?

LENOX. The enemy has lost upwards of 500 in killed and wounded, and several principal officers have been taken prisoners.

GENERAL. In what position were they when the attack became general?

LENOX. The British commander, pressed by our artillery under Towson, issued in all his force from his entrenchments. It was a gallant sight, to see his solid columns and burnished arms advance on the margin of the river, and his cavalry, with lightning's force, dart on our flanks to turn and throw them into confusion: but they were met by the volunteers under the brave Porter, and gallantly repulsed.

GENERAL. Go on.

LENOX. The enemy then condensed his forces and crossed the bridge, and was encountered on the plains of Chippewa by Scott, with his brigade, when the action became severe and general. No ambuscade or masked batteries were held in reserve—the enemy was not a moment concealed from our view—no tangled thicket or umbrageous groves gave effect or facility to our rifles:

the battle was fought on a plain—where man grappled man, force was opposed to force, skill to skill, and eye to eye, in regular, disciplined, and admirable order.

GENERAL. How near were you to the British general?

LENOX. In sight and hearing. Charge the Yankees! said a hoarse voice which I knew to be his. Charge away! said our ardent troops, as they advanced with fixed bayonets; the fire became dreadful, and our stars and stripes were seen waving in the blaze. Scott rode through the lines cheering the men, and gallantly leading them on; Jessup and his third battalion turned the right flank of the enemy after a dreadful conflict; Ketchum had kept up a cross and ruinous fire; and Towson, from his dread artillery, scattered grape like hail amongst them. On, on! cried Leavenworth, the day's our own, my boys! Just then a shot struck down my comrade, Harrison, and shattered his leg.

GENERAL. Well?

LENOX. He grasped his sword and fought on his stump, clinging to the spot like fire-eyed Mars; the enemy, pressed on all sides, gave way; our troops pursued, and the flight became general. At length we drove them to their entrenchments, and remained masters of the field. Our trumpets sounded their retreat; victory perched on our eagles, and our bands struck up the soul-inspiring air of "Hail, Columbia, happy land!"

GENERAL. Well done, my brave fellows! This action will teach the enemy to respect that valour which they cannot subdue. See that the wounded prisoners are taken care of: give them all succor: victory loses half its value, when it is not tempered with mercy. [Exit GENERAL.

LENOX. Now to my dear Christine, to receive from her the reward which I hope I have fairly earned, and seek with her the joys of tranquillity and love.

Enter a SOLDIER.

SOLDIER. Towards the conclusion of the battle we made two Indian warriors prisoners, who were fighting desperately; we have them with us.

LENOX. Bring them in; I will examine them, touching the number and force of their tribe. [Exit SOLDIER, *who returns with* PENDRAGON *and* LAROLE, *with a file of men; both are painted and dressed as Indians;* PENDRAGON *preserves his opera-glass, and* LAROLE *his snuff-box.*]

PENDRAGON. What are we brought here for, fellow?

LENOX. Warriors, the fate of battle has placed you in our power; yet fear nothing, we shall treat you like men and soldiers. Deeply do we regret to see you take up arms against us, instigated by foreign influence, and bribed by foreign gold. How numerous is your tribe?

PENDRAGON. Why what the devil, sir, do you take us for Choctaws? Can't you tell a man of fashion in masquerade?

LENOX. Who and what are you?

PENDRAGON. I am the honourable Captain Pendragon, of his Majesty's Coldstream guards.

LENOX. The *honourable* Captain Pendragon, and taken prisoner fighting in the ranks with Indians, and in disguise? A man of rank and fashion, and a soldier, changing his complexion, his nature and his character—herding with savages—infuriating their horrid passions, and whetting their knives and tomahawks against their defenceless prisoners? Impossible! And who are you, sir? [*To* LAROLE.

LAROLE. [*Taking snuff.*] Begar, sair, I am von man of fashion aussi, I am valet de sham to capitain Pendragoon; ve are in de masquerade, sair.

PENDRAGON. It's very true, sir, 'pon honour—we are in masquerade, though you look as if you doubt it. War, sir, is a kind of a—a singular science, and if you are to be knock'd on the head, 'tis of very little consequence whether your nose is tipped with blue or red, damme. I am in your power, sir, and a man of fashion, 'pon honour.

LENOX. Well, sir, if your example is to govern men of honour or men of fashion, I hope I am ignorant of the attributes of the one, or the eccentricities of the other. However, mercy to prisoners, even when they have forfeited mercy, may teach your nation lessons of toleration and humanity. Your life is safe, sir.

PENDRAGON. Sir, you speak very like a gentleman, and I shall be happy to taste Burgundy with you at the Horse Guards.

LENOX. I thank you, sir.

LAROLE. Par example, dis Yankee Doodel is von very pretti spoken jeune gentiman, I will give him de encouragement. Sair, I vill be ver happy to serve you en my contree, to take un tasse de caffee at de Palais Royale en Paris wid you, to dress your hair, or pull your corset tight.

Enter GENERAL, ADELA *and* OFFICER.

GENERAL. Who have we here?

LENOX. Prisoners, sir, and in disguise.

ADELA. As I live, an Indian dandy!

PENDRAGON. A lady? [*With an air of fashion.*] Ma'am, your most devoted slave—inexpressibly happy to find a beautiful creature in this damn'd wilderness. You see, ma'am, I am a kind of a prisoner, but always at home, always at my ease, *à-la-mode* St. James—extremely rejoiced to have the honour of your acquaintance. A fine girl, LaRole, split me!

LaROLE. Oh, oui, she is very fine, I like her ver mush.

ADELA. Pray, sir, may I ask how came you to fancy that disguise?

PENDRAGON. Oh, it's not my fancy, 'pon honour, though I am one of the fancy; a mere *russe de guerre*. We on the other side of the water, have a kind of floating idea that you North Americans are half savages, and we must fight you after your own fashion.

ADELA. And have you discovered that any difference exists in the last affair in which you have been engaged?

PENDRAGON. Why, 'pon my soul, ma'am, this Yankee kind of warfare is inexpressibly inelegant, without flattery—no order— no military arrangement—no *deploying* in solid columns—but a kind of helter-skelter warfare, like a reel or a country-dance at a village inn, while the house is on fire.

ADELA. Indeed?

PENDRAGON. All true, I assure you. Why, do you know, ma'am, that one of your common soldiers was amusing himself with shooting at me for several minutes, although he saw from my air, and my dodging, that I was a man of fashion? Monstrous assurance! wasn't it?

ADELA. Why ay, it was rather impertinent for a common soldier to attempt to bring down a man of fashion.

LaROLE. Oui—it is dam impertinent, mai par example, de littel bullet of von common soldat, he sometime kill von great general.

PENDRAGON. Pray, ma'am, will you permit me to ask, when you arrived from England, and what family has the honour to boast of so beautiful a representative?

ADELA. Sir, I am not of England, I stand on my native soil.

PENDRAGON. Oh.

ADELA. And much as I esteem English women for their many amiable qualities, I hope that worth and virtue are not wholly centered in that country.

PENDRAGON. Why, 'pon my soul, ma'am, though it is not fashionable this year to be prejudiced, yet were I to admit that I saw any beauty or elegance in America, my Bond-Street friends would cut me—split me!

ADELA. I cannot admire their candour. Merit is the exclusive property of no country, and to form a just estimate of our own advantages, we should be ever prepared to admit the advantages possessed by others.

Enter a SOLDIER.

SOLDIER. We have surprised and made captive the celebrated Indian chief, who fought so desperately against us.

GENERAL. Bring him before us. [*Exit* SOLDIER.] He has long been the terror of the neighbourhood, and the crafty foe of our country.

Enter SOLDIERS *with the* INDIAN CHIEF.

INDIAN. Who among you is the chief of these pale-faced enemies of our race?

GENERAL. I am he.

INDIAN. 'Tis well, sir; behold in me your captive, who has fallen into your power after a resistance becoming a warrior. I am ready to meet that death which I know awaits me.

GENERAL. Chief, your fears are groundless; we intend you no harm, but by our example, teach you the blessings of valour and mercy united.

INDIAN. Wherefore show me mercy? I ask it not of you.— Think you that I cannot bear the flames? that a warrior shrinks from the uplifted tomahawk? Try me—try how a great soul can smile on death. Or do you hope that I will meanly beg a life, which fate and evil fortune has thrown into your hands?

GENERAL. We ask no concessions of you, warrior; we wish to see you sensible of the delusions into which foreign nations have plunged you. We wish to see you our friend.

INDIAN. Your friend? Call back the times which we passed in liberty and happiness, when in the tranquil enjoyment of unrestrained freedom we roved through our forests, and only knew the bears as our enemy; call back our council fires, our fathers and pious priests; call back our brothers, wives and children, which cruel white men have destroyed.—Your friend? You came with the silver smile of peace, and we received you into our cabins; we hunted for you, toiled for you; our wives and daughters cherished and protected you; but when your numbers increased, you rose like wolves upon us, fired our dwellings, drove off our cattle, sent us in tribes to the wilderness, to seek for shelter; and now you ask me, while naked and a prisoner, to be your friend!

GENERAL. We have not done this, deluded man; your pretended advocates, over the great waters, have told you this tale.

INDIAN. Alas! it is a true one; I feel it here; 'tis no fiction: I was the chief of a great and daring tribe, which smiled on death with indifference and contempt; my cabin was the seat of hospitality and of love; I was first in council, and first in the field; my prosperity increased, my prospects brightened; but the white man came, and all was blasted.

GENERAL. What has been done, was the result of war.

INDIAN. Wherefore wage war against us? Was not your territory sufficiently ample, but did you sigh for our possessions? Were you not satisfied with taking our land from us, but would you hunt the lords of the soil into the den of the otter? Why drive to desperation a free and liberal people? Think you I would be your enemy unless urged by powerful wrongs? No, white man, no! the Great Spirit whom we worship, is also the God whom you adore; for friends we cheerfully lay down our lives; but against foes, our lives are staked with desperation. Had I taken you prisoner, death should have been your portion; death in cruel torments. Then why spare me? why spare the man whose knife was whetted against your life?

GENERAL. To show, by contrast, the difference of our principles. You would strike down the captive who implores your protection: we tender life and liberty to the prisoner, who asks himself for death.

INDIAN. Is this your vengeance?

GENERAL. It is. The Great Spirit delights in mercy. Be thou our friend, warrior; bury thy tomahawk deep in earth; let not jealous foreigners excite thy vengeance against us; but living as we do in one territory, let us smoke the calumet of peace, you and all your tribe, and let concord hereafter reign amongst us.—Be this the token. [*Gives a belt of wampum.*

INDIAN. Brother, I accept the token; forgive my rage, and pardon my unjust anger. Protect our warriors and wives; guard their wigwams from destruction; soften their prejudices and remove their jealousies. Do this, and the red man is your friend. I have urged you far to end my life: you have tempered your passions with mercy, and we are no longer foes. Farewell! [*Exit.*

LaROLE. Parbleu, dis general is like von great Roman. I vill speak von vord pour myself, I vill make de speech like de sauvage.

GENERAL. [*To* LA ROLE.] And you, sir, it appears, are in disguise, unlike a civilized soldier; you have been taken in the ranks with Indians.

LaROLE. Sair, mon general, you sall here vat I am goin to say. I am von Frenchiman; in my contree every Frenchiman he is von soldat.

GENERAL. Well?

LaROLE. Begar, sair, I must fight vid somebody, because it is my bisness. In de Egypt I did fight 'gainst de Turc; in Europe I did fight de whole vorld vis de Grand Napoleon, and in Amérique I did fight against you vid myself. Mais, you take a me de prisonier, I can fight no more; I vill trow myself on de protection of dis contree; I vill no more fight contree de Yankee Doodel; I vill stay here and eat de ros beef vid you, and mon capitan là, he may go to de devil.

GENERAL. Admirably concluded. And you, sir, what can we do to lighten your captivity?

PENDRAGON. Why sir, if war was not my profession, I'd sell out; but it's always my maxim to obey orders, whatever they may be: therefore, shall be happy to have a brush with you in war, and equally happy to crack a bottle of Burgundy with you in peace; a flash in the pan in one way, or a puff from a segar in another; a bullet under the ribs in battle, or a country dance in a ball-room; all's one to me, if it's only fashionably conducted.

GENERAL. Well, let's into my tent and partake of some refreshment. We may not always meet as enemies.

PENDRAGON. [*To* ADELA.] Allow me the felicity of your little finger. [*Aside.*] She's struck with my figure, split me! LaRole, take notice.

LaROLE. Oh, you are de littel devil among de ladies. [*Exeunt.*

SCENE II. *A Prison.*

CHRISTINE *seated on a bench; her appearance betrays grief and
despair.*

CHRISTINE. At length the weary night has passed away, and
day dawns, but brings no joy or comfort to my aching heart.
Alas! alas! Christine, where are all the bright visions thy fond
fancy painted? where is that content and love which gleamed
through the casement of our cottage, when my dear father smiled
on his child, and entwined around her his protecting arms: when
the false Lenox, too, with honeyed lips, and tones soft as zephyrs,
vow'd eternal love? Let me not think of them, or I shall go mad.
Oh, what a contrast! pent up in a vile prison, and in disguise!
condemned to die, and perishing unknown and unprotected.
On the one side, my grave yawns for me; and on the other, a
false lover, and a cruel father, drive me to despair. My brain is
on fire! [*Hurries about with rapid strides. Music loud and violent.*]
Ha! what is this? [*Tears the miniature from around her neck.*]
Lenox, these are thy features! thy mild looks beam hope and joy
upon me. [*Kisses it.*] Could such a face be false? Away with
it! even now he weds another. [*Throws the miniature indignantly
from her.*] So, 'tis gone, and I am left alone in darkness and
despair. [*She stands transfixed with grief—muffled drum rolls—
she starts.*] Ha! they come for me! Be firm, my heart!

Enter an OFFICER *and a file of* SOLDIERS.

OFFICER. Young man, your hour has arrived; the detachment
waits without to receive you.
CHRISTINE. [*Faintly.*] I am ready.
OFFICER. Can I serve you in any manner? Is there no letter—
no remembrance that you would wish sent to father or friend?
CHRISTINE. Oh, forbear!
SOLDIER. [*Picking up the miniature.*] See, sir, here is a minia-
ture.
OFFICER. [*Examining it.*] By Heavens, they are the features
of Captain Lenox! How came you by this? What! a thief too?
'Tis well your career is cut short.
CHRISTINE. Oh no, no! Give it me, I implore you; 'tis mine.
OFFICER. I shall restore it to the rightful owner. Come, we wait.
CHRISTINE. Lead on. A few fleeting moments, and all my
troubles will be at an end.   [*Exeunt.*

SCENE III. *Before the Tent.*

Enter GENERAL, SOLDIERS, &c., *with papers.*

GENERAL. He has not confessed who set him on?

OFFICER. He has not, but admits the crime.

GENERAL. [*Returning papers.*] 'Tis well—see him executed according to the sentence. Hard and imperious duty, which, at once, shuts out hope and mercy! [*Exit* GENERAL.

OFFICER. Now to seek for Lenox, and restore to him his miniature. [*Exit.*

SCENE IV. *The Camp, as in Act I, Scene III; the stage is thrown open, drums roll, and the procession enters for the execution of* CHRISTINE; *she is in the centre, between the two detachments; her coat is off, and the stock unloosened from her neck—her step is firm, until she reaches the tent of* LENOX, *when she clasps her hands and hangs down her head in despair. Procession makes the circuit of the stage with slow steps, and when opposite the tent she kneels; an* OFFICER *places the bandage over her eyes, and gives a sign to a detachment of four to advance; they step forward, and level their muskets at her; at the moment,* LENOX *rushes from the tent with the miniature in his hand and strikes up their guns.*

LENOX. Hold! for your lives! [*Rushes down to* CHRISTINE, *and tears the bandage from her eyes.*] 'Tis she! 'tis she! 'tis my own, my beloved Christine! [*Holds her in his arms; she faints.*

2ND OFFICER. What means this?

LENOX. Stand off, ye cruel executioners, would you destroy a woman?

OFFICER. A woman? Heavens! how did this happen?

Enter GENERAL, ADELA, LaROLE, SOLDIERS, &c.

LENOX. Support her, Adela, support my dear Christine! [ADELA *assists.*

CHRISTINE. [*Recovering.*] Where am I? [*Sees* LENOX *and* ADELA.] Hide me, save me from that horrid sight!

LENOX. Do you not know me, dear Christine?

CHRISTINE. Traitor, begone! let me die at once! Is she not your bride?

LENOX. No, by Heavens, no! 'tis my early friend, my dear companion. Could you doubt my love?

CHRISTINE. Not married? not your betrothed? O Lenox, are you then faithful?

LENOX. Could Christine doubt my vows?

CHRISTINE. I see it all—I have been deceived. Pardon me, dear Lenox; but driven to despair by your supposed perfidy, I enlisted, and rushed on my fate—which in a moment (horrid thought!) would have terminated. But you are true, and I am happy. [*Embrace.*

LAROLE. Parbleu! it is a littel voman vidout de petticoat. Suppose she take a me von prisonier, O quell disgrâce!

Enter JASPER, JERRY *and* PEASANTS.

JASPER. Where is she? where is my daughter?

CHRISTINE. My father? I dare not look upon him.

JASPER. Come to my arms, dear wanderer. Could you leave your poor old father thus? You've nearly broke my heart, Christine.

CHRISTINE. My sufferings have been equally severe; but do you pardon your child?

JASPER. I do—I do! and further prove my love, by making you happy. Take her, Lenox, she is yours; and never let father attempt to force his child into a marriage which her heart abhors.

JERRY. Well, I vow, Miss Crissy, you look very pretty in pantaloons, and make a fine soger; but after all, I'm glad to have escaped a wife who wears the breeches before marriage—so I consent that you shall have the infantry ossifer, because I can't help it; and so I'll marry Patty, the weaver's daughter, though she can't crack a bottle nor bring down a buck.

GENERAL. All things have terminated happily. Our arms have been triumphant, and our gallant soldiers rewarded with the approbation of their country. Love has intwined a wreath for your brows, Lenox, and domestic peace and happiness await you; and when old age draws on apace, may you remember the PLAINS OF CHIPPEWA, and feel towards Britain as freemen should feel towards all the world: *"Enemies in war—in peace, friends."*

Finis.